NEGOTIATION

NEGOTIATION
Processes for Problem Solving

Carrie J. Menkel-Meadow

A.B. Chettle, Jr. Professor of Law, Dispute Resolution and Civil Procedure, and Director,
Georgetown-Hewlett Program on Conflict Resolution and Legal Problem Solving
Georgetown University Law Center

Andrea Kupfer Schneider

Professor of Law
Marquette University Law School

Lela Porter Love

Professor of Law and Director, Kukin Program for Conflict Resolution and the Cardozo
Mediation Clinic
Benjamin N. Cardozo Law School, Yeshiva University

111 Eighth Avenue, New York, NY 10011
http://lawschool.aspenpublishers.com

Printed in the United States of America.

1 2 3 4 5 6 7 8 9 0

ISBN 0-7355-4441-7

Library of Congress Cataloging-in-Publication Data

Menkel-Meadow, Carrie J.
   Negotiation : processes for problem solving / Carrie J. Menkel-Meadow, Andrea Kupfer Schneider,
Lela Porter Love. — 1st ed.
     p. cm.
   ISBN 0-7355-4441-7 (alk. paper)
   1. Compromise (Law) — United States — Cases.   2. Dispute resolution (Law) — United States —
Cases.   3. Negotiation — Cases.   I. Love, Lela Porter, 1950-   II. Schneider, Andrea Kupfer.
III. Title.

KF9084.A7M46 2006
347.73'9 — dc22

                                    2005032254

About Aspen Publishers

Aspen Publishers, headquartered in New York City, is a leading information provider for attorneys, business professionals, and law students. Written by preeminent authorities, our products consist of analytical and practical information covering both U.S. and international topics. We publish in the full range of formats, including updated manuals, books, periodicals, CDs, and online products.

Our proprietary content is complemented by 2,500 legal databases, containing over 11 million documents, available through our Loislaw division. Aspen Publishers also offers a wide range of topical legal and business databases linked to Loislaw's primary material. Our mission is to provide accurate, timely, and authoritative content in easily accessible formats, supported by unmatched customer care.

To order any Aspen Publishers title, go to *http://lawschool.aspenpublishers.com* or call 1-800-638-8437.

To reinstate your manual update service, call 1-800-638-8437.

For more information on Loislaw products, go to *www.loislaw.com* or call 1-800-364-2512.

For Customer Care issues, e-mail *CustomerCare@aspenpublishers.com*; call 1-800-234-1660; or fax 1-800-901-9075.

Aspen Publishers
a Wolters Kluwer business

We dedicate this book to those mentors and colleagues from whom and with whom we have learned about negotiation and problem solving, especially Roger Fisher, Howard Raiffa, Larry Susskind, Mike Wheeler, Robert Mnookin, Deborah Kolb, Bruce Patton, Jim Sebenius, Josh Stulberg, Frank Scardilli, and Jim Coben.

We also dedicate this book to the community of negotiation scholars and practitioners who have made our choices in teaching, practice, and scholarship so immensely rewarding.

May we all continue to learn together, with each other, and with the next generation.

Summary of Contents

Contents

Preface

This book is the culmination of decades of work in a field that began with roots in other disciplines and is now an important part of the law school curriculum — as part of an intellectual and pragmatic movement to teach law students about what lawyers actually do.

When the senior author of this book was a legal services attorney over thirty years ago, she noticed that even when she was victorious in litigation — whether in class action law reform or individual cases — the litigation often would not solve the underlying problem presented by the parties to the formal legal dispute. She began to study how negotiated outcomes in a wide variety of matters often were able, through tailored, specific, and consensually arrived at resolutions, to do more for the parties than achieving a legal judgment, which still required enforcement. And so began a lifetime of study of the negotiation process as a problem-solving process for lawyers who were conventionally more oriented to "winning" cases for their clients than to solving clients' underlying problems. This orientation to negotiation — solving problems — also, of course, includes the other work that lawyers do — creating transactions, entities, and new forms of legal reality (for example, constitutions, legislation, organizations, corporations, coops, condominiums, and unions).

The study and teaching of negotiation as a legal process is relatively new and derivative of work done in other disciplines, such as psychology, political science, economics, sociology, anthropology, and other hybrid fields, such as game theory and decision sciences (Carrie Menkel-Meadow, Legal Negotiation: A Study of Strategies in Search of a Theory, 1983 Am. Bar. Found. Res. J. 905). Legal scholars first took note of negotiated processes in the law in the days of Legal Realism, the Legal Process school of the 1950s and 1960s (Henry M. Hart, Jr. & Albert M. Sacks, The Legal Process: Basic Problems in the Making and Application of Law (William N. Eskridge, Jr. & Philip P. Frickey eds., 1994)) and in socio-legal studies, through empirical work done by researchers affiliated with the Law and Society movement, which still flourishes today (and is complemented by new work in behavioral economics and psychology). Then, in the 1960s and 1970s, another effort to transform legal education, the Clinical Education movement, spawned intensive study and teaching of the skills employed by lawyers to do their work. Negotiation was one of several important skills, including interviewing, counseling, trial practice, drafting, and decision making, taught in separate courses, with simulations, case studies, and exercises, transforming the materials through which law is studied. No longer is the appellate case the only text in the classroom.

Much negotiation theory was derived from the intellectually rich era of game theoretic and strategic study in World War II and Cold War simulations of "Prisoner's Dilemma" and other games, intended to map how parties act under conditions of uncertainty and scarce resources. Much of the lawyer's conventional "map" of negotiation (and the businessperson's selling or buying) is based on these early models of competitive bargaining and assumptions of scarce resources.

As economic and political conditions changed during the 1970s and 1980s, offering a potentially more optimistic view of human nature and the ability to create, as well as divide, human resources, a movement of intellectual convergence around a new way to negotiate was born with the publication of several new approaches to negotiation, including the now world-famous *Getting to YES* (Roger Fisher, William Ury & Bruce Patton 2d ed. 1991, first published 1981), Howard Raiffa's *The Art and Science of Negotiation* (1982), David Lax & James Sebenius's *The Manager as Negotiator* (1986), and, applied to legal negotiations specifically, Carrie Menkel-Meadow's Toward Another View of Legal Negotiation: The Structure of Problem Solving, 31 UCLA L. Rev. 485 (1984). These works all expanded on ideas of using more integrative and collaborative processes (using appeals to reason and objective standards, as well as to underlying needs, wants, and desires) to achieve better, that is more Pareto-optimal, outcomes for the parties — giving the parties as much of what they both need without unnecessary loss or harm to either. This pragmatic, principled, and utilitarian model of negotiation then was taught to thousands of law, business, policy, and graduate students as a "corrective" to the overly adversarial and possibly wasteful, but more common, approaches of competitive and distributional bargaining. Courses in negotiation are now required in many business and public policy schools, and they exist in virtually every law school. Modern professionals from many disciplines are learning about the processes that are necessary to design solutions to human problems when consent, not command, is required to achieve good results.

The last few decades have seen an outpouring of work (both scholarly and practical) studying under what conditions, and with what people and issues, different models of negotiation might be appropriately employed. Our second author was an early student of these processes in both international and domestic contexts, studying at one of the premier organizations, the Program on Negotiation at Harvard Law School, with the field's modern founders. Our third author harnessed the early teachings of negotiation theory to become one of the founders of the modern mediation movement in American, now also European, law schools. All three of the authors of this book have studied and practiced negotiation in a wide variety of contexts, both domestic and international, and this book reflects our learning at all of these levels: theoretical, practical, domestic, international, dyadic, multiparty, legal, and personal.

We have dedicated this book to some of the field's founders, with whom we have worked and with whom we have learned. But, rather than only looking backward, we also acknowledge the flowering of a new generation of negotiation scholars who have uncovered new patterns in negotiation behavior, both distortions in the processes that prevent good agreement and incentives that encourage good behaviors to produce better outcomes for parties. You will find their work on these pages.

The use of negotiation in law remains controversial (though it is the mainstay of legal practice). When should parties be permitted to "privatize" their actions and agreements? When should disputes be resolved in the public sphere, creating precedents for the rest of us? When is negotiation more efficient? Whom should negotiation serve: the parties inside the process, or those affected by it? Does negotiation result in unprincipled, transaction cost-reducing compromise, or can it provide solutions more precisely tailored to the needs of the parties and justice for those whose problem it is? When should we negotiate? When should we not negotiate? We explore these critical questions in this book too.

The authors of this book are firmly committed to the notion that negotiation is not only essential in human interaction but that it also promises to promote the best of human flourishing. If we are perceived to be in the "as long as they are talking, they are not killing" school of negotiation, it is because we do hope and believe that with the right intentions and good instruction, we can all learn to be better problem solvers, decision makers, and negotiators by studying this process, practicing it, and looking for new ways to improve human communication.

We begin this book by reviewing basic theoretical concepts and models of conflict, dispute resolution, and negotiation. Next, we focus on the classic models of negotiation: preparing for and conducting integrative and distributive bargaining. Then we turn to the important interpersonal skills required to negotiate, including working with clients and counterparts to create trust and rapport, learn information, and craft good solutions. Next we confront the barriers to reaching good agreements, that is, the variety of social, cognitive, cultural, and material impediments to negotiation. We explore some of the difficult and significant ethical dimensions of negotiating with and on behalf of others and review how various bodies of law constrain negotiation in legal matters. Finally, we provide some examples of modern and sophisticated applications of negotiation processes in multiparty and international settings. And we conclude the book with an introduction to what we treat in more detail in our companion volumes (Menkel-Meadow, Love, Schneider & Sternlight, *Dispute Resolution: Beyond the Adversarial Model* (Aspen 2005), and Menkel-Meadow, Love & Schneider, *Mediation: Practice, Policy, and Ethics* (Aspen 2006)) — facilitated negotiation or mediation. The accompanying *Teacher's Manual* to this book provides one of the largest available collections of negotiation simulations, role-plays, exercises, and case studies. We firmly believe that this is a field of study that must be practiced to be learned and that theory must be developed from its usefulness.

Footnotes by the authors of this book, in both the excerpts and our text, are marked using symbols. The order of the footnote symbols, if more than one symbol appears on a page, is * † ‡. The original footnote numbering in the excerpts has been retained.

* * *

A few thanks before we get started: We begin with some intellectual and foundational thanks to the other negotiation teachers and scholars who have deeply influenced us in a variety of different ways — in addition to those to whom we dedicate this book, we also thank Harry Edwards, James J. White, Bea Moulton, the late Gary Bellow, Jack Himmelstein, Howard Gadlin, Gary Lowenthal, and Paul Brest who also influenced our early thinking in this field. We next thank Jean Sternlight, our coauthor on the larger project who could not participate in this one (due to her other book on mediation) but who remains with us in spirit.

All of us thank various other colleagues in this work. From Carrie, special thanks to Susan Gillig and Peter Reilly for being the best coteachers and cotravelers one could have in this journey of pedagogical innovation; to Vicki Jackson and Carol O'Neil, deans, friends, and supporters extraordinaire; and to the Program on Negotiation at Harvard (and especially Bill Breslin, Mike Wheeler, Frank Sander, Bob Bordone, Bob Mnookin, Larry Susskind, Deborah Kolb, and Susan Hackley) — for being my second home and always the best of audiences.

From Andrea, special thanks to my wonderful colleagues and classmates at the Harvard Negotiation Project who inspired me — Liz Kopelman Borgwardt, Shelley LaGere Carlin, Estie Dallet, Bruce Deming, Kerri Fox, Sheila Heen, William Jackson, Paul Mayer, Michael Moffitt, Erin Monaghan, Linda Netsch, Scott Peppet, Alan Price, John Richardson, Doug Stone, Chris Thorne, Carol Umhoefer, Jeff Wing, Tim Wu, and others — if negotiation had not been so much fun way back when, it would not be nearly as interesting now. And for making it so much fun now, a truly appreciative thanks to my colleague and friend, Joanne Lipo-Zovic.

From Lela, special thanks to those who have helped build an innovative curriculum at Cardozo and around the world — Hal Abramson, Kitty Atkins, Simeon Baum, Jim Coben, Kinga Goncz, James Kornbluh, Michael Lang, Ray Patterson, Dana Potockova, Frank Scardilli, Peggy Sweeney, Josh Stulberg, and Dan Weitz.

Carrie profoundly thanks her able support team, research assistant extraordinaire, David Mattingly; administrative assistants Corrie Mathiowetz and Carolyn Howard; research assistants Bonard Molina, James Bond, and Jaimie Kent; the faculty production team at Georgetown, Sylvia Johnson, Toni Patterson and Ronnie E. Rease, Jr. (I promise I will stop killing trees soon!).

Andrea thanks her fabulous assistant Carrie Kratochvil, who negotiates both the large and small crises in the law school while getting everything done, and her truly devoted research assistants, Anna Coyer and Stacey Meyer, who have done superlative work on this book and the accompanying Teacher's Manual.

Lela is enormously grateful for her wonderful support at Cardozo: Justin Braun, Tracey Pastan, Kaaron Saphir, and Dan Zinn, and also past and present members of the Cardozo Mediation Clinic, whose energy and enthusiasm undergirds this and other efforts.

All of us feel enormously grateful to our home institutions, which gave us support in so many different ways: Thanks to Deans Judith Areen and Alex Aleinikoff and Associate Dean Vicki Jackson at Georgetown University Law Center (and to the donors of the A.B. Chettle, Jr., Chair in Dispute Resolution and Civil

Procedure); to Carol O'Neil, for academic and pedagogical support and interest way beyond the call of duty; thanks to Dean Joseph Kearney and Associate Dean Peter Rofes at Marquette University Law School; and thanks to Dean David Rudenstein and former Dean Monroe Price at Benjamin Cardozo School of Law and to Kaaron Saphir who so cheerfully jumps in whenever a request is made.

We are also appreciative of the various "pushes" and "pulls" of the Aspen team—Melody Davies, Lisa Wehrle, Laurel Ibey, Susan Boulanger, Elsie Starbecker (who guided the first volume with care and beauty), Elizabeth Ricklefs, Richard Mixter, and others behind the pages.

We thank the many reviewers of this text, some known to us (Michael Moffitt, Clark Freshman) and other undisclosed helpers. We hope we have met your needs and answered your concerns.

We thank our families, to whom the larger ADR book was dedicated, Robert Meadow, Peter Popov, Nicole Love Popov, Rodd, Joshua, Noah, and Zachary Schneider for their patience, support, and, on very rare occasions, some opportunity to practice our conflict resolution and negotiation skills!

And mostly, we thank our students whom we hope will use these materials to create a better world—one with peace, sensitive and rigorous problem solving, and justice.

Let us know what you think.

Carrie Menkel-Meadow
Andrea Kupfer Schneider
Lela Porter Love

December 2005

Acknowledgments

The authors wish to express their thanks to the following authors, periodicals, and publishers for their permission to reproduce materials from their publications:

Adler, Robert S., Benson Rosen, and Elliot M. Silverstein, How to Manage Fear and Anger, 14 NEGOTIATION JOURNAL 161, 168-174 (1998). Reprinted with permission from the publisher.

Adler, Robert S., and Elliot M. Silverstein, When David Meets Goliath: Dealing with Power Differentials in Negotiations, 5 HARVARD NEGOTIATION LAW REVIEW 1, 10-28, 69-72, 77-81, 84-86, 88-90, 103-105, 92-103, 106-110 (2000). Reprinted with permission from the publisher.

Albin, Cecilia, The Role of Fairness in Negotiations, 9 NEGOTIATION JOURNAL 223, 225-228, 233-239 (1993). Reprinted with permission from the publisher.

Alfini, James J., Trashing, Bashing, and Hashing It Out: Is This the End of "Good Mediation"? 19 FLORIDA STATE UNIVERSITY LAW REVIEW 47, 66-71, 73 (1991). Reprinted with permission of the Florida State University Law Review.

American Bar Association, Model Rule of Professional Conduct (2004), Rules 1.2, 1.4, 1.6, 1.8(g), 3.3, 4.1, 4.4(a), 5.6, 8.3, and 8.4(a)-(d). Reprinted with permission of the American Bar Association. Copies of ABA Model Rules of Professional Conduct, 2004 are available from Service Center, American Bar Association, 321 North Clark Street, Chicago, IL 60610, 1-800-285-2221.

American Law Institute, Restatement (Second) of Contracts (1981) §161 When Non-Disclosure Is Equivalent to an Assertion. Copyright © 1981 by the American Law Institute. Reprinted with permission. All rights reserved.

American Law Institute, Restatement (Second) of Contracts (1981) §164 When a Misrepresentation Makes a Contract Voidable. Copyright © 1981 by the American Law Institute. Reprinted with permission. All rights reserved.

American Law Institute, Restatement (Second) of Torts (1977) §525 Liability for Fraudulent Misrepresentation. Copyright © 1977 by the American Law Institute. Reprinted with permission. All rights reserved.

Angier, Natalie, Why We're So Nice: We're Wired to Cooperate, N.Y. TIMES, July 23, 2002, at 1. Copyright © 2002 by The New York Times Co. Reprinted with permission.

Applbaum, Arthur, and Richard Zeckhauser, Rules of the Game, Permissible Harms, and the Principle of Fair Play, in WISE CHOICES: DECISIONS, GAMES, AND NEGOTIATIONS 301, 304-305 (Richard J. Zeckhauser, Ralph L. Keeney and James K. Sebenius eds., 1996). Reprinted with permission of the publisher.

Arnold, Tom, 20 Common Errors in Mediation Advocacy, 13 ALTERNATIVES TO THE HIGH COST OF LITIGATION 67-71 (1995). Reprinted by permission of the author and John Wiley & Sons, Inc.

Avruch, Kevin, Culture and Negotiation Pedagogy, 16 NEGOTIATION JOURNAL 339, 340-341, 343-345 (2000). Reprinted with permission from the publisher.

Avruch, Kevin, Culture as Context, Culture as Communication: Considerations for Humanitarian Negotiators, 9 HARVARD NEGOTIATION LAW REVIEW 391, 392-395, 396-399, 400, 404-405, 406, 407 (2004). Reprinted with permission from the publisher.

Axelrod, Robert, THE EVOLUTION OF COOPERATION 3, 7, 9, 30-31, 40-42, 54, 73-87, 110-122 (Basic Books, 1984). Reprinted with permission.

Ayres, Ian, Fair Driving: Gender and Race Discrimination in Retail Car Negotiations, 104 HARVARD LAW REVIEW 817, 818-819 (1991). Reprinted with permission from the publisher.

Ayres, Ian, Further Evidence of Discrimination in New Car Negotiations and Estimates of Its Cause, 94 MICHIGAN LAW REVIEW 109, 109-110, 124, 127-128, 142, 145 (University of Michigan School of Law, 1995). Reprinted by permission of the author.

Babbitt, Eileen F., Challenges for International Diplomatic Agents, in NEGOTIATING ON BEHALF OF OTHERS: ADVICE TO LAWYERS, BUSINESS EXECUTIVES, SPORTS AGENTS, DIPLOMATS, POLITICIANS, AND EVERYBODY ELSE 136-137, 139, 141, 143, 145-146 (Robert H. Mnookin and Lawrence E. Susskind eds., 1999). Reprinted with permission from Sage Publications, Inc.

Babcock, Linda, and Sara Laschever, WOMEN DON'T ASK: NEGOTIATION AND THE GENDER DIVIDE 1-2, 4-6, 8-10 (2003). Reprinted with permission of Princeton University Press.

Bastress, Robert M., and Joseph D. Harbaugh, INTERVIEWING, COUNSELING AND NEGOTIATING: SKILLS FOR EFFECTIVE REPRESENTATION 66, 71, 77-78, 85-86, 92-97, 99, 101, 104, 106, 237-240 (Little, Brown, 1990). Reprinted with permission.

Bazerman, Max H. et al., Negotiating with Yourself and Losing: Making Decisions with Competing Internal Preferences, 23 ACADEMIC MANAGEMENT REVIEW 225, 236-238 (1998). Reprinted with permission from the publisher.

Bazerman, Max H., and Margaret A. Neale, NEGOTIATING RATIONALLY 9-11, 26-28, 49, 54, 62-63 (Free Press, 1992). Reprinted with the permission of The Free Press, a Division of Simon & Schuster Adult Publishing Group. Copyright © 1992 by Max H. Bazerman and Margaret A. Neale. All rights reserved.

Begley, Sharon, The Stereotype Trap, NEWSWEEK, Nov. 6, 2000, at 66-68. Reprinted with permission from the publisher.

Bezanson, Randall, Gilbert Cranberg, and John Soloski, LIBEL LAW AND THE PRESS: MYTH AND REALITY 29-53. Reprinted with permission of the Free Press, a Division of Simon & Schuster Adult Publishing Group. Copyright © 1987 by The Free Press. All rights reserved.

Binder, David A., Paul B. Bergman, Susan C. Price, and Paul K. Tremblay, LAWYERS AS COUNSELORS: A CLIENT-CENTERED APPROACH 2-11, 19-27, 29-31, 306-309, 311-312, 317, 320-321 (2d ed. West 2004). Reprinted with permission.

Birke, Richard, Reconciling Loss Aversion and Guilty Pleas, 1999 UTAH LAW REVIEW 205, 207-209, 209-210. Reprinted with permission from the publisher.

***Bookshop* cartoon.** © Dave Carpenter, dave@cartoons.com. Reprinted by permission of Dave Carpenter.

Brown, Jennifer Gerarda, Creativity and Problem-Solving, 87 MARQUETTE LAW REVIEW 697, 697-705 (2004). Copyright © 2004. Reprinted with permission of the author.

Brown, Jennifer Gerarda, The Role of Apology in Negotiation, 87 MARQUETTE LAW REVIEW 665, 665-673 (2004). Reprinted with permission from the author.

Brown, Jennifer Gerarda, The Role of Hope in Negotiation, 44 UCLA LAW REVIEW 1661, 1669-1670, 1672-1673, 1674-1682, 1684-1686 (1997). Reprinted with permission.

Burger, Warren, The Necessity for Civility, 52 FEDERAL RULES DECISIONS 211, 212-215 (West Publishing 1971). Reprinted with permission.

Bush, Robert A. Baruch, and Joseph P. Folger, THE PROMISE OF MEDIATION: THE TRANSFORMATIVE APPROACH TO CONFLICT 45, 49, 51-53, 65-66 (rev. ed., Jossey-Bass 2005). Reprinted with permission of John Wiley & Sons, Inc.

Calvin and Hobbes **cartoon.** © 1990 Watterson. Dist. By UNIVERSAL PRESS SYNDICATE. Reprinted with permission. All rights reserved.

Calvin and Hobbes **cartoon.** © 1993 Watterson. Dist. By UNIVERSAL PRESS SYNDICATE. Reprinted with permission. All rights reserved.

Calvin and Hobbes **cartoon.** © 1994 Watterson. Dist. By UNIVERSAL PRESS SYNDICATE. Reprinted with permission. All rights reserved.

Candlelight **cartoon.** "Okay, 60 million..." © 2005 Peter Steiner from *Cartoonbank.com*. All rights reserved. Reprinted with permission.

Cialdini, Robert, excerpts from INFLUENCE: THE PSYCHOLOGY OF PERSUASION 15-16, 17-18, 36, 38, 40-42. Copyright © 1993 Robert B. Cialdini. Reprinted by permission of HarperCollins Publishers, Inc.

Cohen, Jonathan R., When People Are the Means: Negotiating with Respect, 14 GEORGETOWN JOURNAL OF LEGAL ETHICS 739, 741-743, 760-763, 766-767. Reprinted with permission of the publisher, GEORGETOWN JOURNAL OF LEGAL ETHICS © 2001.

Cohen, Jonathan R., excerpts from Advising Clients to Apologize, 72 SOUTHERN CALIFORNIA LAW REVIEW 1009, 1013-1015, 1018-1025, 1028-1029, 1031-1034, 1036-1045, 1047, 1053 (1999). Reprinted with the permission of SOUTHERN CALIFORNIA LAW REVIEW.

Cohen, Jonathan R., Adversaries? Partners? How About Counterparts? On Metaphors in the Practice and Teaching of Negotiation and Dispute Resolution, 20 CONFLICT RESOLUTION QUARTERLY 433-436, 438-439. Copyright © 2003 by Jossey-Bass, Inc. This material is used by permission of John Wiley & Sons, Inc.

Cohen, Jonathan R., Apology and Organizations: Exploring an Example from Medical Practice, 27 FORDHAM URBAN LAW JOURNAL 1447. Copyright © 2000. Reprinted by permission of the author.

Coleman, Peter T., Power and Conflict, in THE HANDBOOK OF CONFLICT RESOLUTION: THEORY AND PRACTICE 108-109, 110-111, 113, 121-122, 123, 124, 125, 126-127 (Morton Deutsch and Peter T. Coleman eds., 2000). Reprinted with permission of John Wiley & Sons, Inc.

Cosgrove, Rabbi Elliot, excerpts from a Sermon. Used by permission.

Craver, Charles B., and David W. Barnes, Gender, Risk Taking, and Negotiation Performance, 5 MICHIGAN JOURNAL OF GENDER AND LAW 299, 320-321, 346-347 (1999). Copyright © 1999 by Charles B. Craver and David W. Barnes. Reprinted by permission.

Croson, Rachel, and Robert H. Mnookin, Does Disputing Through Agents Enhance Cooperation? 26 JOURNAL LEGAL STUDIES 331, 344-345 (1997). Reprinted with permission from the publisher.

Curran, Daniel, James K. Sebenius, and Michael Watkins, Two Paths to Peace: Contrasting George Mitchell in Northern Ireland with Richard Holbrooke in Bosnia–Herzegovina, 20 NEGOTIATION JOURNAL 513, 514-525, 530-531 (2004). Reprinted with permission from the publisher.

Docherty, Jayne Seminare, Culture and Negotiation: Symmetrical Anthropology for Negotiators, 87 MARQUETTE LAW REVIEW 711, 712, 713, 714-715, 717, 718, 719 (2004). Reprinted by permission from Jayne Docherty, Associate Professor of Conflict Studies, Center for Justice and Peacebuilding, Eastern Mennonite University.

Docherty, Jayne Seminare, and Marcia Caton Campbell, Teaching Negotiators to Analyze Conflict Structure and Anticipate the Consequences of Principal-Agent Relationships, 87 MARQUETTE LAW REVIEW, 655, 657-659, 662-664. Copyright © 2004 by Brill Academic Publishers. Reprinted by permission from Jayne Docherty, Associate Professor of Conflict Studies, Center for Justice and Peacebuilding, Eastern Mennonite University; and Marcia Caton Campbell, Assistant Professor, University of Wisconsin-Madison.

Doerre, Sharon, Negotiating Gender and Authority in Northern Syria, 6 INTERNATIONAL NEGOTIATION JOURNAL 251, 252-253, 255-261 (2001). Reprinted with permission.

Falk, David B., The Art of Contract Negotiation, 3 MARQUETTE SPORTS LAW JOURNAL 1, 12-14 (© Marquette University, Fall 1992). Reprinted with permission of the publisher.

Family Circus **cartoon.** © Family Circus — Bill Keane, Inc. King Features Syndicate.

Far Side **cartoon.** The Far Side® by Gary Larson © 1984 FarWorks, Inc. All rights reserved. The Far Side® and the Larson® signature are registered trademarks of FarWorks, Inc. Used with permission.

Felstiner, William L.F., and Austin Sarat, Enactments of Power: Negotiating Reality and Responsibility in Lawyer-Client Interactions, 77 CORNELL LAW REVIEW 1447, 1495, 1498 (1992). Reprinted by permission of the publisher.

Final Report of the Committee on Civility of the Seventh Federal Judicial Circuit, 143 FEDERAL RULES DECISIONS 441, 448-449 (West 1992). Reprinted with permission.

Fisher, Roger, William Ury, and Bruce Patton, GETTING TO YES 4-7, 8-9, 10-14, 85-88, 99-103 (2d ed. 1991). Copyright © 1981, 1991 by Roger Fisher and William Ury. Reprinted by permission of Houghton Mifflin Company. All rights reserved.

Fisher, Roger, Elizabeth Kopelman, and Andrea Kupfer Schneider, BEYOND MACHIAVELLI: TOOLS FOR COPING WITH CONFLICT 32-35, 67-94, ch. 4, 123-132, Cambridge, Mass.: Harvard University Press. Copyright © 1994 by the President and Fellows of Harvard College. Reprinted with permission of the publisher.

Fisher, Roger, and Wayne H. Davis, Six Interpersonal Skills for a Negotiator's Repertoire, 3 NEGOTIATION JOURNAL 117, 117-122 (1987). Reprinted with permission from the publisher.

Follett, Mary Parker, Constructive Conflict, in MARY PARKER FOLLETT — PROPHET OF MANAGEMENT: A CELEBRATION OF WRITINGS FROM THE 1920's, at 67-69, 75, 77, 79, 82, 84-86 (Pauline Graham ed., 1995). Reprinted with permission from the publisher.

Forest, Heather, THE WISE MASTER, WISDOM TALES FROM AROUND THE WORLD 15-16 (August House, 1996). Reprinted with permission.

Frank & Ernest **cartoon.** "Of course there are two sides..." Copyright © 1994 by Tom Thaves (*www.thecomics.com*). Used by permission.

Frank & Ernest **cartoon.** "The question of right and wrong..." Copyright © 2005 by Tom Thaves (*www.thecomics.com*). Used by permission.

Freshman, Clark, Adele Hayes, and Greg Feldman, The Lawyer-Negotiator as Mood Scientist: What We Know and Don't Know About How Mood Relates to Successful Negotiation, 2002 JOURNAL OF DISPUTE RESOLUTION 1, 55, 66-69, 73-75. Reprinted with permission of the JOURNAL OF DISPUTE RESOLUTION, University of Missouri-Columbia, Center for the Study of Dispute Resolution, 206 Hulston Hall, Columbia, MO 65211.

Friedman, Gary, and Jack Himmelstein, THE UNDERSTANDING-BASED MODEL OF MEDIATION, The Center for Mediation in Law (2004). Reprinted with permission from the authors.

Fuller, Lon L., Mediation — Its Forms and Functions, 44 SOUTHERN CALIFORNIA LAW REVIEW 305-327 (1971). Reprinted with the permission of the SOUTHERN CALIFORNIA LAW REVIEW.

Galton, Eric, Mediation of Medical Negligence Claims, 28 CAPITAL UNIVERSITY LAW REVIEW 321, 324-325 (2000). Reprinted with permission from the publisher.

Gifford, Donald, The Synthesis of Legal Counseling and Negotiation Models: Preserving Client-Centered Advocacy in the Negotiation Context, 34 UCLA LAW REVIEW 811, 811-844 (1987). Reprinted by permission of the author.

Gilligan, Carol, Reprinted by permission of the publisher from IN A DIFFERENT VOICE: PSYCHOLOGICAL THEORY AND WOMEN'S DEVELOPMENT 25-28, Cambridge, Mass.: Harvard University Press. Copyright © 1982, 1993 by Carol Gilligan.

Gilson, Ronald J., excerpts from Value Creation by Business Lawyers: Legal Skills and Asset Pricing, 94 YALE LAW JOURNAL 239, 243, 246, 252, 293, 303, 309-310 (1984). Reprinted by permission of The Yale Law Journal Company and William S. Hein Company from THE YALE LAW JOURNAL, Vol. 94, 239-313.

Gilson, Ronald J., and Robert H. Mnookin, Disputing Through Agents: Cooperation and Conflict Between Lawyers in Litigation, 94 COLUMBIA LAW REVIEW 509, 510-512, 516, 520, 522-528, 565-566 (1995). Reprinted with permission from the publisher.

Ginsburg, Tom, and Richard H. McAdams, Adjudicating in Anarchy: An Expressive Theory of International Dispute Resolution, 45(4) WILLIAM & MARY LAW REVIEW 1229, 1263-1275 (2004). Reprinted with permission from the publisher.

Gladwell, Malcolm, excerpts from BLINK: THE POWER OF THINKING WITHOUT THINKING 40-42, 90, 95-96. Copyright © 2005 by Malcolm Gladwell. By permission of Little, Brown and Co., Inc.

Glaser, Connie, and Barbara Smalley, Visualizing Your Success, in WHAT QUEEN ESTHER KNEW 29-30, 113, 120-122 (Rodale, 2003). Reprinted with permission.

Glick, Steven, and Rachel Croson, excerpts from Reputations in Negotiation, in WHARTON ON MAKING DECISIONS 178-186 (Stephen J. Hoch, Howard C. Kunreuther, and Robert E. Gunther eds., 2001). Reprinted with permission of John Wiley & Sons, Inc.

Goodpaster, Gary, A Primer on Competitive Bargaining, 1996 JOURNAL OF DISPUTE RESOLUTION 325, 326, 341-42, 370-375. Reprinted with permission of the author and the JOURNAL OF DISPUTE RESOLUTION, University of Missouri-Columbia, Center for the Study of Dispute Resolution, 206 Hulston Hall, Columbia, MO 65211.

Greenhalgh, Leonard, The Case Against Winning in Negotiations, 3 NEGOTIATION JOURNAL 167, 167-172 (1987). Reprinted with permission from the publisher.

Gulliver, Philip H., DISPUTES AND NEGOTIATIONS: A CROSS-CULTURAL PERSPECTIVE 82-86, 88-89 (Academic Press, 1979). Reprinted with permission.

Gurr, Ted Robert, Peoples Against States: Ethnopolitical Conflict and the Changing World System: 1994 Presidential Address, 38 INTERNATIONAL STUDIES QUARTERLY 347, 347-377 (1994). Reprinted with permission from the publisher.

Guthrie, Chris, Panacea or Pandora's Box? The Costs of Options in Negotiation, 88 IOWA LAW REVIEW 601, 604-606, 608-610, 613-615, 617, 621-622, 625, 631-632, 634-636,

638-641, 644 (College of Law, University of Iowa, 2003). Reprinted by permission of the author.

Guthrie, Chris, Principles of Influence in Negotiation, 87 MARQUETTE LAW REVIEW 829, 831, 832, 833-834, 835 (2004). Reprinted with permission from the publisher.

Guthrie, Chris, and David Sally, The Impact of the Impact Bias on Negotiation, 87 MARQUETTE LAW REVIEW 817, 817-818, 821, 827-828 (2004). Reprinted with permission of the authors: Chris Guthrie, Vanderbilt University Law School; and David Sally, Tuck School of Business at Dartmouth, 100 Tuck Hall, Hanover, NH 03755.

Hagar the Horrible **cartoon.** Request a Mediator. © Hagar Cartoon—King Features Syndicate.

Harter, Philip, Negotiating Regulations: A Cure for Malaise, 71 GEORGETOWN LAW JOURNAL 1, 28-31, 33-34, 42, 82-86, 112-113 (1982). Reprinted with permission of the publisher.

Hawkins, Jr., Lee, GM's Finance Arm Is Close to Settling Racial-Bias Lawsuit, WALL STREET JOURNAL, Jan. 30, 2004, at A1. Reprinted with permission from the publisher.

Hegland, Kenny, Why Teach Trial Advocacy? An Essay on Never Ask Why, in HUMANISTIC EDUCATION IN LAW 69 (J. Himmelstein and H. Lesnick eds., Columbia University, 1982). Reprinted with permission.

Hofstadter, Douglas R., METAMAGICAL THEMAS: QUESTING FOR THE ESSENCE OF MIND AND PATTERN 716, 730-731. Copyright © 1985 by Basic Books, Inc. Reprinted by permission of Basic Books, a member of Perseus Books, L.L.C.

Huntington, Samuel P., The Clash of Civilizations? in THE INTERNATIONAL SYSTEM AFTER THE COLLAPSE OF THE EAST-WEST ORDER 7, 8-11 (Armand Clesse et al. eds., 1994). Reprinted with permission from the publisher.

Hurt, Christine, No Harm Intended: Teaching a Torts Class Offered Endless Opportunity for Dark Humor—Until It Became No Laughing Matter, CHRONICLE OF HIGHER EDUCATION, May 27, 2005, at C3. Reprinted with permission from the publisher.

Ignatieff, Michael, BLOOD AND BELONGING: JOURNEYS INTO THE NEW NATIONALISM 11, 13 (AP Watt, 1994). Reprinted with permission of AP Watt Ltd. on behalf of Michael Ignatieff.

Interim Report of the Committee on Civility of the Seventh Federal Judicial Circuit, 143 FEDERAL RULES DECISIONS 371, 385-386 (West Publishing, 1991). Reprinted with permission.

Kahneman, Daniel, and Amos Tversky, Conflict Resolution: A Cognitive Perspective, in BARRIERS TO CONFLICT RESOLUTION 46-47, 54-55 (Kenneth Arrow et al. eds., 1995). Copyright © 1995 by The Stanford Center on Conflict and Negotiation. Used by permission of W.W. Norton & Company, Inc.

Karrass, Chester L., THE NEGOTIATING GAME 8-10 (Thomas Y. Crowell Co., 1970). Reprinted with permission from the author.

Kolb, Deborah, and Judith Williams, EVERYDAY NEGOTIATION: NAVIGATING THE HIDDEN AGENDAS 3-5, 8-13 (Jossey-Bass, 2003). Reprinted with permission of John Wiley & Sons, Inc.

Kolb, Deborah M., Judith Williams, and Carol Frohlinger, HER PLACE AT THE TABLE: A WOMAN'S GUIDE TO NEGOTIATING; FIVE KEY CHALLENGES TO LEADERSHIP SUCCESS 81-82, 234-236 (Jossey-Bass, 2004). Reprinted with the permission of John Wiley & Sons, Inc.

Korobkin, Russell, A Positive Theory of Legal Negotiation, 88 GEORGETOWN LAW JOURNAL 1789, 1791-1794, 1794-1798, 1799, 1816 (2000). Reprinted with permission of the publisher, GEORGETOWN LAW JOURNAL © 2000.

Korobkin, Russell, The Role of Law in Settlements, in THE HANDBOOK OF DISPUTE RESOLUTION (Michael L. Moffitt and Robert C. Bordone eds., 2005). Reprinted by permission.

Korobkin, Russell, Bargaining Power as Threat of Impasse, 87 MARQUETTE LAW REVIEW 867, 867-871 (2004). Reprinted by permission of the author.

Korobkin, Russell, and Chris Guthrie, Heuristics and Biases at the Bargaining Table, 87 MARQUETTE LAW REVIEW 795, 795-808 (2004). Reprinted by permission of the authors.

Korobkin, Russell, and Chris Guthrie, Psychological Barriers to Litigation Settlement: An Experimental Approach, 93 MICHIGAN LAW REVIEW 107, 130-135, 137-138, 144-146 (University of Michigan School of Law, 1994). Reprinted with permission.

Kritek, Phyllis Beck, NEGOTIATING AT AN UNEVEN TABLE: A PRACTICAL APPROACH TO WORKING WITH DIFFERENCE AND DIVERSITY 187, 200, 209-210, 224, 228, 244, 252-253, 261, 281, 292, 298, 314-315 (Jossey-Bass, 1994). Reprinted with permission of John Wiley & Sons, Inc.

Lax, David A., and James K. Sebenius, Interests: The Measure of Negotiation, 2 NEGOTIATION JOURNAL 73, 73-74, 76-77, 78-80, 81, 82, 88-89, 90-91 (1986). Reprinted with permission from the publisher.

Lax, David A., and James K. Sebenius, THE MANAGER AS NEGOTIATOR: BARGAINING FOR COOPERATION AND COMPETITIVE GAIN 11, 29-30, 32, 38-40, 89-90 (The Free Press, 1986). Reprinted with the permission of The Free Press, a Division of Simon & Schuster Adult Publishing Group. Copyright © 1986 by David A. Lax and James K. Sebenius. All rights reserved.

Lederach, John Paul, Cultivating Peace: A Practitioner's View of Deadly Conflict and Negotiation, in CONTEMPORARY PEACEMAKING: CONFLICT, VIOLENCE AND PEACE PROCESSES 33-35, 37 (John Darby and Roger MacGinty eds., 2003). Reprinted with permission from the publisher, Palgrave Macmillan.

Lehman, Warren, The Pursuit of a Client's Interest, 77 MICHIGAN LAW REVIEW 1078, 1079, 1088-1089, 1091-1093 (University of Michigan School of Law, 1979). Reprinted with permission from the publisher.

Lewicki, Roy J., and Barbara Benedict Bunker, Trust in Relationships: A Model of Development and Decline, in CONFLICT, COOPERATION AND JUSTICE 133, 142-143, 145-146, 148-156, 167-169 (Barbara Bunker, Jeffrey Rubin et al. eds., 1995). Reprinted with permission of John Wiley & Sons, Inc.

Lewicki, Roy J., and Carolyn Wiethoff, Trust, Trust Development, and Trust Repair, in THE HANDBOOK OF CONFLICT RESOLUTION: THEORY AND PRACTICE 100-103 (Morton Deutsch and Peter T. Coleman eds., 2000). Reprinted with permission of John Wiley & Sons, Inc.

Love, Lela P., Glen Cove: Mediation Achieves What Litigation Cannot, 20 CONSENSUS 1, 1-2 (1993). Reprinted with permission from the publisher.

Luban, David, Settlement and the Erosion of the Public Realm, 83 GEORGETOWN LAW JOURNAL 2619, 2621-2626, 2642-2646, 2648-2649, 2662 (1995). Reprinted with permission of the publisher, GEORGETOWN LAW JOURNAL © 1995.

Lubet, Steven, Notes on the Bedouin Horse Trade or "Why Won't the Market Clear Daddy?" 74 TEXAS LAW REVIEW 1039 (1996). Reprinted with permission from the publisher.

Machiavelli, Niccolo, THE PRINCE 11, 13, 61, 68-70, 98-100 (H. Mansfield trans., 2d ed. Chicago University Press, 1998). By permission of the publisher.

Meltsner, Michael, and Philip Schrag, Negotiation, in PUBLIC INTEREST ADVOCACY: MATERIALS FOR CLINICAL LEGAL EDUCATION 232-238 (St. Paul, MN: Little, Brown & Company, 1974). Reprinted with permission.

Menkel-Meadow, Carrie, Aha? Is Creativity Possible in Legal Problem Solving and Teachable in Legal Education? 6 HARVARD NEGOTIATION LAW REVIEW 97, 106, 120-123, 125, 127-128, 131, 133, 135-136 (2001). Reprinted with permission.

Menkel-Meadow, Carrie, The Art and Science of Problem Solving Negotiation, TRIAL MAGAZINE, June 1999, at 50-51. Reprinted by permission of the author.

Menkel-Meadow, Carrie, excerpt from Conflict Theory, in ENCYCLOPEDIA OF COMMUNITY: FROM THE VILLAGE TO THE VIRTUAL WORLD, Vol. 1, 323-326 (Karen Christensen and David Levinson eds., 2003). Copyright © 2003 by Sage Publications, Inc. Reprinted with permission.

Menkel-Meadow, Carrie, Ethics, Morality and Professional Responsibility in Negotiation, in DISPUTE RESOLUTION ETHICS 131-139 (Phyllis Bernard and Bryant Garth eds., 2002). Copyright © 2002 by the American Bar Association. Reprinted with permission.

Menkel-Meadow, Carrie, Feminist Discourse, Moral Values and the Law — A Conversation, 34 BUFFALO LAW REVIEW 11, 50-54 (1985). Reprinted with permission from the publisher.

Menkel-Meadow, Carrie, Introduction: From Legal Disputes to Conflict Resolution and Human Problem Solving, in DISPUTE PROCESSING AND CONFLICT RESOLUTION xxxi. Copyright © 2003, Ashgate Publishing Limited. Reprinted with permission.

Menkel-Meadow, Carrie, Introduction, in MEDIATION: THEORY, POLICY AND PRACTICE xiii-xviii, xxix. Copyright © 2001 by Ashgate Publishing Limited. Reprinted by permission of the author.

Menkel-Meadow, Carrie, Public Access to Private Settlements: Conflicting Legal Policies, 11 ALTERNATIVES TO THE HIGH COST OF LITIGATION 85, 85-87 (1993). Reprinted with permission of John Wiley & Sons, Inc.

Menkel-Meadow, Carrie, excerpts from Roots and Inspirations: A Brief History of the Foundations of Dispute Resolution, in THE HANDBOOK OF DISPUTE RESOLU-TION 13, 14-15 (Michael L. Moffitt and Robert C. Bordone eds., 2005). Reprinted with permission from the publisher.

Menkel-Meadow, Carrie, Toward Another View of Legal Negotiation: The Structure of Problem Solving, 31 UCLA LAW REVIEW 754, 754-759, 768-775, 775-781, 794-801 (1984). Reprinted with permission from the publisher and author.

Menkel-Meadow, Carrie, The Trouble with the Adversary System in a Postmodern, Multicultural World, 38 WILLIAM & MARY LAW REVIEW 5, 6-10 (1996). Reprinted with permission from the publisher.

Menkel-Meadow, Carrie, What's Fair in Negotiation? What Is Ethics in Negotiation? in WHAT'S FAIR: ETHICS FOR NEGOTIATORS xiii-xvi (Carrie Menkel-Meadow and Michael Wheeler eds., Jossey-Bass, 2004). Reprinted with permission of John Wiley & Sons, Inc.

Mnookin, Robert H., Strategic Barriers to Dispute Resolution: A Comparison of Bilateral and Multilateral Negotiations, 159(1) JOURNAL OF INSTITUTIONAL & THEORETICAL ECONOMICS 199, 200, 201, 219 (2003). Reprinted with permission from the publisher.

Mnookin, Robert H., When Not to Negotiate: A Negotiation Imperialist Reflects on Appropriate Limits, 74 UNIVERSITY OF COLORADO LAW REVIEW 1077, 1078, 1081-1083, 1085, 1088-1090, 1095-1096, 1106-1107 (2003). Reprinted with permission from the publisher.

Mnookin, Robert H., Why Negotiations Fail: An Exploration of Barriers to Conflict Resolution, 8 OHIO STATE JOURNAL OF DISPUTE RESOLUTION 235, 239-342 (The Ohio State University Moritz College of Law, 1993). Reprinted with permission.

Mnookin, Robert H., Scott Peppet, and Andrew S. Tulumello, BEYOND WINNING: NEGOTIATING TO CREATE VALUE IN DEALS AND DISPUTES 24-25, 27, 40, 42-43, 46-49, 75-76, 83-87, 90, Cambridge, Mass.: The Belknap Press of Harvard University Press. Copyright © 2000 by the President and Fellows of Harvard College. Reprinted by permission of the publisher.

Moffitt, Michael L., Contingent Agreements: Agreeing to Disagree About the Future, 87 MARQUETTE LAW REVIEW 691 (2004). Reprinted with permission from the publisher.

Moffitt, Michael L., Disputes as Opportunities to Create Value, in THE HANDBOOK OF DISPUTE RESOLUTION 173, 173-174 (Michael L. Moffitt and Robert C. Bordone eds., 2005). Reprinted with permission of the author.

Nadler, Janice, Rapport in Negotiation and Conflict Resolution, 87 MARQUETTE LAW REVIEW 875, 875-882 (2004). Reprinted by permission of the author.

Nelken, Melissa, Negotiation and Psychoanalysis: If I'd Wanted to Learn About Feelings, I Wouldn't Have Gone to Law School, 46 JOURNAL OF LEGAL EDUCATION 420, 426 (1996). Reprinted with permission from the publisher.

Noesner, Gary W., and Mike Webster, Crisis Intervention: Using Active Listening Skills in Negotiations, FBI LAW ENFORCEMENT BULLETIN, Aug. 1997, at 13-19. Reprinted with permission from the publisher.

NPR, Morning Edition, PROFILE: SUCCESS OF SOUTHWEST AIRLINES (Dec. 4, 2002). Reprinted with permission.

Peppet, Scott R., Lawyers' Bargaining Ethics, Contract, and Collaboration: The End of the Legal Profession and the Beginning of Professional Pluralism, 90 IOWA LAW REVIEW 475, 523-524 (2005). Reprinted with permission.

Peppet, Scott R., Contract Formation in Imperfect Markets: Should We Use Mediators in Deals? 38 OHIO STATE JOURNAL OF DISPUTE RESOLUTION 283, 298-301 (The Ohio State University Moritz College of Law, 2004). Reprinted with permission from the publisher.

Peppet, Scott R., Six Principles for Using Negotiating Agents to Maximum Advantage, in THE HANDBOOK OF DISPUTE RESOLUTION 194-199 (Michael L. Moffitt and Robert C. Bordone eds., 2005). Reprinted with permission of John Wiley & Sons, Inc.

Pruitt, Dean, Achieving Integrative Agreements, in NEGOTIATION IN ORGANIZA-TIONS 36-41 (Max Bazerman and Roy Lewicki eds., 1983). Reprinted with permission of Sage Publications, Inc.

Putnam, Linda L., Challenging the Assumptions of Traditional Approaches to Negotiation, 10 NEGOTIATION JOURNAL 337, 338-340, 341, 342-344 (1994). Reprinted with permission from the publisher.

Putnam, Robert D., Diplomacy and Domestic Politics: The Logic of Two-Level Games, in DOUBLE-EDGED DIPLOMACY: INTERNATIONAL BARGAINING AND DOMES-TIC POLITICS 436-442, 459-460 (Peter B. Evans, Harold K. Jacobson, and Robert D. Putnam eds., University of California Press, 1993). Reprinted with permission from the University of California Press.

Raiffa, Howard, THE ART AND SCIENCE OF NEGOTIATION: HOW TO RESOLVE CONFLICTS AND GET THE BEST OUT OF BARGAINING 33-34, Cambridge, Mass.: The Belknap Press of Harvard University Press. Copyright © 1982 by the President and Fellows of Harvard College. Reprinted by permission of the publisher.

Reilly, Peter, Teaching Law Students How to Feel: Using Negotiations Training to Increase Emotional Intelligence, 21 NEGOTIATION JOURNAL 301, 303-304, 308-310, 311 (2005). Reprinted with permission from the publisher.

Riskin, Leonard L., Mediator Orientations, Strategies and Techniques, 12 ALTERNATIVES TO THE HIGH COST OF LITIGATION 111, 111-114 (1994). Reprinted with permission of John Wiley & Sons, Inc.

Rose, Carol, Bargaining and Gender, 18 HARVARD JOURNAL OF LAW & PUBLIC POLICY 547, 549-552, 555-557 (1995). Reprinted with permission from the publisher.

Ross, Lee, Reactive Devaluation in Negotiation and Conflict Resolution, in BARRIERS TO CONFLICT RESOLUTION 28-29, 33-35 (Kenneth Arrow et al. eds., 1995). Copyright © 1995 by The Stanford Center on Conflict and Negotiation. Used by permission of W.W. Norton & Company, Inc.

Ross, Rick, The Ladder of Inference, in THE FIFTH DISCIPLINE FIELDBOOK 242-246 (Peter M. Senge et al. eds., 1994). Reprinted with permission from the publisher.

Rubin, Jeffrey Z., and Frank E.A. Sander, Culture, Negotiation, and the Eye of the Beholder, 7 NEGOTIATION JOURNAL 249, 251-253 (1991). Reprinted with permission from the publisher.

Rubin, Jeffrey Z., and Frank E.A. Sander, When Should We Use Agents? Direct vs. Representative Negotiation, 4 NEGOTIATION JOURNAL 395, 396-398 (Program on Negotiation at Harvard Law School and Blackwell Publishing, 1988). Reprinted with permission.

Salacuse, Jeswald W., Ten Ways That Culture Affects Negotiating Style: Some Survey Results, 14 NEGOTIATION JOURNAL 221, 223, 225-238 (1998). Reprinted with permission from the publisher.

Sander, Frank E.A., and Jeffrey Rubin, The Janus Quality of Negotiation: Dealmaking and Dispute Settlement, 4 NEGOTIATION JOURNAL 109, 109-110, 112 (2001). Reprinted with permission.

Scardilli, Frank J., excerpts from *Sisters of the Precious Blood v. Bristol-Myers Co.*: A Shareholder-Management Dispute, in DISPUTE RESOLUTION AND LAWYERS 362-367 (Leonard Riskin and James Westbrook eds. 2d ed. West, 1997). Copyright © 1997 by Thomson West. Reprinted with permission of Thomson West.

Schelling, Thomas C., Reprinted by permission of the publisher from THE STRATEGY OF CONFLICT 21-23, Cambridge, Mass.: Harvard University Press. Copyright © 1960, 1980 by the President and Fellows of Harvard College.

Schiltz, Patrick J., On Being a Happy, Healthy, and Ethical Member of an Unhappy, Unhealthy, and Unethical Profession, 52 VANDERBILT LAW REVIEW 871, 906-912, 915-918 (Vanderbilt University School of Law, 1999). Reprinted with permission.

Schneider, Andrea Kupfer, Aspirations in Negotiation, 87 MARQUETTE LAW REVIEW 675, 675-680 (2004). Reprinted with permission.

Schneider, Andrea Kupfer, Effective Responses to Offensive Comments, 10 NEGOTIATION JOURNAL 107, 108-110, 110-113 (1994). Reprinted with permission from the publisher.

Schneider, Andrea Kupfer, Shattering Negotiation Myths: Empirical Evidence on the Effectiveness of Negotiation Style, 7 HARVARD NEGOTIATION LAW REVIEW 143, 171-175, 181, 183-184 (Students of Harvard Law Review, 2002). Reprinted with permission.

Schneider, Andrea Kupfer, Getting Along: The Evolution of Dispute Resolution Regimes in the International Trade Organizations, 20 MICHIGAN JOURNAL OF INTERNATIONAL LAW 697, 712-725 (1999). Reprinted with permission from the author and publisher.

Sebenius, James K., Caveats for Cross-Border Negotiations, 18 NEGOTIATION JOURNAL 121, 122-128 (2002). Reprinted with permission from the publisher.

Sebenius, James K., Solving Teddy Roosevelt's Negotiation Problem, from SIX HABITS OF MERELY EFFECTIVE NEGOTIATORS (2001). Reprinted by permission of HARVARD BUSINESS REVIEW.

Sebenius, James K., Sequencing to Build Coalitions: With Whom Should I Talk First? in WISE CHOICES: DECISIONS, GAMES, AND NEGOTIATIONS 324-329, 332-333, 335, 337-338, 344-345 (Richard J. Zeckhauser, Ralph L. Keeney, and James K. Sebenius eds., 1996). Reprinted with permission from the publisher.

Senger, Jeffrey M., Decision Analysis in Negotiation, 87 MARQUETTE LAW REVIEW 723, 723-725 (2004). Reprinted with permission from the publisher.

Seul, Jeffrey R., Settling Significant Cases, 79 WASHINGTON LAW REVIEW 881, 887, 889 (2005). Reprinted with permission from the publisher.

Shapiro, Daniel L., Emotions in Negotiation: Peril or Promise? 87 MARQUETTE LAW REVIEW 737, 738-743, 745 (2004). Reprinted with permission from the publisher.

Shell, G. Richard, excerpts from "The Second Foundation: Your Goals and Expectations" and "Bargaining with the Devil Without Losing Your Soul," from BARGAINING FOR ADVANTAGE: NEGOTIATION STRATEGIES FOR REASONABLE PEOPLE 31-34, 208-209, 215-220, by Richard C. Shell. Copyright © 1999 by Richard C. Shell. Used by permission of Viking Penguin, a division of Penguin Group (USA), Inc.

Silbey, Susan S., and Sally E. Merry, Mediator Settlement Strategies, 8 LAW & POLICY QUARTERLY 7, 19-20 (1986). Reprinted with permission from the publisher.

Spinney, Laura, Why We Do What We Do, NEW SCIENTIST, Vol. 183, Issue 2458. Reprinted with permission from the publisher.

Stone, Douglas, Bruce Patton, and Sheila Heen, DIFFICULT CONVERSATIONS: HOW TO DISCUSS WHAT MATTERS MOST 163, 166-167, 169-170, 172-174, 178, 180-183, ch. 10 (Viking Penguin, 1999). Reprinted with permission.

Stone Soup, *http://spanky.triumf.ca/www/fractint/stone_soup.html.*

Straus, David A., Managing Meetings to Build Consensus, in THE CONSENSUS BUILDING HANDBOOK 287-289, 302-304, 310-311, 313-314, 321-322 (Lawrence Susskind, Sarah McKearnan, and Jennifer Thomas-Larmer eds., 1999). Reprinted with permission from Sage Publications, Inc.

Stuntz, William J., Plea Bargaining and Criminal Law's Disappearing Shadow, 117 HARVARD LAW REVIEW 2548, 2548-2550 (2004). Reprinted with permission from the publisher.

Sunstein, Cass R., Deliberative Trouble? Why Groups Go to Extremes. Copyright © 2000 by Yale Law Journal. Reprinted by permission of The Yale Law Journal Company and William S. Hein Company from THE YALE LAW JOURNAL, Vol. 110, 71-119.

Thomas, Kenneth, Conflict and Conflict Management, in HANDBOOK OF INDUSTRIAL AND ORGANIZATIONAL PSYCHOLOGY 889, 900-902 (Marvin D. Dunnette ed., 1976). Reprinted with permission.

Thompson, Leigh L., THE MIND AND HEART OF THE NEGOTIATOR 109, 126-130, 133, 158-159, 162, 164-167, 189-194, 198-203 (3d ed. 2005). Copyright © 2005. Reprinted by permission of Pearson Education, Inc., Upper Saddle River, NJ.

Thompson, Leigh L., Janice Nadler, and Peter H. Kim, Some Like It Hot: The Case for the Emotional Negotiator, in SHARED COGNITION IN ORGANIZATIONS: THE MANAGEMENT OF KNOWLEDGE 157 (Lawrence Erlbaum Associates Publishers, 1999). Reprinted with permission.

Tierney, John, What Women Want, N.Y. TIMES, May 24, 2005, at A25. Copyright © 2005 by The New York Times Co. Reprinted with permission.

Tinsley, Cathy et al., Tough Guys Finish Last: The Perils of a Distributive Reputation, 88 ORGANIZATION BEHAVIOR & HUMAN DECISION PROCESSES 621-642 (2001). Reprinted with permission from the publisher.

Ury, William, excerpts from GETTING PAST NO 143-146. Copyright © 1991 by William Ury. Used by permission of Bantam Books, a division of Random House, Inc.

Watson, Carol, Gender Versus Power as a Predictor of Negotiation Behavior and Outcomes, 10 NEGOTIATION JOURNAL 117 (1994). Reprinted with permission from the publisher.

Weinstein, Janet, and Linda Morton, Stuck in a Rut: The Role of Creative Thinking in Problem Solving and Legal Education, 9 CLINICAL LAW REVIEW 835 (2003). Reprinted by permission of the author.

Wetlaufer, Gerald B., The Ethics of Lying in Negotiations, 75 IOWA LAW REVIEW 1219, 1236-1239, 1241-1243, 1245, 1248, 1250-1251, 1254-1255, 1265, 1270-1271 (1990). Reprinted with permission from the publisher.

Wetlaufer, Gerald B., The Limits of Integrative Bargaining, 85 GEORGETOWN LAW JOURNAL 369, 372-391 (1996). Reprinted with permission from the publisher.

White, James J., Machiavelli and the Bar: Ethical Limitations on Lying in Negotiation, 1980 AMERICAN BAR FOUNDATION RESEARCH JOURNAL 926-928, 931-935.

Williams, Gerald, LEGAL NEGOTIATION AND SETTLEMENT 53, 70, 72-73, 77-81, 84 (West Publishing, 1983). Reprinted with permission from the publisher.

Williams, Gerald, Negotiation as a Healing Process, 1996 JOURNAL OF DISPUTE RESOLUTION 37-45, 50-56. Reprinted with permission of the author and the JOURNAL OF DISPUTE RESOLUTION, University of Missouri-Columbia, Center for the Study of Dispute Resolution, 206 Hulston Hall, Columbia, MO 65211.

Wisconsin Bar Assocation, 1959 Advice in Joseph Goldstein and Jay Katz, THE FAMILY AND THE LAW: PROBLEMS FOR DECISION IN THE FAMILY LAW PROCESS 87 (1965). Reprinted with permission.

Wu, Jianzhong, and Robert Axelrod, Noise Box: How to Cope with Noise in the Iterated Prisoner's Dilemma, 39 JOURNAL OF CONFLICT RESOLUTION 183 (1995). Reprinted with permission from Sage Publications, Inc.

Zartman, William, and Maureen R. Berman, THE PRACTICAL NEGOTIATOR 39-41 (Yale University Press, 1982). Reprinted by permission of the publisher.

Zartman, I. William, The Timing of Peace Initiatives: Hurting Stalemates and Ripe Moments, in CONTEMPORARY PEACEMAKING: CONFLICT, VIOLENCE AND PEACE PROCESSES 19-20, 24, 26 (John Darby and Roger MacGinty eds., 2003). Reprinted with permission from the publisher, Palgrave MacMillan.

NEGOTIATION

PART 1 | CONCEPTS AND MODELS OF NEGOTIATION

Chapter 1 Conflict Theory: Concepts of Conflict and Negotiation

A pessimist sees the difficulty in every opportunity; an optimist sees the opportunity in every difficulty.

— Winston Churchill

In the Chinese language, the character for conflict is two different symbols—one means danger and the other means opportunity.

— Anonymous

The skillful management of conflicts [is] among the highest of human skills.
— Stuart Hampshire, *Justice Is Conflict* 35 (2000)

People negotiate whenever they need someone else to help them accomplish their goals. Sometimes these negotiations are designed to create something new—a new relationship, partnership, entity, transaction—and other times negotiations occur because people are in conflict with each other and hope to resolve whatever dispute lies between them. In this book we offer you the latest materials on negotiating to resolve conflicts and disputes, on planning and negotiating for new transactions and entities, and on considering how negotiation could help you to create new solutions to law's and life's intractable problems.

We begin by introducing you to some basic concepts. The study of negotiation is now part of a larger field known as dispute resolution in law and conflict resolution in the social sciences. The field is concerned with studying and analyzing the human behaviors that enable people to work together to overcome differences, explore new solutions to problems, and seek joint gains from collaboration.

In conventional legal practice many people think of negotiation as necessarily competitive, with arguments about the meanings of law and doctrine, the significance of facts, and the allocation of scarce resources. In the course of reading this book we hope you will come to see that negotiations provide us with a rich opportunity to transform difficult conflicts and troublesome disputes into new relationships, creating value (in both monetary and nonmonetary forms) for all parties. We explore all models of negotiation—both more conventional conceptions and a large body of new work—in theory, practice, empirical study and evaluation, and ethics.

We want you to learn that negotiation is both an analytic "science" of considering what issues are at stake, who the parties are, and what solutions are legally and creatively possible, and a human "art" in the sense that actually doing negotiations involves talking with and doing things with other people. You need conceptual, behavioral, and affective competencies in order to become a good negotiator. We explore the necessary analytic frameworks, the skills you need to master negotiation, ethical issues implicating how you use your skills on behalf of and with others, and finally, some of the different contexts in which negotiation is used. Because legal negotiators are working with clients, as agents, we also provide some guidance about how you can negotiate for others by interviewing, advising, coaching, and otherwise counseling your clients about how they can achieve good outcomes with well-considered processes.

In this first chapter we introduce you to some of the foundational concepts of conflict theory (both constructive and competitive) and negotiation (problem solving for joint gain or individual gain maximization). We introduce you to different models of negotiation and some descriptions of the typical stages most negotiations go through. We hope you will see that there is no one "mind-set" or orientation to all negotiations. Each negotiation must be separately conceptualized:

1. What is at stake?
2. What are the parties trying to achieve?
3. What is the relationship of the parties to each other?
4. What legal constraints are the parties operating under?
5. What behaviors might most effectively be employed to accomplish the goals of the negotiation?
6. How does this single negotiation affect other people or other situations?
7. How can we know we have had a successful negotiation?

A. CONFLICT THEORY: THEORETICAL UNDERPINNINGS OF CONFLICT AND DISPUTE RESOLUTION

Although law school focuses on disputes or cases, the disputes that make it into casebooks represent the tip of the iceberg of all the kinds of conflicts that people have. Lawyers are often called on not only to bring or defend lawsuits, but also to help prevent conflicts from arising or to deal with disputes other than in court. Thus, it is useful for lawyers to have a broad understanding of the types of conflicts that may exist. Scholars in a wide variety of the social sciences have attempted to define and develop taxonomies of different kinds of conflicts so as to better understand the different possible treatments or interventions available in conflict settings. At the same time, it is important to realize that not all conflict is bad or ought to be avoided. Social psychologists and sociologists such as Morton Deutsch, Georg Simmel, and Lewis Coser remind us to think about conflicts that are constructive as well as destructive. Carrie Menkel-Meadow briefly explores these multiple aspects of conflict.

 Carrie Menkel-Meadow, **CONFLICT THEORY**

in Encyclopedia of Community: From the Village to the Virtual World
323-326 (Karen Christensen & David Levinson eds., 2003)

There are many reasons for conflicts to develop, at both the individual and at the group level. Some conflicts are based on belief systems or principles, some are based on personality differences, and others on conflicts about material goods or personal or group status or reputation. Because there are so many different reasons conflicts develop and because much conflict is dangerous and unproductive, the theory of conflict attempts to understand the different sources of conflict, the dynamics of how conflict develops, escalates or declines and how conflict can be managed, reduced or resolved.

At the same time, it must be recognized that conflict can have social utility as well. Many important changes in human society, many for the betterment of human life, have come from hard-fought conflicts that resulted in the change of human institutions, relationships or ideas. The United States Civil War, for example, was a bloody and painful war in which over a million Americans died, but this war eliminated slavery in the United States and ushered in a long period of change in race relations in the United States (which is not yet over and still marked by many different kinds of conflicts, such as whether there should be reparations paid to the descendants of slaves or whether there should be affirmative action in education and employment to compensate for past wrongs of the society). Even small interpersonal conflicts (like between a husband and wife or parent and child) can lead to important changes, not only in relationships between the people in conflict, but in larger social movements, such as the women's rights or feminist movement and the children's rights movement. Conflicts with outsiders often clarify and reinforce commitments and norms of one's own group. And internal conflict within the individual can lead to changed views and intellectual and emotional growth.

Conflict theory tries to explain the types of conflicts that exist and whether they are productive or destructive and then goes on to attempt to explain the ways in which conflict proceeds or is structured (both by internal and external forces) and how it can be managed or resolved.

A conflict can be experienced as a simple disagreement, a feeling of discomfort or opposition, and a perception of difference from others, or a competition or incompatibility with others. Conflicts, then, can be perceptual, emotional or behavioral. When a conflict is actually acted on it becomes a dispute with someone or a group of others. In order for a conflict to fully develop into a dispute we have to experience some sense of wrong to ourselves, someone else to "blame" for that wrong and some way to take action against those we think caused our difficulty—what one set of scholars have called, "naming, blaming and claiming."[*] How the conflict turns into a dispute and how it is labeled ("framing") then may affect how it progresses and how it may either escalate and get worse, leading in extreme cases to war, or how it can be handled, managed or resolved ("reclaiming").

TYPES OF CONFLICTS

Conflict can exist on many different levels, including the intrapersonal, interpersonal, intragroup, intergroup, and international. Conflicts can exist about different subject

---

[*] William L.F. Felstiner, Richard Abel & Austin Sarat, The Emergence and Transformation of Disputes: Naming, Blaming and Claiming . . . , 15 L. & Socy. Rev. 631-654 (1980-1981).

matters—ideational or beliefs, values, materiel and resources, emotions, roles and responsibilities. Conflicts vary in terms of the social contexts in which they are located (two old friends, family members, neighbors, strangers, consumers and merchants, distant nation-states) and in the time span in which they are located ("one-off" or "one-shot" encounters and conflicts, long-standing or "embedded" conflicts, temporary or "repeated" conflicts in ongoing relationships like families and employment settings). Conflicts vary, even within the same social environment or subject matter by how the disputants treat the conflict, in the strategies, tactics and behaviors they employ (avoidance, self-help, peaceful negotiation, argument, escalation, physical violence, peace seeking, mediation or settlement) and how the strategies chosen interact with each other. And conflicts are often classified by how they affect the parties in the conflict (the consequences of the conflict) and those outside of the conflict (the "externalities" of the conflict, like children in a marital argument or divorce and neighbors of warring states who accept refugees).

In an effort to describe and diagnose conflicts so that we can understand and manage them better, social theorist and psychologist Morton Deutsch[*] has developed a useful typology of conflicts which contrasts "objective conditions" with "perceived" concerns of the parties:

Veridical Conflict—"true" conflict with matched perceptions and realities, such as when two or more parties want to use the same scarce resource for different purposes (a piece of land, a room in a house, a finite number of dollars, water).

Contingent Conflict—perceptions here do not match objective reality, such that a change in resources or perceptions of the conflict could readily resolve it. If more land, water or dollars were available or could be created, for example, multiple or shared uses might be possible. Another room or space could be built or found somewhere else. Such conflicts are "resolvable" if the parties can change their perceptions or cognitions or use creativity to expand resources or seek resolution from outside their "limited resources" frame of thinking.

Displaced Conflict—here parties in conflict have manifest or express conflicts about one thing when they are really arguing or caring about something different—the underlying conflict. Parents and children may argue about the use of a car, but the "real" conflict is about separation, responsibility and growing up. Countries will have disputes about borders and land when the "real" dispute is about power, sovereignty, control and economic well-being or identity.

Misattributed Conflict—parties here have conflicts with the wrong "others" or about the wrong issues. Siblings might fight with each other when they are really angry at the control of their parents. Disempowered groups might fight with each other (former colonized groups, racial minorities) rather than take on the powerful party that has dominated both groups. Individuals or groups may feel they are being

[*] The Resolution of Conflict: Constructive and Destructive Processes 12 (1973).

treated differently (and less well) when the real issue might be unavailable resources for all.

Latent Conflict — this is conflict that may be just beneath the surface but is not yet expressed, but perhaps should be. In relationships people may not want to start a fight so they will suppress things that make them angry, or an employee may be afraid to express dissatisfaction with a working condition or assignment. If the "latent" conflict is not expressed, things may actually get worse if the parties are not honest and cannot work out their differences.

False Conflict — parties may create conflicts or disputes where there is no objective reason for them, especially if there are generally bad relations between the parties or if someone prefers "conflictual" states of unrest or activity to relative peace. In situations of opposition (employer-employee, parent-child, academic or sports competition) disputes or conflicts may develop over minor or even major issues when there is no real reason to be in a dispute.

Conflicts have also been classified by various social scientists and conflict theorists by virtue of what is at stake in the conflict such as:

Resources (land, power, property, natural resources like water, oil, minerals, money);
Values or Beliefs (class, religious, nationality, political aspirations and codes that create systemic belief systems for groups or individual members);
Preferences or Interests (incompatible desires, wants or objectives of action);
Relationship (differences in desires or objectives about relationships);
Identity (concerns about recognition of and respect for group memberships).

The theory of such classifications is that if we can analyze different kinds of conflict, we can determine how they might unfold and whether a particular conflict is amenable to a positive outcome (whether harnessing the conflict to constructive solutions or processes) or whether it is likely to become destructive (for the parties or others affected by the parties). . . .

Conflicts often take somewhat predictable turns ranging from precipitating event, response or reaction, development of in-group-out-group loyalties and the development of both offensive and defensive strategies, followed by escalation, impasse or stalemate and then, motivation for resolution, settlement, and solution seeking (or, in highly competitive or violent conflicts, victory or "annihilation" of the other). But while many think of conflicts as necessarily competitive and antagonistic, there really are a wider range of behaviors that occur in most conflict situations, many of them dependent on the situation and social and political environment of the conflict, as well as the sophistication of the parties in using multiple strategies. Many of those who study conflict see a greater variety of possible conflict modes or strategies in handling conflict that can occur at individual, group, organizational, and even nation-state levels of actions. There are those who *compete* (or seek to maximize their own self-interest, even at the expense of others), those who *cooperate* (seeking to work with the other side(s) to find some middle or compromise grounds), those who *accommodate* (who may simply give in to the other party), those who *avoid* (by exiting or absenting themselves from the conflict) and those who *collaborate* (by seeking to work for joint and mutual gains for all parties, without unnecessary harm to others or needless compromise or giving in).*

What makes conflict processes so complex are the strategic interactions that occur when more than one party must interact to start, maintain, interrupt or resolve the conflict. These different conflict management strategies interact with each other and can produce reactive and unproductive responses, such as when competing leads to more competing and escalation of competitive behavior causes more violence, less information sharing and an inability to seek mutual gain possibilities. This "mirroring" effect, when each party merely returns the behavior that is offered to it, often leads to stalemates or the impossibility of achieving some resolution because the parties cannot even see or hear beyond the one strategy they have chosen.

Thus, much recent empirical work in conflict processes has been to study the conditions under which parties in conflict can alter their behavioral or strategy choices and open themselves up to new ways of communicating or testing the possibilities with other parties. Conflicts have been studied at the level of community relations, ethnic-racial conflicts, economic and resource competition, environmental disputes, lawsuits (both individual and class actions) and international conflicts. Parties in conflict are now asked to explore their underlying interests (apart from their conflict-producing "positions"), to consider the needs and interests of other parties ("role-reversals" and other communication technologies) and to develop strategies of collaborative and creative problem solving (by expanding and creating resources and alternatives, by trading non-mutually exclusive preferences or goods, by using contingent or "trial" agreements, rather than permanent solutions, by developing processes and rules for respectful co-existence, such as in Truth and Reconciliation Commissions in politically divided nations).

Both modern research and recent history have demonstrated the importance of third party interveners (mediators, conciliators, fact-finders and facilitators) who can effectively manage processes for productively structuring conflict resolution processes. These third party efforts have been effective at interpersonal (divorce and family), organizational (labor-management), and international (Northern Ireland, Mideast) levels of conflict in developing both interim "cease-fires" and more permanent resolutions or agreements to end conflicts and to attempt to resolve larger and underlying problems and conflicts.

Notes and Questions

1.1 Look through a case reporter or one of your casebooks, or do a random search on a computer service, and choose a reported case or cases. What dispute brought the parties to litigation? What underlying conflicts existed between

---

*Kenneth Thomas, Conflict and Conflict Management, in Handbook of Industrial Organizational Psychology (Marvin V. Dunnette ed., 1976).

the parties or between other people involved in or affected by the dispute? Where do these conflicts fit in the list provided by Menkel-Meadow?

1.2 Read a newspaper or magazine and find a conflict that is reported. How might the disputants (or possibly attorneys) have avoided such a conflict in advance? Do you think that the conflict you identified has positive or negative aspects, or both? What are they?

Conflicts will always exist. While we may prevent and avoid some, clearly we will never succeed in eliminating all of them. The remainder of this section examines how to deal with conflicts that already exist.

In focusing on conflict, it is critically important to examine what it means to "win" in a conflict. While many people assume that someone must lose when another person wins, the following readings show that this either-or mentality is often fallacious. In the first excerpt that follows, Thomas Schelling, a Nobel Prize-winning Harvard economist, examines the nature of conflict from a game theoretic perspective. He explains that while a person who approaches conflict strategically always tries to "win" in the sense of doing as well as possible for herself, that does not mean that other disputants need to lose.

The next excerpt is taken from the work of Mary Parker Follett, an important early theorist (working in the first decades of the last century) in the field of conflict resolution. In many ways Follett is the "mother" of much of what you will learn in this book. A political scientist by training and an early social worker by practice, she worked in labor-management relations, administrative science, and business management. She urges that conflict can lead to a creative process that allows constructive solutions to come from the friction created by conflict. For more background on Follett, see Joan C. Tonn, Mary P. Follett: Creating Democracy, Transforming Management (2003).

Yet the win-lose attitude has permeated both our culture in general and our concept of the legal system in particular. Popular writer and professor of linguistics Deborah Tannen critiques the adversarial mind-set of our society, arguing that it limits the possibilities of better alternatives and also makes for an uncomfortable civil society. Finally, Carrie Menkel-Meadow outlines some of the problems that arise when the legal system is envisioned in purely binary win-lose terms.

 Thomas C. Schelling, **THE STRATEGY OF CONFLICT**

3-5 (1960, 1980)

Among diverse theories of conflict — corresponding to the diverse meanings of the word "conflict" — a main dividing line is between those [who] treat conflict as a pathological state and seek its causes and treatment, and those [who] take conflict for granted and study the behavior associated with it. Among the latter there is a further division between those [who] examine the participants in a conflict in all their complexity — with regard to both "rational" and "irrational" behavior, conscious and unconscious, and to motivations as well as to calculations — and those [who] focus on the more rational, conscious artful kind of behavior. Crudely speaking, the latter treat conflict as a kind of contest, in which the participants are trying to "win." A study of conscious, intelligent, sophisticated conflict behavior — of successful behavior — is like a search for rules of "correct" behavior in a contest-winning sense. We can call this field of study the *strategy* of conflict. . . .

But, in taking conflict for granted, and working with an image of participants who try to "win," a strategy does not deny that there are common as well as conflicting interests among the participants. . . . Pure conflict, in which interests of two antagonists are completely opposed, is a special case. . . . For this reason, "winning" in a conflict does not have a strictly competitive meaning; it is not winning relative to one's adversary. It means gaining relative to one's own value system; and this may be done by bargaining, by mutual accommodation and by the avoidance of mutually damaging behavior.

 Mary Parker Follett, **CONSTRUCTIVE CONFLICT**

in Mary Parker Follett — Prophet of Management: A Celebration of Writings from the 1920s 67-69, 75, 77, 79, 82, 84-86 (Pauline Graham ed., 1995)

At the outset I should like to ask you to agree for the moment to think of conflict as neither good nor bad; to consider it without ethical pre-judgment; to think of it not as warfare, but as the appearance of difference, difference of opinions, of interests. For that is what conflict means — difference. We shall not consider merely the differences between employer and employee, but those between managers, between the directors at the Board meetings, or whatever difference appears.

As conflict — difference — is here in the world, as we cannot avoid it, we should, I think, use it. Instead of condemning it, we should set it to work for us. Why not? What does the mechanical engineer do with friction? Of course, his chief job is to eliminate friction, but it is true that he also capitalizes friction. The transmission of power by belts depends on friction between the belt and the pulley. . . . The music of the violin we get by friction. . . . We talk of the friction of the mind on mind as a good thing. So in business too, we have to know when to try to eliminate friction and when to try to capitalize it, when to see what work we can make it do. That is what I wish to consider here, whether we can set conflict to work and make it *do* something for us.

METHODS OF DEALING WITH CONFLICT

There are three main ways of dealing with conflict: domination, compromise and integration. Domination, obviously, is a victory of one side over the other. This is the easiest way of dealing with conflict, the easiest for the moment but not usually successful in the long run. . . .

The second way of dealing with conflict, that of compromise, we understand well, for it is the way we settle most of our controversies; each side gives up a little in order to have peace, or, to speak more accurately, in order that the activity which has been interrupted by the conflict can go on. Compromise is the basis of trade union tactics. In collective bargaining, the trade unionist asks for more than he expects to get, allows for what is going to be lopped off in the conference. Thus we often do not know what he really thinks he should have, and this ignorance is a great barrier to dealing with conflict fruitfully. . . .

But I certainly ought not to imply that compromise is peculiarly a trade union method. It is the accepted, the approved, way of ending controversy. Yet no one really wants to compromise, because that means a giving up of something. Is there any other method of ending conflict? There is a way now beginning to be recognized at least, and even occasionally followed: when two desires are *integrated*, that means that a solution has been found in which both desires have found a place, that neither side has to sacrifice anything. Let us take some very simple illustration. In the Harvard Library one day, in one of the smaller rooms, someone wanted the window open, I wanted it shut. We opened the window in the next room, where no one was sitting. This was not a compromise because there was no curtailing of desire; we both got what we really wanted. For I did not want a closed room, I simply did not want the north wind to blow directly on me; likewise the other occupant did not want that particular window open, he merely wanted more air in the room. . . .

Let us take another illustration. A Dairymen's Co-operative League almost went to pieces last year on the question of precedence in unloading cans at a creamery platform. The men who came down the hill (the creamery was on a downgrade) thought they should have precedence; the men who came up the hill thought they should unload first. The thinking of both sides in the controversy was thus confined within the walls of these two possibilities, and this prevented their even trying to find a way of settling the dispute which would avoid these alternatives. The solution was obviously to change the position of the platforms so that both up-hillers and down-hillers could unload at the same time. But this solution was not found until they had asked the advice of a more or less professional integrator. When, however, it was pointed out to them, they were quite ready to accept it. Integration involves invention, and the clever thing is to recognize this and not to let one's thinking stay within the boundaries of two alternatives which are mutually exclusive. . . .

(Some people tell me that they like what I have written on integration, but say that I am talking of what ought to be instead of what is. But indeed I am not; I am talking neither of what is, to any great extent, nor of what ought to be merely, but of what perhaps may be. This we can discover only by experiment. That is all I am urging, that we try experiments in methods of resolving differences; differences on the Board of Directors, with fellow managers or heads of departments, with employees, or in other relations. If we do this, we may take a different attitude toward conflict.)

The key-word of psychology today is desire. If we wish to speak of conflict in the language of contemporary psychology, we might call it a moment in the interacting of desires. Thus we take from it any connotation of good or bad. Thus we shall not be afraid of conflict, but shall recognize that there is a destructive way of dealing with such moments and a constructive way. Conflict as the moment of the appearing and focusing of difference may be a sign of health, a prophecy of progress. If the Dairymen's League had not fought over the question of precedence, the improved method of unloading would not have been thought of. The conflict in this case was constructive. And this was because, instead of compromising, they sought a way of integrating. Compromise does not create, it deals with what already exists; integration creates something new, in this case a different way of unloading. And because this not only settled the controversy but was actually better technique, saved time for both the farmers and the creamery, I call this: setting friction to work, making it *do* something. . . .

One advantage of integration over compromise I have not yet mentioned. If we get only compromise, the conflict will come up again and again in some other form, for in compromise we give up part of our desire, and because we shall not be content to rest there, sometime we shall try to get the whole of our desire. . . .

[T]he revaluing of interests on both sides may lead the interests to fit into each other, so that all find some place in the final solution. . . . If the first step is to uncover the real conflict, the next is to take the demands of both sides and break them up into their constituent parts. . . . On the other hand, one often has to do just the opposite; find the whole demand, the real demand, which is being obscured by miscellaneous minor claims or by ineffective presentation. . . .

Finally, let us consider the chief *obstacles to integration*. It requires a high order of intelligence, keen perception and discrimination, more than that, a brilliant *inventiveness*. . . . Another obstacle to integration is that our way of life has habituated many of us to enjoy domination. Integration seems a tamer affair, it leaves no "thrills" of conquest. . . . Finally, perhaps the greatest of all obstacles to integration is our lack of training for it. In our college debates we try always to beat the other side. . . .

I should like to emphasize our responsibility for integration. . . . One test of business administration should be: is the organization such that both employers and employees, or co-managers, co-directors, are stimulated to a reciprocal activity which will give more than mere adjustment, more than in equilibrium? Our outlook is narrowed, our activity restricted, our chances of business success largely diminished when our thinking is constrained within the limits of what has been called an "either-or" situation. We should never allow ourselves to be bullied by an "either-or." There is always the possibility of something better than either of two given alternatives.

 ### *Deborah Tannen*, THE ARGUMENT CULTURE: MOVING FROM DEBATE TO DIALOGUE

3-4, 8, 10 (1998)

The argument culture urges us to approach the world — and the people in it — in an adversarial frame of mind. It rests on the assumption that opposition is the best way to get anything done: The best way to discuss an idea is to set up a debate; the best way to cover news is to find spokespeople who express the most extreme, polarized views and present them as "both sides"; the best way to settle disputes is litigation that pits one party against the other; the best way to begin an essay is to attack someone and the best way to show you're really thinking is to criticize. . . .

In a word the type of opposition I am questioning is what I call "agonism." I use this term, which derives from the Greek word for "contest," *agonia*, to mean an automatic war-like stance — not the literal fighting against an attacker or the unavoidable opposition that arises organically in response to conflicting ideas or actions. An agonistic response, to me, is a kind of programmed contentiousness — a prepatterned, unthinking use of fighting to accomplish goals that do not necessarily require it. . . .

Our determination to pursue truth by setting up a fight between two sides leads us to believe that every issue has two sides — no more, no less: If both sides are given a forum to confront each other, all the relevant information will emerge and the best case will be made for each side. But opposition does not lead to truth when an issue is not composed of two opposing sides but is a crystal of many sides. Often the truth is in the complex middle, not the oversimplified extremes.

 Carrie Menkel-Meadow, **THE TROUBLE WITH THE ADVERSARY SYSTEM IN A POSTMODERN, MULTICULTURAL WORLD**

38 Wm. & Mary L. Rev. 5, 6-10 (1996)

Binary, oppositional presentations of facts in dispute are not the best way for us to learn the truth; polarized debate distorts the truth, leaves out important information, simplifies complexity and often obfuscates rather than clarifies. More significantly, some matters — mostly civil, but occasionally even criminal, cases — are not susceptible to a binary (i.e., right/wrong, win/lose) conclusion or solution. The inability to reach a binary resolution of these disputes may result because in some cases we cannot determine the facts with any degree of accuracy. In other cases the law may be conflicting, though legitimate, legal rights giving some entitlement to both, or all, parties. And, in yet another category of cases, human or emotional equities cannot be sharply divided.

Modern life presents us with complex problems, often requiring complex and multifaceted solutions. Courts, with what I have called their "limited remedial imaginations," may not be the best institutional settings for resolving some of the disputes that we continue to put before them.

Even if some form of the adversary system was defensible in particular settings for purposes of adjudication, the "adversary" model employed in the courtroom has bled inappropriately into and infected other aspects of lawyering, including negotiation carried on both in the "shadow of the court" and outside of it in transactional work. . . .

Furthermore, the complexities of both modern life and modern lawsuits have shown us that disputes often have more than two sides in the sense that legal disputes and transactions involve many more than two parties. Procedures and forms like interpleader, joinder, consolidation, and class actions have attempted to allow for more than just plaintiffs' and defendants' voices to be heard, all the while structuring the discourse so that parties must ultimately align themselves on one side of the adversarial line or the other. Multiparty, multiplex lawsuits or disputes may be distorted when only two sides are possible. Consider all of the multiparty and complex policy issues that courts contend with in environmental clean-up and siting, labor disputes in the public sector, consumer actions, antitrust actions, mass torts, school financing and desegregation and other civil rights issues, to name a few examples.

Finally, scholars have criticized modern adversarialism for the ways it teaches people to act toward each other.

Notes and Questions

1.3 For the next 24 hours, keep a list of all the conflicts, disputes, or disagreements you got (or could have gotten) involved in. What did you do? Argue, compromise, accommodate (give in), get your way, avoid, "integrate"? How? Why?

1.4 Notes and Questions 1.1 asked you to examine a series of reported cases and consider what underlying conflicts brought the parties to litigation. Now consider the following with respect to these cases:

    a. Who were the "real parties in interest," whether they were named in the reported case or not? Who else might be affected by a judicial resolution or settlement of the matter at issue?

    b. How were the issues framed? In terms of perceived wrongs and rights? Legal entitlements? Were there any instances of cases where not all the wrongs or rights existed on one side?

    c. Consider what solutions, other than those ordered by the court, might have resolved the conflict among all interested parties.

1.5 Is the legal system capable of encouraging "reciprocal activity," as Follett suggests should happen in business management, or is it only an either-or process? Is litigation different from transactional settings?

1.6 Consider a current issue of domestic or international policy. What are the sides of the issue? Are there more complicated issues at stake? How should such issues be decided? We discuss the issue of "institutional design" below, but for now think about whether a debate on the issue, whichever one you have chosen, presents the best way to get information, make a decision, or resolve a conflict in policy options.

1.7 Can you think of any other institutions or issues, besides those mentioned by Tannen and Menkel-Meadow, that are characterized by adversarial structures or relations? Are those structures necessary? What other possibilities are there?

B. NEGOTIATION THEORY

When most people are asked about conflict, their immediate reaction is a negative one. The concept of conflict and dealing with that conflict often raises the blood pressure, makes us look for the nearest exit, or want to hide under the bed. Few of us actually rejoice — Yea! There is a difference of opinion! And we all have faced the dreaded words, "We need to talk. . . ." The idea of conflict is bad enough, and now we need to talk about it. The irony, particularly for lawyers, is that we would hardly be needed if there were not conflict — conflict about a past situation or about a potential future situation. Conflict is our bread and butter. Clients come to us in order to solve these conflicts, to deal with these problems, to negotiate a resolution.

If you asked people to draw a picture of a negotiation, they likely would draw a table with two or more people sitting on opposite sides. We visualize a negotiation as something akin to arm wrestling. This chapter tries to expand that picture of negotiation. While it is true that many negotiations occur across large tables in anonymous conference rooms, many others occur in the hallways, on the phone, in the car, and at other everyday locations. We all learn more about the process of negotiation when we view it more broadly. Roger Fisher, coauthor of the bestselling book *Getting to YES*, and a well-known negotiation professor, says that a negotiation occurs every time you are trying to influence someone to do something you want.

1. Concepts of Conflict and Negotiation

The next excerpt helps outline some of the different ways we can view conflict. As you read other excerpts on conflict and negotiation, think about where the writer is coming from and how that influences her views on the uses of negotiation.

Carrie Menkel-Meadow, ROOTS AND INSPIRATIONS: A BRIEF HISTORY OF THE FOUNDATIONS OF DISPUTE RESOLUTION

in The Handbook of Dispute Resolution 13, 14-15 (Michael L. Moffitt & Robert C. Bordone eds., 2005)

EARLY HISTORY: DESCRIPTIONS OF THE FIELD AND FOUNDATIONAL THEORIES

The social sciences now include a field called "conflict resolution," whereas modern legal studies more often describe the field as "dispute resolution." The different terms signal an important distinction between the two approaches.

Nineteenth-century founders of the field of sociology, including Emile Durkheim, Georg Simmel, and Karl Marx, looked at widespread social and political conflicts and sought to understand their origins, trajectories, and impacts on the larger society. Early on, tensions developed about whether conflict was beneficial for social change, whether it should be managed for social stability, or whether it was simply a normal part of human existence. These intellectual tensions remain with us today. Seen as a social phenomenon, conflict exists at many different levels—individual, familial, group, or nation-state. Indeed, as social psychologists have noted, conflict can also be intrapersonal or intrapsychic. Within a single human being one can find conflicts linked to diverging perceptions, values, attitudes, or behavioral choices.

In law and legal studies, the unit of analysis has been the dispute, or "case"—an activated conflict in which someone has experienced a wrong and "named it, blamed someone or [some] entity and claimed against them" in a formal way. This activation process often plays out in a binary or polarized format of plaintiff and defendant, or complainant and respondent. Seeing a dispute as a separate, self-contained unit of social interaction, requiring some form of formal or legal intervention, is different from seeing a dispute as located in a more socially enmeshed world of multiple parties, interconnected issues, and social and relational history.

Thus the very nomenclature or definition of the relevant unit of analysis tells us something about how a conflict or dispute might be handled, treated, or resolved. For the most part, social scientists have focused on the embeddedness of disputes in larger fields or patterns of conflict and social relations, while lawyers and other dispute resolution professionals have focused on the concrete nature of particular disputes, suggesting use of particular techniques for dispute settlement or other resolution.

Socio-legal scholars who are both lawyers and anthropologists have bridged these disciplines by studying disputes in a broader social context, looking at how cases are socially constructed, labeled, and enacted. Scholars and practitioners of the school of "legal realism" were similarly attracted to looking at how disputes were formed and dealt with in particular settings, and so created a "jurisprudence of dispute resolution" and its institutions.

Together, the insights of these different approaches to studying conflict resolution have given us some basic propositions about the field, what some call a canon of dispute resolution. Within these approaches, some have aimed to provide a taxonomy for analyzing conflict. Others have sought to link description and prescription. Some have focused on the "constructive" and "destructive" aspects of conflicts. Still others have aimed to describe the institutionalized processes best suited to deal with particular kinds of disputes.

The next excerpts outline different views of negotiation. First, Jonathan Cohen talks about the different ways we view negotiation and the people with whom we negotiate. Next, Gerald Williams argues in a similar vein to Mary Parker Follett that the negotiation process used to resolve conflict is an opportunity. Finally, Linda Putnam challenges some of the conventional thinking about negotiation as a rational process.

Jonathan R. Cohen, ADVERSARIES? PARTNERS? HOW ABOUT COUNTERPARTS? ON METAPHORS IN THE PRACTICE AND TEACHING OF NEGOTIATION AND DISPUTE RESOLUTION

20 Conflict Resol. Q. 433-436, 438-439 (2003)

A student of negotiation—or of its cousin, the assisted negotiation called mediation—will soon find herself awash in a sea of metaphors. Has she entered the animal kingdom, a dog-eat-dog world where hawks prey on doves and lions occasionally lie down with lambs? Or the kitchen, with pies to be baked and their slices cut, and oranges to be separated peel from fruit? Is she attending a music concert, where discord will be replaced by harmony, or embarking on a journey replete with speed bumps, road blocks, and detours, the negotiation "bicycle" at risk of falling if sufficient momentum is not maintained? Perhaps she is a carpenter carrying a toolbox of options, an engineer building bridges to span differences, or an architect designing a multidoor courthouse. . . .

If she is like most students, she will soon arrive at the competitive metaphors that dominate the field of negotiation, if not our culture. Negotiation is a game of poker in which players must hold the cards close to the chest. Negotiation is a sport like football, where a "level playing field" is required; mediators are thus "umpires" or "referees." Or like basketball, where "timeouts" are sometimes taken, or like baseball where parties sometimes play "hardball." . . .

The student may then realize that there is more to negotiation than competition. Although the adversarial metaphors capture an important piece of negotiation, they do not capture the whole of it. Competition is part of negotiation, but so is cooperation. Negotiation involves both give and take. As Schelling wrote, "the richness of the subject arises from the fact that . . . there is mutual dependence as well as opposition. Pure conflict, in which the interests of two antagonists are completely opposed, is a special case[.] . . . Concepts like . . . negotiation are concerned with the common interest and mutual dependence that can exist between participants in a conflict."

The student may now switch to a second set of metaphors within our field, those of cooperation. Whether through stumble or leap, she may well arrive at the metaphor of dance. The other party in the negotiation is not one's adversary, but one's *partner*. The dance occurs in steps and stages. As with empathy and assertiveness, skill in following one's partner is as important as skill in leading. It is essential to "put yourself in [the other side's] shoes," but hopefully without stepping on their toes. What is needed is to be shoulder to shoulder, side by side. Movement, balance, and trust are critical. Before an impasse is reached, perhaps a "trip to the balcony" can reveal new steps to be taken. As to third-party neutrals, the mediator is no longer an umpire at a sports event, but a choreographer.

Yet using solely cooperative metaphors is also problematic. Recall that when the dance metaphor is invoked, it is usually not the waltz but the aggressive and spicy tango, as in, "It takes two to tango." Schelling's point was that *both* competition and cooperation are present in negotiation. Disclosing one's interests, preferences, and resources may help to "expand the pie" (value creation), but it can also result in one getting a sliver (value distribution). On the other hand, if one refuses to disclose any information one may end up with the lion's share of a minuscule pie, also a poor outcome. Thus, most negotiation involves a blend of competition and cooperation.

How, then, is one to proceed? What language should be used to describe negotiation? If the goal is descriptive accuracy, since most negotiation is neither pure competition nor pure cooperation, I suggest using language that reflects the inherent tensions between competition and cooperation in negotiation and other forms of dispute resolution. Consider two examples: (1) what to call the other party to the negotiation, and (2) what to call negotiation and related dispute resolution processes.

Parties to negotiations are often unsure of how to refer to one another. Those with largely competitive views of negotiation tend to label the other party as their "opponent" or "adversary." Those with largely cooperative views tend to label the other party their "partner." Yet what is needed is a word that captures the tension between these two roles. I suggest the word *counterpart*. As with competition, in negotiation the other party is against, or *counter* to, oneself. As with cooperation, the other party is in *partnership* with oneself. Negotiation involves an element of tension or paradox in one's relationship to the other party, and our language should reflect it. Using *counterpart* to describe such a mixed role has no less than biblical (though quite sexist) precedent. The second creation narrative in Genesis describes the creation of woman to be an "ezer c'negdo" to man. *Ezer* means "helper" and *c'negdo* means "against him." This term is sometimes well-translated as "counterpart." The language seems to suggest that being a good intimate partner involves both supportive and oppositional roles.

And what of negotiation and related dispute resolution processes? Should we not use labels that describe the inherent tension between competition and cooperation within them? Fortunately, history has already done this for us. "Negotiation" is derived from the Latin *neg* (not) and *otium* (leisure or ease). Hence, the word "negotiation" reflects the inherent tension — not leisure — within the activity. Other words in our field reflect similar tensions. Consider the terms "conflict" and "dispute." *Conflict* is derived from the Latin *com* (together) and *fligere* (to strike), meaning "to strike together." This too is a somewhat paradoxical pair, the positive association of unified togetherness juxtaposed with the negative association of violent physical striking. Similarly the more discursive *dispute* derives from the Latin *dis* (apart, two, twain, or separate) and *putare* (to reckon, consider, or think), reflecting the two opposing lines of argument present in a dispute. Consider too the positive and negative valences that attach to the word *compromise*. As Schelling observed, "Compromising *a* principle sounds wrong. Compromising *between* principles is all right." Here the tension lies not within the word's linguistic construction but in its opposed, bivalent connotations. . . .

Raising linguistic awareness can be helpful in addressing this pedagogical challenge. At the start of a negotiation course, competitive students tend to describe their negotiation counterparts as opponents, adversaries, or even enemies, and cooperative students tend to describe them as partners. I use this linguistic divide to prompt a discussion by asking students, "Why do you use the term *opponent* (or *partner*) to describe the other party to the negotiation? What does your selection (whether conscious or unconscious) of terms say about yourself?" Though it usually does not happen instantly, over time students often recognize the interwovenness of their approaches to negotiation and their linguistic framings, thereby developing richer understandings of negotiation. To borrow Riskin's term, "mindfulness" toward one's language can be a helpful path toward self-awareness. Further, attention to the metaphors implicit in others' language can give one insight into their thinking too. . . .

Here I have suggested that, as negotiation involves irreducible elements of competition and cooperation, at least for analytical purposes, it is best to use mixed language that reflects this tension. Most fundamentally, practitioners, both parties and neutrals, should ask themselves questions of linguistic awareness ("What metaphors are being used?") and linguistic change ("Should I attempt to shift the linguistic frame?").

Notes and Questions

1.8 Do you agree with Cohen that "raising linguistic awareness" is important? Why or why not?

1.9 What terms do you use to describe the other party in a negotiation?

 Gerald Williams, **NEGOTIATION AS A HEALING PROCESS**

1996 J. Disp. Resol. 1, 37-45, 50-56

To illustrate what is involved in a healing perspective on negotiation, let us assume a typical lawsuit in which both sides have hired lawyers to represent them, the plaintiff has filed a complaint, the defendant has filed an answer, discovery is proceeding apace, and a trial date has been set. By definition, the parties are now *in conflict*. Once they are fully engaged in the conflict, they confront a far more fateful and hazardous problem, *how to get out of that conflict*.

Once the case has been filed in court, we might say metaphorically that the legal system itself constitutes a kind of vessel or container which holds the two contestants in an uncomfortable relationship with each other until they have resolved their problem. This is a highly paradoxical situation. On the one hand, they see the legal system as the vehicle for obtaining their will over the other party. On the other hand, at the same time, the legal system constitutes a metaphorical vessel which holds the protagonist and antagonist together in the same vessel in a forced relationship with each other until they resolve their conflict or it is resolved for them. By the very act of engaging the legal system, they condemn themselves to be in the legal vessel with the person against whom they hold the hardest of feelings, and to staying together in the heat and discomfort of that vessel until their conflict is resolved. . . .

Once parties are in conflict, there are essentially only two ways out: negotiation or adjudication. Both are ritual processes. Both are intended to end the conflict and permit the parties to get on with their lives. Nevertheless, except for the relatively few cases which require a trial verdict, the most desirable outcome is for both to have a change of heart, to arrive not only at an acceptable compromise, but to also experience a genuine reconciliation. The fundamental principle is this: if both sides do not experience a change of heart, then one or both of them will continue to carry everything that was left unresolved into the indefinite future with little prospect for resolving it short of another conflict. This conclusion is supported by research showing that in many situations, conflicts are not resolved, but continue in an endless cycle until one party or the other is able to "exit," that is, to escape the situation by moving far enough away that the disputants no longer see each other. However, it should be noted that this exit does not really "resolve" the conflict because nothing has really changed in either of the parties. The best prediction is that both parties will soon find themselves in similar conflicts wherever they may end up. More troublesome still, there is research suggesting that even when plaintiffs have retained lawyers and obtained a mutually agreeable settlement (but not a genuine settlement or change of heart), they will continue to suffer from emotional and physical traumas growing out of the original problem.

These residual negative effects may include, for one or both parties, unresolved anger, fear, vengefulness, or feelings of helplessness, victimization, distrust, and alienation. On the part of the antagonist or victimizer, these traumas may evoke responses that vary from denial of responsibility and a pretense that the entire problem was caused by the other (or that the other wholly deserved the bad treatment they received), at one extreme, to feelings of guilt, remorse, and of missed opportunity to make restitution or to do equity.

If their individual situations warrant it, and if the process works well enough, the parties will experience a change of heart. On the other hand, if the situation does not warrant it, or if the negotiation process is not powerful enough, and as a consequence the parties fail to reach a mutually acceptable compromise agreement (much less a change of heart), the traditional fallback position is recourse to a much more formal and explicit ritual, that of a court trial. This is not to say that trial is unimportant, or that it should always be avoided. Rather, it is meant to emphasize that by choosing trial, the parties are giving up substantial benefits to themselves and society, benefits that have not traditionally been included in evaluating the value of negotiated outcomes. As Robert Baruch Bush has so insightfully pointed out, if the parties go to trial, they both give up the possibility of learning things that can only be obtained by submitting themselves to the painful process of working out an appropriate solution to a conflict, namely the possibility of learning more about themselves (becoming more self-aware), more about the other side (becoming more aware of the other), more about their own powers (the capacity for self-transformation by staying with the task), and more about their own ability "to transcend [their] narrow self interest, to realize and recognize — even if only fleetingly — some element of legitimacy in the other side's position, some element of common humanity with the other party."...

THE FIVE STEPS FOR RECOVERING FROM CONFLICT

To articulate more specifically the kinds of changes the negotiation ritual is intended to encourage in disputants, I would like to propose a preliminary five-step model of the stages clients must generally move through in order to shift from being *in* a state of conflict to being healed from the conflict. The stages are: *denial, acceptance, sacrifice, leaps of faith*, and *renewal*....

A. Denial

As a preliminary model of the process of recovering from conflict, the first stage is typically a condition of *denial*.... [T]here is in each of us "a deep-seated human desire *not* to be the one at fault, *not* to be the one who must change." This resistance to being the one at fault, to being the one who must change, is part of what makes conflict so painful and its resolution so difficult. Most conflicts are a story of two parties, both of whom contributed to the problem, and neither of whom wants to admit his or her role in it. In the literature on grieving we gain a broader sense of what is meant by the term *denial* and some of the risks it poses to the parties and others: "The person will strongly deny the reality of what has happened, or search for reasons why it has happened, and take revenge on themselves and others." . . .

From this perspective, we might even say that, in most instances, conflicts are meaningful; they have a purpose. Their purpose is to hold up a mirror so disputants may see themselves in a new light, an experience as painful as it is valuable.

Properly understood, then, conflicts serve as such a mirror. They expose the disputants' weaknesses; the areas in which they have been too much the victim, or too much the exploiter; their complexes, their unresolved angers, and their feelings of specialness and entitlement. Because it is so painful for disputants to see these parts of themselves exposed by their own involvement in the conflict, they need the protection and reinforcement, the containment and channeling, that the lawyer-client relationship provides, and they need the benefit of the full play of the negotiation process to help them gradually face what they see in the mirror and to come to terms with it.

This is why the negotiation ritual must be performed with such understanding and care. It is intended to help the disputants through an extremely painful and threatening process. Seen in this light, conflicts are opportunities to increase in self-knowledge and in an empathetic understanding of the world around us. But it is extremely difficult for disputants to learn from this painful experience without the assistance of experienced, knowledgeable, ritual leaders. In our secular society, it seems as though law is one of the few authentic mediating structures left.

B. Acceptance

The next step is *acceptance*. It may take time, but at some point the parties need to move beyond denial and to *accept the possibility that they themselves are part of the problem*. They do not yet need to *do* anything about it, just to accept the possibility that the problem does not begin and end with the other side, that they themselves may have some complicity in the problem. In some cases, however, it may be that one side actually is wholly innocent and the other wholly to blame for the problem. But even when parties are wholly innocent, they still need to accept the possibility there is *something they could do now to move the situation in the direction of an appropriate resolution*. Again, they don't need to actually take action, they simply need to register a change in attitude that opens them to the possibility of movement in the direction of an appropriate solution.

C. Sacrifice

Assuming the parties have accepted the possibility they are part of the problem, or the possibility there is something they could do now to move in the direction of a resolution, the next step is to consider what they might be willing to do about it. In its starkest form, the principle is that, for the conflict to be resolved, the parties must be willing to make a sacrifice. From a judge's point of view, the minimum sacrifice required for a valid settlement agreement is a compromise by each side, meaning that both parties must make some concession, must move from their original position. But as a general matter, mere concessions or compromises do not require a change of heart. It has been observed that people usually are not willing to make a sacrifice until they have been brought to a more humble attitude. . . .

Assuming that sacrifices need to be made, what should they be? This is an extremely delicate question. We know, for example, that some people have a history of being *too compliant*, of giving away too much, whether motivated by a need for affection and approval, by fear of reprisals, or for some other reason. For those who are too compliant, the sacrifice called for would probably *not* be to make more concessions to their antagonist, but rather to forebear from giving, to reverse themselves, to give up the part of themselves that always wants to please others. For other people, the problem may be just the opposite. They may be exploiters who are too good at looking out for themselves at others' expense. For them, the sacrifice may be to recognize their exploitive patterns and become more conscious of the interests and needs of other people. There are many other possibilities. The answer will depend on the personalities involved and the particularities of their situations. In some situations, parties may need to sacrifice — to let go of — such things as a desire for a total victory, or an impulse for revenge, a mistaken belief that they themselves are faultless and the other side totally to blame, their pride, their unwillingness to acknowledge or appreciate another's point of view, or their unwillingness to forgive another for his or her mistake. In other situations, parties may need to give up the belief that they can get away with exploiting others, their belief that they are better or more deserving than others, or their excessive opinions of their own abilities, worth, privileged status, etc. There may be situations in which parties need to give up their hope of obtaining a windfall or other unearned benefit, or give up their envy or spite or jealousy with respect to possessions, luck, and social position. Before proceeding to the fourth step, there is one final consideration. Is it mandatory that parties make a sacrifice? The answer is a firm "no." There can be no requirement that the client have a change of heart. It is fundamental that, as lawyers, we implicitly and explicitly declare to our clients that they can stay just the way they are, and so long as they do not expect us to do that which is illegal or unethical, we will stand by them. Our willingness to represent our clients should not depend upon their willingness to change, much less to move in directions we think right. As Shaffer and Elkins remind us, "[t]he client has to be free to be wrong." The negotiation process, then, is not intended for lawyers to impose our values upon our clients, but for us to help contain and channel our clients' energies in appropriate ways until they have had enough time to see their own situations more clearly and to discover for themselves what steps they may be willing to make.

D.   Leap of Faith

The fourth stage refers to action or movement, what might be called the *leap of faith*. . . .

A leap of faith is an expressed willingness to make a sacrifice in the hope of moving a conflict toward a meaningful and appropriate resolution. One of the most powerful is an apology sincerely given. The wrongdoer says to the aggrieved person, "I am truly sorry for the trouble I have caused you." In our rights-oriented society, we are quick to justify our own harmful acts, and we are slow to recognize how healing it can be to the injured person for us to acknowledge our fault, to offer an appropriate apology, and, if the situation warrants, to offer to make reparation. Similarly, we usually think the lawyers' role, when representing defendants, is to protect their clients from having to admit wrongdoing or having to make legal compensation for the harms they cause. But as Macaulay and Walster remind us, just as there are negative psychological consequences to people who are harmed, there are also psychological consequences to those who do the harming, whether purposefully or not. There may be an innate human need to be fair, to make reparation for the harms we cause. This fundamental human need — the need to be equitable — has been largely overlooked in the legal literature. [For more on this topic, see Chapter 2.]

Other leaps of faith are to admit one's part in causing the conflict or in making the problem more difficult to resolve. . . . Leaps of faith are inherently risky. This is what gives them their healing power. They open people to danger, exploitation, and ridicule. . . . When one side to a conflict takes a step downward, in the direction of a less demanding or more understanding attitude, the other side has a choice: they may choose to reciprocate with a downward movement of their own, or they may use it as a pretext for stepping up their own demands. Because lawyers have seen the latter response many times before, they are understandably wary about encouraging clients to take steps downward, and often try to shield their clients from this essential part of the healing process. This is good and bad. It is good that lawyers help clients avoid making concessions when those concessions will be used against them. It is bad because, unless both sides are willing to take some risks, there is no chance for mutual agreement and reconciliation. So the question is not *whether* to permit or encourage the client to make leaps of faith, but *when* and *under what circumstances*. . . .

E. Renewal or Healing from Conflict

If the process works well enough, and both parties are willing to move by incremental leaps of faith in the direction of agreement, and if they seek in the process to fathom the underlying problems and address them along the way, the effect can be two-fold: they may reach a mutually acceptable solution and, in the best of circumstances, they may also experience a change of heart, be reconciled to one another and healed and feel renewed as human beings. This is the transformation objective; it is the goal or purpose of all ritual processes, whether it be theater or court trial or graduation exercise or religious rite or negotiated settlement. Rituals are to help prepare the participants, those on whose behalf the ceremony is enacted, to move forward in a new condition, to a new phase of life. *Renewal* or transformation in this context means not simply they are as good as they were before the conflict, but they are better — they are more whole, or more compassionate, or less greedy, or otherwise changed in an important way from their attitude or condition before the crisis began. Certainly, when people experience such a fundamental change through the process of conflict resolution, they will be far less likely to find themselves in a similar conflict again. On the other hand, if they fail at this process, then to the extent the conflict was a product of their own developmental shortcomings, it is likely they will find themselves in similar conflicts in the future, returning again and again until the party acknowledges and addresses the underlying developmental need.

Notes and Questions

1.10 Both Follett and Williams talk about negotiation as providing opportunity. How are these opportunities the same? Different?

1.11 Do you agree that negotiation can heal? How can you, as a lawyer, help your client move through the healing stages?

  Linda L. Putnam, CHALLENGING THE ASSUMPTIONS OF TRADITIONAL APPROACHES TO NEGOTIATION

10 Negot. J. 337, 338-340, 341, 342-344 (1994)

It is not that traditional approaches are bad or necessarily inaccurate, but that they leave critical elements hidden, unexplained, or untouched. They fail to capture the fluidity, ambiguity, and unpredictability that often accompanies negotiation in routine decision making and they draw on a common set of assumptions about conflict and human nature that need to be questioned. What are these assumptions? How can we turn challenges to these assumptions into different conceptual models for negotiation? . . .

My armchair theorizing begins by challenging three assumptions that are embedded in our traditional models: (1) negotiated outcomes are defined by instrumental goals; (2) the individual is the driving force of negotiation; and (3) rationality is the privileged way of knowing.

INSTRUMENTAL GOALS

Instrumentality refers to two characteristics: (1) the use of negotiation as a tool to an end and (2) a concentration on task or substantive issues to the exclusion of other goals. When negotiation is viewed as a tool for conflict management, bargaining becomes an instrument for reaching a desired end. In traditional models, negotiation is a way to reach a settlement or attain a mutually satisfactory agreement. . . .

In effect, the instrumental aims of negotiation shape the way researchers conceive of the process and the way other goals enter into the negotiation. Basically, instrumental ends serve as a template to filter, define, coopt or recast other elements of negotiation, including relational and identity issues.

What options exist for moving away from conceiving of negotiation as primarily an instrumental activity? Are there other outcomes of negotiation that we have ignored because we concentrate on instrumental goals? One outcome that can be drawn from the broad literature on conflict management is *transformation*. That is, negotiation should strive to transform a dispute — not just to reach an instrumental end. By transforming a dispute, I refer to the extent that a conflict has experienced fundamental changes as a result of the negotiation. Fundamental changes might entail transforming the way individuals conceive of the other person, their relationship, the conflict dilemma, or the social-political situation. Negotiations can produce fundamental changes in conflicts at the actor level, issue level, rules, structures, and context of the dispute; however, most normative and descriptive models overlook these changes and center on the settlement itself. In the transformative approach, conflicts are no longer problems to be resolved; rather, they are opportunities to create a new social reality, a new negotiated order, a different definition of relationship, or a transformed situation. . . .

INDIVIDUALISM

Most approaches to negotiation cast the process as an individualistic enterprise. Individualistic models emphasize the autonomy, strategic choice, self-determination, and self-interest of negotiators. Individuals manipulate strategies and tactics to attain instrumental ends. They have motivations and aspirations, make decisions, and make errors in judgment. Individuals also have power, manage face, and handle bargainer-constituent relationships. Thus, even though negotiation scholars recognize that bargaining is a complex dyadic and team-based activity, they continue to house the authority for negotiation in the individual. Basically, the individual is the driving force of negotiation, even though the process may entail multiparty endeavors. . . .

A view of bargaining as relational development houses choice, action, and outcome within the dyad rather than the individual. In the relational model, the major goal or object of negotiation is to form, build, transform, or redefine the relationship. It centers on the way that the task of negotiating can serve the relationship rather than the reverse. This perspective values relationship in its own right, not for instrumental gain. . . .

RATIONALITY

Traditional negotiation models have exalted rationality to a privileged status. Effective negotiators are rational if they anticipate their opponent's moves, select appropriate strategies and tactics, and make logical decisions. Thus, rationality is linked to a priori planning and purposeful action. Rationality underlies the belief that negotiators should be objective in assessing utilities, comparing alternatives, and making strategic choices. Although negotiators exhibit flaws in judgment, biases in thinking, and perceptual distortions, the ultimate goal of a successful bargainer is to become more rational by improving his or her judgment processes. In traditional models, intentions and strategies serve the interests of rational means and instrumental ends. . . .

What alternatives exist for valuing emotions in negotiation and for positioning feelings as legitimate in their own right? A transformative view of negotiation might treat emotion as the critical moment in which the nature of a conflict shifts. Through its chaotic nature, emotion lays the groundwork for periods of ambivalence in which parties can pursue different courses of action. Emotions cast routine patterns into disarray and create space for new forms of action. Thus, emotions can signal shift-points, punctuation, or crisis moments that help negotiators transform issues, interests, positions, and relationships.

A *dialogic view* would shift the goal of negotiation to building mutual understanding and to creating a forum for effective interaction. It would stress relational and emotional aspects of negotiation as genuine in their own right rather than conceived instrumentally through outcome-driven models. Feelings become a source of knowing or understanding through interpreting meanings and values.

Emotion via dialogue becomes a way to learn, appreciate, and honor differences between parties for their own sake. Dialogue also introduces related concepts of intuition and sensing that have remained invisible in traditional models of negotiation. Narrative tales told by a group of exemplary mediators indicate that intuition and sensing are critical components of negotiation, ones tied closely to feelings. New models of negotiation need to find ways of integrating emotions with substantive issues — not to serve the ends of rationality or instrumentality, but to reveal how negotiators come to understand self, the other party, and the connectedness among them.

CONCLUSION

Despite the emergence of different conceptual models in the field, researchers and practitioners continue to embrace a dominant paradigm that governs traditional approaches to negotiation. Three assumptions underlie the roots of this paradigm: (1) negotiated outcomes are defined through instrumental goals; (2) the individual is the driving force in a negotiation; and (3) rationality surfaces as the privileged way of knowing.

By challenging these assumptions, I have tried to expose elements of negotiation that have remained hidden or invisible to traditional models and to explore new horizons that might lead to alternative theories — ones that can flourish and enrich our interdisciplinary work. Among many alternatives, a theorist could approach the subject in the following ways: negotiation as transforming disputes; negotiation as a deliberative process; negotiation as social networks; negotiation as relational development; and negotiation as dialogue. These alternatives are presented here merely as stimuli; they are neither fully developed nor necessarily consistent with one another. However, they do provide direction for embarking on a new journey — one that travels into new terrains.

Notes and Questions

1.12 What is the difference between an instrumental and noninstrumental approach to negotiations? What other goals might negotiators orient themselves to?

The readings up to now have taken a broader overview to conflict and the opportunities it may provide. In this next well-known excerpt, Frank Sander and Jeffrey Rubin take a more legalistic approach to negotiation. The reading after this by Michael Moffitt challenges this division of types of negotiation.

Frank E.A. Sander & Jeffrey Rubin, **THE JANUS QUALITY OF NEGOTIATION: DEALMAKING AND DISPUTE SETTLEMENT**

4 Negot. J. 109, 109-110, 112 (1988)

[W]e will explore the simple difference between negotiation over entry into a relationship (what we will refer to as Deal-Making Negotiation, or DMN) and negotiation over remaining in or leaving a relationship (what we will refer to as Dispute Settlement Negotiation, or DSN). We will first look at the critical distinguishing characteristics between DSN and DMN, and then consider briefly some of the practical consequences of this distinction for more effective negotiation.

By definition, DMN arises when parties embark upon a deal. Typically this means the parties *have had no prior dealings*, and the *focus is on their future relationship* (e.g., A negotiates for the purchase of B's house; C Corp. agrees to sell its business to D Corp.). Although the second factor is critical in this definition, the first is not. The deal-making parties *may* have had a prior relationship. Indeed sometimes the deal grows out of, or is based on, a prior relationship (e.g., Union X makes a new contract with Company Y; Father F enters an arrangement with Son S for shoveling the sidewalk or putting out the trash), but the thrust of the dealmaking—and hence of the negotiations that lead to the deal — is forward-looking. The parties typically have come together in order to reach agreement, and anticipate a future relationship under the umbrella of the deal that has been struck. . . .

By contrast, dispute settlement negotiation (DSN) is a *backward*-looking transaction because dispute settlement, in the sense the term is used here, means a dispute arising under an existing agreement. If a dispute arises in the course of any of the previously described deals (e.g., the house to be sold is damaged in a fire, and the question is who bears the risk of that event), then the resulting negotiation is a DSN. A DSN addresses the rights (both substantive and procedural) established under a previous agreement. For example, the just-mentioned agreement to purchase a house may say nothing specifically on the subject of fire damage but may contain an arbitration clause for the settlement of any dispute arising in the course of the sale. Hence the key distinction: DMN creates the deal and defines the rights that will then be looked to in case of any future dispute under the agreement (DSN). . . .

Table 1
Summary of Differences Between DSN and DMN

DSN	DMN
Looks backward	Looks forward
Focus on claiming	Focus on creating
Focus on rights	Focus on interests
BATNA* poor and similar	BATNA wide open and different for both parties
Adversarial style	Joint problem solving
Constrained by prior deal to remain in relationship	Freedom to enter into negotiation if one chooses

*BATNA stands for "best alternative to a negotiated agreement." This concept is based on the idea that you should reach agreement only if your agreement is better than your alternatives, including your best alternative. See Chapter 2 for more explanation. — EDS.

Table 1 summarizes the major points that we have made concerning the key differences between negotiation in the service of making a deal as compared with settling a dispute. We acknowledge the possibility of oversimplification in the preceding analysis, noting in particular our tendency to portray DMN as the "good guy," and DSN as the "bad." A more sensitive, and probably accurate, analysis of the two forms of negotiation would indicate that each has its virtues and liabilities. Each confers opportunities on the wise negotiator, and each form of negotiation should therefore be understood if both are to be used effectively.

 ### *Michael L. Moffitt*, DISPUTES AS OPPORTUNITIES TO CREATE VALUE

in The Handbook of Dispute Resolution 173, 173-174 (Michael L. Moffitt & Robert C. Bordone eds., 2005)

Some have suggested that negotiations aimed at resolving disputes might be fundamentally different from deal-making negotiations. Business ventures, international treaties, and marriage, such observers say, are *deals* — the product of a different kind of interaction. In such contexts, perhaps, opportunities to create value are conspicuous. The parties can craft an efficient and elegant agreement — one that both would prefer to no agreement. Their agreement can capitalize on the parties' joint interests. It can include value-creating trades that build upon the parties' differences, rather than merely divide a finite resource among the parties. Intuitively, these kinds of value-creating endeavors are easier in a deal-making context.

What this perspective misses is that all interactions involve the potential for disputes. Some disputes relate to past events in the relationship. Who dropped the ball on the marketing plan? Who failed to prevent the environmental damage? Who was supposed to take out the recycling? Other disputes will be more future-oriented. How will we divide the profits? How should we deal with border security? How should we spend Friday night? Disputes and potential disputes are ubiquitous. As a result, even deal-making takes place in the shadow of the prospect of disputes.

Even if it were empirically demonstrable that more value is captured in deal-making contexts than in dispute resolution contexts, dividing negotiations into dispute resolution and deal-making can be unhelpful for negotiators in practice. What the deal-dispute framework suggests is that negotiators who find themselves in a dispute should seek ways to *convert* their context to a deal-making one. The framework calls on negotiators to treat the dispute situation as similar to a deal-making one by searching for joint opportunities to create value. Perhaps for some negotiators, this is a helpful reminder not to ignore the possibility of forward-looking mechanisms for capturing value in disputes.

My concern is that the people who most need to be skilled and aimed at finding value — those who are locked in the most difficult and bitter disputes — are the *most likely* to resist the re-characterization of their dispute as a possible "deal." "Why would I want to think about making another deal with that company? They've already betrayed my trust once." "We do not deal with brutal dictators." "I'm not here to make a deal with that insensitive jerk. I hate him for what he did, and I want him to pay." If value creation is only for deal-making, then, the deal-dispute division risks suggesting to these disputants that they ought not to focus on value creation. And yet they are precisely the parties who would most benefit from such a focus.

A closer look at interactions between people or organizations reveals that differing and conflicting interests are present in virtually all circumstances — even when the parties' relationship bears none of the hallmarks of a dispute. Any two people who spend significant time together quickly discover that not all of their interests are identical or shared. And yet, businesses engage in joint ventures, countries sign treaties, couples marry — and disputants reach resolution.

Disputants need not imagine that in order to create value, they must somehow expend the energy to convert their situation into a deal-making context. Instead, the challenge for negotiators is to recognize the value creation opportunities, along with the dispute resolution opportunities, inherent in virtually all interactions.

Notes and Questions

1.13 How is it helpful to think about negotiation as falling into the two categories outlined above? Would you change the way that you approach the other side based on the type of dispute? Would you change the way that you prepare?

1.14 How does Moffitt disagree with Sander and Rubin?

---

2. Descriptions of the Negotiation Process

Each of the readings in this section describes the author's view of how the negotiation actually proceeds. As you read these, think about which view or views seem to resonate most closely with your own assumptions about how negotiations actually occur. Does this differ depending on context? Does this differ depending on how you view conflict in general?

 Gerald Williams, **LEGAL NEGOTIATION AND SETTLEMENT**

70, 72-73, 77-81, 84 (1983)

Negotiation is a repetitive process that follows reasonably predictable patterns over time. Yet in legal disputes, so much of the attorneys' attention and energy are absorbed by pretrial procedure and the approach of trial that they fail to recognize the identifiable patterns and dynamics of the negotiation process. . . .

DISCUSSION OF THE STAGES

A.   Stage One: Orientation and Positioning

1. Orientation

Stage One of the negotiation process involves two interrelated dynamics, described as orientation and positioning. Orientation is the less obvious of the two. In routine matters it is the natural by-product of the interaction between the attorneys as they begin to work on a case. Letters are exchanged, phone calls are made, and each lawyer becomes oriented to the basic approach and style of the other. . . . In every case, even between very experienced lawyers, the negotiating relationship that emerges will decide whether the negotiators will approach each other as competitive or cooperative negotiators, or a mix of the two, and will determine what strategies and tactics will be used by each attorney in the case. As in political campaigns, the heights or depths to which the opponents will go to gain advantage over each other is strongly influenced by impressions given and received at this stage.

2. Positioning

The second aspect of Stage One is closely related to the first, but also has a dynamic of its own. The lawyers come forward with an opening position. At this early stage in the dispute, that is not as simple as it appears. The facts are not all in, the legal questions are not fully researched, and unforeseen developments loom on the horizon. In the face of these uncertainties, the negotiators must leave themselves a certain amount of latitude, yet they must come up with something. What they come up with is an opening position. . . .

3. Inalterable Commitment to an Opening Position

The next element of Stage One relating to positioning is that each side seeks to establish the illusion that he is inalterably committed to his opening position. The purposes served by this tactic are several. It lends credibility to the demand, and particularly in the case of high opening demands, it gives time for the demand to have its effect on the hopes or expectations of the other side. It gives each negotiator time to make further evaluations of the value of the case and to gain information about what the other side is willing to accept. When the negotiators are ready to begin more serious negotiation, they are better informed and better able to bargain than when the extreme demands were established. As with the other elements of the negotiation process, however, this strategy can easily be overdone. It must be used with judgment, perceptiveness, and flexibility.

4. Duration of Stage One

The final element in Stage One is the observation that it generally continues over a longer period of time than all of the other stages combined. At least one reason for this is that in many actionable cases the attorneys do not begin seriously considering settlement until trial deadlines make themselves felt. . . .

B. Stage Two: Argumentation

1. Overview

It is axiomatic that the opening positions established by negotiation in Stage One will be some distance apart. If not, there would be no controversy and the case would be resolved immediately. Given the distance between the opening positions, some method or procedure is necessary whereby it may be explored and evaluated. These dynamics come into play in Stage Two. Both sides begin to gather information about the real or hidden expectations of the other, while at the same time trying to avoid disclosing information about their own minimum expectations and utilities. A great deal of information may be exchanged, but it is presented in a favorable light. Through this process, the legal and factual issues become better defined and the strengths and weaknesses of each side become more apparent.

2. The Problem of Making Concessions

It is usually in Stage Two that the first concessions are made. Concessions are important devices because they are the primary means by which agreement can be approached. They also have importance as instruments of strategy. The task of the cooperative attorney is to establish a cooperative, trusting atmosphere where a just or equitable outcome can be sought. One of the primary means for doing this is through the selective granting of concessions. By comparison, the task of the competitive or maximalist negotiator is to obtain the maximum number of concessions from his opponent while making the fewest and smallest concessions possible. This is consistent with his goal of obtaining the maximum possible outcome. . . .

C. Stage Three: Emergence and Crisis

1. Effect of a Deadline

As the deadline approaches, a crisis is reached. Concessions have been made, neither side wishes to give anything more, both sides are wary of being exploited, and both sides know that they must stop somewhere. At this point, one party suggests a final offer and says, in effect, that's the best I can do. Take it or else we go to trial. It has been helpfully observed in non-legal literature that this kind of demand actually presents a threefold choice: take it, or leave it, or come up with something else. This acute observation suggests that the attorney who lacks imagination may see only a two-fold choice: take it or leave it. He may decide that since he cannot take it, impasse has been reached, and the negotiation is over. It is important to bear in mind the third alternative, to come up with something else. Furthermore, what the negotiator comes up with does not have to be a significant concession. It can be an integrative proposal, suggesting another alternative or new combinations of alternatives that increase the utility of settlement to the parties without decreasing their total payoffs. . . .

D. Stage Four: Agreement or Final Breakdown

1. Agreement

If the parties come to an agreement, the work is not over. There are important steps yet to be taken. The first of these is to work out the details of the agreement. Some attorneys negotiate in a way that keeps the details alive and active in the ongoing discussion. This is a common feature of integrative bargaining, where alternative solutions to each sub-issue are explored and creative solutions sought.

By contrast, other attorneys prefer to negotiate only the most basic issues, such as money, while leaving the others to be wrapped up after general agreement has been reached. One variation of this strategy is to separate the issues according to how difficult they are to resolve, then to resolve them working from the easiest to the most difficult. Whatever variation or combination is used, the attorneys at some point have an agreement, yet important details may remain to be worked out. These are sometimes known as "Oh, by the ways." These details must be considered important to the overall quality and favorability of the agreement and should be given the attention they deserve....

2. Final Breakdown

If the parties are unable to arrive at a settlement and the negotiations are not revived, a final breakdown has occurred and the case goes to trial for resolution. The term *final breakdown* is used because not all breakdowns in negotiation are final.

Notes and Questions

1.15 Think of the most recent negotiation you engaged in (with friends, family, or colleagues) and apply Williams's stages to that negotiation. Is this framework a useful template?

1.16 Imagine that you are house hunting. You find a house that looks like it meets your needs and is priced fairly based on your look at other houses in the neighborhood. It has the number of bedrooms you need and a lovely backyard. It is listed for $290,000, but your realtor thinks that it probably will go for less. You give an opening bid of $270,000. The realtor for the owners does not respond immediately but instead invites you to come back to see the house again. While there, the owner's realtor points out the newly refurbished kitchen with new appliances and a new floor. Also, he mentions that the owners recently redid much of the outdoor landscaping (which you cannot see because it is winter). You note, and point out to the realtor, that the driveway needs repaving soon. It also appears that the roof needs to be replaced within the next five years. When you ask for a response to your bid, the owners reply with a counteroffer of $285,000. You take your time to counteroffer and note that the house has been on the market for some time. You counteroffer at $280,000 and strongly let the realtor know this is your final bid. The owners accept. Using Williams's stages, at which point does each stage commence in the above scenario? What issues are left for stage four?

1.17 In stage three, Williams notes that the "take it or leave it" option actually is three choices — take it, leave it, or come up with something else. Why do some lawyers see only the first two choices? Using the house-hunting example, how could the owners respond to your final offer?

1.18 To the stages above, Carrie Menkel-Meadow and David Binder add several pre- and post-negotiation steps, including planning for the negotiation, planning with the client on goals and possible solutions, and learning from the negotiation after it is completed. Carrie Menkel-Meadow & David Binder, Lawyering Skills Institute, The Stages and Phases of Negotiation (1983). How does this add to Williams's stages?

This next excerpt from anthropology professor Philip Gulliver explains negotiation as both a cyclical and a developmental process.

 Philip H. Gulliver, **DISPUTES AND NEGOTIATIONS: A CROSS-CULTURAL PERSPECTIVE**

82-86, 88-89 (1979)

In negotiation there are two distinct though interconnected processes going on simultaneously: a repetitive, cyclical one and a developmental one. A simple analogy is a moving automobile. There is a cyclical turning of the wheels (linked to the cyclical action of valves, pistons, etc., in the motor) that enables the vehicle to move, and there is the actual movement of the vehicle from one place to another.... In negotiation, somewhat similarly, there is a cyclical process comprising the repetitive exchange of information between the parties, its assessment, and the resulting adjustments of expectations and preferences; there is also a developmental process involved in the movement from the initiation of the dispute to its conclusion — some outcome — and its implementation....

In negotiation there is a continual need both to give and to receive information. There is a need to give it in order to tell the opponent about one's own demands and strengths and to attempt to induce him to shift his demands toward one's own. There is a need to obtain information in order to get a better understanding of the opponent — his expectations and demands, his attitudes, strategies, strengths, and weaknesses, together with any changes in all these matters. In order to obtain needed information, a party has to give information to his opponent. In order to give information, he needs to receive information from his opponent. Receiving information creates the opportunity, but also the necessity perhaps, to learn and to adjust expectations and demands. That in turn induces the party to offer further information and to seek to obtain more....

An inherent problem in these exchanges is that each party tends to edit in his own favor the information he offers.... Thus he usually stresses and exaggerates the more advantageous features of his case while discounting or ignoring the disadvantageous ones. A party must expect that the messages he receives are similarly edited. The flow of information is therefore distorted in some degree. Moreover, the exchange of messages always carries the possibility that unintended information will be conveyed at the same time. On the one hand, a party may not say what he intended, or he may say more than he intended as information is carried between the lines and, as an affectual penumbra, colors what is said. On the other hand, his opponent may misreceive and misinterpret messages and obtain wrong information.

Information is carried by any and all kinds of messages.... These include both the intended and unintended, the overt and covert, and the linguistic and the nonlinguistic. Silence too sends a message of some kind, according to context and cultural norms....

In terms of the cyclical model, the supply of more or less assessed information can be seen as flowing in two directions. First, received information may affect a party's behavior as a result of causing changes in knowledge, preferences, attitudes, and strategy — in brief, as a result of changes in his preference set. Second, the information may affect a party's behavior as a result of his assessment of his opponent's future behavior — his expectations of his opponent. Both are liable to be affected and changed by each new piece of information received.

Notes and Questions

1.19 Williams views the negotiation process as more linear while Gulliver argues for a more cyclical view of negotiation. Think again about your negotiation experience. Which makes the most sense to you?

1.20 Map the hypothetical house-buying scenario in Notes and Questions 1.16 to Gulliver's ideas of the negotiation process.

1.21 Could a negotiation be both cyclical and linear? Can you resolve the different theories?

1.22 Gulliver bases his cyclical approach to negotiations on extensive cross-cultural research. How might his description of the negotiation process be based on his research locations? Gulliver is also looking at all negotiations whereas Williams is writing about legal disputes. How might a legal dispute differ from other types?

The final excerpt in this section comes from Russell Korobkin. His description of negotiation is neither linear nor cyclical but rather task-oriented.

 Russell Korobkin, **A POSITIVE THEORY OF LEGAL NEGOTIATION**

88 Geo. L.J. 1789, 1791-1794, 1799, 1816 (2000)

This article presents a new dichotomy that creates a clear theoretical structure for viewing the legal negotiation process. This "zone definition/surplus allocation" dichotomy provides a complete description of the negotiation process: *every* action taken by negotiators in preparation for negotiations or at the bargaining table fits into one of these categories.

First, negotiators attempt to define the bargaining zone — the distance between the reservation points (or "walkaway" points) of the two parties — in the manner most advantageous to their respective clients. I call this activity "zone definition." . . .

Second, negotiators attempt to convince their opponent to agree to a single "deal point" within the bargaining zone. I call this activity "surplus allocation." Surplus allocation effectively divides the cooperative surplus that the parties create by reaching an agreement. For both parties, transacting at any point within the bargaining zone is more desirable than not reaching agreement, but each knows that the same is true for the other. Once the bargaining zone is established, there is no economically obvious way for the parties to select a deal point. As a result, surplus allocation usually requires that negotiators appeal to community norms of either procedural or substantive fairness. Consequently, surplus allocation can be understood as an inherently social activity. . . .

I. ZONE DEFINITION

In any negotiation, the maximum amount that a buyer will pay for a good, service, or other legal entitlement is called his "reservation point" or, if the deal being negotiated is a monetary transaction, his "reservation price" (RP). The minimum amount that a seller would accept for that item is her RP. If the buyer's RP is higher than the seller's, the distance between the two points is called the "bargaining zone." [See Figure 1.] . . .

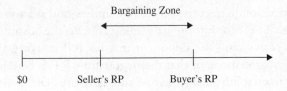

Figure 1
Reservation Points That Create a Bargaining Zone

For example, suppose Esau, looking to get into business for himself, is willing to pay up to $200,000 for Jacob's catering business, while Jacob, interested in retiring, is willing to sell the business for any amount over $150,000. This difference between Esau's and Jacob's RPs creates a $50,000 bargaining zone. At any price between $150,000 and $200,000, both parties are better off agreeing to the sale of the business than they are reaching no agreement and going their separate ways.

The same structure used to describe a transactional negotiation can be used to describe a dispute resolution negotiation. Suppose that Goliath has filed suit against David for battery. David is willing to pay up to $90,000 to settle the case out of court — essentially, to buy Goliath's legal right to bring suit — while Goliath will "sell" his right for any amount over $60,000. These RPs create a $30,000 bargaining zone between $60,000 and $90,000. Any settlement in this range would leave both parties better off than they would be without a settlement.

In contrast, if the seller's RP is higher than the buyer's RP, there is no bargaining zone. In this circumstance, there is no sale price that would make both parties better off than they would be by not reaching a negotiated agreement. Put another way, the parties would be better off not reaching a negotiated agreement. If Jacob will not part with his business for less than $150,000 and Esau will not pay more than $100,000 for it, there is no bargaining zone. If David will pay up to $50,000 to settle Goliath's claim, but Goliath will not accept any amount less than $60,000, again there is no bargaining zone. An agreement in either case would leave at least one party, and possibly both parties, worse off than if they were to decide not to take a deal.

Knowledge of the parameters of the bargaining zone, which is created by the two parties' reservation points, is the most critical information for the negotiator to possess. Those parameters tell the negotiator both whether any agreement is possible and, if so, identify the range of possible deal points. At the same time, the negotiator has an interest in adjusting the parameters of the bargaining zone to his advantage. A buyer not only wants to know his and the seller's RPs, he wishes to make both lower, or at least make both *appear* lower to the seller. . . .

Esau wants to know his and Jacob's RPs, but he also would like to shift both numbers, and therefore the bargaining range, lower. Assuming Esau knows his RP is $200,000 and learns Jacob's is $150,000, Esau knows that an agreement is possible for some amount greater than the latter figure and less than the former. If he could reduce Jacob's RP to $120,000 and his own to $170,000, however, the bargaining zone would remain the same size, but its changed parameters would suggest that Esau would be likely to buy the business for a lower price. Esau could achieve the same advantage if Jacob *believes* the parties' RPs are $120,000 and $170,000 respectively, even if the RPs objectively are $150,000 and $200,000. . . .

Efforts at persuasion in negotiation are best understood as attempts to satisfy one or both of two goals: (1) to shift the bargaining zone to the advantage of the negotiator, either by convincing the opponent that his RP is worse than he believed before beginning negotiations or that the negotiator's RP is better than previously believed; and (2) to establish an objective — and therefore "fair" — method of agreeing on a sale price that falls within the bargaining zone. . . .

II.   SURPLUS ALLOCATION

Through zone definition, negotiators establish a bounded set of possible negotiated outcomes, or "deal points." If the bargaining zone consists of only a single point, it is the only possible deal point. Unless the parties mistakenly believe that there is no bargaining zone at all, they should reach a deal at precisely that point. But in many, and perhaps most, cases in which a bargaining zone exists, the zone will include a range of potential deal points. In this situation, agreement at each possible deal point is superior for both parties to not reaching an agreement, or, put in economic terms, every deal point is Pareto* superior to no deal. The problem is that, in this situation, no potential deal point is obviously superior to any other. If Esau is willing to pay $200,000 for Jacob's business, and Jacob is willing to accept $150,000, a sale clearly should take place, but it is unclear whether the price should be $150,000, $200,000, or any amount in between.

How do negotiators solve this dilemma and agree on a single deal point? This part argues that bargainers usually rely on socially constructed norms of reaching agreement that are based implicitly on notions of fair dealing. Failure to agree on how to fairly allocate the cooperative surplus can, perversely, cause negotiators to fail to consummate a deal even when both would be better off striking a deal than pursuing their BATNAs.

---

* The Pareto frontier refers to economic maximization as in [Figure 2]. For example, assume that X and Y agree on initial solution I. By moving to solution A, X's utility is the same and Y's is increased. A is *Pareto superior* to I since it is better for one party without being worse for the other. If X and Y were able to agree on B, this solution would increase both X and Y's utility — both parties would be better off. On the other hand, C and D are other solutions along the Pareto curve where X or Y would have to give up something in order for the other to gain. The lesson is that either solutions A or B are better for the parties and that it makes sense for parties to push for Pareto optimal solutions.

Many common negotiating tactics are best understood as attempts to establish a procedure that the other party will view as "fair" for agreeing on a deal point within the bargaining zone. In employing such tactics, the negotiator may have either of two motives. He might believe that the procedure is equitable to both parties, and the resulting deal point will thus create a mutually beneficial transaction in which neither side gets the better of the other.

Alternatively, he might attempt to establish procedure that will lead to an agreement that benefits him or his client substantially more than it benefits the other negotiator. Whether the negotiator's motives are communitarian or individualistic, however, the procedures must have the appearance of equity in order to win acceptance. . . .

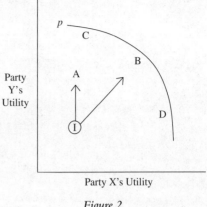

Party Y's Utility

Party X's Utility

Figure 2
[Pareto Frontier]

Singling out a deal point requires the parties to agree on what is fair. In many negotiations, agreement is achieved by the parties acting consistently with procedural norms of bargaining behavior such as reciprocity, splitting the difference, and the selection of prominent focal points. The deal point that emerges from a procedurally fair process is accepted by the parties as itself fair, assuming it lies within the bargaining zone. In other negotiations, the parties instead negotiate over what specific deal point would be most substantively fair. . . .

As is true of any criteria that claims substantive fairness, claims of morality or merit are only as valuable as the similarities in the negotiators' social constructions of fairness. When negotiators share a set of social values, substantive fairness claims are most likely to lead to agreement on a deal point. . . .

Notes and Questions

1.23 Korobkin focuses on the tasks of a negotiation versus stages or other concepts. Does this seem easier to grasp to you? Do these tasks need to occur in a particular order?

1.24 What assumptions about negotiation does Korobkin make by dividing the negotiation process in this way? How does that differ from other concepts of negotiation outlined in this chapter?

Chapter 2 | Preparing and Making Your Case

This second chapter focuses on how negotiators prepare and present their interests to the other side. The first excerpt in the chapter explains the underlying importance of interests — the currency of negotiation. As you read this chapter, you can start to outline specific steps you will need to take both in advance of and during the negotiation in order to be more effective. The particular skills in this chapter focus on persuading your counterpart to take the action you desire. Later chapters will focus on other skills that effective negotiators use, such as consideration of how taking account of the other side will be necessary and important to getting what you want from a negotiation. In planning for any negotiation it is important to analyze what the case or matter is about before deciding on a particular behavioral approach or style. What are the parties seeking to accomplish? What goals are served by what behaviors? What outcomes are produced by particular behaviors? Is joint gain possible, or are parties trying to maximize their individual or self-interested gain? Analysis of the matter to be negotiated, or the "science" of negotiation, is essential before the negotiator meets or does anything else with the other side.

After outlining interests, the first section examines how negotiators set their goals in a negotiation and gives advice that goals should be specific, justifiable, and optimistic. The second section then turns to the reservation points or "bottom lines" negotiators will want to establish based on the alternatives available to them. The third section examines objective criteria — how do we know that both our goals (aspirations) and our bottom lines (limits) are reasonable and fair? Finally, the chapter ends with advice about how to frame our arguments in ways that are most persuasive to our negotiation counterpart. Planning for negotiation involves thinking about the matter from the perspective of all sides — "single-sided" planning (focusing only on what you want) is likely to prevent you from seeing what can actually be achieved in a negotiation.

❖ *David A. Lax & James K. Sebenius*, **INTERESTS: THE MEASURE OF NEGOTIATION**

2 Negot. J. 73, 73-74, 76-77, 78-80, 81, 82, 88-89, 90-91 (1986)

AN EXPANSIVE CONCEPTION OF A NEGOTIATOR'S INTERESTS

In evaluating the interests at stake, a typical negotiator might focus on commodities that can be bought and sold or on concrete terms that can be written into a contract or treaty. And, negotiators definitely have such interests: the crippled plaintiff desperately wants compensation; a sales manager cares intensely about prices, profit margins, return on investment, and personal compensation; managers may derive value from seeing their particular product sweep the market or furthering some vision of the public interest.

Throughout this article, we assume that negotiators want to do well for themselves. Of course, "doing well" is only measured with respect to the things they care about, whether out of direct self-interest or concern for the welfare of others. Thus, doing "better" in a negotiation need not imply pressing for more money or a bigger share; rather, it means advancing the totality of one's interests, which may include money and other intangibles as well as fairness, the well-being of one's counterparts, and the collegiality of the process. . . .

Negotiators' interests can go beyond the obvious and tangible. Take for example the almost universal quest for social approval or the simple pleasure one derives from being treated with respect, even in a one-time encounter. A stockbroker may want to build a relationship with a customer because of the future business it may bring; or a plaintiff, anxious at the thought of a trial, may be willing to take a reduced settlement to avoid courtroom trauma. . . .

TWO HELPFUL DISTINCTIONS

Interests, Issues and Positions

Negotiators seek to reach agreement on specific *positions* on a specific set of *issues*. For example, a potential employee may initially demand $36,000 (the position) for salary (the issue). The job seeker's underlying *interests* may be in financial security, enhanced lifestyle, organizational status, and advanced career prospects. Or, the desire of a Midwestern utility company to build a dam may collide with farmers' needs for water and environmentalists' concern for the downstream habitat of endangered whooping cranes. Increased economic return, irrigated crops, and preserved species are the relevant *interests*; they conflict over the *issue* of the dam's construction, *positions* on which are pro and con. . . .

Many negotiators retard creativity by failing to distinguish the issues under discussion from their underlying interests. When the issues under discussion poorly match the interests at stake, modifications of the issues sometimes enable all parties to satisfy their interests better. For example, recall the conflict between the Midwestern utility company, the farmers, and the environmentalists. After several years of costly and embittering litigation, the parties came to a resolution by a shift to issues that matched their underlying interests in a more fruitful manner. By moving from positions ("yes" and "no") on the issue of the dam's construction to discussions about the nature of downstream water guarantees, the amount of a trust fund to protect the whooping crane habitat, and the size of the dam, the parties reached an agreement that left all of them better off. . . .

Intrinsic and Instrumental Interests

It should be clear that negotiators may have many kinds of interests: money and financial security, a particular conception of the public interest, the quality of products, enhancing a reputation as a skilled bargainer, maintaining a working relationship, precedents, and so on. However, one distinction — between intrinsic and instrumental interests — can provide an economical way to capture some important qualities of interests, call negotiators' attention to often-overlooked, sometimes subtle interests, and lead to improved agreements.

One's interest in an issue is *instrumental* if favorable terms on the issue are valued because of their effect on subsequent dealings. One's interest in an issue is *intrinsic* if one values favorable terms of settlement on the issue independent of any subsequent dealings. Thus, a divorcing parent's interest in gaining custody of his or her child, the farmer's interest in water rights, or a country's interest in secure borders can usefully be thought of as intrinsic interests. . . .

Most issues affect both intrinsic and instrumental interests. Dealings with a subordinate who wants to hire an assistant can arouse an intrinsic interest in the overall size of the budget as well as a concern with the perceived precedent the hiring will set in the eyes of the subordinate's peers — an instrumental interest. Recognizing the distinction may lead to improved agreements; the subordinate who can create a justifiable device to prevent decisions about his or her staff support from setting precedents may well receive authorization to hire a new assistant.

One of the main reasons we focus on the intrinsic-instrumental distinction is for the light it sheds on three often-misunderstood aspects of negotiation: interests in the process, in relationships, and in principles.

"Process" Interests — Intrinsic and Instrumental

Analysts often assume that negotiators evaluate agreements by measuring the value obtained from the outcome. Yet, negotiators may care about the *process* of bargaining as well. Even with no prospect of further interaction, some would prefer a negotiated outcome reached by pleasant, cooperative discussion to the same outcome reached by abusive, threat-filled dealings. Others might even derive value from a strident process that gives them the satisfied feeling of having extracted something from their opponents. Either way, negotiators can have intrinsic interests in the character of the negotiation process itself.

Beyond such intrinsic valuation, an unpleasant process can dramatically affect future dealings; the supplier who is berated and threatened may be unresponsive when cooperation at a later point would help. Indeed, negotiators often have strong instrumental interests in building trust and confidence early in the negotiation process in order to facilitate jointly beneficial agreements.

"Relationship" Interests — Intrinsic and Instrumental

Negotiators often stress the value of their relationships; this interest sometimes achieves an almost transcendent status. For example, Fisher and Ury say that "every negotiator has two kinds of interests: in the substance and in the relationship." Many negotiators derive intrinsic value from developing or furthering a pleasant relationship. Moreover, when repeated dealings are likely, most negotiators perceive the instrumental value of developing an effective working relationship.

Of course, in the dissolution of a partnership or the divorce of a childless couple with few assets, the parties may find no instrumental value in furthering their relationship; that is, the parties would not be willing to trade substantive gains on, say, financial terms, to enhance their future dealings. In fact, a bitter divorcing couple may actually prefer a financial outcome that requires absolutely no future contact over another that is better for both in tax terms but requires them to deal with each other in the future. Similarly, a division head with two valuable but constantly warring employees may have a keen interest in separating them organizationally to prevent *any* active relationship between them. And, when dealing with an obnoxious salesperson who has come to the door or by the office, one's interest in the "relationship" may mainly be to terminate it.

Interest in "Principles" — Intrinsic and Instrumental

Negotiators may discover shared norms or principles relevant to their bargaining problem. Such norms may include equal division, more complex distributive judgments, historical or ethical rationales, objective or accepted standards, as well as notions that simply seem fair or are represented as such. Acting in accord with such a norm or principle may be of intrinsic interest to one or more of the parties; for example, a settlement of $532 — arrived at in accord with the mutually acknowledged principle that each party should be paid in proportion to time worked — may be valued quite differently than the same dollar figure reached by haggling. Of course, an acknowledged norm need not be an absolute value in a negotiation: it may be partly or fully traded off against other interests. . . .

ASSESSING THE INTERESTS OF OTHERS

Finally, it goes almost without saying that negotiators should constantly assess their counterparts' interests and preferences. Obviously, careful listening and clear communication help this process. Uninvolved third parties can render insight not suspected by partisans wrapped up in the negotiation. And some negotiators find that, as part of preparing for the process, actually playing the other party's role can offer deepened perspectives. In various management programs at Harvard, for example, senior industrialists have been assigned the parts of environmentalists and vice versa. To simulate arms talks, high-level U.S. military officers and diplomats have been assigned to play Russian negotiators in intensive simulations. Palestinians and Israelis have had to swap places. After some initial discomfort and reluctance, the most common reaction of participants in these exercises is surprise at how greatly such role-playing enhances their understanding of each side's interests, of why others may seem intransigent, and of unexpected possibilities for agreement.

Beyond various ways of trying to put oneself in the other's shoes, assessment of another's interests may be improved by investigating:

- Their past behavior in related settings, both in style and substance.
- Their training and professional affiliation: engineers and financial analysts will often have quite different modes of perception and approaches to potential conflict from, say, lawyers and insurance adjusters.
- Their organizational position and affiliation. Those in the production department will often see long, predictable manufacturing runs as the company's

dominant interest while marketers will opt for individual tailoring to customer specs and deep inventories for rapid deliveries. This is but one example of the old and wise expression "where you stand depends on where you sit."

- Whom they admire, whose advice carries weight, and to whom they tend to defer on the kind of issues at stake.

A. GOALS — ASPIRATIONS

Business school professor G. Richard Shell explains why goals are important and how a negotiator can make achieving those goals more likely.

 G. Richard Shell, **BARGAINING FOR ADVANTAGE: NEGOTIATION STRATEGIES FOR REASONABLE PEOPLE**

31-34 (1999)

SET AN OPTIMISTIC, JUSTIFIABLE TARGET

When you set goals, think boldly and optimistically about what you would like to see happen. Research has repeatedly shown that people who have higher aspirations in negotiations perform better and get more than people who have modest or "I'll do my best" goals, provided they really believe in their targets.

In one classic study, psychologists Sydney Siegel and Lawrence Fouraker set up a simple buy-sell negotiation experiment. They allowed the negotiators to keep all the profits they achieved but told the subjects they could qualify for a second, "double their-money" round if they met or exceeded certain specified bargaining goals. In other words, Siegel and Fouraker gave their subjects both concrete *incentives* for hitting a certain specified level of performance and, perhaps unintentionally, a hint that the assigned target levels were realistically attainable (why else would subjects be told about the bonus round?). One set of negotiators was told they would have to hit a modest $2.10 target to qualify for the bonus round. Another set of negotiators was told they would have to hit a much more ambitious target of $6.10. Both sides had the same bottom line: They could not accept any deal that involved a loss. The negotiators with the more ambitious $6.10 goal achieved a mean profit of $6.25, far outperforming the median profit of $3.35 achieved by those with the modest $2.10 goal.

My own research has confirmed Siegel's and Fouraker's findings. In our experiment, unlike the one Siegel and Fouraker conducted, negotiation subjects set their own bargaining goals. And instead of letting everyone keep whatever profits they earned, we gave separate $100 prizes to the buyer and the seller with the best individual outcomes. The result was the same, however. Negotiators who reported higher prenegotiation expectations achieved more than those who entered the negotiation with more modest goals.

Why are we tempted to set modest bargaining goals when we can achieve more by raising our sights? There are several possible reasons. First, many people set modest goals to protect their self-esteem. We are less likely to fail if we set our goals low, so we "wing it," telling ourselves that we are doing fine as long as we beat our bottom line. Modest goals thus help us avoid unpleasant feelings of failure and regret.

Second, we may not have enough information about the negotiation to see the full potential for gain; that is, we may fail to appreciate the true worth of what we are selling, not do the research on applicable standards, or fail to note how eager the buyer is for what we have to offer. This usually means we have failed to prepare well enough.

Third, we may lack desire. If the other person wants money, control, or power more urgently than we do, we are unlikely to set a high goal for ourselves. Why look for conflict and trouble over things we care little about?

Research suggests that the self-esteem factor plays a more important role in low goal setting than many of us would care to admit. We once had a negotiation speaker who said that the problem with many reasonable people is that they confuse "win-win" with what he called a "wimp-win" attitude. The "wimp-win" negotiator focuses only on his or her bottom line; the "win-win" negotiator has ambitious goals.

I see further evidence of this in negotiation classes. As students and executives in negotiation workshops start setting more ambitious goals for themselves and strive to improve, they often report feeling more *dissatisfied and discouraged* regarding their performance — even as their objective results get better and better. For this reason, I suggest raising one's goals incrementally, adding risk and difficulty in small steps over a series of negotiations. That way you can maintain your enthusiasm for negotiation as you learn. Research shows that people who succeed in achieving new goals are more likely to raise their goals the next time. Those who fail, however, tend to become discouraged and lower their targets.

Once you have thought about what an optimistic, challenging goal would look like, spend a few minutes permitting realism to dampen your expectations. *Optimistic goals are effective only if they are feasible; that is, only if you believe in them and they can be justified according to some standard or norm.* . . . . [N]egotiation positions must usually be supported by some standard, benchmark, or precedent, or they lose their credibility. No amount of mental goal setting will make your five-year-old car worth more than a brand-new version of the same model. You should also adjust your goal to reflect appropriate relationship concerns. But do not let your ideas of what is appropriate or realistic take over completely. Simply note the reasons you come up with that explain why your optimistic goal may not be possible and look for the next highest, *defendable* target. Your old car may not be worth the same as a new one, but you should be able to find a used-car guide that reports the "average" price for your model. With that foundation, you can justify asking for a premium over that standard based on the tip-top condition of your vehicle.

One danger with being too realistic with your goals is that you may be making unwarranted assumptions about the values and priorities the other side will bring to the deal. Until you know for sure what *the other side* has for goals and what *the other side* thinks is realistic, you should keep your eyes firmly on your own defendable target. The other party will tell you if your optimistic deal isn't possible, and you will not offend him or her by asking for your goal so long as you have some justification to support it, you advance your ideas with courtesy, and you show a concern for his or her perspective.

Keep this point in mind as you progress toward higher goals: A certain amount of dissatisfaction is a good thing when you first start thinking seriously about improving how you negotiate. Dissatisfaction is a sign that you are setting your goals at a high enough level to encounter resistance from other parties and to take the risk that they may walk away. Eventually, you will learn to set targets that are challenging without being unduly discouraging.

BE SPECIFIC

The literature on negotiation goal setting counsels us to be as specific as possible. Clarity drives out fuzziness in negotiations as in many other endeavors. With a definite target, you will begin working on a host of psychological levels to get the job done. For example, when you land your new job, don't just set a goal to "negotiate a fair salary." Push yourself to take aim at a specific target — go for a 10 percent raise over what you made at your last job. Your specific goal will start you thinking about other, comparable jobs that pay your target salary, and you will begin to notice a variety of market standards that support a salary of that amount.

Be especially wary of goals such as "I'll do the best I can" or, worst of all, "I'll just go in and see what I can get." What we are really saying when we enter a negotiation with goals such as these is, "I do not want to take a chance on failing in this negotiation." Fear of failure and our natural desire to avoid feelings of disappointment and regret are legitimate psychological self-protection devices. But effective negotiators do not let these feelings get in the way of setting specific goals.

Notes and Questions

2.1 Why does Shell think that focusing on the bottom line can be inhibiting? What do you think? Shell notes above that negotiators may set modest goals to avoid feelings of regret. Does it make sense to set high aspiration levels if you are more likely to be disappointed?

2.2 What does Shell mean by "justifiable target"? Why should your goal be justifiable? How do you make your goal justifiable (or legitimate)? (Note that we will discuss more about fairness and legitimacy in Section C of this chapter.)

2.3 What is the importance of being specific in setting goals?

The next article outlines some of the theoretical and empirical underpinnings for Shell's advice above. Jennifer Brown uses law and economics theory to explain how hope motivates negotiators to reach their goals — but not necessarily beyond those goals.

❖ *Jennifer Gerarda Brown*, **THE ROLE OF HOPE**
IN NEGOTIATION

44 UCLA L. Rev. 1661, 1669-1670, 1672-1673, 1674-1682, 1684-1686 (1997)

"SATIATION" THEORY OF HOPE: HOPE AS A KINK IN
THE UTILITY CURVE

Most economic models of negotiation present strategy as a function of primitive structural variables. Theses variables typically include reservation price, predictions about the other side's reservation price, and costs of bargaining. A feature common to all of these hopeless economic models is the assumption that negotiators have no satiation point, that their marginal utility of income is constant. But we need not adopt this assumption. Instead, we might entertain the notion that, at some point, negotiators say to themselves: "Enough. I am sated. An additional dollar won't mean as much to me as each dollar I have gained so far." This may be a more realistic approach. Relaxing the assumption that negotiators' utility curves slope constantly upward suggests a way that hope might affect negotiation behavior.

Hope may act as a primitive in negotiation models if we recharacterize the payoff function and give it a kink or satiation point at or beyond which the negotiator's utility rises less steeply or levels completely. The kinking point on the curve might determine the negotiator's aspiration level. The negotiator does not hope to gain surplus beyond this point because each unit gained would be worth little or nothing to the negotiator. Just as it would be irrational to hope for more than the maximum possible payoff, it might also be irrational to hope for more than the negotiator's maximum *utility*. For the seller, the maximum possible utility would be a function not only of the maximum amount the buyer will pay, but also of the seller's satiation point. In other words, the seller's hopes turn on what is feasible from the other side *and* what is desirable given her utility function. Focusing only on what the other side will pay the seller (as most economic models do) is a feasibility-focused approach. Broadening the focus to include the negotiator's own satiation point yields a richer view of the variables that might actually drive negotiation behavior....

AN "OPTIMISM" THEORY OF HOPE: HOPE AS
COGNITIVE DISTORTION

As many critics have observed, economic theory and the models it spawns generally fail to account for the fact that people make distorted assessments of risk, loss, and gain. The "optimism" theory of hope in negotiation, on the other hand, questions economists' assumption that people rationally assess probabilities (such as the probable distribution of an opponent's reservation price or costs of bargaining). It suggests instead that when negotiators predict their opponent's reservation price or costs of bargaining, they are unrealistically optimistic — they may overestimate both to their own potential advantage. "Hope" may represent this unrealistic optimism in negotiation.

Visualizing Your Success

Mentally rehearsing and visualizing success works in a variety of contexts.

In fact, neuroscientists have found compelling new evidence that proves mental practice can actually increase real-world performance. In his book *Mind Sculpture*, author Ian Robertson, Ph.D., describes a recent study in which people who mentally practiced a five-finger piano exercise (their fingers never actually touched any keys) were compared with those who physically practiced. Results? Both groups showed improvements in accuracy. What's more, both showed an increase in size in the areas of the brain that control finger movement.

This means that merely visualizing positive results in our minds actually strengthens our neural circuits — those millions of neurons firing in concert that are involved in successful performance. Thus, if you can generate positive pictures in your mind, this rosy outlook literally gets you positive results — first in your brain, and then in your performance.

In her climb up the ladder to become the first female president of a Hollywood studio, Dawn Steel, former president of Columbia Pictures, often used this technique to boost her confidence. "One of my great tricks was that before I walked into a room, I would picture the people in it applauding me — you know, for whatever — I had done something that made them welcome me into the room. And so when I got to the room, I had made myself more comfortable by that image that I kept in my head. And it always worked. I would take a deep breath and play a part." Connie Glaser & Barbara Smalley, What Queen Esther Knew: Business Strategies from a Biblical Sage 113 (2003).

Hope in this model leads negotiators to distort an element of negotiation that economists and negotiation theorists recognize as significant — the opponent's reservation price — and it does so in a way that might even be quantifiable. Perhaps we could measure hope as the factor by which a negotiator inflates her assessments of these variables. Hope could be a constant that uniformly shifts calculations upward, or it could distort perceptions of probabilities in ways that change the shape of the curve. In this way, hope becomes another primitive for economists to measure and manipulate in models of negotiation. Just as economic models categorize negotiators by reservation price and costs of bargaining, the optimism theory of hope also creates way to categorize negotiators. When planning a negotiation, a seller might predict not only the buyer's reservation price and costs of bargaining, but also the buyer's optimism factor — the extent to which the buyer's corresponding predictions about the seller are likely to be distorted, inflating the buyer's hopes. . . .

POLICY IMPLICATIONS: SHOULD WE MANIPULATE HOPE?

A. Manipulating Optimism

Hopeless economic models assume that a negotiator accurately perceives the distribution of the other side's likely reservation price. In reality, many optimistic negotiators significantly overestimate the value they are likely to extract from the other side. Such optimism inflates expectations and reduces the chance that the parties will come to terms. Optimism can impede agreement, and much of the empirical work on optimism confirms this.

If this were the whole story, advisors and policymakers would not want to raise negotiators' hopes. Hopeful individuals would expect lower payoffs overall because they would reach agreement less frequently. Aggregate welfare would suffer if fewer negotiators made deals and resolved disputes.

The analysis is complicated by the fact that in certain circumstances hope may help individual negotiators. As Kahneman and Tversky explain, "in some competitive situations, the advantages of optimism and overconfidence may stem not from the deception of self, but from the deception of the opponent." Projecting complete confidence in one's position may intimidate the opponent or cause the opponent to reassess earlier estimates of the negotiator's reservation price. Because negotiators may find it difficult to pretend that they are confident, sincere overconfidence can be helpful. In cases of distributional bargaining that reach settlement, a hopeful party is likely to capture more of the surplus than a hopeless negotiator will. . . .

In many bargaining contexts, negotiators similarly must believe that the other party will cooperate in order to depart from the non-optimal strategy of mutual "value claiming." Hope might help negotiators move toward a more optimal strategy of cooperation. If each overestimates the probability of the other side's cooperation, she might risk a departure from the equilibrium of defection and move to an equilibrium of cooperation. Hope could spur one or both of the negotiators to create solutions that boost aggregate welfare and expand, rather than simply divide, the pie.

The hopeful party will not always capture 100% of this increased payoff, and as a result, one party's optimism often will increase payoffs for both parties. As the hopeful party works hard to devise integrative solutions that increase her value from the negotiation, the hopeless party will also benefit because the integrative solution will create value for him as well. In such integrative bargaining contexts, it might be desirable to raise hopes or, if the negotiators are already optimistic, to allow them to maintain these "positive illusions." At least the possibility of increased joint gains for hopeful negotiators undermines the assumption that optimism is always dysfunctional in negotiation.

B. Manipulating Satiation

How, if at all, does introducing the concept of "satiation" affect the probabilities and payoffs of agreement? By rejecting the assumption that marginal utility is constant, a satiation theory of hope reduces parties' incentives to claim a large share of the gains from trade and makes it more likely that they will come to terms. By increasing the likelihood of settlement, hope as satiation would tend to increase both sides' payoffs. If we conceive of hope as a variable that causes negotiators to set their aspiration levels according to a satiation point, then including hope as a variable in models of negotiation might boost our calculations of the probability of settlement and the payoffs from negotiation.

People who are genuinely satisfied with less might spend fewer resources negotiating to reach their satiation points. This, in turn, might leave them resources to spend on other things, with no reduction in satisfaction. Lower satiation points, moreover, would lead bargainers to reach agreement in a greater number of cases. This would increase aggregate welfare, something policymakers should strive to do.

However, some subset of cases will exist in which *individual* negotiators experience lower payoffs in a satiation model than they would in a hopeless economic model. Some sated parties will be satisfied with lower payoffs and will reach settlement at lower values than they might have strived to attain in a hopeless economic model in which marginal utility is constant. Nonetheless, any reduction in welfare for this subset of individual negotiators should be offset by the greater likelihood of settlement overall in the satiation model in which hopes are lowered. . . .

EMPIRICAL QUESTIONS: CAN WE MANIPULATE HOPE?

[S]ome research in the realm of experimental psychology has focused on the extent to which people's aspirations and resulting performance are subject to manipulation. For example, several studies have measured performance at particular tasks when subjects were not striving for specific goals. Subjects were initially given a "do your best" standard, which measured the point at which they were satiated by their own accomplishments. The researchers then assigned the subjects specific, challenging goals and remeasured their performance. These studies consistently found that people perform better when given specific, challenging goals than when they are not striving toward specific goals. Perhaps the assignment of more challenging goals raised the subjects' satiation points. Although such research measures performance outside the context of negotiation, the studies' ability to change goals, and thus change performance, suggests something about the malleability of satiation points. Just as subjects seem to have successfully adopted and acted upon the raised expectations inherent in a more specific, challenging goal, so too might negotiators adopt higher hopes and act upon them in negotiation. . . .

CONCLUSION

Hope may not be easily subject to manipulation. Even if hope is not fixed, we may be unable to find and operate the mechanism that moves hope up or down. So if hope is not malleable — or if we are unable to change malleable hopes — why focus on it? Why not just take hope as a psychological wildcard — like pride, anger, or love — that may affect the negotiation, but not in a manner that economists would study or care about?

Even if we cannot manipulate hope, we might want to include it in models of negotiation because more inclusive models will be better predictors of negotiation because more inclusive models will be better predictors of negotiation process and outcomes. For example, this Article has argued that hope might be set by parties' satiation levels. This theory of hope challenges the assumption that negotiators' marginal utility is constant and instead suggests that some point exists on a marginal utility curve beyond which each additional unit of value gained is worth less to the negotiator than those gained before it. Hopeless models that admit no possibility of satiation will conclude that a party's drive to acquire value will find an upper limit only in the amount she can get from the other side, rather than also finding some constraint in what she herself would find valuable. Realizing that in some cases negotiators will find little or no value in additional gain — even if the other side is willing to surrender it — might suggest that the chances of settlement are greater than hopeless models would predict.

Similarly, hopeless models that fail to incorporate optimism will overestimate the probability of settlement, because they will wrongly assume that negotiators accurately calculate the probable distribution of the other side's reservation price. Realizing that an optimistic seller might inflate the range of the buyer's possible reservation prices will show that such parties are less likely to come to terms than we might at first predict.

Measuring hope — even if we cannot manipulate it — might also be useful. Negotiators should try to assess the other side's optimism or satiation point if these variables might affect behavior in negotiation. For example, if a buyer was able to discover that a seller might be sated easily, this could affect the buyer's first and subsequent offers. Or if the buyer knew that the seller had an unrealistically optimistic view of the buyer's reservation price, the buyer might plan to bring to the negotiation some "proof" that would educate the seller away from her optimism. In either case, measuring hope prior to negotiation might help a negotiator prepare more thoroughly.

In this last excerpt in the section, Andrea Kupfer Schneider summarizes the arguments for setting high aspirations and then explains why negotiators often do not follow this advice.

 Andrea Kupfer Schneider, **ASPIRATIONS IN NEGOTIATION**

87 Marq. L. Rev. 675, 675–680 (2004)

INTRODUCTION

Aspirations are the specific goals in a negotiation that a negotiator wishes to achieve as part of an agreement. Aspirations can be monetary, as in, "He doesn't want to pay more than $50,000 to settle this case," or "She'd like to receive $300,000 for this house." Aspirations can also be non-monetary as in "He'd like to feel fairly treated" or "She wants the painting over the fireplace from her grandmother's estate," and they can often be a combination of monetary and non-monetary goals such as "He'd like to receive an apology and $75,000 to cover medical expenses plus pain and suffering." Aspirations are based on the underlying needs and interests of the negotiator, and they are conceptually independent of the negotiator's bottom line. . . .

OPTIMISTIC ASPIRATIONS

Negotiators should establish optimistic aspirations because empirical evidence has shown that negotiators with higher aspirations tend to achieve better bargaining results. The classic study demonstrating this proposition was run by psychologists Sidney Siegel and Lawrence Fouraker in 1960. One set of negotiators [was] given a modest goal of $2.10 profit in a buy-sell negotiation and the other set [was] given the "high aspirations" of $6.10. Both sets were told that they could keep any profits they made and could qualify for a second, "double-their-money" round if they met or exceeded their specified bargaining goals. The negotiators with the more ambitious $6.10 goal achieved a mean profit of $6.25, far outperforming the median profit of $3.35 achieved by those with the modest $2.10 goal.

There are different explanations for this effect. First, a negotiator's aspirations help to determine the outer limit of what she will request. Because a negotiator will almost never achieve more than what she asks for, setting relatively high goals is important so that the negotiator makes suitable aggressive demands.

Second, optimistic aspirations can cause negotiators to work harder at bargaining than they otherwise might, increasing the likelihood of achieving a desirable outcome. . . .

JUSTIFIABLE ASPIRATIONS

While negotiators should set relatively aggressive aspirations, those aspirations should be reasonable enough to be justifiable for several important reasons. First, aspirations should be consistent with other aspects of effective negotiation behavior. Assuming that demands are based on aspirations, negotiators will be more likely to succeed in convincing their adversary to reach an agreement based on their aspiration level if they can argue that such an outcome is derived from objective criteria. . . .

An additional reason that aspirations should be modest enough to be justifiable is that overly aggressive aspirations can lead to negotiation impasse when mutually beneficial agreements are possible. Korobkin argues that aspirations can act as an "anchor" that skews a negotiator's bottom line. In circumstances in which determining where to set one's bottom line is especially difficult, aggressive aspirations are likely to cause a negotiator to set his bottom line higher than an objective analysis of his alternatives to reaching a negotiated agreement would indicate is appropriate. Thus, aspirations that are too high can indirectly lead the negotiator to reject proposed agreements that are actually within an objectively acceptable range.

WHY DON'T NEGOTIATORS DO THIS?

Negotiators often fail to follow the "optimistic but justifiable" approach to setting aspirations, instead setting vague goals such as "achieving a good deal" or aspiring to relatively low, easy-to-achieve results. Why? One reason is that specific, optimistic aspirations can result in disappointment when they are not achieved. Setting low or non-specific goals — what Shell calls a "wimp-win" approach — maximizes the likelihood of success and protects the self-esteem. If a negotiator sets his goals low, as in a car buyer who is willing to pay up to list price for a car, this "low aspirations" negotiator is more likely to accomplish his goals. After all, it is a rare car dealer who is not happy to accept list price! On the other hand, if a negotiator sets his goal high, as in a car buyer who is aiming to pay up to $500 over the dealer's invoice for a particular car, that "high aspirations" negotiator may be disappointed in himself when he can only negotiate a deal at $1000 over the dealer's invoice — $500 over his original goal. The "high aspirations" car buyer may well have paid $2000 less than the "low aspirations" car buyer, but he may be more focused on his perceived aspirations-based loss of $500. In order to avoid this disappointment, negotiators often set low goals. A related risk is that this disappointment from one negotiation can lead negotiators to set lower goals in future negotiations, again in a self-protective response.

Another circumstance in which negotiators set low aspirations is when the negotiator feels that she lacks enough information about the other side's interests and bottom line to confidently predict what results are possible. A negotiator may assume that she needs the deal more than her counterpart or may not understand why reaching a settlement is important to the other side. Without this information, she may set her goals lower than the goals should be from an objective perspective. For example, if a house seller receives an offer that is $20,000 below the listed price after the house has been on the market for several weeks without any interest, the seller's response depends, to a great extent, on the information the seller has about the buyer. Without any information, the seller might be so excited to get an offer that she accepts the offer immediately. On the other hand, if the seller learns that the buyer needs to move next month or has told his realtor that this was his favorite house, the seller may be more willing to hold on to high aspirations. Just as setting aspirations takes preparation and the appropriate criteria, it also requires preparation about the other side.

Finally, a negotiator may set low goals when she is relatively uninterested in the result or wants to avoid conflict with another person who seems more concerned than she is about the money, power, or other issues at stake. These low goals may be appropriate as long as the negotiator makes a rational decision about this.

Notes and Questions

2.4   When movers moved your furniture into your new home, they scratched the existing kitchen floor by dragging all of the furniture. Because the pattern of the floor had been discontinued, you had to replace the entire kitchen floor. Assume that you are now negotiating with the movers for damages. What is your goal?

2.5   Goals and aspirations can sometimes be limited by court rules, such as caps on punitive damages. Placing a cap on punitive damages tends to affect the size and variability of the awards. Higher caps lead to greater size and variability of awards. Lower caps tend to narrow the range of awards. See Jennifer K. Robbennolt & Christine A. Studebaker, Anchoring in the Courtroom: The Effects of Caps on Punitive Damages, 23 Law & Hum. Behav. 353 (1999).

B.   LIMITS — BATNA AND RESERVATION POINT

This next section in the chapter turns to the other side of setting goals — that of setting your bottom line by understanding both the alternatives to an agreement and how to set your reservation point.

This first excerpt is from the international bestseller on negotiation, *Getting to YES*, which first introduced the concept of BATNA.

Roger Fisher, William Ury & Bruce Patton, **GETTING TO YES:**
NEGOTIATING AGREEMENT WITHOUT GIVING IN

99-103 (2d ed. 1991)

KNOW YOUR BATNA...

The reason you negotiate is to produce something better than the results you can obtain without negotiating. What are those results? What is that alternative? What is your BATNA—your Best Alternative to a Negotiated Agreement? That is the standard against which any proposed agreement should be measured. That is the only standard which can protect you both from accepting terms that are too unfavorable and from rejecting terms it would be in your interest to accept.

Your BATNA not only is a better measure but also has the advantage of being flexible enough to permit the exploration of imaginative solutions. Instead of ruling out any solution which does not meet your bottom line, you can compare a proposal with your BATNA to see whether it better satisfies your interest.

THE INSECURITY OF AN UNKNOWN BATNA

If you have not thought carefully about what you will do if you fail to reach an agreement, you are negotiating with your eyes closed. You may, for instance, be too optimistic and assume that you have many other choices: other houses for sale, other buyers for your secondhand car, other plumbers, other jobs available, other wholesalers, and so on. Even when your alternative is fixed, you may be taking too rosy a view of the consequences of not reaching agreement. . . .

In most circumstances, however, the greater danger is that you are *too* committed to reaching agreement. Not having developed any alternative to a negotiated solution, you are unduly pessimistic about what would happen if negotiations broke off.

DEVELOP YOUR BATNA

Vigorous exploration of what you will do if you do not reach agreement can greatly strengthen your hand. Attractive alternatives are not just sitting there waiting for you; you usually have to develop them. Generating possible BATNAs requires three distinct operations: (1) inventing a list of actions you might conceivably take if no agreement is reached; (2) improving some of the more promising ideas and converting them into practical alternatives; and (3) selecting, tentatively, the one alternative that seems best.

A NOTE ON BATNA

Using your BATNA to protect yourself from unwise agreements takes several steps. First, you need to brainstorm all of your alternatives to an agreement. This might include going to court in certain kinds of situations. Or your alternatives might include making an agreement with another company or buying a different house. Second, you choose your best alternative—the one that leaves you in the best situation. Finally, you translate this BATNA into a reservation price. The reservation price is the point at which you would be better off going to your BATNA.

For example, assume you are purchasing a home. Your first-choice home is priced at $300,000. Your second-choice home is priced at $250,000 and you have a good sense from the real estate agent that you could probably purchase it for $240,000. How do you decide when buying your second choice makes more sense? You need to value the difference between the homes — what makes your first-choice home your preferred choice? List these out: (1) attached garage; (2) better school district; (3) larger backyard; (4) does not need to be painted before moving in. Next, attach values to each of these items. For some differences between the properties, like the garage and the backyard, you might check with your real estate agent to get a sense of how others might value particular items. For others, like the school district, you are attaching a tangible number to an intangible item. Ask yourself how much more you would pay for the exact same house in one neighborhood versus the other. For the last item, painting, you can price this with some research of your own.

Now assume you've done the research and have attached the following values for your items: (1) attached garage ($10,000); (2) better school district ($15,000); (3) larger backyard ($5,000); and (4) not having to paint ($5,000 — for paint, the painter, and the inconvenience). The first-choice home is worth about $35,000 more to you. Therefore, your reservation price is $240,000 plus $35,000 = $275,000. This means that if you can't negotiate the price on the more expensive house down to $275,000, you would be better off, given your preferences, buying the less expensive home.

The next excerpt from Russell Korobkin provides more specific advice on how to use your BATNA — best alternative to negotiated agreement — to ensure you achieve a wise agreement. Your BATNA and reservation price should set the parameters of the bargaining zone.

 Russell Korobkin, **A POSITIVE THEORY OF LEGAL NEGOTIATION**

88 Geo. L.J. 1789, 1794-1798 (2000)

[P]ainstaking preparation is critical to success at the bargaining table. . . . [T]horough preparation is a prerequisite for the negotiator to accomplish zone definition as advantageously as possible. . . . "Internal" preparation refers to research that the negotiator does to set and adjust his own RP [Reservation Point]. "External" preparation refers to research that the negotiator does to estimate and manipulate the other party's RP.

INTERNAL PREPARATION

A negotiator cannot determine his RP without first understanding his substitutes for and the opportunity costs of reaching a negotiated agreement. This, of course, requires research. . . .

After identifying the various alternatives to reaching a negotiated agreement, the negotiator needs to determine which alternative is most desirable. Fisher and his coauthors coined the appropriate term "BATNA" — "best alternative to a negotiated agreement" — to identify this choice. The identity and quality of a negotiator's BATNA is the primary input into his RP.

If the negotiator's BATNA and the subject of the negotiation are perfectly interchangeable, determining the reservation price is quite simple: the reservation price is merely the value of the BATNA. For example, if Esau's BATNA is buying another catering business for $190,000 that is identical to Jacob's in terms of quality, earnings potential, and all other factors that are important to Esau, then his RP is $190,000. If Jacob will sell for some amount less than that, Esau will be better off buying Jacob's company than he would pursuing his best alternative. If Jacob demands more than $190,000, Esau is better off buying the alternative company and not reaching an agreement with Jacob.

In most circumstances, however, the subject of a negotiation and the negotiator's BATNA are not perfect substitutes. If Jacob's business is of higher quality, has a higher earnings potential, or is located closer to Esau's home, he would probably be willing to pay a premium for it over what he would pay for the alternative choice. For example, if the alternative business is selling for $190,000, Esau might determine he would be willing to pay up to a $10,000 premium over the alternative for Jacob's business and thus set his RP at $200,000. On the other hand, if Esau's BATNA is more desirable to him than Jacob's business, Esau will discount the value of his BATNA by the amount necessary to make the two alternatives equally desirable values for the money; perhaps he will set his RP at $180,000 in recognition that his BATNA is $10,000 more desirable than Jacob's business, and Jacob's business would be equally desirable only at a $10,000 discount. . . .

The relationship between a party's BATNA and his RP can be generalized in the following way. A party's RP has two components: (1) the market value of his BATNA; and (2) the difference to *him* between the value of his BATNA and the value of the subject of the negotiation. A seller sets his RP by calculating (1) and either *subtracting* (2) if the subject of the negotiation is more valuable than his BATNA (and therefore he is willing to accept less to reach an agreement) or *adding* (2) if the BATNA is more valuable than the subject of the negotiation (and therefore, he would demand more to reach an agreement and give up his BATNA). A buyer sets his RP by calculating (1) and either *adding* (2) if the subject of the negotiation is more valuable than his BATNA (and therefore he would pay a premium to reach an agreement) or *subtracting* (2) if his BATNA is more valuable than the subject of the negotiation (and therefore he would demand a discount to give up the BATNA). . . .

By investigating an even wider range of alternatives to reaching agreement, and by more thoroughly investigating the value of obvious alternatives, the negotiator can alter his RP in a way that will shift the bargaining zone to his advantage. . . .

EXTERNAL PREPARATION

External preparation allows the negotiator to estimate his opponent's RP . . . [t]o accurately predict Jacob's RP and therefore pinpoint the low end of the bargaining zone. This information will also prepare Esau to attempt to persuade Jacob during the course of negotiations to lower his RP, a point discussed in detail below.

It is worth noting that in the litigation context both parties often have the same alternatives and the same BATNA. If plaintiff Goliath determines that his BATNA is going to trial, then defendant David's only alternative — and therefore his BATNA default — is going to trial as well. In this circumstance, internal preparation and external preparations merge. Research suggests that an "egocentric bias" is likely to cause litigants to interpret material facts in a light favorable to their legal position, thus causing them to overestimate the expected value of an adjudicated outcome. Consequently, it is likely that, examining the same operative facts and legal precedent, plaintiff Goliath will place a higher value on the BATNA of trial than defendant David. This difference in perception often will be offset, however, by the fact that plaintiff Goliath is likely to set his RP, or the minimum settlement he will accept, below his perceived expected value of trial to account for the higher costs and higher risk associated with trial, while defendant David is likely to set his RP, or the maximum settlement he will agree to pay, above the expected value of trial for the same reasons. . . . [L]ess confident the parties are in the value that they place on the BATNA of trial, the larger the bargaining zone between their RPs is likely to be.

PERSUASION

Efforts at persuasion in negotiation are best understood as attempts to satisfy one or both of two goals: (1) to shift the bargaining zone to the advantage of the negotiator, either by convincing the opponent that his RP is worse than he believed before beginning negotiations or that the negotiator's RP is better than previously believed; and (2) to establish an objective — and therefore "fair" — method of agreeing on a sale price that falls within the bargaining zone. [Only the] first point is considered here. . . . In either case, the importance of persuasion demonstrates that both zone definition and surplus allocation are dynamic activities, dependent not only on negotiators' individual prebargaining analysis but also on their interaction.

Notes and Questions

2.6 What is the difference between a BATNA and a reservation point? Why is this important? In what context might the difference not be useful?

2.7 Why does Korobkin suggest preparing with respect to your counterpart's BATNA and reservation point? How can you do this?

2.8 What if, in the course of the negotiation, you find out that your assumptions about your counterpart's BATNA are mistaken? What if, for example, you thought the people placing a bid on your house also were very interested in another house? How would that affect your negotiation? What if you found out, instead, they loved your house?

2.9 Assume again that when movers moved your furniture into your new home, they scratched the existing kitchen floor by dragging all of the furniture. Because the pattern of the floor had been discontinued, you had to replace the entire kitchen floor. Assume that you are now negotiating with the movers for damages. What are your alternatives to an agreement with them? Which of these is your BATNA? How would you determine your reservation point? What other information might you need? How is this different from setting your goals in the negotiation?

2.10 Assume that a local sandwich shop is negotiating with a national coffee franchise, Morebucks, to serve Morebucks coffee. The sandwich shop is interested in serving Morebucks so that it can bring in more customers and make more money. What else can the sandwich shop do to improve its financial situation? These are all alternatives to a negotiated agreement. Note that some of these alternatives may make sense to do anyway. What type of research would you perform in advance of the negotiations with Morebucks? Based on your research and your other alternatives to this agreement, you can choose your BATNA. The BATNA is an action plan. The next step is to translate this BATNA into a reservation price. For example, assume you find out that (1) the other national coffee franchise, Coffeebest, usually charges $3 per pound of coffee to its franchisees; (2) the standard price from Morebucks to outside vendors is usually $4 per pound; and (3) Morebucks has been known to give discounts for long-term contracts, for large volume, and in new areas where it is trying to get a niche. How do you set your reservation point?

2.11 Some authors believe that BATNA is not useful in all negotiations:

> [T]he notion of commitment to a relationship limits the usefulness of the "best alternative to a negotiated agreement" (BATNA) concept. Inherent in the BATNA idea is the assumption that negotiators will walk away from an agreement if there is a higher-utility alternative outside the relationship. This concept, in my opinion, assumes that either the parties' commitment to the relationship is zero, or that the parties factor the cost of sacrificing the relationship when assessing the utility of offers. Both assumptions seem unrealistic when applied to day-to-day negotiations in the real world. Imagine, for instance, a dispute between a woman and her husband. He wants her companionship in social and leisure events, but she is too busy with her medical practice. The BATNA concept assumes the husband will seriously consider meeting his social needs outside the marriage when evaluating her counteroffers. Examples involving others with whom one frequently negotiates show similar shortcomings of the BATNA concept — for example, negotiations with one's boss, children, key customers, social organizations, and any other entity to which one has a strong, ongoing relationship.

Leonard Greenhalgh, Relationships in Negotiation, 3 Negot. J. 235, 238 (1987). How does Greenhalgh seem to define BATNA in his example? Do you agree with his argument that BATNA is not a useful concept in this context? Can you think of other BATNAs for the husband? How can BATNAs be used in negotiations where strong relationships exist?

2.12 For a recent literature review on first offers in negotiation, see John M. Oesch & Adam D. Galinsky, First Offers in Negotiations: Determinants and Effects, 16th Annual IACM Conference Melbourne, Australia, at *http://ssrn.com/abstract=399722* (offers often reflect both information on goals and limits; whether to make the first offer is often debated in negotiation advice books, but, unfortunately, the answer is the ever helpful "it depends").

The next excerpt discusses decision analysis as a tool for preparing both your goals and your BATNA in a negotiation, particularly as to deciding whether to settle or to pursue litigation. Jeffrey Senger, senior counsel in the Office of Dispute Resolution for the U.S. Department of Justice, examines how decision analysis works. After his excerpt, this section then demonstrates how to use decision analysis in a particular case.

 Jeffrey M. Senger, **DECISION ANALYSIS IN NEGOTIATION**

87 Marq. L. Rev. 723, 723-725 (2004)

Imagine a United States President facing a decision on whether to attempt a military mission to rescue Americans trapped in a hostile country. In a meeting in the White House Situation Room, top military advisers describe a possible plan. The President asks about the chances of success for the mission. The advisers respond that there are six crucial stages of the plan, and all have to go smoothly in order for the mission to work. They state that the overall chances for the plan are good because each individual stage has an eighty percent chance of success. What should the President do?

A field known as "decision analysis" can help answer this type of question and many others in a wide range of situations. When parties understand what their chances of success are for each of several possible choices, they can make better decisions on how to proceed. The tools of decision analysis are particularly useful for negotiators. People who are negotiating need to be able to evaluate what is likely to happen to them if they accept a deal and what will occur if they do not.

In the rescue example above, it is easy to see how a President might be tempted to authorize the plan. If the chances of success at each stage of a mission are eighty percent, it may seem that the chances of success for the overall mission would be reasonably good. However, decision analysis shows that the mission is much more likely to fail than succeed. The statistical method used to calculate the overall likelihood of success in this situation requires multiplying the chances of success of each individual stage. Thus the President should multiply 0.80 (the chance of succeeding in the first stage) by 0.80 (the chance of the second stage), then multiply this result by 0.80 for the third stage, and so on, all the way through the six stages of the mission. This total, $0.80 \times 0.80 \times 0.80 \times 0.80 \times 0.80 \times 0.80$, (or 0.80 to the sixth power), is 0.26. Thus, the overall chances of success for the mission are only twenty-six percent, or slightly better than one in four.

EXAMPLES OF DECISION ANALYSIS

The mathematical processes used in risk analysis may be explained further with several examples. Imagine going to a local carnival and approaching a midway booth with a giant "Wheel of Chance." The wheel has many spaces on it, half colored blue and half yellow. The carnival operator tells you that if you spin and the wheel lands on a blue space, you will win $20.[3] If it lands on a yellow space, you win nothing. How much would you pay to play this game?

Many people can answer this question intuitively, without having to use a mathematical approach. However, following the math in this example can be helpful to understanding what happens in more complicated situations. Decision analysis principles state that the expected outcome of a situation like this is found by multiplying the probabilities of each possible outcome by the result of that outcome (called

---

[3] Assume for purposes of the example that the carnival operator has not rigged the wheel to give an unfair result.

the payoff), and then summing these products. In the Wheel of Chance example, the probability of landing on blue is 0.50, and the payoff for landing on blue is $20. Multiplying these numbers yields $10. The probability of landing on yellow is 0.50, the payoff for this is $0, and multiplying these numbers yields $0. Adding these two results, $10 plus $0, gives the expected result of the game: $10.

Figure 1 shows a graphical representation of this situation, which is a simple example of a "decision tree."[4] The trunk of the tree (entitled "Wheel of Chance") breaks off into two branches, representing the two possible outcomes of the game, blue or yellow. This juncture is marked with a circle (called a "chance node"), indicating that the results at this point cannot be controlled. The probabilities of each outcome (0.50) are written below each branch. Each branch ends in a triangle (called a "terminal node"), indicating that the game is over at that point, with payoffs of $20 for blue and $0 for yellow. A computer can be used to "roll back" the tree, which gives the expected value of the tree at the chance node. The box next to the chance node in Figure 1 shows the expected value of $10.

It is worth noting that $10 is not a possible outcome from playing a single game (which yields either $20 or $0). Instead, it is a mathematical construct providing a sense of what the game is worth, in a theoretical sense, to someone who plays it. One way of explaining this is that the expected value represents the average payoff for someone who played the game many times.

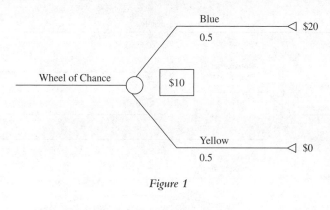

Figure 1

A NOTE ON DECISION TREE ANALYSIS IN ACTION

Assume that Brooks and Smith are involved in a car accident. Brooks was recklessly speeding on Main Street when he collided with Smith's vehicle after she unexpectedly braked for a squirrel in the road. You, as Smith's attorney, conclude that Smith was contributorily negligent and is at least potentially liable for Brooks's damages. You believe that Smith has a 50 percent chance of withstanding a motion to dismiss. If you proceed to trial, you believe there is a 50 percent chance of winning and a 50 percent chance of losing. Smith's attorneys' fees are estimated as nominal if you settle

---

[4] Technically, this figure would be called a "chance tree" or an "event tree," as a decision tree would include another branch to indicate the option not to play the game at all.

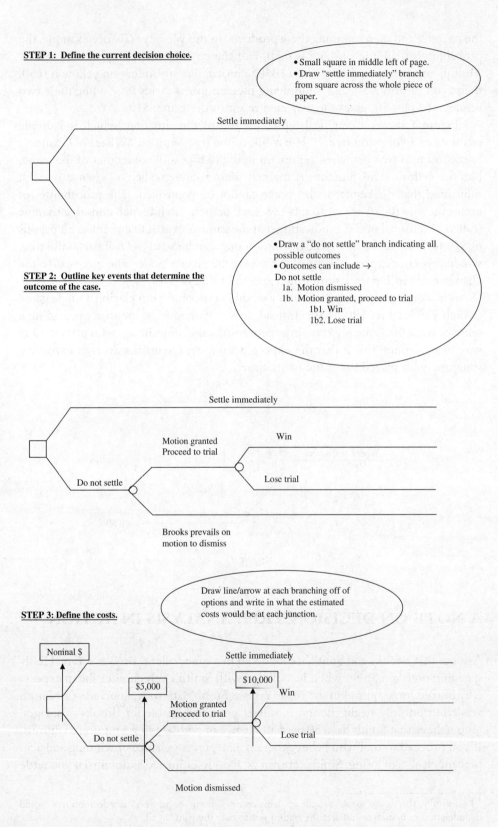

STEP 1: Define the current decision choice.

- Small square in middle left of page.
- Draw "settle immediately" branch from square across the whole piece of paper.

Settle immediately

STEP 2: Outline key events that determine the outcome of the case.

- Draw a "do not settle" branch indicating all possible outcomes
- Outcomes can include →
  Do not settle
  1a. Motion dismissed
  1b. Motion granted, proceed to trial
      1b1. Win
      1b2. Lose trial

Settle immediately

Motion granted
Proceed to trial

Win

Do not settle

Lose trial

Brooks prevails on
motion to dismiss

STEP 3: Define the costs.

Draw line/arrow at each branching off of options and write in what the estimated costs would be at each junction.

Nominal $

Settle immediately

$5,000

$10,000

Win

Motion granted
Proceed to trial

Do not settle

Lose trial

Motion dismissed

STEP 4: Confirm that the diagram of the case is adequate.

No additional drawing.

STEP 5: Define the possible outcomes of the case.

Assign dollar values to the probable outcomes on each of the branches of the diagram (actual damages, punitive damages, losing, etc.).

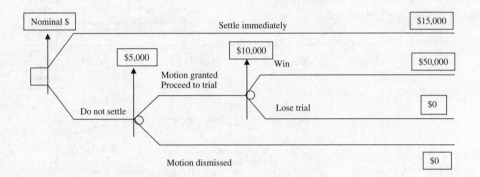

STEP 6: Assign probabilities to each possibility.

For each branch off of a chance node, assign the possibility of that outcome.

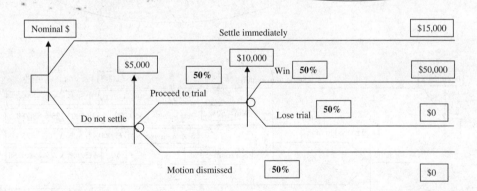

STEP 7: Estimate the amount of time the case will take.

Indicate estimates of time delays and how much the additional time will incur costs.

STEP 8: Subtract the costs from each possible outcome.

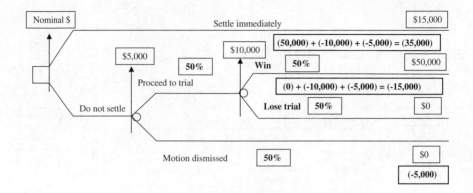

STEP 9: Calculate the final value of each outcome.

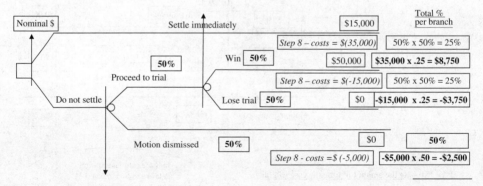

So, Smith should accept the settlement offer.

the case immediately, $5,000 if you argue a motion to dismiss, and an additional $10,000 if you go to trial.

You draw a decision tree to show Smith your analysis as to what amount she should settle for. Should Smith accept Brooks's offer to settle for $15,000?

Notes and Questions

2.13 What is the minimum you would advise your client to accept as a settlement offer if, having taken all factors into account, you think you have a 60 percent chance of winning $150,000 and a 40 percent chance of losing? (Ignore any adjustment for time value of money.)

2.14 What is the minimum you would advise your client to accept in settlement if you think you have a 10 percent chance of winning $1 million in punitive and actual damages, and a 50 percent chance of winning $150,000 in actual damages, and a 40 percent chance of losing? (Ignore any adjustment for time value of money.)

C. CRITERIA AND FAIRNESS

A crucial part of setting your goals and limits and of convincing others to respect them, as discussed in the preceding section, depends on establishing the relevant criteria. This first excerpt from research scholar Cecilia Albin focuses broadly on different types of fairness in a negotiation.

 Cecilia Albin, **THE ROLE OF FAIRNESS IN NEGOTIATIONS**

9 Negot. J. 223, 225-228, 233-239 (1993)

[T]he actual practice of negotiation . . . suggests that concepts of fairness are often an influential factor. They influence the "give-and-take" in the bargaining process, help parties to forge agreement, and help to determine whether a particular outcome will be viewed as satisfactory, and thus be honored in the long run. Notions of fairness may create a motivation to resolve a particular problem through negotiation in the first place, and thus have an impact on the positions and expectations which parties bring to the table. A limited body of research on negotiation, experimental and social psychological in particular, supports these propositions. . . .

This study identifies and analyzes four types of fairness which have an impact on negotiation: structural fairness, process fairness, procedural fairness, and outcome fairness. In any one case, all four types of fairness will not necessarily be significant nor even present. While concerns about outcome fairness are commonly thought to dominate negotiations, in some contexts no outcome can be quite fair — e.g., in the allocation of a single indivisible good or burden for which there is no adequate compensation, such as a death mission or a child in a custody dispute. Parties may then agree to use a procedure viewed as fair for settling the issue, and to accept whatever (unfair) solution it produces. Similarly, when a negotiation process cannot be fair in important respects (e.g., permit participation by all parties or public scrutiny), greater demands will often be advanced regarding the fairness of its outcome.

While analytically useful, the four categories are not always distinct from one another, even conceptually. An outcome viewed as fair may, in effect, be a fair procedure (e.g., for allocating a scarce resource on a continuous basis). Elements of structural fairness, such as the grouping of issues, influence outcome fairness; notions of outcome fairness often influence the choice of "fair" procedures; and particular procedures will, in turn, have an impact on the outcome. Some procedures (e.g., problem-solving techniques) may help to "neutralize" structural variables such as power asymmetry, or may be part of the structure themselves.

STRUCTURAL FAIRNESS

We commonly think of fairness as relating to the outcome, and perhaps also the process, of negotiations. Yet an important class of fairness issues concerns the overarching structure of the negotiation process which, in turn, reflects more or less the structure of the dispute and overall relations between parties. . . .

A major set of structural components concerns the parties to the negotiations, including any third parties: their identity; number; attributes (e.g., interests, amount of resources); representation; and relations, including the distribution of resources between them. . . . The idea that every major party to a conflict, or groups most affected by the outcome should be given a genuine opportunity to be represented in the negotiations is regarded as a key element of fairness which significantly influences perceptions of the legitimacy of the outcome and the chances of its implementation. An example is negotiations over the siting of hazardous waste treatment plants, prisons, and other unwanted facilities. . . .

A second group of structural elements concerns the issues to be negotiated — their number and grouping as they appear on the agenda when negotiations begin; their complexity and "sums" (degree to which they are, or are perceived as, zero-sum or positive sum); and relationships between them (e.g., degree to which they are separate or intertwined). . . .

Another category of structural fairness elements is the rules and codes of conduct to govern the negotiations, and ways in which these are established. These elements include agenda-setting (e.g., issues to be negotiated, their order on the agenda, and time allowed for each issue); communication procedures between parties and with the outside world (e.g., use of press conferences to report on progress or deadlocks); voting procedures; and the use of deadlines and other time limits. A common notion of fairness is that parties, whether equal or not in power, should have an *equal* chance to determine the agenda, equal control over the use of deadlines, and so forth.

Finally, a major set of structural elements involving fairness issues concerns the physical features of the negotiations: the location; the presence and degree of access of various audiences to the negotiations; the availability of communication channels between parties; and access to information and technical support. . . .

PROCESS FAIRNESS

Process fairness concerns two broad issues: the extent to which parties in the process of negotiating relate to and treat each other "fairly"; and how parties' notions of (outcome) fairness influence the dynamics of the negotiation process, including their choice of procedures for arriving at an agreement.

"Fair behavior" in negotiations can be defined as the extent to which parties actually honor agreements reached on many structural issues before the process began and the degree to which they use procedures without deception in the effort to find a solution. The first criterion to assess fair behavior leads to questions such as[:] Is every party to the

> **Mind Your Manners**
>
> A study of libel litigation found that the primary goals of plaintiffs — restoring reputation, correcting a falsehood, and vengeance — had little to do with money or even their chance of success. The way that plaintiffs were treated when they called to complain of libel was directly connected to whether they chose to sue. The Iowa study of libel litigation found that some plaintiffs who were initially unsure about whether to sue only initiated lawsuits after being treated rudely by the media defendant. Randall Bezanson et al., Libel Law and the Press: Myth and Reality 29-53 (1987).

negotiation or affected groups given an adequate chance to be heard and have an input into the process at each stage — from framing the problem, identifying and assessing alternative solutions, to making the final decision? . . .

The proposition that specifically divergent concepts of fairness could provide terms of trade and facilitate agreement in predominantly integrative negotiations deserves more testing on actual cases. One illustrative example of a formula for an agreement incorporating divergent fairness concepts which increased joint gains is the 1987 Montreal Protocol on Substances That Deplete the Ozone Layer. For the developing countries, a fair solution must not penalize them for a problem caused essentially by the industrialized world. At the heart of the developing countries' notion of a fair agreement was the principle of need — of compensating them through technical and financial assistance and other special provisions for accepting regulation of emissions which could hamper their development. At the core of the North's notion of fairness was equity — expressed in the proposed reductions in chlorofluorocarbons (CFCs) proportionally to each country's emission level, and the foreseen final regime accepting the North's much higher emission levels and keeping those of the South low. The equality norm was expressed in the long term goal of the North and the South sharing the cost of regulation on a basis of parity. . . .

PROCEDURAL FAIRNESS

Procedural fairness concerns specific mechanisms used for arriving at an agreement. These mechanisms are considered fair because of some intrinsic value (e.g., they give parties an equal chance to "win" or demand equal concessions from them), because they tend to produce fair outcomes, or because of both of the qualities. Thus procedural fairness concerns the features of the mechanisms themselves, while process fairness refers to larger issues, such as how the mechanisms are actually used in the negotiation process (e.g., if in good faith, without bluffing) and the substance of parties' concessions.

Fair procedures may be diffuse and difficult to observe, such as reciprocation, or more clearly defined and manifest, such as tossing a coin and divide-and-choose. They may be determined prior to the talks, and considered part of the established "rules of the game" and overall structure of the negotiations. For example, the reciprocity norm is incorporated in the General Agreement on Tariffs and Trade (GATT), which provides much of the structure for negotiations over trade liberalization. It permits protectionist measures against countries which subsidize their exports or engage in other trade practices deemed unfair, and holds that a cut in any country's import tariffs should be balanced fairly with equivalent foreign tariff cuts. Distributive procedures may be distinguished from integrative procedures. Particularly in complex negotiations involving multiple issues and parties, procedures of both kinds are used.

Many fair procedures serve as mechanisms which govern the exchange of concessions leading to a division of a limited bundle of goods. Often, these mechanisms are based on variations of the principle of reciprocity, and tend to be used when parties view themselves as equal in power, recognize a mutually prominent solution, and/or foresee an agreement based on equality.

Reciprocity procedures are perceived as fair because they supposedly lead to a fair outcome. For example, when parties foresee or favor a split-the-difference agreement, equal concessions tend to be exchanged. But even in the absence of agreement on a predicted outcome, the reciprocity norm is widely regarded as intrinsically fair — even as "one of the universal 'principal components' of moral codes" (Ikle, How Nations Negotiate, 1964). . . .

Another major category of distributive procedures grants parties a fair (often equal) chance to win the disputed resource, or be relieved of it in the case of a burden. . . .

These kinds of procedures are often used when parties cannot agree on a fair solution; when no solution can be quite fair (e.g., the allocation of a mission involving high risks of death); when a solution is needed quickly; when the stakes are relatively low so that it is not worth using a more time consuming procedure; when the stakes are so high that full-fledged bargaining would seem inappropriate or involve too many pressures and pain; and when the greater ambiguity or manipulability of other procedures are to be avoided.

Some procedures are "random methods" — e.g., tossing a die, flipping a coin, or arranging a lottery. They usually reflect fairness understood specifically as equality: Initial equal entitlements to the resources and no (or equal) information about the other's evaluations are assumed, and parties are given an equal chance to win. . . .

Another type of procedure is to arrange an "auction" to determine which party values the disputed resources the most. . . .

Still another procedure is "divide-and-choose." It refers to the old custom of how to deal with two children fighting over a cake they both want. Their parents decide that one of them will cut the cake and then the other will choose the first piece, thus inducing the child cutting the cake to do so fairly. The mechanism was used successfully in the complex Law of the Sea negotiations to determine the allocation of mining sites in the deep seabed. . . .

The fairness issues raised by integrative procedures are subtle and difficult to define. Yet they have an intrinsic value of fairness in seeking to elicit balanced, truthful information about core concerns underlying stated positions, and/or in producing new options which can better meet all parties' essential concerns. When used successfully, integrative procedures also tend to bring about fair outcomes by virtue of satisfying all vital interests involved, although parties do not necessarily gain to the same extent.

One group of integrative procedures consists of more-or-less structured approaches for improving communication and trust between parties, changing their zero-sum perceptions of the conflict, and building confidence in the possibility of mutually satisfactory solutions. Examples are "controlled communication" and "problem-solving workshops" and the introduction of "superordinate goals." The second group consists of specific techniques for reframing conflict situations and creating solutions of high joint benefit. They include "expanding the pie," linkage of issues, and compensation; functional strategies; "dovetailing"; and formula construction. The formula not only serves as a framework for the substance of a fair outcome, but also as a procedure for increasing joint gains and allocating them fairly. . . .

OUTCOME FAIRNESS

Outcome fairness refers to the principles underlying the allocation (exchange or division) of benefits and burdens in negotiated agreements, and the extent to which parties actually consider that allocation fair after the fact.

Three major principles will be discussed, with brief references to ethnic conflict in which outcome fairness issues figure prominently: equity, equality, and need.

Equity

Originating in Aristotle's notion of justice as rooted in "balance" and "proportion," the equity principle holds that resources (rewards) should be distributed proportionally to relevant contributions (inputs). Fairness is achieved when each party's ratio of inputs to rewards is the same, and injustice is experienced in relation to these ratios rather than in absolute terms. Relevant contributions may be qualities and endowments (e.g., status, power, skills, wealth, intelligence), or actions and efforts (e.g., hours worked, tasks completed, leadership exercised). . . .

Equality

The principle of equality, also termed "impartial justice," holds that parties should receive the same or comparable rewards, irrespective of their contributions or needs. The norm finds its origins in the Enlightenment and the philosophy of Jean-Jacques Rousseau, which regarded individual differences as environmental products and equal treatment of all people as the natural and preferred type of human relationships. . . .

Need

A third major principle of outcome fairness is need, also termed compensatory or redistributive justice. This principle stipulates that resources should be allocated proportionally based on the strength of need alone, so that the least endowed party gets the greatest share.

Factors such as age, status, gender, type of relationship between parties, goals, culture, and type of issue(s) may influence perceptions of fairness, and the choice and particular interpretation of fairness principles, in the settlement of distributive issues. . . .

The principles reviewed often pose questions of interpretation and operationalization. Thus negotiations often revolve around reaching agreement on the application, as much as the choice, of the principle(s) to guide the resource allocation. Furthermore, outcome fairness in many contexts must involve a balance between a combination of principles, all of which may appear equally applicable, which accounts for a wider range of factors and circumstances than any single norm can do. . . .

This article has analyzed four classes of fairness issues, all of which affect the process and outcome of negotiations under different conditions. It has proposed that when a common notion of outcome fairness exists at an early stage in the talks, that notion will tend to coordinate concessions and facilitate agreement. When parties are entrenched in opposing notions of fairness, a solution may still be reached. In integrative negotiations, divergent concepts of fairness become part of the bargaining itself, and may help to provide terms of trade. A fair outcome in many real-world situations cannot rely on a single norm, but only on a balance between a number of principles. A concluded agreement may become viewed as unfair and thus call for renegotiation. . . .

Negotiations are not driven by requests for fairness alone. Nor is there, for sure, a single universal concept or application of fairness which reflects itself in negotiations. Notions of fairness are extremely diverse and vary with the context. But in response to the introductory question, on what (if any) role notions of fairness play in negotiations, it must be concluded that the issue is not *whether* but *how* they have an impact.

Notes and Questions

2.15 Albin suggests that another type of fairness can substitute for outcome fairness if the latter is not available. Do you think this makes sense? How would this actually work?

2.16 There has been a long-running national debate over where to locate the nation's nuclear waste. In 2002, Congress approved burying the nuclear waste in Yucca Mountain in Nevada. The state of Nevada filed a lawsuit to block this. What issues of fairness does this raise? Who should determine where the waste is buried? Who should be at the table?

2.17 One student shared the following story in class. It is a great example of a negotiation based on criteria and fairness. "I was selling my used car and the person I was dealing with was more of a haggling than problem-solving type. She asked if the car passed emission standards. I said I didn't know because it was never tested. She didn't believe me. Instead of arguing with her about whether or not I was lying, I offered to take her to the emissions test center so we would both know whether it passed. It did and she bought it." Which of Albin's fairness issues is raised here? How do the parties resolve it?

This next excerpt addresses Albin's point of outcome fairness — the principles underlying the resolution. Earlier in this chapter, we read excerpts from *Getting to YES* that outlined BATNA. This excerpt focuses on the use of objective criteria.

 Roger Fisher, William Ury & Bruce Patton, GETTING TO YES: NEGOTIATING AGREEMENT WITHOUT GIVING IN

85-88 (2d ed. 1991)

DEVELOPING OBJECTIVE CRITERIA

Carrying on a principled negotiation involves two questions: How do you develop objective criteria, and how do you use them in negotiating?

Whatever method of negotiation you use, you will do better if you prepare in advance. This certainly holds true of principled negotiation. So develop some alternative standards beforehand and think through their application to your case.

Fair Standards

You will usually find more than one objective criterion available as a basis for agreement. Suppose, for example, your car is demolished and you file a claim with an insurance company. In your discussion with the adjuster, you might take into account such measures of the car's value as (1) the original cost of the car less depreciation; (2) what the car could have been sold for; (3) the standard "blue book" value for a car of that year and model; (4) what it would cost to replace the car with a comparable one; and (5) what a court might award as the value of the car. . . .

At a minimum, objective criteria need to be independent of each side's will. Ideally, to assure a wise agreement, objective criteria should be not only independent of will but also both legitimate and practical. In a

> **Moneyball**
>
> The use of objective criteria can be seen in many different ways as a method of persuasion. Consider new criteria used by Billy Beane, general manager of the Oakland A's baseball club, to evaluate and choose new players. For example, rather than equating on-base percentage with a player's slugging percentage, he valued on-base percentage at three times the value of the slugging percentage, thus giving more weight to walks and a general ability to get on base. Ultimately, a follower of Beane's method, Theo Epstein, became general manager for the Boston Red Sox and, using these new criteria, helped build a team that won its first World Series in 86 years. See Michael Lewis, Moneyball: The Art of Winning an Unfair Game (2003).

boundary dispute, for example, you may find it easier to agree on a physically salient feature such as a river than on a line three yards to the east of the riverbank. . . .

Fair Procedures

To produce an outcome independent of will, you can use either fair standards for the substantive question or, for example, the age-old way to divide a piece of cake between two children: one cuts and the other chooses. Neither can complain about an unfair division. . . .

As you consider procedural solutions, look at other basic means of settling differences: taking turns, drawing lots, letting someone else decide, and so on.

Frequently, taking turns presents the best way for heirs to divide a large number of heirlooms left to them collectively. Afterwards, they can do some trading if they want. Or they can make the selection tentative so they see how it comes out before committing themselves to accept it. Drawing lots, flipping a coin, and other forms of chance have an inherent fairness. The results may be unequal, but each side had an equal opportunity. . . .

NEGOTIATING WITH OBJECTIVE CRITERIA

Having identified some objective criteria and procedures, how do you go about discussing them with the other side?

There are three basic points to remember:

1. Frame each issue as a joint search for objective criteria.
2. Reason and be open to reason as to which standards are most appropriate and how they should be applied.
3. Never yield to pressure, only to principle.

Notes and Questions

2.18 The use of objective criteria is often cited as one of the most powerful tools of principled negotiation. Why do you think this is so? How does the use of objective criteria make your argument stronger?

2.19 In an analysis of fairness, where do objective criteria fit — structure, process, procedure, or outcome?

2.20 How can you use objective criteria against a "hard" bargainer to avoid being taken advantage of?

2.21 If you are trying to settle a case for medical malpractice, what objective criteria could you look to? How would you find these?

The next excerpt discusses the idea of fairness related to how one side feels about the other side. A party who feels poorly treated is less likely to settle, even when that does not make economic sense. This suggests that fairness or equity is an independent variable that influences bargaining outcomes.

 Russell Korobkin & Chris Guthrie, **PSYCHOLOGICAL BARRIERS TO LITIGATION SETTLEMENT: AN EXPERIMENTAL APPROACH**

93 Mich. L. Rev. 107, 144-146 (1994)

We provided subjects with a simple landlord-tenant dispute. Subjects were told that they signed a six-month lease to live in an off-campus apartment beginning September 1. After two months the heater broke down. Although they immediately notified the landlord and requested repair, the landlord failed to fix the heater. As a result, according to the scenario, the subjects spent four winter months in a cold apartment attempting to keep warm with a space heater before moving out at the end of the lease period. Throughout this time period, the subjects had continued to pay $1,000 per month in rent. After moving out, they learned from a student legal service lawyer that "there was a good chance" of recovering a portion of the $4,000 in rent paid over that four-month period of time. The lawyer gave neither a specific prediction of the likelihood of success nor any estimate of the exact magnitude of a judgment. Subjects learned that, with the assistance of their attorney, they had filed an action in small claims court against the landlord. Prior to the court date, the landlord offered to settle the case out of court for $900.

Start Walking!

A favorite story about this phenomenon of caring about the treatment of the other side comes from Steve Lubet's story of his family trip to Petra in Jordan. Tourists can either walk over a mile to the ruins at Petra or hire a Bedouin guide and horse for the ride. Tourists can either hire a horse round trip (for 7 dinars) or one way (guides would demand 7 dinars and would reluctantly lower to 4 dinars). In an experiment over three days, Professor Lubet tried unsuccessfully to negotiate a lower price than 4 dinars for just the return trip each day from Petra. His theory was that (a) by the end of the day there were more horses than tourists and that (b) guides would prefer to use their horses as much as possible in order to make money. As he wrote, "So we walked. Four of us. Three times. . . . The result was clearly suboptimal. My family walked instead of riding; the horses idled instead of working." Why did the Bedouin horse owners refuse to bargain lower with Lubet? Lubet finally asked his children why. "'Because you didn't offer them enough money Daddy, and they thought that you didn't respect them.' But they still should have preferred the money to just standing around not working. 'No, Daddy, they would rather stand around than take less than they thought they were worth.'" Steven Lubet, Notes on the Bedouin Horse Trade or "Why Won't the Market Clear Daddy?," 74 Tex. L. Rev. 1039 (1996).

The variable tested in this scenario was the landlord's reason for failing to repair the heater in spite of the tenant's prompt request that he do so. Group *A* subjects learned that they had made a number of calls to the landlord, to no avail. "The landlord promised to fix your heater, but he never did. A week later, you called him again. Again, he promised to fix it, but he never did. Over the next several weeks, you called him a half-dozen times, but he did not return your calls." Group *B* participants received a different explanation: After the second call to the landlord, "[y]ou learned that he had left the country unexpectedly due to a family emergency and that he was expected to be gone for several months." Both Group *A* and Group *B* subjects chose one of the five usual answer choices to indicate their likelihood of accepting the $900 settlement offer.

The given explanation had a significant impact on how likely subjects were to accept the settlement offer and forgo their day in court. Knowing that the landlord did not fix the heater because he was out of the country due to a family emergency, most Group *B* (Family Emergency) subjects were willing to accept the landlord's offer and let the matter rest. Their mean response was 3.41 (n = 58). Group *A* subjects (Broken Promise), in contrast, were more likely to reject the $900 offer and risk a less favorable decision in small claims court than to accept the offer. Their average score was 2.60 (n = 60). The difference between the two groups is highly significant. Fifty-nine percent of the Family Emergency subjects said they would "definitely" or "probably" accept the settlement offer, while only 35 percent of the Broken Promise subjects provided those same responses. Thirty percent of the Broken Promise subjects said they would "definitely reject" the $900 settlement offer in favor of small claims court, while only 9 percent of the Family Emergency subjects would "definitely reject" the offer.

Notes and Questions

2.22 Should you care about how the other side treats you in a dispute? Should that impact your willingness to settle?

2.23 How can attorneys help their clients avoid this situation? What would you suggest?

Often, there are psychological factors that negotiators use to help determine fairness and can be persuasive in a negotiation. The next excerpt from Chris Guthrie outlines some of these factors.

 Chris Guthrie, **PRINCIPLES OF INFLUENCE IN NEGOTIATION**

87 Marq. L. Rev. 829, 831, 832, 833-834, 835 (2004)

A. LIKING

The first principle of influence that a lawyer might use to her client's advantage is the "liking" rule. According to this principle, individuals prefer to comply with requests made by those they know and like. Individuals tend to like those who are physically attractive, those with whom they share something in common, and those with whom they are familiar. . . .

B. SOCIAL PROOF

The second principle of influence that a lawyer might use to her client's advantage is "social proof." According to this principle, individuals "view a behavior as correct in a given situation to the degree that we see others performing it." . . .

Social proof is most likely to prove persuasive when two conditions are obtained. First, social proof is more influential under conditions of uncertainty. "In general, when we are unsure of ourselves, when the situation is unclear or ambiguous, when uncertainty reigns, we are most likely to look to and accept the actions of others as correct." Second, social proof is more influential when the observer perceives similarities between herself and the party she is observing. . . .

> **Planning Ahead to Sell Yourself**
>
> When trying to land a position as director of human resources for a multibillion-dollar firm, Virginia Means knew she faced an uphill battle because of her young age — 32. "Once I had made it through the interviews with the executive search firm, I was scheduled to meet with the CEO and his top team," she recalls. "I was incredibly nervous and knew that to be successful, I had to project the confidence of someone a decade my senior. So, I sought counsel from a male mentor, who served as my 'image consultant.' He gave me great advice far beyond the 'polish your shoes' and 'wear a suit that's in sync with the company's culture.'"
>
> That advice included doing her homework on each executive in the company — "finding out as much as I could about their hot buttons, then mapping my skills and experience to their concerns," she says. "The internet is a great place to begin that kind of research, and if you believe in six degrees of separation, you are bound to have a connection with someone in the company who can act as an information source." Connie Glaser & Barbara Smalley, What Queen Esther Knew: Business Strategies from a Biblical Sage 29-30 (2003).

C. COMMITMENT AND CONSISTENCY

The third principle of influence that a lawyer might use to her client's advantage is the "commitment and consistency" principle. According to this principle, "[o]nce we make a choice or take a stand, we will encounter personal and interpersonal pressures to behave consistently with that commitment." . . .

D. RECIPROCITY

The fourth principle of influence that a lawyer might use to her client's advantage is the "reciprocity rule" or "reciprocity norm." According to this rule or norm, one "should try to repay, in kind, what another person has provided us." . . .

A lawyer can use the reciprocity rule in two ways to persuade her counterpart to make a meaningful concession at the bargaining table. First, and most obviously, she can make a concession herself, and this can create in her counterpart a sense of obligation to respond similarly. . . .

Second, and more subtly, a lawyer can request a substantial concession, get turned down, and then make a more modest request. In many instances, the lawyer's counterpart will feel obligated to respond to this ostensible concession. . . .

E. AUTHORITY

The fifth principle of influence that a lawyer might use to her client's advantage is "authority." According to this principle, individuals feel an obligation to comply with those who are in real or perceived authority positions. . . .

F. SCARCITY

The sixth principle of influence a lawyer might use to her client's advantage is "scarcity." According to this principle, "opportunities seem more valuable to us when they are less available." Scarcity induces compliance in large part because it threatens our freedom of choice ("if I do not act now, I will lose the opportunity to do so"). . . .

[A] lawyer can use these principles of influence to induce her counterpart in negotiation to settle on terms that are favorable to her client. Simply because a lawyer *can* use these principles, however, does not necessarily mean she *should*. A lawyer should try to obtain the best possible outcome for her client, but she should do so in ways that comport not only with the formal ethical rules, but also with her own sense of professional responsibility and personal ethics. (Would I want my mother to know I used that tactic? Would I want my counterpart to use that tactic? How would I feel if the local newspaper ran a story about the negotiation?)

Next, psychology professor Robert Cialdini shows how the idea of reciprocity — one of the basic concepts of fairness — can be used positively and negatively to persuade people.

 Robert B. Cialdini, **INFLUENCE: THE PSYCHOLOGY OF PERSUASION**

17-18, 36, 38, 40-42 (rev. ed, 1993)

The rule [of reciprocation] says that we should try to repay, in kind, what another person has provided us. If a woman does us a favor, we should do her one in return; if a man sends us a birthday present, we should remember his birthday with a gift of our own; if a couple invites us to a party, we should be sure to invite them to one of ours. By virtue of the reciprocity rule, then, we are *obligated* to the future repayment of favors, gifts, invitations, and the like. So typical is it for indebtedness to accompany the receipt of such things that a term like "much obliged" has become a synonym for "thank you," not only in the English language but in others as well.

The impressive aspect of the rule for reciprocation and the sense of obligation that goes with it is its pervasiveness in human culture. It is so widespread that after intensive study, sociologists such as Alvin Gouldner can report that there is no human society that does not subscribe to the rule. . . .

I know of no better illustration of how reciprocal obligations can reach long and powerfully into the future than the perplexing story of five thousand dollars of relief aid that was sent in 1985 between Mexico and the impoverished people of Ethiopia. In 1985 Ethiopia could justly lay claim to the greatest suffering and privation in the world. Its economy was in ruin. Its food supply had been ravaged by years of drought and internal war. Its inhabitants were dying by the thousands from disease and starvation. Under these circumstances, I would not have been surprised to learn of a five-thousand-dollar relief donation from Mexico to that wrenchingly needy country. I remember my chin hitting my chest, though, when a brief newspaper item I was reading insisted that the aid had gone in the opposite direction. Native officials of the Ethiopian Red Cross had decided to send the money to help the victims of that year's earthquakes in Mexico City. . . .

Despite the enormous needs prevailing in Ethiopia, the money was being sent because Mexico had sent aid to Ethiopia in 1935, when it was invaded by Italy. So informed, I remained awed, but I was no longer puzzled. The need to reciprocate had transcended great cultural differences, long distances, acute famine, and immediate self-interest. Quite simply, a half century later, against all countervailing forces, obligation triumphed. . . .

THE RULE IS OVERPOWERING

One of the reasons reciprocation can be used so effectively as a device for gaining other's compliance is its power. The rule possesses awesome strength, often producing a "yes" response to a request that, except for an existing feeling of indebtedness, would have surely been refused.

Reciprocal Concessions

I was walking down the street when I was approached by an eleven- or twelve-year-old boy. He introduced himself and said that he was selling tickets to the annual Boy Scouts circus to be held on the upcoming Saturday night. He asked if I wished to buy any at five dollars apiece. Since one of the last places I wanted to spend Saturday evening was with the Boy Scouts, I declined. "Well," he said, "if you don't want to buy any tickets, how about buying some of our big chocolate bars? They're only a dollar each." I bought a couple and, right away, realized that something noteworthy had happened. I knew that to be the case because: (a) I do not like chocolate bars; (b) I do like dollars; (c) I was standing there with two of his chocolate bars; and (d) he was walking away with two of my dollars. . . .

Because the rule for reciprocation governs the compromise process, it is possible to use an initial concession as part of a highly effective compliance technique. The technique is a simple one that we can call the rejection-then-retreat technique. Suppose you want me to agree to a certain request. One way to increase your chances would be first to make a larger request of me, one that I will most likely turn down.

Then, after I have refused, you would make the smaller request that you were really interested in all along. Provided that you have structured your requests skillfully, I should view your second request as a concession to me and should feel inclined to respond with a concession of my own, the only one I would have immediately open to me — compliance with your second request. . . .

THE FAMILY CIRCUS   By Bil Keane

© 2004 Bil Keane, Inc.
Dist. by King Features Synd.
www.familycircus.com

"Ask Mommy for ten cookies, but then
tell her you'll settle for two."

It seems that certain of the most successful television producers, such as Grant Tinker and Gary Marshall, are masters of this art in their negotiations with network censors. In a candid interview with *TV Guide* writer Dick Russell, both admitted to "deliberately inserting lines into scripts that a censor's sure to ax" so that they could then retreat to the lines they really wanted included. Marshall appears especially active in this regard. Consider, for example, the following quotes from Russell's article:

> But Marshall . . . not only admits his tricks . . . he seems to revel in them. On one episode of his [then] top-rated *Laverne and Shirley* series, for example, he says, "We had a situation where Squiggy's in a rush to get out of his apartment and meet some girls upstairs. He says: 'Will you hurry up before I lose my lust?' But in the script we put something even stronger, knowing the censors would cut it. They did; so we asked innocently, well, how about 'lose my lust'? 'That's good,' they said. Sometimes you gotta go at 'em backward."
>
>   On the *Happy Days* series, the biggest censorship fight was over the word "virgin." That time, says Marshall, "I knew we'd have trouble, so we put the word in seven times, hoping they'd cut six and keep one. It worked. We used the same pattern again with the word 'pregnant.'" . . .

The desirable side effects of making a concession during an interaction with another person are nicely shown in studies of the way people bargain with each other. One experiment, conducted by social psychologists at UCLA, offers an especially apt demonstration. A subject in that study faced a "negotiation opponent" and was told to bargain with the opponent concerning how to divide between themselves a certain amount of money provided by the experimenters. The subject was also informed that if no mutual agreement could be reached after a certain period of bargaining, no one would get any money. Unknown to the subjects, the opponent was really an experimental assistant who had been previously instructed to bargain with the subject in one of three ways. With some of the subjects, the opponent made an extreme first demand, assigning virtually all of the money to himself, and stubbornly persisted in that demand throughout the negotiations. With another group of subjects, the opponent began with a demand that was moderately favorable to himself; he, too, steadfastly refused to move from that position during the negotiations. With a third group, the opponent began with the extreme demand and then gradually retreated to the more moderate one during the course of the bargaining.

There were three important findings in this experiment that help us to understand why the rejection-then-retreat technique is so effective. First, compared to the two other approaches, the strategy of starting with an extreme demand and then retreating to the more moderate one produced the most money for the person using it. But this result is not very surprising in light of the previous evidence we have seen of the power of larger-then-smaller-request tactics to bring about profitable agreements. It is the two additional findings of the study that are more striking.

Responsibility. Those subjects facing the opponent who used the retreating strategy felt most responsible for the final deal. Much more than the subjects who faced a nonchanging negotiation opponent, these subjects reported that they had successfully influenced the opponent to take less money for himself. Of course, we know that they hadn't done any such thing. The experimenter had instructed their opponent to retreat gradually from his initial demand no matter what the subjects did. But it appeared to these subjects that they had made the opponent change, that they had *produced* his concessions. The result was that they felt more responsible for the final outcome of the negotiations. It does not require much of a leap from this finding to clarify the previous mystery of why the rejection-then-retreat technique causes its targets to live up to their agreements with such astounding frequency. The requester's concession within the technique not only causes targets to say yes more often, it also causes them to feel more responsible for having "dictated" the final agreement. Thus the uncanny ability of the rejection-then-retreat technique to make its targets meet their commitments becomes understandable: A person who feels responsible for the terms of a contract will be more likely to live up to that contract.

Satisfaction. Even though, on the average, they gave the most money to the opponent who used the concessions strategy, the subjects who were the targets of this strategy were the most satisfied with the final arrangement. It appears that an agreement that has been forged through the concessions of one's opponent is quite satisfying. With this in mind, we can begin to explain the second previously puzzling feature of the rejection-then-retreat tactic — the ability to prompt its victims to agree to further requests. Since the tactic uses a concession to bring about compliance, the victim is likely to feel more satisfied with the arrangement as a result. And it stands to reason that people who are satisfied with a given arrangement are more likely to be willing to agree to further such arrangements. . . .

Notes and Questions

2.24 Cialdini explains that the reciprocity technique is used in hundreds of different contexts. Have you seen this technique yourself? Did you feel compelled to reciprocate (the invitation, the gift, help on homework, the free address labels, and so on)? Why do you think people feel compelled to reciprocate something even if they do not want the item in the first place (for example, the chocolate bar)?

2.25 Cialdini seems to describe reciprocity as a strategy in negotiation while Albin earlier uses it as an example of procedural fairness. Is this contradictory? Why or why not? How can the concept of reciprocal concessions be used in a negotiation? How can you protect yourself against conceding too much if this is used unfairly?

2.26 One night during dinner, a charity called to ask if Rodd would be willing to send out letters to his neighbors asking for donations (invoking another method of persuading people to do something called the familiarity principle). When Rodd refused, the charity asked him if he would be willing to increase his gift from last year. He agreed, even though he was not planning on raising it previously. What did the charity do so well?

2.27 This reading makes an argument for the often-used competitive bargaining tactic of starting with an outrageously high demand. In fact, some research supports that further. What are the advantages and disadvantages of that tactic? Why might it be counterproductive even if your opponent does not walk away? What about the ethics of false demands?

D. TALKING PERSUASIVELY

This last section moves from preparing your case to talking about your case. Before making your argument to your counterpart in the negotiation, you need to think about how to make the most persuasive case. This is not unlike a trial lawyer's task when preparing to make arguments in front of a jury. What is likely to convince them that you are right?

One of the ways to make your argument more persuasive is to tell a coherent story about what you want. For example, in addition to your legal arguments, you might also base your argument on good policy, a principle to be upheld, the better consequences of your agreement, or the general custom in that type of business (and these can also be your objective criteria).

Additional methods to bolster your argument include framing and analogy. Negotiators sometimes use metaphors and labeling to make their arguments more persuasive. In a negotiation, are we partners or opponents, as Jonathan Cohen outlined in the previous chapter? When trying to motivate U.S. involvement in Kosovo, was this another Vietnam or was Milosevic another Hitler? Similar metaphors were used with the Iraq war in 2003. In another case, were the people who took 700 hostages in a Moscow theater in October 2002 terrorists or Chechen freedom fighters? The label simplifies a complex situation to convince and persuade the recipient. How you view the situation clearly affects what action you think is appropriate.

Other framing occurs through the use of specifics and detail. You can use statistics or expert authority to provide specific support for your argument. Sometimes this experience is personal — if you can tell a story about how your motorcycle helmet saved your life, you might be better able to persuade a legislator to change the law. Many congressional hearings focus on this type of framing. Other times you can tell the story using vivid detail to describe what has happened and bring the listener into the situation. Excellent trial attorneys often use this type of framing with the jury. In fact, in a study comparing the use of pallid information ("The defendant staggered against a serving table, knocking a bowl to the floor") versus vivid information ("The defendant staggered against a serving table, knocking a bowl of guacamole dip to the floor and splattering guacamole on the white shag carpet"), members of the mock jury were more likely to find the latter defendant guilty.*

Notes and Questions

2.28 Think of a recent case you studied in another law class. Suppose you are arguing that case to a jury or to a negotiation counterpart. What are your top three arguments? Are these based in law, in policy, on consequences, on detail? What makes these arguments persuasive?

2.29 Assume that you are arguing for increased funding of art and music programs in the public education system in your hometown. What arguments would you make from the perspective of policy? Of principle? Of consequences? What details or statistics might you want to know?

2.30 Robert Condlin states that legal arguments tend to be the least persuasive to law students or practicing attorneys. Robert Condlin, "Cases on Both Sides": Patterns of Argument in Legal Dispute Negotiation, 44 Md. L. Rev. 65 (1985). Why do you think this might be the case?

Psychologists, management consultants, and communications experts talk about the importance of "framing" (a "stable, coherent cognitive structure that organizes and simplifies the complex reality that a manager operates in. Many frames reside in memory and are usually evoked or triggered automatically"). Paul J.H. Shoemaker & J. Edward Russo, Managing Frames to Make Better Decisions, in *Wharton on Making*

---

*R.M. Reyes, W.C. Thompson & G.H. Bower, Judgmental Biases Resulting from Differing Availabilities of Arguments, 39 J. Personality & Soc. Psychol. 2 (1980), cited in Scott Plous, The Psychology of Judgment and Decision Making 127-128 (1993).

Decisions 134 (Stephen J. Hoch, Howard C. Kunreuther & Robert E. Gunther eds., 2001). Those who negotiate may need to think about the frames they create to structure the thinking of others, the frames they may be applying to their own matters, and the "decision frames" by which parties come together, cognitively, to agree. The use of particular concepts, images, metaphors, and even simple words can both create "frames" or organizing principles, and also demolish or "reframe" the way we think about a problem.

Consider how the author of this letter sent to author Robert Cialdini masterfully frames her message. The context, placing, and timing of information become critical to how the readers/listeners receive the information.

 Robert B. Cialdini, INFLUENCE: THE PSYCHOLOGY OF PERSUASION

15-16 (1993)

READER'S REPORT FROM THE PARENT OF A COLLEGE COED

Dear Mother and Dad:

Since I left for college I have been remiss in writing and I am sorry for my thoughtlessness in not having written before. I will bring you up to date now, but before you read on, please sit down. You are not to read any further unless you are sitting down, okay?

Well, then, I am getting along pretty well now. The skull fracture and the concussion I got when I jumped out the window of my dormitory when it caught on fire shortly after my arrival here is pretty well healed now. I only spent two weeks in the hospital and now I can see almost normally and only get those sick headaches once a day. Fortunately, the fire in the dormitory, and my jump, was witnessed by an attendant at the gas station near the dorm, and he was the one who called the Fire Department and the ambulance. He also visited me in the hospital and since I had nowhere to live because of the burnt-out dormitory, he was kind enough to invite me to share his apartment with him. It's really a basement room, but it's kind of cute. He is a very fine boy and we have fallen deeply in love and are planning to get married. We haven't got the exact date yet, but it will be before my pregnancy begins to show.

Yes, Mother and Dad, I am pregnant. I know how much you are looking forward to being grandparents and I know you will welcome the baby and give it the same love and devotion and tender care you gave me when I was a child. The reason for the delay in our marriage is that my boyfriend has a minor infection which prevents us from passing our pre-marital blood tests and I carelessly caught it from him.

Now that I have brought you up to date, I want to tell you that there was no dormitory fire, I did not have a concussion or skull fracture, I was not in the hospital, I am not pregnant, I am not engaged, I am not infected, and there is no boyfriend. However, I am getting a "D" in American History, and an "F" in Chemistry and I want you to see those marks in their proper perspective.

Your loving daughter,
Sharon

Sharon may be failing chemistry, but she gets an "A" in psychology.

Another example of framing is the following ad from World War II. New Haven Railroad was being used to transport troops to ship out for the war. Regular travelers of the railroad were faced with delays, dirty trains, lack of seats, and other inconveniences. Customers were bombarding the railroad with complaints. The railroad approached an advertising agency to come up with an ad on troop transportation to explain what was going on.

The Kid in Upper 4
It is 3:42 A.M. on a troop train.
Men wrapped in blankets are breathing heavily.
Two in every lower berth. One in every upper.
This is no ordinary trip. It may be their last in the U.S.A. till the end of the war.
Tomorrow they will be on the high seas.
One is wide awake . . . listening . . . staring into the blackness.
It is the kid in Upper 4.
Tonight, he knows, he is leaving behind a lot of little things — and big ones.
The taste of hamburgers and pop . . . the feel of driving a roadster over a
six-lane highway . . . a dog named Shucks, or Sport, or Barnacle Bill.
The pretty girl who writes so often . . . that gray haired man, so proud and
awkward at the station . . . the mother who knit the socks he'll wear soon.
Tonight he's thinking them over.
There's a lump in his throat. And maybe — a tear fills his eye. *It doesn't matter,*
Kid.
Nobody will see . . . it's too dark.

A couple of thousand miles away, where he's going, they don't know him very
well.
But people all over the world are waiting, praying for him to come.
And he will come, this kid in Upper 4.
With new hope, peace and freedom for a tired, bleeding world.

Next time you are on the train, *remember the kid in Upper 4.*
If you have to stand enroute — *it is so he may have a seat.*
If there is no berth for you — *it is so that he may sleep.*
If you have to wait for a seat in the diner — *it is so he . . . and thousands like him*
. . . may have a meal they won't forget in the days to come.
For to treat him as our most honored guest is the least we can do to pay a mighty
debt of gratitude.

In a poll by *Advertising Age*, "The Kid" was ranked among the all-time top
advertisements and is written about in numerous advertising books. Nelson Metcalf,
Jr., The Kid in Upper 4, Harv. Mag., Jan.-Feb. 1992, at 76.

Notes and Questions

2.31   What does Sharon do that is so effective? How could a negotiator use Sharon's
technique?

2.32   Advertising is one of the best venues to see good framing and storytelling in
action. What gives the New Haven Railroad ad its impact?

2.33   Think of other successful ads. What type of framing do they use? Think of a
particular policy you support. How can you frame that story?

2.34   Consider how the campaign manager framed the following problem:

> Theodore Roosevelt, nearing the end of a hard-fought presidential election
> campaign in 1912, scheduled a final whistle-stop journey. At each stop, Roo-
> sevelt planned to clinch the crowd's votes by distributing an elegant pamphlet

with a stern presidential portrait on the cover and a stirring speech, "Confession of Faith," inside. Some three million copies had been printed when a campaign worker noticed a small line under the photograph on each brochure that read, "Moffett Studios, Chicago." Since Moffett held the copyright, the unauthorized used of the photo could cost the campaign one dollar per reproduction. With no time to reprint the brochure, what was the campaign to do?

Not using the pamphlets at all would damage Roosevelt's election prospects. Yet, if they went ahead, a scandal could easily erupt very close to the election, and the campaign could be liable for an unaffordable sum. Campaign workers quickly realized they would have to negotiate with Moffett. But research by their Chicago operatives turned up bad news: although early in his career as a photographer, Moffett had been taken with the potential of this new artistic medium, he had received little recognition. Now, Moffett was financially hard up and bitterly approaching retirement with a single-minded focus on money.

Dispirited, the campaign workers approached campaign manager George Perkins, a former partner of J.P. Morgan. Perkins lost no time in summoning his stenographer to dispatch the following cable to Moffett Studios: "We are planning to distribute millions of pamphlets with Roosevelt's picture on the cover. It will be great publicity for the studio whose photograph we use. How much will you pay us to use yours? Respond immediately." Shortly, Moffett replied: "We've never done this before, but under the circumstances we'd be pleased to offer you $250." Reportedly, Perkins accepted — without dickering for more.

Perkins's misleading approach raises ethical yellow flags and is anything but a model negotiation on how to enhance working relationships. Yet this case raises a very interesting question: why did the campaign workers find the prospect of this negotiation so difficult? Their inability to see what Perkins immediately perceived flowed from their anxious obsession with their own side's problem: their blunders so far, the high risk of losing the election, a potential $3 million exposure, an urgent deadline, and no cash to meet Moffett's likely demands for something the campaign vitally needed. . . . Perkins's tactical genius was to recognize the essence of the negotiator's central task: shape how your counterpart sees its problem such that it chooses what you want.

The campaign workers were paralyzed in the face of what they saw as sharply conflicting monetary interests and their pathetic BATNA. From their perspective, Moffett's only choice was how to exploit their desperation at the prospect of losing the presidency. . . . Perkins immediately grasped the importance of favorably shaping Moffett's BATNA perceptions, both of the campaign's (awful) no-deal options and Moffett's (powerful) one. Perkins looked beyond price positions, and common ground . . . and used Moffett's different interest to frame the photographer's choice as "the value of publicity and recognition." Had he assumed this would be a standard, hardball price deal by offering a small amount to start, not only would this assumption have been dead wrong but, worse, it would have been self-fulfilling. . . .

Solving Teddy Roosevelt's Negotiation Problem, from James K. Sebenius, Six Habits of Merely Effective Negotiators, Harv. Bus. Rev., Apr. 2001, at 92-93.

Although not every negotiation ends up being a difficult one, negotiators need a set of tools to deal with more challenging situations as they arise. Three negotiation trainers and researchers advise in the next excerpt how to deal with or even prevent a difficult conversation.

 Douglas Stone, Bruce Patton & Sheila Heen, **DIFFICULT CONVERSATIONS: HOW TO DISCUSS WHAT MATTERS MOST**

186, 189, 190, 191, 195-198 (1999)

ORATORS NEED NOT APPLY

In a difficult conversation your primary task is not to persuade, impress, trick, outwit, convert, or win over the other person. It is to express what you see and why you see it that way, how you feel, and maybe who you are. Self-knowledge and the belief that what you want to share is important will take you significantly further than eloquence and wit. . . .

SPEAK THE HEART OF THE MATTER

The first step toward expressing yourself is finding your sense of entitlement to speak up; the next step is figuring out what, exactly, you want to say.

START WITH WHAT MATTERS MOST

There's no better place to begin your story than with what is at the very heart of the matter for you: "For me, what this is really about is. . . . What I'm feeling is. . . . What is important to me is. . . ."

Sharing what is important to you is common sense, and yet it's advice we often neglect. . . .

As you embark upon a difficult conversation, ask yourself, "Have I said what is at the heart of the matter for me? Have I shared what is at stake?" If not, ask yourself why, and see if you can find the courage to try.

SAY WHAT YOU MEAN: DON'T MAKE THEM GUESS

One way we often skirt sharing things that are important to us is by embedding them in the subtext of the conversation rather than simply stating them outright.

Don't Rely on Subtext. . . . One common way to manage [the dilemma of whether to engage in a conversation or to try to avoid it] — especially when you're not sure you're really entitled to bring something up — is to communicate through subtext. You try to get your message across indirectly, through jokes, questions, offhand comments, or body language.

Bringing it up by not quite bringing it up seems a happy medium between avoiding and engaging. It is a way of doing neither and doing both. The problem is, to the extent you are doing both, you're doing both badly. You end up triggering all of the problems you worried you'd create by bringing it up, without getting the benefit of clearly saying what you want to say....

To do better, you need to figure out what you are really thinking and feeling, and then say it directly: "I'd like to spend more time with you, and Saturday morning was one of the few times we had to spend together. As a result, I'm finding your interest in golf irritating...."

Avoid Easing In.   Easing in is where you try to soften a message by delivering it indirectly through hints and leading questions....

Easing in conveys three messages: "I have a view," "This is too embarrassing to discuss directly," and "I'm not going to be straight with you." Not surprisingly, these messages increase both sides' anxiety and defensiveness. And the recipient's imagination almost always conjures up a message worse than the real one.

A better approach is to make the subject clear and discussable by stating your thoughts straight out....

TELLING YOUR STORY WITH CLARITY: THREE GUIDELINES

Obviously, how you express yourself makes a difference. How you say what you want to say will determine, in part, how others respond to you, and how the conversation will go. So when you choose to share something important, you'll want to do so in a way that will maximize the chance that the other person will understand and respond productively. Clarity is the key.

1.   Don't Present Your Conclusions as *the* Truth

Some aspects of difficult conversations will continue to be rough even when you communicate with great skill: sharing feelings of vulnerability, delivering bad news, learning something painful about how others see you. But presenting your story as the truth — which creates resentment, defensiveness, and leads to arguments — is a wholly avoidable disaster....

Some words — like "attractive," "ugly," "good," and "bad" — carry judgments that are obvious. But be careful with words like "inappropriate," "should," or "professional." The judgments contained in these words are less obvious, but can still provoke the "Who are you to tell me?!" response. If you want to say something is "inappropriate," preface your judgment with "My view is that...." Better still, avoid these words altogether.

2.   Share Where Your Conclusions Come From

The first step toward clarity, then, is to share your conclusions and opinions as *your* conclusions and opinions and not as the truth. The second step is to share what's beneath your conclusions — the information you have and how you have interpreted it....

3. Don't Exaggerate with "Always" and "Never": Give Them Room to Change

In the heat of the moment, it's easy to express frustration through a bit of exaggeration: "Why do you *always* criticize my clothes?" "You *never* give one word of appreciation or encouragement. The only time anyone hears anything from you is when there's something wrong!"

"Always" and "never" do a pretty good job of conveying frustration, but they have two serious drawbacks. First, it is seldom strictly accurate that someone criticizes *every* time, or that they haven't at some point said *something* positive....

"Always" and "never" also make it harder — rather than easier — for the other person to consider changing [her] behavior. In fact, "always" and "never" suggest that change will be difficult or impossible. The implicit message is, "What is wrong with you such that you are driven to criticize my clothes?" or even "You are obviously incapable of acting like a normal person." ...

The key is to communicate your feelings in a way that invites and encourages the recipient to consider new ways of behaving, rather than suggesting [he's] a schmuck and it's too bad there's nothing [he] can do about it....

The secret of powerful expression is recognizing that you are the ultimate authority on you. You are an expert on what you think, how you feel, and why you've come to this place. If you think it or feel it, you are entitled to say it, and no one can legitimately contradict you. You only get in trouble if you try to assert what you are *not* the final authority on — who is right, who intended what, what happened. Speak fully the range of your experience and you will be clear. Speak for yourself and you can speak with power.

Notes and Questions

2.35 You work for a large international bank and have been pleased with the company's treatment of women. For example, the bank has generous maternity leave provisions, permits part-time work, and has a number of female executives. Recently, however, you have become worried about a particular situation in your department, which establishes new branches overseas. The bank has been working with a country whose representatives have said that their country's cultural norms will make it difficult for their government and banking officials to work with women in the bank. By coincidence, no women were working on setting up that branch at the time these preferences became known.

But things have changed recently. As you've moved up, this project represents a next logical step for you. Yet so far, you have not been asked to work on the project, although several of your male colleagues with the same level of experience have been. When you initially raised the issue with your supervisor, she recommended that you "give it time, and not rock the boat." You felt surprised, let down, and even somewhat hurt to hear this, but didn't push the matter. On reflection, you've decided to talk with her again and let her know how strongly you feel about this. Give three different ways to frame this conversation as you begin talking with your supervisor.

2.36 Based on the above facts, rephrase in a sentence or sequence of sentences the following statements to make them more clear, accurate, and conducive to facilitating dialogue. The phrases may conflict slightly from what appears to be true based on the discussion problem. Part of your task is to bring them back in line with what is true in the discussion problem.

    a. "If I can't work on the project, my career will really be damaged."
    b. "I appreciated that you took the time to talk about this before, but I found our conversation really disturbing."
    c. "It seems to me that the bank is acquiescing to the country too easily. We need to put up more of a fight."
    d. "This bank just doesn't seem to care about its female employees."
    e. "Your attempt to set the matter aside really hurt me."
    f. "Do you think that delaying this is the best way to handle the situation?"

2.37 It is the beginning of April in your first year as a law student. You have been desperately searching for a summer job for several months now. Two days ago, you finally got a call from the hiring partner of a law firm in your hometown, Green Bay. You interviewed with this firm over spring break. You liked them and know that the summer would be educational and pleasant enough there. On the other hand, this is not a firm at which you would want to work at after graduation; it has no national reputation, and you are more interested in major league corporate work. The hiring partner made you an offer over the phone. He didn't say when exactly he was expecting an answer, but left a significant pause after the offer. You didn't know what to do. After a nervous silence you blurted out, "Well, uh, I accept." The partner was delighted, and you were feeling pretty good about it too. After all, you told yourself, this was a job, and probably the only one you could get. Besides, you told yourself, it's for good money, and you probably won't have to work as hard as in Milwaukee. Then the unexpected happened. This morning, as you checked your cell phone after class, you got a call from Foley, Brady & Friedrich — practically your ideal firm. You'd talked to them a month ago and assumed nothing would come of it, but here they were with an offer. You were so excited, you accepted practically without pausing for breath. A few hours later, you still think you made the right decision, but you're dreading having to call the firm in Green Bay. You know what you should do immediately, especially since you have just discovered a message on your answering machine from the hiring partner in Green Bay. He said he wanted to get your input whether to visit the Packers' preseason practices. What are some ways to approach this conversation?*

---

* Questions 2.35, 2.36, and 2.37 are from "Discussion Problems on Difficult Conversations" by Bruce Patton, Douglas Stone & Sheila Heen of the Harvard Negotiation Project (1993).

 **Chapter 3** | Integrative Negotiation: Expanding the Pie and Solving the Problem

Many beginning negotiators assume that there are only two approaches — adversarial and accommodating — as primary choices of strategy in a negotiation. *This is a false choice.* Both of these strategies focus only on one part of the negotiation — behaviors for dividing the resources available (or "dividing the pie") as discussed in the next chapter — rather than on the other activities that can increase the resources, or create new solutions, to "expand the pie" in a negotiation. When choosing the adversarial or competitive model negotiators assume that scarce resources must always be divided and allocated, in a "zero-sum" game. Instead, integrative negotiation (taking account of the real needs and interests of all parties) can actually lead to "expanded pies," increased resources, added value, and often, creative and new solutions to negotiation problems. This chapter will focus on the analysis, activities, and behaviors that foster an integrative approach to negotiation. Integrative negotiation has also been called problem solving and principled negotiation, referencing both its conceptual or analytic features, as well as the different behaviors that might be necessary for collaborative processes to produce better solutions. The latter part of this chapter outlines skills and tools that negotiators can use to be more integrative. To be effective at finding integrative outcomes, negotiators should prepare in advance, using creativity (analysis and synthesis), as well as thinking about how to work with negotiation counterparts in a different way.

A. THEORY

In the first chapter, Jonathan Cohen outlined different language choices we can make in negotiation. This article continues that analysis, arguing that the win-lose metaphor in negotiation may be crippling.

 Leonard Greenhalgh, **THE CASE AGAINST WINNING IN NEGOTIATIONS**

3 Negot. J. 167, 167-172 (1987)

Making a case against "winning" seems heretical, like attacking patriotic ideals or revered institutions. Nevertheless, my aim in this article is to point out that the metaphor of winning is not only inappropriate in most situations, but is actually dangerous when used to characterize negotiations. In a nutshell, winning implies losing, and this dichotomy is inherently zero-sum in nature. The metaphor of winning is appropriate for describing power struggles, but inappropriate for describing other means of resolving apparent conflicts, particularly cooperative solutions such as problem-solving or other forms of integrative bargaining.

Sports metaphors are somewhat interchangeable with military metaphors, as is evident from the prevalence of hybrid metaphors. We speak of war games, the arms race, tennis volleys, shots on goal, knocking out a machine gun emplacement, and designation of players as lines, forwards, captains, guards, and so on. Thus it is not always possible to tell precisely when someone using win-lose metaphors is visualizing sports or war, and harder still to tell what imagery those metaphors evoke in the listener or reader. Either way, the win-lose metaphor is limiting when used uncritically to characterize negotiations.

Sometimes win-lose metaphors are appropriate, such as when describing the relationship between two businesses attempting to gain sales among a limited set of customers. Indeed, it is difficult to avoid describing firms in such circumstances as "competing." However, more often than not, the application of the win-lose metaphor is inappropriate to describe the interaction situation.

It appears, first of all, that a focus on rules easily can lead to attempts to exploit rather than negotiate fairly. If management conceives of the interaction as a rules-bounded game, management's tactics may be to cooperate as little as possible without violating "the letter of the law"; there will be little emphasis on mutual accommodation and the development of goodwill. This situation actually happens with surprising frequency. Almost inevitably, management's relationship with the union suffers as a result of such treatment, and managers subsequently blame the union for not cooperating for the good of all, as if their own behavior had nothing to do with the outcome.

Another disadvantage of having one's thinking shaped by sports metaphors is that they induce disputants to focus on the immediate conflict episode rather than take a longer-term perspective. Sports contests are discrete, independent events. Irrespective of who won or lost the last game, the scores are set at zero at the beginning of the next game. Furthermore, sports norms would not permit players to let one team win this week in exchange for reciprocal leniency by the other team the next week. Thus, the history and future of the ongoing relationship between contestants is irrelevant in sports.

When this same short-term perspective is applied to negotiation situations, the conflict becomes much more difficult to deal with than it would be otherwise. Negotiators with a short-term perspective can choose harsh or exploitive tactics without fear of repercussions, because they view any future interaction as "a new game." Likewise, there is nothing to gain in the future from being accommodating in the current interaction, since anything "given up" is perceived as forever lost. From this standpoint, intransigence — and even aggression — is rational.

For instance, imagine a salesman with a short-term perspective engaged in a dispute over the interpretation of ambiguous terms in a sales contract. Let's say, furthermore, that the purchasing agent is predisposed to avoid conflicts. The salesman acts on his belief that he can "win" the dispute by applying pressure: browbeating, ad hominem attacks, threats, withholding or distorting information, and other aggressive behaviors. This approach does indeed result in the predicted concessions from the purchasing agent. However, any winning in this scenario is likely to be a Pyrrhic victory: The purchasing agent will subsequently go to great lengths to avoid doing business with this abrasive salesman, and will no doubt tell other purchasing agents — and possibly the salesman's superior — about the experience. Thus the long-term cost in terms of relationships and reputation offsets the short-term gain.

Notes and Questions

3.1 Why is negotiation not like sports or war? Why do you think we tend to think of it that way?

3.2 When one of the authors got engaged, the best advice she received was from Roger Fisher. He told her that there would be times when she would argue with her husband. If she walked away from the negotiation thinking to herself, "Ha, I won!", she missed the primary point of the negotiation. Why does marriage not fit the win-lose metaphor? What relationships are similar?

This next excerpt begins to outline the differences in approaches to negotiation. Principled negotiation, as explained in the classic negotiation bestseller *Getting to YES*, is one way of exemplifying integrative negotiation.

 Roger Fisher, William Ury & Bruce Patton, GETTING TO YES: NEGOTIATING AGREEMENT WITHOUT GIVING IN

4-7, 10-14 (2d ed. 1991)

Any method of negotiation may be fairly judged by three criteria: It should produce a wise agreement if agreement is possible. It should be efficient. And it should improve or at least not damage the relationship between the parties. (A wise agreement can be defined as one that meets the legitimate interests of each side to the extent possible, resolves conflicting interests fairly, is durable, and takes community interest into account.)

Taking positions, as the customer and storekeeper do, serves some useful purposes in a negotiation. It tells the other side what you want; it provides an anchor in an uncertain and pressured situation; and it can eventually produce the terms of an acceptable agreement. But those purposes can be served in other ways. And positional bargaining fails to meet the basic criteria of producing a wise agreement, efficiently and amicably.

ARGUING OVER POSITIONS PRODUCES UNWISE AGREEMENTS

When negotiators bargain over positions, they tend to lock themselves into those positions. The more you clarify your position and defend it against attack, the more committed you become to it. The more you try to convince the other side of the impossibility of changing your opening position, the more difficult it becomes to do so. Your ego becomes identified with your position. You now have a new interest in "saving face" — in reconciling future action with past positions — making it less and less likely that any agreement will wisely reconcile the parties' original interests.

The danger that positional bargaining will impede a negotiation is well illustrated by the breakdown of the talks under President Kennedy for a comprehensive ban on nuclear testing. A critical question arose: How many onsite inspections per year should the Soviet Union and the United States be permitted to make within the other's territory to investigate suspicious seismic events? The Soviet Union finally agreed to three inspections. The United States insisted on no less than ten. And there the talks broke down — over positions — despite the fact that no one understood whether an "inspection" would involve a person looking around for one day, or a hundred people prying indiscriminately for a month. The parties had made little attempt to design an inspection procedure that would reconcile the United States' interest in verification with the desire of both countries for minimal intrusion.

As more attention is paid to positions, less attention is devoted to meeting the underlying concerns of the parties. Agreement becomes less likely. Any agreement reached may reflect a mechanical splitting of the difference between final positions rather than a solution carefully crafted to meet the legitimate interests of the parties. The result is frequently an agreement less satisfactory to each side than it could have been.

ARGUING OVER POSITIONS IS INEFFICIENT

The standard method of negotiation may produce either agreement . . . or break-down, as with the number of onsite inspections. In either event, the process takes a lot of time.

Bargaining over positions creates incentives that stall settlement. In positional bargaining you try to improve the chance that any settlement reached is favorable to you by starting with an extreme position, by stubbornly holding to it, by deceiving the other party as to your true views, and by making small concessions only as necessary to keep the negotiation going. The same is true for the other side. Each of those factors tends to interfere with reaching a settlement promptly. The more extreme the opening positions and the smaller the concessions; the more time and effort it will take to discover whether or not agreement is possible. . . . Dragging one's feet, threatening to walk out, stonewalling, and other such tactics become common-place. They all increase the time and costs of reaching agreement as well as the risk that no agreement will be reached at all.

ARGUING OVER POSITIONS ENDANGERS AN ONGOING RELATIONSHIP

Positional bargaining becomes a contest of will. . . . Anger and resentment often result as one side sees itself bending to the rigid will of the other while its own legitimate concerns go unaddressed. Positional bargaining thus strains and sometimes shatters the relationship between the parties. . . .

WHEN THERE ARE MANY PARTIES POSITIONAL BARGAINING IS EVEN WORSE

Although it is convenient to discuss negotiation in terms of two persons, you and "the other side," in fact, almost every negotiation involves more than two persons. Several different parties may sit at the table, or each side may have constituents, higher-ups, boards of directors, or committees with whom they must deal. The more people involved in a negotiation the more serious the drawbacks to positional bargaining.

If some 150 countries are negotiating, as in various United Nations conferences, positional bargaining is next to impossible. It may take all to say yes, but only one to say no. Reciprocal concessions are difficult: to whom do you make a concession?... What is worse, once they have painfully developed and agreed upon a position, it becomes much harder to change it. Altering a position becomes equally difficult when additional participants are higher authorities who, while absent from the table, must nevertheless give their approval.

BEING NICE IS NO ANSWER

Many people recognize the high costs of hard positional bargaining, particularly on the parties and their relationship. They hope to avoid them by following a more gentle style of negotiation. Instead of seeing the other side as adversaries, they prefer to see them as friends. Rather than emphasizing a goal of victory, they emphasize the necessity of reaching agreement. In a soft negotiating game the standard moves are to make offers and concessions, to trust the other side, to be friendly, and to yield as necessary to avoid confrontation. . . .

Most people see their choice of negotiating strategies as between these two styles [hard or soft bargaining]. . . .

THERE IS AN ALTERNATIVE...

The answer to the question of whether to use soft positional bargaining or hard is "neither." Change the game. At the Harvard Negotiation Project we have been developing an alternative to positional bargaining: a method of negotiation explicitly designed to produce wise outcomes efficiently and amicably. This method, called *principled negotiation* or *negotiation on the merits*, can be boiled down to four basic points.

These four points define a straightforward method of negotiation that can be used under almost any circumstance. Each point deals with a basic element of negotiation, and suggests what you should do about it.

People:	Separate the people from the problem.
Interests:	Focus on interests, not positions.
Options:	Generate a variety of possibilities before deciding what to do.
Criteria:	Insist that the result be based on some objective standard. . . .

[E]motions typically become entangled with the objective merits of the problem. Taking positions just makes this worse because people's egos become identified with their positions. Hence, before working on the substantive problem, the "people problem" should be disentangled from it and dealt with separately. Figuratively if not literally, the participants should come to see themselves as working side by side, attacking the problem, not each other. Hence the first proposition: *Separate the people from the problem.*

The second point is designed to overcome the drawback of focusing on people's stated positions when the object of a negotiation is to satisfy their underlying interests. A negotiating position often obscures what you really want. Compromising between positions is not likely to produce an agreement which will effectively take care of the human needs that led people to adopt those positions. The second basic element of the method is: *Focus on interests, not positions.*

The third point responds to the difficulty of designing optimal solutions while under pressure. Trying to decide in the presence of an adversary narrows your vision. Having a lot at stake inhibits creativity. So does searching for the one right solution. You can offset these constraints by setting aside a designated time within which to think up a wide range of possible solutions that advance shared interests and creatively reconcile differing interests. Hence the third basic point: Before trying to reach agreement, *invent options for mutual gain.*

Where interests are directly opposed, a negotiator may be able to obtain a favorable result simply by being stubborn. . . . However you can counter such a negotiator by insisting that this single say-so is not enough and that the agreement must reflect some fair standard independent of the naked will of the other side. This does not mean insisting that the terms be based on the standard you select, but only that some fair standard such as market value, expert opinion, custom, or law determine the outcome. By discussing such criteria rather than what the parties are willing or unwilling to do, neither party need give in to the other; both can defer to a fair solution. Hence the fourth basic point: *Insist on using objective criteria.* . . .

PROBLEM		SOLUTION
Positional Bargaining: Which Game Should You Play?		Change the Game — **Negotiate on the Merits**
SOFT	**HARD**	**PRINCIPLED**
Participants are friends.	Participants are adversaries.	Participants are problem-solvers.
The goal is agreement.	The goal is victory.	The goal is a wise outcome reached efficiently and amicably.
Make concessions to cultivate the relationship.	Demand concessions as a condition of the relationship.	**Separate the people from the problem.**
Be soft on the people and the problem.	Be hard on the problem and the people.	Be soft on the people, hard on the problem.
Trust others.	Distrust others.	Proceed independent of trust.
Change your position easily.	Dig in to your position.	**Focus on interests, not positions.**

PROBLEM		SOLUTION
		Change the Game—
Positional Bargaining: Which Game Should You Play?		**Negotiate on the Merits**
SOFT	**HARD**	**PRINCIPLED**
Make offers.	Make threats.	Explore interests.
Disclose your bottom line.	Mislead as to your bottom line.	Avoid having a bottom line.
Accept one-side losses to reach agreement.	Demand one-sided gains as the price of agreement.	**Invent options for mutual gain.**
Search for the single answer: the one *they* will accept.	Search for the single answer: the one *you* will accept.	Develop multiple options to choose from; decide later.
Insist on agreement.	Insist on your position.	**Insist on using objective criteria.**
Try to avoid a contest of will.	Try to win a contest of will.	Try to reach a result based on standards independent of will.
Yield to pressure.	Apply pressure.	Reason and be open to reason; yield to principle, not pressure.

To sum up, in contrast to positional bargaining, the principled negotiation method of focusing on basic interests, mutually satisfying options, and fair standards typically results in a *wise* agreement. The method permits you to reach a gradual consensus on a joint decision *efficiently* without all the transactional costs of digging into positions only to have to dig yourself out of them. And separating the people from the problem allows you to deal directly and emphatically with the other negotiator as a human being, thus making possible an *amicable* agreement.

Notes and Questions

3.3 Do you agree that principled bargaining is more effective against hard bargaining than soft bargaining? Why or why not?

3.4 After reading this excerpt, what skills do you believe are required in problem solving?

3.5 Think of the last argument you had. What did the other side want? Why? What was the interest behind your counterpart's position?

This next excerpt is from Carrie Menkel-Meadow's article on negotiation as problem solving. The combination of *Getting to YES*'s publication and this law review article focused negotiation scholars for the next two decades on problem solving, as contrasted to competitive approaches to negotiation.

Carrie Menkel-Meadow, TOWARD ANOTHER VIEW OF
LEGAL NEGOTIATION: THE STRUCTURE OF
PROBLEM SOLVING

31 UCLA L. Rev. 754, 754-759, 794-801 (1984)

TOWARD A MODEL OF PROBLEM SOLVING NEGOTIATION: A THEORY OF NEEDS

Problem solving is an orientation to negotiation which focuses on finding solutions to the parties' sets of underlying needs and objectives. The problem-solving conception subordinates strategies and tactics to the process of identifying possible solutions and therefore allows a broader range of outcomes to negotiation problems. . . .

The Underlying Principles of Problem Solving: Meeting Varied and Complementary Needs

Parties to a negotiation typically have underlying needs or objectives — what they hope to achieve, accomplish, and/or be compensated for as a result of the dispute or transaction. Although litigants typically ask for relief in the form of damages, this relief is actually a proxy for more basic needs or objectives. By attempting to uncover those underlying needs, the problem-solving model presents opportunities for discovering greater numbers of and better quality solutions. It offers the possibility of meeting a greater variety of needs both directly and by trading off different needs, rather than forcing a zero-sum battle over a single item.

The principle underlying such an approach is that unearthing a greater number of the actual needs of the parties will create more possible solutions because not all needs will be mutually exclusive. As a corollary, because not all individuals value the same things in the same way, the exploitation of differential or complementary needs will produce a wider variety of solutions which more closely meet the parties' needs.

A few examples may illustrate these points. In personal injury actions courts usually award monetary damages. Plaintiffs, however, commonly want this money for specific purposes. For instance, an individual who has been injured in a car accident may desire compensation for any or all of the following items: past and future medical expenses, rehabilitation and compensation for the cost of rehabilitation, replacement of damaged property such as a car and the costs of such replacement, lost income, compensation for lost time, pain and suffering, the loss of companionship with one's family, friends and fellow employees and employer, lost opportunities to engage in activities which may no longer be possible, such as backpacking or playing basketball with one's children, vindication or acknowledgment of fault by the responsible party, and retribution or punishment of the person who was at fault. In short, the injured person seeks to be returned to the same physical, psychological, social and economic state she was in before the accident occurred. Because this may be impossible, the plaintiff needs money in order to buy back as many of these things as possible. . . .

In the commercial context, a breach of contract for failure to supply goods might involve compensation for the following: the cost of obtaining substitute goods, psychological damage resulting from loss of a steady source of supply, lost sales, loss of goodwill, any disruption in business which may have occurred, having to lay off employees as a result of decreased business, restoration of good business relationships, and retribution or punishment of the defaulting party. In the Brown and Snead case described [on pages 154-155 in this textbook], the litigation model structured the parties' goals in terms of the payment of money, when in fact one party sought to purchase and own a reliable form of transportation and the other sought a profit. It may be more useful in any contract case to think of the parties' needs in terms of what originally brought them together — the purpose of their relationship. Can the parties still realize their original goals? Charles Fried describes the classic function of contracts as attempts by the parties to mutually meet each other's needs:

You want to accomplish purpose A and I want to accomplish purpose B. Neither of us can succeed without the cooperation of the other. Thus, I want to be able to commit myself to help you achieve A so that you will commit yourself to help me achieve B.

Some of the parties' needs may not be compensable, directly or indirectly. For example, some injuries may be impossible to fully rehabilitate. A physical disability, a scar, or damage to a personal or business reputation may never be fully eradicated. Thus, the underlying needs produced by these injuries may not be susceptible to full and/or monetary satisfaction. The need to be regarded as totally normal or completely honorable can probably never be met, but the party in a negotiation will be motivated by the desire to satisfy as fully as possible these underlying human needs. Some parties may have a need to get "as much X as possible," such as in demands for money for pain and suffering. This demand simply may represent the best proxy available for satisfying the unsatisfiable desire to be made truly whole — that is to be put back in the position of no accident at all. It also may represent a desire to save for a rainy day or to maximize power, fame or love.

It is also important to recognize that *both* parties have such needs. For example, in the personal injury case above, the defendant may have the same need for vindication or retribution if he believes he was not responsible for the accident. In addition, the defendant may need to be compensated for his damaged car and injured body. He will also have needs with respect to how much, when and how he may be able to pay the monetary damages because of other uses for the money. A contract breaching defendant may have specific financial needs such as payroll, advertising, purchases of supplies, etc.; defendants are not always simply trying to avoid paying a certain sum of money to plaintiffs. In the commercial case, the defendant may have needs similar to those of the plaintiff: lost income due to the plaintiff's failure to pay on the contract, and, to the extent the plaintiff may seek to terminate the relationship with the defendant, a steady source of future business. . . .

To the extent that negotiators focus exclusively on "winning" the greatest amount of money, they focus on only one form of need. The only flexibility in tailoring an agreement may lie in the choice of ways to structure monetary solutions, including one shot payments, installments, and structured settlements. By looking, however, at what the parties desire money for, there may be a variety of solutions that will satisfy the parties more fully and directly. For example, when an injured plaintiff needs physical rehabilitation, if the defendant can provide the plaintiff directly with rehabilitation services, the defendant may save money and the plaintiff may gain the needed rehabilitation at lower cost. In addition, if the defendant can provide the plaintiff with a job that provides physical rehabilitation, the plaintiff may not only receive income which could be used to purchase more rehabilitation, but be further rehabilitated in the form of the psychological self-worth which accompanies such employment. Admittedly, none of these solutions may fully satisfy the injured plaintiff, but some or all may be equally beneficial to the plaintiff, and the latter two may be preferable to the defendant because they are less costly.

Understanding that the other party's needs are not necessarily as assumed may present an opportunity for arriving at creative solutions. Traditionally, lawyers approaching negotiations from the adversarial model view the other side as an enemy to be defeated. By examining the underlying needs of the other side, the lawyer may instead see opportunities for solutions that would not have existed before based upon the recognition of different, but not conflicting, preferences.

An example from the psychological literature illustrates this point.[167] Suppose that a husband and wife have two weeks in which to take their vacation. The husband prefers the mountains and the wife prefers the seaside. If vacation time is limited and thus a scarce resource, the couple may engage in adversarial negotiation about where they should go. The simple compromise situation, if they engage in distributive bargaining, would be to split the two weeks of vacation time spending one week in the mountains and one week at the ocean. This solution is not likely to be satisfying, however, because of the lost time and money in moving from place to place and in getting used to a new hotel room and locale. In addition to being happy only half of the time, each party to the negotiation has incurred transaction costs associated with this solution. Other "compromise" solutions might include alternating preferences on a year to year basis, taking separate vacations, or taking a longer vacation at a loss of pay. Assuming that husband and wife want to vacation together, all of these solutions may leave something to be desired by at least one of the parties.

By examining their underlying preferences, however, the parties might find additional solutions that could make both happy at less cost. Perhaps the husband prefers the mountains because he likes to hike and engage in stream fishing. Perhaps the wife enjoys swimming, sunbathing and seafood. By exploring these underlying preferences the couple might find vacation spots that permit all of these activities: a mountain resort on a large lake, or a seaside resort at the foot of mountains. By examining their underlying needs the parties can see solutions that satisfy many more of their preferences, and the "sum of the utilities" to the couple as a whole is greater than what they would have achieved by compromising.

In addition, by exploring whether they attach different values to their preferences they may be able to arrive at other solutions by trading items. The wife in our example might be willing to give up ocean fresh seafood if she can have fresh stream or lake trout, and so, with very little cost to her, the couple can choose another waterspot where the hikes might be better for the husband. By examining the weight or value given to certain preferences the parties may realize that some desires are easily attainable because they are not of equal importance to the other side. Thus, one party can increase its utilities without reducing the other's. This differs from a zero-sum conception of negotiation because of the recognition that preferences may be

---

[167] Dean G. Pruitt & Steven A. Lewis, "The Psychology of Integrative Bargaining" in *Negotiations: Social-Psychological Perspectives* 169-170 (Daniel Druckman ed., 1977).

totally different and are, therefore, neither scarce nor in competition with each other. In addition, if a preference is not used to "force" a concession from the other party (which as the example shows is not necessary), there are none of the forced reciprocal concessions of adversarial negotiation.

The exploitation of complementary interests occurs frequently in the legal context. For example, in a child custody case the lawyers may learn that both parties desire to have the children some of the time and neither of the parties wishes to have the children all of the time. It will be easy, therefore, to arrange for a joint custody agreement that satisfies the needs of both parties. Similarly, in a commercial matter, the defendant may want to make payment over time and the plaintiff, for tax purposes or to increase interest income, may desire deferred income.

STONE SOUP

There is a story of stone soup told in many cultures which exemplifies the idea of working together and the principle that the benefit of enticing/persuading others to work together is often more than the sum of its parts:

Once upon a time, somewhere in Eastern Europe, there was a great famine. People jealously hoarded whatever food they could find, hiding it even from their friends and neighbors. One day a peddler drove his wagon into a village, sold a few of his wares, and began asking questions as if he planned to stay for the night. "There's not a bite to eat in the whole province," he was told. "Better keep moving on."

"Oh, I have everything I need," he said. "In fact, I was thinking of making some stone soup to share with all of you." He pulled an iron cauldron from his wagon, filled it with water, and built a fire under it. Then, with great ceremony, he drew an ordinary-looking stone from a velvet bag and dropped it into the water.

By now, hearing the rumor of food, most of the villagers had come to the square or watched from their windows. As the peddler sniffed the "broth" and licked his lips in anticipation, hunger began to overcome their skepticism. "Ahh," the peddler said to himself rather loudly, "I do like a tasty stone soup. Of course, stone soup with *Cabbage*—that's hard to beat."

Soon a villager approached hesitantly, holding a cabbage he'd retrieved from its hiding place, and added it to the pot. "Capital!" cried the peddler. "You know, I once had stone soup with cabbage and a bit of salt beef as well, and it was fit for a king."

The village butcher managed to find some salt beef...and so it went, through potatoes, onions, carrots, mushrooms, and so on, until there was indeed a delicious meal for all. The villagers offered the peddler a great deal of money for the magic stone, but he refused to sell and traveled on the next day. And from that time on, long after the famine had ended, they reminisced about the finest soup they'd ever had.

This excerpt is adapted from a version found on the Internet at *http:// spanky.triumf.ca/www/fractint/stone_soup.html*. The story is so ubiquitous that it is also acted out on the PBS television show Barney for small children and is the name of a creative writing magazine!

Notes and Questions

3.6 How does problem solving actually work in a negotiation? Must the parties work together? Can one party "solve the problem" without the other?

3.7 Why does Menkel-Meadow argue that problem solving is more likely to meet a client's needs than compromise?

B. STRATEGY

The most common short-hand expression for integrative negotiating is to talk about value creation or expanding the pie. This next excerpt discusses the concept of value creation in negotiation and why it is important.

 David A. Lax & James K. Sebenius, **THE MANAGER AS NEGOTIATOR: BARGAINING FOR COOPERATION AND COMPETITIVE GAIN**

11, 89-90 (1986)

[W]e characterize negotiation as a process of potentially opportunistic interaction by which two or more parties, with some apparent conflict, seek to do better through jointly decided action than they could otherwise. . . .

We can now be more precise about what we mean by discovering joint gains and "creating value." By this, we have three kinds of actions in mind. First, reaching any agreement that exceeds the parties' no-agreement possibilities creates value relative to the alternatives. Second, negotiators create potential value with respect to one negotiated outcome by finding another that all prefer. And, third, negotiators create potential value by discovering that more is jointly feasible than previously was thought. That is, without necessarily reaching agreement, they discover a way — whether a new trade, a different option, a changed schedule of payments, or the like — to push the perceived Pareto frontier northeasterly, to reduce the apparent conflict of interest.

Negotiators can create two distinct kinds of value. [We] will consider each in turn. The first kind — what we will call "private value" — includes profits to be split, land to be parceled out, goods to be allocated, and, generally, results of negotiation that one party can consume, use, or enjoy while excluding others from the benefits. Those who mainly think of negotiation as the process of working out mutually beneficial exchanges have traditionally focused on private value. . . .

Yet negotiators can also create "common value," which is exceedingly important but often neglected in thinking about the process. Common value can be shared by all parties simultaneously; no one can be excluded unless all are. . . . For example, suppose that two graphic designers are each committed to a different logo. They bargain for days over which one they will jointly recommend to top management.

But suppose they discover a new logo that both prefer to their original choices. Their agreement to recommend it is good for both at the same time. . . .

The parties must explore — imperfectly — the arrangements they may jointly be able to create. In practice many gains go unrealized. Inferior agreements are made. Impasse results and conflict escalates when cooperative action might have been far better for all. Understanding where private and common value really come from should make jointly creating it more likely. [There are] three primary sources: (1) the key role of *differences* among the participants in creating private (and common) value [i.e., when one person values X highly and the other does not]; (2) the often-misunderstood role of *shared interests* in creating common value [i.e., when both parties want the venture to succeed or want to avoid a strike]; and (3) how *economies of scale* can create both kinds of value without requiring differences or shared interests [i.e., when merging companies can save on overhead].

Notes and Questions

3.8 What do Lax and Sebenius suggest are the advantages of value creation? Do you agree? Are there any disadvantages of seeking to create value? What might they be?

3.9 The classic example of value creation is the story of two siblings fighting over an orange. They agree to split it in half. One throws out the peel and eats her half of the orange. The other uses her half of the peel in a recipe and throws out the rest of the orange. How could these siblings have better resolved this dispute? On the other hand, what arguments could you make that the resolution between the siblings is a good one?

The following excerpt is based on an empirical study that asked lawyers how during their most recent negotiation they perceived the other side's negotiation strategy. Over 700 lawyers (out of 2,500) sent back a mailed questionnaire that asked lawyers to rate their counterpart attorneys using 89 adjectives, 60 negotiation techniques, and 14 goals. The attorneys also rated their counterparts for effectiveness. The studied attorneys were grouped in two, three, and four styles based on statistical analysis. It discusses the division of attorneys into three groups — true problem solvers, cautious problem solvers, and adversarials. It then outlines the differences among the groups, both in the description of the groups and each group's respective effectiveness. Note particularly the difference between true problem-solving negotiators — those who truly engage in the behavior described in the previous excerpts on integrative bargaining — and "cautious" problem solvers — those who don't fully use the range of problem-solving behavior. Also, think about what adjectives most closely describe your approach to negotiation.

Andrea Kupfer Schneider, **SHATTERING NEGOTIATION MYTHS: EMPIRICAL EVIDENCE ON THE EFFECTIVENESS OF NEGOTIATION STYLE**

7 Harv. Negot. L. Rev. 143, 171-175 (2002)

[We] can also separate negotiation styles into three clusters, which I have labeled true problem-solving, cautious problem-solving, and adversarial.... [L]awyers were divided far more evenly among the three clusters with approximately 36% in the true problem-solving group, 36% in the cautious problem-solving group, and 28% in the adversarial group. The new middle group appears to have come primarily from the original problem-solving group that consisted of 64% of lawyers. This suggestion is reinforced since the cautious problem-solving group's adjectives overlap with the problem-solving group. Therefore, rather than a separate style of negotiation, it appears that the third group is really just comprised of lawyers who are relatively nondescript and average in terms of effectiveness.

ADJECTIVE RATINGS

When compiling the list of adjectives to describe each group, we looked for ratings of three or higher on the five-point scale. The following table shows the top twenty adjectives for the three new clusters.

Top 20 Adjectives for Three Clusters

	TRUE PROBLEM-SOLVING	CAUTIOUS PROBLEM-SOLVING	ADVERSARIAL
1	Ethical	Ethical	Irritating
2	Personable	Experienced	Headstrong
3	Experienced	Confident	Stubborn
4	Trustworthy	Personable	Arrogant
5	Rational	Self-controlled	Egotistical
6	Agreeable	Rational	Argumentative
7	Fair-minded	Sociable	Assertive
8	Communicative	Dignified	Demanding
9	Realistic	Trustworthy	Quarrelsome
10	Accommodating		Confident
11	Perceptive		Ambitious
12	Sociable		Manipulative
13	Adaptable		Experienced
14	Confident		Hostile
15	Dignified		Forceful
16	Self-controlled		Tough
17	Helpful		Suspicious
18	Astute about the law		Firm
19	Poised		Complaining
20	Flexible		Rude

The most interesting result in this analysis is the middle category. Clearly this middle group is comprised of "good" lawyers in that all of the adjectives are positive. Again, all nine are included in the true problem-solving group. In comparison, however, the true problem-solving group had forty-nine highly rated adjectives. Consequently, I have labeled the middle group "cautious problem-solvers" to highlight the fact that most of these traits are problem-solving, yet this group seems hesitant to utilize all of the problem-solving attributes. By "cautious," I do not mean to suggest that these negotiators are themselves cautious, but rather they are cautious about adopting a completely problem-solving approach to the negotiation. . . .

The bipolar descriptions reveal more about the differences among these three types of negotiators. . . .

Three Cluster Bipolars		
TRUE PROBLEM-SOLVING	**CAUTIOUS PROBLEM-SOLVING**	**ADVERSARIAL**
1 Did not use derogatory personal references	Did not use derogatory personal references	Aggressive
2 Honest	Interested in my client's needs	Not interested in my client's needs
3 Courteous	Zealous representation within bounds	Arrogant
4 Interested in my client's needs	Courteous	Extreme opening demand
5 Friendly	Intelligent	Rigid
6 Best interests of client	Honest	Unrealistic
7 Intelligent	Adhered to legal courtesies	Unconcerned how I look
8 Zealous representation within bounds	Best interests of client	Interested in my client's needs
9 Reasonable		Negotiation = Win/Lose
10 Prepared		Narrow view of problem
11 Adhered to legal courtesies		Fixed conception of problem
12 Tactful		Narrow range of strategies
13 Accurate representation of position		Fixed on a single solution
14 Cooperative		Uncooperative
15 Forthright		Did not consider my needs
16 Trustful		
17 Sincere		
18 Facilitated		
19 Viewed negotiation as possibly having mutual benefits		
20 Did not make unwarranted claims		

The true problem-solving negotiator understands the case well (reasonable, prepared, accurate representation of client's position, did own factual investigation) and wanted to work with the other side (friendly, tactful, cooperative, facilitated the negotiation, viewed the negotiation process as one with mutual benefits, understood my client's interests). This negotiator was flexible (movable position, did not use take-it-or-leave-it) and did not engage in manipulative tactics (did not make unwarranted claims, did not use threats, avoided needless harm to my client). The true problem-solving negotiator believed in the good faith exchange of information (cooperative, forthright, trustful, sincere, shared information, probed). . . .

The cautious problem-solving group, as in the adjectives ratings, did not stand out in most of the characteristics and is only rated more than slightly characteristic in eight descriptions. These eight are all positive and also appear on the problem-solving list, but the cautious problem-solving category lacks twenty-two descriptions that true problem-solvers display. As described above, these absent characteristics describe negotiation qualities that add depth and breadth to a negotiator's skills. . . .

Top Three Cluster Goals

	TRUE PROBLEM-SOLVING	CAUTIOUS PROBLEM-SOLVING	ADVERSARIAL
1	Ethical conduct	Maximizing settlement	Maximizing settlement
2	Fair settlement	Ethical conduct	Outdoing you
3	Maximizing settlement	Fair settlement	Profitable fee
4	Meet both sides' interests	Meeting client's needs	Meeting client's needs
5	Meeting client's needs	Avoiding litigation	Use legal skills well
6	Avoiding litigation	Meet both sides' interests	Improving firm reputation
7	Good relations with you	Good relations with you	Ethical conduct
8	Use legal skills well	Use legal skills well	Fair settlement
9	Good relations between parties	Profitable fee	Improving bar reputation
10	Improving reputation with you	Good relations between parties	Avoiding litigation
11		Outdoing you	
12		Improving firm reputation	

True problem-solvers also have different goals than cautious problem-solvers. Both ethical conduct and a fair settlement are higher goals for the problem-solver than maximizing settlement, which is the highest goal for cautious problem-solvers.

In this vein, the cautious problem-solver is more like the adversarial bargainer in terms of their first priority. Further demonstrating this negotiator's ambivalence about style is the fact that the cautious problem-solver was also perceived as having goals such as obtaining a profitable fee and outdoing his opponent.

The study of effectiveness can demonstrate the impact of these differences in the rating-scale.

Number of Lawyers per Group by Effectiveness			
	INEFFECTIVE	AVERAGE	EFFECTIVE
True Problem-Solving	3	53	164
Cautious Problem-Solving	29	139	55
Adversarial	102	58	15

First, approximately 25% of the negotiators in the new cautious problem-solving group are effective, whereas 75% of the true problem-solvers are described as effective. The missing negotiation elements between the groups must cause this difference. Adjectives found in true problem-solving but not in cautious problem-solving highlight empathy (communicative, accommodating, perceptive, helpful), option creation (adaptable, flexible), personality (agreeable, poised), and preparation (fair-minded, realistic, astute about the law). These skills make the difference between average skills and truly effective skills. Contrary to popular belief, behaviors described by these adjectives are not risky at all. The traditional fear of problem-solving is that problem-solvers will be taken advantage of by more adversarial bargainers, yet only 1% of true problem-solving negotiators were considered ineffective.

Notes and Questions

3.10 One way of thinking about the difference between true problem solvers and cautious problem solvers is as three clusters of skills under assertiveness, empathy, and flexibility with ethics and a pleasant personality as a base. What seem to be the primary differences between true and cautious problem solvers? Which of these do you think is the most important?

3.11 How do you think these differences matter in terms of effectiveness?

C. CONCERNS

The next two articles present some thoughtful critiques of integrative negotiation.

Gerald B. Wetlaufer, **THE LIMITS OF INTEGRATIVE BARGAINING**

85 Geo. L.J. 369, 372-391 (1996)

My essay has two purposes. One is to take a fresh look at the claims concerning the pervasiveness of opportunities for integrative bargaining. The other is to re-examine the argument that the tactics of cooperation, openness, and truthtelling are in the immediate pecuniary self-interest of the parties to a negotiation. In pursuing these objectives, I will seek to specify the exact nature of the self-interest and of the joint gains (or "pie expansion") that are being invoked. I will then test certain claims regarding the circumstances that create opportunities for integrative bargaining. I will also assess the case that has, or has not, been made in favor of cooperation, openness, and truthtelling.

I reach three conclusions. First, opportunities for integrative bargaining are not nearly as pervasive as is sometimes authoritatively asserted. Second, the claim that opportunities for integrative bargaining make good behavior a simple matter of rational, pecuniary self-interest is not nearly as strong as is sometimes claimed, both because opportunities for integrative bargaining are less pervasive than has been asserted and because, even when such opportunities may exist, the case for good behavior is weaker than has been claimed. Third, and accordingly, the case for good behavior cannot rest entirely on pecuniary self-interest. . . .

DISTINCTIONS IN THE DOMAIN OF JOINT GAINS

A good deal of confusion arises from the assertion that opportunities for integrative or "win-win" bargaining are distinguishable from opportunities for "distributive" or "win-lose" bargaining in that the former can "create value" and "expand the pie" while the latter cannot. Characterizing the distinction in this way causes confusion because, in fact, all opportunities for bargaining, including opportunities that are solely win-lose or zero-sum games, present opportunities to "create value" and to "expand the pie."

For purposes of clarification, I will distinguish three forms of value creation, only one of which constitutes an opportunity for integrative or win-win bargaining. The first of these forms is found where the pie can be made larger only in the sense that is true of all bargaining including all bargaining that is merely distributive. In such circumstances, there is a zone of agreement (i.e., a range of possible agreement) within which both parties will be better off than they would have been in the absence of the agreement. Thus, in this minimal sense, purely distributive bargaining can be said to "create value" or "expand the pie." I shall call this "Form I" value creation. Though it involves the "creation" of value, Form I does not involve integrative bargaining and is not a situation in which the more open tactics associated with integrative bargaining will promote the immediate pecuniary self-interest of a party.

The same can also be said of opportunities for "Form II" value creation. Form II value creation is possible when there is one issue (e.g., the amount of money to be paid for some product), and one party cares more about that issue than does the other. This is a situation in which, assuming there is a range of possible agreements that would leave both parties better off, there is an opportunity for Form I value creation in that the aggregate benefits to the parties will vary depending on whether or not they can reach agreement. Also, and this is what distinguishes Form II value creation, this is a situation in which the aggregate benefits to the parties, the size of the pie, will vary across the range of possible agreements. Thus, the total value created by the agreement will be relatively large if most of that over which the parties are negotiating (e.g., surplus as measured in dollars) is captured by the party who cares more about that issue. Similarly, the total value created by the agreement will be relatively small if most of the surplus is captured by the party who cares less about that issue. . . .

Only what I shall call "Form III" value creation offers an opportunity for integrative or win-win bargaining. Unlike Forms I and II, Form III value creation involves that kind of pie-expansion or value creation in which the parties can reach a range of different agreements, in which the size of the pie will vary across the range of possible agreements (also true of Form II), but in which some of those agreements leave both parties better off than do others. If there are some possible agreements that both parties would regard as better than others, then the size of the pie created by the agreement depends both upon the parties' ability to reach some agreement (Form I value creation) and upon their wit and ability to arrive at one of the better agreements. It is in this sense that a situation presenting an opportunity for Form III value creation is a non-zero-sum game and an opportunity for integrative or win-win bargaining. . . .

DIFFERING INTERESTS, INCLUDING MULTIPLE ISSUES DIFFERENTLY VALUED

We might begin with the situation in which the parties have differing interests and with the question whether, under all or some such circumstances, those differences in interests create opportunities for integrative bargaining. While I shall argue that opportunities for integrative bargaining do not exist in all such circumstances, they do appear to exist in some. Imagine, for instance, that a corporate plaintiff sues an airline, that the parties have been exploring the possibility of settlement, and that they have reached a tentative agreement on $80,000. Next assume that the defendant, just back from a seminar on win-win negotiation, proposes an in-kind settlement in which the defendant would provide the plaintiff with $120,000 worth of air travel. Because of the airline's high fixed costs and the frequency with which it carries empty seats, the cost to the airline will be only $30,000. Both parties find the in-kind settlement to be highly preferable to the cash agreement they had tentatively reached. In this sense, the parties have found themselves in a situation where there is a range of possible agreements and some of those agreements are better than others for both parties. Thus there is an opportunity for Form III value creation and for integrative bargaining.

If this is a situation in which differences in the parties' interests present an opportunity for integrative bargaining, attention must be paid to a range of circumstances that appear similar to our example, yet do not present opportunities for integrative bargaining. One set of cases to be excluded from our category includes all exchange transactions in which two parties simply exchange one thing for another, say for instance money for a used car. We may assume, at a minimum, that such transactions occur only when the car is more highly valued by the buyer than by the seller. This difference in valuation, while it could be characterized as a "difference in interests" between the parties, does nothing more than create the possibility of a mutual beneficial agreement and, with that, the possibility of Form I value creation. It merely satisfies the minimal conditions necessary for distributive bargaining. It is distinctly not an opportunity for Form III value creation, and thus it is not an opportunity for integrative bargaining. . . .

Lax and Sebenius . . . assert that differences in probabilistic assessments create opportunities for integrative bargaining. It would be more accurate, however, to say that these circumstances will sometimes present opportunities for a particular kind of integrative bargaining if, but only if, the parties are both willing to bet on their differing assessments. The differences being exploited here are differences in the parties' predictions concerning future events. More specifically, they are either differing probabilistic assessments of the likelihood of some future event or differing assessments of the likely future value of some variable. . . .

A common example of an opportunity for integrative bargaining involves a situation in which the parties have, and then exploit, different assessments of the likelihood that some tangible device (e.g., a used car or a new technology) will work. . . . Absent a contingent agreement, there was no possibility of agreement at all. But once the parties identified and exploited the opportunity for a contingent agreement, a mutually advantageous transaction became possible. The possibility of a contingent agreement allows the parties to transform their situation from one presenting no zone of agreement to one presenting a sizable zone of agreement, thereby expanding the size of the pie. [But] [t]here is nothing inherent about the possibility of placing a bet that would cause people, even people in business, to place that bet. Surely some are in the business of speculating and betting on their projections. Most, however, are in the business of providing goods and services at a reasonable price. Many, if not most, in this second group are not looking for opportunities to roll the dice. If, however, what is offered is an opportunity to bet on one's product (or invention), I assume the number of people willing to gamble will go up. But as a general matter, among businessmen and others, people seeking out opportunities to bet on their projections are probably the exception and not the rule. . . .

If the parties to a negotiation have different aversions to risk, and if the negotiation involves something that carries a risk, then there may (but also may not) be an opportunity for integrative bargaining in the sense that an agreement, reached without regard to the allocation of risk, may be modified so as to leave both parties better off. Such an opportunity will exist when, and only when, the preliminary agreement leaves the risk in the wrong hands. Under those circumstances, the party who is not left bearing the risk can be given the risk, the party who will thus get rid of the risk will be better off in more than the amount by which the party acquiring the risk will be worse off, and the party getting rid of the risk will be in a position to compensate the party acquiring the risk in an amount that will leave both parties better off than they were before the compensated shifting of the risk.

There is then the question of whether all such differences constitute opportunities for integrative bargaining. They do not. Thus, if in the normal course of the negotiation the risk ends up with the party who assigns to it the lower negative value, the risk is already where it ought to be and transferring it to the other party would not increase the aggregate value arising from the transaction but would, instead, decrease it. Such a transfer would not cause the pie to expand, but rather to contract. . . .

Differences in capabilities and possible economies of scale may create opportunities for joint gains, but not for the Form III gains that distinguish integrative bargaining. Rather, they create opportunities for the Form I joint gains that arise any time two parties enter into a mutually beneficial agreement. Such differences may create or expand the possibility of a distributive agreement by which both parties may make themselves better off than they otherwise would have been. But that is simply to say that these circumstances create an opportunity for bargaining. They do not create an opportunity for Form III joint gains and for integrative bargaining.

Considerations related to continuing relationships or to reputational effects may provide a negotiator with a good reason to be cooperative, to be open and truthful, or otherwise to moderate her reliance upon the tactics (e.g., misrepresentation) associated with distributive bargaining. But the fact that she has found reason to alter her tactics in the direction of cooperation, openness, and truthtelling does not mean that she has done so because there exists an opportunity for Form III value creation. No such opportunity exists. Although the parties face a series of negotiations, nothing in this circumstance indicates the presence of anything other than Form I joint gains. It is certainly not a situation, as it must be for there to be an opportunity for integrative bargaining, in which the size of the pie may vary and in which both parties will be better off with some of the possible agreements than they would have been with others. . . .

 Chris Guthrie, **PANACEA OR PANDORA'S BOX? THE COSTS OF OPTIONS IN NEGOTIATION**

88 Iowa L. Rev. 601, 604-606, 608-610, 613-615, 617, 621-622, 625, 631-632, 634-636, 638-641, 644 (2003)

At first glance, the option-generation prescription seems unassailable. After all, negotiators can include in their agreements only those options that they actually consider, and the more options they will have to choose from at the bargaining table [the better]. . . .

Upon closer inspection, however, the option-generation prescription begins to appear vulnerable, for it rests on a questionable premise about the behavior of negotiators. It assumes that negotiators will make rational decisions when selecting from multiple options. Regardless of the number of options available or the manner in which they are presented, it assumes that negotiators will independently assess the subjective value of each option, rank-order them, and then select the one that offers the most value. In reality, however, people often have great difficulty selecting the value-maximizing option when multiple options are on the table; that is, the very presence of multiple options has a tendency to induce people to make suboptimal decisions.

The purpose of this Article is to describe some of the predictable problems that may arise as a consequence of option generation in negotiation. Relying on existing experimental research, new experimental research, and "real-world" empirical evidence, the Article identifies four potential costs associated with option generation: option devaluation, context dependence (both contrast and compromise), non-compensatory decision making, and decision regret. Taken together, these "option costs" stand for the ironic proposition that negotiators who heed the option-generation prescription may be more likely than those who ignore it to enter into inferior agreements with which they may be less satisfied. In short, option generation may not be the panacea its proponents imagine, but rather a Pandora's box that can lead negotiators astray.

The purpose of this Article is *not* to argue that negotiators should cease option generation. As its proponents have observed, option generation may enable negotiators to identify novel alternatives that "effectively reconcile the differing interests of the parties." The problem, however, is that this very same process can also induce negotiators to make suboptimal decisions at the bargaining table. Thus, this Article's more modest goal is merely to delineate some of the potential pitfalls that can accompany option generation. . . .

The Article argues that *lawyer*-negotiators, acting on behalf of clients, are more likely than *non-lawyer*-negotiators, acting on their own behalf, to maximize the benefits and minimize the costs of option generation in negotiation. . . . First, lawyers, in contrast to their clients, are likely to assess decision options according to rational principles of choice (and evidence suggests that principals want their agents to evaluate decision options in this fashion). Second, because lawyers can assess decision options rationally, they can help clients faced with multiple options make "better" decisions at the bargaining table. Finally, and perhaps more controversially, sophisticated lawyers can use decision options strategically in negotiation to induce their counterparts to make desired concessions. . . .

OPTION COST #1 (OPTION DEVALUATION)

The first phenomenon that may negatively influence decision making in multiple-option negotiation is "option devaluation." That is, negotiators may unwittingly devalue an option once it becomes part of a set of options because options that look attractive by themselves often look less attractive when compared to others.

1. Option Devaluation Explained

Rational models of decision making generally assume that people assess the subjective value of an option based solely on the value of that option. According to the rational model, "an option's attractiveness does not depend on comparisons drawn between it and other alternatives." Contrary to the rational model, however, some psychologists have found that comparisons do influence the way people evaluate an option. In fact, "comparisons typically serve to decrease the attractiveness of the options being compared." . . .

Suppose, for example, that [a] college student prefers to attend a law school with a large enrollment located in a temperate climate. When she compares the two schools, she will deem Harvard's size to be an advantage relative to Stanford, and Stanford's location to be an advantage relative to Harvard; at the same time, she will perceive Stanford's size to be a *dis*advantage relative to Harvard, and Harvard's location to be a *dis*advantage relative to Stanford. . . .

In fact, in experimental investigations of this "loss aversion" phenomenon, psychologists have found that people find disadvantages or losses *at least* twice as painful as they find advantages or gains of the same magnitude pleasurable. Because the process of comparison brings to mind the relative advantages and disadvantages of the options under consideration, and because each option's disadvantages are likely to loom larger than its advantages, loss aversion implies that comparisons will decrease the attractiveness of *every* option under consideration. When our college student compares Harvard and Stanford Law Schools, for example, Harvard's location in a harsh climate will decrease its attractiveness more than its size will increase its attractiveness; likewise, Stanford's small enrollment will decrease its attractiveness more than its location will increase its attractiveness. In short, *both* Harvard and Stanford will seem less attractive when compared to one another than when evaluated independently. . . .

2. Option Devaluation in Negotiation

[S]ubjects [in two groups] anticipated negotiating with a seller to purchase one small sedan. I asked the subjects in both groups to indicate how much they would pay for a Toyota Corolla. The only difference between the two groups was that I asked subjects in the three-car group to consider two other small sedans as well, a Honda Civic and a Mazda Protégé.

Because the subjects were randomly assigned to the two groups, there was no reason to expect them to evaluate the Toyota Corolla differently. Nonetheless, I found that the mere presence of the additional options prompted subjects in the three-car group to evaluate the Corolla less favorably. Subjects in the one-car group indicated they would pay an average amount of $13,125 for the Corolla, while subjects in the three-car group indicated that they would pay only $11,447.37 for the very same car. Even though the additional options presented to the three-car group conveyed no information about the value of the Toyota Corolla, their very presence depressed average valuations by $1,677.63 or 12.8%.

In negotiation, as well as consumer decision making, people seem to devalue options when comparing them to others. When the "other" options provide relevant information about the value of the options already under consideration, this is quite reasonable; however, this phenomenon seems to occur even when the added options do not provide relevant contextual information. This is because the very process of comparison "emphasize[s] the advantages and disadvantages of options under consideration" and "disadvantages are given greater weight than advantages" in the evaluation. Thus, "whenever the options under consideration have both meaningful advantages and meaningful disadvantages, comparisons hurt."

OPTION COST #2 (CONTEXT DEPENDENCE)

The second phenomenon that can induce suboptimal decision making in multiple-option negotiation arises when a new option is added to an existing choice set. . . .

Psychologists have discovered, however, that people's assessments of initially considered options are often systematically influenced by the emergence of an additional, irrelevant option. People "make context-based inferences about the worth of alternatives whether or not the context provides a valid basis for such inferences." Researchers have documented two distinct types of "context-dependent" decision effects: "contrast" and "compromise." . . .

1.   Contrast Explained

In one simple experiment, for example, Itamar Simonson and Amos Tversky randomly assigned subjects to a two-option group or a three-option group and asked the subjects in each group to select either cash or a pen. The subjects in the two-option group could choose to receive $6 or an elegant Cross pen. Subjects in the three-option group could choose $6, the elegant Cross pen, or a lesser known, unattractive pen. The researchers found that 36% of the subjects in the two-option group, as compared to 46% of the subjects in the three-option group, selected the Cross pen. Despite the fact that subjects in the latter group chose from among three options rather than two, 27.8% more of them selected the Cross pen. The availability of the inferior option, i.e., the unattractive pen, substantially increased the likelihood that subjects would select the superior option, i.e., the Cross pen.

2.   Contrast in Negotiation

This work suggests that negotiators may alter their evaluations in predictably non-normative ways when an inferior option is added to the choice set. Although negotiators are unlikely to select the inferior option, its presence is likely to make the similar, superior option seem more attractive than it appeared before.

3.   Compromise Explained

Compromise or "extremeness aversion" is another form of context dependence. Research on compromise suggests that people are likely to evaluate an option more favorably when it appears to be intermediate, rather than extreme, in a choice set. . . .

To illustrate this phenomenon, suppose our college student has established state residency in Virginia. Suppose further that she has applied to, and been accepted by, the law schools at the University of Virginia and William & Mary and that the two factors most relevant to her decision are prestige and cost. She knows that Virginia generally ranks higher than William & Mary (currently 7th versus 32nd in the *U.S. News* rankings), but William & Mary is much less expensive (currently $10,400 tuition versus $18,090 at Virginia), so she is not sure which school she prefers.

Now suppose our college student has just learned that she has been admitted to Columbia, which is more prestigious (currently ranked 4th) but also more expensive ($30,868 tuition). From a rational perspective, her admission to Columbia should not have any effect on her preference for Virginia or William & Mary. Research on compromise suggests, however, that her admission to Columbia is likely to make Virginia seem relatively more attractive than William & Mary because it renders Virginia an intermediate or compromise option. Columbia is the most prestigious of the three schools but is also the most expensive; William & Mary is the least expensive but also the least prestigious; Virginia is in between on both dimensions. Although counterintuitive, the research on compromise suggests that our college student is more likely to select Virginia when she gets into both William & Mary and Columbia than when she gets into William & Mary alone. . . .

4.   Compromise in Negotiation

This research suggests that negotiators may alter their evaluations in non-normative ways when an extreme option is added to the choice set. Although negotiators are unlikely to select that option, its presence is likely to make the intermediate option appear more attractive than it appeared before. . . . [See treatment of noncompensatory decision making and decision regret discussed in this article in Chapter 8.]

THE ROLE OF THE LAWYER-NEGOTIATOR

The prescriptive negotiation literature advises negotiators to generate, evaluate, and select from as many options as possible, yet this Article has argued that the presence of multiple options in a choice set can lead negotiators to make suboptimal decisions. Which is right? Is option generation a panacea, as the prescriptive negotiation literature claims, or is it a Pandora's box, as this Article has suggested?

Negotiators can surely benefit from considering and evaluating multiple options. Negotiators can select only those options they actually consider, so the more options they consider, the more likely it seems they will reach an agreement that maximizes their preferences. Moreover, in some circumstances, the emergence of a "new" option can provide relevant information about the other options under consideration so that negotiators might actually make better decisions. As this Article has sought to demonstrate, however, there is a potential downside to option generation. Negotiators who generate and evaluate multiple options are susceptible to decision-making errors that may lead them to enter into agreements that are inferior to those they would have entered into had they not considered multiple options in the first place.

Thus, option generation is *neither* a panacea *nor* a Pandora's box; rather, it has the potential to be *either* a panacea *or* a Pandora's box. In other words, option generation offers significant potential benefits to negotiators, but it can also impose predictable potential costs. How then can those attempting to settle a dispute or close a deal obtain the benefits of option generation (i.e., identifying creative options that might facilitate the attainment of a better outcome) without incurring the costs (i.e., making non-value maximizing decisions because of the presence of irrelevant options)?

This Article argues that people can maximize the benefits and minimize the costs of option generation by hiring lawyers to negotiate for them. . . .

First, lawyers are more likely than their clients to evaluate negotiation options "rationally" or "normatively" (and evidence suggests this is what clients often want). Second, because lawyers are likely to evaluate options rationally, they can help their clients make "better" decisions in negotiation. Finally, lawyers can also use options strategically in negotiation to gain advantage for their clients.

Notes and Questions

3.12 Do you agree with Wetlaufer's critiques of integrative bargaining? How would you respond to his critique?

3.13 What do you think the primary risks of problem-solving behavior are? How can you help your client avoid these?

3.14 Even under highly competitive situations, police working in hostage negotiations use integrative approaches to problem-solve and move negotiations from competitive to integrative. See William A. Donohue & Anthony J. Roberto, Relational Development as Negotiated Order in Hostage Negotiation, 20 Hum. Comm. Res. 175-198 (1993).

D. SKILL BUILDING FOR CREATIVE PROBLEM SOLVING

As any parent of young children will know, children are far better at being creative than their parents. What to adult eyes looks like a basic shoebox can actually be a house for dinosaurs, a bookcase for baby books, the first block in a tower, or a hat, all depending how you look at it. After years of being told to color in the lines (and that the grass should be green and the sky should be blue), answer only the question asked, and play games only by the rules printed on the box, we all lose much of our natural creativity. Yet the need to be creative hardly decreases with age. In fact, certain successful companies incorporate "creative conflict" into the very structure of the company.[*] Procter and Gamble, for example, fosters competition among its various brands. Nissan has used this method for designing new car models. Other companies use the model of brainteaser questions in their interviewing process in order to find creative people. Microsoft's methodology has spawned not only a book, *How Would You Move Mount Fuji?*,[†] but also multiple Web sites to help potential employees prepare for the interview.

(Lehman Brothers apparently also followed this methodology of asking interviewees tough questions. In response to an interviewer's request to open a window in an office on the forty-third floor, the interviewee tossed a chair through the window![‡] While we don't recommend this approach to law students or others, we do appreciate the ability of this particular person to let no barrier to creativity stand in the way.)

The value of creative thinking also applies to effective negotiation where the ability to "think outside the box" is quite valuable. This chapter focuses on the advantage that creative thinking can bring to a negotiation and then provides some specific ideas to increase creativity.

In this next excerpt, Jennifer Brown explains several different creativity techniques that can be useful in negotiation. These include transfer, visualization, and entry points.

---

[*] Sy Landau, Barbara Landau & Daryl Landau, From Conflict to Creativity 97-98 (2001).
[†] William Poundstone, How Would You Move Mount Fuji? (2003).
[‡] Michael Lewis, Liar's Poker: Rising Through the Wreckage on Wall Street (1989).

Jennifer Gerarda Brown, **CREATIVITY AND PROBLEM-SOLVING**

87 Marq. L. Rev. 697, 697–705 (2004)

Negotiation experts seem to agree that creative solutions are often the key to reaching value-maximizing outcomes in integrative, interest based bargaining. Sticking to the problem as it is initially framed and considering only the solutions that most readily present themselves will sometimes yield the optimal result, but more often the situation will require the parties and their representatives to think more expansively. This process of thinking more expansively — thinking "that ventures out from the accustomed way of considering a problem, to find something else that might work" — is often referred to as creativity or creative thinking. Some commentators distinguish creative thinking from creativity, arguing that creativity "is more value-laden and tends to be often linked with art (in its broad sense)." Creativity might seem to resemble any other artistic quality, something people lack or possess as much as a matter of genetics as anything

> **Stuck, Stuck, Stuck**
>
> Stuck, stuck, stuck in a rut;
> Solving a problem's like cracking a nut.
> Without the right tools
> You can't do the work —
> You'll stress and waste time
> And look like a jerk.
> It's time we admit our long-standing denial.
> Treading one path will impede our survival.
> By connecting synapses
> We'll end mental lapses,
> So in rut-jumping we'll not have a rival.
>
> Janet Weinstein & Linda Morton, Stuck in a Rut: The Role of Creative Thinking in Problem Solving and Legal Education, 9 Clinical L. Rev. 835 (2003).

else. And yet, like other artistic qualities (observation, hand-eye coordination, vocabulary, or writing skills), creativity may be teachable — or at least, whatever quantity one has as a matter of natural endowment might be enhanced with the right training. On the theory that both creativity and creative thinking can be enhanced with some training and work, this essay will use the terms interchangeably. . . .

I. BEYOND BRAINSTORMING

Most teachers and trainers of interest-based negotiation will spend some time teaching creative thinking. Following the template set forth in *Getting to YES*, they will encourage their students to "brainstorm." Brainstorming, as most readers of this essay know, is a somewhat formalized process in which participants work together to generate ideas. I say that it is formalized because it proceeds according to two important ground rules: participants agree not to evaluate the ideas while they are brainstorming, and they agree not to take "ownership" of the ideas. They strive to generate options and put them on the table, no matter how wacky or far-fetched they may seem. The "no evaluation" rule encourages participants to suspend their natural urge to criticize, edit, or censor the ideas. Evaluation can come later, but the notion here is that solutions will flow more easily if people are not assessing even as they articulate them. The "no ownership" rule also facilitates innovation because participants are encouraged to feel free to propose an idea or solution without endorsing it — no one can later attribute the idea to the person who proposed it, or try to hold it against that person. People can therefore propose ideas that might actually disadvantage them and benefit their counterparts without conceding that they would actually agree to such proposals in the final analysis. The ground rules for brainstorming constrain the natural inclination to criticize, so that participants are free to imagine, envision, and play with ideas, even though these processes come less easily to them. Why is brainstorming so popular, both in practice and in negotiation training? Perhaps the answer lies not so much in what it activates, but in what it disables. What I mean is that it may be easier to teach people what *not* to do — rather than what to do affirmatively — in order to enhance their creative thinking. We may not know much about how to unleash new sources of creativity for negotiators, but we are pretty sure about some things that impede creative thinking. Theory and practice suggest that creative thinking is difficult when people jump to conclusions, close off discussion, or seize upon an answer prematurely. Indeed, the very heuristics that make decisionmaking possible — those pathways that permit people to make positive and sometimes normative judgments — can also lead people astray. One of the ways they may be led astray is that the heuristic prompts them to decide too quickly what something is or should be. Once judgment has occurred, it is tough to justify the expenditure of additional energy that creative thinking would require. Creativity could be considered the "anti-heuristic"; it keeps multiple pathways of perception and decision-making open, even when people are tempted to choose a single, one-way route to a solution. If we do nothing else, we can attempt to delay this kind of judgment until negotiators have considered multiple options. Brainstorming provides the structure for this kind of delay. . . .

Wordplay

Once an issue or problem is articulated, it is possible to play with the words expressing that problem in order to improve understanding and sometimes to yield new solutions.

1. Shifting Emphasis

To take a fairly simple example, suppose that two neighbors are in a dispute because cigarette butts and other small pieces of trash, deposited by Mr. Smith in his own front yard, are blowing into Mr. Jones's yard, and those that remain in Mr. Smith's yard are detracting from the appearance of the neighborhood (at least as Mr. Jones sees it). Mr. Jones might ask himself (or a mediator at the neighborhood justice center), "How can I get Mr. Smith to stop littering in his yard?" Shifting the emphasis in this sentence brings into focus various aspects of the problem and suggests possible solutions addressing those specific aspects. Consider the different meanings of the following sentences:

"How can *I* get Mr. Smith to stop littering in his yard?"
"How can I get *Mr. Smith* to stop littering in his yard?"

"How can I get Mr. Smith to stop *littering* in his yard?"
"How can I get Mr. Smith to stop littering in *his* yard?"
"How can I get Mr. Smith to stop littering in his *yard*?"

As the focus of the problem shifts, so too different potential solutions might emerge to address the problem as specifically articulated.

2. Changing a Word
Sometimes changing a word in the sentence helps to reformulate the problem in a way that suggests new solutions. In the example above, Mr. Jones might change the phrase "littering in his yard" to something else, such as "neglecting his yard" or "hanging out in his yard." It may be that something besides littering lies at the root of the problem, and a solution will be found, for example, not in stopping the littering, but in more regularized yard work.

3. Deleting a Word
Through word play, parties can delete words or phrases to see whether broadening the statement of the problem more accurately or helpfully captures its essence. Mr. Jones might delete the phrase "Mr. Smith" from his formulation of the problem, and thereby discover that it is not just Mr. Smith's yard, but the entire street, that is looking bad. Focusing on Mr. Smith as the source of the problem may be counterproductive; Mr. Jones might discover that he needs to organize all of the homeowners on his block to battle littering in order to make a difference. Deleting words sometimes spurs creativity by removing an overly restrictive focus on the issue or problem.

4. Adding a New Word
A final form of word play that can spur creative thinking is sometimes called "random word association." Through this process, participants choose a word randomly and then think of ways to associate it with the problem. Suppose Mr. Jones and Mr. Smith were given the word "work" and asked how it might relate to their dispute. Here are some possible results:

Work (time, effort): Mr. Smith will try to work harder to keep his yard looking nice, and he will check Mr. Jones's yard every Saturday to make sure there are no cigarette butts or other pieces of trash in it.

Work (being operational or functional): What the neighborhood needs is a sense of cohesion; Mr. Jones and Mr. Smith will organize a neighborhood beautification project to try to instill a sense of community among their neighbors.

Work (job): Although Mr. Smith's odd working hours sometimes lead him to smoke on his front porch and chat with his friends or family late at night (after Mr. Jones has gone to bed), Mr. Smith will stay in the back of his house after 10 P.M., further from Mr. Jones's bedroom window.

As the different meanings and resulting associations of "work" are explored by the parties, they discover new ways to solve their shared problem. Other seemingly unrelated words might trigger still more associations and more potential solutions. . . .

De Bono's "Six Hats" Technique

Edward de Bono has proposed a technique he calls "Six Thinking Hats," in which six aspects of a problem are assessed independently. As problem solvers symbolically don each of six differently colored hats, they focus on an aspect of the problem associated with each color: red for emotions, white for facts, yellow for positive aspects of the situation, green for future implications, black for critique, and blue for process.[22] As Weinstein and Morton point out, the technique of isolating the black/critique hat may be especially important for lawyers, whose tendency to move quickly into a critical mode may prevent them from seeing other important aspects of a problem. If the black hat is worn at or near the end of the process, the Six Hats technique displays a characteristic shared by brainstorming: it delays critique and judgment until other approaches can be tried. And shutting down judgment may enable creativity, as suggested above. By forcing themselves to address separately the emotional, factual, and process issues at stake in a problem, parties may discover room for creative solutions. Similarly, creative solutions are sometimes found in the terms of a future relationship between the parties. Wearing the green hat may force participants to come to terms with a future they would rather ignore.

The prospect of changing hats, even (perhaps especially) if it is done symbolically, could make some participants uncomfortable. Negotiators and neutrals should bear in mind that age, sex, ethnicity and other cultural specifics may create dignitary interests for some participants that would be threatened or compromised by some techniques for boosting creative thought. Some people would feel embarrassed or humiliated if they were asked to engage in the theatrics required by some of these exercises. For others, the chance to pretend or play might be just the prod they need to open new avenues of thought. In a spirit of flexibility (surely a necessary condition for creativity), therefore, one should be thinking of ways to modify these techniques to fit other needs of the parties.[26]

Atlas of Approaches

Another technique for stimulating creative ideas about a problem from a variety of perspectives is called the "Atlas of Approaches." Roger Fisher, Elizabeth Kopelman and Andrea Kupfer Schneider propose this approach in *Beyond Machiavelli*, their book on international negotiation.[27] Using the Atlas of Approaches technique, participants adopt the perspectives of professionals from a variety of fields. By asking themselves, for example, "What would a journalist do?," "What would an economist do?," "How would a psychologist view this?," and so on, negotiators are able to form a more interdisciplinary view of their problem. With this more complete picture of the issues and potential outcomes, they might be able to connect disciplines in ways that give rise to creative solutions....

---

[22] Edward de Bono, Six Thinking Hats (rev. ed. 1999).

[26] For example, the Six Hats technique could be transformed into a "Six Flip Charts" exercise, still using differently colored paper or markers to signal the different focus of each inquiry.

[27] Roger Fisher et al., Beyond Machiavelli: Tools for Coping with Conflict 67 (1994).

"WWCD": What Would Croeses[30] Do?

This process requires a participant to take the perspective of an unconstrained actor. What solutions suggest themselves if we assume no limit to available money, time, talent, technology, or effort? In some ways, one could think of the WWCD method as a more specific application of brainstorming. As the proponents of brainstorming are quick to point out, creativity and the free flow of ideas can be impeded by criticism or assessment. WWCD takes off the table any assessment based on constraints—financial, technological, etc. If we assume that we can afford and operationalize any solution we can come up with, what might we discover?

A second phase of this approach requires participants to think about the extent to which their unconstrained solution might be modified to make it workable given the existing constraints. . . .

Flipping or Reversal

With this technique, one asks whether flipping or reversing a given situation will work. As Edward de Bono explains:

> In the reversal method, one takes things as they are and then turns them round, inside out, upside down, back to front. Then one sees what happens . . . one is not looking for the right answer but for a different arrangement of information which will provoke a different way of looking at the situation.

Chris Honeyman sometimes uses this technique in his work as a neutral when he asks the parties to put forward some really *bad* ideas for resolving the conflict. When people offer ideas in response to a call for "bad" ideas, they may free themselves to offer the ideas they partially or secretly support; again, as in brainstorming, they disclaim ownership of the ideas. It is also possible that the instruction to offer bad ideas stimulates creative thinking because it can seem *funny* to people. Humor is a good stimulant for creativity.

Notes and Questions

3.15 Creativity is even being used in advertisements. The following is from an advertisement in *Vanity Fair* magazine:

> Two women apply for jobs. They look exactly alike. On their applications they list the same last name, address and phone number. They were born to the same parents, on the same day, same month, same year. Everything is identical. The receptionist says, "You must be twins." They say "no." How is that possible?

---

[30] Nalebuff and Ayers explain: "Croesus (rhymes with Jesus) was the supremely rich king of Lydia (modern Turkey), reigning from 560 to 546 B.C. His wealth came from mining gold. . . . His lavish gifts and sacrifices made his name synonymous with wealth. Even today we say 'rich as Croesus.'" Barry Nalebuff & Ian Ayres, Why Not? How to Use Everyday Ingenuity to Solve Problems Big and Small (2003).

What do you think the answer is?

The reader then turns the page over to find the answer.* The ad continues:

> If the answer wasn't obvious, start thinking differently. Which is exactly the strategy behind the totally new 2003 Ford Expedition. Brilliant solutions are easy to see in hindsight. But, having the foresight to come up with one is something completely different. Smart, innovative ideas require unconventional thinking. You have to think without boundaries.

This could be an ad for creative thinking in general. Why does Ford think this will help sell more cars? What do you think about the ad?

3.16 Another example of creativity demonstrates a different method of influence. In the 1970s, U.S. physician Bernard Lown visited the Soviet Union and formed lasting relationships with his Soviet counterparts, one such physician being Evgenii Chazov. The Lown-Chazov connection paved the way for the Boston-based Physicians for Social Responsibility to evolve into a transnational network that eventually became the International Physicians for the Prevention of Nuclear War (IPPNW). Comprising some 200,000 members from 80 countries, the IPPNW won the Nobel Peace Prize in 1985. While none of these doctors could have individually persuaded his or her own government to change its arms policy, this group was very persuasive in helping the United States and the Soviet Union sign arms control agreements. What type of creativity does this demonstrate?

3.17 Days before her wedding, a bride was contacted by her bakery. An employee of the bakery wanted to ask a few questions about her already-paid-for wedding cake. The employee pulled out the magazine page the bride had given them several months ago with the picture of the cake she wanted. The picture showed a chocolate-frosted cake with ornate white trim between each of the layers. On top of the cake was a heart, made out of cake, leaning on its side with the initials of the bride and groom, which could be cut off and frozen for the bride and groom to eat on their anniversary. The employee started the conversation by informing the bride that they could not duplicate the white edging between the layers, for they didn't have that trim. Nor could they do the heart cake top because the weight of the cake could actually cause the whole cake to collapse. The employee then explained that the woman who had promised that they could make the cake in the picture had recently been fired! After contacting another bakery the bride discovered it would be difficult to find another baker this close to the wedding and that the concerns voiced by the first bakery about the weight of the heart were legitimate. The second baker, however, suggested that using a Styrofoam heart and covering it with icing could achieve the same look. The bride took the information back to the original bakery and told them that she wanted a cake that looked like the cake in the picture, even if the heart top was not made out of cake. They agreed to make such a top and do a decorative white "S" trim around each layer to achieve as close to the "look" of the picture as possible.

---

*The women are from a set of triplets.

Why didn't the first bakery suggest the Styrofoam substitute as an option for the bride? What benefit was offered by calling the other baker? How can other professionals or experts help you expand the pie, or cake as it were?

3.18 Creativity can be found to solve all sorts of problems. For another treatment of creativity devices to be used in problem solving, see Janet Weinstein & Linda Morton, Stuck in a Rut: The Role of Creative Thinking in Problem Solving and Legal Education, 9 Clinical L. Rev. 835 (2003), in which they suggest some techniques, like visualization, incubation, and relaxation, in addition to those suggested above and below.

This next excerpt raises a number of issues in regard to creativity. First, Carrie Menkel-Meadow discusses the importance of creativity in successful problem solving and gives you a chance to test your own creativity with a few problems and brain-teasers. She then describes another set of creativity techniques. Then she highlights some past examples of legal creativity. Finally, she asks whether creativity is even teachable and then provides some pointers for how to teach and learn more about creativity in law schools.

 Carrie Menkel-Meadow, **AHA? IS CREATIVITY POSSIBLE IN LEGAL PROBLEM SOLVING AND TEACHABLE IN LEGAL EDUCATION?**

6 Harv. Negot. L. Rev. 97, 106, 120-123, 125, 127-128, 131, 133, 135-136 (2001)

Dispute negotiation too often looks for its solutions among legal precedents or outcomes thought likely in the "shadow of the courthouse" (these days most often [a] compromise of some monetary values), and deal negotiations too often seek solutions in the boilerplate language of form contracts for transactions. Ironically, these litigated outcomes and boilerplate clauses were once the creative ideas of some lawyers who developed a new reading of a statute, a novel argument before a common law or Constitutional court, developed a new scheme of risk allocation, or found a new source of capital or drafted a new clause for a deal document.

Solutions to legal problems, then, come from creative lawyers, as well as legal or practice precedent. The challenge for negotiation theorists, practitioners and teachers is to find systematic ways to teach solution devising, short of reading thousands of cases, transactional documents, statutes or other legal documents that will show us not only what already has been done, but also what might be done. Are there ways of learning or thinking about solutions to legal problems that are generic or are there only substantive (domain based) solutions? Here the teachings of other disciplines may be useful. Some researchers focus on the positive solution-seeking side of cognition and creativity; others focus on the negative side of impediments to good or, as they define it, rational decision making or problem solving. . . .

A few . . . exercises follow below. As you attempt to solve these problems, pay attention to your own thinking processes — how are you trying to solve the problem? What problem or domain space are you searching? What do you call on, from what you already know, to try to solve these problems?

1. In what has become the canonical problem for literally, and figuratively, demonstrating this point, consider the following: Connect the three rows of dots below with four straight lines without moving your pen off the page:

       ●   ●   ●

       ●   ●   ●

       ●   ●   ●

Now, try connecting the dots with three lines.

Now, try one.

The solution to the first problem involves "thinking out of the box" and by realizing that most people imagine a closed box or frame within which they think the lines must be drawn. Those with both spatial and some forms of linguistic intelligence may solve this problem more quickly than others by not feeling so constrained by what they hear as the instructions. The next two problems involve some manipulation of the media or problem materials. The dots must be made a bit larger to use three lines and we must stretch our sense of "line" to imagine one large line to cover all the dots. Or, we must change the paper on which the lines are drawn in order to line them up one by one. Law students, and even some law professors, resist the manipulation of words or material that is required by this problem. Is this teaching people to manipulate rules, instructions and to transgress the "box" of laws that comprise our legal system?

2. Now, take a piece of paper and put your body through the page. The solution to this problem requires some alteration of the media in which you are working. Word manipulation? Creative use of spatial intelligence?

3. You have four cows in a field. How can you arrange those cows so they are equidistant from each other? (Hint, this too calls on spatial intelligence and manipulation of media).

4. A taxi-driver becomes annoyed with a particularly loquacious passenger. He realizes he has not said a word during the whole trip so he signals to his ears to indicate he is deaf. The passenger quiets down. Later, after the passenger has left the cab, she realizes a trick has been played on her. How does she know?

5. A surgeon is asked to rush to the operating room after a car accident. The surgeon is told a father and his son have been brought in, but the father has died and the son needs emergency surgery. Upon entering the Operating Room the surgeon gasps, "Oh my God, that's my son!" How can this be?

6. You are in a hotel going to a cocktail party during a conference and have no pockets or handbag. Where can you put your key so both your hands are free to hold drinks and hors d'oeuvres? (There are many solutions to this problem.)

These examples illustrate just a few points about creative problem solving in negotiation. Framing, creating and implementing solutions can be done in many ways, so focus on precedents, standard clauses, conventional solutions and a limited defined problem space can actually hinder what we think is possible in solving legal problems. By using puzzles and brainteasers of various kinds, students and negotiators are forced to confront their own processes of cognition or problem solving and expand the realms of possible information and solutions they seek. After being stuck in an impasse in a negotiation, students who stop and do a few brainteasers will often re-approach a problem with new ideas, insights, and often, different ways of looking at the problem. . . .

In this literature, the following techniques are suggested as formal ways of enhancing creativity, solving problems and suggesting new ideas, some as separate individual cognitive processes, and others as structured processes to be used in multi-party settings. . . .

1. Uses of analogy (direct, fanciful) and use of metaphor;
2. Aggregation/disaggregation/re-combination of elements of a problem;
3. Transfer (cross-disciplinary use of concepts, ideas, information, solutions from other fields);
4. Reversal (either extreme polarization or gradual modification of ideas) — which is done both in cognitive and in personal forms (as in role-reversal efforts to understand the point of view of others in the situation);
5. Extension — extending a line of reasoning, principle or solution beyond its original purpose;
6. Challenging assumptions — re-examining givens or problem statements and unpacking clichéd, conventional solutions or stereotypes;
7. Narrative — fully describing facts and problems to elaborate on complexity, and producing alternative endings;
8. Backward/forward thinking — focusing on how we came to a particular situation (reasons why, causes) in order to figure out how we get to desired end-state(s);
9. Design — plan for desired future end-state, structures, means;
10. Random stimulation/brainstorming — separation of idea generation, randomly generated, from judgment and evaluation. . . .
11. Visualization — use of different competencies and modes of thinking and processing information; this includes efforts at altered states (e.g., retreats and meditations);
12. Entry points — explicit reframing of problems and solutions from different perspectives. . . .

Law as a discipline had contributed to the solution of human problems with the creation of institutions designed to preserve order and reduce or eliminate violence through the development of both governing principles and processes. Whether particular regimes or institutions are legitimate within a particular society, law and the institutions it creates are the glue which holds the society together by resolving disputes at both system-wide and individual levels. . . .

Lawyers work with words, so most of our creative acts involve the construction of new language and interpretation of existing language, creating new concepts from whole cloth or from the interstices of statutory, regulatory or contractual gaps. Our words have the force of law behind them, however, so that powerfully creative words in law have been known to create whole new institutions. Examples of new legal and real entities that have been created are corporations, trusts, regulatory agencies, condominiums, unions and tax shelters. In addition, our words have created new legal rights and constructs like leases, sexual harassment, probation — and also have recognized (sometimes from conflicting ideologies) new claims like civil rights, privacy, free speech and emotional distress. . . .

One of the major legally creative acts in modern times was Charles Reich's "new property,"* an application or extension of traditional property principles to the new forms of property — employment expectations, welfare and other entitlements provided by the government. Current efforts to expand the Nuremberg War Tribunals and the current War Crimes Tribunal to build an International Criminal Court demonstrate the expansion of an entire legal institution by changing levels of regulation and exposing the difficulties and opportunities of creating legal institutions and laws across jurisdictional domains.

Related to expansion of legal concepts is the common legal creative act of transfer from one legal domain to another. Another important creative act is the variety of contributions made to legal scholarship by Joseph Sax† — the use of public trust doctrine in environmental law, the treatment of "slumlordism" as a tort, both of which were developed by exporting or importing one area of the law to another. The juxtaposition of seemingly unrelated things, or combining, explains much of innovative product development. . . .

A form of creativity somewhat unique to legal reasoning, though similar to our related linguistic intelligences, is the process of characterization or argumentation in which we use our words to re-categorize facts, claims, arguments and rules, which disturb the linguistic purity desired by those outside of our domain. Consider how patent lawyers successfully assimilated the architecture of software to the vocabulary of a machine in order to obtain patent protection for what were thought to be unpatentable "mental processes, abstract intellectual concepts" or ideas. . . .

Similarly, alterations (in the form of aggregations or disaggregations) of concepts is a common legal trope, particularly in transactional legal work. Using basic property principles which combine space and time (time bounded estates in land), creative lawyers created co-ops, condominiums and time shares. . . .

Law's creativity may be somewhat limited by the bounds of law and legal ethics rules, but there still remains a fair amount of problem space to be manipulated within our adversarial culture. At the same time, the adversarial culture may also constrain and cabin our thinking unnecessarily by structuring it in polarized and oppositional terms. Are transactional lawyers more creative by being less constrained? Corporations and trusts, for example, were created legally to accomplish many different goals, some adversarial (tax delay, minimization or avoidance), but also to permit different

---

* Charles Reich, "The New Property," 73 Yale L.J. 733 (1964).
† Joseph Sax, "Slumlordism As a Tort," 65 Mich. L. Rev. 869 (1967),

power and control arrangements and to bundle and unbundle interests of wealth, time and assets to permit great flexibility of action. . . .

Legal creativity is necessarily limited by its need to work within the law, or at least within the foreseeable boundaries of legal change, but for optimal problem solving it would seem we should try to push the boundaries of little "c" creativity as much as we can to produce at least a greater number of choices about how best to accomplish legal results.

At the level of conventional case instruction, it is possible to teach alternative ways of structuring and solving legal problems at the same time that students are learning to brief a case, make arguments and discover the relevant facts and holdings. As described elsewhere, a series of questions could be asked of students of each case read to encourage creative thinking. This would push students to look for multiple possibilities and directions that the case could have taken, before it hardened into its appellate form. In addition to the stated facts and legal issues, one should ask the following questions:

What are the "real" issues between the parties?

What were the parties trying to accomplish?

Who else is, or was, involved in the transaction, dispute or underlying issue?

How else might the parties have dealt with or managed their problem aside from the lawsuit at hand?

What other solutions, proposals or resolutions of their matter would have been possible?

Answering these questions allows students to see how much more might be at stake than what the court fixes on; that other people may be involved and that other resources might have been mobilized to deal with the problem. Such readings of cases open up other possible readings of a case, perhaps to "creative misreadings" and to other possible solutions. I often ask students to re-think a case or problem for new possibilities after they have worked on some of the brainteasers or other problems described above. This might be a good empirical testing ground of the effectiveness of creativity teaching and training—can students or lawyers see more possibilities in legal problems after they have had the opportunity to use some other intelligences?

In the previous article, Carrie Menkel-Meadow outlines 12 different ways to be more creative. This next excerpt from psychology professor Dean Pruitt focuses on how to achieve integrative agreements primarily using her second point: aggregation/disaggregation and recombination.

 Dean Pruitt, **ACHIEVING INTEGRATIVE AGREEMENTS**

in Negotiation in Organizations 36-41 (Max Bazerman & Roy Lewicki eds., 1983)

METHODS FOR ACHIEVING INTEGRATIVE AGREEMENTS

Five methods for achieving integrative agreements will now be described. These are means by which the parties' initially opposing demands can be transformed into alternatives that reconcile their interests. They can be used by one party, both parties working together, or a third party such as a mediator. Each method involves a different way of refocusing the issues under dispute. Hence potentially useful refocusing questions will be provided under each heading. Information that is useful for implementing each method will also be mentioned, and the methods will be listed in order of increasing difficulty of getting this information.

The methods will be illustrated by a running example concerning a husband and wife who are trying to decide where to go on a two-week vacation. [Also used by Carrie Menkel-Meadow in her article, Toward Another View of Legal Negotiation: The Structure of Problem Solving.] The husband wants to go to the mountains, his wife to the seashore. They have considered the compromise of spending one week in each location but are hoping for something better. What approach should they take?

Expanding the Pie

Some conflicts hinge on a resource shortage. For example, time, money, space, and automobiles are in short supply but long demand. In such circumstances, integrative agreements can be devised by increasing the available resources. This is called expanding the pie. For example, our married couple might solve their problems by persuading their employers to give them four weeks of vacation so that they can take two in the mountains and two at the seashore. . . .

Expanding the pie is a useful formula when the parties reject one another's demands because of opportunity costs; for example, if the husband rejects the seashore because it keeps him away from the mountains and the wife rejects the mountains because they deny her the pleasure of the seashore. But it is by no means a universal remedy. Expanding the pie may yield strikingly poor benefits if there are inherent costs in the other's proposal, e.g., the husband cannot stand the seashore or the wife the mountains. Other methods are better in such cases.

Expanding the pie requires no analysis of the interests underlying the parties' demands. Hence its information requirements are slim. However, this does not mean that a solution by this method is always easy to find. There may be no resource shortage, or the shortage may not be easy to see or to remedy.

Refocusing questions that can be useful in seeking a solution by pie expansion include: How can both parties get what they want? Does the conflict hinge on a resource shortage? How can the critical resource be expanded?

Nonspecific Compensation

In nonspecific compensation, one party gets what he or she wants and the other is repaid in some unrelated coin. Compensation is nonspecific if it does not deal with the precise costs incurred by the other party. For example, the wife in our example might agree to go to the mountains, even though she finds them boring, if her husband promises her a fur coat. Another example would be giving an employee a bonus for going without dinner.

Compensation usually comes from the party whose demands are granted. But it can also originate with a third party or even with the party who is compensated. An example of the latter would be an employee who pampers him- or herself by finding a nice office to work in while going without dinner.

Two kinds of information are useful for devising a solution by nonspecific compensation: (a) information about what is valuable to the other party; for example, knowledge that he or she values love, attention, or money; (b) information about how badly the other party is hurting by making concessions. This is useful for devising adequate compensation for these concessions. If such information is not available, it may be possible to conduct an "auction" for the other party's acquiescence, changing the sort of benefit offered or raising one's offer, in trial-and-error fashion, until an acceptable formula is found.

Refocusing questions that can help locate a means of compensation include: How much is the other party hurting in conceding to me? What does the other party value that I can supply? How valuable is this to the other party?

Logrolling

Logrolling is possible in complex agendas where several issues are under consideration and the parties have differing priorities among these issues. Each party concedes on low priority issues in exchange for concessions on issues of higher priority to itself. Each gets that part of its demands that it finds most important. For example, suppose that in addition to disagreeing about where to go on vacation, the wife in our example wants to go to a first-class hotel while her husband prefers a tourist home. If accommodations are a high priority issue for the wife and location for the husband, they can reach a fairly integrative solution by agreeing to go to a first-class hotel in the mountains. Logrolling can be viewed as a variant of nonspecific compensation in which both parties instead of one are compensated for making concessions desired by the other.

To develop solutions by logrolling, it is useful to have information about the two parties' priorities so that exchangeable concessions can be identified. But it is not necessary to have information about the interests (e.g., the aspirations, values) underlying these priorities. Solutions by logrolling can also be developed by a process of trial and error in which one party moves systematically through a series of possible packages, keeping his or her own outcomes as high as possible, until an alternative is found that is acceptable to the other party.

Refocusing questions that can be useful for developing solutions by logrolling include: Which issues are of higher and lower priority to myself? Which issues are of higher and lower priority to the other party? Are some of my high-priority issues of low priority to the other party and vice versa?

Cost Cutting

In solutions by cost cutting, one party gets what he or she wants and the other's costs are reduced or eliminated. The result is high joint benefit, not because the first party has changed his or her demands but because the second party suffers less. For instance, suppose that the husband in our example dislikes the beach because of the hustle and bustle. He may be quite willing to go there on vacation if his costs are cut by renting a house with a quiet inner courtyard where he can read while his wife goes out among the crowds.

Cost cutting often takes the form of specific compensation in which the party who concedes receives something in return that satisfies the precise values frustrated. For example, the employee who must work through dinner time can be specifically compensated by provision of a meal in a box. Specific compensation differs from nonspecific compensation in dealing with the precise costs incurred rather than providing repayment in an unrelated coin. The costs are actually canceled out rather than overbalanced by benefits experienced in some other realm.

Information about the nature of one of the parties' costs is, of course, helpful for developing solutions by cost cutting. This is a deeper kind of information than knowledge of that party's priorities. It involves knowing something about the interests — the values, aspirations, and standards — underlying that party's overt position.

Refocusing questions for developing solutions by cost cutting include: What costs are posed for the other party by our proposal? How can these costs be mitigated or eliminated?

Bridging

In bridging, neither party achieves its initial demands but a new option is devised that satisfies the most important interests underlying these demands. For example, suppose that the husband in our vacation example is mainly interested in fishing and hunting and the wife in swimming and sunbathing. Their interests might be bridged by finding an inland resort with a lake and a beach that is close to woods and streams. . . .

Bridging typically involves a reformulation of the issue(s) based on an analysis of the underlying interests on both sides. For example, a critical turning point in our vacation example is likely to come when the initial formulation, "Shall we go to the mountains or the seashore?" is replaced by "Where can we find fishing, hunting, swimming, and sunbathing?" . . . This new formulation can be done by either or both parties or by a third party who is trying to help.

People who seek to develop solutions by bridging need information about the nature of the two parties' interests and their priorities among these interests. . . . More often, higher-priority interests are served while lower-priority interests are discarded. For example, the wife who agrees to go to an inland lake may have forgone the lesser value of smelling the sea air and the husband may have forgone his preference for spectacular mountain vistas.

In the initial phase of the search for a solution by bridging, the search model can include all of the interests on both sides. But if this does not generate a mutually acceptable alternative, some of the lower-priority interests must be discarded from the model and the search begun anew. The result will not be an ideal solution but, it is hoped, one that is mutually acceptable. Dropping low-priority interests in the development of a solution by bridging is similar to dropping low-priority demands in the search for a solution by logrolling. However, the latter is in the realm of concrete proposals, while the former is in the realm of the interests underlying these proposals.

Refocusing questions that can be raised in search of a solution by bridging include: What are the two parties' basic interests? What are their priorities among these interests? How can the two sets of high priority interests be reconciled?

Notes and Questions

3.19 Pruitt spends much time outlining the questions to ask for each type of creative solution. Note that these questions need to be asked *both* of your client *and* the other side to be successful.

3.20 Which strategies for creating value outlined by Pruitt are consistent with the idea of procedural fairness (procedures for arriving at a solution that are intrinsically fair and/or likely to arrive at a fair outcome) outlined in Chapter 2, Section C on fairness?

3.21 Another example of nonspecific compensation is provided by Leigh Thompson. Phil Jones, managing director of Real Time, the London-based interactive design studio, recalls an instance where he used nonspecific compensation in his negotiations. The problem was that his client, a Formula 1 motor-racing team, wanted to launch Internet Web sites but did not have the budget to pay him. However, in Jones's eyes, the client was high profile and had creative, challenging projects that Real Time wanted to get involved with. Formula 1 came up with a nonspecific compensation offer to make the deal go through: tickets to some of the major Formula 1 meetings. It worked. Says Jones: "The tickets are like gold dust . . . and can be used as a pat on the back for staff or as an opportunity to pamper existing clients or woo new ones." Leigh Thompson, The Mind and Heart of the Negotiator 163-164 (2001).

3.22 A law student had chronic medical problems. Unfortunately, she was also uninsured. The good news was that she was a fabulous cook. The first time she saw the doctor she explained her financial situation. She was able to work out with her doctor a payment plan for services over time. What kind of solution is this? After they negotiated the first time, she delivered a chocolate chip cheesecake to the doctor in appreciation for his understanding. The next time she needed the doctor, the doctor requested payment in cheesecakes! What kind of solution is this?

The next excerpt by Leigh Thompson is from a business school text on negotiation. As we have seen, businesspeople clearly recognize the importance of creative thinking for new products. The first part talks about breaking apart the problem, as suggested by Pruitt, and also challenging assumptions. The second part of the excerpt outlines one idea under Carrie Menkel-Meadow's ninth point, focusing on the design of the agreement.

 Leigh Thompson, **THE MIND AND HEART OF THE NEGOTIATOR**

158-159, 162, 164-167 (2d ed. 2001)

The creative aspect of negotiation is too often ignored or downplayed by negotiators, who fixate on the competitive aspect of negotiation. This tendency is largely driven by pervasive *fixed-pie perception*, or the belief that negotiation is a win or lose enter-prise. Even negotiators who believe in win-win potential frequently misconstrue "expanding the pie" to mean compromising or feeling good, rather than a true joint gain process. Successful negotiation requires a great deal of creativity and problem solving, and the process of slicing the pie can be a lot easier when the pie has been enlarged via creative and insightful problem solving strategies.

FRACTIONING PROBLEMS INTO SOLVABLE PARTS

Fractioning problems into solvable parts and creating multiple-issue negotiations from what appear to be single-issue negotiations is probably the most important aspect of creative negotiation. We consistently find that people are very good at solving problems when the problems are presented directly to them: however, people are not very good at *defining* problems. Negotiation is mostly about defining a problem rather than solving it (i.e., searching for differences in such a way that trade-offs can be creative). Psychologists call this *problem representation*, as opposed to prob-lem solving. This is not to say that problem solving is not an important skill. Rather, how a negotiator frames a problem can either set limits or create important oppor-tunities in the problem-solving process.

STRUCTURING CONTINGENCIES

Often, a major obstacle to reaching negotiated agreements concerns negotiators' beliefs about some future event or outcome. Impasses often result from conflicting beliefs that are difficult to surmount, especially when each side is confident about the accuracy of his or her own prediction and consequently suspicious of the other side's forecasts. Often, compromise is not a viable solution, and each party may be reluctant to change his or her point of view. Fortunately, contingent contracts can provide a way out of the mire. With a *contingent contract*, differences of opinion among nego-tiators concerning future events do not have to be bridged; they become the core of the agreement. According to Bazerman and Gillespie, companies can bet on the future rather than argue about it. In some areas of business, contingent contracts are commonplace. For example, CEOs regularly agree to tie their salary to [their] com-pany's stock price, and, in the textbook publishing business, royalty rates to authors are often tied to sales.

However, in many business negotiations, contingency contracts are either ignored or rejected out of hand. There are several key reasons for this: First, people are unaware of the possibility for contingent contracts. It often never occurs to people to bet on their differences when they are embroiled in conflict. Second, contingency contracts are often seen as a form of gambling, which is not good business. Third, there is often no systematic way of thinking about the formulation of such contracts, meaning that they *appear* to be a good idea, but how to formalize and act upon them remains an enigma. Fourth, many negotiators have a "getting to yes" bias, meaning that they focus on reaching common ground with the other party and are reluctant to accept differences of interest, even when this might create viable options for joint gain. In fact, most negotiators believe that differences in belief are a source of problems in a negotiation. The paradoxical view suggested by the contingency contract, negotiators can focus on their real mutual interests, not on their speculative disagreements. When companies fail to find their way out of differences in beliefs, they will often wind up in court, creating expensive delays, litigation costs, loss of control by both parties, and deteriorating BATNAs.

Another wonderful feature of contingency contracts is that they provide a nearly perfect lie-detection device. In business negotiations, the fear of being deceived can be a major impediment to reaching agreements. Contingency contracts are a powerful method for uncovering deceit and neutralizing its consequences; they are particularly useful because they allow negotiators to test the opponent's veracity in a nonconfrontational manner, thereby allowing parties to save face. Contingency contracts also allow parties who are concerned about being cheated to safeguard themselves. . . .

By the same token, contingency contracts can build trust and good faith between negotiators, because incentives can be provided for each company to deliver exceptional performance. For example, Phil Jones, Real Time's managing director, was negotiating a deal with the Football Association (FA) for an e-commerce Web site dedicated to the U.K. bid for the 2006 World Cup. Real Time was responsible for the bid's logo and original Web site. "The FA have a limited budget to spend across a range of media, so I'm talking to them about perhaps receiving a percentage of what's sold from the new site. . . . That's really putting your money where your mouth is." Therefore, contingency contracts provide a safety net, limiting each company's losses should an agreement unexpectedly go awry.

Although we believe that contingency contracts can be valuable in many kinds of business negotiations, they are not always the right strategy to use. Bazerman and Gillespie suggest three key criteria for assessing the viability and usefulness of the contingency contracts in negotiation.

1. Contingency contracts require *some degree of continued interaction between the parties.* Because the final terms of the contract will not be determined until sometime after the initial agreement is signed, there must be some amount of future interaction between parties, thereby allowing them to assess the terms of their agreement. Therefore, if the future seems highly uncertain, or if one of the parties is suspected of preparing to leave the situation permanently, contingency contracts may not be wise.

2. Parties need to think about the *enforceability* of the contingency contract. Under a contingency contract, one or more of the parties will probably not be correct about the outcome because the contract often functions as a bet. This creates a problem for the "loser" of the bet, who may be reluctant to reimburse the other party when things do not go his or her way. For this reason, the money in question might well be placed in escrow, thereby removing each party's temptation to defect.

3. Contingency contracts require a high degree of *clarity* and *measurability*. If an event is ambiguous, nonmeasurable, or of a subjective nature, overconfidence, egocentric bias, and a variety of other self-serving biases can make the objective appraisal of a contingency contract a matter of some opinion. Thus, we strongly suggest the parties agree up-front on clear, specific measures concerning how the contract will be evaluated. For this reason, it is often wise to consult with a third party.

Notes and Questions

3.23 One other aspect of contingent agreements that may affect the way people consider them (and possibly one part of the explanation for why people don't use them more often) is that they may affect perceptions about "winners" and "losers" in agreements:

> Contingent agreements may affect negotiators' perceptions of "winning" and "losing." Classical negotiation advice counsels negotiators to conceive of negotiations in terms other than win-lose, pointing to the risk that competitive behavior may cloud opportunities for joint gains. In one respect, contingent agreements may present an opportunity for negotiators to avoid the necessity of identifying a winner. Rather than forcing one side to concede on its forecast, contingent agreements permit (in fact, require) both sides to maintain their conflicting predictions about the future. At the time of the agreement, therefore, each side can declare "victory," to the extent such a declaration is important. On the other hand, contingent agreements have the nature of a wager or a bet. Unless one counts the sheer joy of gambling as a victory, *both* sides cannot win a wager. The contingent event either happens or it does not. Either way, one side may be disappointed. In some organizational cultures, failure is punished more harshly than success is rewarded. A negotiator fearful of identifiable failure (for example, a wager that visibly did not pay off) may forgo an elegant contingent agreement in favor of a less efficient non-contingent deal. Elegantly structured contingent deals may help to reduce the risk of visibly "losing." For example, if the plaintiff fears that a jury may award him nothing, and a defendant fears a runaway jury award of millions, the two could agree to a small guaranteed recovery in exchange for a cap on the maximum recovery. The losing party at trial will then be grateful to have made the contingent agreement, and the winner's regret will be dampened by having won a favorable verdict.

Michael Moffitt, Contingent Agreements: Agreeing to Disagree About the Future, 87 Marq. L. Rev. 691, 695-696 (2004).

3.24 Many authors use Mary Parker Follett's example of the library window as the classic integrative solution. You'll recall that one library patron wanted fresh air while the other did not want the wind blowing her papers around. The solution was to open the window in the next room. As a modern day update, in the movie *A Beautiful Mind*, there is a somewhat similar scene where the students in Professor Nash's class want the window open for fresh air. He wanted the window closed because the construction crew outside was making too much noise for him to be heard giving his lecture. In the movie, Alicia Nash (to be) leans out the window and asks the construction crew if they could take a break during class. Both professor and students are happy with the open window on a quiet campus. What type of solution is this?

3.25 In 1991, two West Coast energy producers found a new way to help Columbia River salmon and improve Southern California's dirty air without spending a dime. Southern California Edison Co. and the Bonneville Power Administration entered into an agreement in 1991 that helped to protect young salmon in the Pacific Northwest. Under the agreement, Bonneville Power increased its release of water in the Columbia River during the summer, and Edison accepted the hydroelectric power that was generated. The flows helped young salmon swim through reservoirs more quickly, as large numbers of these fish get lost or eaten in slack water. In the fall and winter, Edison returned the power it borrowed from Bonneville. This meant that the company would not need to run oil and coal-fired plants during the summer. This exchange of about 200 megawatts of power, enough for about 100,000 households, improved the downstream migration of young salmon in the river. It enhanced Southern California's air quality by reducing the need to operate fossil fuel power plants during the smoggy summer months. Edison said that the arrangement cut the amount of pollution entering the Los Angeles basin by about 46 tons, the equivalent of taking about 5,000 cars off the highways. In this creative agreement, no money changed hands. Leigh Thompson, The Mind and Heart of the Negotiator 158 (2001).

3.26 As we read in Chapter 1, Mary Parker Follett suggests that the best way to find integrative agreements is to bring differences into the open. Why do negotiators fear that? What are the risks? What can be accomplished by bringing out the differences?

The following excerpt gives some more specific ideas toward carrying out Menkel-Meadow's suggestions above, such as backward/forward thinking, brainstorming, visualization and retreats, and using different intelligences.

 Roger Fisher, Elizabeth Kopelman & Andrea Kupfer Schneider, **BEYOND MACHIAVELLI: TOOLS FOR COPING WITH CONFLICT**

68-71, 82-83, 86 (1994)

THINK SYSTEMATICALLY

Four-Quadrant Analysis has turned out to be a powerful and basic aid to clear thinking in all kinds of conflict situations. It helps people understand where they agree and where they disagree, it helps multiply good ideas, and it helps people think about whether what they propose makes sense. We often use this tool to structure the brainstorming process, to help us figure out where we are stuck and why, or to analyze a success in the hopes of replicating it.

The analytical thinking involved in dealing with a problem can be sorted into four categories shown in Chart 16: *What is wrong?* (Quadrant I), *General diagnoses* (Quadrant II), *General approaches* (Quadrant III), and *Action ideas* (Quadrant IV). Busy practitioners, who often feel that they do not have the luxury of analysis, tend to jump from problem to response (from Quadrant I to Quadrant IV), without a cogent theory of why they are doing what they are doing. Academics, in contrast, often theorize about why in general certain problems occur (Quadrant II) and what in general might be done about them (Quadrant III). Looking forward to developing an action plan for a specific conflict, we want to merge the approach of a busy practitioner, who has little time for theory, with that of an academic, who may have limited interest in a practical outcome.

[Chart] 16 A Four-Quadrant Analysis for Problem-Solving			
QUADRANT I **WHAT IS WRONG?**	**QUADRANT II** **GENERAL DIAGNOSES**	**QUADRANT III** **GENERAL APPROACHES**	**QUADRANT IV** **ACTION IDEAS**
Perceptions of: • disliked symptoms; • a preferred situation; and the gap between them.	Possible reasons why the problem hasn't been resolved or the conflict settled. Possible causes (about which somebody could do something) of the gap in Quadrant I.	Possible strategies for overcoming the identified diagnoses.	Ideas about who might do what tomorrow to put a general approach into action.

A Four-Quadrant Analysis [as shown in Chart 17] encourages systematic yet creative problem solving. . . .

[Chart] 17 A Four-Quadrant Analysis Case: Negotiating a New Constitution, South Africa, February 1993			
PROBLEM	**DIAGNOSIS**	**APPROACH**	**ACTION PLAN**
Many decisions need to be made.	The process of first agreeing in principle, and later on implementation is causing extensive delay.	Need a process which minimizes delays and works when: • there are many parties • and many public constituents • a low level of trust • parties see each other as adversaries	Stimulate a parallel process: government and ANC, without commitment, start producing a working draft of a comprehensive, operational document that can be enacted when needed.
Risk of delay. Rising tide of violence.	That process is useful when: • there are few parties • few constituents • much trust • parties have worked cooperatively before		
Political leaders losing control. Need for swift action.			
The analysis suggested that the process then being used (which works well in some situations) should be supplemented by a process that tends to work better between perceived adversaries.			

[It] is sufficiently simple to be quickly accepted by diverse members of a group and sufficiently basic to be applicable to almost any situation. It is also useful for multiplying good ideas by allowing participants to go backward and forward from one quadrant to another. If a specific idea (in Quadrant IV) seems promising, what is the general approach (Quadrant III) of which that specific idea is an example? Can we think of other specific ways in which that general approach might be implemented? If a general approach seems sound, what is the diagnosis (Quadrant II) to which that is an appropriate response? Can we think of other ways in which we might respond to that diagnosis? And so forth. . . .

USE SOME ADDITIONAL MAPS

Once we have a sense of the obstacles to progress, we can generate fresh approaches by employing the specialized perspectives of a variety of academic and professional disciplines, using a tool we call the Atlas of Approaches. Collecting many different maps into an atlas reduces the danger that we will be misled by the distortions of any one of them. Academic disciplines and professional points of view can provide us with insights about what is wrong, what is causing it, who could make a difference, and what variables may be manipulated. The list presented in Chart 19 can get us started. . . .

[Chart] 19 **An Atlas of Approaches** **Maps for Understanding a Conflict**	
ACADEMIC DISCIPLINES	**PROFESSIONAL POINTS OF VIEW**
Economics	Religious leader
Political science	Lawyer
Psychology	Doctor
Anthropology	Military officer
History	Journalist
Sociology	Public health official
Business	Diplomat
Ethics	Educator
Engineering	Bank-investor
Geography	Social worker

Adding additional maps or points of view to our atlas helps us better understand a conflict. By identifying the choices available to people who may be able to bring about change, an atlas may help us develop an action plan. Whether we are reading books or speaking with professionals, two kinds of questions are useful to ask: "Why is the conflict not being settled?" and "Who do you think might be able to do what in order to help resolve it?" These questions are sufficiently open-ended to avoid prejudging what we need to learn and at the same time produce ideas of practical use. . . .

[Chart] 23
Some Guidelines for Brainstorming

Schedule a special occasion, assemble a few people (between five and ten is ideal), and identify the time as a session to be devoted solely to coming up with new ideas.

Make it clear that it is to be a meeting at which no proposals are to be agreed upon nor decisions made.

The circumstances of the session should be substantially different from those of routine meetings. It may be held, for example, at an unusual time (evening, all day, a weekend), at an unusual place (country house, outdoors, social club), or under unusual conditions (no scheduled breaks for coffee or meals, participants stand or sit on the floor).

Consider breaking a large group down into smaller working groups tackling different aspects of the problem simultaneously.

The rules of discussion should preclude negative comments. This should be strictly enforced, especially in the early part of a session.

It should be clear that value is placed on developing many new and different ideas. Consider devising incentives to reward abundant creative thinking.

Ideas are recorded on one central list, such as a whiteboard or flip chart, where they are visible to all (so that they may stimulate other ideas), but they are "off the record" and listed without attribution — no list is kept of who came up with what idea.

Use a facilitator and someone to record every idea on the board or flip chart. (These roles can be filled by one person, but it is easier with two.) They can step out of role temporarily to contribute their own ideas to the list.

Schedule a separate session for evaluating and criticizing ideas and selecting the most promising ones for follow-up discussions.

Notes and Questions

3.27 Steven Brams and Alan Taylor have spent more than a decade working on how to eliminate envy through the use of procedural devices to achieve fair division. This work has yielded a series of mathematical equations and increased study in how fair division can be achieved. This work has been applied to various arenas of disputing, including divorce, labor relations, and international relations. One interesting aspect to come out of this is the adjusted winner. In the adjusted winner procedure, one party wins on each issue. For example, in the following chart Brams applies adjusted winning to the divorce of Donald and Ivana Trump.

PROPERTY	DONALD	IVANA
Connecticut estate	10	<u>40</u>
Palm Beach mansion	<u>40</u>	20
Plaza apartment	10	<u>30</u>
Tower triplex	<u>40</u>	10

Each party is given 100 points to allocate as they choose. Donald will receive the Palm Beach mansion and the Tower triplex because he placed a higher value on those than did Ivana. Similarly, Ivana will receive the Connecticut estate and the Plaza apartment. If the total outcome of this is unfair (that is, one party unfairly receives more than the other after every issue is decided), an adjustment is made on one issue to make the two sides equitable. Here, the total points for Donald's properties are 80 (40 + 40), while Ivana's total is only 70 (40 + 30). To achieve fair division, one of Donald's items must be equitably adjusted so that both parties achieve the same total. Because Ivana valued the Palm Beach mansion closer to what Donald did than the Tower triplex, Ivana should receive a portion of this or compensation for it. Thus, both parties will receive an equitable share and get what they value most. The total value of the pie will be expanded because each party will value their share more than if the pie were simply divided into shares with no regard for personal value. For Donald and Ivana, each has a total of more than the 50 points they would have gotten had a judge simply ordered division because each got the properties that had more value to them. Steven J. Brams, Fair Division, in Oxford Handbook of Political Economy (Barry R. Weingast & Donald Wittman eds., 2006). See also Steven J. Brams & Alan D. Taylor, Fair Division: From Cake-Cutting to Dispute Resolution (1996). Note the methods suggested by Brams and Taylor also are linked with the ideas of procedural fairness discussed in Chapter 2.

3.28 Brams and another colleague have also used this method to suggest a way for dealing with the dispute over the Spratly Islands in the South China Sea. The Spratly Islands are a grouping of over 230 small islands claimed by six different countries — China, Taiwan, Vietnam, the Philippines, Malaysia, and Brunei. Because of the strategic placement of the islands in important shipping lanes, as well as the oil and gas deposits on the islands, no country has backed off. At the same time, because of overlapping claims and the lack of continuous control by any one country, international law does not designate a clear winner. Brams and his coauthor suggest that the Fair Division method could be used in order to allocate the islands peacefully. David B.H. Denoon & Steven J. Brams, Fair Division: A New Approach to the Spratly Islands Controversy, 2 Intl. Negot. 303 (1997). Would this method allow for useful groupings of islands under different regimes?

This next excerpt by sports agent and lawyer David Falk gives specific examples of value creation in the sports context. Think of how this advice translates into other contexts with which you are familiar.

David B. Falk, THE ART OF CONTRACT NEGOTIATION

3 Marq. Sports L.J. 1, 12-14 (1992)

Every deal has trade-offs; they are the essence of the bargaining process. You can call it bargaining, negotiating, or horse-trading. There are some basic trade-offs I use when I am negotiating a deal. The first is the length of the contract. You must understand the needs and goals of your client. Does he want security? Does he want to maximize the amount of dollars protected in case he fails to reach an expected level of performance? Or does he want flexibility, so if the market changes substantially in the first two or three years of his contract, he has the ability to renegotiate as a free agent? . . . But the first issue is length, or what I call aggregate dollars and flexibility, so you can come back and renegotiate. I mentioned the case of Stanley Roberts, which is a very interesting one because he was the twenty-third pick in the 1991 draft, and because of the salary cap, he signed a one-year contract. Most general managers thought that he was overweight, was not a very hard worker, and therefore was a risky pick. Roberts averaged ten points and six rebounds a game as a rookie. But he was a center, and centers are extremely hard to obtain in the NBA. As a result, at the conclusion of his one-year contract, four or five teams bid for him. He signed a contract averaging in excess of $3 million a year. Had he come out of school and signed a great contract for the twenty-third pick, let's say $1 million a year, but locked himself up for five years, he would have cost himself a tremendous amount of money. Because he was in a position to get only a one-year deal, it ended up working to his benefit. The decision whether to sign long-term or short-term is a critical one that demands full discussion with your client. You cannot make judgments *for* your client. You have to make judgments *with* your client. You have to point out the benefits of security and the detriments of locking him in for a long period of time and having to renegotiate a contract when you do not have a lot of leverage.

The second trade-off is guarantees. In basketball, eighty-three percent of all contracts are guaranteed for either skill or injury. This means that if the club terminates the contract, it remains obligated to pay the player. In football, a very small percentage of contracts are guaranteed. Since guarantees provide security, teams will often pay a player more dollars if he will take fewer guarantees. Conversely, teams may propose that the player sacrifice dollars in order to get the entire contract guaranteed.

The third trade-off is current cash dollars versus deferred money. I believe deferred money is one of the most abused areas in professional sports contracts. That is why I like to call it "funny money." . . . Many players negotiate deals with money deferred as many as twenty to thirty years out. As interest rates climb, the deferred monies are worth as little as one-fourth of what they are worth today.

Sometimes there are pressures on player representatives to try to obtain a certain amount of money for a client. This pressure may force the representative to make a bad deal by signing an unduly long contract, or deferring large amounts of money, or both. . . . When they agree to defer large amounts of money in their contracts and they receive it many years later, it is literally like Monopoly money. Obviously, a team would much prefer to pay a player in deferred dollars than in cash today. In the

NBA, this trade-off is affected by the salary cap. For purposes of the cap, a dollar deferred is not discounted and is treated the same as a cash dollar. Thus, suppose two players make . . . $1 million a year, one all current, and the other $800,000 current and $200,000 deferred. For purposes of the salary cap, they would both be treated as making $1 million. Therefore, there is a disincentive for a team to defer money from a salary cap standpoint, but a strong incentive for the team to do so from a financial standpoint.

Another area of trade-offs is incentive bonuses. As with deferred compensation, incentive bonuses represent an area of abuse. Obviously, if a player could choose between earning a dollar guaranteed or a dollar in incentive bonuses, always insist on getting the dollar guaranteed. However, when you are negotiating a contract and you are apart in your positions, one area available to you to close the deal is incentive bonuses. I am not against bonuses, but I always recommend to a client that we try to maximize the amount of guaranteed current dollars. When you have "maxed out" guaranteed cash, but you have not closed the deal, bonuses are a creative trade-off in closing the gap.

Notes and Questions

3.29 What specific ideas does Falk suggest for value creation? Which of these translate into other contract negotiations? For those who think of athletes' contract negotiations as being only about a salary amount, appreciate how Falk "expands the pie" in multiple ways.

3.30 Another great example of an incentive contract at work occurred in 2004 as part of the College Bowl Championship Series. In his last contract, the former coach of the Louisiana State University football team, Nick Saban, had negotiated a clause that provided that if Saban won the national title in the Sugar Bowl, he was guaranteed $1 more than the highest paid college football coach. At first, this clause does not appear to provide Saban with all that much incentive given the odds that LSU would both be invited to the Sugar Bowl and then win it. In fact, when LSU won the Sugar Bowl against Oklahoma University on January 4, 2004, this clause entitled Saban to receive a raise from his previous salary of $1.2 million to $1 more than the highest paid coach's salary of $2.3 million — a raise of over $1 million! Nice clause after all. (Ironically, the highest paid coach had been Oklahoma's coach, Bob Stoops.) Also, the raise was merely the baseline. With a national championship under his belt, Saban's salary ultimately went even higher. At the end of 2004, Saban opted to leave LSU to become the head coach of the Miami Dolphins of the NFL, where he will make nearly $5 million.

While many negotiators and scholars find value creation in deal making compelling, Michael Moffitt demonstrates how value creation is also useful in dispute resolution situations.

Michael L. Moffitt, **DISPUTES AS OPPORTUNITIES TO CREATE VALUE**

in The Handbook of Dispute Resolution 173, 176–181 (Michael L. Moffitt & Robert C. Bordone eds., 2005)

SHARED INTERESTS

Much of the dispute resolution literature includes the assumption that disputants are motivated by a complex set of interests, even when each party articulates one very simple-sounding position. Assuming that disputants hold multiple interests, it is reasonable to expect that sometimes they will have some interests that are opposed. (You want to pay less and I want to receive more from you.) Disputants may have other interests that are differing, but not opposing. (I care about a change in policy and you care about confidentiality.) Finally, it is reasonable to assume that some of the disputants' interests are shared. (You and I both want the project to be completed on time. You would prefer a cleaner environment and so would I. Both divorcing parents want their children to receive a quality education. And so on.) Shared interests present the opportunity for crafting arrangements that make both sides better off in a noncompetitive way.

Even in circumstances in which most of the disputants' interests are conspicuously opposed, the disputants may also have shared interests. A group of college seniors are outraged at what they perceive as the college administration's lack of responsiveness to the needs and concerns of female students. They file a lawsuit alleging gender discrimination, demanding a considerable cash payment and a change in specific college policies. The college denies all of the allegations contained in the lawsuit. The students and the college administration do not have identical sets of interests. Yet they have at least some shared interests. The college administration wants to maintain the reputation of the school. It wants to attract high quality students and to provide students with a first-class education. It wants happy alumni. The soon-to-be-graduates share these interests. The seniors do not want to receive a diploma from a discredited institution that attracts a weaker pool of students, has a soiled reputation, and is unable to provide a top-notch education. Building on their shared interests, the students and the administration might undertake a comprehensive review of policies. They might agree to a process for addressing future issues. They might jointly agree to the allocation of funds to a gender studies program. Disputants will virtually never have identical interests, but focusing on interests in common presents the opportunity to discover mutually attractive settlement options.

REDUCING TRANSACTION COSTS

Unresolved disputes can be costly. In some cases, the continually growing expenses associated with an unresolved dispute are easy to identify and quantify. As the landlord and tenant fight over who will pay to repair the leaky plumbing, the water bill continues to rise, as does the risk of permanent water damage. In other cases, the costs associated with an ongoing dispute may not be quantifiable, but they are nonetheless real. Two neighbors who are bitter over an unresolved issue about noise may lose sleep because of the stress involved in the dispute. They may also miss out on opportunities to socialize or to share expenses on things like lawn care. Being in a dispute takes a toll. Resolving disputes earlier at least helps to preserve whatever value remains to be captured.

Transaction costs are not just about resolving a dispute sooner, however. In order to minimize unwanted transaction costs, disputants should also consider carefully the process they choose for resolving their dispute. The process of negotiating can be costly. Negotiating takes time and often creates stress. In many contexts, agents get involved in negotiations, adding further direct expenses. Other dispute resolution mechanisms may have additional direct costs, ranging from mediators' fees, to filing fees in arbitration or in court, to discovery and more. Disputants may be able to find ways to structure dispute resolution processes in ways that minimize these expenses. For example, disputants involved in complex litigation might jointly agree on limited discovery, or on a strict timetable for the various stages of the process, or even on a process for resolving the dispute quickly if no agreement is reached by a certain deadline. I know one married couple who decided to set a limit on how long they would argue over the division of household chores. After the expiration of that time, if they had not come to a resolution, they would always do rock-paper-scissors to resolve their dispute. This process occasionally yielded inelegant outcomes, but by cutting off the transaction costs involved in further argument, they captured value — or at least prevented its further destruction.

REDUCING IMPLEMENTATION PROBLEMS

In some circumstances, the resolution of a dispute is self-executing. One side hands some money to the other side, ending the dispute. Often, though, an agreement requires more complex implementation, raising the prospect of implementation problems. No perfect system of implementation monitoring exists, and disputants therefore face the prospect of moral hazard. Moral hazard is a condition in which one party might act in a way that harms the interests of the other party during implementation, but does so in a way that is difficult for the other party to recognize or prevent. Consider a construction dispute between a homeowner and a contractor. If the two sides begin to consider an agreement that has a contractor rebuilding a structure for a fixed sum, several implementation risks arise. The contractor might not use the highest quality materials, might not prioritize the job, or might not assign the most competent workers to the project. If the homeowner does not have a sophisticated understanding of construction, he has no real chance of spotting defects in the contractor's implementation of the deal. Even if the homeowner had the expertise, monitoring would require time and expense. Anxious about this prospect, the homeowner may pass up an agreement that captures the potential benefit of having the contractor do the rebuilding. If disputants recognize the possibility of moral hazard in implementation, they may be able to structure the agreement to manage those risks and create an acceptable deal for all parties. The homeowner and the contractor might agree to a timeline; they might jointly share the expense of hiring an independent contractor to inspect the site unannounced three times during construction; and the contractor might agree to a penalty clause in the event any defects are found within three years of construction.

DIFFERENCES IN PRIORITIES

In rare circumstances, a dispute is all about one issue — for example, who gets how many dollars. In most disputes, multiple issues are on the table, or lurk somewhere just beneath it. Any time there are multiple issues, it stands to reason that disputants are likely to value them differently. The plaintiff wants more money, sooner, with greater publicity. The defendant wants to pay less, later, and with less fanfare. Yet each may put different weight on these three issues. For example, the plaintiff may care most about the short-term payout, while the defendant cares most about how the settlement is presented to the public. If the disputants can recognize these differences in relative valuation, they can structure a resolution that captures the value of trading off the issues. The plaintiff gives the defendant the non-disclosure assurances it seeks in exchange for a greater immediate payout.

DIFFERENCES IN TIMEFRAME

People value things differently at different times. Most of us would prefer a dollar today over a dollar next year. Yet we may differ in how much more attractive a dollar today is. Installment contracts and structured payments are the vehicles for capturing value when disputants have different preferences regarding time horizons. If a small business has a short-term cash flow problem, it might offer to settle a dispute with one of its suppliers by promising to pay the supplier a sum well above the nominal amount of the dispute, provided it need not make the payment until two years from now. Assuming the supplier has no short term need for cash, and that the supplier is confident that it will receive the payment at the proposed time, the offer could be value creating when compared with a straight exchange of dollars today. Opportunities to create value out of differences in timeframe are not limited to financial exchanges. For example, the issue of cattle grazing near rivers can create considerable disagreement between ranchers and environmental groups. In some areas, disputing parties have discovered that they have different timelines and have crafted value-creating solutions based on those differences. The traditional method of ranching allowed cattle onto large tracts of land, without respect to the season. Because cattle are drawn to water, they would spend much of the spring eating every new plant shoot that came up near the river. Pursuant to an agreement between ranchers and environmentalists in some places, cattle are now fenced out of the areas directly connected to the streams during the spring season. As a result, the plants have a chance to grow to maturity, birds have time to nest, and flowers can go to seed before the cattle are let in. And it turns out that this arrangement not only has had a more beneficial impact on the ecosystem, but also has produced greater total forage for the cattle because the plants were able to grow to maturity.

DIFFERENCES IN PREDICTION

Some disputes hinge not on differing perceptions about what has already happened, but rather on differing perceptions about what will happen in the future. A man driving a rental truck runs into a car driven by a woman who was stopped at a stop sign. She has some bruises, but otherwise appears fine. Will the victim develop further injuries later on? If the victim believes that more serious injuries may manifest themselves down the road, she may demand a high price to settle the claim today for a flat fee. If the truck driver believes that the minor injuries currently visible are all that will result from the accident, he is unlikely to accept such a high demand. The two may be unable to persuade each other about the likelihood of further injuries, but they have the opportunity to craft a contingent agreement, capitalizing on their differing predictions about the future. They could craft a settlement that includes a modest payment for current injuries, medical monitoring for a period of time, and a contingent clause that provides the accident victim with a large payout if future injuries are discovered. Because the victim believes injuries will appear, she will be excited about the prospect of a large payout. Because the driver believes no injuries will occur, he will view his costs to resolve the dispute as relatively modest.

DIFFERENCES IN RISK TOLERANCE

Some people love taking risks and some try generally to avoid them. In certain circumstances, the stakes are low enough that even those who are generally risk averse can tolerate a risk. In others, most are willing to pay a premium not to bear any risk. Out of this basic dynamic, insurance companies do business, and disputants can find opportunities to create value. For example, two business partners fighting over ownership of a product may eventually decide to send the product to market, rather than have it languish during a protracted ownership dispute. Yet they still must decide on how they will split the uncertain future profits. If one partner has a real need for financial security, while the other is more secure and better able to take on the risk, the two can structure an arrangement in which the less nervous party takes on the risk of the product failing, in exchange for a greater percentage of the profits if the product succeeds.

Disputants' risk tolerances play a role even in cases that proceed to trial. The plaintiff dreams of a lottery-sized payout, and the defendant hopes that the jury will award the plaintiff nothing. Yet each party may fear the "bad" outcome even more than it wants the "good" outcome. If the plaintiff does not receive any award, she will be unable to afford the ongoing medical care she requires. If the jury hits the defendant with a heavily punitive award, it will send the company into bankruptcy. Even if these two parties are unable to agree to a settlement package before trial, they could form a so-called "high-low" agreement, creating a floor and a ceiling on the plaintiff's eventual recovery. For example, the disputants might agree to a "low" of $500,000 and a "high" of $2 million. Having signed their high-low agreement, the parties would take the case to trial, and the jury would make its award. If the jury award fell below $500,000, the defendant would pay the plaintiff the agreed-upon "low" number of $500,000. If the jury award came in above $2 million, the defendant would pay the plaintiff $2 million. If the jury award fell between the two figures, the jury award would stand as the award. Such high-low agreements can help to create more attractive settlement options than would otherwise be possible in conditions of high risk.

DIFFERENCES IN CAPABILITIES

Disputants rarely enter a dispute with identical skills, resources, and abilities. If they are able to identify the ways in which they have different capabilities, they may be able to craft agreements that capitalize on the combination of their relative strengths and weaknesses. The authors of *Beyond Winning* describe the 1997 dispute between Intel and Digital Equipment Corporation over Intel's alleged misappropriation of Digital's intellectual property when it created a new computer chip. Intel and Digital settled the multi-million dollar claim and counterclaim with a series of agreements that involved the sale of existing manufacturing facilities, the licensing of current technology, and agreements for future work over the coming decade. The disputants were able to capitalize on the resources and capabilities each brought to the table, treating the settlement negotiations much like potential business partners exploring a possible joint venture.

Notes and Questions

3.31 Moffitt discusses integrative ideas in settling disputes. How are these ideas similar or dissimilar to ideas about creating value in deals? For some other useful ideas for how to create value in negotiation, see the now classic book, David Lax & James Sebenius, The Manager as Negotiator: Bargaining for Cooperation and Competitive Gain 90-102 (1986), discussing the value of trading on differences, unbundling differences of interests, using differences in probability and risk assessments to form contingent agreements, using altered payment schemes, and capitalizing on complementary capabilities.

3.32 Moffitt argues elsewhere (in Chapter 1) that dividing the world into deals versus disputes ignores the potential for value creation in disputes. Do you agree?

3.33 In many contexts, participants assume they have conflicting interests.

> In 1999 Jeanne Lewis was appointed president of staples.com. [T]o compete effectively — and for the online enterprise to have any credibility — Jeanne needed two things: an ability to attract dot-com talent and a way to defuse potential opposition from the bricks-and-mortar side [who thought online shopping would take business away from them]. . . . Jeanne set out to prove that they were not playing a zero-sum game. "Many of our customers shop across all three channels — stores, catalogue, and Web site. And, when they do, they spend on average 4.5 times as much per year as customers who shop only in the stores. . . ." Moreover, the online site could help the stores and merchandising, whose biggest headache was old stock. . . . [Jeanne] wanted to prove that "they were in this all together." Right after she took over at staples.com, she gave a speech to three thousand general managers.
>
> "I talked about the Internet and then I told them to look under their chairs. I had had chocolate boats made — half said Staples, the other half staples.com — and put one under each chair. I asked everyone to pick up

their boat and see if they had the right one. There was a lot of confusion. I let it go on for a bit, then said: 'Stop. We are all in the same boat.' It was a real Aha! moment. People saw how silly the worries about cannibalization were."

Deborah M. Kolb, Judith Williams & Carol Frohlinger, Her Place at the Table: A Woman's Guide to Negotiating Five Key Challenges to Leadership Success 234-236 (2004).

 **Chapter 4** | # Distributive Bargaining: Dividing the Pie and Mixed Models

All polishing is achieved by friction.

— Mary Parker Follett

This chapter discusses the interaction among different approaches to negotiation. The first approach discussed in the previous chapter is problem solving, also called integrative, collaborative, or principled bargaining. A problem-solving approach to a negotiation is one in which the negotiator is interested in doing well for herself and her client and in working with the other side to meet that party's interests and to attempt to achieve joint gains or to "solve the problem" between the parties. The second approach discussed in this chapter is competitive bargaining or, as it is sometimes called, adversarial or positional negotiation. Most of these labels refer to a negotiator who is primarily concerned with "winning" the negotiation for the client and for him- or herself, or maximizing individual gain. Distributive bargaining refers to the fact, perception, or belief that limited resources will be divided during the negotiation. A competitive negotiator is often seen as more likely to engage in deceptive, manipulative, or "power" tactics, less likely to be interested in the other side's point of view, and perhaps, but not always, likely to seem more unpleasant to deal with.

At the other end of the spectrum is so-called soft bargaining, also known as accommodative or cooperative bargaining. As the readings highlight, this approach focuses on relationships and on working with the other side. A cooperative negotiator is likely to be more pleasant, trusting, and friendly. One risk of a cooperative negotiation style is being taken advantage of by a competitive negotiator. The last part of the chapter more specifically discusses the interaction of different approaches using the classic Prisoner's Dilemma model (where parties have to decide whether to "cooperate" or "defect" in each interaction).

In the first excerpt below, two other styles are also discussed. A sharing approach is a splitting-the-difference or compromise style of negotiation. The final approach is avoiding. Avoiding is exactly as it sounds—a negotiator who tries to avoid conflict. This person either does not raise the conflict at all or tries to avoid discussing it if approached; if forced to deal with the conflict, an avoider tries to resolve it as quickly as possible.

Because each approach has strengths and weaknesses in choosing a negotiation strategy, negotiators should first identify what behaviors might be most effective for accomplishing particular goals in each matter, and then assess their natural tendencies or "default" behaviors. Second, negotiators should recognize that most people use elements of each approach at different times. Third, by understanding each of the approaches to negotiation, negotiators can start to understand when using each model makes the most sense, depending on a variety of variables, including what is at stake for the parties and who the other parties are. Fourth, understanding the common approaches to negotiation can help negotiators recognize the "moves" of the other side and learn constructive ways to respond.

 Kenneth Thomas, **CONFLICT AND CONFLICT MANAGEMENT**

in **Handbook of Industrial and Organizational Psychology** 889, 900-902
(**Marvin D. Dunnette ed., 1976**)

Conflict, like power, is one of those fascinating but frequently abused and misunderstood subjects. Like any potent force, conflict generates ambivalence by virtue of its ability to do great injury or, if harnessed, great good. Until recently, social scientists have been most aware of conflict's destructive capability — epitomized by strikes, wars, interracial hostility, and so on. This awareness seems to have given conflict an overwhelming connotation of danger and to have created a bias toward harmony and peacemaking in the social sciences. However, a more balanced view of conflict seems to be emerging. More and more, social scientists are coming to realize — and to demonstrate — that conflict itself is no evil, but rather a phenomenon which can have constructive or destructive effects depending upon its management....

[A] party's perceptions of stakes and conflict of interest have an important influence on his behavior....

ORIENTATION

The model categorizes a party's orientation on the basis of the degree to which he would like to satisfy his own concern and the degree to which he would like to satisfy the concern of the other. Figure 4-1 uses the joint outcome space to plot five such orientations — competitive, collaborative, avoidant, accommodative, and sharing — together with their preferred outcomes....

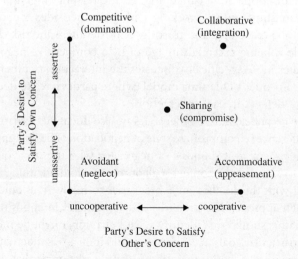

Figure 4-1
Five Conflict Handling Orientations

Before discussing the orientations in Figure 4 individually, some comments on the complexity of this scheme are in order. A five-category scheme is obviously more complicated and difficult to master than a dichotomous differentiation like cooperative-uncooperative. The latter is appealing in its simplicity and is still used extensively in the experimental game approach to conflict research. However, the cooperative-uncooperative dichotomy appears to greatly oversimplify the more complex range of options available to the conflict party.

A stronger case can be made for the present two-dimensional scheme. The cooperative-uncooperative distinction represents one dimension which might accurately reflect the thinking of Party's opponent: "Does he want to cooperate and help me satisfy my concerns, or doesn't he?" However, a different distinction is more likely to be reflected in the thinking of Party and his constituents, namely, "Does Party actively strive to achieve his own concerns, or doesn't he?" Both distinctions in fact reflect important dimensions which are analytically independent: the degree to which one attempts to satisfy the other's concern and the degree to which one assertively pursues one's own concerns.

A great deal of unnecessary sacrifice or competition seems to stem from confusing these two dimensions or reducing them to a single dimension. When cooperation is assumed to be in opposition to pursuing one's own concerns, cooperation comes to mean sacrifice, and asserting one's needs ("standing up for one's rights") comes to mean putting up a fight.

Returning to the five orientations in Figure 4, the competitive orientation represents a desire to win one's own concerns at the other's expense, namely, to dominate.... Blake ... refer[s] to such relationships as "win-lose power struggles."[*]

By contrast, an accommodative orientation focuses upon appeasement— satisfying the other's concerns without attending to one's own. Under such an orientation, a party may be generous or self-sacrificing for the sake of their relationship....

The sharing orientation is intermediate between domination and appeasement. It is a preference for moderate but incomplete satisfaction for both parties—for compromise. Party gives up something and keeps something.... Blake ... refer[s] to this as "splitting the difference," since Party seeks an outcome which is intermediate between the preferred outcomes of both parties.

In contrast to sharing, the collaborative orientation represents a desire to *fully* satisfy the concerns of both parties—to integrate their concerns....

The remaining orientation, avoidance, reflects indifference to the concerns of either party. Blake ... describe[s] this orientation as an instance of withdrawal, isolation, indifference, ignorance, or reliance upon fate. The words "evasion," "flight," and "apathy" have also been used to describe this orientation....

Let us now consider the cooperative dimension in Figure 4 in more detail.... Cooperation involves movement toward the other—attempts to satisfy the other's concerns. Collaboration and accommodation are certainly cooperative in this regard. By contrast, competition and avoidance are uncooperative, involving movement

---

[*] R.R. Blake, H.A. Shepard & J.S. Mouton, Managing Intergroup Conflict in Industry (1964).

against and away from the other, respectively. Sharing is moderately cooperative, since it contains a limited amount of movement toward the other as well as a limited amount of competitive movement against. . . .

The cooperativeness of Party toward Other is to a large extent a function of his identification with Other. Party's identification may range from positive identification through indifference to hostility. Attention to Other's satisfaction through collaboration or accommodation appears to be a manifestation of identification. If two parties have agreed upon important issues in the past or agree on common ends, then they may feel sufficient goodwill toward each other to approach disagreement cooperatively. An uncooperative orientation, on the other hand, may stem from indifference to the other's outcomes or from a desire to injure the other. . . .

The second dimension in Figure 4, assertiveness . . . represents the extent to which Party is interested in satisfying his own concerns. The assertiveness of Party's orientation is in part a result of the strength of Party's concern, or [the] Party's "stakes" in the conflict. The most assertive orientations, competition and collaboration, require the greatest immediate outlay of energy — to compete and problem solve, respectively. Hence, they require some degree of commitment to one's concern. By contrast, avoidance and accommodation require less energy — Party has only to do nothing or go along with Other. In matters of little import to Party, he is, therefore, apt to drift into avoidance or accommodation. Sharing is intermediate in assertiveness and energy expenditure.

Notes and Questions

4.1 Which orientation do you use when negotiating with your family? With your friends? With your romantic interest? With someone at work?

4.2 Should your orientation change depending on the context? On the other side's approach? On your interests? Why or why not?

4.3 Thomas describes the avoider as someone who has both low interest for himself and low interest in the other side. In the writings on legal negotiation, the avoidance orientation is usually ignored. Why do you think this is so?

4.4 Given that lawyers act as agents for clients, should lawyers ask clients to approve their orientation?

4.5 For a different way of categorizing personality types in negotiation, see Don Peters, Forever Jung: Psychological Type Theory, the Myers-Briggs Type Indicator and Learning Negotiation, 42 Drake L. Rev. 1 (1993).

This next excerpt describes distributive bargaining.

Howard Raiffa, **THE ART AND SCIENCE OF NEGOTIATION**

33-34 (1982)

Two-party bargaining can be divided into two types: distributive and integrative. . . . In the distributive case one single issue, such as money, is under contention and the parties have almost strictly opposing interests on that issue: the more you get, the less the other party gets, and — with some exceptions and provisos — you want as much as you can get. Of course, if you are too greedy or if your adversary is too greedy, or if you both are too greedy, you will both fail to come to an agreement that would mean profits for both of you (that is why I speak of "almost" strictly opposing interests). Benjamin Franklin aptly summed it up: "Trades would not take place unless it were advantageous to the parties concerned. Of course, it is better to strike as good a bargain as one's bargaining position permits. The worst outcome is when, by over-reaching greed, no bargain is struck, and a trade that could have been advantageous to both parties does not come off at all."

Two disputants bargain over a price; one wants the price to be high, whereas the other wants it low. One wants to maximize the agreed-upon price, the other to minimize as a buyer. This interpretation is extremely narrow: The ex-wife who is arguing over alimony in a divorce case does not want to view herself as a seller, and the plaintiff who is suing a negligent party doesn't think of himself as a seller. But still, for the most part, you will not go too far astray if you think of the prototypical problem . . . as the problem of a seller and a buyer haggling over a single price.

Sometimes the single commodity in contention may be something like time instead of money. The contractor wants more time, the "contractee" less time. A bride-to-be, for instance, may want the proposed marriage to take place in June, so she says April; her fiancé starts the bidding in August and they settle for June. Or the disputed commodity may be a particular amount of effort or attention, or the number of days of someone's vacation, or the percentage of a harvest, and so on. The important thing to remember is that in distributive bargaining only one issue is being negotiated.

A. ADVERSARIAL APPROACHES

In this section, we review strategies and tactics used to divide the limited resources at stake in a negotiation, when resources or the "res" (or thing) being negotiated are limited or scarce. The first part discusses adversarial approaches, also known as competitive bargaining. Remember to keep separate in your analysis when resources are actually limited and need to be divided (distributive bargaining) from competitive or adversarial behaviors, which are sometimes used (inappropriately) in situations where scarcity is assumed, but not real.

1. Theory

 Gary Goodpaster, **A PRIMER ON COMPETITIVE BARGAINING**

1996 J. Disp. Resol. 325, 326, 341–342

COMPETING

Competitive bargaining, sometimes called hard, distributive, positional, zero-sum or win-lose bargaining, has the purpose of maximizing the competitive bargainer's gain over the gain of those with whom he negotiates. He is, in effect, trying to "come out ahead of," or "do better than," all other parties in the negotiation. For this reason, we sometimes refer to this competitive bargaining strategy as a *domination* strategy, meaning that the competitive bargainer tends to treat negotiations as a kind of contest to win.

The competitive negotiator tends to define success in negotiation rather narrowly. It is simply getting as much as possible for himself: the cheapest price, the most profit, the least cost, the best terms and so on. In its simplest form, this strategy focuses on immediate gain and is not much concerned with the relationship between the negotiating parties. A more complex version of this strategy focuses on long-term gain. This focus usually requires some effort to maintain or further a relationship and usually moderates the competitive, often aggressive, behavior that jeopardizes relationships and possibilities of long-term gain. . . .

WHY PEOPLE BARGAIN COMPETITIVELY

People bargain competitively essentially for three reasons, which often overlap. First, by inclination or calculation, they view the negotiation as a kind of competition, in which they wish to win or gain as much as possible. Secondly, they do not trust the other party. Where parties are non-trusting, they are non-disclosing and withhold information, which leads to further distrust and defensive or self-protective moves. Parties may be non-trusting because they are unfamiliar with the other party or because they are generally or situationally non-trusting. Finally, a party may bargain competitively as a defense to, or retaliation for, competitive moves directed at it.

This next description of adversarial bargaining is from Carrie Menkel-Meadow's article on problem solving.

 Carrie Menkel-Meadow, **TOWARD ANOTHER VIEW OF LEGAL NEGOTIATION: THE STRUCTURE OF PROBLEM SOLVING**

31 UCLA L. Rev. 754, 768–775 (1984)

THE STRUCTURE OF ADVERSARIAL NEGOTIATION: LINEAR CONCESSIONS ON THE ROAD TO COMPROMISE

Most disputes are settled out of court. Describing how this majority of cases is settled, writers depict a remarkably uniform negotiation model. Because the parties fear the cost, the length of time to judicial resolution, and the winner-take-all quality of the judicial result, most cases are settled somewhere mid-range between each party's initial demand. Thus, the structure of adversarial negotiation consists of: (1) the setting of "target points" or "aspiration levels" — what the parties would like to achieve (target points may be set at the initial demand in the complaint or reduced slightly by a more realistic appraisal of what is possible); (2) the setting of "resistance points" or "reservation points," the points below which the party seeks not to go (preferring to risk the possibility of winning the polarized game in court); and (3) the ritual of offer and demand with patterns of "reciprocal concessions." The process results in (4) a compromise solution at some point along the scale where target or resistance points overlap for the two parties. This structure . . . expresses graphically the assumption that negotiations are linear win/lose games where X's gain is Y's loss:

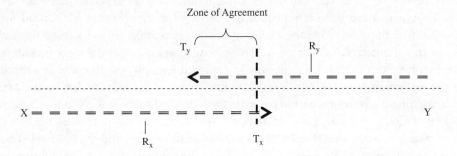

T = Target point (or aspiration point)
R = Resistance point (or reservation level)

Figure 1

In this negotiation game, X and Y attempt to assess each other's "target points" and "resistance points" in order to determine whether there is a "bargaining range." The resemblance of adversarial negotiations to a football field and goals is hardly coincidental. . . . Following "resolution" of the first offer controversy, the parties proceed in a pattern of offer-counteroffer or demand-response resulting in "reciprocal concessions" which can be analyzed to give each party information about the other's target and resistance points. The process continues until a compromise solution is reached somewhere within the bargaining range.

Given this linear conception of the structure of negotiation it is easy to see why results are perceived as compromises along this linear scale and why "split the difference" solutions are so common in conventional negotiations. In order to avoid the costs and risk of polarized results in court the parties choose compromise, after a culturally appropriate time of debate and concessions.

Although such a model encourages compromise at some midway point, it frequently fails to provide a satisfactory solution for the parties. Consider the example of two children arguing over a piece of chocolate cake. The parental compromise solution, cutting the piece in half, will not be satisfactory to either child if one prefers the cake and the other the icing. Compromises may be highly dysfunctional in cases where one needs a pair, rather than a single shoe to do the necessary walking.

A linear negotiation structure might work in those few cases where there is really only one issue, but it is clearly insufficient when the issues in a negotiation are many and varied. For instance, in negotiating a personal injury case one party may seek an apology, as well as lost earnings, rehabilitation costs, and pain and suffering damages. The "concession" of an apology from the other side may or may not reduce the amount of money to be negotiated as compensation for the other things. Similarly, in the formation of a partnership, a "concession" on one issue of control does not necessarily move the "result" away from or toward one of the parties, especially if unaccompanied by an equivalent "trade" of contribution. Indeed, it may be impossible to represent graphically the negotiation of a complex, multi-issue transaction as a two dimensional structure, without imagining a many-planed axis with hundreds of potential coordinates. . . .

[For example] Ms. Brown buys a car from Mr. Snead, a used car salesman. After a short period of time the car ceases to function, despite repeated attempts by Ms. Brown to have the car repaired. Ms. Brown, therefore, sues Mr. Snead for rescission of the sales contract, claiming misrepresentation in the sale of the car or, in the alternative, breach of warranty, with consequential damages including lost income from the loss of a job due to repeated lateness and absences as a result of the malfunctioning car. Mr. Snead counterclaims for the balance due on the car, claiming that the warranty period has ended and the dealership was given insufficient time in which to cure any possible defects. Suppose the car was purchased for a total of $2500, Ms. Brown received $500 as a trade-in allowance, and she has made one monthly payment of $50. Her lost income from losing time at work, and ultimately her job, is approximately $2000, and she has spent approximately $400 in her attempts to repair the car. By the terms of the sales contract, Mr. Snead is entitled not only to the unpaid balance on the car but to attorneys fees for any collection action required to recover the unpaid balance.

Following the filing of the lawsuits described above, the parties, if engaged in conventional adversarial negotiation, would structure their negotiations around the value of their respective monetary claims. Ms. Brown's attorney would evaluate the amount her client had spent on the car, how much she has lost in income and repairs, and the cost of the lawsuit itself. Mr. Snead's attorney would compute the balance due on the car, subtract payments made, and add the fees to recover the balance due. Both parties might then discount their target and resistance points by an estimate of how likely it is that they would prevail in court, subject to a further discount of the cost of achieving that result through adjudication. The attorneys would then engage in a bargaining process of reciprocal concessions based on their assessments of the values and probabilities of recovery on each of the claims, until they reached some dollar amount on which they might agree. Such a settlement would be a compromise with respect to the "scarce" resource in this case — money. In addition to the money, the parties might also negotiate to return their relationship to the *status quo ante*. The difficulty with this solution is that the real goals or objectives sought by the parties might not be accomplished at all. Ms. Brown wants a reliable car to take her to work and Mr. Snead a profitable sale and a satisfied customer who will make recommendations to her friends.

If, however, the parties considered what they had initially desired from this transaction, they might arrive at other solutions. Alternatives could be found that would more completely and efficiently satisfy their needs, solutions not necessarily arising from compromise. If, for example, Ms. Brown's problem is transportation to work, Snead might repair her present car or substitute another car at little or low cost to a dealer who has large inventory. At the same time, Snead could continue to hold Ms. Brown to her contract, or a new contract could be negotiated. With this solution, both parties meet their objectives — a car for Ms. Brown and a continued profit for Mr. Snead — at considerably less legal expense, lower transaction cost in the negotiation, and avoidance of litigation. Note how in the compromise solution above, Ms. Brown could receive a settlement dollar amount that would be insufficient to permit her to buy a new car and Mr. Snead would receive less than an adequate profit, either by having to pay Ms. Brown or by receiving less than the contract price as his settlement. Note also that most courts would not be authorized to order the non-compromise arrangement, although particular judges or settlement officers in some courts might encourage the parties to "work out" such a settlement in private where the court does not have the authority to order such relief.

Notes and Questions

4.6 What assumptions does a competitive approach make about the negotiation? About the other side?

4.7 If the linear competitive approach is limited in the way Menkel-Meadow suggests, why do you suppose it is used so often in resolving legal disputes?

2. Strategy

This excerpt is a more detailed report on the specific tactics often used in competitive bargaining. It is taken from a handbook for public interest lawyers authored by Michael Meltsner and Philip Schrag.

 Michael Meltsner & Philip G. Schrag, NEGOTIATION

> **in Public Interest Advocacy: Materials for Clinical Legal Education 232-238 (1974)**

This section catalogs a number of successful negotiating tactics. Of course, not every tactic described is appropriate for every negotiation; the use of each depends on the particular case and especially upon the perceived relative strengths of the parties during the bargaining process. In general, a party who appears to himself and to his adversary to be strongly desirous of negotiations is less able to use the more powerful tactics set forth. Of course, even the attorney who must negotiate from a position of perceived weakness should be familiar with the tactics that may be used against him, so that he may defend himself as best he can. . . .

A. PREPARATORY TACTICS

1. *Arrange to negotiate on your own turf.* Whenever possible, insist that the meeting be held in your office, or in another setting where you will feel more comfortable

than your adversary; and where he will be at a psychological disadvantage because he has had to come to you. . . .

Neighborhood poverty lawyers who negotiate with attorneys for banks, realty corporations, and other large firms have added a new twist to the "home base" tactic by attempting to maneuver their adversaries into entering the ghetto, sometimes for the first time in their lives. Their fears for their physical safety and their shock at viewing local housing conditions may reduce their bargaining effectiveness. . . .

2. *Balance or slightly outnumber the other side.* Attempt to ascertain or to estimate the number of persons the other side is bringing to the meeting, and do your best to ensure that your side is represented by the same number of persons, or by exactly one more person. In a bargaining session where two negotiate against one or three against two, the side with fewer representatives is usually at a disadvantage: it will tire more readily, and the other side will be better able to control the flow of discussion. . . . On the other hand, an adversary who feels cornered because he is substantially out-numbered may feel too insecure to bargain seriously. Be prepared therefore to justify the presence of additional representatives on the ground that they have technical expertise necessary to successful completion of the settlement.

3. *Time the negotiations to advantage.* When one side wants to get the discussion over with quickly, it usually loses. . . . Some public interest lawyers make it a point to schedule negotiations with government attorneys at 4:00 P.M., on the assumption that civil service lawyers expect to go home at 5:00 and will bargain much more quickly and carelessly at that hour than they would in the morning. Similarly, a lawyer who is not used to working on weekends will probably negotiate more poorly on a Saturday or Sunday than during the week.

4. *Know the facts thoroughly.* An unprepared lawyer is usually at a severe disadvantage (unless he is deliberately unprepared so that the negotiations will be delayed). He will constantly have to apologize for his ignorance and his apologies often create a subtle pressure to concede points as to which his adversary is better informed. In addition, an unprepared lawyer may feel inner pressure to compromise because he does not wish to reveal his ignorance by participation in an extended discussion.

5. *Lock yourself in.* This is a risky but powerful prenegotiation tactic and should be used only with the greatest care. In cases that have attracted public attention, an attorney can increase his bargaining power by announcing publicly a position from which he will not retreat so that his adversary knows that he will lose face if he does in fact retreat. . . .

6. *Designate one of your demands a "precondition."* If the other side wants to talk (for example, if it requested the negotiations), a lawyer can often improve the chances of favorable outcome by calling one of his demands a "precondition" to negotiations. . . .

B. INITIAL TACTICS

7. *When it is in your interest, make the other side tender the first offer.* The party making the first offer suffers the disadvantage of conceding that it really wants to settle. Furthermore, it may make an offer that actually concedes more than the other side thought it could get at the end of the negotiating process. Of course, the attorney who receives such a surprising offer will declare his shock that so little is being tendered,

and will demand much more. One surprisingly successful technique for evoking the first offer is to remain silent. Few people can tolerate more than a few seconds of silence during a negotiation; most feel compelled to say something to break the ice. Or you might simply say to your adversary, "Why don't you start by giving us an idea of your position." There are situations, however, where by making the first offer a party advantageously sets the bounds for the entire discussion. The negotiations may never leave the questions raised initially; other questions, which may be the weakest from your point of view, will fall into place as part of a general wrap up of the deal.

8. *Make your first demand very high.* Outrageously unreasonable demands become more justifiable after substantial discussion. And even if an initially high demand is rejected, it makes a subsequent demand that is almost as high appear to be a more reasonable compromise. . . . Nevertheless, some demands are too outrageous to make. They will encourage your adversary to believe that you are not seriously interested in bargaining despite your protestation to the contrary.

9. *Place your major demands at the beginning of the agenda.* There seems to be a "honeymoon" period, in which negotiators make compromises more freely, at the outset of a negotiation, and another such period at the very conclusion. By forcing your adversary to deal at the outset, when he wants most to compromise, with the items of greatest interest to you, or at the end, when he has invested many hours or weeks of time in negotiating and wants a return on his investment, you can improve your client's position.

10. *Make the other side make the first compromise.* There is a psychological advantage in benefiting from the first concession. Studies indicate that losers generally make the first concessions in negotiating a dispute.

C.   TACTICS GENERALLY

11. *Use two negotiators who play different roles.* The famous "Mutt and Jeff" technique, in which police use one friendly and one nasty interrogator to extract a statement from a reluctant defendant, works very well in negotiation. Two lawyers for the same side feign an internal dispute concerning their position; one takes the hard line, offering almost no compromise, while the other appears to desire to make small concessions, and occasionally he prevails. . . .

12. *Invoke law or justice.* To a surprising extent, lawyers are impressed with the citation of authority and laymen tend to be overwhelmed by a reference to a case or statute. If your adversary seems to react to it, quote or advert to legal authority as often as possible, particularly if you can assert that the position you urge is legally compelled, or that the one he desires is legally prohibited, or at least troublesome. . . . If the law is not on your side, avoid using it. Instead, invoke more general principles of justice, or whatever other kind of authority (for example, public pressure) seems to support your position.

13. *Be tough — especially against a patsy.* Unfortunately, when one party is conciliatory and the other cantankerous, the imbalance usually favors the competitive player in the short run. . . .

14. *Appear irrational when it seems helpful.* This is a dangerous but often successful tactic. An adversary who is himself an expert negotiator can be thrown off base

considerably by a lawyer who doesn't seem to play the same game; for example, one who seems to behave irrationally. Premier Nikita Khrushchev significantly increased the deterrent power of the relatively small Soviet nuclear force by banging his shoe on the table at the United Nations in 1960; he gave the impression of being somewhat imbalanced — a man who might unleash nuclear weapons upon even a slight provocation.

15. *Raise some of your demands as the negotiations progress.* The conventional model of negotiation contemplates both sides lowering their demands until a compromise is finally reached. But the highly successful negotiator backtracks; he raises one of his demands for every two concessions he makes and occasionally reopens for further discussion topics that everyone thought had been settled and laid aside. . . .

16. *Claim that you do not have authority to compromise.* You can make a topic non-negotiable by persuading your adversary that you do not have, and cannot obtain, the authority to go beyond a certain point. The freshman negotiator sometimes makes the mistake of trying to impress the other side with his authority; the expert modestly explains that he has very little authority, and that his client is adamant. . . .

17. *Clear the agreement with your client before signing it.* Before you reach final agreement, you will want to consult with your client. Checking with the client is not only an obligation that you owe to him, it is an important bargaining tactic. It enables you to delay the proceedings while you check, and it gives you a chance to consider any errors you might have made before you sign.

D. POST-NEGOTIATION TACTICS

18. *Make your adversary feel good.* Never gloat over the terms of a settlement. Not only is such behavior boorish, but it may provoke an adversary to reopen negotiations or to adopt a different and stronger negotiating posture the next time you deal with him. If you can do so with candor, feel free to tell opposing counsel what a hard bargain he drove and what a good job he did for his client. If you meet an adversary and his client together, tell the client what a good job his lawyer did for him. This may please the client, but it certainly will please the lawyer and perhaps make him look forward to doing business with you again. . . .

19. *After agreement has been reached, have your client reject it and raise his demands.* This is the most ethically dubious of the tactics listed here, but there will be occasions where a lawyer will have to defend against it or even to employ it. After laboring for hours, days, or weeks to work out a settlement, a negotiator is likely to be dismayed by the prospect of the agreement falling through. As a result, his adversary may be able to obtain last-minute concessions. Of course, such a strategy can boomerang. It may so anger an adversary that he simply refuses to bargain, even though bargaining is still in his interest, or he may fight fire with fire by increasing his own demands.

20. *Reduce the agreement to writing yourself and except in special circumstances do it promptly.* Unless the terms of settlement are reduced to writing a lawyer can never be certain that he has an agreement. Counsel may be laboring under a mistaken impression that they have settled when in fact they have not resolved all of the questions that divided them. Reduction of terms to writing is an effective means of discovering whether there is actual agreement. Not only is the written instrument evidence of the

agreement, but the formulation of its terms will tend to govern the conduct of the parties in the future. Quite often the terms that have been agreed upon will be subject to differing interpretations, some of which favor your side, some of which favor your adversary's side. You should, therefore, volunteer to undertake the labor of drafting the agreement. By doing so, you can choose language which reflects your interpretation of the terms agreed upon. . . . If an adversary writes the first draft, you should be prepared to go over it line by line and to rewrite every word, if necessary.

This next excerpt is from *Beyond Winning*. The authors conclude this section on competitive bargaining by listing the top ten tactics their readers and clients have reported to them. Have you ever used any of these tactics? Have they been used on you? How did you react?

 Robert H. Mnookin, Scott R. Peppet & Andrew S. Tulumello,
**BEYOND WINNING: NEGOTIATING TO CREATE VALUE
IN DEALS AND DISPUTES**

24-25 (2000)

(1) *Extreme claims followed by small, slow concessions:* Aiming high (or low) and conceding slowly. This may be the most common of all hard-bargaining tactics, and it has undeniable advantages. Chiefly, it protects the user from giving away too much surplus at the start. Experimental research also suggests that an ambitious initial demand tends to anchor the other negotiator's perceptions of the bargaining range — even though the other side knows full well that the opening demand is probably a self-serving gambit that conceals the offerer's true reservation value. But this tactic has two disadvantages: it lessens the chances that any deal may be made and invites protracted haggling.

(2) *Commitment tactics:* Committing to a course of action that ties one's hands, thus forcing the other side to accommodate; limiting one's freedom of action in order to influence the other side's view of what agreements are possible. To be effective, a commitment must seem "binding, credible, visible, and irreversible."

(3) *Take-it-or-leave-it offers:* Stating that one's offer is non-negotiable — that the negotiation will end if it is not accepted. Like commitment strategies, the risk is that no deal will be made if both parties play chicken. Moreover, take-it-or-leave-it offers can often be countered simply by making some other offer.

(4) *Inviting unreciprocated offers:* Asking the offerer to bid against himself. Instead of meeting an offer with a counter offer, the hard bargainer indicates that the first offer is insufficient and requests a better offer.

(5) *Flinch:* Piling one demand on top of another until the other side makes a visible sign that the demands have reached her breaking point.

(6) *Personal insults and feather ruffling:* Using personal attacks to play on the other side's insecurities, fluster him, throw him off balance, and otherwise gain psychological advantage.

(7) *Bluffing, puffing, and lying:* Trying to influence the other side's perception of what would be acceptable by exaggerating or misrepresenting facts.

(8) ***Threats and warnings:*** Promise drastic consequences if one's demands are not met.

(9) ***Belittling the other party's alternatives:*** Trying to influence the other side's reservation value by bashing their BATNA.

(10) ***Good cop, bad cop:*** Designating one person in a two-negotiator team as the reasonable person who is supposedly trying to help the other side out, while the other negotiator adopts a tough, abrasive manner and pushes for concessions.

Notes and Questions

4.8   Which of Meltsner and Schrag's tactics seem to be good advice regardless of which approach to negotiation you choose? Why? Which of the tactics seem to be the most risky? Why?

4.9   Meltsner and Schrag are writing for a certain set of lawyers. How might this affect their advice? Do you think their advice applies to all lawyers? Why or why not?

4.10 The excerpt from Meltsner and Schrag is from the 1970s, while *Beyond Winning* was published in 2000. Note that some of the new tactics in *Beyond Winning* — bidding against yourself, personal insults, and belittling — seem to reflect a shift in some negotiation tactics to more personal tactics. One study of negotiators found that adversarial negotiators had become nastier and more negative in the last 25 years. Furthermore, these current adversarial negotiators also were viewed by their peers as far less effective (25 percent down to 9 percent) than adversarial negotiators 25 years ago. Andrea Kupfer Schneider, Shattering Negotiation Myths: Empirical Evidence on the Effectiveness of Negotiation Style, 7 Harv. Negot. L. Rev. 143 (2002). Note that in Chapter 7, we will spend time discussing how to counter many of these tactics.

4.11 Which tactics would you fear facing the most? How could you respond to them? (We will discuss more about responding to tactics in Chapters 6, 7, and 8.)

3. Concerns

This next excerpt discusses some of the risks associated with adversarial bargaining.

 Carrie Menkel-Meadow, TOWARD ANOTHER VIEW OF LEGAL NEGOTIATION: THE STRUCTURE OF PROBLEM SOLVING

31 UCLA L. Rev. 754, 775-781 (1984)

Adversarial assumptions affect not only the quality of solutions to negotiated problems but also the process by which these solutions are reached. This is especially important because the type and quality of solutions may depend a great deal on the process used. The adversarial conception of negotiation produces a particular mind-set concerning possible solutions which then tend to produce a competitive process. This, in turn, may cause the parties to miss opportunities for expanding the range of solutions. Thus, by encouraging competitive strategies important information may not be communicated and the parties may arrive at unsatisfactory and inefficient solutions. . . .

What is astounding about the conventional literature on tactics and strategies is the assumption of universal applicability. Strategic exhortations are offered without reference to how negotiations might vary in different contexts or under different circumstances, such as under the influence of various clients' desires. Negotiators are admonished to never make the first offer and to always draft the final agreement as if there were a few simple rules negotiators should obey in order always to maximize individual gain.

Commentators on the adversarial negotiation process have described a remarkable uniformity of stages and phases of negotiation that all appear to be derived from the linear negotiation structure described above. Thus, . . . the phases of an adversarial negotiation will generally proceed along these lines: (1) prenegotiation strategizing or planning to determine target and resistance points, location, and timing of negotiation . . . ; (2) offers and responses (expression of differences and issue definitions); (3) information exchange (positions, arguments and objectives "presented"); (4) bargaining . . . , where concessions are made and analyzed; (5) closure or agreement, where agreements are made and parties allocate final responsibilities for negotiated relations. These stages and phases of negotiation are intended to lead negotiators of divergent and polarized objectives through the process of argument and concession, to the point of compromise and agreement.

The difficulty with such a description of the stages and phases of negotiation is not one of accuracy. The problem is that the stylized ritual of offer/response, counteroffer/counterresponse and concessions may not be of assistance when the issues are multi-dimensional and the parties seek to discuss a variety of solutions at the same time. Furthermore, these descriptions of negotiations emphasize an argumentative, debate form of discussion that may force the parties into attack and defensive postures which then may inhibit creativity in finding solutions. In short, this form of negotiation debate may lead to competitive reactive dynamics rather than to creative proactive dynamics. For example, commitment to a particular offer may keep the adversarial negotiator from seeing variations of that offer that might be more advantageous for the parties. By arguing for a particular proposal the adversarial negotiator may lock himself into a "mind-set" about why that offer must be accepted. Adversarial negotiation processes are frequently characterized by arguments and statements rather than questions and searches for new information.

The recommended strategies may not work even on their own terms. Many commentators have offered a number of competitive strategies designed to force the other side to capitulate. The difficulty with all of these strategic exhortations is the assumption that the other side can be bullied, manipulated or deceived. It is true, for example, that some will wilt under pressure, but others are likely to respond in kind.

Moreover, even those who wilt at the negotiation table may be resentful later and exercise their power either by failing to follow through on the agreement or by seeking revenge the next time the parties meet.

Many of these strategic exhortations may work against the negotiator, even in an adversarial negotiation. For example, if as Meltsner & Schrag suggest, the negotiator chooses his own office for greater comfort in negotiating, the other side may be less comfortable and less amenable to open discussions. In addition, choosing one's own office for comfort minimizes the chances of learning about the other party by not negotiating on their "turf" or by keeping the other party from its sources of information, such as office files. On a more mundane level, the choice of one's own office for comfort may actually increase discomfort by encouraging interruptions from co-workers and telephone calls. Thus, these strategic exhortations, designed to put the other party at a disadvantage, may not even be effective on their own terms.

The literature is replete with advice to overpower and take advantage of the other side. But as one of the popular guides to negotiation has so wisely stated, "a tactic perceived is no tactic." If two competitive negotiators read the same literature it is difficult to see how these strategies will be employed to maximize individual gain. Who will win when both sides know all the same tricks?

The one strategic exhortation that seems to dominate most descriptions of adversarial negotiation is the admonition that the negotiator should never reveal what is really desired. . . .

The principle that one should hide information about one's real preferences is based on unexplored assumptions of human behavior that negotiators are manipulative, competitive and adversarial. The danger of acting on such assumptions is that opportunities for better solutions may be lost (remember the chocolate cake!) and that when one party behaves in this way, the other side may be more likely to reciprocate with competitive and manipulative conduct of its own. Like many of the other assumptions of the adversarial model, the notion that one should hide information is based on a conception of the court outcome. Trial lawyers may fear releasing information in pre-trial negotiations because of the presumed loss of advantage at trial. In this era of discovery, however, this fear may be misplaced. Although thoughtless revelation of "all the facts" may not lead to satisfactory solutions either, failure to disclose real preferences has been shown to foreclose some of the most efficient and mutually satisfactory solutions. Moreover, revealing preferences or needs is not the same thing as revealing "evidence."

This particular excerpt from the Schneider study on how lawyers negotiate shows a distinct difference between perceived ethical and unethical adversarial negotiators. Both categories of adversarial bargainers are more likely than not to be perceived as ineffective. However, being adversarial and unethical compounds the likelihood of being perceived as ineffective.

Andrea Kupfer Schneider, **SHATTERING NEGOTIATION MYTHS: EMPIRICAL EVIDENCE ON THE EFFECTIVENESS OF NEGOTIATION STYLE**

7 Harv. Negot. L. Rev. 143, 181, 183-184 (2002)

The more revealing result from [dividing lawyers into four groups] concerns the further division of lawyers in adversarial behavior. The unethical adversarial [is] deceptive, loud, and foolish. On the other hand, the new cluster labeled ethical adversarial has some important differences from . . . the . . . unethical adversarial group. . . . Though many of the adjectives do overlap, the rankings of adjectives are ordered differently. The top five adjectives in the ethical group are confident, assertive, arrogant, headstrong, and experienced. Furthermore, unlike the [unethical adversarial], the ethical group is *not* described as manipulative, conniving, deceptive, evasive, complaining, rude, angry, intolerant, sarcastic, greedy or stern. The ethical adjectives therefore are not particularly negative nor do they suggest the table-banging style of negotiation.

A review of the bipolar pairs [polar opposite negotiation techniques] further shows the difference between the two adversarial groups. Attorneys falling in the unethical adversarial group had numerous adjectives and behavior ascribed to them that were not ascribed to attorneys in the ethical adversarial group. First, attorneys in the unethical adversarial group were unpleasant: discourteous, unfriendly, and tactless. Second, they were untrustworthy: insincere, devious, dishonest and distrustful. Third, these attorneys were uninterested in the client or lawyer on the other side: no understanding of the opposing client, unconcerned how opposing counsel would look, no consideration of opposing counsel's needs, infliction of needless harm. Fourth, these attorneys were inflexible in their view of the case and their strategies: narrow view of case, rigid, took one position, narrow range of strategies, focused on a single solution, fixed concept of negotiation. Fifth, they used manipulative tactics: attacked, used take it or leave it, inaccurate case estimate, advanced unwarranted claims. Finally, their general view of the negotiation process was competitive: uncooperative, unreasonable, viewed negotiation as win-lose, obstructed the negotiation. The ethical adversarials, as compared to the unethical adversarials, had a broader view of the case, a different negotiation style, and were more pleasant. . . .

Top 20 Adjectives for Adversarials

	ETHICAL ADVERSARIAL	UNETHICAL ADVERSARIAL
1	Confident	Irritating
2	Assertive	Stubborn
3	Arrogant	Headstrong
4	Headstrong	Argumentative
5	Experienced	Quarrelsome
6	Demanding	Arrogant
7	Egotistical	Egotistical
8	Ambitious	Manipulative

	ETHICAL ADVERSARIAL	UNETHICAL ADVERSARIAL
9	Stubborn	Assertive
10	Argumentative	Demanding
11	Tough	Complaining
12	Irritating	Hostile
13	Forceful	Suspicious
14	Firm	Conniving
15	Quarrelsome	Greedy
16	Masculine	Rude
17	Dominant	Angry
18	Ethical	Confident
19	Deliberate	Ambitious
20	Hostile	Deceptive

The further breakdown of numbers in each cluster and effectiveness help to identify these clusters even more. The effectiveness rating of the unethical adversarial cluster compared to the effectiveness rating of the ethical adversarial cluster completes the story. Seventy-five percent of the unethical adversarial group is considered ineffective. Only two attorneys out of the seventy-seven attorneys in this group, 2.5%, were considered effective. In comparison, the ethical adversarial bargainer is more likely to be average if not effective. Forty percent of ethical adversarials were ineffective, 44% were average and 16% were effective. These are still clearly lower ratios for effective and average behavior than the [true] problem-solving negotiator and even the cautious problem-solving negotiator. On the other hand, they are notably better than the unethical adversarial bargainer is.

Effectiveness in Four Clusters

Effectiveness x Clusters	Ineffective	Average	Effective	Totals by Cluster
Problem-Solving (PS)	1% of PS	27% of PS	72% of PS	PS = 238
Cautious Problem-Solving (CPS)	12% of CPS	65% of CPS	23.5% of CPS	CPS = 170
Ethical Adversarial (EA)	40% of EA	44% of EA	16% of EA	EA = 133
Unethical Adversarial (UA)	75% of UA	22% of UA	3% of UA	UA = 77
Totals by Effectiveness	Total = 134	Total = 250	Total = 234	Total = 618

Notes and Questions

4.12 The study indicates it is most dangerous in terms of ineffectiveness to be both adversarial and unethical, but it is also dangerous to be simply adversarial (compared to other approaches). Do these results mesh with images from television and movies? With the culture portrayed in law school?

4.13 What are the key perceived behavioral differences between these two types of adversarial negotiators?

4.14 How closely does the description of adversarial lawyer behavior mirror the advice that Meltsner and Schrag give? Are Meltsner and Schrag advocating for ethical or unethical adversarial bargaining? Explain your answer.

B. ACCOMMODATING

A different approach to a negotiation when there are limited resources to divide is to be more concerned with the other side's needs than your own. Some authors describe this orientation as "accommodative." Other authors refer to this approach as "soft bargaining" or as "cooperative." While this approach is completely different from the adversarial approach, it often shares the assumption that a distributional negotiation exists. This soft approach is used when the relationship is *so* important that accommodating your counterpart is more important than your own interests.

1. Theory and Strategies

These next excerpts outline the theories of an accommodating or soft approach to negotiation. The first excerpt from *Getting to YES* outlines the differences between hard and soft bargaining. Gerald Williams outlines some specific strategies for a cooperative approach.

 Roger Fisher, William Ury & Bruce Patton, **GETTING TO YES: NEGOTIATING AGREEMENT WITHOUT GIVING IN**

8-9 (2d ed. 1991)

The . . . table [shown] illustrates two styles of positional bargaining, soft and hard. Most people see their choice of negotiating strategies as between these two styles. . . . The soft negotiating game emphasizes the importance of building and maintaining a relationship. Within families and among friends much negotiation takes place in this way. The process tends to be efficient, at least to the extent of producing results quickly. As each party competes with the other in being more generous and more forthcoming, an agreement becomes highly likely. But it may not be a wise one. The results may not be as tragic as in the O. Henry story about an impoverished couple in which the loving wife sells her hair in order to buy a handsome chain for her husband's watch, and the unknowing husband sells his watch in order to buy beautiful combs for his wife's hair. However, any negotiation primarily concerned with the relationship runs the risk of producing a sloppy agreement.

PROBLEM
Positional Bargaining: Which Game Should You Play?

SOFT	HARD
Participants are friends.	Participants are adversaries.
The goal is agreement.	The goal is victory.
Make concessions to cultivate the relationship.	Demand concessions as a condition of the relationship.
Be soft on the people and the problem.	Be hard on the problem and the people.
Trust others.	Distrust others.
Change your position easily.	Dig in to your position.
Make offers.	Make threats.
Disclose your bottom line.	Mislead as to your bottom line.
Accept one-sided losses to reach agreement.	Demand one-sided gains as the price of agreement.
Search for the single answer: the one *they* will accept.	Search for the single answer: the one *you* will accept.
Insist on agreement.	Insist on your position.
Try to avoid a contest of will.	Try to win a contest of will.
Yield to pressure.	Apply pressure.

More seriously, pursuing a soft and friendly form of positional bargaining makes you vulnerable to someone who plays a hard game of positional bargaining. In positional bargaining, a hard game dominates a soft one. If the hard bargainer insists on concessions and makes threats while the soft bargainer yields in order to avoid confrontation and insists on agreement, the negotiating game is biased in favor of the hard player. The process will produce an agreement, although it may not be a wise one. It will certainly be more favorable to the hard positional bargainer than to the soft one. If your response to sustained, hard positional bargaining is soft positional bargaining, you will probably lose your shirt.

 Gerald R. Williams, **LEGAL NEGOTIATION AND SETTLEMENT**

53 (1983)

The basic dynamic of the cooperative negotiator is to move psychologically *toward* the opposing attorney. Cooperative negotiators seek a common ground. They communicate a sense of shared interests, values, and attitudes using rational, logical persuasion as a means of seeking cooperation. They promote a trusting atmosphere appearing to seek no special advantage for self or client. The explicit goal is to reach a fair resolution of the conflict based on an objective analysis of facts and law.

Osgood observed a crucial dynamic here: the cooperative negotiator shows his own trust and good faith by making unilateral concessions. Making unilateral concessions is risky, but cooperative negotiators believe it creates a moral obligation in the other to reciprocate. The cooperative strategy is calculated (subconsciously) to induce the other party to reciprocate: to cooperate in openly and objectively resolving the problem; to forego aggression, and to make reciprocal concessions until a solution is reached.

Cooperative negotiators feel a high commitment to fairness, objecting to the competitive view of negotiation as a game. To a cooperative, the gamesmanship view is ethically suspect. They feel that to move psychologically *against* another person to promote one's own interest is manipulative and an affront to human dignity. On the other hand, cooperatives move psychologically *toward* other people to achieve their preferred outcome. Competitive negotiators have reason to ask whether this is in any way less manipulative. Their manipulation is designed to induce or permit the opponent to trust, cooperate with, and make concessions to the manipulator.

Notes and Questions

4.15 When does the accommodating approach make the most sense? Think of a negotiation in which you adopted the accommodating approach. Did your choice make sense? Why or why not?

4.16 How does a cooperative approach fit into the linear view of the negotiation ritual of offer/counteroffer? For an explanation of the theory behind what a more accommodating approach can do, see Donald Gifford, A Context-Based Theory of Strategy Selection in Legal Negotiation, 46 Ohio St. L.J. 41, 52-54 (1985).

2. Concerns

 Chester L. Karrass, **THE NEGOTIATING GAME**

  8-10 (1970)

THE RAPE OF CZECHOSLOVAKIA

The inability to bargain effectively can result in consequences far beyond the mere loss of money. In 1938, Prime Minister Chamberlain did an incredibly poor job at Munich. For three years Hitler had taken spectacular gambles and won. Against the advice of his generals, he had rearmed the country, rebuilt the navy and established a powerful air force. Hitler correctly sensed that the British and French wanted peace desperately, for they had chosen to overlook German rearmament and expansionism. Encouraged by success, Germany applied pressure on Austria and occupied the country early in 1938. Czechoslovakia was next.

Hitler was not fully satisfied with earlier victories, as they had been bloodless. He yearned to show the world how powerful Germany was by provoking a shooting war, and he did this by making impossibly high demands on the Czech Government for German minority rights and by establishing an October 1, 1938, war deadline. It was a ridiculous gamble.

As shown in [the following table], relative bargaining strength was overwhelmingly in favor of the Allies on September 27, 1938. Hitler was aware of his weakness and chose to win by negotiation what could not be won by war. The following events indicate why he was optimistic:

1. On September 13, Chamberlain announced a willingness to grant large concessions if Hitler would agree to discuss issues.
2. On September 15, the aged Prime Minister of Great Britain made a grueling journey to meet Hitler deep in eastern Germany. Hitler had refused to meet him halfway.
3. Hitler opened the conference by abusing Chamberlain and by making outrageously large demands for territory, to which the leader of the Western world *immediately agreed.*
4. Hitler was aware that Chamberlain spent the next four days convincing the French that Germany could be trusted. The Czechs were bluntly told not to be *unreasonable* by fighting back.
5. On September 22, Chamberlain flew back to Germany and offered Hitler *more* than he asked for. Hitler was astounded but nonplussed. *He raised his demands.*
6. Chamberlain returned home to argue Hitler's cause while the German leader made public announcements that war would start October 1 if his *moderate demands* were not granted.

When the two men met on September 29, Hitler had little doubt of victory. Mussolini acted as mediator (imagine that!) and proposed a small compromise, which was quickly accepted by both parties. And in a few months Czechoslovakia ceased to exist. Chamberlain, businessman turned politician had lost the greatest negotiation of all time. As a consequence, 25 million people were soon to lose their lives.

GERMANY vs. ALLIES
Relative Bargaining Strength

THE GERMAN POSITION	THE ALLIED POSITION
1. German generals reported that the Czechs were determined to fight. They told Hitler that Czech fortifications were sufficiently strong to repulse the Germans even without military help from France and England.	1. A million Czechs were ready to fight from strong mountain fortresses.
2. German intelligence reported that French and Czech together outnumbered the Nazis two to one.	2. The French were prepared to place 100 divisions in the field.
	3. Anti-Nazi generals in Germany were prepared to destroy Hitler if the Allies would commit themselves to resist the Czech takeover.
	4. British and French public opinion was stiffening against Germany's

THE GERMAN POSITION	THE ALLIED POSITION
3. The General Staff reported only twelve German divisions available to fight the French in the west.	outrageous demands.
	5. The British fleet, largest in the world, was fully mobilized for action.
4. In Berlin a massive parade was staged. William L. Shirer reports that less than 200 Germans watched. Hitler attended and was infuriated by the lack of interest.	6. President Roosevelt pledged aid to the Allies.
5. German Intelligence reported that Mussolini had privately decided not to assist Hitler.	
6. German diplomats reported that world opinion was overwhelmingly pro-Czechoslovakian.	

Notes and Questions

4.17 What advice would you give to Chamberlain now? Admittedly, hindsight is 20/20. How could Chamberlain have better prepared for his negotiation?

4.18 What advice would you give to someone using an accommodating approach? How could that person avoid being taken advantage of? Is accommodation ever appropriate? When? Have we come to fear the "Chamberlain effect" too much?

C. MIXED MODELS AND PRISONER'S DILEMMA

Chapter 3 discusses integrative negotiation while, thus far, this chapter has discussed distributive negotiation with either the competitive or accommodating approach. In fact, many negotiations have both elements of potentially expanding the pie and dividing it. This next section examines the Prisoner's Dilemma, a classic scenario from economic game theory (taken from our own world of law enforcement) that is often applied to the negotiation context. The following section examines the Negotiator's Dilemma, the choice of which strategy to choose and how this choice may affect the outcome of the negotiation.

 Douglas R. Hofstadter, METAMAGICAL THEMAS: QUESTING FOR THE ESSENCE OF MIND AND PATTERN

716 (1985)

In case you're wondering why it is called "Prisoner's Dilemma," here's the reason. Imagine that you and an accomplice (someone you have no feelings for one way or the other) committed a crime, and now you've both been apprehended and thrown in jail, and are fearfully awaiting trials. You are being held in separate cells with no way to communicate. The prosecutor offers each of you the following deal (and informs you both that the identical deal is being offered to each of you — and that you both know *that* as well!): "We have a lot of circumstantial evidence on you both. So if you both claim innocence, we will convict you anyway and you'll both get two years in jail. But if you will help us out by admitting your guilt and making it easier for us to convict your accomplice — oh, pardon me, your *alleged* accomplice — why, then, we'll let you out free. And don't worry about revenge — your accomplice will be in for five years! How about it?" Warily you ask, "But what if we *both* say we're guilty?" "Ah, well, my friend — I'm afraid you'll both get four-year sentences, then."

Now you're in a pickle! Clearly, you don't want to claim innocence if your partner has sung, for then you're in for five long years. Better you should both have sung — then you'll only get four. On the other hand, if your partner claims innocence, then the best possible thing for you to do is sing, since then you're out scot-free! So at first sight, it seems obvious what you should do: Sing! But what is obvious to you is equally obvious to your opposite number, so now it looks like you both ought to sing, which means — Sing Sing for four years! At least that's what *logic* tells you to do. Funny, since if both of you had just been *illogical* and maintained innocence, you'd both be in for only half as long! Ah, logic does it again.

Notes and Questions

4.19 If one of the prisoners was your client, how would you advise him or her? If both of the prisoners were your clients, how would you advise them? Does your advice differ? Why or why not?

4.20 Assume that the prisoners know each other. How would you advise your client now? Is this different advice than above? Why or why not? Assume that the prisoners are married. How would you advise your client now?

4.21 The Prisoner's Dilemma is a highly stylized interaction. Yet some legal scholars have analogized this situation to discovery prior to trial. See Ronald J. Gilson & Robert H. Mnookin, Disputing Through Agents: Cooperation and Conflict Between Lawyers in Litigation, 94 Colum. L. Rev. 509 (1995). Each side has the choice whether to cooperate in discovery (to turn over requested documents easily, to schedule depositions conveniently, to answer interrogatories fully) or to be more adversarial (to fight document requests, to make depositions a true inconvenience, to evade answering interrogatories). If both sides cooperate, discovery moves forward quickly and relatively inexpensively. If both sides are adversarial, discovery is delayed and is far more costly as the parties file additional motions. If one side is cooperative while the other is adversarial, then the cooperative side ends up spending more money and getting less information. The adversarial side saves money and gets the information it needs. How would you decide what to do? What if the opposing side has a reputation for fairness? What if the opposing side has a reputation for hard bargaining? What if you deal with the opposing side regularly? Note that we will discuss reputation and this article in the next chapter.

What if the prisoners in the Prisoner's Dilemma were going to find themselves in the same situation next week? Does the idea of repeat interactions change behavior? The next excerpt explains a computer tournament run on that assumption and the lessons that can be drawn from the winning entry.

 Robert Axelrod, THE EVOLUTION OF COOPERATION

3, 7, 9, 30-31, 40-42, 54, 110-122 (1984)

Under what conditions will cooperation emerge in a world of egoists without central authority? This question has intrigued people for a long time. And for good reason. We all know that people are not angels, and that they tend to look after themselves and their own first. Yet we also know that cooperation does occur and that our civilization is based upon it. But, in situations where each individual has an incentive to be selfish, how can cooperation ever develop? . . .

A good example of the fundamental problem of cooperation is the case where two industrial nations have erected trade barriers to each other's exports. Because of the mutual advantages of free trade, both countries would be better off if these barriers were eliminated. But if either country were to unilaterally eliminate its barriers, it would find itself facing terms of trade that hurt its own economy. In fact, whatever one country does, the other country is better off retaining its own trade barriers. Therefore, the problem is that each country has an incentive to retain trade barriers, leading to a worse outcome than would have been possible had both counties cooperated with each other.

This basic problem occurs when the pursuit of self-interest by each leads to a poor outcome for all. To make headway in understanding the vast array of specific situations which have this property, a way is needed to represent what is common to these situations without becoming bogged down in the details unique to each. Fortunately, there is such a representation available: the famous *Prisoner's Dilemma* game.

In the Prisoner's Dilemma game, there are two players. Each has two choices, namely cooperate or defect. Each must make the choice without knowing what the other will do. No matter what the other does, defection yields a higher payoff than cooperation. The dilemma is that if both defect, both do worse than if both had cooperated. . . .

The way the game works is shown in figure 1. One player chooses a row, either cooperating or defecting. The other player simultaneously chooses a column, either cooperating or defecting. Together, these choices result in one of the four possible outcomes shown in that matrix. If both players cooperate, both do fairly well. Both get R, the *reward for mutual cooperation*. In the concrete illustration of figure 1 the reward is 3 points. This number might, for example, be a payoff in dollars that each player gets for that outcome. If one player cooperates but the other defects, the defecting player gets the *temptation to defect*, while the cooperating player gets the *sucker's payoff*. In the example, these are 5 points and 0 points respectively. If both defect, both get 1 point, the *punishment for mutual defection*.

Column Player

		Cooperate	Defect
	Cooperate	$R = 3, R = 3$ Reward for mutual cooperation	$S = 0, T = 5$ Sucker's payoff and temptation to defect
Row Player	Defect	$T = 5, S = 0$ Temptation to defect and sucker's payoff	$P = 1, P = 1$ Punishment for mutual defection

Figure 1
The Prisoner's Dilemma
Note: The payoffs to the row chooser are listed first.

What should you do in such a game? Suppose you are the row player, and you think the column player will cooperate. This means that you will get one of the two outcomes in the first column of figure 1. You have a choice. You can cooperate as well, getting the 3 points of the reward for mutual cooperation. Or you can defect, getting the 5 points of the temptation payoff. So it pays to defect if you think the other player will cooperate. But now suppose that you think the other player will defect. Now you are in the second column of figure 1, and you have a choice between cooperating, which would make you a sucker and give you 0 points, and defecting, which would result in mutual punishment giving you 1 point. So it pays to defect if you think the other player will defect. This means that it is better to defect if you think the other player will cooperate, *and* it is better to defect if you think the other player will defect. So no matter what the other player does, it pays for you to defect.

So far, so good. But the same logic holds for the other player too. Therefore, the other player should defect no matter what you are expected to do. So you should both defect. But then you both get 1 point which is worse than the 3 points of the reward that you both could have gotten had you both cooperated. Individual rationality leads to a worse outcome for both than is possible. Hence the dilemma....

Wanting to find out what would happen [in an iterated game], I invited professional game theorists to send in entries to just such a computer tournament. It was structured as a round robin, meaning that each entry was paired with each other entry. As announced in the rules of the tournament, each entry was also paired with its own twin and with RANDOM, a program that randomly cooperates and defects with equal probability....

TIT FOR TAT ... won the tournament. This was the simplest of all submitted programs and it turned out to be the best! TIT FOR TAT, of course, starts with a cooperative choice, and thereafter does what the other player did on the previous move. . . .

The analysis of the tournament results indicate[s] that there is a lot to be learned about coping in an environment of mutual power. Even expert strategists from political science, sociology, economics, psychology, and mathematics made the systematic errors of being too competitive for their own good, not being forgiving enough, and being too pessimistic about the responsiveness of the other side.

The effectiveness of a particular strategy depends not only on its own character- istics, but also on the nature of the other strategies with which it must interact. For this reason, the results of a single tournament are not definitive. Therefore, a second round of the tournament was conducted.

The results of the second round provide substantially better grounds for insight into the nature of effective choice in the Prisoner's Dilemma. The reason is that the entrants to the second round were all given the detailed analysis of the first round, including a discussion of the supplemental rules that would have done very well in the environment of the first round. . . .

The second round was also a dramatic improvement over the first round in sheer size of the tournament. The response was far greater than anticipated. There was a total of sixty-two entries from six countries. . . . The contestants ranged from a ten-year-old computer hobbyist to professors of computer science, physics, economics, psychology, mathematics, sociology, political science, and evolutionary biology. . . .

TIT FOR TAT was the simplest program submitted in the first round, and it won the first round. It was the simplest submission in the second round, and it won the second round. Even though all the entrants to the second round knew that TIT FOR TAT had won the first round, no one was able to design an entry that did any better. . . .

TIT FOR TAT won the tournament because it did well in its interactions with a wide variety of other strategies. On average, it did better than any other rule with the other strategies in the tournament. Yet TIT FOR TAT never once scored better in a game than the other player! In fact, it can't. It lets the other player defect first, and it never defects more times than the other player has defected. Therefore, TIT FOR TAT achieves either the same score as the other player, or a little less. TIT FOR TAT won the tournament, not by beating the other player, but by eliciting behavior from the other player which allowed both to do well. TIT FOR TAT was so consistent at eliciting mutually rewarding outcomes that it attained a higher overall score than any other strategy. . . .

The purpose of this chapter is to translate these findings into advice for a player.

The advice takes the form of four simple suggestions for how to do well in a durable iterated Prisoner's Dilemma:

1. Don't be envious.
2. Don't be the first to defect.
3. Reciprocate both cooperation and defection.
4. Don't be too clever.

1. DON'T BE ENVIOUS . . .

People tend to resort to the standard of comparison that they have available — and this standard is often the success of the other player relative to their own success. This standard leads to envy. And envy leads to attempts to rectify any advantage the other player has attained. In this form of Prisoner's Dilemma, rectification of the other's advantage can only be done by defection. But defection leads to more defection and to mutual punishment. So envy is self-destructive.

Asking how well you are doing compared to how well the other player is doing is not a good standard unless your goal is to destroy the other player. In most situations, such a goal is impossible to achieve, or likely to lead to such costly conflict as to be very dangerous to pursue. When you are not trying to destroy the other player, comparing your score to the other's score simply risks the development of self-destructive envy. A better standard of comparison is how well you are doing relative to how well someone else could be doing in your shoes. Given the strategy of the other player, are you doing as well as possible? Could someone else in your situation have done better with this other player? This is the proper test of successful performance. . . .

2. DON'T BE THE FIRST TO DEFECT

Both the tournament and the theoretical results show that it pays to cooperate as long as the other player is cooperating. . . . The single best predictor of how well a rule performed was whether or not it was nice, which is to say, whether or not it would ever be the first to defect. In the first round, each of the top eight rules were nice, and not one of the bottom seven were nice. In the second round, all but one of the top fifteen rules were nice (and that one ranked eighth). Of the bottom fifteen rules, all but one were not nice. . . .

When the future of the interaction is not important enough relative to immediate gains from defection, then simply waiting for the other to defect is not such a good idea. . . . [I]f the other player is not likely to be seen again, defecting right away is better than being nice. . . . Short interactions are not the only condition which would make it pay to be the first to defect. The other possibility is that cooperation will simply not be reciprocated. If everyone else is using a strategy of always defecting, then a single individual can do no better than to use this same strategy. . . .

Of course, one could try to "play it safe" by defecting until the other player cooperates, and only then starting to cooperate. The tournament results show, however, that this is actually a very risky strategy. The reason is that your own initial defection is likely to set off a retaliation by the other player. This will put the two of you in the difficult position of trying to extricate yourselves from an initial pattern of exploitation or mutual defection. If you punish the other's retaliation, the problem can echo into the future. And if you forgive the other, you risk appearing to be exploitable. Even if you can avoid these long-term problems, a prompt retaliation against your initial defection can make you wish that you had been nice from the start. . . .

The lesson is that not being nice may look promising at first, but in the long run it can destroy the very environment it needs for its own success.

3. RECIPROCATE BOTH COOPERATION AND DEFECTION

The extraordinary success of TIT FOR TAT leads to some simple, but powerful advice: practice reciprocity. After cooperating on the first move, TIT FOR TAT simply reciprocates whatever the other player did on the previous move....

In responding to a defection from the other player, TIT FOR TAT represents a balance between punishing and being forgiving. TIT FOR TAT always defects exactly once after each defection by the other.... What is clear is that extracting more than one defection for each defection of the other side risks escalation. On the other hand, extracting less than one-for-one risks exploitation....

The moral of the story is that the precise level of forgiveness that is optimal depends upon the environment. In particular, if the main danger is unending mutual recriminations, then a generous level of forgiveness is appropriate. But, if the main danger is from strategies that are good at exploiting easygoing rules, then an excess of forgiveness is costly. While the exact balance will be hard to determine in a given environment, the evidence of the tournament suggests that something approaching a one-for-one response to defection is likely to be quite effective in a wide range of settings. Therefore it is good advice to a player to reciprocate defection as well as cooperation.

4. DON'T BE TOO CLEVER

The tournament results show that in a Prisoner's Dilemma situation it is easy to be *too* clever. The very sophisticated rules did not do better than the simple ones. In fact, the so-called maximizing rules often did poorly because they got into a rut of mutual defection. A common problem with these rules is that they used complex methods of making inferences about the other player — and these inferences were wrong....

In deciding whether to carry an umbrella, we do not have to worry that the clouds will take our behavior into account. We can do a calculation about the chance of rain based on past experience. Likewise in a zero-sum game, such as chess, we can safely use the assumption that the other player will pick the most dangerous move that can be found, and we can act accordingly. Therefore it pays for us to be as sophisticated and as complex in our analysis as we can.

Non-zero-sum games, such as the Prisoner's Dilemma, are not like this. Unlike the clouds, the other player can respond to your own choices. And unlike the chess opponent, the other player in a Prisoner's Dilemma should not be regarded as someone who is out to defeat you. The other player will be watching your behavior for signs of whether you will reciprocate cooperation or not, and therefore your own behavior is likely to be echoed back to you.

Rules that try to maximize their own score while treating the other player as a fixed part of the environment ignore this aspect of the interaction, no matter how clever they are in calculating under their limiting assumptions. Therefore, it does not pay to be clever in modeling the other player if you leave out the reverberating process in which the other player is adapting to you, you are adapting to the other, and then the other player is adapting to your adaptation and so on....

In other words, too much complexity can appear to be total chaos. If you are using a strategy which appears random, then you also appear unresponsive to the other player. If you are unresponsive, then the other player has no incentive to cooperate with you. So being so complex as to be incomprehensible is very dangerous.... Once again, there is an important contrast between a zero-sum game like chess and a non–zero-sum game like the iterated Prisoner's Dilemma. In chess, it is useful to keep the other player guessing about your intentions. The more the other player is in doubt, the less efficient will be his or her strategy. Keeping one's intentions hidden is useful in a zero-sum setting where any inefficiency in the other player's behavior will be to your benefit. But in a non–zero-sum setting it does not always pay to be so clever. In the iterated Prisoner's Dilemma, you benefit from the other player's cooperation. The trick is to encourage that cooperation. A good way to do it is to make it clear that you will reciprocate. Words can help here, but as everyone knows, actions speak louder than words. That is why the easily understood actions of TIT FOR TAT are so effective.

> ## "NOISE"
>
> What happens in a Prisoner's Dilemma when communication between the parties is unclear? Researchers hypothesize that the Soviet shooting down of a South Korean airliner in 1983 (killing all 269 people aboard) could have been a result of this miscommunication (or "noise" as it is called in a Prisoner's Dilemma game). Why did the airliner stray off course? What was the Soviet Union conveying when it shot it down? Jianzhong Wu and Robert Axelrod conducted additional experiments in 1995 to determine the most effective strategy in Prisoner's Dilemma when there is noise. Their conclusion is that it still pays to reciprocate provided that it is accompanied by either some generosity (immediately forgiving a defection rather than responding in kind) or contrition (cooperating after the other player defects in response to *your* own defection). Generosity allows for the correction of the other player's errors and contrition corrects for your own errors in communication. Jianzhong Wu & Robert Axelrod, How to Cope with Noise in the Iterated Prisoner's Dilemma, 39 J. Conflict Res. 183 (1995).

What accounts for TIT FOR TAT's robust success is its combination of being nice, retaliatory, forgiving, and clear. Its niceness prevents it from getting into unnecessary trouble. Its retaliation discourages the other side from persisting whenever defection is tried. Its forgiveness helps restore mutual cooperation. And its clarity makes it intelligible to the other player, thereby eliciting long-term cooperation.

Notes and Questions

4.22 Do the results of the computer tournament surprise you? Why or why not?

4.23 What lessons do you draw from TIT FOR TAT? How would you use those lessons in the litigation discovery scenario? In negotiations?

4.24 How would you compare Axelrod's advice to the negotiation approaches discussed in this chapter?

4.25 For a review of recent advances in game theory as applied to negotiations, see David Sally, Game Theory Behaves, 87 Marq. L. Rev. 783 (2004).

How realistic is the Prisoner's Dilemma as applied to real life? This next excerpt explains both the attraction and drawbacks of using Prisoner's Dilemma in a model for negotiation.

 Michael L. Moffitt, **DISPUTES AS OPPORTUNITIES TO CREATE VALUE**

in The Handbook of Dispute Resolution 173, 182-183
(Michael L. Moffitt & Robert C. Bordone eds., 2005)

The prisoner's dilemma model holds two attractive features for theorists wishing to model disputants' bargaining behavior. First, the model captures part of the tension many negotiators experience around issues of cooperation and disclosure. Most negotiators recognize that if both sides fail to disclose important information, the likelihood of solving the problem in a jointly satisfactory manner is greatly reduced. At the same time, most negotiators recognize that unilateral disclosure creates a risk of exploitation. So it is with the prisoner's dilemma. Both might recognize the stable benefits of a good/good payout, and both fear being the lone cooperator who receives the awful payout. The second attractive aspect of the prisoner's dilemma is that, with its variable payouts, the prisoner's dilemma is a model of bargaining that does not assume a fixed pie. There are more total benefits to be divided among the negotiators in a condition of joint cooperation than in a condition of mutual defection. Negotiators receive more or less favorable results based on their behavior and on the behavior of their counterparts, and yet cooperation is not necessarily without risks. In these senses, the prisoner's dilemma is a reasonable model of certain aspects of bargaining.

Nevertheless, the prisoner's dilemma model is limited in its descriptive and prescriptive utility. One obvious drawback is that it assumes only two disputants or participants. While such conditions are clean and easy for economists to analyze, real world disputes rarely reflect the sterile condition in which only two people are affected by a dispute or its resolution. If one person injures another, many different parties may be affected by the injury or by a proposed resolution. The victim's family, the victim's employer, the injurer's family and employer, insurance companies for the various actors, and possibly society at large may be affected in ways that would be ignored if the only perspectives considered were the victim and the injurer.

Even more troubling from the perspective of modeling disputes, the prisoner's dilemma assumes that negotiators have a binary choice: cooperate or defect. This construction of negotiation poses two problems. First, as a descriptive matter, disputing conditions are rarely so straightforward. Much of what a negotiator does is neither purely cooperative nor purely the opposite. When I asked that careful question, was I cooperating or defecting? If I make a forceful, principled argument for my side, does that constitute cooperation or defection? How about when I made a generous counter-offer? Second, even if it were possible to discern cooperation from defection, the model is utterly silent on how it is that real world negotiators translate "cooperation" into value creation. Only by building on one or more of the value creating opportunities listed above can the two sides reap the rewards of cooperation.

So what actually happens when parties in the real world are given the choice to cooperate or defect? While rational actors often argue that negotiators should defect, in fact, there are numerous reasons that real-world negotiators cooperate. First, some negotiators will find defection as immoral, illegal or demonstrating bad character. Consider the following excerpt from physicist, game theorist, and Pulitzer Prize winner Douglas Hofstadter.

 Douglas R. Hofstadter, **METAMAGICAL THEMAS: QUESTING FOR THE ESSENCE OF MIND AND PATTERN**

730–731 (1985)

In the course of writing this column and thinking the ideas through, I was forced to confront over and over again the paradox that the Prisoner's Dilemma presents. I found that I simply could not accept the seemingly flawless logical conclusion that says that a rational player in a *non*iterated situation will always defect. . . .

Suppose I take my car in to get the oil changed. I know little about auto mechanics, so when I come in to pick it up, I really have no way to verify if they've done the job. For all I know, it's been sitting untouched in their parking lot all day, and as I drive off they may be snickering behind my back. On the other hand, maybe *I've* got the last laugh, for how do *they* know if that check I gave them will bounce?

This is a perfect example of how either of us *could* defect, but because the situation is iterated, neither of us is likely to do so. On the other hand, suppose I'm on my way across the country and have some radiator trouble near Gillette, Wyoming, and stop in town to get my radiator repaired there. There is a decent chance now that one party or the other will attempt to defect, because this kind of situation is not an iterated one. I'll probably never again need the services of this garage, and they'll never get another check from me. In the most crude sense, then, it's not in my interest to give them a good check, nor is it in theirs to fix my car. But do I really defect? Do I give out bad checks? No. Why not?

Notes and Questions

4.26 If you were in the same situation as Hofstadter — you were in a town where you would not return — would you write a bad check for a radiator repair? Why or why not? How is this scenario the same or different from the Prisoner's Dilemma?

4.27 Philosopher and moral theorist David Gauthier argues that people can make a rational choice (in addition to a moral one) to become "constrained maximizers," that is, someone who sacrifices short-term self-interest for a longer-term commitment to keep agreements. Gauthier reasons as follows: "A straight-forward maximizer, who is disposed to make maximizing choices [that is, defect in the Prisoner's Dilemma], must expect to be excluded from co-operative arrangements which he would find advantageous. A constrained maximizer may expect to be included in such arrangements. She benefits from her disposition, not in the choices she makes, but in her opportunities to choose." David Gauthier, Morals by Agreement 183 (1986). What do you think about this argument? Do people cooperate because it is the moral thing to do or the rational thing to do? Is it both? Is it neither?

A second reason that parties do not defect in a Prisoner's Dilemma is the repeated interaction between them. Either because of reputation, consequences, or the recognition that defection would lead to escalation, parties choose to cooperate. In this next excerpt, Professor Ronald Gilson explains the Japanese business community as an iterated Prisoner's Dilemma situation.

 Ronald J. Gilson, **VALUE CREATION BY BUSINESS LAWYERS: LEGAL SKILLS AND ASSET PRICING**

94 Yale L.J. 239, 309-310 (1984)

The picture I offer is of individuals in one company compelled to deal with the same individuals in other companies over their entire professional lives. Indeed, the Nenko system not only results in a continuity of contracts across companies, but also ensures that by the time a manager has reached the stage in his career when he has significant transactional authority, he will have dealt with his counterparts at other companies for a long period of time. This, together with the anticipation of repeated dealings with the same parties over an entire career, puts each manager in a situation where a significant penalty can be imposed if that individual behaves opportunistically. During the period in which a manager accrues the seniority necessary to a position of major transactional responsibility, repeated dealings with cohorts in other companies on smaller transactions result in an individual's developing a substantial stake in his own reputation for cooperative behavior. If the individual behaves opportunistically in one transaction, his credibility in future transactions with the same parties, and therefore the value of his human capital—his value to his employer—is reduced. The result is that a manager can expect personally to bear the cost of his opportunistic behavior, and the incentive to take advantage of a situation is therefore drastically reduced. The individual's long-earned reputation functions, in effect, as a bond that is forfeit if misbehavior occurs.

While I have no evidence of how much of the Japanese approach to contracting my analysis might explain, I find some support in the fact that, in those business settings in the United States where conditions resemble those in Japan, the approach to contracting is also somewhat similar. One example that comes to mind is Stewart Macaulay's classic study of the importance of the terms and conditions printed on the backs of purchase orders and acceptances to the way sellers and buyers behaved when a dispute arose.* Macaulay concluded that the formal terms had little impact; the parties worked out their problems in light of the conditions then existing largely without reference to the pre-existing formal agreement. My own anecdotal experience suggest that the point can be generalized. The lengthy, detailed documents Morita associates with the American approach to contracting largely involve situations, like an acquisition, where there is little anticipation of future transactions between the parties — where, in other words, final-period problems will exist in the absence of the transactional engineering of an artificial second round and other contractual restrictions on opportunism. In contrast, where repeated future dealings are anticipated, as in the small world of Macaulay's Wisconsin businessmen, patterns of transacting more closely resemble the Japanese approach.

Notes and Questions

4.28   In a similar example, lawyers who frequently litigate against one another are more likely to pursue cooperative litigation strategies and, thus, less likely to go to trial. See Jason Scott Johnston & Joel Waldfogel, Does Repeat Play Elicit Cooperation? Evidence from Federal Civil Litigation, 31 J. Legal Stud. 39 (2002). Why do you think this is so?

4.29   For additional discussion of how other influential factors, such as the payoffs of past decisions, affect decision makers in making their current choice, see Colin F. Camerer & Teck H. Ho, Strategic Learning and Teaching, in Wharton on Making Decisions (Stephen J. Hoch et al. eds., 2001).

A third reason that we cooperate is potentially due to biology — it is in human nature to cooperate rather than defect. Researchers have recently found a biological reason that we cooperate.

 Natalie Angier, **WHY WE'RE SO NICE: WE'RE WIRED TO COOPERATE**

N.Y. Times, July 23, 2002, at 1

What feels as good as chocolate on the tongue or money in the bank but won't make you fat or risk a subpoena from the Securities and Exchange Commission?

Hard as it may be to believe in these days of infectious greed and sabers unsheathed, scientists have discovered that the small, brave act of cooperating with another person, of choosing trust over cynicism, generosity over selfishness, makes the brain light up with quiet joy.

---

* Stewart Macaulay, Non-contractual Relations in Business, 28 Am. Soc. Rev. 55 (1963).

Studying neural activity in young women who were playing a classic laboratory game called the Prisoner's Dilemma, in which participants can select from a number of greedy or cooperative strategies as they pursue financial gain, researchers found that when the women chose mutualism over "me-ism," the mental circuitry normally associated with reward-seeking behavior swelled to life.

And the longer the women engaged in a cooperative strategy, the more strongly flowed the blood to the pathways of pleasure.

The researchers had thought that the biggest response would occur in cases where one person cooperated and the other defected, when the cooperator might feel that she was being treated unjustly.

Instead, the brightest signals arose in cooperative alliances and in those neighborhoods of the brain already known to respond to desserts, pictures of pretty faces, money, cocaine and any number of licit or illicit delights.

Notes and Questions

4.30 Although the experiment was only performed on women, the researchers predicted that these findings would be the same for both genders. The researchers thought that this push to cooperate might explain why humans behave better than other species. What do you think? How did you feel playing a Prisoner's Dilemma game?

4.31 Empathy for the other side in a negotiation can reduce the impetus to defect, even when the other side has already done so. In an experiment using a single round of Prisoner's Dilemma, almost half of the participants (45 percent) did not defect despite the other side's defection, when induced to feel empathy for them because of a recent romantic breakup. C. Daniel Batson & Nadia Ahmad, Empathy-Induced Altruism in a Prisoner's Dilemma II: What if the Target of Empathy Has Defected?, 31 Eur. J. Soc. Psychol. 25-36 (2001). How can negotiators use this information?

Finally, another reason that negotiators may cooperate is that defection costs lives.

> Back in the 1950s at the height of the cold war, President Truman got an alarming piece of advice from the scientists at his military think-tank, the RAND corporation. The Soviets have nuclear capability, they said, we have nuclear capability, better nuke them before they nuke us. This, according to game theory, their latest piece of mathematical wizardry, was the only rational course of action. While an agreement not to push the button would benefit both parties, cooperation is also the riskiest strategy because you stand to lose everything if the other guy gets in there first. Better, then, to act — and hang the consequences.
>
> History records that Truman made a different choice, and that the Soviets also kept their nuclear arsenal in check. How could RAND mathematicians have got it so wrong?... [W]here Truman's advisers went wrong was in assuming that the best decisions are totally rational....

It is clear that when we weigh up the costs and benefits of various courses of action, we do not just consider the material gains but also the social and emotional ones.... Each of us puts a different value on the various components we must consider to reach our final decision. "Individually, it comes down to the personal motivations of each person: more money or be a nice person?"... This might suggest that you can never reduce decision making down to a mathematical formula, but the neuroscientists are not daunted. On the surface, the problem looks like comparing apples and pears, but the brain must use a common currency to encode all the different elements of cost and benefit so that they can be weighed up. If you can find the part of the brain where this common currency is computed, perhaps then you'll have the key to predicting the choices people make.

Laura Spinney, Why We Do What We Do, 183 New Scientist 32, 32-33 (2004).

This next excerpt from Robert Axelrod is one of his applications of the Prisoner's Dilemma to real life where defection would cost lives. Amazingly, he found that cooperation occurred between combatants in war.

 Robert Axelrod, THE EVOLUTION OF COOPERATION

73-87 (1984)

Sometimes cooperation emerges where it is least expected. During World War I, the Western Front was the scene of horrible battles for a few yards of territory. But between these battles, and even during them at other places along the five-hundred-mile line in France and Belgium, the enemy soldiers often exercised considerable restraint. A British staff officer on a tour of the trenches remarked that he was "astonished to observe German soldiers walking about within rifle range behind their own line. Our men appeared to take no notice.... These people evidently did not know there was a war on. Both sides apparently believed in the policy of 'live and let live.'"

This is not an isolated example. The live-and-let-live system was endemic in trench warfare. It flourished despite the best efforts of senior officers to stop it, despite the passions aroused by combat, despite the military logic of kill or be killed, and despite the ease with which the high command was able to repress any local efforts to arrange a direct truce....

[A]t the national level, World War I approximated a zero-sum game in which losses for one side represented gains for the other side. But at the local level, along the front line, mutual restraint was much preferred to mutual punishment.

The first stage of the war, which began in August 1914, was highly mobile and very bloody. But as the lines stabilized, nonaggression between troops emerged spontaneously in many places along the front. The earliest instances may have been associated with meals which were served at the same times on both sides of no-man's land.

By Christmas there was extensive fraternization, a practice which the headquarters frowned upon. In the following months, direct truces were occasionally arranged by shouts or by signals.

A key factor was the realization that if one side would exercise restraint, then the other might reciprocate. Similarities in basic needs and activities let the soldiers appreciate that the other side would probably not be following a strategy of unconditional defection. For example, in the summer of 1915, a soldier saw that the enemy would be likely to reciprocate cooperation based on the desire for fresh rations.

It would be child's play to shell the road behind the enemy's trenches crowded as it must be with ration wagons and water carts, into a bloodstained wilderness . . . but on the whole there is silence. After all, if you prevent your enemy from drawing his rations, his remedy is simple; he will prevent you from drawing yours.

During the periods of mutual restraint, the enemy soldiers took pains to show each other that they could indeed retaliate if necessary. . . . These demonstrations of retaliatory capabilities helped police the system by showing that restraint was not due to weakness, and that defection would be self defeating.

When a defection actually occurred, the retaliation was often more than would be called for by TIT FOR TAT. Two-for-one or three-for-one was a common response to an act that went beyond what was considered acceptable.

Another problem that had to be overcome to maintain the stability of cooperation was the rotation of troops. . . . But sometimes it was quite sufficient for an old timer to point out to a newcomer that "Mr. Bosche ain't a bad fellow. You leave 'em alone; he'll leave you alone." This socialization allowed one unit to pick up the game right where the other left it.

What finally destroyed the live-and-let-live system was the institution of a type of incessant aggression that the headquarters *could* monitor. This was the raid. . . . There was no effective way to pretend that a raid had been undertaken when it had not. The live-and-let-live system could not cope with the disruption caused by the hundreds of small raids. After a raid neither side knew what to expect next. The side that had raided could expect retaliation but could not predict when, where or how.

The mechanism for evolution involved neither blind mutation nor survival of the fittest. Unlike blind mutation, the soldiers understood their situation and actively tried to make the most of it. They understood the indirect consequences of their acts as embodied in what I call the echo principle: "To provide discomfort for the other is but a roundabout way of providing it for themselves." . . . They learned that cooperation had to be based upon reciprocity.

The live-and-let-live system that emerged in the bitter trench warfare of World War I demonstrates that friendship is hardly necessary for cooperation based upon reciprocity to get started. Under suitable circumstances, cooperation can develop even between antagonists.

Notes and Questions

4.32 Recognizing that companies often negotiate with the same vendors, suppliers, and partners repeatedly, Danny Ertel argues that executives need to move to a long-term view from a situational view of negotiation by creating a negotiation infrastructure for a coordinated approach. See Danny Ertel, Turning Negotiation into a Corporate Capability, Harv. Bus. Rev., May-June 1999, at 55.

4.33 Scholars have noted increased collaboration among businesses rather than competition. Barbara Gray argues that collaboration is a necessary response to turbulent conditions. Six contextual factors are associated with increased environmental turbulence and are creating powerful incentives to collaborate:

1. Rapid economic and technological change
2. Declining productivity growth and increasing competitive pressures
3. Global interdependence
4. Blurring of boundaries between business, government, and labor
5. Shrinking federal revenues for social programs
6. Dissatisfaction with the judicial process for solving problems

Barbara Gray, The Impetus to Collaborate, in Collaborating: Finding Common Ground for Multi-Party Problems 26, 29 (1989).

D. NEGOTIATOR'S DILEMMA

The next two excerpts discuss the similarity between the Prisoner's Dilemma and the Negotiator's Dilemma.

 David A. Lax & James K. Sebenius, **THE MANAGER AS NEGOTIATOR: BARGAINING FOR COOPERATION AND COMPETITIVE GAIN**

29-30, 32, 38-40 (1986)

Negotiators and analysts tend to fall into two groups that are guided by warring conceptions of the bargaining process. In the left-hand corner are the "value creators" and in the right-hand corner are the "value claimers." Value creators tend to believe that, above all, successful negotiators must be inventive and cooperative enough to devise an agreement that yields considerable gain to each party, relative to no-agreement possibilities. Some speak about the need for replacing the "win-lose" image of negotiation with "win-win" negotiation, from which all parties presumably derive great value. . . .

Value claimers, on the other hand, tend to see this drive for joint gain as naïve and weak-minded. For them, negotiation is hard, tough bargaining. The object of negotiation is to convince the other guy that he wants what you have to offer much more than you want what he has. . . . To "win" at negotiation — and thus make the other fellow "lose" — one must start high, concede slowly, exaggerate the value of concessions, minimize the benefits of the other's concessions, conceal information, argue forcefully on behalf of principles that imply favorable settlement, make commitments to accept only highly favorable agreements, and be willing to outwait the other fellow. . . .

Both of these images of negotiation are incomplete and inadequate. Value creating and value claiming are linked parts of negotiation. Both processes are present. No matter how much creative problem solving enlarges the pie, it must still be divided;

value that has been created must be claimed. And, if the pie is not enlarged, there will be less to divide; there is more value to be claimed if one has helped create it first. An essential tension in negotiation exists between cooperative moves to create value and competitive moves to claim it. . . .

Consider two negotiators (. . . named Ward and Stone) each of whom can choose between two negotiating styles: creating value (being open, sharing information about preferences and beliefs, not being misleading about minimum requirements, and so forth) and claiming value (being cagey and misleading about preferences, beliefs, and minimum requirements; making commitments and threats, and so forth). Each has the same two options for any tactical choice. If both choose to create value, they each receive a good outcome, which we will call GOOD for each. If Ward chooses to create value and Stone chooses to claim value, then Stone does even better than if he had chosen to create value — rank this outcome GREAT for Stone — but Ward does much worse — rank this outcome TERRIBLE for him. Similarly, if Stone is the creative one and Ward is the claimer, then Ward does well — rank this outcome for him as GREAT — while Stone's outcome is TERRIBLE. If both claim, they fail to find joint gains and come up with a mediocre outcome, which we call ME-DIOCRE for both. . . . In each box, Ward's payoff is in the lower left corner and Stone's is in the upper right. Thus, when Ward claims and Stone creates, Ward's outcome is GREAT while Stone's is TERRIBLE. [See Figure 2.1.]

		Stone's Choice	
		Create	Claim
	Create	GOOD GOOD	GREAT TERRIBLE
Ward's Choice	**Claim**	TERRIBLE GREAT	MEDIOCRE MEDIOCRE

Figure 2.1
Negotiator's Dilemma
The lower left entry in each cell is Ward's outcome; the second entry is Stone's.

Now, if Ward were going to create, Stone would prefer the GREAT outcome obtained by claiming to the GOOD outcome he could have obtained by creating; so, Stone should claim. If, on the other hand, Ward were going to claim, Stone would prefer the MEDIOCRE outcome from claiming to the TERRIBLE outcome he would receive from creating. In fact, no matter what Ward does, it seems that Stone would be better off trying to claim value!

Similarly, Ward should also prefer to claim. By symmetric reasoning, if Stone chooses to create, Ward prefers the GREAT outcome he gets by claiming to the GOOD outcome he gets from creating. If Stone claims, Ward prefers the MEDIOCRE outcome he gets from claiming to the TERRIBLE outcome he gets from creating.

Both negotiators choose to claim. They land in the lower-right-hand box and receive MEDIOCRE outcomes. They leave joint gains on the table, since both would prefer the GOOD outcomes they could have received had they both chosen to create value and ended up in the upper-left-hand box.

This is the crux of the Negotiator's Dilemma. Individually rational decisions to emphasize claiming tactics by being cagey and misleading lead to a mutually undesirable outcome. As described, this situation has the structure of the famous "Prisoner's Dilemma." In such situations, the motivation to protect oneself and employ tactics for claiming value is compelling.

 Robert H. Mnookin, Scott R. Peppet & Andrew S. Tulumello,
BEYOND WINNING: NEGOTIATING TO CREATE VALUE IN DEALS AND DISPUTES

27, 40, 42-43 (2000)

We have now arrived at the core of the problem. How can you create value while minimizing the risks of exploitation in the distributive aspects of negotiation?

The challenge of problem-solving negotiation is to acknowledge and manage this tension. Keep in mind that this tension *cannot be resolved*. It can only be managed. The goal is to design processes for negotiation that allow value creation to occur, when possible, while minimizing the risks of exploitation. . . .

No matter how good you are at brainstorming and no matter how carefully you search out value-creating trades, at some point the pie has to be sliced.

What happens to interest-based, collaborative problem-solving when you turn to distributive issues? Some negotiators act as if problem-solving has to be tossed overboard when the going gets tough. We could not disagree more. In our experience, it's when distributive issues are at the forefront that problem-solving skills are most desperately needed. [The] goal at this point is to treat distributive issues as a shared problem. Both sides know that distributive issues exist. She knows that, other things being equal, she'd like to earn more and [he] would like to pay less. There's no getting around it. At the same time, however, she doesn't want to behave in a way that would damage her relationship. . . .

Sometimes, of course, you won't be able to find a solution that satisfies both sides. No matter how hard you try, you will continue to disagree about salary, the amount to be paid in a bonus, or some aspect of a dispute settlement. Norms may have helped move you closer together, but there's still a big gap between the two sides. What should you do?

Think about process. How can you design a process that would fairly resolve this impasse? In a dispute settlement, you might be able to hire a mediator to address the distributive issues that are still open. Is there anyone both sides trust enough to decide the issue? Could you put five possible agreements into a hat and pick one at random? Procedural solutions can often rescue a distributive negotiation that has reached an impasse. They need not involve complicated alternative dispute resolution procedures that cost money and time. Instead, you can often come up with simple process solutions that will resolve a distributive deadlock and allow you to move forward. . . .

CONCLUSION

The tension between value creation and value distribution exists in almost all negotiations. But as our teaching and consulting have shown us, many people tend to see negotiation as purely one or the other. Some people see the world in zero-sum terms — as solely distributive. We work hard to demonstrate to people that there are nearly always opportunities to create value. Others believe that, with cooperation, the pie can be made so large that distributive questions will disappear. For these negotiators, we emphasize that there are always distributive issues to address. . . .

The problem-solving approach we have suggested here will not make distributive issues go away or this first tension of negotiation disappear. But it does outline an approach that will help you find value-creating opportunities when they exist and resolve distributive issues efficiently and as a shared problem.

Notes and Questions

4.34 In what negotiation scenarios would you expect to face the Negotiator's Dilemma? In what scenarios would you not expect to?

4.35 How would you apply the lessons learned in TIT FOR TAT to the Negotiator's Dilemma?

4.36 Hofstader writes that he would not write a bad check even if he could get away with it. What would he likely say about the Negotiator's Dilemma? Should we make discovery more difficult for the other side in litigation even if the judge is unlikely to sanction us? Should we refuse to share information about a negotiation even if the other side shares information with us?

E. CHOOSING AMONG NEGOTIATION APPROACHES

You have now seen that there are a variety of different approaches to negotiation — including both the analysis of what is at stake and the behaviors or styles that negotiators use to approach each other. Consider what happens when negotiators choose different models or approaches with which to work with each other. What happens when the negotiators are on different parts of the Thomas map at the beginning of this chapter? Carrie Menkel-Meadow has suggested some variables or factors that might be useful in considering which approach to negotiation might be appropriate in a particular case.

Carrie Menkel-Meadow, THE ART AND SCIENCE OF PROBLEM SOLVING NEGOTIATION

Trial Mag., June 1999, at 50-51

Rather than employing a uniform behavioral repertoire in all cases, the good problem solver considers at least these factors, which may affect how the negotiation should be conducted:

- *Subject matter:* Is this a business transaction? A tort suit?
- *Issues involved:* Is the dispute over an indivisible item? Is there a principle involved, such as a constitutional claim?
- *Voluntariness:* Has the negotiation been required by a court, law or contract, or is purely voluntary?
- *Relationship of the parties and/or lawyers:* Is the relationship ongoing, or is there potential for relations sometime in the future?
- *Visibility:* How much publicity surrounds the case? Who else will "view" the negotiations or the outcome?
- *Accountability:* To whom is the negotiator or party accountable? Family members of clients? Members of organizations? The public?
- *Stake:* Who has most to gain or lose? What is most important to whom?
- *Routineness:* Will the outcome resolve a lot of similar problems? Are there expectations about "common ways" to solve the problem, and, if that is so, are they appropriate?
- *Power:* Who has it? Is it variable? Can power or its perception be altered in the negotiation?
- *Personalities:* What are the personality traits of the lawyers and clients? Should other principals or agents be used if there are known personality conflicts?
- *Culture:* Are there differences in expectations due to the nationality, ethnicity, or gender of the parties or the geographical location of the negotiation?

Notes and Questions

4.37 Can you think of any other specific factors that might influence which negotiation approach would be appropriate in particular settings?

4.38 Do all parties in a negotiation have to "share" their assessments of these factors to choose a negotiation model together? Or, can each party make its own choice, based on its analysis?

PART II | SKILLS FOR NEGOTIATION

 **Chapter 5** | # Working with Your Client: Interviewing, Counseling, and Representing

Negotiation begins with learning what your client hopes to accomplish in a negotiation. This chapter discusses how lawyers, as legal problem solvers and agents for their clients, discover what clients need and hope to gain in negotiation. The chapter also discusses how lawyers counsel their clients about changing expectations and outcomes as the dynamic process of negotiation unfolds. Many of the skills presented in this chapter (for example, interviewing and questioning clients) are also useful when working with the other parties in negotiation.

A. INTERVIEWING AND COUNSELING

1. Learning Your Client's Needs

Problem solving is based on the idea of truly meeting your client's needs. Clearly the first step in that process is finding out what those needs are. This begins with the client interview and then continues throughout the negotiation process.

 David A. Binder, Paul B. Bergman, Susan C. Price & Paul K. Tremblay, **LAWYERS AS COUNSELORS: A CLIENT-CENTERED APPROACH**

2-11 (2d ed. 2004)

Clients come to lawyers seeking help in solving problems. . . . [T]he range of people and problems that you are likely to encounter as a lawyer is enormous. The array embraces differences in size, complexity, emotional content and legal status. Some problems involve disputes over past events and others focus on planning for the future. Nonetheless, all of the problems have something in common — the clients hope that satisfactory solutions can be achieved with the aid of your lawyerly knowledge, skills and judgment.

Thus, no matter who your client, what the substantive legal issues or whether a situation involves litigation or planning, your principal role as a lawyer will almost always be the same — to help clients achieve satisfactory and effective solutions to problems. . . .

This [approach] sets forth a "client-centered" approach to counseling. The client-centered conception has its source in a perspective that legal problems typically raise both legal and non-legal concerns for clients, that collaboration between attorneys and clients is likely to enhance the effectiveness of problem-solving, and that clients ordinarily are in the best position to make important decisions. . . .

CLIENTS ARE AUTONOMOUS "OWNERS" OF THEIR PROBLEMS

Underlying client-centeredness is the philosophy that clients are autonomous and therefore deserving of making important decisions that lead to resolution of their legal problems. Whether a client is a labor organization involved in negotiations for a new contract, a parent with an abusive spouse, a young couple who want an estate plan that will protect their young children or a developer seeking permission to demolish an existing building, clients do not give up the right to shape their destinies simply because they seek the help of lawyers. . . . After all, clients, and not lawyers, live with decisions' consequences. For example, if a plaintiff in a wrongful termination matter decides to accept a sum of money in settlement rather than pursue reinstatement through trial, it is the plaintiff and not the lawyer whose future life the decision helps to shape. . . .

CLIENTS ARE GENERALLY IN A BETTER POSITION THAN LAWYERS TO IDENTIFY AND ASSESS THE IMPORTANCE OF SOLUTIONS' NON-LEGAL CONSEQUENCES

Clients consult lawyers rather than other helping professionals when they recognize that problems have important legal dimensions. For example, people who want to leave property to relatives and friends while minimizing the impact of taxes and other expenses will go to a lawyer because they realize that if their wishes are to be carried out, their estate planning documents must comply with legal requirements. . . .

However, a second justification for client-centeredness emanates from the reality that the satisfactoriness of solutions often depends on how well they respond to clients' concerns about non-legal consequences. Significant non-legal ramifications are typically embedded in solutions to legal problems. . . .

The significance and frequency of non-legal ramifications that necessarily attach to potential solutions to legal problems affect your approach to counseling because clients are almost always in a better position than you to identify non-legal consequences. This is especially likely to be true because clients with similar legal problems may have very different non-legal concerns. That is, two clients' matters may concern the same legal *issues*, but their legal *problems* may be very different because of differences in the clients' circumstances, personalities and values. . . .

Moreover, clients are typically in a better position than lawyers to assess the importance of the potential non-legal consequences of proposed solutions. For instance, the business executive faced with the decision to fire an employee will undoubtedly be in a better position than you to assess the importance of the harm to company morale and the effect of that harm on the company's operations when it comes time to decide whether to actually fire the employee.

In sum, clients are typically in the best position to identify non-legal conse-quences and assess their importance. Because such consequences significantly affect the determination of what solutions are most satisfactory, it makes sense for clients to play an active role in developing and analyzing potential solutions and to have the final say in deciding what course(s) of action to choose when trying to resolve legal problems. . . .

CLIENTS ARE NORMALLY IN A BETTER POSITION THAN LAWYERS TO DETERMINE WHAT RISKS ARE WORTH TAKING

A third primary justification for client-centered counseling emanates from the fact that decisions in legal matters (as in most other aspects of life) are almost always made under conditions of uncertainty. . . . For example, neither you nor clients can know for certain whether a client who settles a lawsuit will suffer "buyer's remorse," what the costs of complying with environmental requirements will be, or the extent to which firing a popular employee will harm employee morale.

However, as a few minutes observing the action at a Las Vegas blackjack table will verify, people vary enormously in their willingness to take risks. Some people are by dint of their personalities more willing to take risks than are other people. More-over, risk-taking is often situational; people may take risks in some situations that they would be unwilling to take in others. For example, clients' readiness to take risks may be influenced by the importance they attach to the gains they foresee if their predictions are correct or to the losses they fear will ensue if their predictions are wrong. . . .

CLIENTS ARE CAPABLE OF AND INTERESTED IN PARTICIPATING IN THE COUNSELING PROCESS AND MAKING IMPORTANT DECISIONS

Other justifications for client-centeredness would mean little if clients typically were incapable of making important decisions or rarely were willing to participate in the counseling process. However, quite the opposite is likely to be true. That is, most clients are quite capable of actively participating in the effort to resolve important problems. Moreover, clients typically want to participate in counseling, though of course their level of interest is likely to vary according to such factors as the relative importance of decisions and the time available to decide. . . .

ACTIVE LAWYER-CLIENT COLLABORATION PROMOTES EFFECTIVE IMPLEMENTATION OF DECISIONS

Once decisions are made, clients often have to implement them. In such situations, clients' active participation in the counseling process enhances the likelihood that they will effectively carry out the tasks necessary to implement decisions.

For example, assume that your client is involved in a dispute that the client hopes to resolve through mediation. You will not participate in the mediation, and the client has consulted you so as to go into mediation with an understanding of potential legal rights, solutions and pitfalls. Surely the client's ability to achieve a satisfactory outcome through mediation is enhanced if you and the client have collaborated in an analysis of potential outcomes and their likely consequences.

SEEK OUT POTENTIAL NON-LEGAL CONSEQUENCES

Helping clients develop satisfactory solutions requires you not only to uncover information that is relevant to legal *issues*, but also to help clients identify non-legal ramifications that are embedded in solutions to their legal *problems*. Hence, one hallmark of your counseling conversations is to actively encourage clients to identify potential non-legal consequences. With potential non-legal consequences on the table, you can assist clients in evaluating their likely impact on potential solutions. Actively encouraging clients to talk about non-legal concerns is often necessary because clients may not on their own identify and evaluate the non-legal ramifications that may legitimately bear on the problem-solving process. . . .

With experience, you will no doubt anticipate possible non-legal ramifications that tend to accompany particular types of legal problems. You may certainly raise such non-legal possibilities in the course of counseling conversations. At the same time, you will also need to encourage clients to identify non-legal concerns that may not be on your "radar screen" because no amount of experience and legal expertise can enable you to fully recognize or evaluate all the non-legal consequences that may attend a given client's situation.

ASK CLIENTS TO SUGGEST POTENTIAL SOLUTIONS

Clients reasonably expect you to develop potential solutions to their legal problems, and client-centered counseling is certainly consistent with your doing so. However, a second hallmark of client-centered counseling is that you encourage clients to identify potential solutions as well. Clients' backgrounds and experiences may lead them to suggest sensible options that you might have overlooked. At the very least, clients' suggested solutions may suggest concerns that you can account for in solutions that you devise.

By way of illustration, consider a situation in which you represent a building contractor who has been sued by a residents' association for alleged construction defects in a large apartment complex. The residents contend among other things that a basement laundry facility floods as a result of the contractor's failure to properly seal the foundation walls. The contractor is probably more likely than you to identify a solution that includes a repair process that will cure the flooding. Thus, asking the contractor to suggest possible solutions promotes the likelihood that the contractor is satisfied with the eventual outcome.

ENCOURAGE CLIENTS TO MAKE IMPORTANT DECISIONS

A third hallmark of client-centered counseling is that you encourage clients to make important decisions. The strategies and techniques that constitute a client-centered approach put clients in a position to make knowledgeable decisions by facilitating identification of possible outcomes and their likely consequences. At the end of the day, however, the factors described above, such as the inevitable presence of non-legal ramifications and variations in values and risk-aversion, suggest that important decisions are for clients to make....

PROVIDE ADVICE BASED ON CLIENTS' VALUES

Within the universe of decision-makers are clients who may require that you take a more active role in decision-making. For example, even experienced and sophisticated clients may not want to make decisions until hearing your advice. Other clients may be "socially disempowered" from decision-making. That is, because of mental impairment or social economic or cultural disadvantage, some clients may need your advice as to the solution that you think is in their best interests....

Sometimes law school can inadvertently reinforce the lack of understanding we show to clients. Consider the following story from Professor Christine Hurt's tort class (no pun intended!).

 Christine Hurt, NO HARM INTENDED: TEACHING A TORTS CLASS OFFERED ENDLESS OPPORTUNITY FOR DARK HUMOR — UNTIL IT BECAME NO LAUGHING MATTER

Chron. Higher Educ., May 27, 2005, at C3

At the beginning of the semester, I would have told you that "Torts" was an incredibly fun class to teach. The facts are fascinating and often gruesome; the cases we discussed had blood and guts and crazy freak accidents. We had a lot of guffaws at the expense of some of the plaintiffs and defendants in our cases, who either undertook actions that were incredibly ill-conceived or who met with unpredictable consequences.

One case involved a service-station waiting room and a cast of characters including a dim-witted attendant, a space heater, and a customer wearing a purple fake-fur coat. When the gas attendant decided to blow gasoline out of a hose in front of the space heater, that action produced ghastly results for the coat wearer, whom we then referred to as the "human torch." Other cases involved car wrecks, train wrecks, gun accidents, swimming accidents, staircase accidents, fraternity parties, medical malpractice, and mean dogs. We laughed and laughed, in the way that people do when they spend large amounts of time talking about horrible tragedies.

It might not sound like it, but I was very conscientious in teaching my class. We discussed legal doctrine, but we also discussed underlying public policy. I wanted my students to be aware of the economic effect of assigning liability to classes of individuals, businesses, or industries and also the personal effect of limiting liability. I wanted my students to be able to discuss these topics openly and well, without reliance on general propositions made either by tort-reform or by plaintiffs'-rights groups....

By midsemester, I thought things were going great. I loved my students, they seemed to love me, and everyone was learning. I had accommodated several students who ran into problems, including one with a chronic illness and another who told me the first week of class that he had had a "tragedy in his immediate family." In the latter case, I didn't want to pry, so I had assured the student that he was needed more at home than at law school at that time and patted myself on the back for being so understanding.

The last week of the semester, I found out the nature of the student's tragedy and was floored by my inadvertent, semester-long insensitivity to him.

I had negligently injured my student every time he came to class. Let me explain. My student (I'll call him David) had two siblings. In August both siblings were in a car accident. One died instantly. The other remained in a coma until he died two months later. Between the two deaths, David sat through my class four hours a week while I made up an infinite number of hypotheticals beginning with "Say you hit someone in your car, and they die/they are in a coma/they are paralyzed/they are disabled...."

For four hours a week, David heard me and the rest of the class speak in embarrassingly cold terms about what the value of a life is in calculating damages: Can someone in a coma recover damages for pain and suffering when the person has no awareness of pain? How much are the expected lost wages of a college student when we don't know for sure if he would have graduated or been successful in a particular field? Should a parent who loses a child recover damages for the mental anguish?...

On the last day of class, as I was wrapping up, I attempted to rectify the situation somewhat. I reminded my students that every person in our textbook's cases, whether plaintiff or defendant, was a real person who had either been injured, or caused injury to others, and would therefore never be the same.

I admitted that in the interest of being able to discuss theoretically the issues posed by the cases that we had distanced ourselves from these people and had even used humor to disarm both the physically grisly and emotionally wrenching scenarios. However, as lawyers, we have to be sensitive to the fact that we are not dealing with fictional characters but real human beings. No one ever anticipates being a tort victim, I told them, but obviously some of us will be.

New professors learn a lot the first time that they teach a course, and my first semester in "Torts" was no exception. So as I swap topics around in my syllabus for next year, I am putting that speech into my notes for the first day of class.

––––––––––––––––

In this next article, Warren Lehman demonstrates that a client's interest, *as the client defines it*, must be the goal of the lawyer. In the article that follows, Chris Guthrie and David Sally point out some of the problems with determining the client's interests.

 Warren Lehman, **THE PURSUIT OF A CLIENT'S INTEREST**

77 Mich. L. Rev. 1078, 1079, 1088-1089, 1091-1093 (1979)

Clients come to lawyers for help with important decisions in their business and private lives. How do lawyers respond to these requests, and how ought they?

Doubtless many clients, thinking they know what they want — or wishing to appear to know — encourage the lawyer to believe he is consulted solely for a technical expertise, for a knowledge of how to do legal things, for his ability to interpret legal words, or for the objective way he looks at legal and practical outcomes. . . .

What I want to discuss in the balance of this Article is how utilitarianism in specific kinds of familiar counseling situations leads to giving clients bad advice, advice that sacrifices their humanity in the name of seemingly self-evident goods.

My father-in-law, Charles Wooster, tells of clients of his, a husband and wife, who had been moved to give a sizeable gift to a friend who had shown them care and love. Mr. Wooster encouraged them to put off giving until the next year because a gift given that year would have been taxed less heavily. The following January, husband and wife were killed in the same accident, before the gift was delivered; there was thereafter no way to transfer the gift. The intended donee had lost out because of Mr. Wooster's tax advice. So, too, the donors had been denied the pleasure of bestowing the gift. The event suggests to a nice conscience that perhaps the advice had been wrong in the first place. Mr. Wooster was unhappy with the result, but could see nothing else — with the clients alive before him and no crystal ball — that would have been right for him to have done. . . .

A practicing lawyer, call him Doe, who also teaches client counseling, said that he is very concerned, in doing estate matters, with the possibility that a client will be overborne by information about tax consequences. His tactic to avoid that result is to persuade his client — before there is any mention of those consequences — to expand in as much detail as possible upon what it is he wants to do. Only after that does Doe point out costs and mention ways the client's plan could be changed to save money. In teaching as well as practice, Doe is trying to take account of the power a lawyer has to impress upon a client the importance of his lawyerly considerations. The progress represented by Doe's concerned approach is the recognition that the client's values may not be the lawyer's, or more precisely, that the real, live client's interests may not match those of the "standard client" for whom lawyers are wont to model their services. . . .

I told Doe of a friend of mine, a widow recovering from alcoholism, who is fifty-four years old. Her house has become a burden to her, perhaps even a threat to her sobriety, although it might seem overly dramatic to say as much to a stranger. If she waits until she is fifty-five, the better part of a year, the large capital gain on the house will be tax free. She decided she did not want to go to a lawyer for fear he might talk her into putting off the sale. I asked Doe if that were realistic. He said her fear was well grounded; a lawyer might well give her the impression that another year in the house ought to be suffered for the tax saving. (I expect a lawyer's inclination to press the merits of his money-saving advice reflects, among other things, a desire to feel that his expertise is really useful. We may know no other way to judge our own usefulness.)

One possible analysis of these cases is that suggested by Doe: that the lawyer needs to be careful to discover what it is the client is really about, to give fullest possible opportunity for her interests to be explored, and to avoid the over-bearing assertion of simple money saving. . . .

The objection to utilitarian advice that we have been talking about is that there is a need to insert moral values into the calculation utilitarianism urges us to make. Once the choice of values comes out into the open, the question is whether it is to be done by the lawyer alone, by the client alone, or jointly. Once the choice comes out into the open the attractive apparent neutrality of utilitarian consequentialism disappears. The value questions must finally be faced. It is possible through self-awareness and honesty, which is the important basis of Doe's style of advice, to reduce the likelihood of the lawyer's imposing either his own values or the set presumed to be adopted by the standard, rationally self-interested ego. But there is an even more general problem with the utilitarian giving of advice that is independent of the values we assign to specific outcomes. That general problem is consequentialism itself: the idea that the way to decide how to act now is not to consider one's present disposition and the merit of the act in question, but to consider the value of the consequences of doing the act. . . .

So little are we allowed to regard the present that a client is likely to have difficulty even expressing the wise, human inclination to do the presently right-seeming and satisfying thing, especially if the lawyer is telling him how this or that will be saved or protected by deferral. The lawyer becomes an ally of the mean spirit that tells us we ought to live in and for the future; we ought to suffer and deprive ourselves of the only gratification possible — that which occurs presently. Present gratification in the law office is the prerogative of the eccentric client, the crotchety and willful. The solid everyday client does not do that kind of thing, and the lawyer will not let him.

 Chris Guthrie & David Sally, **THE IMPACT OF THE IMPACT BIAS ON NEGOTIATION**

87 Marq. L. Rev. 817, 817-818, 821, 827-828 (2004)

The defining feature of "principled" or "problem-solving" negotiation is its emphasis on "interests" rather than "positions." In negotiation parlance, "positions" are what disputants declare they want. "Interests," on the other hand, "are the silent movers behind the hubbub of positions." They are the "needs, desires, concerns, and fears" that underlie stated positions. . . .

Indeed, according to the proponents of this approach to negotiation, "the object of a negotiation is to satisfy underlying interests." On this view, disputants should try to get what they *really* want at the bargaining table.

But what if they do not know what they *really* want?

I.   IMPACT BIAS

Researchers from an emerging movement within psychology — variously labeled "positive psychology" or "hedonic psychology" or "affective forecasting" — have learned a great deal in recent years about what people really want. Of greatest relevance to this essay, researchers studying affective forecasting have discovered that people are often mistaken about what they want or what will make them happy. In more technical terms, people often find that what they predict they want or how they predict they will feel — i.e., their "predicted utility" — is different from their actual experience — i.e., their "experienced utility. . . . "

II. "MISWANTING" IN NEGOTIATION

The potential impact of the impact bias on negotiation is straightforward. If people in general are likely to have difficulty determining what they really want because of a tendency to overestimate how attaining that item will affect their sense of well-being, disputants are also likely to have difficulty identifying what they really want in negotiation for the very same reason. Just like the consumer who erroneously believes he will be much happier if he purchases a new BMW, the disputant seeking to obtain vindication from the other side or financial security or whatever else may very well overestimate how much obtaining it will contribute to her sense of well-being. Indeed, it seems reasonable to speculate that the added complexity of a negotiation — in particular, the tension and conflict between the negotiators — will make it even more difficult for disputants to discern what they really want. . . .

Research on the impact bias gives one pause, however, because it suggests that clients may have great difficulty predicting accurately what they want out of a negotiation. Even given this difficulty, the client will generally know better than anyone else what she wants. But in some circumstances, her lawyer may have insight into her wants that even she does not. Namely, in those cases where the client is a "one-shotter" (perhaps in a divorce case or a personal injury suit), and the lawyer is a "repeat player" who has represented dozens or even hundreds of similarly situated clients in like cases, it seems *possible* that the lawyer might know better than the client what the client really wants. . . .

III. CONCLUSION

Negotiation scholars and practitioners have long known that disputants may not get what they want at the bargaining table. Perhaps what they want is unreasonable, unavailable, or even unlawful; perhaps they will commit decision errors in the negotiation process due to "heuristics and biases"; perhaps their counterparts will simply "out-negotiate" them using successful "hard-ball" negotiation tactics or the more subtle but still effective "principles of influence" employed by advertisers and retailers; perhaps any number of "barriers" might prevent them from getting what they want.

What negotiation scholars and practitioners have generally assumed, however, is that disputants know what they want. The work reported in this essay calls this assumption into question. [T]he most significant problem plaguing disputants may very well be that they cannot always know what they want.

The dilemma for lawyers (who are susceptible to the impact bias in their own right, of course) is what to do with this insight. In our view, the lawyer who is truly client-centered will neither substitute her judgment for that of her client, nor will she turn a blind eye to the very real possibility that her client is mistaken about what he really wants. Client-centeredness requires her to eschew extreme paternalism on the one hand and extreme anti-paternalism on the other in favor of a more balanced approach to legal counseling.

Notes and Questions

5.1 Lehman notes that most lawyers use a morally neutral utilitarian model in counseling their clients. From a utilitarian approach, lawyers give advice based on practicality or long-run consequences rather than morality. Lehman argues that such an approach is problematic for a number of reasons. First, the lawyer considers a hypothetical, standardized client rather than the specific client. This results in advice that does not account for controversial or undesirable outcomes. Second, the lawyer may encourage the client to put off present gratification to the future. To suggest otherwise would be bending to the whims of the "eccentric" or "crotchety" client. The result is that the client does not realize his own interests because the lawyer views the alternative act as more rational. On what basis should lawyers be counseling clients? Morality? Practicality? What do you think of Lehman's argument?

5.2 How should lawyers value nonlegal concerns compared to legal ones? How should lawyers help their clients compare these?

5.3 How can lawyers help their clients deal with impact bias and the problem of "miswanting"?

2. Interviewing Skills

Interviewing skills are critical in helping clients choose a dispute resolution process and, once representation is under way, in making sure client goals and needs are being met. To ensure this, regular communication with the client is necessary. The lawyer who either assumes she knows what the client wants or, even more troublesome, substitutes her own judgment for the client's, is failing the client. Yet communication between lawyer and client does not always occur as often or as well as it should. This first summary explains the goal of interviewing and how the actual interview progresses.

 Robert M. Bastress & Joseph D. Harbaugh, **INTERVIEWING, COUNSELING AND NEGOTIATING: SKILLS FOR EFFECTIVE REPRESENTATION**

66-68, 71, 77-78, 85-86, 92-97, 99, 101, 104, 106 (1990)

THE GOALS OF INTERVIEWING

1. Attorney-Client Rapport

From your first contact with a client, a relationship forms that will grow throughout the period of representation. The kind and quality of the relationship ultimately needed to effectively represent a client in a substantial case is likely beyond attaining in the initial interview. But the initial interview is essential to cementing the foundation for the lawyer-client relationship. If the job is poorly done, the foundation will be unable to support the construction of the complex professional relationship needed to conduct a long or emotionally difficult case. Therefore, your initial telephone contact or face-to-face meeting with the client is the moment to begin to establish the appropriate professional rapport.

"Rapport" here has a twofold significance. First, it connotes a certain personal regard between you and the client. . . . Rapport also means that the client respects you as a competent professional who is truly interested in the client's problem. . . .

Second, "rapport" means mutual trust. . . .

2. Goals of the Attorney-Client Relationship During the Interview Stage

In the initial phases of representation, you want to establish a relationship with the client that facilitates information flow, encourages assignment of responsibility, and fosters a willingness in the client to seriously consider your advice and engage in frank discussion of alternatives.

Information, whether it be helpful or damaging to the case, is the cornerstone of a lawyer's work and the primary goal of interviewing. . . . With an attitude that encourages, supports, and accepts the client, you make the client more comfortable and facilitate information flow. . . .

Assignment of responsibility in the client interview is a two-way street. Clients normally assign to you the overall handling of their legal problems. You, in turn, will more likely assign to the client additional information functions. . . . To facilitate this cross-assignment of duties, clients should have confidence in you as a competent professional and as a caring, considerate human being. With that confidence, clients are more likely to assign to you all facets of the legal problem and to accept your assignment of necessary fact-finding tasks.

Finally, lawyers are givers of advice. This advice, of course, is worthless if the client is unwilling to consider it seriously. . . . A relationship with the client must be established that encourages understanding of your role in advice-giving and the client's role in receiving and acting on that advice. Such a relationship demands

"Would you carry a Lawyer-Client/Client-Lawyer Dictionary?"

Reprinted by permission of Dave Carpenter.

your candor and honesty in evaluating alternatives and consequences and your patience and assistance as the client works through the available options. . . .

THE ANATOMY OF THE INITIAL CLIENT INTERVIEW

The initial interview with the client is an obviously important — and particularly difficult — stage of the lawyer-client relationship. . . . Because little or no information about the client's problem and goals has been exchanged, the lawyer must operate without a detailed agenda and the structure it provides.

Despite the apparent absence of information, you can nevertheless efficiently structure initial client interviews. . . . Those parts include planning for the interview, "ice-breaking," problem identification, problem overview, verification, and closure. . . .

Introductory Ice-Breaking

Most clients, from the experienced business client who routinely deals with attorneys to an unsophisticated person seeking a lawyer's advice for the first time, are apprehensive about the initial meeting with their new lawyer. Except for the most gregarious of us, people generally are discomforted by the process of formally meeting another person who, like a lawyer, represents power and authority. That discomfort is exacerbated by the fact that clients seeking legal counsel are usually troubled and concerned about the problem confronting them. Finally, because many clients visit a lawyer to seek help in a matter over which they have little control, they consciously or unconsciously experience a sense of dependency. The combination of these three factors produces people who approach their initial interviews with trepidation. . . .

By their very nature, feelings of apprehension, discomfort, and anxiety are inhibitors of open communication. Since these emotional conditions can interfere with the flow of information and the establishment of a trusting relationship between the attorney and the client, it is your responsibility to alleviate the apprehension and diminish the discomfort.

> **Ice-breaking**
>
> To appreciate the range of client reactions to the initial interview, picture yourself about to visit a doctor with whom you have never consulted. Compare how you would feel if your visit were occasioned by your discovery of two or three of the classic warning signals of heart disease or cancer with how you would feel if, instead, you were going for an annual checkup. Though your anxiety would be higher in the first situation, both occasions are likely to produce tension. If you are like most people, you would appreciate the opportunity to adjust to your surroundings and to get comfortable before the doctor begins testing and probing. It is unlikely to relax you if you are coldly escorted to a small, sterile examining room, left alone for some time, and then immediately upon the doctor's arrival subjected to questioning about your physical condition.
>
> Bastress & Harbaugh, Interviewing, Counseling and Negotiating: Skills for Effective Representation, at 87.

Effective use of your introductory interaction with the new (or old) client and the application of "ice-breaking" techniques should help to reduce client anxiety and allow the client to feel more comfortable in the professional setting. . . .

Problem Identification

Your goal during the problem identification stage of the initial interview is to obtain the client's perception of the problem without imposing your own structure on the client. To achieve this goal, begin with an open-ended question or statement that calls for a narrative response from the client and that contains only general guidance on the direction his or her response should take. . . .

First, the client is asked to identify the problem in his or her own terms. . . . Second, by suggesting there is a beginning of the problem, the client is reminded of the importance of chronological order. . . . By allowing the client to decide where along the time continuum to begin, you are more apt to get the client's uninfluenced view of which facts are critical. Third, the client should be told to isolate his or her preferred solutions to the identified problems. In this way, you obtain valuable information about the client's goals and are in a position to evaluate whether the client's expectations are realistic or unrealistic. . . .

Clients, from the most sophisticated businessperson with extensive experience with lawyers to the most naïve layperson with no prior legal contacts, usually have prepared for their initial encounter with counsel. Consciously or unconsciously, most clients review and organize the facts of their problems, think through their goals and options, and even select the words they will use in telling the lawyer about their problems and solutions. . . .

Given these likelihoods, you should listen carefully to the client's response to the initial open-ended question. . . . During your clients' narratives, you should encourage their elaboration with body language (maintaining eye contact, leaning forward slightly holding your arms in an open position, and nodding) and positive oral signals (e.g., "uh-huh" and "I see").

Lawyers often err in interviews by failing to allow the clients to complete their description of the problem, their perceptions, and their proposed solutions. Two reasons explain this common failure: premature diagnosis and fear of wasted time. . . .

If the attorney focuses too early on what appears to be the crux of the client's problem, the lawyer may impose this snap judgment on the rest of the interview. If this occurs, subtle facts can be missed, important emotions can be ignored, and unique solutions can be discarded. . . .

The first step in avoiding these interviewing errors is simple: Do not interrupt the client's rendition of the problem. . . .

Problem Overview

Once you gain an understanding of the problem as the client sees it and of the solution the client wants, you are ready to move to the heart of the interview: the overview. . . . By overview, we mean you should carefully scrutinize the whole of the client's problem during this stage. . . .

You must determine three important issues during the problem overview portion of the initial client interview: (1) the sequencing of topics; (2) the nature of the questions put by the client; and (3) the techniques of following up initial topic questions. . . .

The process of topic identification involves determining which events mentioned by the client are significant to the solution of the client's problem. . . . The primary means of obtaining information during the overview phase of the interview is the posing of a series of questions to the client. . . . An inverted funnel approach begins with specific, narrow questions and leads toward inquiries of a broad, general nature. . . .

As the interview progresses, particularly during the later stages of the problem overview, you develop some tentative hypotheses about how the client's problem may be resolved. As these alternative solutions evolve in your mind, you encounter a growing need to confirm pivotal facts, corroborate the important feelings of the client, and clarify the client's real goals. In short, you must verify those factors upon which identification of likely alternatives will depend.

Notes and Questions

5.4 How do Bastress and Harbaugh suggest that you start the interview? What do you consider typical "ice-breaker" topics? Why do they think it is important to include such topics?

5.5 Bastress and Harbaugh outline the client-centered approach to interviewing. The alternative to this is often called the hierarchical approach to lawyer-client relations. For example, the Wisconsin Bar Association in 1959 offered this advice:

> Most lawyers spend too much time in interviewing clients. This is very wasteful and costly to the lawyer. . . . Get at the client's problem immediately and stick to it. Don't bother to explain the reasoning processes by which you arrive at your advice. The client expects you to be an expert. This not only prolongs the interview, but generally confuses the client. The client will feel better and more secure if told in simple straightforward language what to do and how to do it, without an explanation of how you reached your conclusions.

Quoted in Joseph Goldstein & Jay Katz, The Family and the Law: Problems for Decision in the Family Law Process 87 (1965). What are the advantages to you as a lawyer of the hierarchical approach? What are the advantages to the client? What are the disadvantages to you and to the client?

5.6 What differences do you imagine between clients making deals and clients facing litigation? Should these clients be counseled differently? Why or why not?

This next excerpt also takes the client-centered approach to client counseling and explains several key points raised earlier. First, it lists "inhibitors" — situations that make it more difficult to interview a client. Second, the authors review "facilitators" — techniques lawyers can use to help the interview process. Finally, it reviews important questioning techniques.

David A. Binder, Paul B. Bergman, Susan C. Price & Paul K. Tremblay,
LAWYERS AS COUNSELORS: A CLIENT-CENTERED APPROACH

19-27, 29-31 (2d ed. 2004)

INHIBITORS

The seven inhibitors that this section describes are common in lawyer-client dialogues. While other phenomena may also inhibit active client participation, these seven operate across a wide range of client personality types. Though the discussion treats each inhibitor as a separate phenomenon, in practice each often intertwines with others.

Of the seven inhibitors, the first two — ego threat and case threat — probably play the most pervasive role in blocking full communication.

A. Ego Threat

Clients tend to withhold information which they perceive as threatening to their self-esteem. The requested information may relate either to past or anticipated behavior, and the feelings that a question may arouse can range from mild embarrassment to a strong sense of guilt or shame. If a client believes that a truthful response will lead you to evaluate the client negatively, such a response threatens the client's self-esteem; the response is "ego threatening." Rather than risk your negative evaluation, the client may answer falsely or evasively, or become reluctant to participate in that part of the conversation. . . .

B. Case Threat

A second major factor tending to inhibit client communication is "case threat." As the term suggests, "case threat" may arise when clients believe that revealing information will hurt their case. For example, Susan may not want to reveal to you that she was near the scene of a crime because she fears that if the judge and jurors were to find out she will be convicted even though she is not guilty. Alternatively, Susan may fear that revealing the information will cause you to believe that the case is a loser and therefore fail to pursue it zealously. In either event, "case threat" is present. Similarly, assume that in a civil matter you ask Ernesto about the whereabouts of a business document. If Ernesto fears that information on the document contains damaging information, case threat may lead him not to reveal its whereabouts.

C. Role Expectations

Role expectations often affect communication between lawyers and clients. Most of us have sets of beliefs about what kind of behavior is appropriate within the confines of particular roles in relationships. . . .

The "role expectations" phenomenon means that clients will frequently enter your law office with a set of expectations about what constitutes appropriate "client behavior." For some clients, those expectations will be that lawyers occupy positions of authority. Such clients may be somewhat reluctant to communicate fully in the belief that you know what subjects are deserving of inquiry. Thus, if you fail to broach a topic that a client feels is important, the client may assume (again, either consciously or intuitively) that the topic is not a significant one. Similarly, such clients may think it outside their role to suggest potential solutions to their problems. . . .

Interestingly, many clients have an opposite set of beliefs. This second group of clients tends to believe that a lawyer's role is limited to carrying out their wishes and that it is their privilege to speak their minds about any and all topics. In short, these clients see themselves in a dominant position vis à vis their counsel, and they are often not interested in fully responding to inquiries they perceive as unimportant. . . .

D. Etiquette Barrier

A fourth inhibitor is the "etiquette barrier." Often, individuals have information that they will freely provide to persons in a similar peer group but not to "outsiders." . . .

E. Trauma

This phenomenon occurs when you ask clients to recall experiences that evoke unpleasant feelings. Many events (especially those that clients relate to lawyers) cause people to experience such negative feelings as fear, anger, humiliation, and sadness. When you ask clients to recall such events, they may re-experience the negative feelings. Consequently, clients may avoid thinking and talking about unpleasant events. . . .

F. Perceived Irrelevancy

This inhibitor is often difficult to recognize, as clients may not signal feelings of discomfort or threat. The attitude involved here is a client's feeling that there exists "no good reason to provide that information." Clients who feel that they have nothing to gain by providing information may be reluctant to provide it. . . .

G. Greater Need

The last of the common inhibitors is "greater need." This situation arises from the clients' needs or desires to talk about subjects other than the one that is of immediate interest to you. . . .

FACILITATORS

The five facilitators described below encourage clients to participate fully in counseling dialogues. This section describes the facilitators and offers illustrations of how to employ them effectively. You may choose to employ facilitators without waiting for client reluctance to rear its annoying head. That is, you can incorporate facilitators into all counseling conversations, as part of your routine style, whether clients are enthusiastic or reluctant participants.

A. Empathic Understanding

Empathic understanding may arouse in clients feelings of trust and confidence and thereby motivates clients to participate fully in conversations. Empathy probably cannot be defined or precisely described. Perhaps the following comments by Carl Rogers give some sense of what empathy involves:

> Empathy in its most fundamental sense . . . involves understanding the experiences, behaviors, and feelings of others as they experience them. It means that [lawyers] must, to the best of their abilities, put aside their own biases, prejudices, and points of view in order to understand as clearly as possible the points of view of their clients. It means entering into the experience of clients in order to develop a feeling for their inner world and how they view both this inner world and the world of people and [events] around them.[27]

People have limited opportunities in our society to express their thoughts and feelings to someone who is willing to (1) listen, (2) understand, and (3) at the same time, not judge. . . .

"Listening Matters!"

Believe it or not, the risk of being sued for malpractice has very little to do with how many mistakes a doctor makes. . . .

Recently the medical researcher Wendy Levinson recorded hundreds of conversations between a group of physicians and their patients. Roughly half of the doctors had never been sued. The other half had been sued at least twice, and Levinson found that just on the basis of those conversations, she could find clear differences between the two groups. The surgeons who had never been sued spent more than 3 minutes longer with each patient than those who had been sued did (18.3 minutes versus 15 minutes). They were more likely to make "orienting" comments, such as "First I'll examine you, and then we will talk the problem over" or "I will leave time for your questions" — which help patients get a sense of what the visit is supposed to accomplish and when they ought to ask questions. They were more likely to engage in active listening, saying such things as, "Go on, tell me more about that," and they were far more likely to laugh and be funny during the visit. Interestingly, there was no difference in the amount or quality of information they gave their patients; they didn't provide more details about medication or the patient's condition. The difference was entirely in how they talked to their patients.

Malcolm Gladwell, Blink: The Power of Thinking Without Thinking 40-42 (2005).

B. Fulfilling Expectations

The phenomenon of "fulfilling expectations" refers to people's tendencies to want to satisfy the perceived expectations of those with whom they interact. . . .

---

[27] Gerald Egan, The Skilled Helper 87 (3d ed. 1986). In general, see also Davis, Empathy: A Social Psychological Approach 7-12 (1994).

C.   Recognition

Human beings often need attention and recognition from people outside their close circle of family and friends. They enjoy feeling important and seek the attention and esteem of outsiders.

D.   Altruistic Appeals

People often need to identify with a "higher value" or cause that is beyond their immediate self-interest. This need may be a form of identification with the objectives of a large social group. A person's performance of altruistic deeds usually increases their self-esteem. Thus, clients are often motivated to participate fully when doing so makes them feel altruistic. . . .

E.   Extrinsic Reward

You are undoubtedly aware from everyday experience that people tend to act in their self-interest. Thus, you can often motivate clients to participate actively by pointing out how disclosure of the information is likely to help them achieve more satisfactory outcomes. . . .

A NOTE ON LISTENING

Before continuing, it might be helpful to read the listening materials in Chapter 7. Using the listening concepts described there is not at all limited to conversations with the other side. In fact, many attorneys report more difficulty in conversations with their clients than with their opponents. As you will see later in Chapter 7, the readings on listening provide specific advice on how to confirm that you have understood the speaker and that you are aware of underlying emotions in the conversation. The readings also discuss the importance of building empathy and provide ways to do that.

Notes and Questions

5.7 How do the lessons from listening tie in with the readings on interviewing?

5.8 Why would lawyers want to demonstrate empathy with their clients? Why may lawyers feel hesitant to show empathy?

5.9 The listening readings in Chapter 7 discuss some of the typical barriers to listening well when people are in conflict (for example, people are busy coming up with a response, people are defending themselves, or people are distracted). How might similar barriers to listening arise when lawyers are interviewing clients?

3. Counseling Skills

After a lawyer interviews a client, it is time to use whatever legal and nonlegal information is learned to help the client decide what to try to accomplish in a negotiation and how to pursue those goals. This section discusses how those conversations between lawyer and client should be conducted to ensure that the client makes the best choice.

 David A. Binder, Paul B. Bergman, Susan C. Price & Paul K. Tremblay, **LAWYERS AS COUNSELORS: A CLIENT-CENTERED APPROACH**

306-309, 311-312, 317, 320-321 (2d ed. 2004)

[After step one of clarifying objectives and step two of identifying alternatives,] the *third step* is to identify the likely consequences of each. Since, as you know, solutions carry nonlegal consequences, you must explore likely nonlegal as well as legal consequences. . . .

A. THE NECESSITY TO PREDICT

Assessing the consequences involves predictions about future events. . . . Predictions are, by and large, statements of probability. . . . The predictions that you and your clients make almost always center on the behavior of a variety of actors, such as adversaries, judges and juries, government officials, and consumers, for which accurate data bases are not available. . . . Any data bases you and a client have individually acquired for predicting future consequences have usually been arrived at by a highly selective and intuitive process in which seeming similarities tend to mask important differences, and thus introduce uncertainty into your data base.

However, those imperfect data bases are often all that you and your clients will have available for making predictions. The question, then, is on whose data base should a prediction be made — yours or a client's?

B. PREDICTING LEGAL CONSEQUENCES

Predicting legal consequences is the essence of providing legal advice. That is, responsibility for predicting legal consequences rests primarily on you. Clients generally expect you to have a better data base for predicting such matters as how a jury is likely to rule, what legal consequences attach to doing business as a corporation rather than a sole proprietorship, how acquiring a trademark might protect a company's product, and whether a corporation's omission of information from a securities prospectus might subject the corporate officers to criminal or civil liability.

C. PREDICTING NONLEGAL CONSEQUENCES

Nonlegal consequences, as you know, consist of the likely economic, social, psychological, political and moral ramifications that may flow from adopting a particular solution. And just as you generally have the better data base for predicting legal consequences, clients often have the better data base for predicting nonlegal ones.... Therefore, you typically rely on clients to predict nonlegal consequences.

At the same time, your own experiences may enable you to predict (or at least inquire about) common nonlegal consequences....

D. ORGANIZING THE DISCUSSION OF CONSEQUENCES

The subsections below examine techniques for counseling clients with respect to likely consequences.

1. Review Options Separately

Many people have difficulty making decisions because they cannot focus on discrete options and their attendant advantages and disadvantages.... Thus, an effective strategy for analyzing options and their consequences is to focus on options separately.

2. Ask Clients to Choose a Starting Place

To maintain a client-centered approach, ask clients which option they want to discuss first.... This approach builds on the advantages of neutrality, as you leave to a client the choice of which option to discuss first. This technique also tends to encourage clients to participate actively in counseling discussions.

Preparation for Counseling

Step 1. Research the law and investigate the facts ....

Step 2. Clarify your goals for the counseling session ....

Step 3. Scan your research, investigation, and experience to identify alternatives for the client....

Step 4. Note the positive and negative consequences of each alternative to ensure that the client fully considers the total impact of his or her decision. Your explanation should include legal and nonlegal consequences....

Step 5. Plan for in-session probing to accomplish three interrelated objectives...: (a) ...clarify the client's priorities, (b) ascertain the client's reactions to the possible consequences of the identified alternatives, and (c) cure informational gaps and ambiguities....

Step 6. Plan the format for the counseling session....

Step 7. Think through what [communication] techniques might be appropriate during the counseling session....

Step 8. Prepare visual aids for the client.

Robert M. Bastress & Joseph D. Harbaugh, Interviewing, Counseling and Negotiating 237-240 (1990).

---

3. Adopt the Role of Information Seeker

After a client selects an option, you may continue to place a client in the figurative limelight by asking the client to identify the pros and cons of the chosen option....

You can seek a clients' thoughts about consequences in one of three ways. You can ask a client only about advantages, about both advantages and disadvantages, or only about disadvantages. . . .

4. The Cross Over Phenomenon

[R]arely will it be possible or desirable to systematically run through each alternative individually, taking up pros and then cons. Rather, clients tend to "cross over" from one alternative to another. Within a single alternative, they often jump back and forth between "pros" and "cons." . . .

5. Discuss Consequences You Foresee

Discussions of likely consequences usually include advising clients of potential legal and nonlegal consequences that you foresee. If, as will often be the case, you first ask a client to predict consequences, you might then either (1) integrate the consequences you foresee into the client's discussion, or (2) wait until the client concludes and supplement the client's list with your own. . . .

6. Identify Downstream Consequences

[A]n important contribution you can often make to the counseling process is to point out that a "pro" of an option is that it leaves open future possibilities, while a "con" is that it is likely to foreclose future possibilities. . . .

7. Chart Alternatives and Consequences

Writing down consequences as they emerge is often essential because discussions of alternatives and consequences are often characterized by "cross-overs" between options, advantages and disadvantages. . . . First, a chart is often essential for carrying out the goal of fully exploring each alternative. Because of cross over, a discussion of alternatives and consequences rarely proceeds in a straightforward manner. Without a written record, it is hard for both you and a client to remember what territory has already been covered. Also, seeing consequences in writing may stimulate both you and a client to recall additional ones. . . .

Sometimes you may have to re-review the options and their likely consequences, perhaps asking a client to think carefully about how likely a consequence really is and how much importance a consequence carries as you do so. Referring to a chart and summarizing its contents will often help you carry out the re-review.

Notes and Questions

5.10 Robert Dinerstein proposes that one aspect of the client-centered model, identifying alternatives, is too law- and lawyer-centered. Dinerstein states that by suggesting alternatives first, the lawyer focuses on the standard approaches of litigation, settlement, or doing nothing, which may not be the most effective alternatives. To develop more effective alternatives, Diner-stein suggests that the lawyer should brainstorm with the client about the client's goals and ideas before considering the lawyer's ideas. Robert D. Diner-stein, Client-Centered Counseling: Reappraisal and Refinement, 32 Ariz. L. Rev. 504, 584-597 (1990). Is the discussion about alternatives, even dispute resolution alternatives, too driven by law and lawyers? Is this inevitable or avoidable? How would Dinerstein's ideas help?

5.11 Stephen Ellmann argues that while the client-centered model appears to give more power to the client, lawyers using these techniques actually gain more power over their clients. Ellmann believes that a client-centered approach is manipulative since the techniques create a seemingly intimate relationship that then allows the lawyer to undercut the client's ability to make her own deci-sions. For instance, techniques such as active listening, where the lawyer con-veys back in a nonjudgmental manner the essence of what the client has said, encourage the client to speak freely with a false sense of the lawyer's accep-tance. When the counseling turns to discussing alternatives, a lawyer who does not state opinions can still have a significant influence in defining alternatives and identifying their consequences. Ellmann addresses whether the manipu-lative aspect of client-centered counseling can be avoided and comes to the ultimate conclusion that lawyers cannot assist clients' decision making without the risk of manipulating their decisions. Stephen Ellmann, Lawyers and Clients, 34 UCLA L. Rev. 717 (1987). What do you think about this con-clusion? Is focusing on the clients also controlling them? Has Ellmann created a definition of "manipulation" so expansive as to render it irrelevant? Can you envision an attorney doing anything that would not conceivably constitute manipulation? Even doing nothing?

5.12 Another concern in counseling is the power balance (or imbalance) between lawyers and clients. Professors Felstiner and Sarat discuss this further:

> [P]ower in lawyer-client interaction is not the straightforward phenomenon generally depicted in the literature, but a more subtle and complicated con-struct enacted through often ambiguous and conflicted behavior. Some of the more important respects in which power in lawyer-client relations differs from the conventional picture are that it is enacted through implicit negotiation as well as overt action; that motives, goals and data are often deliberately con-cealed; that power can be elusive, even to the point of disappearing; that assertions of power may be resisted openly or covertly; that the locus and nature of power changes over time; and that lawyer-client differences, even on matters of great moment in a client's affairs, rarely result in open con-frontation. . . .
>
> Only on rare occasions . . . does interaction between lawyers and clients resemble a straightforward provision of technical services to a generally com-placent, dependent and weak laity. The interaction is more often complex, shifting, frequently conflicted, and negotiated. In the relationship between lawyer and client, the professional, like it or not, shares power and resources with the client. It is a relationship where the knowledge and experience of each may be challenged by the other; where the economic investment of the

lawyer in any particular client may equal or out-strip the client's investment in the lawyer; where lawyers have conflicts of interest that clients seek to identify and protect against; and where the humanity of each may be constantly under the scrutiny of the other. Thus, the nature of lawyer-client relationships beyond the context of divorce cannot be captured by simple models of professional or lay dominance, or by simple estimates of lawyer and client resources. Power in those relationships is, like power everywhere, deeply embedded in complex and changing processes of negotiation.

William L.F. Felstiner & Austin Sarat, Enactments of Power: Negotiating Reality and Responsibility in Lawyer-Client Interactions, 77 Cornell L. Rev. 1447, 1495, 1498 (1992).

Donald Gifford examines the impact of the strategy choices in negotiation and how a client should be counseled both before and during the negotiation process.

 Donald Gifford, **THE SYNTHESIS OF LEGAL COUNSELING AND NEGOTIATION MODELS: PRESERVING CLIENT-CENTERED ADVOCACY IN THE NEGOTIATION CONTEXT**

34 UCLA L. Rev. 811, 811-844 (1987)

PRENEGOTIATION COUNSELING CONFERENCE

The lawyer should provide the client with a realistic description of the client's BATNA [best alternative to negotiated agreement] and the prospects for a satisfactory negotiated result at the earliest possible time. This lessens the likelihood that after negotiations, the lawyer and client will have vastly different opinions on the advisability of accepting or rejecting the settlement offer. Lawyers often quite naturally postpone bad news until the last possible moment, and, as a result, they allow their clients to entertain unrealistically optimistic expectations until the negotiations conclude. Reality then intrudes when the lawyer believes settlement is justified, and the client dismisses the option because he still possesses unrealistic expectations about what will happen at trial or about the viability of his other nonlitigation BATNA. . . .

The second issue to be discussed during the prenegotiation conference is which negotiation strategy best serves the client's interests. As previously mentioned, the Model Rules of Professional Conduct require the attorney to consult her client regarding the "means" of representation; this requirement suggests that the attorney should consult with the client regarding the negotiation strategy she intends to use. Some clients will decline any interest in their lawyers' negotiating tactics, but each client should reach this decision only after the lawyer outlines how negotiation tactics can affect the client. In particular, the lawyer and client should explore the implications of the lawyer's intended negotiation strategy on future relationships between her client and the other party. If the parties have a continuing relationship, a noncompetitive negotiation strategy is usually preferred. The competitive strategy often generates distrust and ill-will and may alienate other lawyers and invite retaliation for violating fairness norms. On the other hand, some clients prefer the competitive strategy in negotiating with a party with whom they have a continuing relationship, because it establishes a strong bargaining image and discourages future attempts at exploitation by the other party. Because clients have different concerns about how their lawyer's negotiating behavior affects their own relationships with other parties, their input should be solicited prior to the negotiations.

The lawyer and the client also should consider the lawyer's authority to enter into an agreement binding on the client. . . . The type of authority affects both the negotiation process and the prospects for a client-centered counseling process. . . .

Restricting the lawyer's authority to enter into a binding agreement also aids client-centered advocacy because the client retains greater control over his attorney's conduct during the negotiation. A series of incrementally increasing grants of authority over the course of the negotiation guarantees that the attorney must consult regularly with the client. Presumably, lawyers preface such requests for additional authority with reports on the current status of the negotiations, and thus keep the client better informed about the negotiations and more directly involved in them.

The lawyer and client also should consider together whether they can devise solutions that satisfy the underlying interests of both the client and the other party. . . . During these planning sessions, lawyer and client should develop proposed solutions to the problem[s] facing the parties, which then will be considered with the other party's lawyer during negotiations. . . .

Brainstorming prior to the negotiations significantly contributes to both client centered counseling and negotiation results. Brainstorming actively involves the client in the negotiation process, builds rapport, and often provides the client with a more realistic picture of the difficulties to be faced during the negotiation. Brainstorming with the client also increases the likelihood that negotiations will yield desirable results. . . .

CLIENT-COUNSELING CONFERENCES DURING THE COURSE OF NEGOTIATIONS

The lawyer should confer often with her client during the course of the negotiations, preferably after each contact with the other lawyer. Frequent client contacts between negotiation sessions facilitate both client-centered advocacy and negotiation results which maximize the interests of parties. . . .

POSTNEGOTIATION COUNSELING CONFERENCE

Following the repetition of the alternating negotiation and counseling sessions, the lawyer concludes at some point that she has received the last, best possible outcome from the negotiations and that further bargaining will not yield better results for her client. At this time . . . the lawyer and client are now ready to discuss together the advantages and disadvantages of the negotiated agreement and the alternatives to agreement to enable the client to make an informed decision. . . .

When the lawyer and the client confer regularly before the negotiations begin and between negotiation sessions, the client is better informed about the substance of the negotiations and more accustomed to participating in the decision-making process. By the time of the postnegotiation conference, the client already should be aware of his nonsettlement alternatives, because his lawyer has discussed these with him prior to the negotiations and kept him informed during the negotiations of any new information affecting his BATNA. Further, because the lawyer constantly updated the client on the actual content of the negotiations, the client has become gradually aware of the substance of the negotiated option.

The client's greater understanding of the alternatives available to him, prior to the postnegotiation counseling conference, favorably affects the counseling conference and makes the client-centered decisionmaking more feasible. First, the amount of new information the lawyer must convey to the client regarding the available alternatives and the consequences of each option is considerably less, because of the client's familiarity with most of this information. . . .

The second advantage of the ongoing counseling process is that it is less likely the lawyer and client will disagree vehemently and unexpectedly about the relative desirability of the remaining alternatives. . . . [O]ngoing counseling makes it less likely the client will form unrealistic expectations about the results of either the negotiation or the alternatives to negotiations. . . .

Finally, counseling sessions with the client during the negotiation process contribute to client-centered advocacy by building a relationship with the lawyer in which the client actively participates in the decisionmaking process.

Notes and Questions

5.13 What advantages does Gifford outline regarding the final settlement if an attorney has met with the client regularly throughout the negotiation? What is the process Gifford suggests for meeting with the client at the conclusion of the negotiation?

5.14 What if, in the process of a bitter divorce, the client wants you to negotiate in a highly adversarial manner? How do you counsel your client? What if you agree with that choice? What if you do not?

5.15 What if your client, a victim of a car accident, wants you to accept an offer from the insurance company as quickly as possible, and you know that this company usually only offers low-balls until the month before trial? How do you counsel your client?

5.16 In counseling about accepting a settlement, the decision tree outlined in Chapter 2 could be particularly useful.

B. ATTORNEY-CLIENT ISSUES

This section examines negotiation behavior when another layer, that of legal representation, is added onto the communication. Much of the theory and advice provided about negotiation assumes that the negotiator is the principal party. Lawyers, however, most often represent a client. This relationship creates an agent-principal relationship that brings additional questions and concerns about negotiation strategy and legal liability (see Chapter 11). This section discusses how lawyers can be particularly useful in negotiation. At the same time, there are additional concerns raised when communication and interests of the client are filtered through another party (the lawyer) to another lawyer and then back to the client on the other side. Abram Chayes writes that the agency issue is always at hand in a negotiation — even when one is negotiating on one's own behalf, there are inevitably other constituencies (spouse, employees, and so on) to which one must answer. Abram J. Chayes, Preface, Negotiating on Behalf of Others: Advice to Lawyers, Business Executives, Sports Agents, Diplomats, Politicians, and Everybody Else (Robert H. Mnookin & Lawrence E. Susskind eds., 1999). In what ways do you think the use of agents in negotiation helps or hurts the process?

This next excerpt deals specifically with the question of why people (called principals) hire agents (the lawyers) in negotiation.

 Jeffrey Z. Rubin & Frank E.A. Sander, **WHEN SHOULD WE USE AGENTS? DIRECT VS. REPRESENTATIVE NEGOTIATION**

4 Negot. J. 395, 396-398 (1988)

EXPERTISE

One of the primary reasons that principals choose to negotiate through agents is that the latter possess expertise that makes agreement — particularly favorable agreement — more likely. This expertise is likely to be of three different stripes:

Substantive knowledge. A tax attorney or accountant knows things about the current tax code that make it more likely that negotiations with an IRS auditor will benefit the client as much as possible. Similarly, a divorce lawyer, an engineering consultant, and a real estate agent may have substantive knowledge in a rather narrow domain of expertise, and this expertise may redound to the client's benefit.

Process expertise. Quite apart from the specific expertise they may have in particular content areas, agents may have skill at the negotiation *process*, per se, thereby enhancing the prospects of a favorable agreement. A skillful negotiator — someone who understands how to obtain and reveal information about preferences, who is inventive, resourceful, firm on goals but flexible on means, etc. — is a valuable resource. Wise principals would do well to utilize the services of such skilled negotiators, unless they can find ways of developing such process skills themselves.

Special influence. A Washington lobbyist is paid to know the "right" people, to have access to the "corridors of power" that the principals themselves are unlikely to possess. Such "pull" can certainly help immensely, and is yet another form of expertise that agents may possess, although the lure of this "access" often outweighs in promise the special benefits that are confirmed in reality. . . .

DETACHMENT

Another important reason for using an agent to do the actual negotiation is that the principals may be too emotionally entangled in the subject of the dispute. A classic example is divorce. A husband and wife, caught in the throes of a bitter fight over the end of their marriage, may benefit from the "buffering" that agents can provide. Rather than confront each other with the depth of their anger and bitterness, the principals . . . may do far better by communicating only *indirectly*, via their respective representatives. . . . Stated most generally, when the negotiating climate is adversarial — when the disputants are confrontational rather than collaborative — it may be wiser to manage the conflict through intermediaries than run the risk of an impasse or explosion resulting from direct exchange.

Sometimes, however, it is the *agents* who are too intensely entangled. What is needed then is the detachment and rationality that only the principals can bring to the exchange. . . .

Note, however, that the very "detachment" we are touting as a virtue of negotiation through agents can also be a liability. For example, in some interpersonal negotiations, apology and reconciliation may be an important ingredient of any resolution. Surrogates who are primarily technicians may not be able to bring to bear these empathetic qualities.

TACTICAL FLEXIBILITY

The use of agents allows various gambits to be played out by the principals, in an effort to ratchet as much as possible from the other side. For example, if a seller asserts that the bottom line is $100,000, the buyer can try to haggle, albeit at the risk of losing the deal. If the buyer employs an agent, however, the agent can profess willingness to pay that sum but plead lack of authority, thereby gaining valuable time and opportunity for fuller consideration of the situation together with the principal. Or an agent for the seller who senses that the buyer may be especially eager to buy the property can claim that it is necessary to go back to the seller for ratification of the deal, only to return and up the price, profusely apologizing all the while for the behavior of an "unreasonable" client. The client and agent can thus together play the hard-hearted partner game.

Conversely, an agent may be used in order to push the other side in tough, even obnoxious, fashion, making it possible — in the best tradition of the "good cop/bad cop" ploy — for the client to intercede at last, and seem the essence of sweet reason in comparison with the agent. Or the agent may be used as a "stalking horse," to gather as much information about the adversary as possible, opening the way to proposals by the client that exploit the intelligence gathered.

Notes and Questions

5.17 Which of these reasons to use a lawyer-agent make the most sense to you? Which reasons would you use to persuade a skeptical client that you are useful?

5.18 What concerns might you have about hiring a lawyer? How would you decide
when to hire a lawyer? On what factors would your decision depend?

The following excerpt examines the classic tension between lawyer and client in
a negotiation.

 Robert H. Mnookin, Scott R. Peppet & Andrew S. Tulumello, **BEYOND
WINNING: NEGOTIATING TO CREATE VALUE IN DEALS
AND DISPUTES**

75-76, 83-87, 90 (2000)

THE PROBLEM: AGENCY COSTS

Hiring an agent is not a simple matter. Bringing an agent into a negotiation introduces a third tension: between the principal and the agent. Because agents often have
expert knowledge, substantial experience and special resources that the principal
lacks, the relationship can create value. At the same time, however, because the
agent's interests may not align with those of the principal, a number of unique
and intensely stubborn problems can arise. . . .

THE SOURCES OF THE TENSION

Agency costs are not limited to the amount of money that a principal pays an agent as
compensation for doing the job. They also include the money and time the principal
spends trying to ensure that the agent does not exploit him but instead serves his
interests well. To understand why agency costs exist, consider that principals and
agents may differ in three general ways:

- Preferences
- Incentives
- Information

Different Preferences

First, the preferences, or interest, of an agent are rarely identical to those of the
principal. Consider their economic interest. Betty's primary economic interest is
in her own earnings as a real estate agent. In this transaction, Sam's primary economic
interest is in the net sale price for his house. Betty may have other interests as well.
She has a strong interest in her reputation and in securing future clients. She has an
interest in maintaining good relationships with other agents, banks, home inspectors,
and insurance agencies. Betty is a repeat player in this game, while Sam, particularly if
he intends to leave the community, is a one-shot player who might be more than
willing to sacrifice Betty's reputation in order to get a better deal for himself.

Conversely, Betty may be reluctant to bargain hard for certain advantages for Sam because of her desire to maintain a congenial relationship with the buyer's agent, who may be a source of future client referrals.

Different Incentives

Agency problems may also arise because the *incentives* of the principal and the agent are imperfectly aligned. The culprit is typically the agent's fee structure, which may create perverse incentives for the agent to act contrary to the principal's interests. This discrepancy is sometimes called an incentive gap.

For example, Sam wants an arrangement that maximizes his expected net sale proceeds after her fee. Betty, on the other hand, wants a fee structure that yields her the highest expected return *for her time spent*. If they agree to a percentage fee, Betty may prefer a quick and easy sale at a lower price to a difficult sale at a higher price because with the former she will get more return for hours spent working. Indeed, a recent study suggests that when realtors put their *own* homes on the market, they tend to get higher-than-average prices, because they get the entire benefit of their additional hours of work, not just 6 percent of it.

Different Information

The information available to the principal and the agent may differ. We are speaking here of kinds of information that either side may have an incentive to keep to itself. Betty may know that market conditions are improving, for example, but she may be reluctant to share this with Sam for fear of inflating his expectations. Similarly, it may be difficult to know how much effort an agent is actually putting in on the principal's behalf. Because the principal cannot readily discover this information, the agent might shirk her responsibilities and earn pay without expending effort.

MANAGEMENT MECHANISMS AND THEIR LIMITATIONS

These potential conflicts can be controlled somewhat, through three basic management mechanisms:

- Incentive contracts
- Monitoring systems
- Bonding . . .

Principal-Agent Problems in the Legal Context

The principal-agent relationship of most interest to us here is the relationship between a lawyer and a client who are involved in a legal negotiation. Like all other agency relationships, this one poses problems for both parties, owing to difference in preferences, information and incentives. Here, we briefly outline some management mechanisms that can dampen the principal-agent tension when it arises in the context of a legal negotiation.

Incentives

To tackle incentive problems, lawyers and clients have developed an array of fee structures—all inevitably flawed. The most common of these are:

- Contingency fee
- Hourly fee
- Fixed fee
- Mixed fee
- Salary...

Monitoring Systems

The principal-agent tension may be dampened by monitoring the agent's activities. This is difficult and expensive in the legal context, with respect to both inputs and outputs. To know whether a lawyer is acting solely in his client's interests, the client must possess enough knowledge to evaluate the lawyer's decisions and must be able to observe the lawyer's behavior. There may be no easy way for a client to verify information about a lawyer's true work habits, diligence, or timekeeping practices. Similarly, it may be quite expensive for a client to monitor the quality of her lawyer's work, unless the client is herself an attorney. Often in-house corporate counsel can monitor the activities of outside counsel, but this is hardly a cost-free solution.

Reputational Bonding

To the extent that potential clients have access to accurate information about an attorney's reputation, the attorney will have more incentive to build and maintain a reputation for trustworthiness and hard work. If an unsatisfied client can go elsewhere in the market for legal services, a lawyer is more likely to act loyally and diligently to keep that client....

But this constraint is an imperfect one. Once a lawyer-client relationship has been established, it is often very costly for the client to leave one lawyer and start a new relationship with another. In the middle of a lawsuit or a complicated transaction, for example, a new lawyer would have to invest a great deal of time to learn what the old lawyer already knows about the matter. Because the client will typically have to pay to educate his new lawyer, these extra costs of switching lawyers midstream mean the market cannot completely constrain opportunism. For this market constraint to operate most effectively, moreover, clients must be able to evaluate the performance of their lawyers, which, as noted above, is no simple matter....

THE APPROACH: MANAGING THE TENSION

The central challenge in agency relationships is to capture the benefits while minimizing agency costs. Our approach requires the tension be acknowledged and managed explicitly; that principals and agents use the concept of comparative advantage to structure their roles and responsibilities; and that they aim to form a partnership based on reciprocal candor and respect.... Here we outline general advice.

Create a Collaborative Relationship That Minimizes Agency Costs

The principal-agent tension should be acknowledged, not avoided, and treated as a shared problem. Fees and monitoring should be addressed explicitly, not left lurking under the table. . . . [P]rincipals and agents should search together for ways to reassure the principal without overburdening the agent. In our experience, openness and candor build trust. . . .

The goal should be to find fee arrangements and monitoring mechanisms that are thoughtfully tailored to a given context. One size does not fit all. If a principal wants an agent exhaustively to research an issue where a lot is at stake, compensation by the hour may create a better incentive than a fixed fee. On the other hand, if a principal is worried about controlling costs and thinks she is in a position to monitor the quality effectively, a fixed fee may be better. . . .

Consider Comparative Advantage and Strategy in Allocating Roles

A principal and agent may allocate negotiation roles in a variety of ways. At one extreme, the principal may do all the negotiating herself, using the agent as a coach and consultant behind the scenes. At the other extreme, the agent alone may be at the bargaining table and may not even disclose the principal's identity to the other side. There are many options in between. . . .

Sometimes conventions influence who is at the table and how roles are allocated. . . .

Principals and agents obviously should take such conventions into account, but they also must consider comparative advantage and may even want to challenge assumptions about who should be at the table. . . . The preferences, skills, knowledge, and resources of the principal and agent must be considered. What is the agent particularly good at? What about the principal? Who has more information that will be relevant to the upcoming negotiation? Who is more skilled at negotiating? Who has more time or desire to engage in various tasks needed to prepare for the negotiation? By thinking carefully about their relationship and about what each can bring to the table, a principal and agent can structure their roles so that each does those things for which he is particularly suited.

Strategic implications must also be taken into account. Who your side sends to the table can depend on, and influence, who the other side sends. . . .

If an agent plays a role at the bargaining table, what is the scope of the agent's authority or mandate, and what information is the agent authorized to share with the other side? If a principal is fearful that his agent will disclose too much, this worry can inhibit the principal from sharing necessary information with his agent. On the other hand, by sending only the agent to the bargaining table, a principal may be able to avoid having to answer awkward questions that might be posed by the other side.

The most salient question is whether the agent has the authority within a particular range to settle a dispute or make a deal. This is an important issue for principals and agents to discuss in allocating roles. Too often, however, an agent will simply ask the principal for her bottom line or reservation value to make clear just how far the agent can go. . . .

Rather than ask for the principal's bottom line, the more appropriate, and subtle, question is how the agent's authority should be adjusted during the course of a negotiation. Paradoxically, limiting the authority of agents may facilitate brainstorming and the development of creative solutions because neither agent has power to bind. At the outset of a negotiation, it may be best for the agent to have no authority to make a binding commitment on substantive issues but instead to have a broad mandate to design a negotiation process, discuss interest, and generate options.

Consider the Incentives Created by Agency Relationships on the Other Side

In addition to thinking through principal-agent issues on your side, you should consider the relationships on the other side as well. Do not naively assume that the other side is a "unified actor" with a single set of interests. What are the agent's incentives? A broker or a sales agent may get paid only if the deal goes through. A contingent-fee lawyer who is very pressed for time because of other commitments may be eager to settle. An executive on the other side may either support or oppose a merger, depending on how his career will be affected. In crafting proposals, it is not enough to consider only the interests of the principal on the other side. The agent's incentives and interests should be taken into account as well.

Beware of the Tactical Use of Agents

The agency relationship can be used to implement a variety of hard-bargaining tactics. An agent can play the bad cop to his client's good cop, or vice versa. Ambiguities about authority can be exploited to take two bites of the apple: the agent at the table might extract a final concession from you in order to strike a deal, only to report subsequently that his principal demands more — he really had no authority to commit. A problem-solving negotiator must be able to recognize these tactics and deploy effective counter measures. Naming their game and being explicit about process and authority can help....

Notes and Questions

5.19 What are the primary differences that might occur between a lawyer and her client? How should the lawyer manage these? What advice would you give to a client to manage these differences?

5.20 If you were hiring a lawyer, how would you prefer to be billed? Hourly? On contingency? Why? On what factors would your decision depend?

5.21 See also Neil E. Fassina, Constraining a Principal's Choice: Outcome Versus Behavior Contingent Agency Contracts in Representative Negotiations, 20 Negot. J. 435 (2004), for a discussion of how the factors leading to the decision to enter into a principal-agent relationship determine whether the contract formed between the agent and principal is outcome contingent (a commissioned real estate agent or a lawyer who earns a percentage of punitive damages) or behavior contingent (a noncommissioned salesperson or a human resources manager who is responsible for making job offers).

5.22 There is an old saying that only a fool represents himself. In what type of cases would you want to represent yourself? Never? Why?

5.23 In the International War Crimes Tribunal for Former Yugoslavia, former Serbian leader Slobodon Milosevic insisted on representing himself. In addition to his numerous political reasons for doing this, what concerns about agency might he have had?

The next excerpt looks more broadly at some of the communication issues that can arise when negotiating with agents.

Jayne Seminare Docherty & Marcia Caton Campbell, TEACHING NEGOTIATORS TO ANALYZE CONFLICT STRUCTURE AND ANTICIPATE THE CONSEQUENCES OF PRINCIPAL-AGENT RELATIONSHIPS

87 Marq. L. Rev. 655, 657-659, 662-664 (2004)

Negotiation courses usually focus primary attention on the interactions among the parties involved in the actual negotiation. Such courses also tend to either isolate the negotiation process from the social context within which it is embedded, or assume that students need only know about one small piece of the social context (e.g., the legal system or the business world). Students of negotiation should be encouraged to step back from the negotiation process and think more broadly about the social context within which they are operating. To this end, it is useful to consider how the structure of the larger social conflict or social problem affects the negotiation process....

Because negotiation is a process driven by communication, any increase in the number of persons involved—adding more parties or involving agents acting on behalf of principals—complicates the process. We all know what happens in the game of telephone: the more a message gets passed around, the more likely it is to be distorted. When messages must go from principal A to agent A, from agent A to agent B, from agent B to principal B and back again, we have more places where messages can get distorted. If we throw in principal C and agent C, or even more parties and their agents, the communication problems become daunting indeed. Figure 1 diagrams a relatively simple negotiation with two parties represented by agents.

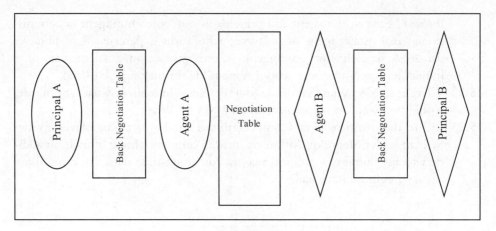

Figure 1
Interconnected or Embedded Negotiations

When teaching students the art of negotiating on behalf of others, we can focus on the problems that might arise between agents and principals and give the students skills to prevent or overcome those problems. Thus, noting that an agent who does not understand her client's interests and positions might miss opportunities for an integrative agreement, we can make our students practice interviewing skills that will help them uncover the client's interests. Noting the serious problem of poor communication between principal and agent, we can teach active listening, clear presentation, and other communication techniques. Similarly, recognizing that the interests of the agent and the principal sometimes differ, we can familiarize students with the ethical and professional standards regulating their relationships with clients.

These are all valid parts of a good negotiation curriculum, but they are not enough to develop highly skilled, reflective practitioners of negotiation. Students also need to learn that introducing principal–agent relationships into a negotiation establishes a set of interconnected negotiations. Principal A and agent A have a set of "back table negotiations" and so do principal B and agent B. The negotiations at the table intersect with and impact the negotiations behind the table and vice versa. Put another way, conflicts between principals and their agents impact the conflicts between the parties to the central conflict and vice versa.

Sometimes agents and their principals use this structure of interconnected negotiations for strategic purposes. Parties can buy time in the primary negotiation by dragging out their back table negotiations. The agent can also use an absent principal as an excuse for taking actions ("my client made me say this") or declining offers from the other party ("I'm sorry, but my client won't let me accept this offer."). On the other hand, there are times when problems with the behind the table negotiations actually jeopardize the central negotiation. Highly skilled negotiators need to understand why this happens and how they can work with these problems. . . .

Two structural factors can increase or decrease the possibility that conflicts between parties and their representatives will negatively affect the main negotiation.

Negotiators should learn to ask the following questions about each representative in a negotiation:

- How formal and structured is the relationship between the principal and the agent?
- How much legitimacy does the agent have?

In addition to the legitimacy of other representatives and the formality of their relationships with their respective parties, good negotiators should have some understanding of the way the *nature* of the party impacts their back table negotiations. Some parties can move quickly, while others need significantly more time to validate or reject proposed agreements. This is not *always* a stalling tactic; it may be an honest reflection of the complexity of the party's internal organization or a reflection of the party's culture. . . .

Developing a table such as the following can help a negotiator pay attention to the structural factors that shape back table negotiations between a representative and his party. A blank version of this chart can be filled in for a particular case. The negotiator should always remember to map her own party on this diagram so that she examines the structural factors that are shaping her own back table negotiation.

TYPE OF PARTY	NATURE OF STRUCTURE	SPEED WITH WHICH IT CAN ACT	COHERENCE OF GOALS
Corporation	Highly Organized Hierarchical	Quickly — once the necessary component parts become involved	Very coherent — clear, widely shared standards for measuring success (i.e., bottom line)
Government Agency	Hierarchical Organized, but may have some incoherence in the system because of competing mandates and the influence of political actors on policies and Standard Operating Procedures	Slowly compared to corporations Quickly compared to community organizations and other political groups	May be confused by competing mandates and shifting political scene

TYPE OF PARTY	NATURE OF STRUCTURE	SPEED WITH WHICH IT CAN ACT	COHERENCE OF GOALS
Community Organization — e.g., Neighborhood Association	Semi-structured Democratic and therefore open to change	Relatively slowly — needs time to build consensus through democratic processes	May not be fully coherent and may lack shared standards for measuring success
Native American Tribe	Frequently subject to internal conflicts between "progressive" and "traditional" factions Culturally more likely to work by consensus rather than majority vote	May be very slow, particularly if tribe works by consensus and deliberation	May be difficult to discern because of internal conflicts

There are many negotiations that do not require the level of analysis outlined in this essay. However, when faced with a complex negotiation involving different types of parties using representatives, looking at the structure of the larger conflict and the nature of the parties can be a very helpful process. It assists a negotiator in setting realistic expectations about such basic factors as how long a negotiation will probably take and the likelihood of ratification of an agreement reached at the primary negotiation table. A negotiator who understands the pressures and opportunities created by a counterpart's back table negotiations can also craft more creative proposals by incorporating the needs and interests of the agent and her principals into an agreement.

Notes and Questions

5.24 Docherty and Campbell use complex negotiations to make the point that you need to understand the internal structure of your counterpart. How could you apply these lessons even in the simpler context of two lawyers with two clients?

This next excerpt discusses a more direct approach to consider whether business lawyers are worth it. In other words, does the money you save in a deal by hiring a lawyer outweigh the money you spend on that lawyer?

 Ronald J. Gilson, **VALUE CREATION BY BUSINESS LAWYERS: LEGAL SKILLS AND ASSET PRICING**

94 Yale L.J. 243, 246, 252, 293, 303 (1984)

To be sure, the unfavorable views ascribed to the client reflect the view that business lawyers *reduce* the value of a transaction, while both the quite favorable view held by business lawyers themselves and the more neutral but still positive view offered in the academic literature assume that business lawyers *increase* the value of a transaction. But both sides do seem to agree on the appropriate standard by which the performance of business lawyers should be judged: *If what a business lawyer does has value, a transaction must be worth more, net of legal fees as a result of the lawyer's participation.* And the common failure of all of these views is not their differing conclusions. Rather, it is the absence of an explanation of the *relation* between the business lawyers' participation in a transaction and the value of the transaction to the clients. In other words, precisely *how* do the activities of business lawyers affect transaction value? . . .

We can thus add on a condition to the proposition that business lawyers have potential to add value to a transaction: The increase must be in the overall value of the transaction, not merely in the distributive share of one of the parties. That is, a business lawyer must show the potential to enlarge the entire pie, not just to increase the size of one piece at the expense of another. . . .

At this point we need to look more carefully at the assumptions on which capital asset pricing theory is built. Of particular importance to our inquiry are four:

1. All investors have a common time horizon — *i.e.*, they measure the return to be earned from the asset in question over the same period of time.
2. All investors have the same expectations about the future, in particular, about the future risk and return associated with the asset in question.
3. There are no transaction costs.
4. All information is costlessly available to all investors.

These assumptions, of course, do not describe the real world. Investors do not have the same time horizons; indeed, it is often precisely because they do not — for example, an older person may wish to alter the composition of his portfolio in favor of assets whose earnings patterns more closely match his remaining life span — that a transaction occurs in the first place. Similarly, investors do not have homogeneous expectations; the phenomenon of conflicting forecasts of earnings or value even among reputed experts is too familiar for that assumption to stand. Transaction costs, of course, are pervasive. Finally, information is often one of the most expensive and poorly distributed commodities. In short, the world in which capital assets are priced and transactions actually carried out differs in critical respects from the world of perfect markets in which capital asset pricing theory operates.

For a business lawyer, however, the unreality of these perfect market assumptions is not cause for despair. Rather, it is in the very failure of these assumptions to describe the real world that I find the potential for value creation by lawyers. When markets fall short of perfection, incentives exist for private innovations that improve market performance. As long as the costs of innovation are less than the resulting gains, private innovation to reduce the extent of market failure creates value. It is in precisely this fashion that opportunity exists for business lawyers to create value. . . .

I suggest that the tie between legal skills and transaction value is the business lawyer's ability to create a transactional structure which reduces transaction costs and therefore results in more accurate asset pricing. Put in terms of capital asset pricing theory, the business lawyer acts to constrain the extent to which conditions in the real world deviate from the theoretical assumptions of capital asset pricing. My hypothesis about what business lawyers *really* do — their potential to create value — is simply this: Lawyers function as *transaction cost engineers*, devising efficient mechanisms which bridge the gap between capital asset pricing theory's hypothetical world of perfect markets and the less-than-perfect reality of effecting transaction in this world. Value is created when the transactional structure designed by the business lawyer allows the parties to act, *for that transaction*, as if the assumptions on which capital asset pricing theory is based were accurate. . . .

I think the core of my hypothesis has been established: Important elements of the acquisition agreement serve to remedy failures of the perfect market assumptions on which capital asset pricing theory is based. Earnout or contingent-pricing techniques respond to the failure of the homogeneous expectations assumption; controls over operation of the seller's business during the period in which the determinants of the contingent price are measured respond to the failure of the common-time-horizon assumption; and the panoply of representations and warranties, together with provisions for indemnification and other verification techniques, respond to the failure of the costless-information, or as I have characterized it, the homogeneous-retrospection assumption. . . .

As my analysis of the contents of an acquisition agreement demonstrated, the fact is that, under the circumstances, business lawyers have done an awfully good job at something that law schools did not and, for the most part, still do not teach: helping people arrange their relationships in the absence of governmental intervention; facilitating *private ordering*.

Notes and Questions

5.25 How do lawyers help manage the four flaws of capital markets?

5.26 At the end of the article, Gilson argues that law schools really don't teach these skills — how to facilitate private ordering. What do you think?

Several years later, Gilson joined with Bob Mnookin to examine the value of lawyers in litigation. The same question was raised: What value do lawyers add to their clients' activities?

 Ronald J. Gilson & Robert H. Mnookin, **DISPUTING THROUGH AGENTS: COOPERATION AND CONFLICT BETWEEN LAWYERS IN LITIGATION**

94 Colum. L. Rev. 509, 510-512, 516, 520, 522-528, 565-566 (1995)

Today, the dominant popular view is that lawyers magnify the inherent divisiveness of dispute resolution. According to this vision, litigators rarely cooperate to resolve disputes efficiently. Instead, shielded by a professional ideology that is said to require zealous advocacy, they endlessly and wastefully fight in ways that enrich themselves but rarely advantage the clients. . . .

Purveyor of needless conflict need not be the only vision of the lawyer's role in litigation. Over a century ago, Abraham Lincoln suggested that lawyers can play an extraordinarily constructive role in disputes — as peacemakers who facilitate efficient and fair resolution of conflict when their clients could not do so for themselves. From this perspective, a central characteristic of the formal legal system — that clients carry on their dispute through lawyers who are their agents — has the potential for damping rather than exacerbating the conflictual character of litigation. In this Article we offer a conceptual foundation for this alternative perspective — a foundation that rests on the idea that lawyers may allow clients to cooperate in circumstances when their clients could not do so on their own. We construct this foundation using basic notions drawn from game theory and agency theory. . . .

Is the Prisoner's Dilemma an Appropriate Model for Litigation?

To what extent does the prisoner's dilemma represent an appropriate, albeit highly simplified, model of the litigation process? Focus first on the payoff structure. In a prisoner's dilemma, the best payoff for a player occurs when that player defects and the other player cooperates. The worst payoff results when a player cooperates while the other player defects. The other two outcomes fall between these extremes, with the reward for mutual cooperation better than the payoff for mutual defection. This means that a prisoner's dilemma cannot be a zero sum or purely distributive game: the total combined payoff from mutual cooperation must exceed the total combined payoff from mutual defection. Indeed, in a symmetric prisoner's dilemma, each player's payoff from mutual cooperation must be greater than each player's payoff from mutual defection. . . .

[T]he payoff structure specified for a prisoner's dilemma seems appropriate for many disputes. Moreover, verification problems make the adequate enforcement of binding general commitments to cooperate in litigation (whether imposed by contract or rule) highly problematic. Therefore, despite its restrictive assumptions about payoffs and blind action, the prisoner's dilemma game is a powerful heuristic for understanding the barriers to cooperation in litigation.

THE ROLE LAWYERS MIGHT PLAY IN OVERCOMING THE PRISONER'S DILEMMA

We are now ready to introduce individual lawyers into the clients' prisoner's dilemma model of litigation. Assuming the particular litigation game has the payoff structure of a prisoner's dilemma, each client would prefer mutual cooperation to mutual defection. However, each lacks the means credibly to commit to her good intentions. In this Part, we show how disputing through lawyers may provide a means to make such a commitment: Lawyers, acting as agents, have the potential to solve the game theoretic problem of mutual defection. We then consider the first level of the game theory-agency theory dialectic: how use of an agent to precommit to cooperate creates its own set of agency problems. Initially we consider a world of sole practitioners — all lawyers practice alone. Later we consider representation by firms of lawyers. . . .

A.   The Pre-Litigation Game: Choosing Lawyers

Assume that both clients must litigate through a lawyer (an assumption that, for a change, is descriptively accurate). Further suppose that there exists a class of sole practitioners who have reputations for cooperation which assure that, once retained, they will conduct the litigation in a cooperative fashion. Three final assumptions define our "pre-litigation game." First, clients disclose their choice of lawyer — and thus, whether they have chosen a cooperative lawyer — prior to the beginning of the litigation game. Second, if one client chooses a cooperative lawyer and her opponent does not, the client choosing a cooperative lawyer can change her mind without cost before the litigation game begins. Third, after the litigation game begins, clients cannot change lawyers.

Under these assumptions, disputing through lawyers provides an escape from the prisoner's dilemma. As we have defined the pre-litigation game, each client's dominant strategy is to choose a cooperative lawyer because the choice of a cooperative lawyer binds each client to a cooperative strategy. If client A chooses a cooperative lawyer and client B also chooses a cooperative lawyer, both clients receive the higher cooperative payoff. Alternatively, if client B does not choose a cooperative lawyer, client A is no worse off having initially chosen to cooperate. In that event, client A replaces her cooperative lawyer with a gladiator and is in the same position as if she had chosen a gladiator in the first instance. Thus, her dominant strategy is to choose a cooperative lawyer and to switch if her opponent does not adopt a parallel strategy. Of course, client B confronts the same choices and has the same dominant strategy. The result is a cooperative equilibrium because the introduction of lawyers has transformed the prisoner's dilemma payoff structure into a game in which the only choices are mutual cooperation or mutual defection. Mutual cooperation obviously has the higher payoff for each party.

This is the easy part. Designing a game in which the players can credibly commit is not difficult if one assumes the availability of commitment techniques. What makes the game interesting from a policy perspective is the extent to which its assumptions are consistent with institutional patterns. This consistency is what interests us about lawyers as sources of credible commitments: We believe the assumptions that define the pre-litigation game are roughly consistent with the way litigation occurs.

In the pre-litigation game, we first required clients to disclose their choice of lawyer before the game began. In real litigation, plaintiffs must typically disclose their choice of lawyer at the outset of litigation: the lawyer's name is, quite literally, the first thing that appears on the complaint. Similarly, the defendant must have a lawyer to respond to the complaint, and even to request an extension of the time in which to file an answer to the complaint. Again, this discloses the identity of the lawyer chosen.

We next assumed that a plaintiff choosing a cooperative lawyer could costlessly switch to a gladiator upon learning that her opponent had chosen a gladiator. In the real world, there are costs in switching lawyers, but these costs are likely to be low at the outset. A client will have expended little on her lawyer by the time the identity of her opponent's lawyer is revealed. Thus, for practical purposes, the game's assumption of a costless opportunity to switch lawyers on the disclosure of opposing counsel is roughly consistent with real litigation patterns.

The third assumption — that clients cannot change lawyers during the litigation game — is more problematic. At first glance, the assumption seems patently false; a client may discharge counsel at any time. On closer examination, the presence of substantial switching costs may provide a reasonable proxy for a prohibition against discharging cooperative counsel once the litigation is well underway. As litigation proceeds, a lawyer expends substantial time becoming familiar with the law and especially the facts of the case. The client pays for the lawyer's acquisition of this knowledge. The client's investment in the lawyer's knowledge is relationship-specific in the extreme; that is, it is of no value to the client if the lawyer is fired. Thus, the price of firing the lawyer is the cost of bringing another lawyer up to speed in the litigation. While not a prohibition on changing lawyers, switching costs impose a substantial penalty on defection. Indeed, the longer the litigation continues, the more switching will cost.

Thus, the special assumptions underlying our pre-litigation game are not implausible. What remains, however, is the most critical of the assumptions on which lawyers' potential to facilitate cooperation depends: the existence of lawyers with reputations for cooperation. How and why are such reputations created and sustained? How do clients learn which lawyers are cooperative? . . .

B.   A Reputation Market for Cooperative Lawyers

The preceding discussion suggests why there might be a demand for cooperative lawyers. Both parties to a lawsuit with a prisoner's dilemma payoff schedule would like to hire cooperative lawyers because that allows them to commit to a cooperative strategy. Clients should therefore be willing to pay a premium for such lawyers, reflecting a portion of the amount by which the cooperative payoff exceeds the noncooperative payoff.

Establishing the supply side is also straightforward. Lawyers would be willing to invest in achieving a reputation for cooperation because they would receive a return on that investment by virtue of the premium fees clients would be willing to pay. As in standard reputation models, the lawyer's investment in reputation serves two functions. First, it identifies the lawyer as one who possesses the desired, but otherwise unobservable, attribute; the client must be able to find a cooperative lawyer. Second, it represents the penalty that the market will impose if the lawyer treats his reputation as bait rather than as bond by turning into a gladiator at the request of an opportunistic client. Noncooperative behavior would forfeit the lawyer's investment in a cooperative reputation. Thus, so long as the lawyer's possible loss of investment in reputation exceeds the size of the bribe an opportunistic client would be willing to pay, cooperative lawyers will not be suborned and a market for cooperative lawyers should be available.

In our case, noncooperative conduct by one client's lawyer may not be verifiable, but may nonetheless be readily observable by the lawyer on the other side. Recall that the outcome of the pre-litigation game is that both clients retain cooperative lawyers. Thus, one lawyer's subsequent misconduct must, in the first instance, be observable only to the opposing lawyer, not to the client. A trained litigator, himself pursuing a cooperative strategy and completely familiar with the facts of the case, should be able to detect a change in the behavior of opposing counsel. After all, in litigation, noncooperative behavior by one lawyer must operate initially through its impact on the other side's lawyer. The lawyer can then pass on to the client the fact of noncooperative conduct — the reputation violation — following which both lawyer and client can impose the penalty of lost reputation on the misbehaving lawyer by distributing the information to the legal community.

Thus, the conditions necessary for the operation of a reputation market for cooperative lawyers are plausible, at least at this level of abstraction.

C. Agency Problems That May Subvert Cooperation

The employment of lawyers with identifiable reputations does have the potential to facilitate cooperation between clients in litigation. However, the use of agents to make credible the commitment to cooperate itself poses two potential agency problems. First, the two lawyer-agents may "conspire" to maximize their incomes at the expense of their clients through noncooperative behavior that prolongs the litigation and increases legal fees. When each lawyer stands as gatekeeper against the other lawyer's individual noncooperative misconduct, what protects both clients from the lawyers' joint determination to behave noncooperatively? Second, a client may subvert a lawyer with a reputation for cooperation. This second problem represents the converse of the first. For a lawyer with a limited number of clients, a particular client may be so important that the threat of withdrawn patronage may induce the lawyer to risk his cooperative reputation by behaving noncooperatively. In other words, there may be circumstances in which incentives may induce a lawyer to abandon his cooperative reputation.

CONCLUSION

Our story weaves together three principal ideas: (a) the prisoner's dilemma offers a suggestive and powerful metaphor for some aspects of litigation; (b) a lawyer's reputation may serve to bond a client's cooperation in the litigation process, thereby resolving the prisoner's dilemma; and (c) principal-agent conflicts (whether between lawyers and clients, or between lawyers and their firms) create incentives that sometimes facilitate cooperation in litigation but that, at other times, undermine cooperation. Our message is that the relationship between opposing lawyers and their capacity to establish credible reputations for cooperation have profound implications for dispute resolution: if the payoff structure establishes cooperation as the most desirable strategy and supportive institutional structures exist, lawyers may be able to damp conflict, reduce transaction costs, and facilitate dispute resolution.

Our story rests fundamentally on the idea that lawyers develop reputations, and that the reputation for being a cooperative problem-solver may be a valuable asset. When opposing lawyers know and trust each other, we believe there often will be substantial opportunities for both parties to benefit by reducing transaction costs. . . .

Theory suggests that a reputational market would operate most effectively when the size of the legal community is comparatively small. The actions of lawyers can then be well publicized, and lawyers can expect to face each other repeatedly in the future. Thus our analysis at least suggests why small-town lawyers may be less prone to exacerbate disputes with one another than are big-city lawyers, and also why one might expect to see a greater degree of cooperation within certain specialties than within the general community of attorneys.

Notes and Questions

5.27 What are the weaknesses in assuming that lawyers can build and use their litigation reputations? We discuss the impact of reputation in negotiation further in the next chapter.

5.28 In Saskatchawan, almost every single family lawyer has converted to collaborative lawyering (in which the parties and lawyers agree to work things out without litigation). Julie Macfarlane, Experiences of Collaborative Law: Preliminary Results from the Collaborative Lawyering Research Project, 2004 J. Disp. Res. 179. How does this evolution relate to the arguments made here?

This next excerpt describes an empirical test of the hypothesis above.

 Rachel Croson & Robert H. Mnookin, **DOES DISPUTING THROUGH AGENTS ENHANCE COOPERATION? EXPERIMENTAL EVIDENCE**

26 J. Legal Stud. 331, 344-345 (1997)

[I]n a recent article, Ronald Gilson and Robert Mnookin suggested . . . by choosing lawyers with reputations for cooperation, clients might be able to commit to cooperative litigation strategies in circumstances where the clients themselves would not otherwise trust each other. Using the methodology of experimental economics, this article presents the results of our test of their idea that, by choosing agents under well-specified procedures, principals may be able to cooperate more often than they could without such procedures. . . .

[Our] experiment involved two different treatments of a finitely repeated Prisoner's Dilemma game, one with the prelitigation game and one without. We derive the equilibria for our experimental games and discuss some important experimental procedures. . . . We find that significantly more cooperative agents are chosen (and cooperative moves made) in the prelitigation game than in the litigation game. These results are also compared with slightly different earlier Prisoner's Dilemma experiments. . . .

EXPERIMENTAL IMPLEMENTATION

The Games and Equilibria

The Gilson/Mnookin model predicts that there will be more cooperation in the prelitigation game than in the litigation game. The experiment designed to test this prediction involves two treatments of a finitely repeated Prisoner's Dilemma game.

In both treatments, subjects are shown a standard Prisoner's Dilemma matrix and asked to choose an agent to play this game 10 times in a row for them (to represent them in a lawsuit). Agent A (the cooperative lawyer) always plays A (the cooperative move). . . . Agent B (the gladiator lawyer) always plays B (the noncooperative move). . . . The experiment used to test this model introduces a third sort of lawyer, who is a mix between the two; the gladiator lawyer remains weakly dominant. Agent C (the lawyer without a reputation) will play any prespecified combination of A and B in periods 1-10. For simplicity, agent C's choices are assumed to be strict mixtures of moves A and B (subjects choosing agent C and specifying all A moves are treated as having chosen agent A).

In the treatment without the prelitigation game, subjects choose lawyers who then go on to represent them. In this game, the dominant strategy equilibrium is to choose a gladiator lawyer (agent B).

In the prelitigation game treatment, subjects choose a lawyer and are then matched. Any subject who chooses a cooperative lawyer (agent A) and faces a lawyer who is not cooperative (agents B or C) is given the option to change his choice. This two-stage game . . . has a Pareto-optimal sub-game perfect Nash equilibrium of always choosing agent A (cooperate throughout). In this equilibrium both players choose agent A (neither has the opportunity to switch), and both earn $5. To see that this is an equilibrium we show no player can be made better off by playing some other move. This game also has a (weak) Nash equilibrium of always choosing agent B. . . . The results of this experiment strongly supported the predictions of Gilson and Mnookin. As predicted, subjects in the prelitigation game were significantly more likely to choose cooperative lawyers than were subjects in the litigation game. . . .

In conclusion, two important but obvious points bear emphasis. First, as Gilson and Mnookin themselves point out, the real world of litigation is much more complicated than their model. They suggest that not all litigation has a payoff structure consistent with a Prisoner's Dilemma game. Moreover, the assumptions of the prelitigation game (and the rules governing our experiment) are demanding: reputations are known in advance, and stable; a client can costlessly switch from a cooperative attorney to a gladiatorial one if the other side fails to choose a cooperative attorney; and no changes in attorneys are permitted once the litigation game begins. A similar point was also made by Russell Korobkin, who suggested that in the real world litigants may not know or understand the payoffs involved with their choice of lawyers.

The realism or appropriateness of these (demanding) assumptions are not tested in the experiment presented in this article. Rather, the experiment provides a test of the *implications* of these assumptions. If all these conditions are met, is the outcome we observe the outcome we expect—more cooperation? The answer from this experiment is a conclusive yes.

The second point is equally obvious but also important. To the extent there are real-world institutions that facilitate and promote the efficiency of reputational markets, it would seem that cooperation might well be enhanced. These results pose an interesting question—well beyond the scope of this article—about what institutional arrangements might best support and promote the existence of reputational markets. Other sorts of research—empirical rather than experimental—might usefully explore the complex set of puzzles concerning how reputations are developed and are sustained, and how lawyers actually cooperate in the litigation process.

This section concludes with some practical advice that might be most useful to practitioners when dealing with lawyer-client issues.

 Scott Peppet, **SIX PRINCIPLES FOR USING NEGOTIATING AGENTS TO MAXIMUM ADVANTAGE**

in The Handbook of Dispute Resolution 189, 194-199 (Michael L. Moffitt & Robert C. Bordone eds., 2005)

Principle One: If Possible, Use Agents (and work for principals) Whose Preferences Are Known and Acceptable to You.   A simple first principle is to use agents, and to work for principals, [whom] you know or whose reputations you can discover. Agency relationships can easily go awry because of basic differences in orientation, perspective, or ideology. In the legal context, a client can be unpleasantly surprised to discover herself in a war of attrition when she simply sought legal advice and problem-solving counsel. Conversely, a lawyer may be confronted with a client who demands unsavory tactics or unethical behavior. As a result, just as clients screen their attorneys, lawyers sometimes try to screen potential clients by asking colleagues or friends for information about the client's history.

Finding out about your agent or principal before entering into an agency relationship is wise. Because of both monitoring and incentive-based solutions to agency problems, principals will be best served if they initially choose like-minded agents, and vice versa. In the negotiation context, this means asking about an agent's negotiation approach, experience, and philosophy. Does the agent have a reputation as an adversarial or hard bargainer? Is the principal likely to require deceptive or dishonest tactics? What stance does each take towards the risks inherent in trying to problem-solve or collaborate? Do they have similar goals and reputations? These questions are fundamental to establishing a successful principal-agent relationship in the negotiation context.

   Principle Two: If Possible, Use Agents (and work for principals) Whose Preferences are Known to the Other Side.   Negotiation can be roughly analogized to the famous Prisoner's Dilemma game. If two negotiators collaborate and share information openly (i.e., they "cooperate" in the game), they each benefit. Their ability to trust one another often will facilitate finding mutually-advantageous or "joint gain" solutions, and they are thus likely to reach more economically beneficial bargaining outcomes than they would if forced to deal with a hard-bargaining counterpart. Conversely, two hard-bargainers (or "defectors" in a Prisoner's Dilemma game) may each suffer. They may engage in difficult and adversarial tactics that increase transaction costs, decrease the odds of settlement, and lessen the chance of finding joint gains.

   To the extent that parties can separate out honest collaborators from deceptive hard-bargainers, collaborators will deal only with other collaborators, thus avoiding the possibility of exploitation and increasing the likelihood of a successful negotiation. Unfortunately, it may be difficult or impossible to be certain about a counterpart's type.

   This uncertainty imposes costs. To the extent that a party cannot sort collaborators from hard bargainers, she will enter a negotiation with trepidation. If she treats an undetectable hard bargainer as an honest collaborator, a negotiator may fare badly. As a result, she may choose to protect herself by limiting herself to "safe" strategies that protect against exploitation. She may withhold information about her needs and priorities from the other side, fearing that her counterpart will try to use that information to extract concessions. This can lead to failed negotiations — the negotiating parties may not reach agreement even though an agreement is possible. It may also cause inefficient outcomes — the parties may reach a deal, but it may not be the most economically beneficial deal possible.

   Ronald Gilson and Robert Mnookin have proposed an ingenious solution to this problem by analyzing the dynamics of negotiations in the legal context. Although they recognize that many clients, or principals, do not know each other and thus cannot sort hard bargainers from collaborators, they also realize that often an *attorney* does know opposing counsel. In a given city, for example, all of the family lawyers may know each other, and thus two divorce attorneys may be acquainted. As a result, a client can use her choice of agent — in this case, her choice of lawyer — to *signal* collaborative intent (or an intent to hard bargain) to the other side. If a client hires an attorney with a solid reputation for collaboration, it may facilitate pursuing that approach by indicating the client's preference for collaboration.

   This signal is not perfect. But it is certainly better than no signal at all, and worth serious consideration by a principal contemplating hiring a negotiating agent. Whenever possible, Principle Two suggests hiring a well-known agent [who] can serve as a strong signal of the principal's intentions. Whether hiring a sports agent, diplomat, political representative, or attorney, a principal should consider that agent's reputation and whether it will help to move the negotiation forward. I do not assume that all principals will want to pursue collaborative strategies. Some may want to hire an agent known as a hard bargainer. Regardless of strategy, however, a principal should ensure that her agent shares her orientation, strategy preferences, and approach, and that the agent has a reputation in line with the strategic signals that the principal seeks to send.

Principle Three: If Possible, Change the Structure of the Negotiation to Align the Incentives of Principal and Agent.   As discussed above, the incentives of principals and agents may diverge, leading an agent to act contrary to his principal's interests. Principals and agents must therefore try to arrange fee structures and other incentives to align their interests. Contingent fees can help. Bonuses for reaching a negotiated agreement also may incentivize a negotiating agent, as may bonuses for achieving certain performance objectives (such as settling for more or less than a given amount, creating certain types of value, or meeting certain of the principal's key interests). The point is that fees can help to minimize incentive divergence between principals and agents.

Principals and agents should also look beyond these basic fee arrangements and ask whether there are ways to change the basic structure of their negotiation for mutual advantage. The effort of the nascent "Collaborative Law" movement to change the traditional adversarial style of lawyers illustrates this process of structural adjustment. To date Collaborative Law has been used primarily in the family or divorce law context. The basic idea is simple. Both divorcing parties agree to hire self-identified "collaborative lawyers" to handle their case. The lawyers and parties then agree that, so long as each side is represented by a collaborative lawyer, the attorneys will serve their clients *only* during negotiations. In other words, if the attorneys fail to settle the case, they will withdraw. The parties and their lawyers sign limited retention agreements (LRAs) that limit the scope of the lawyer-client relationships and require the lawyers to withdraw if they cannot reach settlement. These agreements explain the lawyers' limited role and the mandatory mutual with-drawal provisions. In addition, the parties and their lawyers sign a collaborative law participation agreement (CLPA) at the start of their negotiations. This is a contract with the other side that signifies mutual interest in the Collaborative Law process.

Collaborative Law practitioners describe this contractual modification of the traditional lawyer-client relationship, and of the traditional lawyer-lawyer negotia-tion process, as a huge benefit for all involved. Collaborative Law practice is touted as more cost-effective, more creative, and less damaging to the clients' relationship than traditional adversarial litigation. It has become fashionable in the family law context — there are now at least eighty-seven local and regional Collaborative Law groups in twenty-five states.

Mandatory mutual withdrawal provisions are a clever alteration of the structure of the traditional lawyer-client principal-agent relationship. If the parties do not settle, the client loses because she must expend the costs necessary to find, hire, and train new counsel. This gives the client incentive to be reasonable. The lawyer, meanwhile, will lose the fees that the lawyer would normally receive for litigating the matter. This signals the lawyer's intent to collaborate and reach agreement.

Collaborative Law is a useful example of how a principal-agent relationship can be structured to meet the interests of both the principal and the agent. By signing an

LRA, both the lawyer and the client signal an intention to collaborate — to each other, and to the other side. These signals facilitate their working relationship, and make it more likely that they will productively negotiate for the principal. To the extent possible, principals and agents should consider such incentive-aligning, game-changing moves.

Principle Four: Share Information Between Principal and Agent to the Extent Necessary to Effect the Principal's Strategy.   As discussed above, coordinating information exchange between a principal and an agent can pose challenges. How much time should a principal spend educating her agent about her interests, priorities, and strategy preferences prior to a negotiation? Educating to the point that the agent is a functional equivalent of the principal is both unrealistic and unwise — such extensive information exchange would take so much time that it would eviscerate the efficiencies of using an agent in the first place. Yet this leaves a principal and agent having to decide how much information to share, and when, to prepare the agent to negotiate on the principal's behalf.

The challenge is that for two agents to negotiate successfully they must understand the strategy preferences of their principals *and* learn sufficient information from those principals to be able to interact without the principals present. In particular, if an agent hopes to problem-solve on his client's behalf, he must have more and different information than if he simply hopes to haggle. To problem-solve requires understanding his client's interests, priorities, risk preferences, and alternatives, as well as his client's perceptions, emotions, and sense of fairness. To haggle, an agent needs only to know more basic information such as his client's bottom line and aspirations.

Thus, Principle Four simply states that principals and agents should structure their information exchange to make it possible for the agent to enact the principal's choice of strategy in the principal's absence. In practice this means that discussion about strategy choice must be explicit, early, and ongoing during the principal-agent relationship. Only if the agent really understands the principal's preferred strategy can the agent know the sorts of questions to ask of the principal and the kind of information to insist upon.

One challenge, of course, is that in many negotiations the principal may not be able to determine beforehand what strategy to use. Strategy selection depends in part on sizing up the other side and how it seems inclined to negotiate. Principle Four thus requires an ongoing conversation between principal and client to coordinate information exchange based on lessons learned during interaction with the other side. If a negotiation seems to have the potential for complex, interest-based problem-solving, an agent should probably begin prepared to pursue such avenues at least to some limited degree. The agent can then return to the principal for more information if necessary.

Principle Five: Treat Role Coordination and Authority Delegation as an Ongoing Negotiation, Not a One-Time Event.   Principals often worry about how much authority to delegate to an agent. The problem is obvious — too much and the agent may make unwanted commitments for the principal, too little and the agent's freedom of action may be too restricted to permit a successful negotiation. This is one manifestation of the monitoring, incentive, and coordination problems in the negotiation context. Because principals cannot perfectly trust or monitor agents, they seek to control agents by restricting their agents' authority.

Roger Fisher and Wayne Davis have persuasively argued for a different approach to authority delegation. They advocate for principals and agents to conceive of authority allocation as an ongoing task that proceeds throughout the negotiation process. The question to ask, in other words, is not how *much* authority to delegate, but *when* to delegate authority. At the start of a negotiation, an agent should not have authority to make substantive commitments, but instead should only be able to establish a negotiation process and begin discussion with the other side. As bargaining progresses and both principal and agent learn more about the other side, the negotiation itself, and the agent's performance, the principal should begin to give the agent more leeway. Eventually, assuming that performance satisfies the principal, the agent should be given sufficient authority to negotiate a final settlement package and recommend it to the principal for approval.

One can complicate and challenge this approach. At the same time, it is fundamentally good advice, and a useful revision to the common approach to negotiation authority.

Principle Six: Rely Most Heavily on an Agent When Psychological Biases or Emotional Risks Cloud the Principal's Decision Making.   Negotiators are often subject to various cognitive and emotional heuristics or "biases" that can prevent rational decision-making and thus prevent reaching agreement. Sometimes agents can help. Research on how these cognitive, social, and emotional biases impact agents is still in its infancy, and it is important not to assume that agents are a panacea for these problematic effects. At the same time, some evidence suggests that agents may dampen these biases. At least in some instances, an agent may be less susceptible to these psychological phenomena, and thus able to balance out a principal's questionable tendencies. For example, an agent may be less prone than a principal to discount or misconstrue information learned from the other side.

At the very least, principals and agents should be attuned to the ways in which a principal's reasoning may be compromised or her thinking impacted by psychological biases. If a principal's emotions may cloud her decision-making, an agent can and should use his perspective, expertise, and judgment to help the principal reason more clearly. This is a benefit of agency and one way in which principals and agents can structure their relations to maximum advantage.

Notes and Questions

5.29 Having read all of the advice on principal–agent relationships, how should you prepare for a negotiation with your client?

5.30 Given that as lawyers we are often the agents rather than the principals in a negotiation, how does Peppet's advice to principals help us as agents?

Chapter 6

Relating to Your Counterpart: Reputation, Trust, Rapport, and Power

In the next set of chapters we turn to how a negotiator should think about and work with the other parties or "counterparts" to a negotiation. We begin with some of the interpersonal aspects of negotiation — building trust and rapport from known reputations or actual behavior, and the power relations between the parties that may be dynamic during the negotiation. Next we turn to the importance of the feeling or affective side of negotiation (Chapter 7). Then we explore the barriers to reaching agreements in negotiation (Chapter 8), including the cultural and demographic differences that may exist between the negotiators or parties (Chapter 9). We then examine the ethical (Chapter 10) and legal (Chapter 11) constraints on legal negotiations in Part III of this book.

This chapter tackles some of the most important elements in working with your negotiation counterpart. We begin with reputation and how reputation affects negotiation assumptions and strategies. Closely linked to reputation is the question of how trust and rapport are built or destroyed during negotiations. Finally, we explore how perceptions of power affect negotiation.

A. REPUTATION

 Steven Glick & Rachel Croson, **REPUTATIONS IN NEGOTIATION**

> in **Wharton on Making Decisions 178-186 (Stephen J. Hoch, Howard C. Kunreuther & Robert E. Gunther eds., 2001)**

Real estate developer Donald Trump has a well-publicized reputation as a hard-line negotiator. In an article describing his negotiations with the Taj Mahal Casino Resort's bondholders, Trump's advisors tell how after a deal is agreed upon, he always comes back requesting something more. Well-informed counterparts, familiar with his reputation, are prepared for this tactic and anticipate it in deciding how many concessions to make during the preagreement stage. Similarly, Trump has a reputation for storming out of negotiations in the middle of talks. An anonymous participant in the bondholders negotiation said, "You know Donald's going to get up and leave, you just don't know when." Once negotiators develop reputations for hardball tactics like these, counterparts change their tactics and strategies to accommodate. . . .

YOU HAVE A REPUTATION—WHETHER YOU KNOW IT OR NOT

In negotiation communities, almost everyone has a reputation, even if it is sketchy and second hand. This prevalence of reputations is a direct result of the degree of information exchanged within the community. "If you are hooked into the right network, and have the right people on your side, you can find out an incredible amount about the person you are negotiating with," noted [one] Silicon Valley entrepreneur.

A study of 105 graduate and undergraduate students enrolled in a negotiations course at the Wharton School demonstrated the speed with which reputations are established within a negotiation community. As part of the course, students negotiated with each other and conducted debriefing sessions with their classmates. Reputations quickly developed and spread among the students as to who was what type of negotiator. Clearly, the classroom setting and prescribed pattern of interaction accelerated information sharing and reputation development. However, in other key dimensions, the negotiation community created in the classroom closely mirrors those found in the business world.

In this study, we asked students to rate their negotiating partners based on five reputation types. They were organized from least cooperative (most confrontational or toughest) to most cooperative (softest):

1. Liar/Manipulator: Will do anything to gain an advantage
2. Tough but Honest: Very tough negotiator but doesn't lie, makes few concessions
3. Nice and Reasonable: Will make concessions/be conciliatory
4. Cream Puff: Will make concessions/be conciliatory regardless of what you do
5. No Particular Reputation

Reputations can be formed based on either first-hand experience or second-hand experience. First-hand reputations come from negotiating yourself with the person in question; second-hand reputations are based on information about the negotiating experiences of others. Since we are interested in both types of reputations, we did not distinguish between the two....

This first study demonstrates the existence of negotiation reputations within a group of individuals. But what impact do these reputations have on the actions of partners? In a second study, we examined the effect of these reputations on the negotiation process and the tactics used.

HOW REPUTATIONS AFFECT NEGOTIATING TACTICS

A subset of 75 of the business students who had participated in the first study on reputation communities participated in a second study on the impact of these reputations. Negotiators were provided with a list of tactics and asked to indicate which of those they would use or had used against counterparts of varying reputations:

1. Beginning with extreme demands
2. Threatening to walk away from the negotiation
3. Evading the questions of your counterpart

4. Asking pointed questions of your counterpart
5. Sharing information voluntarily
6. Making unilateral concessions

The first four of these tactics are "hardball" tactics, typically used in distributive (win-lose) negotiations—beginning with extreme demands, threatening to walk, asking pointed questions of your counterpart, and evading your partner's questions. The last two are tactics more appropriate for integrative (win-win) negotiations—sharing information voluntarily or offering unilateral concessions. . . .

Interestingly, however, reputations did not influence the tactics used in a uniform way. Confrontational tactics were more likely to be used against "tough" negotiators (for defensive reasons), but *also* against "soft" negotiating types (for offensive reasons). These tactics were not often used against participants with reputations for moderate negotiating styles. Similarly, integrative (win-win) tactics were used more often against participants with moderate negotiation styles than against either tough or soft negotiators. For example, 53 percent of the respondents said they begin with an extreme demand when facing a liar/manipulator and 40 percent against a tough but fair negotiator. Subjects were statistically significantly less likely to use this tactic against negotiators who were nice and reasonable (20 percent). However, the incidence of using this tactic rose to 47 percent against a cream puff negotiator.

We speculate that the first two uses of this tactic are defensive; in order to hold your own against a liar or tough negotiator you need to begin with extreme demands. In contrast, the latter use of this tactic is offensive; starting with an extreme demand will often yield benefits against a cream puff. Against a nice and reasonable negotiator, however, beginning with extreme demands may spoil the negotiation atmosphere.

We found a similar but inverted relationship between tactics and reputations for integrative tactics. For example, subjects were reluctant to share information voluntarily with either tough negotiators or with cream puffs (44 percent and 33 percent respectively). Significantly more subjects (83 percent) were willing to share information with nice and reasonable negotiating partners. Here, we speculate that the reluctance to share information with tough or manipulative negotiators is defensive, and the reluctance to share information with cream puffs is offensive. . . .

Cathy Tinsley et al., TOUGH GUYS FINISH LAST: THE PERILS OF A DISTRIBUTIVE REPUTATION

88 Org. Behav. & Hum. Decision Processes 621, 621-642 (2001)

One hundred and twenty MBA students from two eastern U.S. universities participated as part of a course on negotiations. Participants were paired across universities to negotiate a multi-issue buyer-seller agreement over email. The negotiation involved the potential sale of a TV show into syndication and had one distributive issue (price), two integrative issues that can be traded (payment schedule and number of runs), one compatible issue (juniors), and the possibility for a contingency contract (projected ratings). Students were given 10 days in which to negotiate. They were told to keep a running log of their dialogue over email and to forward this process to their respective professors once agreement was reached or time had run out. Although negotiators typically try to maximize their final outcomes, the process by which final outcomes are maximized is mixed motive in nature, meaning that each negotiator is trying to both create value (integrate) and claim value (distribute). Uncertainty abounds in that a negotiator rarely knows for sure what his counterpart cares about, what his alternatives might be, and thus whether his counterpart's behavior is an attempt to create value or claim value. . . .

Because reputations provide negotiators with a schema for understanding the counterpart's character, they help a negotiator "identify" (i.e., interpret the meaning of) a counterpart's action. . . .

[W]hen negotiations are more distributive than integrative in nature, parties with a distributive reputation (i.e., those who are generally characterized as being skilled value claimers) may reap significant rewards regardless of whether they actually employ these tactics. However, when negotiations have a significant integrative potential, as most do, then having a reputation as a skilled distributive negotiator might be a handicap. To achieve a negotiation's integrative potential, negotiators must, among other things, make tradeoffs among issues and add issues that might address the other party's interests. The success of these tactics lies in sharing information to develop an accurate understanding of the parties' interests and priorities. For example, if a party understands what her counterpart cares about, she can propose trades that will meet her counterpart's interests, or she can offer other resources that may not otherwise be considered. An accurate understanding of each other's interests requires negotiators to build rapport and create an environment of trust at the table. Shared trust engenders a cooperative orientation, which encourages parties to share specific information about their interests, preferences, and priorities.

These tactics — building rapport, trust, and sharing information — are likely to be undercut by a negotiator's distributive reputation. The discovery that one's counterpart has a distributive reputation is likely to bring to mind a schema of a typical hard bargainer. This would likely be an image of someone who is singularly focused on maximizing his/her own gain by making extreme offers, conceding little, threatening the other party's resistance point, and employing other tough tactics. Although these hard bargaining tactics can maximize individual profit on distributive issues, they can interfere for issues that provide opportunities for joint gain. To the extent that negotiations have an integrative potential, a negotiator's distributive reputation is likely to undercut his profit. Specifically, we expect that negotiators who face counterparts with a distributive reputation will develop relatively negative perceptions of the counterpart's intentions which will affect the focal negotiator's willingness to be vulnerable and share information about interests and priorities. This lack of information will constrain the parties' abilities to find joint benefit, hurting both individual and dyadic outcomes. . . .

We sought to investigate whether and how reputational information about one's counterpart would affect the process and outcomes of negotiation. Generally, our data confirmed our hypotheses that a distributive reputation hurts a party because the negotiator facing that party forms negative prejudices of that party's intentions . . . , which then affect the subsequent interaction. The negotiator becomes reluctant to share information . . . and is sensitive to controlling the interaction. . . . As a result, the party with the distributive reputation, despite his or her relative expertise, is unable to create joint value . . . or claim individual value. . . . Although the relative experts . . . [who were given no reputation information] . . . were able to achieve significantly more value than their novice counterparts, for those experts assigned a distributive reputation, the advantages of their relative expertise were outweighed by the disadvantages of their distributive reputation. As a result, they did no better than their novice opponents.

We also found that the schematic interpretations and reciprocity might create a "Pygmalion" effect. Specifically, negotiators' expectations and interpretations of their "distributive" counterparts' behaviors, and their own distributive behavior, induced their counterparts to behave more distributively than counterparts in the control condition. . . .

Given the powerful effects of reputations, it seems critical for negotiators to attend to them. Although all negotiations ultimately require value-claiming skills, negotiators should be wary of developing a reputation for being a bargainer who prizes claiming value over other goals, as this is likely to undercut profits when integrative issues are on the table. Similarly, the findings suggest that negotiators carefully attend to their behavior at the table to avoid evoking in their counterparts a schema of a distributive bargainer, especially when a negotiation has integrative potential. Simply expressing a willingness to cooperate with the other side to create value may help avoid elicitation of such a schema.

It also would behoove negotiators to avoid prejudging their counterparts based on limited reputation information. Our results show that a "distributive reputation" label, even one that was unjustified, negatively influenced negotiators' perceptions and behaviors, which, in turn, caused the labeled party to behave more distributively. Here, both minimal and incorrect information about a counterpart's distributive reputation created a harmful self-fulfilling prophesy that constrained both parties' actions and limited both parties' profits. We would advise negotiators to attend to information about their counterparts' reputations, but they should be vigilant about verifying and falsifying this information during the initial stages of the negotiation. That is, negotiators should look for both confirming and disconfirming evidence of their early impressions of the counterpart. . . .

While research in the cognitive tradition shows how judgment errors (such as fixed pie bias) limit joint gain, our study shows how social information (negotiator reputation) *shapes* these judgments. Parties attend to social information (here, reputations) to shape their judgments about the opponent's intentions; these judgments affect the negotiator's behavior, the counterpart's responses, and the outcome. This implies that reputations are likely to be a critical antecedent to the kinds of cognitive biases and errors that have been found to limit outcomes. Moreover, it suggests that reputations may be a mechanism by which negotiators construct or enact their own negotiation situation.

Similarly, past research has established that when negotiators discuss their interests, they make fewer decision errors and reach more integrative agreements. Negotiators' motives (e.g., individualistic versus prosocial) have been shown to affect

246 *Part II* Skills for Negotiation

whether negotiators will risk exploitation and divulge information. Our study offers another antecedent variable to determining whether negotiators will risk exploitation in pursuit of high joint gains — namely, the reputation of the counterpart. A counterpart's distributive reputation appears to inhibit negotiators from taking the risks necessary to achieve high quality agreements.

Finally, our results showed that one's own unjustified reputation can create a self-fulfilling prophecy that may be difficult to avoid. This suggests that the degree to which negotiators are interwoven at the table goes beyond simple behavioral reciprocity. Rather parties' cognitions and behaviors may be intertwined such that one party's *perceptions* of the other side can affect the other side's *actual behavior*. This level of reciprocity might explain why parties get started down a distributive power spiral, even though neither intended to start this destructive cycle. . . .

Having a distributive reputation, whether deserved or not, hurts negotiators in an integrative exchange because their counterparts infer relatively more sinister intentions, fostering a pattern of avoidance and control behavior, which decreases negotiators' individual and joint gain. Finding that reputations matter suggests that negotiations should be conceptualized as exchanges embedded in a longer chain of exchanges rather than as discrete transactions. . . .

Notes and Questions

6.1 What lessons do the empirical studies tell you about the impact of reputation? What kind of reputation would you want to cultivate as a negotiator?

6.2 If this is a negotiation class with exercises in class, what type of reputation do you think you have thus far among your classmates? Why should this matter?

6.3 Outside of class or empirical studies, how can lawyers build their reputations in negotiation? Are there ways to build your reputation outside of negotiation? See Kathleen M. O'Connor & Catherine Tinsley, Looking for an Edge in Negotiations? Cultivate an Integrative Reputation (2005), for an empirical study of differing reputations among business school negotiators.

B. TRUST

Any negotiation involves an element of trust — whether to trust the other side, how to verify their statements, how to get over hurdles of mistrust, how to continue to build trust. In the Prisoner's Dilemma, discussed earlier, trust is at the core of the dilemma: with trust, we cooperate to reach mutual goals; without trust, we enter into a cycle of defection and lost opportunity. This next excerpt from business school professor Roy Lewicki and psychology professor Barbara Bunker discusses the different types of trust and how to build trust in a relationship.

Roy J. Lewicki & Barbara Benedict Bunker, **TRUST IN RELATIONSHIPS: A MODEL OF DEVELOPMENT AND DECLINE**

**in Conflict Cooperation and Justice 133, 142-143, 145-146, 148-156, 167-169
(Barbara Benedict Bunker, Jeffrey Rubin et al. eds., 1995)**

Is trust easier to destroy than it is to build? The presumption that the answer to this question is a resounding yes has been prevalent in cooperation and conflict management research for over thirty years. Observation of the relationship development process between subjects in simple experimental research game paradigms (for example, Prisoner's Dilemma . . .) shows that cooperative behavior can be developed over a long series of predictable moves by the parties. But this cooperation can be rapidly destroyed if one party decides to defect — if the defection violates the expectations of the other — and can be even more destructive if the defection occurs after the parties have made some explicit agreement to coordinate their moves. Similarly, friends, spouses, and business partners may take months or years to learn how to cooperate with each other; yet the foundations of their cooperation can be destroyed in a heartbeat if one party engages in behavior destructive to that cooperation. . . .

CALCULUS-BASED TRUST

[T]he first kind of trust [is] deterrence-based trust: individuals will do what they say because they fear the consequences of not doing what they say. Like any behavior based on a theory of deterrence, trust is sustained to the degree that the deterrent (punishment) is clear, possible, and likely to occur if the trust is violated. Thus, the threat of punishment is likely to be a more significant motivator than the promise of reward.

A broader view of deterrence-based trust is that this form is grounded not only in the fear of punishment for violating the trust but also in the rewards to be derived from preserving it. At this level, trust is an ongoing, market-oriented, economic calculation whose value is derived by comparing the outcomes resulting from creating and sustaining the relationship to the costs of maintaining or severing it. This transactional view of trust is based on concepts used to describe the economic behavior of actors in a firm, only applied at the interpersonal transaction level. Based on these concepts, calculus-based trust in any given transaction with another may be derived by determining:

- Benefits to be derived from staying in the relationship
- Benefits to be derived from cheating on the relationship
- Costs of staying in the relationship
- Costs of breaking the relationship

For multiple transactions in a relationship — more typical of human interaction — we may develop a broader set of calculations that includes the number of different types of interdependence, the costs and benefits derived from cheating (breaking those interdependencies), and the associated costs and benefits of seeking other relationships. . . .

In summary, for the threat of deterrence to be effective, the following conditions must exist:

- The potential loss of future interaction with the other must outweigh the profit potential that comes from defecting from the relationship. The short-term temptation to cheat, and the gains accruing from such behavior, must be overshadowed by the long-term costs if one is caught.
- Deterrence requires monitoring to work; the parties must monitor each other and be willing to tell each other when a trust violation has been noted.
- An injured party must be willing to withdraw benefits from — or harm — the person acting distrustfully. In short, threats must be credible and must be executed, even if their execution destroys the relationship. . . .
- Finally, the calculations of calculus-based trust may be shaped by the actor's orientation toward risk. . . .

KNOWLEDGE-BASED TRUST

The second form of trust is knowledge-based trust. This form of trust is grounded in the other's predictability; we can anticipate his or her behavior. Knowledge-based trust relies on information rather than deterrence. The better we know the other individual, the more accurately we can predict what he or she will do; as long as the other remains predictable (that is, confirming our knowledge and acting consistently with that knowledge), trust will endure.

There are several dimensions to this knowledge-based trust. First, and most simple, information contributes to predictability of the other, which contributes to trust. The better I know the other, the better I can trust what the other will do because I can accurately predict how they will respond in most situations.

Second, predictability enhances trust even if the other is predictably untrustworthy because we can predict the ways that the other will violate the trust. Brothers who are always competing with each other learn to anticipate the other's tactics so well that they can predict exactly how one will attempt to cheat and therefore take measures to ensure that cheating isn't attempted.

Third, accurate prediction requires an understanding that develops over repeated interactions in multidimensional relationships (similar to calculus-based trust) plus two additional factors: regular communication and courtship. Regular communication puts a party in constant contact with the other, which allows for exchanging information about wants, preferences, and approaches to problems. Regular communication enhances our ability to understand the way the other approaches the world and allows us to compare it with our own. Without regular communication, we lose touch with each other — not only emotionally but in our ability to think like and react like the other. Courtship is behavior specifically directed at relationship development, at learning more about a possible partner. Courtship is conducted by "interviewing" the other, watching the other perform in social situations, experiencing the other in a variety of emotional states, and learning how other people view the other's behavior. Courtship permits actors to gain enough information to determine whether the parties can work together well, whether compatibility in style, approach, and preferences exist. . . .

IDENTIFICATION-BASED TRUST

The third type of trust is based on identification, that is, a full internalization of the other's desires and intentions. At this third level, trust exists because the parties effectively understand, agree with, and endorse each other's wants; this mutual understanding is developed to the point that each can effectively act for the other. Identification-based trust thus permits a party to serve as the other's agent and to substitute for the other in interpersonal transactions. The other can be confident that his or her interests will be fully defended and protected, without surveillance or monitoring of the actor. A true affirmation of the strength of identification-based trust between parties is found when one party acts for the other even more zealously than the other might. For example, if [P]arty A is hesitant to defend himself against criticism from an outsider but Party B is willing to take on the outsider and aggressively protect A, A's trust in B may be affirmed and enhanced by B's willingness to do for A what A could not do for himself. . . .

A corollary of this acting for each other in identification-based trust is that as both knowledge and identification develop, a party not only knows and identifies with the other but comes to understand what the party herself must do to sustain the other's trust. This process might be described as second-order learning. A learns what really matters to B and comes to place the same importance on those behaviors as B does. For example, Spouse A comes to learn how critical Spouse B believes it is to pick up the children from day care at the appointed hour. Spouse B is concerned for the children, who have been at day care all day, and also has high empathy for the teachers in the day-care center, who want to go home on time. Spouse A knows that if he is late, Spouse B will become very angry and take this lateness as evidence that Spouse A can't be trusted to pick up the children on time. Thus, Spouse A has internalized the same sense of urgency as Spouse B and regularly makes sure that he is not late to pick up the children. . . .

[Four activities serve to develop identification-based trust.]

- *Commonalty in name* (collective identity). One vehicle to create common identification is a joint name or identity. Mergers, strategic alliances, and joint ventures create new company names and identities — buildings, logos, mission statements, slogans, trademarks, colors, and so on — to constantly remind themselves and others of their collective intentions. . . .
- *Colocation.* A second way to create a common identification is to colocate — the same city, same building, same room — or to share some linking vehicle, such as a communication tool, work flow system, meeting structure, or even bathroom or coffee pot. . . .
- *Creation of joint products and goals.* When people work to create joint products and goals, they strengthen their identification with each other. . . .
- *Shared values.* Finally, over time, the parties can actually come to believe in and stand for the same core values, beliefs, and concerns. To the degree that this actually happens, one partner can effectively stand in for the other. . . .

The next excerpt continues the analysis of how different types of trust affect behavior and rebuilding trust.

 Roy J. Lewicki & Carolyn Wiethoff, **TRUST, TRUST DEVELOP-MENT, AND TRUST REPAIR**

in The Handbook of Conflict Resolution: Theory and Practice 100-103 (Morton Deutsch & Peter T. Coleman eds., 2000)

Strategies of trust restoration necessarily differ with the kind of relationship the parties have. . . .

1. *The existence of trust between individuals makes conflict resolution easier and more effective.* This point is obvious to anyone who has been in a conflict. A party who trusts another is likely to believe the other's words and assume that the other will act out of good intentions, and probably look for productive ways to resolve a conflict should one occur. Conversely, if one distrusts another, one might disbelieve the other's words, assume that the other is acting out of bad intentions, and defend oneself against the other or attempt to beat and conquer the other. As we have tried to indicate several times in this chapter, the level of trust or distrust in a relationship therefore definitively shapes emergent conflict dynamics.

2. *Trust is often the first casualty in conflict.* If trust makes conflict resolution easier and more effective, eruption of conflict usually injures trust and builds distrust. It does so because it violates the trust expectations, creates the perception of unreliability in the other party, and breaks promises that have been broken. Moreover, the conflict may serve to undermine the foundations of identification-based trust that may exist between the parties. Thus, as conflict escalates — for whatever reason or cause — it serves to decrease trust and increase distrust. The deeper the distrust that is developed, the more the parties focus on defending themselves against the other or attempting to win the conflict, which further serves to increase the focus on distrust and decrease actions that might rebuild trust.

3. *Creating trust in a relationship is initially a matter of building calculus-based trust.* Many of those writing on trust have suggested that one of the objectives in resolving a conflict is to "build trust." Yet in spite of these glib recommendations, few authors are sufficiently detailed and descriptive of those actions required to actually do so. From our review of the literature and the research we have reported in this chapter, it is clear to us that to build trust a party must begin with those actions we outline in this chapter: act consistently and reliably, meet deadlines and commitments, and repeatedly do so over time or over several bands of activity in the relationship.

4. *Relationships can be further strengthened if the parties are able to build identification-based trust.* Strong calculus-based trust is critical to any stable relationship, but IBT (based on perceived common goals and purposes, common values, and

common identity) is likely to strengthen the overall trust between the parties and enhance the ability of the relationship to withstand conflict that may be relationship fracturing. If the parties perceive themselves as having strong common goals, values, and identities, they are motivated to sustain the relationship and find productive ways to resolve the conflict so that it does not damage the relationship.

5. *Relationships characterized by calculus-based or identification-based distrust are likely to be conflict laden, and eruption of conflict within that relationship is likely to feed and encourage further distrust.* At the calculus-based level, the actor finds the other's behavior (at least) unreliable and unpredictable, and the other's intentions and motivations might be seen as intentionally malevolent in nature. At the identification-based level, the actor believes that he and the other are committed to dissimilar goals, values, and purposes and might thus attribute hostile motives and intentions to the other. Once such negative expectations are created, actions by the other become negative self-fulfilling prophecies (I expect the worst of the other and his behavior confirms my worst fears), which often leads the conflict into greater scope, intensity, and even intractability.

6. *As we have noted, most relationships are not purely trust and distrust but contain elements of both.* As a result, we have positive and negative feelings about the other, which produces another level of conflict: an intraphysic conflict often called "ambivalence." States of ambivalence are characterized by elements of both trust and distrust for another; the internal conflict created by that ambivalence serves to undermine clear expectations of the other's behavior and force the actor to scrutinize every action by the other to determine whether it should be counted in the trust or the distrust column. Ambivalent relationships are often finely grained and finely differentiated because the actor is forced to determine the contexts in which the other can be trusted and those in which the other should be distrusted. As noted elsewhere, ambivalence can lead actors to become incapacitated in further action, or to modify strategies of influence with the other party. Thus, an actor's internal conflict between trust and distrust probably also affects how he handles the interpersonal conflict between himself and the other party. Because of the number of bands in the bandwidth of a relationship, and the ways in which trust and distrust can mix in any given relationship, we also argue that relationships holding varied degrees of ambivalence are far more common than relationships characterized by "pure" high trust or high distrust.

7. *Finally, it is possible to repair trust — although it is easier to write about the steps of such repair than to actually perform it.* Effective trust repair is often a key part of effective conflict resolution. In the preceding section of this chapter, we have talked about some of the steps that are necessary to repair trust.

However, as we noted, repairing trust may take a long time, because the parties have to reestablish reliability and dependability that can only occur over time. Therefore, although rebuilding trust may be necessary for effective conflict resolution in the relationship over the long run, addressing and managing the distrust may be the most effective strategy for short-term containment of conflict. By managing distrust, as noted earlier, we engage in certain activities.

1. We explicitly address the behaviors that created the distrust. These may be actions of unreliability and undependability, harsh comments and criticism, or aggressive and antagonistic activities occurring as the conflict escalated.
2. If possible, each person responsible for a trust violation or an act of distrust should apologize and give a full account of the reasons for the trust violation. Acknowledging responsibility for actions that created the trust violation, and expressing regret for harm or damage caused by the violation, is often a necessary step in reducing distrust.
3. We restate and renegotiate the expectations for the other's conduct in the future. The parties have to articulate expectations about the behavior that needs to occur, and commit to those behaviors in future interactions.
4. We agree on procedures for monitoring and verifying the designated actions, to ensure that commitments are being met.
5. We simultaneously create ways to minimize our vulnerability or dependence on the other party in areas where distrust has developed. This often occurs as the vulnerable parties find ways to ensure that they are no longer vulnerable to the other's exploitation or identify alternative ways to have their needs met. If one person depends on another for a ride to work and the driver is consistently late or occasionally forgets, then even if the actor accepts the other's apology and commitment to be more reliable, the actor may also explore alternative ways to get to work.

Notes and Questions

6.4 Think of relationships you have at each level of trust. What types of relationships are these?

6.5 How does one move from one level of trust to another? Can you think of your own examples of this happening?

In the best relationships, the relationship helps facilitate the negotiation and makes the negotiation itself more efficient. In the best negotiations, the negotiation improves the relationship. At the heart of relationship building is the idea of trust.

Trust at the United Nations

There are many instances when the element of trust between negotiators — even those coming from countries that are not allies — has made a difference. Lord Caradon, formerly British Permanent Representative to the United Nations, recalls such an incident:

> In 1967 when we put forward a British resolution, 242, on the Middle East . . . I thought we had the nine votes in the [Security] Council and we had worked for it and we thought we had got it. We were going in to take the vote on the Monday, when on the Sunday night they called up from my delegation and said, "It's no use." I said, "What's happened?" They said, "At this last moment there is a Russian resolution put down, clearly a wrecking resolution, an extreme resolution." . . .
>
> Then Deputy Foreign Minister Kuznetzov wants to see me. I greatly respect him. Could he see me alone? Certainly. So we go into a little room by the Security Council, and he says at once, "I want you to give me two days." And I say, "Look, ask me anything else, but don't ask me that. We haven't been to bed for several nights and I don't suppose you have either. We've got the nine votes, I think." . . .
>
> And then he said, "I am not sure you understand what I am saying to you. I am personally asking you for two days."
>
> So I wonder what my delegation will think or what my Government will think about it, but I go back into the Council and say that at this last moment a request has been made for a postponement of this all-important vote, and I ask for an adjournment till Wednesday evening.
>
> On the Wednesday you go down — there can't be any postponements now. . . .
>
> You proceed to the vote, and you vote by raising your hand as you know. You raise your right hand in support of the British resolution because it was down first. Then there is a sort of ragged cheer from the back of the press gallery, and then you realize that it's a unanimous vote. The Russians too voted for the British resolution; that's why he was asking me for the two days. He couldn't have asked me in those terms unless he was going to work with the rest of the delegates; actually I didn't expect him to do more than to abstain. But when he said, "I am personally asking you for two days," he meant that he was not out to wreck my own initiative; he wanted time to refer back to his government to get support for our resolution. What he was saying to me was a question of trust; it all depended on working together.

William Zartman & Maureen R. Berman, The Practical Negotiator, 39-41 (1982).

In this last excerpt, business school professor Leigh Thompson provides some specific advice on how to build trust and how to rebuild trust if it has been broken. Note how many of these ideas are similar to the ideas needed to influence others outlined by Guthrie and Cialdini in Chapter 2.

Leigh Thompson, THE MIND AND HEART OF
THE NEGOTIATOR

131–136, 138 (3d ed. 2005)

BUILDING TRUST: PSYCHOLOGICAL STRATEGIES

A variety of psychological tools can be used to enhance and build trust between people....

Similarity. People who are similar to each other like one another. The *similarity-attraction effect* may occur on the basis of little, and sometimes downright trivial, information.... Negotiators are more likely to make concessions when negotiating with people they know and like. Savvy negotiators increase their effectiveness by making themselves similar to the other party....

Mere Exposure. The more we are exposed to something — a person, object, or idea — the more we come to like it.... Savvy negotiators increase their effectiveness by making themselves familiar to the other party. Instead of having a single-shot negotiation, they suggest a preliminary meeting over drinks and follow with a few phone calls and unexpected gifts....

Good Mood. People in a good mood are more agreeable. Funny cartoons, unexpected little gifts, small strokes of fortune, and thinking positive thoughts all engender a good mood....

Physical Presence. People form both personal and business relationships to others who are literally physically close to them. For example, when students are seated alphabetically in a classroom, friendships are significantly more likely to form between those whose last names begin with the same or nearby letter.... This point may not seen important until you consider the fact that you may meet some of your closest colleagues,

---

Trust in Football

Superagent and attorney Leigh Steinberg negotiated quarterback Drew Bledsoe's multiyear contract with New England Patriots owner Bob Kraft. The two of them were sitting in a loud, crowded hotel lobby during the National Football League (NFL) Owners' Conference. As they led up to their bargaining positions, other people were interrupting them, thus making it difficult to talk or build a connection. In the midst of the interruptions and chaos, Kraft proposed $29 million over 7 years. Steinberg countered with $51 million. Insulted, angry, and shaking his head, Kraft got up and walked out. Steinberg had made a mistake, but instead of inflaming the situation, he gave it more time. Six months later, Steinberg asked Kraft to dinner at a quiet Italian restaurant. He let Kraft vent anger and frustration over Bledsoe's proposed salary. It came out that Kraft had interpreted the high counteroffer as a signal that Bledsoe wanted nothing to do with the team and instead wanted to be a free agent. Calmly, Steinberg assured Kraft that Bledsoe wanted to stay. He explained that in the hubbub of the lobby six months earlier, Steinberg had not been able to create the solid rapport that they had that evening and had not been able to establish an atmosphere of trust. That night, they settled on $42 million. Says Steinberg, "The key to successful negotiations is to develop relationships, not conquests."...

Leigh Thompson, The Mind and Heart of the Negotiator 133 (3d ed. 2005).

and perhaps even a future business partner, merely because of an instructor's seating chart! . . .

Reciprocity. According to the *reciprocity principle*, we feel obligated to return in kind what others have offered or given to us. . . . People feel upset and distressed if they have received a favor from another person and are prevented from returning it. . . .

Don't Gloat. Negotiators should resist the urge to gloat or show signs of smugness following negotiations. In one investigation, some negotiators gloated following their negotiation. Other negotiators made self-effacing remarks. . . . Later, negotiators who overheard the other party gloat or make self-effacing remarks were given the opportunity to provide valuable stock options to these same parties. Those parties who gloated received significantly fewer stock options than those who made self-effacing remarks.

Schmoozing. Small talk often seems to serve no obvious function. . . . However, on a *preconscious* level, schmoozing has a dramatic impact on our liking and trust of others. . . .

Flattery. People like others who appreciate and admire them. People are more likely to trust others who like them, and respond more favorably when they are flattered. . . .

Self-Disclosure. Self-disclosure means sharing information about oneself with another person. It is a way of building a relationship with another person by making oneself vulnerable, in that the self-disclosing negotiator is providing information that could potentially be exploited. . . .

STEPS TOWARD REPAIRING BROKEN TRUST

1. Suggest a personal meeting.
2. Put the focus on the relationship.
3. Apologize.
4. Let them vent.
5. Do not get defensive.
6. Ask for clarifying information.
7. Test your understanding.
8. Formulate a plan.
9. Think about ways to prevent a future problem.
10. Do a relationship checkup.

Notes and Questions

6.6 In which of Thompson's steps to repair broken trust did sports agent Steinberg engage? How do these steps compare to Lewicki and Wiethoff's ideas for building trust?

6.7 Thompson also suggests reciprocity, which is discussed earlier in this chapter, and being in a good mood, which is discussed in the next chapter.

6.8 Trust and relationships after World War II actually helped Japanese women get equal rights. American Beate Sirota Gordon found herself in Japan in 1946 working with the U.S. military and the Japanese government to draft the new Japanese constitution after World War II. Gordon had lived in Japan for much of her childhood before going to the United States for college and understood the Japanese language as well as the culture. In many of the negotiations over particular articles in the constitution, she had supported the Japanese leadership in previous disagreements with the Americans. Gordon then drafted Article 24 of the Japanese Constitution granting Japanese women equal rights. After the Japanese committee read her article, they protested, arguing that it did not conform to their way of life. However, U.S. Colonel Kades, the head of the constitutional steering committee, simply stated to the committee that because Gordon had her heart set on this provision, the committee should pass it. Because Gordon developed a solid reputation in her time on the committee, the chair of the committee acknowledged this and helped pass Article 24. See James Brooke, Fighting to Protect Her Gift to Japanese Women, N.Y. Times, May 28, 2005, at A4. Also see Beate Sirota Gordon's memoir, The Only Woman in the Room (2001).

C. RAPPORT

In the following excerpt Janice Nadler outlines how to create rapport and its beneficial impact.

 Janice Nadler, **RAPPORT IN NEGOTIATION AND CONFLICT RESOLUTION**

87 Marq. L. Rev. 875, 875–882 (2004)

In negotiation, rapport is a powerful determinant of the extent to which negotiators develop the trust necessary to reach integrative agreements. Rapport between negotiators is linked to negotiators' willingness to cooperate, to share crucial information, to make fewer ultimatums and threats, and to a reduction of the risk of impasse. This essay first outlines the general concept of rapport and how it develops between people in social interactions. This essay then focuses on key implications of rapport for negotiations.

I. WHAT IS RAPPORT?

Interpersonal rapport has been described as a state of mutual positivity and interest. The development of rapport has been characterized by three dynamic components: (1) mutual attention and involvement; (2) positivity; and (3) coordination. These will be considered in turn.

First, mutual attention and involvement are exemplified by the simple idea that my focusing attention on you makes you feel involved in the interaction, and vice versa. An important component of rapport is when we both simultaneously attend to one another and both feel involved in the interaction. Mutual attention and involvement are signaled by the physical orientation of participants in the interaction. For example, spontaneous formation of a circular or semi-circular configuration in a group, forward lean, uncrossed arms, and eye contact are all signals of attention, and, in turn, foster feelings of involvement in the interaction.

Second, rapport is characterized by participants in an interaction having positive attitudes toward one another. Such mutual positivity is signaled by particular non-verbal behaviors such as forward lean, eye contact, smiling, and gestures.

Third, most definitions of rapport include in their descriptions the feeling of being "in sync" with the other persons in the interaction. Rapport-related coordination includes smooth turn taking in conversation, in which the listener acknowledges under-standing, agreement, or attention with forward lean, head nods, and brief verbal responses (e.g., "uh-huh"). In addition to smooth turn taking, rapport-related coordi-nation is characterized by nonconscious mimicry, which occurs when one person imitates the behaviors of another. Without even realizing it, when people interact they tend to mirror one another in posture, facial expression, tone of voice, and man-nerisms. On the surface, it might seem that mimicking would be annoying—almost like a form of mockery. The type of mimicry that is involved in everyday social encounters, however, is quite subtle—people do not usually recognize when it is happening. At the same time, powerful effects of mimicry result in greater liking and rapport in an interaction. For example, in one study, half the participants were mimicked by the other person in the interaction and half were not. Participants who were mimicked rated the interaction as more smooth and harmonious than those who were not. Additionally, when people are motivated to create an affiliation with another person, they automatically and unconsciously increase their mimicry behavior to accomplish this goal. When two people are mirroring one another, their movements become a choreographed dance. To the extent that our behaviors are synchronized with those of others, we feel more rapport, and this increases our trust in those with whom we communicate. Such rapport-based trust is particularly useful during negotiation.

II. THE ROLE OF RAPPORT IN NEGOTIATION

Frequently, negotiations involve mixed-motive conflicts in which negotiators are motivated to cooperate just enough to ensure a settlement is reached, but at the same time, each negotiator is motivated to compete with each other to claim the greatest possible bargaining surplus for themselves. In mixed-motive conflicts where the collec-tively optimal outcome requires cooperation, it is often the case that each party would prefer to cooperate if the other party does, but not otherwise. To reach a collectively optimal outcome in such situations, parties must coordinate on cooperation.

There is now considerable empirical evidence suggesting that the development of rapport fosters cooperative behavior necessary for efficient negotiated outcomes in mixed-motive conflicts. Some of this evidence derives from experimental investiga-tions in which bargainers communicate in intentionally impoverished environments (e.g., side by side, intercom, telephone, email) in order to systematically examine the extent to which stifling rapport development hinders efficient conflict resolution. Other studies examining various aspects of bargainers' social relationships (e.g., social affiliation, affect, identification with an in-group) produce evidence consistent with the possibility that rapport facilitates conflict resolution by encouraging cooperative behavior. In this section, I will review briefly both literatures.

A. Visual Access and Rapport in Conflict Resolution

Because important components of rapport are linked with nonverbal expression and because most channels of nonverbal expression are accessible only visually, we would expect that the efficacy of conflict resolution would be reduced by limited visual access. For example, mutual attention and involvement requires that I know that you are attending to me and vice versa; in the absence of visual cues this can be difficult. Similarly, most forms of mimicry require visual access.

How does lack of visual access affect rapport and cooperation in conflict resolution? Several studies show that visual access enhances cooperation among players in a Prisoner's Dilemma and other social dilemmas. For example, in one game, players are asked to make a decision on behalf of a small company regarding the advertising of a product sold by only one other small company. The task is structured as a Prisoner's Dilemma, and the decision to cooperate or compete is made by the two parties simultaneously and separately. Cooperation by both parties yields the highest collective outcome; however, individual incentives favor competition regardless of the other party's decision. In a study where participants played the advertising game seven times, there was one condition in which players were not permitted to communicate prior to making their decision; in the second condition, players were permitted a brief face-to-face meeting prior to each round; in the third condition, players did not communicate, but instead envisioned a meeting with the opponent prior to each round and recorded in a journal what they would say to each other. Results indicate that during the first six rounds, no communication resulted in the lowest rates of cooperation, and the face-to-face meeting resulted in the highest. Interestingly, imagining the face-to-face meeting boosted the cooperation rate above that of the no communication group, although not as high as the actual face-to-face group.

In another study using the same advertising Prisoner's Dilemma game, participants engaged in a brief introductory conversation prior to playing the game. The conversation took place either face-to-face or via speakerphone. After the conversation, subjects rated the extent to which they felt rapport during the conversation. In addition, independent coders later viewed videotapes of the conversation and rated the extent to which the participants displayed mutual interest and gestural synchrony. Both the coders and the participants themselves reported higher rapport when the conversation took place face-to-face compared to speakerphone. Higher rapport in the face-to-face condition proved to be a crucial element in the decision to cooperate in the advertising game that followed: participants who had met face-to-face were significantly more likely to cooperate in the advertising conflict than were participants who talked via speakerphone. Most important, rapport ratings (both subjective and objective) mediated the relationship between visual access and cooperation: i.e., visual access led to higher rapport, which in turn led to more cooperation in the advertising conflict.

B.   Relationships and Cooperation in Conflict Resolution

Apart from visual access, cooperative behavior is also facilitated by the perceived affiliation of the participants in a conflict or negotiation. In general, people often use noticed similarities between themselves and the other person as a basis for categorizing the other as an in-group member. Once we decide that we share an affiliation with another person, many consequences follow: we evaluate members of our own group more favorably; we allocate more rewards to members of our own group; and we are more cooperative when dealing with in-group members. The special treatment of and affinity for in-group members can arise from even the most superficial basis (e.g., we both like the same artist). Even the mere act of communication leads to feelings of affiliation that promotes cooperation in a social dilemma. In these circumstances cooperation arises from not simply the formation of commitments (i.e., "I promise to cooperate if you do"), but rather from an emotional social aspect of communication (e.g., "I like you because we are alike, so I will cooperate with you"). Feelings of liking toward another person can lead to an increase in perception of similarity and convergence of attitudes, and similarity in attitudes can, in turn, lead to more cooperation.

The greater likelihood of cooperation stemming from the perception of an affiliation or a prior relationship has been confirmed in the context of legal settlement negotiations. In a study of actual legal disputes, Johnston and Waldfogel examined whether the existence of a prior relationship between opposing counsel would affect the likelihood of settlement in civil lawsuits. After examining thousands of cases, they found that cases were resolved more quickly and were less likely to go to trial when opposing counsel had faced each other in the past, than when the attorneys did not know each other. Johnston and Waldfogel argue that when attorneys have repeated interactions, they learn how to communicate in a way that promotes the cooperative sharing of crucial information. The elimination of information asymmetries allows attorneys who know each other to converge on a settlement that is perceived as acceptable to both sides. But why would attorneys be more willing to share private information simply because they have faced their opponent in the past? This question is especially puzzling in light of the adversarial context of the interactions of litigation counsel.

A laboratory study of group affiliation among negotiators provides insight. In this study, business students negotiated either with students from their own school or students from a different school. Consistent with Johnston and Waldfogel's theory, those who negotiated with an in-group member revealed more about their own preferences, asked more information-seeking questions, and in the end, were more likely to achieve a negotiated agreement compared to those who negotiated with an outgroup member. However, a key finding uncovered in the laboratory study is that affiliation produces rapport, which in turn, reduces the likelihood of impasse. Thus, in the absence of a basis for a positive relationship, such as shared group affiliation, negotiators do not express much positive affect, do not develop as much rapport, and are less likely to come to an agreement.

III.   DEVELOPING RAPPORT WHEN VISUAL ACCESS AND RELATIONSHIPS ARE LIMITED

In the absence of visual access or a basis for a positive relationship, negotiators are less likely to develop the kind of rapport that promotes the cooperation necessary to reach efficient agreements in mixed-motive negotiations. Can negotiators working under these circumstances take steps to develop rapport on their own initiative? Even though rapport normally develops in social interactions without social actors even being aware of it, several studies have identified methods that can be used by negotiators who wish to develop rapport to enhance negotiation processes and outcomes.

Sometimes we must negotiate with people we do not know and have never met. Moreover, the advent of communication technologies, like email, means that sometimes the negotiation itself does not provide the opportunity for a face-to-face meeting with our counterpart. Negotiating with someone with whom we have no prior relationship, and using a communication medium that provides no visual access (e.g., telephone, email), makes it more likely that rapport will not sufficiently develop, that cooperative information exchange will be insufficient, and that the result will be an impasse rather than a mutually beneficial agreement. How can this undesirable state of affairs be avoided in a world in which negotiation with strangers using information technology is taken as a given?

First, negotiators who make an effort to create a basis for a positive relationship by engaging in a short, get-acquainted conversation create a basis for smooth negotiation processes that follow. For example, in two studies, some negotiators who used email to negotiate a transaction with a stranger were instructed to talk on the telephone and schmooze for ten minutes in an effort to get to know one another. Other negotiators were not given this opportunity. Engaging in small talk enabled negotiators who were strangers to affiliate in a fashion that did not spontaneously occur during the process of email exchange. The seemingly inert act of schmoozing facilitated cooperation during the negotiation, leading to the sharing of crucial information with the other part, and resulting in favorable impressions of the counterpart after the negotiation.

By contrast, negotiators who did not chat with their counterpart prior to negotiation either failed to exchange the kind of information that would lead to identification of mutually beneficial solutions, or failed to recognize as beneficial the solutions which arose, leading to a greater likelihood of impasse. In the absence of the preliminary chat, the two negotiation counterparts were complete strangers, never having seen one another or heard one another's voice, hindering the development of rapport. By failing to reach agreement, pairs that reached an impasse settled for a result that was economically worse than any of the many possible agreements that would have resulted in a profitable outcome for each party. The prenegotiation, getting-to-know-you chat allowed the negotiation to proceed more smoothly by creating rapport before the negotiation began. This rapport helped negotiators approach the negotiation with a more cooperative mental model, thereby trusting in each others' good intentions. This mental model, in turn, led to a successful negotiation that concluded with a contract and engendered positive feelings about one another. Adopting an attitude that was more cooperative than competitive allowed negotiators to trust the other party enough to share with them relevant private information, and to expect the other party to reciprocate by sharing their own relevant private information, which, in turn, resulted in identification of and agreement to efficient solutions.

If preliminary small talk is not possible, there are other means for creating the basis for a rapport-promoting positive relationship. For example, in the [business school] study discussed earlier, negotiators who were students at the same school (but did not necessarily know one another) were more successful at generating rapport than students at different schools. As a result, their impasse rate was lower (especially when their email exchanges contained mutual self-disclosures). In addition, other negotiators who exchanged pictures and personal biographical information (such as alma mater, interests, hobbies) generated more affect-based rapport. The absence of either of these factors (in-group identification or mutual self-disclosure) led to a much higher impasse rate than when negotiators had a basis for a positive relationship. Thus, prior to negotiation, strangers who negotiate can try to create a basis for affiliation, through identification of shared interests, group memberships, and so forth. This shared affiliation will then create the basis for affect-based rapport that leads to cooperation, information exchange, and mutually beneficial agreements.

IV. CONCLUSION

In a face-to-face negotiation, nonverbal (e.g., body orientation, gestures, eye contact, head nodding) and paraverbal (e.g., the use of "uh-huhs") behaviors are important building blocks of rapport. Face-to-face contact contributes to smooth negotiations because, although seldom consciously recognized, people rely heavily on nonverbal signals and mimicry to help them conduct social interactions. In face-to-face negotiation, rapport tends to develop quite naturally, resulting in the feeling of being "in sync" or "on the same wavelength" with another person. In negotiation, the rapport that results from visual access facilitates cooperation and mutually beneficial negotiation outcomes.

In the absence of face-to-face communication, negotiators can rely upon noticed similarities between themselves and their counterpart as a basis for generating affect-based rapport to facilitate a smooth negotiation process. In the absence of either visual access or a positive relationship, negotiators can create rapport synthetically by means of a prenegotiation, a getting-to-know-you chat, or a mutual self-disclosure. These simple steps are likely to facilitate conflict resolution in mixed-motive negotiations.

Notes and Questions

6.9   For a study applying these principles about rapport to e-mail negotiations, see Michael Morris, Janice Nadler, Teri Kurtzberg & Leigh Thompson, Schmooze or Lose: Social Friction and Lubrication in E-Mail Negotiations, 6 Group Dynamics 89 (2002) (finding that the absence of face-to-face negotiation "schmoozing" can have deleterious effects on negotiation). Janice Nadler repeated a similar experiment with negotiation students at two law schools. Each student conducted a negotiation about a company car via e-mail. One group of students also engaged in small talk via telephone that lasted about five minutes before their negotiations began. The group that engaged in small talk was four times more likely to reach an agreement than those who did not. Janice Nadler, Rapport in Legal Negotiation: How Small Talk Can Facilitate E-Mail Dealmaking, 9 Harv. Negot. L. Rev. 223 (2004). Why do you think this is?

6.10   While e-mail bargaining can be very useful and help parties quickly move through the process, there are also pitfalls associated with this method. To avoid these pitfalls, G. Richard Shell has tips for electronic bargainers:

1.   Think before you click. E-mail may not be the best negotiation medium for resolving sensitive matters. . . .

2. Remember, human beings with feelings will receive your message. Go out of your way to soften your language. Refer to personal information and/or compliment the other party, if appropriate. . . .

3. Take advantage of the broadcast feature of e-mail to build coalitions and keep your allies informed about what is going on. . . .

4. Everyone can benefit from becoming more skilled at e-mail negotiations. But shy people, those at lower rungs in corporate hierarchies, and those who strongly dislike interpersonal confrontation may benefit most from learning to rely more on e-mail to conduct negotiations. . . .

G. Richard Shell, Electronic Bargaining: The Perils of E-Mail and the Promise of Computer-Assisted Negotiations, in Wharton on Making Decisions 219 (J. Hoch, Howard C. Kunreuther & Robert E. Gunther eds., 2001).

D. POWER

In this next section, we tackle the issue of power in negotiation. Simplistically, some assume that more power leads to success. In fact, power is far more complex. The next two articles start by discussing how we get power in a negotiation and what this means for how we negotiate.

 Robert S. Adler & Elliot M. Silverstein, **WHEN DAVID MEETS GOLIATH: DEALING WITH POWER DIFFERENTIALS IN NEGOTIATIONS**

5 Harv. Negot. L. Rev. 1, 10-28 (2000)

THE NATURE OF POWER

Having defined power and having narrowed our inquiry to social interactions, we now advance several principles that are critical to a proper understanding of power differentials in negotiation. . . .

1.   Power Is Complex and Situational . . .

Power's complexity stems no doubt from its highly situational nature — even slight changes in a setting may substantially affect the underlying power dynamics. For example, the chief executive officer of a large multinational corporation will likely have little power over a state trooper who has stopped the CEO for speeding. . . .

2.   Perceptions Play a Key Role in Power Dynamics

The critical test of one's effectiveness in a negotiation is what one has convinced an opponent that one can do, whether or not one can actually do it. Unless exposed as bluffers, parties [who] convince their opponents that they have more power than they really do will generally be able to exercise the power they have asserted. . . .

Perceptions can also play a critical and confounding role even when no bluffing occurs. One of the most common and deadly perception traps is what we call a "negotiator's bias" in bargaining situations. By this, we mean that the natural tendency of negotiators to enter deliberations with trepidation often leads to judgments, based on little or no evidence, that their opponents are negotiating aggressively and competitively, despite the negotiators' sincere efforts to bargain cooperatively. These judgments, in turn, may be used to rationalize combative behavior against an opponent that would otherwise not be justifiable. . . .

3.   To Have Effective Power, One Must Be Willing to Use It or be Able to Convince an Opponent That One Will Use It

For example, a compassionate boss who feels unable to fire a malingering employee or a timid judge who shies away from disciplining disruptive attorneys in the courtroom cannot be said to be powerful figures despite holding powerful positions. This point is particularly important in negotiation settings.

4.   Having Greater Power Does Not Guarantee Successful Bargaining Outcomes

Repeated studies confirm that power symmetry, rather than disproportionate power, is the most favorable condition for reaching agreement. Disproportionately greater power on the part of one party in a negotiation often reduces the likelihood of a favorable outcome for the powerful party, producing what Professor William Ury calls the "power paradox": "[t]he harder you make it for them to say no, the harder you make it for them to say yes." Several reasons seem to account for this phenomenon. First, parties with greater power are often tempted to achieve their goals through coercion rather than persuasion, and this leads to resistance from those with less power. Second, those with less power and under pressure to acquiesce often will scuttle agreements perceived to be demeaning—even to the point of rejecting deals that give them more benefits than no agreement. Third, while weaker parties are initially more likely to employ conciliatory tactics in negotiation, they may feel provoked to shore up their positions by making threats, adopting stubborn positions, or using punitive tactics in response to power plays by stronger parties. Finally, weaker parties may be so suspicious of the stronger parties' intentions that they will refuse to agree even to terms that most observers would characterize as reasonable. . . .

5.   Power in Negotiations Typically Arises from the Dependence That Each Party Has on the Other

Most power involves the dependence of parties on one another. . . .

6. Negotiation Power Depends Less on the Other Side's Strength Than on One's Own Needs, Fears, and Available Options

As a corollary to the previous point, we note that the essence of determining the relative power of the parties in a negotiation depends less on how powerful each party is in any absolute sense than on how badly each party needs or fears the other. This is where the concept of BATNA (Best Alternative to a Negotiated Agreement) proves useful. If one has a number of attractive alternatives to a deal with one's opponent, one has great power regardless of the tremendous resources that the other side might have within its control. . . .

7. Power Is Neither Inherently Good Nor Bad. . . .

SOURCES OF POWER

Before entering into a negotiation, parties to the process should always assess the power both they and their opponents bring to the table. Without a clear picture of the power dynamic, parties will either underestimate or overestimate the degree of flexibility they have in bargaining. . . .

1. Personal Power

When we refer to personal power, we mean the inherent individual traits that a person brings to a negotiation not directly associated with his or her organizational status. We include things such as a person's intelligence, persistence, courage, physical strength, appearance, celebrity, memory, confidence, awareness, education, interpersonal skills, emotional control, intuition, friendliness, and willingness to take risks. . . .

2. Organizational Power

Given the situational nature of power, it should surprise no one that organizations, which by their very nature are hierarchical and interactive (with power typically concentrated at the top and flowing downward), should play as large a role in power dynamics as personal power does. . . .

3. Information Power

We give special attention to information power because it so often tips the scales in favor of one party and because it is the power source most easily increased in negotiations. Negotiators may not change their looks, personality, job, wealth or strength overnight, but they can often obtain information that dramatically changes the negotiation dynamic in a relatively short time. The more information that a party has, the more likely it is that he or she can see the context of a given situation clearly and respond accordingly. . . . For example, a buyer who knows an automobile dealer's costs for a car and a sense of what a reasonable markup on the vehicle is stands a substantially better chance of obtaining a good deal than one who lacks this information. . . .

4. Moral Power

We use the term "moral power" to refer to those instances in which negotiators achieve gains through appeals to fairness or morality. In some instances, moral claims may be the only source of leverage available against those with greater power. . . . Moral appeals seem likely to carry the greatest impact when they employ empathy to persuade opponents to place themselves in one's shoes. . . .

 Peter T. Coleman, **POWER AND CONFLICT**

> **in The Handbook of Conflict Resolution 108-109, 110-111, 113, 121-122, 123, 124, 125, 126-127 (Morton Deutsch & Peter T. Coleman eds., 2000)**

In the Sonagachi red-light district in Calcutta, India, prostitutes have organized to mobilize against AIDS, altering the power structure by challenging any pimp or madam who would insist on a customer's right to sex without a condom.

At a company in the United States, in an attempt to avoid layoffs, the great majority of employees agreed to cut their own salaries by 20 percent; the offer was rejected by the CEO, who chose instead to fire 20 percent of the workforce, stating that "it was very important that management's prerogative to manage as it saw fit not be compromised by sentimental human considerations."

In the wilds of Wyoming, groups of ranchers and environmentalists, who historically were bitter adversaries, have teamed up to fight a proposal by the federal Department of the Interior to reintroduce wolves into their national parks.

All of these conflicts have one basic element in common: power. Power to challenge, power to resist, and power through cooperating together. Most conflicts directly or indirectly concern power, either as leverage for achieving one's goals, as a means of seeking or maintaining the balance or imbalance of power in a relationship, or as a symbolic expression of one's identity. Scholars propose that the "deep structure" of most conflicts is dictated by preexisting power relations. This structure, established through the history of relations between the parties, their differential access to resources, or the existing social norms and roles, drives the issues in their conflicts and largely influences what is considered to be important, feasible, and fair in these situations. Of course, there are also many overt conflicts about power, as for example between the haves and have-nots or between competing power seekers. Because of its ubiquity, it is paramount that when we address conflict, we consider power. . . .

FOUR PERSPECTIVES ON POWER

[F]our common themes or perspectives on power are found in the social science literature:

- "Power over"
- "Power with"

- "Powerlessness and dependence"
- "Empowered and independent"

Power Over

[P]ower involves "an ability to get another person to do something that he or she would not otherwise have done. . . ." This conception of power was evident in the earlier example of the CEO and his response to the employees' initiative. The implicit assumption in this type of conceptualization is that power relations are inherently coercive and competitive; the more power A has, the less power available for B. Though this is sometimes the case, it is a limited perspective.

Power With

A different outlook on power was offered by Mary Parker Follett in the 1920s. She proposed that even though power was usually conceived of as power over others, it would also be possible to develop the conception of "power with" others. She envisioned this type as jointly developed, coactive, and noncoercive. This is the form of power illustrated in the vignette about partnership between ranchers and environmentalists. . . .

Powerlessness and Dependence

A third perspective that has received some attention in the literature, and is particularly relevant to our discussion of conflict, approaches power from the experience and expression of powerlessness and dependence. The negative physical and psychological impact of a prolonged experience of powerlessness has been shown to be dire and can lead to a tendency to become more rigid, critical, controlling of others in low power, and, ultimately, more irrational and violent. . . .

Empowered and Independent

The flip side of powerlessness is, of course, having power or being empowered with a concomitant sense of independence. Scholars have referred to this view of power as having "power to" or "power from," in the sense that one has enough power to achieve one's objectives without being unduly constrained by someone or something else. . . .

A WORKING DEFINITION OF POWER

[P]ower can be usefully conceptualized as a mutual interaction between the characteristics of a person and the characteristics of a situation, where the person has access to valued resources and uses them to achieve personal, relational, or environmental goals, often through using various strategies of influence. . . .

IMPLICATIONS FOR CONFLICT

This discussion has several major implications for power and conflict. A sample conflict between an adolescent girl, Hannah, and her parents over weekend curfews offers a good illustration. Hannah recently turned sixteen and has argued that having reached that milestone, she should be allowed to stay out later on weekend nights than the 10:30 curfew previously established by her parents. Hannah's parents strongly disagree and have informed her that there will be no change in her curfew until she turns eighteen.

THE PREVAILING APPROACH TO POWER

A competitive orientation to power currently dominates the approach to power of social scientists, as well as of power holders. The majority of scholars in the social sciences investigate power through the competitive lens. Analysis of family conflict from this perspective emphasizes the imbalance of power inherent in the conflict and the various resources available to each side for purposes of altering the balance in their favor, thereby gaining the necessary leverage to prevail in the dispute. It would also be oriented to the many strategies, tactics, and countertactics that the parties could use to gain the upper hand in the situation. Although useful, this perspective ignores many other critical aspects of power, particularly the potential for the parents and adolescent to develop power with each other by approaching their dilemma as a mutual problem for the family to solve. The field of conflict resolution would be well served if scholar-practitioners developed enhanced understanding and improved methods for the cooperative, dependent, and independent approaches to power in conflict. . . .

THE INFLUENCE OF PERSPECTIVE ON STRATEGY

Our perspectives on power influence our strategies in conflict. As previously indicated, how we think about power affects how we perceive conflict and how we respond to it.

COOPERATIVE CONFLICT AND POWER WITH

Cooperative conflict leads to power with. When conflicts occur in situations that have cooperative task, reward, or outcome interdependence structures, or between disputants sharing a cooperative psychological orientation, there is more cooperative power. In other words, in these situations conflict is probably framed as a mutual problem to be solved by both parties, which leads to an increased tendency to minimize power differences between the disputants and to mutually enhance each other's power in order to work together effectively to achieve their shared goals. Thus, if the parents can recognize that their daughter's social needs and their own needs to have a close family life are positively linked, then they may be more likely to involve her in the problem-solving and decision-making processes, thereby enhancing her power and their ability to find mutually satisfying solutions to the conflict.

Some Advice for the "Powerful"

We offer three pieces of advice to more powerful parties to negotiations. First, do not always press advantages to the fullest. In a gracious manner, let the weaker party realize some gains that one could have taken for himself or herself, especially if there is even a slight possibility that one will do business with the weaker party in the future. We urge this both on ethical and prudential grounds. Not only do we find overreaching to be unfair, but also we suggest that those who oppress today will find few supporters when the tables are turned — as often they are. Moreover, oppressive agreements are inherently unstable. To be successful in business, one needs not only to be viewed as tough and shrewd, but also as fair.

Second, when one has done well in a negotiation, without appearing obsequious or patronizing, one should go out of his or her way to reassure the other side how well they have done. One of the secrets of being a "powerful" negotiator is convincing opponents to trust you during the negotiation and then showing them that they also have done well.

Finally, we remind those with more power about the critical need to permit the weaker negotiators to "save face." Fisher and Ury make a compelling argument that preserving each side's dignity in a negotiation should be one of the main goals of a successful interaction. Time after time, they argue, individuals in the midst of a bargain will refuse to agree to terms they otherwise find acceptable because they cannot accept the perceived humiliation of backing down in front of an opponent. Accordingly, one of the most important steps one can take is to assist the other side in accepting the terms one has sought without losing face.

Robert S. Adler & Elliot M. Silverstein, When David Meets Goliath: Dealing with Power Differentials in Negotiations, 5 Harv. Negot. L. Rev. 1, 110-112 (2000).

PERCEPTION OF POWER

Perception of power matters. Saul Alinksy said, "Power is not only what you have, but what the enemy thinks you have...."

EFFECTIVE POWER

The most critical questions to ask in any conflict situation are: "What do I really want or need in this situation?" and "How can I use the power available to me effectively here?" This may mean restraining one's chronic impulses and stopping to assess such things as short-term and long-term objectives, the realm of power that is of primary concern to oneself (personal, relational, environmental), the types of power resource available that are relevant to a given situation, the best strategy given one's objectives, and the likely responses of the other party to using such strategies. If the mother's desire is to improve her strained relationship with her daughter by spending more time together on the weekends, then using a coercive strategy to keep her at home is sure to prove largely ineffective.

CONTEXT AND POWER

The context drives the person, who drives the context. It is critical to bear in mind that power is typically context-dependent and that even the most powerful people are powerless under certain conditions....

TENDENCIES AND STRATEGIES FOR MEMBERS OF
HIGH-POWER GROUPS

The overwhelming evidence seems to indicate that the powerful tend to like power, use it, justify having it, and attempt to keep it. The powerful also tend to be more satisfied and less personally discontent than those not enjoying high power; they have a longer time perspective and more freedom to act and therefore can plan further into the future. These higher levels of satisfaction lead to vested interests in the status quo and development of rationales for maintaining power, such as the power holders' belief in their own superior competence and superior moral value. . . .

Thus, in conflict situations high power holders and members of high-power groups (HPGs) often neglect to analyze — as well as underestimate — the power of low power holders and members of low-power groups (LPGs). Additionally, they usually attempt to dominate the relationship, to use pressure tactics, to offer few concessions, to have high aspirations and to use contentious tactics. HPGs, therefore, make it difficult to arrive at negotiated agreements that are satisfactory to all parties. . . .

TENDENCIES AND STRATEGIES FOR MEMBERS OF
LOW-POWER GROUPS

Not surprisingly, the tendencies for members of LPGs are opposite to those of members of HPGs, with one exception. LPG members tend to be dependent on others, to have short time perspectives, to be unable to plan far ahead, and to be generally discontent. Often, the LPG members attempt to rid themselves of the negative feelings associated with their experiences of powerlessness and dependence (such as rage and fear) by projecting blame onto even less powerful groups or onto relatively safe in-group targets. The latter can result in a breakdown of LPG in-group solidarity. Intense negative feeling may also limit the LPG members' capacity to respond constructively in conflict with HPGs and impel such destructive impulses as violent destruction of property. . . .

IMPLICATIONS FOR TRAINING IN CONFLICT RESOLUTION

In conclusion, we offer a few propositions . . . for use in designing training approaches for power and conflict. The general goals of such training are to enhance people's understanding of power, to facilitate reflection of their own tendencies when in low or high power, and to increase their ability to use it effectively when in conflict.

- Training should help students understand and reflect critically on their commonly held images of and assumptions about power, as well as the sources of these assumptions and images.
- Students should become aware of their own chronic tendencies to react in situations in which they have superior or inferior power to others.
- Students should become emotionally and cognitively aware of the privileges or injustices they and others experience as a result of their skin color, gender, economics, class, age, religion, sexual orientation, physical status, and the like.

- In a conflict situation, students should be able to analyze for the other as well as themselves the resources of power, their orientation to power, and the strategies and tactics for effectively implementing their available power. Students should also be able to identify and develop the necessary skills for implementing their available power in the conflict.
- Students should also be able to distinguish between conflicts in which power with, power from, and power under, rather than power over, are appropriate orientations to the conflict.

Notes and Questions

6.11 Consider the power amassed by Gandhi and his followers in nonviolent resistance. The same moral power was used effectively by Martin Luther King, Jr. Can you think of other powerful historical figures who did not use conventional sources of power?

6.12 What power do law students have vis-à-vis their law professors? How can students enhance their sources of power? If you were going to bargain with your professor regarding the extension of an announced deadline for a paper, what might you do with respect to power differentials?

This next excerpt examines power more narrowly as a function of BATNA—how good are your alternatives, and how good are theirs?

 Russell Korobkin, **BARGAINING POWER AS THREAT OF IMPASSE**

87 Marq. L. Rev. 867, 867-871 (2004)

In an ideal world, all negotiators would have what are sometimes called "common interests." The old chandelier that to me is clutter in the basement would be an antique to you, and your pleasure in receiving it would be outweighed only by my joy in getting rid of it. In most bargaining situations, however, negotiators' interests are in conflict. You might like the chandelier more than I do, which makes a mutually advantageous bargain possible, but it is currently lighting my dining room and I would prefer to keep it rather than give it away. You are interested in buying the chandelier from me, but you want to pay a low price. I will consider selling it to you, but I want a high price. Who will succeed in achieving his goal will most likely depend on who has more bargaining power, defined as the ability to convince the other negotiator to give us what we want even when the other would prefer not to do so.

The source of bargaining power is misunderstood by many negotiators, who wrongly assume that the indicia of success in other realms of life are directly related to power at the negotiating table. Wealth, brains, beauty, political power, prestige, and social influence are nice to have, but none of these items guarantee you the ability to exercise power in any particular negotiation. Bargaining power is situational, not personal. In some labor disputes, unions have more power than management; in others, management has more power than unions. In some merger negotiations, the target company enjoys more power than the suitor; in others, the dynamic is reversed. In some litigation settlement negotiations, the plaintiff has more power than the defendant; in others, the defendant enjoys the advantage. An employee seeking a raise from his boss might enjoy a relative power advantage, or he might not.

In each of these situations, relative bargaining power stems entirely from the negotiator's ability to, explicitly or implicitly, make a single threat credibly: "*I will walk away from the negotiating table without agreeing to a deal if you do not give me what I demand.*" The source of the ability to make such a threat, and therefore the source of bargaining power, is the ability to project that he has a desirable alternative to reaching an agreement, often referred to as a "BATNA." This essay elaborates on this claim.

I. BATNA STRENGTH

What you will do in the case of impasse determines your relative power in the negotiation. In market situations with fungible buyers and sellers, your BATNA is to enter into a similar transaction with someone other than your negotiating counterpart and, thus, your power depends implicitly on the forces of supply and demand. Imagine that you arrive at an automobile dealership hoping to pay "dealer invoice" for the car of your choice and begin to negotiate with a dealer who hopes to charge the "sticker price." Your BATNA is to buy the same car from another dealer. The dealer's BATNA is to wait for the next customer to enter the showroom and attempt to sell the car to that customer. If the model you have selected is in short supply and all of the other dealers in town have a waiting list of purchasers, your BATNA is relatively weak (you will have to wait for a car and probably pay a premium) and the dealer's BATNA is relatively strong (he is confident that another customer will be willing to pay the sticker price). The dealer enjoys substantial power because he can threaten impasse if you do not agree to pay the sticker price, and that threat would be credible because impasse would be in his best interest. In contrast, if all dealers are overstocked and the new year's models are soon to arrive, you will enjoy power. You can credibly threaten to walk away if the dealer will not agree to a handsome discount because the chances are good that another dealer anxious to reduce inventory would likely agree to a discount, meaning that impasse would be in your best interest if you do not receive the price that you demand. . . .

II. PERCEPTION IS REALITY

Strictly speaking, it is not the actual, objective quality of the negotiator's BATNA that determines his degree of bargaining power, but what the counterpart believes that the negotiator believes about the quality of his BATNA. For example, when an employee receives a job offer from a competing firm and asks his boss for a raise, whether the employee has power depends on whether the boss believes that the employee believes it is in the employee's best interest to accept the competing offer if the demand for a raise is not met. The credibility of the employee's threat to walk away from the negotiation and accept the competing offer if his demand is not met is unaffected by the fact that neither the boss nor any of the employee's colleagues would prefer the competing offer to the employee's current job at his current salary. Where power is concerned, the beauty of a BATNA is in the eye of the beholder, and eccentricity is not penalized as long as it is perceived to be genuine. The employee's threat of impasse will be credible to the boss, thus giving the employee power, even if the employee himself actually would not prefer the competing offer, so long as the boss thinks that the employee would prefer that offer. . . .

III. PATIENCE AND POWER

In many bargaining contexts, especially those involving bilateral monopoly, the BATNA of both parties, at least in the short term, will be to continue to negotiate not to pursue a substitute transaction. In this situation, a negotiator's threat not to agree unless her demands are met is in essence a threat of *temporary* rather than permanent impasse. When both parties have a BATNA of temporary impasse, the negotiator for whom temporary impasse is less costly has the strongest BATNA and thus the lion's share of bargaining power. If you have a low cost of temporary impasse, you have the ability to be patient in the negotiations. Thus, it follows that patience translates into bargaining power.

When a union and management meet to attempt to negotiate a settlement of a strike, union members rarely threaten to find substitute employment, and management is precluded by law from firing the striking workers. The union's threat is that if management does not meet its demands, it will continue to strike. Management's threat is that, if the union does not accede to its terms, it will continue to permit the strike to go on. If the union has a large strike fund and if management cannot fill its orders with the labor of replacement workers, the union can be more patient in reaching an agreement and will enjoy superior bargaining power. In contrast, if the union's strike fund is empty and its members cannot pay their rents while management has a large quantity of inventory in storage, temporary impasse will be relatively more costly to the union, giving management power.

IV. THE RISKS OF POWER

In a world in which opposing negotiators had perfect information about the other's alternatives and preferences and both made all negotiating decisions with cold rationality, attempts to exercise bargaining power would never cause impasse. In any situation in which a mutually beneficial agreement were possible, the party with relatively less power would yield to the party with relatively more.

Few negotiations, however, are characterized by perfect information and lack of emotion. If both negotiators believe that they have a strong BATNA but that their counterpart does not, each might try to exercise power while neither yields. Thus, lawsuits go to trial, labor strikes drag on, and ethnic warfare continues, even when agreements that would make both sides better off are feasible. Alternatively, or in addition, the less powerful party might resent the sense of coercion or inequity inherent in the more powerful negotiator's demands and refuse to yield, even knowing that this course of action will cause harm to both sides. These twin possibilities make the exercise of bargaining power as potentially risky as it is potentially rewarding.

This last excerpt provides some specific advice for how to bargain with more powerful negotiators.

 Robert S. Adler & Elliot M. Silverstein, **WHEN DAVID MEETS GOLIATH: DEALING WITH POWER DIFFERENTIALS IN NEGOTIATIONS**

5 Harv. Negot. L. Rev. 1, 77-81, 84-86, 88-90, 103, 105, 106-110 (2000)

We now turn to specific advice for those facing opponents with greater power. As a starting point, we stress several thoughts about this negotiation challenge. First, our suggestions cannot change certain features of the bargaining landscape. Although taking particular steps, such as acquiring greater information, can enhance one's leverage in a given situation, there are usually aspects of the underlying power differential that remain fixed. This means that even when optimizing opportunities in a negotiation, one may still end up with an agreement that tilts substantially in the other side's favor when substantial power disparities exist. A "weak" agreement may be the best obtainable option under this circumstance — perhaps better than no agreement. This result does not necessarily mean that one is a poor negotiator. Conversely, merely because one is able to force a one-sided deal on a relatively weaker party does not mean that one is a good negotiator. What matters in these situations is whether one has achieved the optimal agreement under the circumstances.

Moreover, our suggestions do not guarantee a "happy" ending to most negotiations. In fact, paradoxically, they may lead to less contentment than not following them. For instance, we advise negotiators to raise their aspirations, which is an approach that may produce fewer joyous bargaining moments, but better overall deals. In this sense, happiness will depend more on achieving one's goals than on attaining a particular objective outcome.

Further, everyone approaches negotiation with a unique personal style, which he or she must strive to understand and master. To be an effective bargainer, one must work within one's given personality and negotiation style. But, one must be careful not to make hasty or unduly pessimistic judgments about style and one's ability to improve it. Aside from the fact that negotiators sometimes do not truly understand how others perceive them, they also do not always realize the capacity that they have for improvement. It is possible for those who believe themselves timid to become more assertive and for those who view themselves as aggressive to become more sensitive.

Finally, we note that there is no omniscient scorekeeper who will blow a whistle when one has underperformed or ring a bell when one has done well. Once a deal has been struck, asking the other side whether we have extracted all of the concessions they were prepared to give is unlikely to trigger a full and honest response. In short, one has to operate somewhat blindly in the real world when it comes to assessing success or failure.

With these caveats in mind, we now turn to a set of suggestions for negotiators facing more powerful opponents.

A.   DETERMINE WHETHER THE OTHER SIDE REALLY IS MORE POWERFUL

How does one make this determination? As a starting point, one must set aside any tendency to translate his or her anxiety about negotiating into an unproven assumption that the other side carries greater power. Moreover, even if the other side is powerful, we must still decide whether the opponent has power *over us*. To make this judgment, one must ask the following questions:

- What is it that I want and need from the other side?
- What negative action can the other side take against me if no agreement is reached?
- What alternatives do I have to entering into this agreement? . . .

Equally important, but often overlooked by nervous bargainers, is an assessment of the other side's dependence on us. . . .

- How badly does the other side want or need something that I have?
- What negative action can I take against the other side if no agreement is reached?
- What alternatives does the other side have to reaching an agreement with me? . . .

B.   DETERMINE WHETHER ADVERSARIES UNDERSTAND AND WILL USE THEIR POWER

Given what we believe to be a negotiator's natural tendency to assume that the other side has superior power in a given situation, negotiators should look to whether their opponent has entered into the bargaining in an extremely fearful or awed manner. This possibility seems so far-fetched to some bargainers that they miss obvious signs of their opponents' anxiety or misread them as indicators of hostility. At such moments, opportunities for gain will be missed if one fails to assess the other side's perception of the power dynamics accurately. What is critical is not just a reading of the opponent's power in a given negotiation, but also of his or her *perception* of the power dynamic. . . .

C.   USE OPENING MOVES TO SET THE TONE AND TO DEFLECT POWER PLOYS

First impressions matter. Research suggests that parties typically establish the entire tone of a negotiation through the first array of moves and gestures. . . .

D. USE INFORMATION STRATEGICALLY TO INCREASE POWER

Properly gathered information permits negotiators to discern their opponents' weaknesses, vulnerabilities, likes, dislikes, strategies, and aspirations. This permits negotiators to meet the other side's needs effectively, and to anticipate and block power plays by the other side.... For example, consider the impact of careful preparation in a negotiation between a South African coal company and Nippon Steel Company, as reported by one of the coal company executives:

> We arrived at the venue well prepared (we thought) and soon got down to business, quoting our price, which we knew was cheaper than anything else in the world. Then the dreaded words from Mr. Shibuya that I'll remember until my retirement.... "Please, Mr. Smith, explain to us how you worked out your price, because we also worked out your price for you and get a different figure.... Shibuya then commenced to put an impressive document on the table:... they had detailed figures [on] ... tariffs, on tonnage, on insurance, on the cost of *our* administration. What audacity! Yet they were right: on closer inspection we could not fault them on a single point. Their figures were even more recent than ours. They had better information on our own product than we ourselves! How on earth do you counter this across a table?

What makes this example so illustrative of the strategic use of information is that, prior to entering the negotiation, the South African coal company appeared to enjoy a substantial power advantage, given that it could offer Nippon Steel the lowest price of coal obtainable in the world. Notwithstanding that, Nippon Steel, invoking its research results, seized the power advantage....

E. DEVELOP ADDITIONAL ALTERNATIVES TO IMPROVE ONE'S "WALKAWAY POINT"

As we have discussed, one extremely effective way of dealing with more powerful parties is by creating attractive alternatives to an agreement with the stronger party....

F. RESEARCH AVAILABLE LEGAL PROTECTIONS

As we have discussed, although common law protections for weaker parties exist, they typically require the stronger party to have inflicted some form of overreaching or abuse. While our review suggests that the number of instances in which courts will invalidate agreements is limited, we still counsel a careful examination of existing law when one confronts a more powerful party — particularly when one is a consumer facing a commercial entity....

G. EXPLORE INTERESTS AS ALTERNATIVES TO POWER PLOYS

As unabashed admirers of Fisher and Ury's "principled negotiation" model, we endorse the approach of actively seeking to satisfy mutual interests, whenever possible, over engaging in power displays. Under a principled negotiation approach, bargainers seek ways, regardless of which side holds a power advantage, to sidestep conflict and to focus on exploring and meeting each other's needs. . . .

H.   AVOID UNNECESSARY CONFLICT, BUT RETALIATE IF NECESSARY

[O]ne should try to avoid reacting destructively to another's annoying style, especially when the other side attempts to play a power game. One generally needs to react, but in a way that promotes positive movement. Rather than accuse, one should describe the situation and one's feelings to alert the other side that the bargaining has become more tense. We offer the following advice for communicating displeasure to another:

- Explain the behavior that upsets you in specific and objective terms;
- Describe your feelings about what bothers you;
- Try to get your opponent to view the matter from your perspective;
- Do not accuse your opponent of misbehavior;
- Show respect for your opponent; and
- Apologize for any misunderstanding that your own behavior might have caused if that will help move the discussion without making you appear weak.

What is critical in situations where one party has unleashed a power play or has acted in a way that offends an opponent is to provide feedback that the behavior will not be tolerated, but to do so in a manner that does not begin a cycle of attack and retaliation. . . .

I.   IDENTIFY AND COUNTER POWER PLOYS . . .

[This section of Adler and Silverstein's article is excerpted in Chapter 7.]

J.   INVOLVE MEDIATORS TO BALANCE POWER DIFFERENTIALS

Once a party . . . has agreed to participate in a mediation, he or she has ceded [some] power to the process and to the mediator. . . .

K.   FORM AN ALLIANCE AGAINST THE MORE POWERFUL PARTY

The adage that there is strength in numbers holds particularly true for negotiations. One way to equalize or exceed the power of a stronger party is to form an alliance with others who share an interest in working against the stronger party. . . .

L. APPEAL TO A POWERFUL ADVERSARY'S SENSE OF JUSTICE AND FAIRNESS

People do not operate exclusively on the basis of economic efficiency, notwithstanding the economic models that would suggest otherwise. . . .

As we earlier discussed, moral power can function as effectively in negotiation settings as other, rawer forms of power. The fact that one has the ability to overwhelm the other side does not automatically mean that one will do so. Appeals to fairness and justice can operate powerfully under the proper circumstances. In fact, we suspect that most negotiations involve elements of moral appeals to a greater or lesser extent.

In some cases, virtually an entire claim rests upon a moral foundation. For example, fifty years after the end of World War II, a number of Nazi-era slave laborers have pressed claims for compensation against the corporations (or their successor entities) that "employed" them during the war. Given the passage of time, one might consider these demands legally dubious, but the horror of the practice, as well as the moral stigma that companies would suffer from rejecting the claims, has led a group of roughly sixty-five companies to contribute to a 10 billion mark ($5.19 billion) fund to compensate the laborers.

M. USE WEAKNESS AS A SOURCE OF STRENGTH

Few things better illustrate the situational nature of power than the point that weakness can sometimes be a source of power. Weakness provides substantial leverage in several situations. First, a weak party with little or nothing to lose can bring a powerful weapon — indifference — to bear. . . . Second, the plight of a weaker party may trigger feelings of sympathy and concern in the stronger party. This may lead the stronger party to forbear from taking action against the weaker person. . . .

Third, weakness can trump a stronger party's power if the powerful party faces public criticism for taking action against the weaker. . . .

Finally, weakness can lead to desperate acts, which in turn may make coercive behaviors by powerful parties very costly — so much that the battle may not be worth it. Rosa Parks, a black woman in Montgomery whose refusal to move from her seat to permit a white man to sit down triggered the historic boycott, had not sought a confrontation on the day that she was arrested. She was just tired and frustrated. As David Halberstam describes it:

> Perhaps the most interesting thing about her was how ordinary she was, at least on the surface, almost the prototype of the black woman who toiled so hard and had so little to show for it. She had not, she later explained, thought about getting arrested that day. Later, the stunned white leaders of Montgomery repeatedly charged that Park's refusal was part of a carefully orchestrated plan on the part of the local NAACP, of which she was an officer. But that was not true; what she did represented one person's exhaustion with a system that dehumanized all black people. Something inside her finally snapped.

In such acts of desperation by the oppressed are sometimes born mighty movements that forever shift the power dynamics of a community, a city, and, ultimately, a nation. It, therefore, should not surprise that they can easily change the dynamics of a negotiation. . . .

Notes and Questions

6.13 The readings outline many different definitions of power. Which seem most important to you?

6.14 How can you use Adler and Silverstein's advice to deal with powerful negotiation counterparts? Consider a situation in which you felt overpowered by the other side. In retrospect, what might you have done to achieve a better outcome for yourself?

6.15 A recent example of the use of moral power is the agreement between Australia and East Timor to equally divide revenue from a gasfield in the waters between the two countries. In 1989, Australia had signed a treaty with Indonesia giving Australia extensive rights in the Timor Sea for gas and oil exploration. Upon East Timor's independence from Indonesia, East Timor requested that the boundary be moved to the halfway mark (a more traditional legal standard) between Australia and East Timor rather than the one agreed upon by Indonesia. A new boundary would give East Timor control over much of the oil and gas resources under the ocean. Australia had all the power in this relationship — more wealth, more military — and had even helped East Timor gain its independence in 2002 from Indonesia. But, after a creative solution was proposed that delayed talks upon the boundary for 50 years while agreeing to split revenue from the Greater Sunrise gasfield, Australia finally agreed to give East Timor more money. This agreement could result in upwards of $5 billion for struggling East Timor. As the subtititle in *The Economist* stated, "Australia, at long last, does the right thing by East Timor." Fair Dinkum, The Economist, May 21, 2005, at 46.

6.16 For further reading on coercive social power, see Jayne Seminare Docherty, Power in the Social/Political Realm, 87 Marq. L. Rev. 861 (2004). See also Christopher Honeyman, The Physics of Power, 87 Marq. L. Rev. 871 (2004). Coercive power and other categorizations of power are also discussed in Bertran H. Raven, The Bases of Power: Origins and Recent Developments, 49 J. Soc. Issues 227 (1993).

6.17 For a discussion of how power in a given relationship affects the parties' use of conciliatory and hostile tactics in bargaining, see Edward J. Lawler, Power Process in Bargaining, 33 Soc. Q. 17 (1992).

Chapter 7 | Working with Your Counterpart: Understanding, Listening, Emotions, and Apology

Moderate your desire of victory over your adversary, and be pleased with the one over yourself.

— Benjamin Franklin

This chapter focuses on some of the important interpersonal and affective issues that you will have to deal with when negotiating. No matter how good your analysis and legal arguments, negotiation is a process you engage in with other people. This chapter will help you learn, develop, and improve on skills necessary for you to know yourself and your negotiation counterparts. Whether you are a novice or an expert, focusing on skills can yield improved results. As Roger Fisher says, "Even the tennis professionals at Wimbledon bring their coaches with them."

The first excerpt, from Melissa Nelken, discusses the importance of self-awareness in skill building and the effect this can have as students take negotiation classes. The excerpt that follows by Roger Fisher and Wayne Davis outlines some basic skills for negotiators.

❖ *Melissa Nelken*, NEGOTIATION AND PSYCHOANALYSIS: IF I'D WANTED TO LEARN ABOUT FEELINGS, I WOULDN'T HAVE GONE TO LAW SCHOOL

46 J. Legal Educ. 420, 426 (1996)

A PSYCHOANALYTIC APPROACH TO NEGOTIATION

Introducing psychoanalytic ideas in a legal setting poses a challenge...to the received wisdom of the lawyer. As one student said to me many years ago: "If I'd wanted to learn about feelings, I wouldn't have gone to law school." Her comment reflected not only personal discomfort with the inquiry I was encouraging, but also a sense that such an inquiry was out of place in legal education. Yet the process of lawyering, as distinct from legal theory, inevitably involves the lawyer deeply in the hopes, fears, and conflicts of her clients; and these inevitably arouse responses in the lawyer, no matter how much the professional ideal would have us believe otherwise.

In addition, in representing her clients, the lawyer has no choice but to be who she is: her own conflicts, and attitudes toward conflict, will inform every task she undertakes on a client's behalf.

Negotiation, for example, is at the heart of what lawyers do. Since more than 90 percent of civil lawsuits never go to trial, even those lawyers who handle lawsuits and not business deals spend a significant amount of time negotiating — not just details like the timing of discovery but the ultimate resolution of the dispute itself. Lawyers tend to think that they will somehow be able to stay out of the way when they negotiate, that the process will go on outside of them. In fact, most are unaware of the extent to which their own needs and conflicts enter into the negotiation process. Everyone has heard stories of lawyers so competitive that they poison deals that could have been made to the benefit of their clients; there are also lawyers whose need to accommodate those they negotiate with leads them to give away the store, to the detriment of their clients. Without some degree of self-understanding, then, some attention to feelings, lawyers run the risk of missing much that is central to competent representation. . . .

By developing a capacity for such self-observation, a negotiator becomes more aware of the dynamics of negotiation, of how her and her opponent's responses to each other and to the conflict embodied in the negotiation affect what both of them do and say on behalf of their clients. This increased self-awareness enables her to make choices about how to handle the negotiation that would not otherwise be open: to behave, in fact, more rationally, more like the ideal lawyer. . . .

An understanding of the interpersonal dynamics of conflict has benefits as well for the lawyer-client relationship, since clients inevitably suffer when their lawyers insist on divorcing the professional encounter from the emotional underpinnings of the dispute involved. Client dissatisfaction with legal representation often results from the lawyer's inability to see the client's emotional self as anything but an impediment to sensible, rational management of the legal problem the client brings. . . .

Thinking about how her approach to negotiation as well as her negotiation style have been shaped by past experiences helps a lawyer to organize her present experience in a way that maximizes the possibilities for learning. Since she herself is the one negotiator she can't walk away from, the more she can become aware of what motivates her own behavior in negotiations, the more able she will be to step back in the heat of the moment and to reflect on whether what is happening really serves the interests of her client. Along the way, she will also gain considerable skill in reading what is going on in her opponents. . . .

 Roger Fisher & Wayne H. Davis, **SIX BASIC INTERPERSONAL SKILLS FOR A NEGOTIATOR'S REPERTOIRE**

3 Negot. J. 117, 117-122 (1987)

There is an infinite range and variety in interpersonal skills. Many of these skills can be seen as attractive opposites, such as being independent and being cooperative, or being pragmatic and being imaginative, or being controlled and being expressive. We would like to be good at both but tend to be stronger in one than the other.

These desirable qualities can be visualized as lying on the circumference of a circle, so that becoming more skillful is seen as extending our skills in all directions. Improving our skills can be recognized not as correcting a fault (such as "I am too flexible"), but rather as becoming more skillful at its attractive opposite (e.g., "I want to become better at being firm when that is appropriate").

To broaden one's repertoire, it may help to think of these qualities as falling into six basic categories of interpersonal skills in which each effective negotiator enjoys some competence and confidence. . . .

EXPRESSING STRONG FEELINGS APPROPRIATELY

- *Recognize feelings.* A negotiator needs to recognize that feelings are a natural human phenomenon. They exist. There is nothing wrong with *having* emotions, although *expressing* them in particular ways may be costly or counterproductive.
- *Be aware.* It is a wise practice to become *aware* of the emotions — both our own and those of the other side — that are involved in any given negotiation. . . .
- *Develop a range of expression.* When it comes to communicating feelings to someone else, it is well to recognize that there is a spectrum of ways to do so, ranging from talking rationally about them, through increasing the emotional content of verbal and nonverbal communication, to letting the emotions take charge. . . .
- *Relate tone to substance.* Too often we fail to relate the emotional content of a communication to the substantive issue being discussed. It is far easier to be assertive — and certainly more effective — if we have something sensible to assert. Key to an effective communication of feeling is likely to be some well-prepared substantive content that identifies the purpose of the communication, justifies the feeling, and enlists its expression in the furtherance of that purpose.

REMAINING RATIONAL IN THE FACE
OF STRONG FEELINGS

- *Acknowledge their feelings.*
- *Step above the fray.* When the discussion turns so emotional that rational discussion seems pointless, we might withdraw from the discussion long enough for us and others to regain some composure. State frankly our reasons for withdrawing, and couple that with a commitment to return.
- *Step aside; let their emotions hit the problem.* If they're expressing an emotion, encourage them to express it fully and completely — so they can feel that they've "got it all out."
- *Separate the causes of their feelings from the substantive problem, and deal with them in parallel.* Once feelings have been fully expressed and acknowledged, it may be

appropriate to analyze what engendered the feelings and take steps to alleviate those causes.

- *Be positive.* At the outset, consciously consider and decide on the purpose of the negotiation. Then, when emotions run too strong, we can ask the parties to question whether or not the direction of the discussion serves the agreed-upon purposes of the meeting.

BEING ASSERTIVE WITHIN A NEGOTIATION WITHOUT DAMAGING THE RELATIONSHIP

With or without increasing the emotional content of our expressions, it is possible to be assertive without damage to a relationship. The suggested general strategy:

- *Disentangle relationship issues from substantive ones and work on them in parallel.* Although substantive disagreements can make a working relationship more difficult, and although a good working relationship can make it easier to reach agreement, the process of dealing with differences is usefully treated as a subject quite distinct and separate from the content and extent of those differences.
- *Be "soft on the people."* Avoid personal judgments. Acknowledge some merit in what the other side has said or done. Be open, polite, courteous, and considerate.
- *Have something to assert.* Know the purpose of the session in terms of some product that it is reasonable to expect.
- *Be firm and open.* Be prepared to remain firm as long as that appears . . . to make sense on the substance of the negotiation. At the same time, be open — both in words and thought — to alternative views that are truly persuasive.

IMPROVING A RELATIONSHIP WITHOUT DAMAGE TO A PARTICULAR NEGOTIATION

- *Good relations help reach good outcomes.* It is important to recognize that relationship-building moves tend to strengthen rather than weaken our chances for achieving a good agreement.
- *Acknowledge merit in something they have done.* It is almost always possible to find something meritorious that the other side has done — perhaps in an area apart from what is being negotiated. By acknowledging that, we can communicate that we recognize and respect their worth as people.
- *Acknowledge a need on our part.* Relationships tend to be stronger when there is some interdependence: both sides feel and recognize their need or reliance on the other side in order to achieve mutually desired ends.
- *Take steps outside the negotiation to improve the relationship.* We can concentrate our relationship-building actions in temporally discrete segments of the negotiation, or when we are physically away from the table.

SPEAKING CLEARLY IN WAYS THAT PROMOTE LISTENING

- *Speak for yourself.* Phrase statements about their behavior, motives, statements, etc. in first-person terms of our perceptions and feelings. They may deny the accusation, "You're a bigot!" They can't deny the statement, "I'm feeling discriminated against."

- *Avoid attribution and check assumptions.* Recognize when we make assumptions about their thoughts, feelings, motives, and so on, and try to verify those assumptions with the other side before acting on them. Inquire about their understanding of the background issues or information.
- *Use short, clear statements.*
- *Ask them to repeat back what we've said.* In effect, encourage them to be active listeners by asking them to confirm in their own words what they've heard us say.

ACTIVELY INQUIRING AND LISTENING

- *Explicitly allocate time to listen and understand the other side.*
- *Separate understanding their arguments from judging and responding to them.* Make sure that their full argument has been stated, and that we understand it before trying to respond.
- *Repeat back their statements in our own words.*
- *Inquire actively about the reasoning behind their statements.* Even if we repeat back what they said, often they haven't said all they were thinking. There will be some implicit reasoning or logic underlying their statements. It's helpful to ask them to make that reasoning explicit, and then to repeat back their explanation.

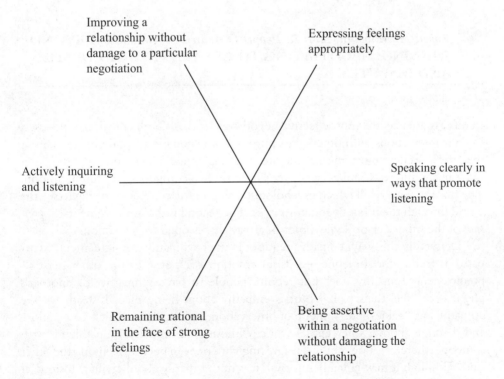

Notes and Questions

7.1 What do you think are your main strengths as a negotiator? Where do you think these come from? What do you think are your main fears and weaknesses as a negotiator? Where do you think these come from? Plot your own skills in the pie chart illustration above. What does this reveal about you?

7.2 Fisher and Davis place each pair of skills on a related opposing spectrum. Do you agree that typically people find one or the other side easier for them?

7.3 For more on how self-awareness and learning occur in adults, see Michael Moffitt & Scott R. Peppet, Action Science and Negotiation, 87 Marq. L. Rev. 649 (2004).

7.4 If you recall, being assertive and speaking clearly are also discussed in Chapter 2.

A. UNDERSTANDING YOUR COUNTERPART

We don't see things as they are, we see things as we are.

— Anais Nin

The next section should help you to understand the other side's or client's point of view. The first excerpt discusses the skill of empathy — one of the key ingredients in effective negotiation. The second provides further tools for creating this empathy and double-checking your assumptions.

 Robert H. Mnookin, Scott R. Peppet & Andrew S. Tulumello, **BEYOND WINNING: NEGOTIATING TO CREATE VALUE IN DEALS AND DISPUTES**

46-49 (2000)

In our experience, the most effective negotiators try . . . to both empathize and assert in their interactions with others. For purposes of negotiation, we define *empathy* as the process of demonstrating an accurate, nonjudgmental understanding of the other side's needs, interests, and perspective. There are two components to this definition. The first involves a skill which psychologists call *perspective-taking* — trying to see the world through the other negotiator's eyes. The second is the nonjudgmental *expression* of the other person's viewpoint in a way that is open to correction.

Defined in this way, empathy requires neither sympathy nor agreement. Sympathy is feeling for someone — it is an emotional response to the other person's predicament. Empathy does not require people to have sympathy for another's plight — to "feel their pain." Nor is empathy about being nice. Instead, we see empathy as a "value-neutral mode of observation," a journey in which you explore and describe another's perceptual world without commitment. Empathizing with someone, therefore, does not mean agreeing with or even necessarily liking the other side. Although it may entail being civil, it is not primarily about civility. Instead, it simply requires the expression of how the world looks to the other person. . . .

Three main points about empathy and assertiveness are central:

- Problem-solving negotiations go better for everyone when each side has well-honed empathy and assertiveness skills.

- Problem-solving negotiations go better for an individual negotiator if she both empathizes and asserts, even if the other side does not follow her lead.
- Empathy and assertiveness make problem-solving easier in both the value creation and the value-distribution aspects of negotiation.

Empathy and assertiveness are aspects of good communication. When people communicate well with each other, problem-solving is easier. . . .

First, [in a dispute between Susan and Martin,] regardless of how Susan is behaving, Martin really *does* need to understand her point of view. . . . This will help him both when he's trying to create value from the deal and when he faces any dispute over how that value should be distributed. . . . [T]o the extent that Martin can clarify *for himself* what Susan's motives and goals are, he will be better equipped to find value-creating trades. Indeed, research confirms that negotiators with higher perspective-taking ability negotiate agreements of higher value than those with lower perspective-taking ability. . . .

The better Martin understands Susan's thinking, the better he will be able to anticipate the strategic problems and opportunities that may crop up in the negotiation — and to prepare for them.

A second benefit of empathy is that it allows Martin to correct any misperceptions *he* may have about Susan's thinking. . . . Indeed, regardless of the emotional content of a negotiation, research has shown that negotiators routinely jump to mistaken conclusions about their counterparts' motivations, usually because their information is limited. Such mistakes are a major reason why negotiations and relationships break down. For example, negotiators often make *attributional* errors — they attribute to their counterparts incorrect or exaggerated intentions or characteristics. If a counterpart is late to a meeting, we might assume either that he intended to make us wait or that he is chronically tardy, even though we may be meeting him for the first time. . . .

A third benefit of combining assertion with empathy is that Martin may be able to loosen Susan up — and gain her trust. . . . Most people have a need to tell their story and to feel that it has been understood. Meeting this need can dramatically shift the tone of a relationship. . . . Even if you are not interested in sharing a deeply soulful moment with your counterpart, remember that empathizing has highly practical benefits. It conveys concern and respect, which tend to defuse anger and mistrust, especially where these emotions stem from feeling unappreciated or exploited.

Finally, your empathy may inspire openness in others and may make you more persuasive.

Notes and Questions

7.5 Mnookin et al. write about empathy in tension with the skill of assertiveness. Why might there be a tension between empathy and assertiveness? Which skill, empathy or assertiveness, are you more comfortable with? What does this tell you about yourself as a negotiator?

7.6 Thinking back to the styles of negotiation outlined by Andrea Kupfer Schneider in her study in Chapter 3 — true problem solver, cautious problem solver, and adversarial — how important is the skill of empathy? Which type of negotiators uses this the most? The least?

 Roger Fisher, Elizabeth Kopelman & Andrea Kupfer Schneider, **BEYOND MACHIAVELLI: TOOLS FOR COPING WITH CONFLICT**

32-35 (1996)

EXPLORE PARTISAN PERCEPTIONS

We all face a complex world. To make sense of it, we develop perceptions that work as a kind of shorthand, a template that we impose on what would otherwise be a welter of chaotic data. When we see a woman holding a child, we perceive that woman as a mother. We are unlikely to ask her about it; we just assume. We question these perceptions only when we recognize disconfirming data; say the woman and the child have different skin color, then we might assume that we were wrong and that they are not mother and child. If these two are then greeted by a man of different skin color than the woman, our perception might change again, and so on.

There is a Russian saying that everyone looks at the world from the belltower of his own village. Perceptions differ because our experiences differ, and because we select from among our experiences. Each of us observes different data in part because we are all interested in different things. Depending on our specific perspective, our perceptions vary. . . .

Coping with conflict means coping with the way people think and feel. In any conflict people think and feel differently from one another, and the issue is not whose perceptions are "true" and whose are "false." To provide us with a foundation for dealing with a conflict, we would like to disaggregate the perceptions on all sides — our own as well as those of others — to understand them, and be fully in touch with them. The better we understand the way people see things, the better we will be able to change them. . . .

Speaking in another's voice — or writing out perceptions from that person's point of view — accomplishes two tasks at once. It helps free us from our own partisan perceptions. It also helps us see how the perceptions of others, while seemingly intractable may contain some seeds of flexibility. . . .

OBSERVE FROM DIFFERENT POINTS OF VIEW

To understand a conflict in which we are a party, we will want to observe it from at least three points of view. First, we want to be aware of ourselves (Are we angry? Losing control? Reacting? Drifting?) and to consider the conflict from our own point of view (What are our goals? What are our interests? What risks do we see? And so forth). Our point of view is an important starting point. It is, however, only a starting point.

We will also want to observe the situation from the point of view of the other parties to this conflict. Putting ourselves hypothetically in their shoes, what would we see? How does everything look from that vantage point? If we were there, what would be our goals, our interests, our concerns? Would we feel justifiably angry? How does the conflict look from there?

And finally, to gain a more balanced view, how would the situation look from the point of view of a neutral third party? How would a "fly on the wall" describe things? How are the parties behaving? Do they seem to be quarreling, debating, scoring points, bickering, and attacking each other, or are they jointly attacking the problem? Are they wasting time or using it well?

THE FAR SIDE® BY GARY LARSON

How birds see the world

To understand conflict well we want to observe it from all three positions. (If there are several parties to a conflict, we will want to understand how each sees it.) One who is skilled at dealing with conflict is likely to be adept at jumping back and forth, observing what is going on from each of these three positions, even "on line," while participating in a discussion. . . .

> ### 3. Three Positions for Observing a Conflict
>
> **First Position (Mine)**: How I see the problem, from my own perspective.
>
> **Second Position (Theirs)**: How I see the problem when I stand in the shoes of the other party to the dispute.
>
> **Third Position ("Fly on the Wall")**: How a neutral third party would assess the conflict.
>
> *These three distinct points of view illuminate a variety of dimensions of a conflict.*

TO GAIN EMPATHY, REVERSE ROLES

Understanding is not simply an intellectual activity. Feeling empathetically how others may feel can be as important as thinking clearly about how others may think.

There is a lot of truth in the old saying that "where you stand depends upon where you sit." Another way of trying to understand the other side's perceptions is literally to sit in a different chair, pretend to be someone on the other side, and try to see the situation from that vantage point.

The chairman of a company held liable for a patent infringement had called in a consultant to advise about the negotiation of a possible settlement on the dollar amount of damages. The case had been in litigation for years. The chairman had been told that if the worst happened, and he should be held liable, he could always settle — but he had little appreciation of how much the other side would expect.

Encouraged by the consultant, the executive agreed to switch seats, moving from his own chair to a chair the consultant had designated as that of the president of the plaintiff company. While the executive initially resisted "playing games," he was eventually persuaded to assume the role of that president and to state the plaintiff's case in the first person as forcefully as he could. Within a few minutes he was playing the role well. Asked how much he might accept in settlement (an amount that, in real life, would be paid out by this executive's own company) he replied (still in his role as the opposing company's president), "Why, I wouldn't take their whole damn company!" Shaken by this experience, and with new insight into what might be required to settle this case, his company raised its settlement offer by one hundred fold. It was rejected, and the judgment was ultimately settled for even more. An earlier attempt to appreciate the other side's partisan perceptions would no doubt have led him to pursue a wiser strategy from the outset. . . .

To gain insight by reversing roles, we first identify the person whom we expect to be attempting to persuade (the "absent party") and find a friend or colleague to help us. Our helper is someone who either already knows our side of the conflict or will quickly learn the points we currently plan to make. Then we sit in the chair labeled "absent party," and with the assistance of the helper, come to think of ourselves as being that person. Finally, our helper sits in our chair, assumes our role, and presents our side of the case. While playing the part of someone on the other side of a conflict, we hear our own arguments come back at us. Through such role reversal we can often gain insight and empathy for the other side—sometimes dramatically so—in a way that helps us tailor our arguments to make them more persuasive. . . .

Focus on Their Choice

Every event has a history. . . . [W]e would like to have some useful ways of capturing the interactions between us to date, ways to integrate relevant events and important economic, legal, and other considerations. We propose two such ways, each of which puts us into the shoes of the other party. The first is to analyze past events in terms of the message we have been sending, as it has been received by the other side. The second is to analyze the resulting choice that the other decision-makers have seen themselves as facing. Together, these two techniques help explain why other parties are doing what they are doing, and point toward what will be needed to overcome barriers to progress. . . .

Understand the Message as They Hear It

. . . A useful way of figuring out what this message looks like to the other party in the dispute is to examine three basic elements of our communication. As of this moment, what is the net effect of everything we have said and done (or not said and not done) in terms of:

- **A demand:** What they hear us asking for;
- **A threat:** What they hear us threatening if our demand is not met;
- **An offer:** What they hear us offering if they meet our demand.

What we call the demand is what we want them to do in the future. . . . What we call the threat is the consequence of not doing as we would like—an action we will deliberately take that may make them unhappy. Sometimes instead of a threat, perhaps what we have been sending is a warning of events beyond our control that could result from their failure to take appropriate action. In either case, whether we have been sending a threat or a warning, the effectiveness of this part of the message depends not only upon its content (What are the consequences? When will they occur? Who will impose them? And what makes them legitimate?) but upon the clarity with which those elements are communicated, their credibility, and their probability.

Similar considerations apply to an offer. The impact of the "good" consequences that we are saying will follow if they do take the desired action depends upon answers to the same set of subsidiary questions: Who? When? What? And why are those consequences legitimate?

Consider the Other Side's Choice

While message analysis helps us estimate what other players are currently hearing, it is usually insufficient to explain why they are acting the way they are. To pursue that issue, we ask: What is the primary decision those on the other side see themselves as facing? Taking into account not only the message we have been sending but all other factors as well, how do the pros and cons of that decision appear to them? To understand the question to which the other side has been saying no thus far, and to be able to present them later with a more persuasive choice, we again want to analyze the existing situation as it appears to them today.

See Changing Their Choice as Our Problem

... Coping effectively with a conflict means being persuasive to the players on the other side — and on our side. Being persuasive requires us to think clearly about changing how people see their choice. In doing so, we do not want to treat any aspect of that choice as fixed and immutable, be it the decisionmaker, the proposed decision, the elements that influence his or her decision, or perceptions that may effect the weighing of those elements. All are potentially subject to change. As we develop a new plan of action for ourselves, we greatly benefit from having set out the other side's currently perceived choice and important parameters of a preferred future choice.

Notes and Questions

7.7 What are partisan perceptions? Think of an issue about which you have strong feelings. Outline your point of view in one column of a piece of paper. Outline the other side's point of view as best you can on the other side of paper. Are there any similarities?

7.8 Why do people all view the world from their own perspectives? This rabbi's sermon points out, in a very funny way, how people each can interpret the same events differently:

> If you were to walk into our home, the first book you would see on the coffee table is our wedding album. That's right, finally, after three years of marriage, two children, a change of city and much procrastination, the proofs were distributed to me, to my wife's parents, to my parents — and at long last the albums are finally complete. Over this past summer, as I have had a chance to review the completed copies in my home, my parent's home and the edition in my in-law's home, I have discovered something very interesting about these albums — each one tells a very different story. Let me explain.
>
> If you were to look at our edition — the first page is a photograph of our wedding invitation, followed by a picture of Debbie and then me. This is followed by pictures of our families, me and Debbie under the huppah, the party, and a final picture of the happy couple. However, if you went to Pittsburgh to see the album at my in-laws, you would begin with a picture of Debbie, then Debbie and her mother, then Debbie and her siblings and then her grandmother, and eventually around page six — you catch a glimpse of me — the groom.
>
> And, the rewriting of history is no less startling at my parent's place in Los Angeles. It begins with the primary male/female relationship, the groom and his mother, followed by the mother and the father, and then almost as an afterthought you meet the son stealer — my bride. And so it is throughout. . . .

And as I looked at these albums this past summer—I was struck by their differences, which until now I kept to myself. It is fascinating really, I am positive I was at the wedding, and yet there exist very different records of the event. Each tells a different story, each constructs a different reality. Each family had the identical set of pictures to choose from and yet each book, the order, the emphasis, the beginnings and the endings lead to very different narratives of that wonderful day.

Courtesy of Rabbi Elliot Cosgrove.

7.9 Similarly, *Wittgenstein's Poker* tells the story of a famous argument between philosophers Ludwig Wittgenstein and Karl Popper at a Cambridge University meeting in 1946. According to the version Popper published in his autobiography, Wittgenstein threatened him with a poker when Popper challenged Wittgenstein on a philosophical point. As the authors write in the book, each of the nine surviving audience members remembers the events differently: whether Wittgenstein was merely gesturing or actually threatening with the poker; if, in response to Wittgenstein's demand for a moral rule, Popper's witty response of "Not to threaten visiting lecturers with pokers" actually caused Wittgenstein to walk out or if Popper replied after Wittgenstein had left the room. It is a fascinating collection of stories, all purportedly retelling the same event. David Edmonds & John Eidinow, Wittgenstein's Poker: The Story of a Ten-Minute Argument Between Two Great Philosophers (2001).

The next several excerpts focus on different tools that help us understand how parties to a negotiation can end up misunderstanding each other. The first is the ladder of inference—how two people can come to different conclusions based on the same experience or data. The second helps us to deal with the assumptions made by others and to analyze the relationship of data to assumptions.

 Rick Ross, **THE LADDER OF INFERENCE**

in The Fifth Discipline Fieldbook 242-246 (Peter M. Senge et al. ed., 1994)

We live in a world of self-generating beliefs which remain largely untested. We adopt those beliefs because they are based on conclusions, which are inferred from what we observe, plus our past experience. Our ability to achieve the results we truly desire is eroded by our feelings that:

- Our beliefs are *the* truth.
- The truth is obvious.
- Our beliefs are based on real data.
- The data we select are the real data.

For example: I am standing before the executive team, making a presentation. They all seem engaged and alert, except for Larry, at the end of the table, who seems bored out of his mind. He turns his dark, morose eyes away from me and puts his hand to his mouth. He doesn't ask any questions until I'm almost done, when he breaks in: "I think we should ask for a full report." In this culture, that typically means, "Let's move on." Everyone starts to shuffle their papers and put their notes away. Larry obviously thinks that I'm incompetent—which is a shame, because these ideas are exactly what his department needs. Now that I think of it, he's never liked my ideas. Clearly, Larry is a power-hungry jerk. By the time I've returned to my seat, I've made a decision: I'm not going to include anything in my report that Larry can use. He wouldn't read it, or, worse still, he'd just use it against me. It's too bad I have an enemy who's so prominent in the company.

In those few seconds before I take my seat, I have climbed up what Chris Argyris calls a "ladder of inference"—a common mental pathway of increasing abstraction, often leading to misguided beliefs:

- I started with the observable data: Larry's comment, which is so self-evident that it would show up on a videotape recorder. . . .
- . . . I selected some details about Larry's behavior: his glance away from me and apparent yawn. (I didn't notice him listening intently one moment before). . . .
- . . . I added some meanings of my own, based on the culture around me (that Larry wanted me to finish up). . . .
- . . . I moved rapidly up to assumptions about Larry's current state (he's bored). . . .
- . . . and I concluded that Larry, in general, thinks I'm incompetent. In fact, I now believe that Larry (and probably everyone whom I associate with Larry) is dangerously opposed to me. . . .
- . . . thus, as I reach the top of the ladder, I'm plotting against him.

It all seems so reasonable, and it happens so quickly, that I'm not even aware I've done it. Moreover, all the rungs of the ladder take place in my head. The only parts visible to anyone else are the directly observable data at the bottom, and my own decision to take action at the top.

The rest of the trip, the ladder where I spend most of my time, is unseen, unquestioned, not considered fit for discussion, and enormously abstract. (These leaps up the ladder are sometimes called "leaps of abstraction.")

I've probably leaped up that ladder of inference many times before. The more I believe that Larry is an evil guy, the more I reinforce my tendency to notice his malevolent behavior in the future. This phenomenon is known as the "reflexive loop": our beliefs influence what data we select next time. And there is a counterpart reflexive loop in

LADDER OF INFERENCE
I take ACTIONS based on my beliefs
I adopt BELIEFS about the world
I draw CONCLUSIONS
I make ASSUMPTIONS based on the meanings I added
I add MEANINGS (cultural and personal)
I select "DATA" from what I observe
Observable DATA and EXPERIENCES (as a videotape recorder might capture them)

Larry's mind: as he reacts to my strangely antagonistic behavior, he's probably jumping up some rungs on his own ladder. For no apparent reason, before too long, we could find ourselves becoming bitter enemies.

Larry might indeed have been bored by my presentation — or he might have been eager to read the report on paper. He might think I'm incompetent, he might be shy, or he might be afraid to embarrass me. More likely than not, he has inferred that I think *he's* incompetent. We can't know, until we find a way to check our conclusions.

Unfortunately, assumptions and conclusions are particularly difficult to test. For instance, suppose I wanted to find out if Larry *really* thought I was incompetent. I would have to pull him aside and ask him, "Larry, do you think I'm an idiot?" Even if I could find a way to phrase the question, how could I believe the answer? Would *I* answer *him* honestly? No, I'd tell him I thought he was a terrific colleague, while privately thinking worse of him for asking me.

Now imagine me, Larry, and three others in a senior management team, with our untested assumptions and beliefs. When we meet to deal with a concrete problem, the air is filled with misunderstandings, communication breakdowns, and feeble compromises. Thus, while our individual IQs average 140, our team has a collective IQ of 85.

The ladder of inference explains why most people don't usually remember where their deepest attitudes came from. The date is long since lost to memory, after years of inferential leaps. Sometimes I find myself arguing that "The Republicans are so-and-so," and someone asks me why I believe that. My immediate, intuitive answer is, "I don't know. But I've believed it for years." In the meantime, other people are saying, "The Democrats are so-and-so," and they can't tell you why, either. Instead, they may drudge up an old platitude which once was an assumption. Before long, we come to think of our longstanding assumptions as data ("Well, I know the Republicans are such-and-such because they're so-and-so"), but we're several steps removed from the data.

USING THE LADDER OF INFERENCE

You can't live your life without adding meaning or drawing conclusions. It would be an inefficient, tedious way to live. But you *can* improve your communications through reflection, and by using the ladder of inference in three ways:

- Becoming more aware of your own thinking and reasoning (reflection);
- Making your thinking and reasoning more visible to others (advocacy);
- Inquiring into others' thinking and reasoning (inquiry).

Once Larry and I understand the concepts behind the "ladder of inference," we have a safe way to stop a conversation in its tracks and ask several questions:

- What is the observable data behind that statement?
- Does everyone agree on what the data is?
- Can you run me through your reasoning?
- How did we get from that data to these abstract assumptions?
- When you said "[your inference]," did you mean "[my interpretation of it]"?

I can ask for data in an open-ended way: "Larry, what was your reaction to this presentation?" I can test my assumptions: "Larry, are you bored?" Or I can simply test the observable data: "You've been quiet, Larry." To which he might reply: "Yeah, I'm taking notes; I love this stuff."

Note that I don't say, "Larry, I think you've moved way up the ladder of inference. Here's what you need to do to get down." The point of this method is not to nail Larry (or even to diagnose Larry), but to make our thinking processes visible, to see what the differences are in our perceptions and what we have in common. (You might say, "I notice I'm moving up the ladder of inference, and maybe we all are. What's the data here?")

This type of conversation is not easy. For example, as Chris Argyris cautions people, when a fact seems especially self-evident, be careful. If your manner suggests that it must be equally self-evident to everyone else, you may cut off the chance to test it. A fact, no matter how obvious it seems, isn't really substantiated until it's verified independently — by more than one person's observation, or by a technological record (a tape recording or photograph).

Embedded into team practice, the ladder becomes a very healthy tool. There's something exhilarating about showing other people the links of your reasoning. They may or may not agree with you, but they can see how you got there. And you're often surprised yourself to see how you got there, once you trace out the links.

CALVIN AND HOBBES © 1990 Watterson. Dist. by **UNIVERSAL PRESS SYNDICATE.**

Andrea Kupfer Schneider, **EFFECTIVE RESPONSES TO OFFENSIVE COMMENTS**

10 Negot. J. 107, 108-110 (1994)

CHECK YOUR ASSUMPTIONS

"Will you get me some coffee?" or "Are *you* the only lawyer for this case?" are only two of the plethora of questions that could be seen as either sexist or racist, depending on the person to whom they are directed. Questions such as, "Is this your first contract (or labor or environmental or . . .) dispute?" or "When did you graduate law school?" to a young lawyer or "Where are you from?" to an Asian-American can also be troubling. Similarly, many "compliments" are often offensively condescending. "You speak English so well" to an Asian-American or "Your family must be so proud of you for finishing college" to a black person are only two examples of people who may mean well but end up offending their listeners.

One of the interesting things to note about such comments is that the inference of bias depends wholly on the person *to* whom they are directed and not *from* whom they come. The same request for coffee or inquiry about the number of lawyers on a case will often not have the same implication of bias if directed to a white male. (The questions, however, still could be evidence of gamesmanship and an attempt to denigrate.)

Because most negotiation situations are fraught with tension, negotiators frequently attribute bad motives to the other side. ("For them to say *that* proves how horrible they are!") The problem with attributing bias or other character flaws to the other side is that we will often change our own behavior toward them in a negative way—perhaps we become more stubborn, more hostile, or more suspicious. The other side will, in turn, perceive this changed behavior and react similarly. We will then perceive their worsened behavior as confirming our suspicions of their biases and react even more. Thus the escalation of tensions and the spiral toward a breakdown in the negotiation begins.

One way to diminish the spiral of escalating tensions is to analyze comments and questions from the other side thoroughly before imputing motives to them. Interpretations of the other sides' questions often stem from our own assumptions about them, their beliefs, and their biases. Negotiators can analyze their assumptions using several tools, one of which is the "Assumptions—Data Chart" shown in Table 1.

Table 1
Assumptions—Data Chart

I. Assumptions *What are your assumptions about the other side's biases?*	II. Data *On what data do you base your assumptions?*
IV. New Conclusion? *Given this new data, what might a new conclusion be?*	**III. Other Data** *Is there additional nonconforming data which you have not considered?*

To use this [table], begin in the upper left quadrant by asking about your own assumptions. For example, you may assume that an older white male is probably prone to sexism. You then move to the upper right quadrant and ask for the data on which your assumption is based. This could, for example, be the inquiry to a woman as to whether she is the *only* lawyer handling this case. Her assumptions would probably be based on interactions with other men in this situation and whether or not they exhibited sexist behavior by such a remark.

To continue, you then move to the lower right quadrant and look for nonconforming data, that is, experiences or comments which do *not* support your assumptions. Commonly in negotiations and interactions with other parties, we filter out the information that does not agree with our belief. And, once we reach a conclusion about a person or situation, we ignore new information that may not support the conclusion. Our assumptions become even more one-sided over time as we notice only that information which conforms with our preconceived opinion. By bringing in nonconforming data, we force ourselves to look beyond our prefabricated assumptions and question them. In the example of the woman lawyer, she may recall a prior discussion with this person during which he displayed no signs of sexism. Or she may acknowledge to herself that not all older white men have acted in a sexist manner.

Moving to the fourth quadrant, you may arrive at a new conclusion different from your original assumption. Based on the totality of information, you may conclude that the question or comment was gamesmanship, an honest inquiry, or that it was indeed insensitive, but not made with a malevolent intent. And you may re-evaluate your perception of the other side's character. Table 2 shows how the woman lawyer faced with the "Are-you-the-only-lawyer-handling-this-case?" comment could analyze this kind of situation.

A significant element of the Assumptions — Data Chart is that it attempts to separate exactly what has occurred from your character judgment. Many good people say and do inappropriate things every day. This tool tries first to separate the actions of the person from his or her character, and second, to ensure that you evaluate the character with all of the relevant data, not just the particular comment that has so annoyed you.

Table 2
Assumptions — Data Chart on a "Sexist" Remark

I. Assumptions	II. Data
He is sexist.	*He asked me if I was the only lawyer handling this case.* *Many older men are uncomfortable dealing with young women in positions of responsibility.*
IV. New Conclusion?	**III. Other Data**
He is merely curious if I am handling this by myself.	*He has never insinuated anything during our phone conversations before the negotiation.* *There are many young women in his law firm and it has a good reputation in dealing with female associates.*

Frank and Ernest

OF COURSE THERE ARE TWO SIDES TO EVERY QUESTION, ERNIE. OTHERWISE, YOU WOULDN'T BE WRONG ALL THE TIME.

BEER 50¢

Notes and Questions

7.10 Think of a particular remark that has offended you. Can you separate the data from your inferences and assumptions?

7.11 Perhaps more challenging, can you recall a remark that you made that was taken the wrong way? Were you able to get the conversation back on a positive track? How?

B. LISTENING

One of the most important ways to find out when we are jumping to conclusions is to listen more carefully to the other side. This gives us information, builds empathy and trust, and makes it more likely that the other side will listen to us. These next two excerpts focus on the skill of listening to the other side and asking good questions.

Douglas Stone, Bruce Patton & Sheila Heen, **DIFFICULT CONVERSATIONS: HOW TO DISCUSS WHAT MATTERS MOST**

163, 166-167, 169-170, 172-174, 178, 180-183 (1999)

Andrew is visiting his Uncle Doug. While Doug is on the phone, Andrew tugs on his uncle's pant leg, saying, "Uncle Doug, I want to go outside."

"Not now, Andrew, I'm on the phone," says Doug.

Andrew persists: "But Uncle Doug, I want to go outside!"

"Not now Andrew!" comes Doug's response.

"But I want to go out!" Andrew repeats.

After several more rounds, Doug tries a different approach: "Hey, Andrew. You really want to go outside, don't you?"

"Yes," says Andrew. Then without further comment, Andrew walks off and begins playing by himself. Andrew, it turns out, just wanted to know that his uncle understood him. He wanted to know he'd been heard.

Andrew's story demonstrates something that is true for all of us: we have a deep desire to feel heard, and to know that others care enough to listen. . . .

LISTENING TO THEM HELPS THEM LISTEN TO YOU

When the other person is not listening, you may imagine it is because they're stubborn or don't understand what you're trying to say. (If they did, they'd understand why they should listen to it.) So you may try to break through that by repeating, trying new ways to explain yourself, talking more loudly, and so forth.

On the face of it, these would seem to be good strategies. But they're not. Why? Because in the great majority of cases, the reason the other person is not listening to you is not because they are stubborn, but because *they* don't feel heard. In other words, they aren't listening to you for the same reason you aren't listening to them: they think *you* are slow or stubborn. So they repeat themselves, find new ways to say things, talk more loudly, and so forth.

If the block to their listening is that they don't feel heard, then the way to remove that block is by helping them feel heard — by bending over backwards to listen to what they have to say, and perhaps most important, by demonstrating that you understand what they are saying and how they are feeling.

If you don't quite believe this, try it. Find the most stubborn person you know, the person who never seems to take in anything you say, the person who repeats himself or herself in every conversation you ever have — and listen to them. Especially, listen for feelings, like frustration or pride or fear, and acknowledge those feelings. See whether that person doesn't become a better listener after all. . . .

THREE SKILLS: INQUIRY, PARAPHRASING, AND ACKNOWLEDGMENT

Inquire to Learn

The heading says it all: inquire to learn. And only to learn. You can tell whether a question will help the conversation or hurt it by thinking about why you asked it. The only good answer is "To learn."

Anyone who has ever been a kid in a car has uttered the cranky words "Are we there yet?" You know you're not there yet, and your parents know you know, and so they respond in a tone as cranky as yours. What you really meant was "I'm feeling restless" or "I wish we were there" or "This is a long trip for me." Any of these would likely elicit a more productive response from Mom and Dad.

This illustrates an important rule about inquiry: If you don't have a question, don't ask a question. Never dress up an assertion as a question. Doing so creates confusion and resentment, because such questions are inevitably heard as sarcastic and sometimes mean-spirited. . . .

Sharing our feelings and making requests are two things that many of us have difficulty doing directly. They can make us feel vulnerable. Turning what we have to say into an attack — a sarcastic question — can feel safer. But this safety is an illusion, and we lose more than we gain. Saying "I'd like you to pay more attention to me" is more likely to produce a conversation (a satisfying outcome) than "Is it impossible for you to focus on me just once?"...

A second error that gets us into trouble is using questions to shoot holes in the other person's argument....

Open-ended questions are questions that give the other person broad latitude in how to answer.... To understand where the other person's conclusions came from and enrich your understanding of what they envision going forward, it helps to ask them to be more explicit about their reasoning and their vision. "What leads you to say that?" "Can you give me an example?" "What would that look like?" "How would that work?" "How would we test that hypothesis?"...

Paraphrase for Clarity

The second skill a good listener brings to the conversation is paraphrasing....

First, paraphrasing gives you a chance to check your understanding. Difficult conversations are made harder when an important misunderstanding exists, and such misunderstandings are more common than we imagine. Paraphrasing gives the other person the chance to say, "No, that's not quite what I meant. What I really meant was...."

Second, paraphrasing lets the other person know that they've been heard. Usually the reason someone repeats himself or herself in a conversation is because they have no indication that you've actually taken in what they've said. If you notice that the other person is saying the same thing over and over again, take it as a signal that you need to paraphrase more. Once they feel heard, they are significantly more likely to listen to *you*....

Acknowledge Their Feelings

Why is acknowledgment so important? Because attached to each expression of feelings is a set of invisible questions: "Are my feelings okay?" "Do you understand them?" "Do you care about them?" "Do you care about me?" These questions are important, and we have trouble moving on in the conversation until we know the answers. Taking time to acknowledge the other person's feelings says loud and clear that the answer to each question is yes.

An acknowledgment is simply this: any indication that you are struggling to understand the emotional content of what the other person is saying....

While you may not agree with the substance of what the other person is saying, you can still acknowledge the importance of their feeling....

Remind yourself that the task of understanding the other person's world is always harder than it seems. Remind yourself that if you think you already understand how someone else feels or what they are trying to say, it is a delusion. Remember a time when you were *sure* you were right and then discovered one little fact that changed everything. There is always more to learn. Remind yourself of the depth, complexities, contradictions, and nuances that make up the stories of each of our lives.

Robert S. Adler & Elliot M. Silverstein, WHEN DAVID MEETS GOLIATH: DEALING WITH POWER DIFFERENTIALS IN NEGOTIATIONS

5 Harv. Negot. L. Rev. 1, 69-72 (2000)

How does one go about seeking information in a negotiation? Before entering into the bargaining, a party should have independently sought as much information about the other side's situation, interests and goals as possible. This should be done from all available sources, including the Internet, newspapers, books, as well as the opponent's friends and enemies. With this pre-negotiation research completed, one should next identify the information to be sought from the opponent during the negotiation. For example, one might know that the other party wishes to sell a house because he or she plans to move to another state. Knowing this, one might then seek information during the bargaining process about when and why the other side wishes to move.

Other things being equal, we advise asking for information directly (politely, in most cases). In doing so, one should generally begin with broad, open-ended questions such as "Will you tell me about this property?" rather than more closed, narrow questions such as "Does the basement flood when it rains?" Open-ended questions prompt the respondent to talk, and permit the questioner to acquire more information than narrow inquiries. Only after the open-ended questions have raised or eliminated issues should one move to more specific queries. Moreover, one should always be prepared to return to open-ended questions as new information needs arise or as promising information trails emerge.

Some open-ended questions work better near the end of a negotiation than at the beginning. For example, on those occasions where one has developed a sense of unease about whether the other side has been forthcoming, we suggest asking what we call the "Come Clean" question: "Is there something important known to you, but not to me, that needs to be revealed at this point?" Because of its all-encompassing nature, this question used at a critical moment can surface vital information. Even if the other party deflects the question, his or her body language may speak volumes.

Although there are times when indirection is called for, we suspect that excessive subtlety in questioning caused by a reluctance to offend too often leads to misunderstanding and a lack of effectiveness. So long as one asks for information in a friendly and non-threatening way, he or she is unlikely to trigger a hostile response. And one needs particularly not only to listen to the answer, but also to observe the other side's body language during responses. Body language sometimes conveys more useful information than spoken words because it is often involuntary and, therefore, revealing. In some cases, the nervous refusal to answer or the inability to give direct eye contact when stating a demand discloses more than the actual words of the response.

Another reason that negotiators refrain from aggressive questioning is because they fear triggering equally aggressive questioning in return. But timidity provides no guarantee that one will be spared a grilling — it may happen anyway. Accordingly, one should always prepare to be questioned exhaustively even if one has no plans for questioning the other party. And, in anticipation of being interrogated, one should determine what information he or she is willing to disclose and under what conditions.

Notes and Questions

7.12 Any parent or babysitter can relate to the story at the beginning of the first excerpt regarding Uncle Doug and his nephew Andrew who wants to go outside to play. How do you explain this phenomenon of wanting to be heard? How does this differ from wanting the result (actually going outside)?

7.13 If wanting to be heard is different from wanting the result, how can you use this in a negotiation? Procedural justice literature discusses the importance that participants attach to the opportunity to voice their opinions and have those opinions heard during mediation, arbitration, and litigation processes. See Tom R. Tyler, Why People Obey the Law (1990); Nancy A. Welsh, Making Deals in Court-Connected Mediation: What's Justice Got to Do with It?, 79 Wash. U. L.Q. 787 (2001).

7.14 In recent years, a growing number of law enforcement agencies, including the FBI, have used active listening to successfully resolve volatile confrontations. These positive results have led the FBI to incorporate and emphasize active listening skills in its crisis negotiation training. As an FBI special agent and a police researcher write,

> Despite the popular notion that listening is a passive behavior, abundant clinical evidence and research suggest that active listening is an effective way to induce behavioral change in others. When listened to by others, individuals tend to listen to themselves more carefully and to evaluate and clarify their own thoughts and feelings. In addition, they tend to become better problem solvers, growing less defensive and oppositional and more accepting of other points of view. Subjects who are met with an empathetic ear also become less fearful of being criticized and grow more inclined to adopt a realistic appraisal of their own position. . . . By applying active listening skills, negotiators demonstrate that they are not a threat to the subject and that their goal is to help rather than harm. When negotiators demonstrate empathy and understanding, they build rapport, which, in turn, enables them to influence the subject's actions by providing nonviolent problem-solving alternatives. In short, by demonstrating support and empathy, negotiators often can talk an expressive subject into surrendering largely by listening.

> Gary W. Noesner & Mike Webster, Crisis Intervention: Using Active Listening Skills in Negotiations, FBI L. Enforcement Bull., Aug. 1997, at 13-19. Does this advice surprise you?

7.15 How many people try the familiar tactic of raising their voices when someone does not appear to understand them? If the speaker was unclear or speaking in a foreign language the first time, what makes the speaker believe speaking *louder* will actually help?

A NOTE ON ACTIVE LISTENING

Active listening—the skill of summarizing back the content or feeling of the speaker—takes a certain amount of discipline. All people are distracted by their internal voice — the one that is planning dinner, becoming defensive, judging the other side, or figuring out the solution. If this internal voice becomes too loud, you may need to manage this by writing down your running commentary and ideas, taking a break to call for dinner reservations, or taking a turn talking and then returning to actively listening.

The following student's story offers one very persuasive reason to improve this skill. The student was interviewing for a job with a commercial real estate firm for an in-house counsel position. The student had been a realtor for a number of years prior to coming to law school. Here is what he wrote in his journal:

> [The] Partner went on a ten minute tangent about how first year associates were basically "useless" and a dime a dozen. Given I was not happy at the time, and I did not think my chances of getting the job were too positive, I let him go on and kept my thoughts to myself. Thank god for my improvements in listening — old John would have interrupted and clarified that I was not a recent grad, rather I have six years of real estate experience and am now a law school graduate.... However, because I politely let him finish he thanked me and said, "I know you're different. I could tell by the way you actively listened to me." I'm not kidding. I got an offer.... Thank you for including listening in your class agenda. It not only saved my marriage, but gave me this amazing job opportunity.

C. EMOTIONS AND MOOD

We are not in charge of what happens in the world; we are in charge of how we respond to what happens.

— **Anonymous**

Traditional theories of negotiation often argue that emotion is the opposite of rationality and, therefore, should be removed from negotiation considerations. In fact, as the next several excerpts point out, we should not, and really cannot, remove emotion from negotiation. Our best advice is to be aware of its impact and be aware of yourself.

 Daniel L. Shapiro, **EMOTIONS IN NEGOTIATION: PERIL OR PROMISE?**

87 Marq. L. Rev. 737, 738-743, 745 (2004)

EMOTIONS CAN OBSTRUCT A NEGOTIATED AGREEMENT

There are a number of ways in which emotions can hinder the ability of negotiators to reach a wise agreement in a fair and amicable way. First, emotions may divert our attention from substantive matters. If we or others are angry or upset, both of us will have to deal with the hassle of emotions. Whether we decide to yell back, to sit quietly and ignore the outburst, or to storm out of the room, somehow we will need to respond.

Second, revelation of emotions can open us up to being manipulated. If we blush with embarrassment or flinch with surprise, these observable reactions offer the other party hints about our "true" concerns. A careful observer of our emotional reactions may learn which issues we value most and least, and could use that information to try to extract concessions from us. . . .

Third, thinking may take a subordinate role to feeling. Emotions are desirable for falling in love, but they make it difficult to think precisely in a negotiation. Because we cannot easily quantify or measure emotions, talking about emotions reduces the role of hard data, facts, and logic. It makes little sense to try to negotiate quantitatively over emotions: "I'll give you 10% more respect if you give me 20% less resentment."

Fourth, unless we are careful, emotions will take charge of us. They may cause us to lose our temper, to stumble anxiously over our words, or to sulk uncontrollably in self-pity. We may neglect even our own substantive goals. In anger, we may reject an agreement that is superior to our alternatives. Or we may focus not on our substantive goals at all, but rather on hurting the negotiator whose actions triggered our anger.

Thus, it is not surprising that a negotiator may fear the power of emotions. They are dangerous and can be destructive. However, this analysis is only a partial picture of the role that emotions play in a negotiation.

GET RID OF EMOTIONS?

Folk wisdom offers clear advice about how to deal with emotions in negotiation: Do not get emotional. Negotiators commonly are encouraged to "Swallow your pride," "Do not worry," and "Keep a straight face." For a negotiator, emotions are seen as an impediment to avoid at all costs. However, this advice is untenable and often makes things worse.

A. Emotions Are Unavoidable

Human beings are in a state of "perpetual emotion." Whether negotiating with another lawyer or with a friend, we constantly experience affective states of some type or another, such as anger, boredom, nostalgia, or anxiety. Emotions are stimulated by the context surrounding us (e.g., walking into another lawyer's office), by our own actions and thoughts (e.g., worrying about one's junior status), and by the actions of the other negotiator toward us (e.g., their demeaning behavior toward us).

Negotiators can be personally affected in many different ways — by impulses, emotions, moods, and attitudes. An *impulse* is a strong desire to do a particular behavior now, without much thought about possible consequences. If the young lawyer experiences feelings of mistreatment by the older lawyer, she may have an impulse to storm out of the room, ruining the possibility of a negotiated agreement.

Negotiators often feel the more generalized pushes and pulls of *emotions*, which are short-lived reactions to thoughts and behaviors of ourselves or others. In contrast to impulses, which propel us to do a *particular* behavior now, such as to tear up the "biased" proposal drafted by the other side, emotions motivate us toward general kinds of behavior, such as to attack the other party in *some way* for their self-serving behavior. An important part of an emotion is its action tendency, which is the type of behavioral urge associated with that emotion. In anger, for example, the action tendency is to strike out or attack. In guilt, the action tendency is to repent. Of course, a person may not act upon the action tendency; that is why it is called a tendency and not an actuality.

Moods are low intensity affective states, background music to our thoughts and actions. Whether you experience a positive mood due to your pay raise or a negative mood due to the rainy weather, your mood may have an effect on your negotiating behavior.

Attitudes are positive or negative evaluations of a person, institution, policy, or event. If the young lawyer learns that her counterpart is deceiving her, she may develop a negative attitude toward him.

B.   Suppressing Emotions Can Make Things Worse

It is not possible to suppress one's actual feelings. An emotion is a "lived experience." We feel some particular emotion, and then we come to realize the emotion which we are experiencing.

It is possible, however, to suppress the expression of those feelings. A negotiator may feel angry toward another without expressing that anger through words, tone of voice, or body language.... First, the negative emotional experience remains, leaving the negotiator in an internal state of tension. This agitated state may motivate us to act in ways that do not serve our short- or long-term interests. ... Second, the effort to suppress the display of emotions consumes important cognitive energy. People are limited in their cognitive capacity to process information, so additional cognitive tasks decrease a negotiator's ability to think about important substantive or process issues. Third, a negotiator who suppresses his or her emotions may be more likely to stereotype that counterpart as an "adversary," leading to competitive behavior....

Positive Versus Negative Emotion

Sometimes, negative emotion is expected — and when it does not occur, the other side may make false assumptions. "[J]ust prior to the Gulf War in 1991, U.S. Secretary of State James Baker met with the foreign minister of Iraq, Tariq Aziz, and Saddam Hussein's half brother, Barzan al-Tikriti. Baker stated his position very clearly to his opponents: If Iraq did not move out of Kuwait, the United States would attack. Barzan al-Tikriti telephoned Hussein and told him, 'The Americans will not attack. They are weak. They are calm. They are not angry. They are only talking.' Six days later, the United States went to war against Iraq, resulting in the death of about 175,000 Iraqi citizens and property damage in the amount of about $200 billion." Leigh L. Thompson, Janice Nadler & Peter H. Kim, Some Like It Hot: The Case for the Emotional Negotiator, in Shared Cognition in Organizations: The Management of Knowledge 157 (1999).

EMOTIONS CAN HELP YOU REACH YOUR
NEGOTIATION GOALS

Emotions affect our ability to reach negotiation goals. In most negotiations, each party has two goals: affective satisfaction and instrumental satisfaction. The ability to deal effectively with emotions increases the likelihood of attaining those goals.

A. Affective Satisfaction

Affective satisfaction is my general level of satisfaction with the emotions I experienced during an interaction. Affective satisfaction focuses on my feelings about my feelings — my "meta-emotions" for short. How do I feel about the feelings I experienced in the negotiation? In reflecting upon my interaction with the other party, do I generally feel satisfied with my emotional experience, or do I feel angry, upset, and dissatisfied?

B. Instrumental Satisfaction

The second goal focuses on instrumental satisfaction, the extent to which substantive work requirements are fulfilled. If two lawyers walk away from a week-long negotiation with plenty of good feelings but no new ideas about how to deal effectively with their differences, the meeting might be considered an affective success but an instrumental failure. . . .

Hence, awareness of emotions, one's own and those of others, provides a negotiator with an understanding of the importance of each person's interests and concerns. A negotiator may come to realize the extent to which she wants a particular object (instrumental satisfaction) or a particular kind of treatment and deference (affective satisfaction). With expanded information about the relative importance of interests, parties are more capable of devising options for mutual gain.

Emotions are not only internal; they may have a communicative function. If the other negotiator says something that offends you, the look on your face may change. Your eyebrows may furrow and your lips may pucker. Your voice may become deeper, and the rhythm of your speech may turn more abrupt. Through these behaviors, you are communicating to the other negotiator that you are angry. By expressing your emotion, you provide the other negotiator with important information about how you want to be treated.

Even if you suppress the expression of your own emotions, they are still communicating information to at least one person: you. The feeling of butterflies in your stomach signals to you that you may be anxious. The feeling of heaviness throughout your body signals that you may be disappointed. Although some negotiators are very good at hiding the expression of their "true" feelings from others, it is much more complicated to hide your own feelings from yourself. . . .

VI. SUMMARY

While it is true that emotions can be a barrier to a value-maximizing agreement, the common advice to "get rid of emotions" is infeasible and unwise. On the contrary, research suggests that negotiators can improve the efficiency and effectiveness of a negotiation by gaining an understanding of the information communicated by emotions, their own and those of others, and enlisting positive emotions into the negotiation.

 Peter Reilly, **TEACHING LAW STUDENTS HOW TO FEEL: USING NEGOTIATIONS TRAINING TO INCREASE EMOTIONAL INTELLIGENCE**

21 Negot. J. 301, 303-304, 308-310, 311 (2005)

WHAT IS EMOTION AND WHAT IS "EMOTIONAL INTELLIGENCE"?

[E]motional intelligence can be divided into four "branches": (1) emotional perception and expression (or the ability to correctly identify how people are feeling); (2) emotional facilitation of thought (or the ability to create emotions and to integrate one's feelings into the way one thinks); (3) emotional understanding (or the ability to understand the causes of emotions); and (4) emotional management (or the ability to discover and implement effective strategies utilizing one's emotions to assist in goal achievement, rather than being used by one's emotions).

Emotional Perception and Expression

This first branch begins with the capacity to perceive and express feelings. Developing emotional intelligence is impossible without developing competencies from this branch. Emotional perception involves registering, deciphering, and attending to emotional messages as they are expressed in facial expressions and voice tone. An example of this capacity would be to see and understand the fleeting expression of fear in the face of another person. This capacity provides one with the ability to: (1) identify emotions in oneself; (2) identify emotions in other people; (3) express emotions accurately; and (4) discriminate between real and phony emotional expressions.

Emotional Facilitation of Thought

The second branch concerns emotional facilitation of cognitive activities. While cognitive activities can be interrupted by emotion, such as fear or anxiety, emotions can also "prioritize" the cognitive system to address what is important and even to focus on what it does best in a given mood. The emotional facilitation of thought focuses on how emotion affects the cognitive system and can thereby lead to more effective reasoning, decision making, problem solving, and creative expression. Emotional facilitation of thought provides one with the ability to: (1) use emotions to redirect attention to important events; (2) generate emotions that facilitate judgment, memory, and decision making; (3) use mood swings as a way to consider and appreciate multiple points of view; and (4) use different emotions to encourage creativity and different approaches to problem solving.

Emotional Understanding

The third branch involves understanding emotion. The most fundamental competency at this level is the ability to label emotions (e.g., "annoyance," "irritation," "rage") and then to deduce the *relationship* among them — how they blend together and how they transition from one state to another and progress over time. For example, a person who understands that annoyance and irritation can lead to rage if the offending stimulus is not eliminated will be able to understand important aspects of interpersonal relationships. Emotional understanding, then, provides one with the ability to: (1) understand relationships among various emotions; (2) perceive the causes and consequences of emotions; (3) understand complex feelings and emotional blends; and (4) understand transitions among emotions.

Emotional Management

The fourth branch, emotional management, is sometimes referred to as emotional regulation. While some believe that mastering this branch of emotional intelligence will allow them to control their emotions or even eliminate the more troublesome emotions (like envy or jealousy), [others] warn that "attempts to minimize or eliminate emotion completely may stifle emotional intelligence" [and] suggest that the regulation of emotion in *other* people is less likely to involve suppressing their emotions and more likely to involve "the harnessing of them, as when a persuasive speaker is said to 'move' his or her audience." Emotional management provides the ability to: (1) be open to one's feelings, both pleasant and unpleasant; (2) stay aware of, monitor, and reflect upon one's emotions; (3) engage, prolong, or detach from an emotional state; (4) manage emotions in one's self; and (5) manage emotions in others. While the skills of reflecting upon and managing one's emotions can be difficult to develop and hone, one researcher suggests that disclosing emotional experiences in writing can assist in the endeavor and also lead to improved physical and mental health. . . .

ON BUILDING EMOTIONAL INTELLIGENCE

The Problem

[I]n 1955, Harvard Law School Dean Erwin Griswold called upon the bar and the legal academy to recognize the need for human relations training in law school. Griswold said that such training could help lawyers better understand their own emotional needs and that of their clients; he also noted that the average lawyer spent far more time interacting with *people* than reading and arguing appellate cases. Stated Griswold:

> [L]awyers constantly deal with people. They deal with people far more than they do with appellate courts. They deal with clients; they deal with witnesses; they deal with persons against whom demands are made; they carry on negotiations; they are constantly endeavoring to come to agreements of one sort or another with people, to persuade people, sometimes when they are reluctant to be persuaded. Lawyers are constantly dealing with people who are under stress or strain of one sort or another. . . .

The Solution

The current situation, then, requires the nation's law schools to: (1) supplement students' analytic orientation; (2) soften students' tendency toward being adversarial; and (3) address student shortcomings in the areas of interpersonal skills and emotional intelligence. . . .

Such training might include the following:

1. *Training law students to be more sensitive to the subtle signs of emotions in others* — in their faces, voices, and postures. Experts in emotion suggest that techniques are available to teach such skills, and students can become quite proficient in the skill in just a few hours of training.

2. *Training law students in the internal sensation of emotion,* so they become more aware when emotions are beginning. Emotions feel quite different from each other physically, and people could be educated about these bodily sensations, developing a greater self-awareness.

3. *Training law students how to determine why they feel the way they do,* how to express those emotions, and how to use all this information in making more informed decisions.

4. *Training law students how to deal with emotional conflict.* This would include both understanding the theory and process of conflict, as well as the practical skills and means that can be implemented to manage and productively harness strong emotions on *all* sides of the negotiation table (including one's own).

Training in emotions will provide law students with a greater capacity to *connect* with their clients — to see, hear, and understand their clients completely and thoroughly, with focus and intention. This is necessary to form a relationship of trust, cooperation, and collaboration, which, in turn, is necessary to effectively (or even adequately) represent a client through litigation, mediation, facilitation, negotiation, or any other legal or quasi-legal process.

Moreover, training in emotions will enable law students to make this essential connection with their clients immediately upon meeting them, which empirical evidence shows can be a crucial time (and perhaps the *only* time) for attorneys to learn vital information about the matter at hand. . . .

Notes and Questions

7.16 How can you learn to use emotions positively in a negotiation? When can they hinder you? See Roger Fisher & Daniel Shapiro, Beyond Reason: Using Emotions as you Negotiate (2005).

7.17 What situations tend to make you emotional (angry, sad, frustrated) in a negotiation? Do these depend on context or on the person on the other side? Note that we will discuss responding to specific tactics in Chapter 8.

7.18 Recent research into the brain demonstrates the connection between emotion and decision making. One famous story demonstrates the importance of this research. In 1848, Phineas Gage was involved in a construction accident, which caused severe trauma to his frontal lobe. Although the rest of the brain was not affected and Gage survived that accident with all of his faculties,

Gage's emotions and, therefore, his reasoning were never the same. His accident and the subsequent research on his and other cases led to breakthroughs on understanding how human emotions work and are controlled. See Antonio R. Damasio, Descartes' Error: Emotion, Reason, and the Human Brain (1994). Based on this research, we can see that it is *not* that emotions hinder decision making. In fact, without emotions, we cannot make good decisions.

Like emotions, mood affects negotiations. A number of key findings from social psychology studies translate into suggested negotiation strategies. Studies show, for instance, that less rapport develops between parties when they conduct the negotiation via e-mail or through another physical barrier rather than face to face. Peter J.D. Carnevale & Alice M. Isen, The Influence of Positive Affect and Visual Access on the Discovery of Integrative Solutions in Bilateral Negotiation, 37 Org. Behav. & Hum. Decision Processes 1 (1986); Michael Morris et al., Schmooze or Lose: Social Friction and Lubrication in E-Mail Negotiations, 6 Group Dynamics 89 (2002). If contentious tactics are then used in the negotiation, trust breaks down between the negotiators much faster than in the face-to-face negotiations. This lack of rapport can be counteracted, however, using specific relationship-building techniques in advance. In the studies, when negotiators talk first on the phone and are given a photo and a few biographical details of each other, this increases the rapport between the negotiators and leads to better outcomes.

A second area of study examines how mood affects negotiation behavior by demonstrating that positive moods make people more creative. The interesting thing is how little it takes to create this positive mood. In two studies, participants are given a bag of candy. Alice M. Isen et al., Positive Affect Facilitates Creative Problem Solving, 52 J. Personality & Soc. Psychol. 112 (1987); Alice M. Isen et al., Positive Affect Facilitates Creative Problem Solving: An Influence of Positive Affect on Social Categorization, 16 Motivation & Emotion 65 (1992).

In other studies, participants watch a comedy film or read comic strips. In all of these, participants in good moods, the "positive affect" group, are more creative than those participants who are in neutral moods. Alice M. Isen et al., Positive Affect Facilitates Creative Problem Solving, 52 J. Personality & Soc. Psychol. 112 (1987). In another study, positive affect created by pleasant scents results in negotiators who set higher goals and are more efficient. Robert A. Baron, Environmentally Induced Positive Affect: Its Impact on Self-Efficacy, Task Performance, Negotiation, and Conflict, 20 J. App. Soc. Psychol. 368 (1990). Another study shows that negotiators who are in good moods are more likely to use cooperative, integrative bargaining strategies and less likely to adopt competitive bargaining strategies than the control groups. Negotiators in bad moods are less likely to use cooperative strategies and more likely to use competitive strategies. Joseph P. Forgas, On Feeling Good and Getting Your Way: Mood Effects on Cognition and Bargaining Strategies, 74 J. Personality & Soc. Psychol. 565 (1998).

Finally, other studies look at how negative moods and anger play out in negotiations. In one experiment studying anger and compassion, negotiators who are very angry and have low compassion for the other side reach fewer joint gains in the negotiation. Although these individuals may feel as though they have an advantage in claiming value in the negotiation, this does not actually happen. Instead, the more anger and less compassion negotiators have for one another, the less willing they are to work with each other in the future. As the authors write, "[O]ur results suggest that high anger and low compassion toward the other party pose serious disadvantages to negotiators without providing any clear advantages." Keith G. Allred et al., The Influence of Anger and Compassion on Negotiation Performance, 70 Org. Behav. & Hum. Decision Processes 175, 184 (1997).

In a very comprehensive article reviewing the literature on negotiators' moods, the authors begin by noting how much we still need to learn about mood and how it applies to legal negotiations. At the end of the article, they suggest how the studies cited above and others translate into specific suggestions for lawyers.

© 2005 Peter Steiner from *Cartoonbank.com.*

"Okay, 60 million. But only because of the candlelight."

 Clark Freshman, Adele Hayes & Greg Feldman, THE LAWYER-NEGOTIATOR AS MOOD SCIENTIST: WHAT WE KNOW AND DON'T KNOW ABOUT HOW MOOD RELATES TO SUCCESSFUL NEGOTIATION

2002 J. Disp. Resol. 1, 55, 66-69, 73-75

The more novel a solution, the more that the expertise and Forgas* theories converge to suggest mood may play a role. Perhaps the greatest potential for mood effects

---

*Joseph P. Forgas, On Feeling Good and Getting Your Way: Mood Effects on Negotiator Cognition and Bargaining Strategies, 74 J. Personality & Soc. Psychol. 565 (1998).

in law and elsewhere is simply not studied: the creation not merely of tradeoffs but novel solutions. In the familiar scenario in *Getting to YES*, the creative solution to Mideast peace is not a tradeoff between Israelis and Egyptians both seeking the Sinai; it is a creative solution: the Sinai will be under the sovereignty of Egypt, thus satisfying Egyptian pride, but it shall be demilitarized, thus satisfying Israeli security interests. In a classic example used by Menkel-Meadow, the husband who wants to vacation in the mountains and the wife who wants to vacation by the sea can both get exactly what they want by vacationing in Santa Barbara, which has both mountains and the Pacific Ocean.[259] In the terminology of Pruitt, these types of creative solutions are bridging agreements; the simple tradeoffs studied in the mood and negotiation studies, however, are simply logrolling.[260] It is likely that mood would affect these novel bridging agreements most....

A. WHAT WE KNOW: POPULAR STRATEGIES DON'T WORK

1. Avoiding and Suppressing Emotion Don't Work

The advice to try to ignore or suppress emotion comes in several different variations. In its crudest form, some negotiators simply think it is best to ignore emotion as something that is simply irrational and therefore irrelevant. In a less crude form, some people might think emotion in negotiation is important, but not to the negotiation itself; the emotion can simply be ignored during the negotiation and dealt with later....

This strategy does not work for at least four sets of reasons. First the attempt to suppress emotions simply may not work at all — the emotions will still exist....

Second, apart from the research on how mood affects negotiation, ... other research [shows] that attempting to suppress emotions impairs one's cognitive skills, particularly memory....

Third, established research shows that attempts to suppress emotion are associated with worse physical and mental health in the long run. These worse base line mental health conditions, in turn, may make it more likely in future negotiations that negotiators will be in the kind of negative moods that we saw led to worse results.

Finally, although there are not empirical data to support this directly, suppressing emotions may lead to worse negotiation outcomes if suppressed conflict leads to conflict later and therefore less compliance with agreements. One of the major claims made by supporters of ADR is that parties comply more with agreements reached in ADR than with agreements imposed by court. Moreover, there is at least some evidence that positive mood increases the likelihood that parties will honor agreements they make. It is plausible to suppose that parties [who] suppress their emotions, particularly if it is suppressed by the pressure from lawyers or other agents, may find that, when these suppressed emotions surface later on, they are less satisfied with their agreements and therefore less likely to comply with them....

---

[259] Carrie Menkel-Meadow, Toward Another View of Legal Negotiation: The Structure of Problem Solving, 31 UCLA L. Rev. 754 (1984).
[260] Dean G. Pruitt, Negotiation Behavior 155 (1981) ("[L]ogrolling involves a simple additive combination of demands previously endorsed by each party, whereas a solution by bridging entails some novel substantive element not previously under consideration").

2. Merely Venting Emotion Doesn't Work Either

At the opposite end of the spectrum from denying, avoiding, and suppressing emotion, venting emotion is perhaps one of the most frequently listed approaches to emotion in popular negotiation literature. Again, this includes a relatively unsophisticated claim that mere venting will sometimes be a phase that allows parties to somehow move on—seemingly as if an emotional analog to the way vomiting up some difficult to ingest food may be one way to calm one's digestion.

As with the popular advice to suppress emotions, however, research shows that venting emotions—at least in the relatively unregulated and spontaneous way discussed in popular negotiation advice—also is often not effective. Most importantly, Allred's study of anger, empathy, and negotiation shows that those who are angry actually have less accurate views of what other parties want.[320] . . .

Finally, we acknowledge that venting in conjunction with processing of emotion may work. Complex processing seems relatively unavailable in most legal settings. This kind of processing is unlikely to occur in a simple discussion between either parties to a case or between lawyers. It may be worth exploring whether such processing might be possible in negotiations that involve persons trained in relatively advanced therapeutic skills, and such processing may be plausible with the presence of properly trained professionals, such as some mediators.

B. MORE PROMISING STRATEGIES FOR MOOD MANAGEMENT

3. Short Term Strategies: Corrections for the Effect of Mood May Work

First, one may try to correct for the way that mood affects strategy. [M]ost people negotiate more cooperatively when in a better mood and more competitively when in a worse mood. . . .

Once an individual decides on one kind of strategy, he should consider how his present mood may undermine or bolster that strategy. If, for example, he decides the settlement of a billing dispute is really about the payment of money (perhaps because, despite consultation, his client explicitly instructs him only to concentrate on maximizing the collection of money at this point), then he should be aware of how his positive mood may undermine that strategy. Such a positive mood might incline him to lose sight of his client's explicit instructions and be more cooperative, as Forgas's[*] study suggested; worse, as Baron's[†] study showed, a positive mood might induce him to make more concessions. Exactly how he corrected for this danger might involve a variety of possibilities. For example, if he fears he is in such a good mood that he might be tempted to concede in person, he might conduct the negotiation by email.

Consider a quite different scenario: a somewhat unhappy or even angry person has been asked to collect on a debt owed by a producer to an actor. The actor may be

---

[320] [Keith G. Allred et al., The Influence of Anger and Compassion on Negotiation Performance, 70 Org. Behav. & Hum. Decision Processes 175, 184 (1997).]

[*] Joseph P. Forgas, On Feeling Good and Getting Your Way: Mood Effects on Negotiator Cognition and Bargaining Strategies, 74 J. Personality & Soc. Psychol. 565 (1998).

[†] Robert A. Baron, Environmentally Induced Positive Affect: Its Impact on Self-Efficacy, Task Performance, Negotiation and Conflict, 20 J. App. Soc. Psychol. 368 (1990).

somewhat satisfied with receiving the money, but he might well instruct his attorney that he has other goals as well: he may be concerned about his long-term reputation in a close industry, or he may even be interested in pursuing some further acting job with this particular producer. In that case, the lawyer would want to correct for the way that his negative mood might make him tend to be more adversarial and tightly focused. Therefore, based on research that direct email further promotes adversarial negotiations, he might choose to meet with the producer in person. If he negotiated by email, he would make a deliberate effort to include some personal chit-chat in the beginning of the email exchange. In addition, to correct for the tendency to be competitive and narrow, he might try in advance to come up with a variety of potential options, such as paying money over time, paying in other forms of goods, taking a share in some future productions' revenue, and so on.

Second, individuals may want to correct for the way that mood shapes perception of information. When angry, individuals often make incorrect assumptions about what matters to other persons. When happy, persons often think that they may have done better than they did, and unhappy persons may not realize quite how well they did.[342] In addition, research outside negotiation shows that happy persons may actually have positive illusions about how good reality is. . . .

Third, negotiators may attempt to correct for the way that mood may affect bargaining intensity, both in terms of initial goals and persistence. Here, the evidence is more mixed: some research suggests those in more positive moods may set higher goals, but others suggest those in persistently worse moods may also set higher goals. Accordingly, one potential source of correction may be for negotiators to be aware of whether their mood is either better or worse — either than their typical mood or of typical negotiators. . . .

As with goals, our best advice, on the evidence now available, is that, if negotiators notice a significant variation in their mood, they pay careful attention before they finalize a deal. Again, different negotiators may implement this in different ways: some may state early on that they need to consult a client before finalizing a deal; others may make a note to themselves; others may bring along someone who is instructed to stop him before he reaches a final agreement.

Notes and Questions

7.19 How do you think your mood affects your negotiations? Think of a time when you were angry, tired, or hungry. How did this affect your preparation? Your goals? Your tone?

7.20 In a study of lawyer negotiations, 66 percent of attorneys were perceived as pleasant and personable. However, the 50 percent of those attorneys who were *also* described as agreeable, helpful, perceptive, poised, and smooth were considered much more effective. Andrea Schneider, Shattering Negotiation

---

[342] See Roderick Kramer, et al., Self-enhancement Biases and Negotiator Judgment: Effects of Self-esteem and Mood, 56 Org. Behav. & Hum. Decision Processes 122 (1993).

Myths: Empirical Evidence on the Effectiveness of Negotiation Style, 7 Harv. Negot. L. Rev. 143 (2002). What do the extra adjectives seem to describe?

7.21 For an in-depth look at measuring happiness and the effects of these measurements, see Daniel Kahneman, Objective Happiness, in Well-Being: The Foundations of Hedonic Psychology 330 (Daniel Kahneman et al. eds., 1999).

D. APOLOGY

The topic of apology has received much attention in recent negotiation literature. Both theoretical and empirical studies argue that apology and accepting responsibility for wrongs can be extremely powerful in negotiations. The following excerpts first outline the impact of apology in negotiation, then discuss whether and how lawyers can advise their clients to negotiate, examine empirical work on what makes an apology effective, and, finally, discuss whether laws need to be changed in order to encourage apology.

 Jennifer Gerarda Brown, **THE ROLE OF APOLOGY IN NEGOTIATION**

87 Marq. L. Rev. 665, 665–673 (2004)

One topic that has received increased attention recently is the role that apology might properly play in negotiation and conflict resolution. From a practical perspective, the central goal seems to be identifying the crucial elements of an effective apology. But to script an effective apology, one must first consider more theoretical matters, including these important questions:

> What is an apology, and what is the purpose of making one?
> Who should make an apology, and who should receive it?
> When is the optimal time for making an apology?

What negative consequences (especially legal consequences, such as civil or criminal liability) might flow from the apology, and is it a good thing for the law to eliminate or mitigate these negative consequences? . . .

I. THE PURPOSES OF APOLOGY

Apology has been defined as "an acknowledgment intended as an atonement for some improper or injurious remark or act: an admission to another of a wrong or discourtesy done him accompanied by an expression of regret," or "[a]n explanation offered to a person affected by one's action that no offence was intended, coupled with the expression of regret for any that may have been given; or, a frank acknowledgment of the offence with expression of regret for it, by way of reparation." As Erving Goffman[*] has explained, apology is a process through which a person

---

[*] Erving Goffman, Relations in Public 113 (1971).

symbolically splits "into two parts, the part that is guilty of an offense and the part that dissociates itself from the delict and affirms a belief in the offended rule."

It is important to think about purposes, because the effectiveness of an apology can only be measured with reference to its goals. The purposes of apologies may be as numerous as the people who make them. Deborah Levi[*] has analyzed categories of apology in mediation, and explained that there are four types: "tactical" (acknowledging the victim's suffering in order to gain credibility and influence the victim's bargaining behavior); "explanation" (attempting to excuse the offender's behavior and make the other party understand that behavior); "formalistic" (capitulating to the demand of an authority figure); and "happy-ending" (accepting responsibility and expressing regret for the bad act). Levi's analysis turns upon the words that are said and the specific speech acts that are performed with each type of apology.

Another approach is to tease out the audience for the apology — whose regard is the central concern for the person who is apologizing? We could think of apology as an essentially self-regarding process. Goffman's description of apology set forth above focuses largely upon the wrongdoer's self-perception or her relationship to the offended rule. Lee Taft[†] articulates a precise formula for this type of apology: "[T]he offender acknowledges through speech the legitimacy of the violated rule, admits fault for its violation, and expresses genuine remorse and regret for the harm caused by his violation." Such apologies can in some ways be viewed as self-serving, not in the sense that they result from selfishness, but that the offender's moral rehabilitation is paramount. The purpose of the apology is to regain moral integrity.

A conception of apology more focused on the recipient is one that strives to console or comfort. The words spoken might be very much the same as a self-regarding apology, but the primary goal of the speaker is not to affirm his own integrity. Instead, the purpose of accepting blame is primarily to assure the other party of her virtue — that it was the offender (or some other entity), and not the victim, who bore responsibility for the harm that occurred. Also, by sincerely apologizing for the harm caused, the offender recognizes, and, in a sense, empathizes with the victim's pain.

Still another approach to apology places third-party effects at the forefront. Here, the primary audience for the apology is not so much the victim of the wrongdoing as it is a third party, often an authority figure. In this case, the obligation to apologize is externally imposed rather than internally driven. Parents of young children may fear that they generate such apologies when they insist that their misbehaving children "say they are sorry," but the instrumental effect can also be seen in adults who hope to reduce criminal sentences by apologizing to their victims.

In addition to the benefits of apology in some criminal law contexts, it is clear that apology can yield advantages in civil lawsuits as well. Sometimes, defendants in civil cases will seek to reduce expected liability by apologizing in mediation or settlement negotiations. Such "tactical" apologies . . . are self-regarding in the sense that their central aim is defensive, but they are simultaneously attuned to the effect the apology will have on the recipient, for they are at least partially motivated by a desire to elicit specific action (concession) on the part of the other person. . . .

[*] Deborah Levi, The Role of Apology in Mediation, 72 N.Y.U. L. Rev. 1165 (1997).
[†] Lee Taft, Apology Subverted: The Commodification of Apology, 109 Yale L.J. 1135, 1140 (2000).

II. THE QUALITIES OF AN EFFECTIVE APOLOGY

This section will synthesize some of the literature on apology to suggest essential elements of an apology. Not only purpose, as outlined above, but also context (including the prior relationship between the parties) will exert strong influence on the formulation of a good apology. In addition, there are important questions about legitimacy in those who deliver and receive apologies. When the offense is specific, short-running, or has occurred within the context of a single relationship . . . , the answers to these questions will be fairly straightforward. It will not be difficult to identify an offender who might apologize and a victim who might receive the apology. This is not to say that it is always easy to identify victim and offender; in some relationships each person will play both roles. But if the harm has occurred on a small scale or in an interpersonal context, we can usually identify people who, if willing, could legitimately apologize or receive an apology on their own behalf.

When the offense is more complex, more historical, or has occurred on a grander scale, the situation becomes much more difficult. Perhaps it is clear that the Pope can legitimately speak for the Roman Catholic Church and apologize for complicity in the Holocaust, and any living Holocaust survivors are the clear recipients of that apology. But are they the only ones? Can the victims' descendants also be recipients of the apology? Are current-day Roman Catholics, while not perhaps the intended recipients, nonetheless an important audience for this apology?

A Child's Wisdom

Another favorite story also deals with the wisdom of children:

In my first year Contracts class, I wished to review various doctrines we had recently studied. I put the following [problem to the students]:

In a long-term installment contract, Seller promises Buyer to deliver widgets at the rate of 1,000 a month. The first two deliveries are perfect. However, in the third month Seller delivers only 990 widgets. Buyer becomes so incensed that he rejects delivery and refuses to pay for the widgets already delivered.

After stating the problem, I asked, "If you were Seller, what would you say?" What I was looking for was a discussion of the various common law theories which would force the buyer to pay for the widgets delivered and those which would throw Buyer into breach for canceling the remaining deliveries. In short, I wanted the class to come up with the legal doctrines which would allow Seller to crush Buyer.

After asking the question, I looked around the room for a volunteer. As is so often the case with first year students, I found there were [none]. There was, however, one eager face, that of an eight-year-old son of one of my students. It seems that he was suffering through Contracts due to his mother's sin of failing to find a sitter. Suddenly, he raised his hand. Such behavior, even from an eight-year-old, must be rewarded.

"OK," I said, "What would you say if you were the seller?"

"I'd say, 'I'm sorry.'"

Kenny Hegland, Why Teach Trial Advocacy? An Essay on Never Ask Why, in Humanistic Education Law 69 (J. Himmelstein & H. Lesnick eds., 1982).

Consider groups that lack a central and authoritative leader such as the Pope. Is it possible for such groups or institutions to apologize authentically?

Almost everyone seems to agree that an apology should be the result of some analysis and introspection on the part of the offender — if it comes too spontaneously or off-the-cuff it loses power and legitimacy. This can create a tension. The offender may need time in order to reflect upon the harm done, form true remorse for the offense, and prepare a heartfelt apology, but the more an apology is delayed the more profound the offense may seem in the eyes of the victim. . . .

Does one apologize for the harm that has occurred — the outcome of one's acts — or for the acts themselves? Lee Taft and others have argued that in order to be effective, an apology must articulate the norm that has been violated and . . . "affirm a belief in the offended rule." Sometimes the offended standard is a personal one — a sense of oneself that has been compromised by errant behavior. In other cases, it will be a rule, policy, or social norm of the organization or group of which the offender is a part. In some cases, it will be a legal standard or rule, and it is the breaking of that rule that may give rise to liability.

Others contend that something short of a "full apology" (one that admits fault and expresses regret) can be effective and helpful to the recipient. For example, Jonathan Cohen argues that even though "a full apology will usually be most powerful,"[25] it can also be constructive to simply express sympathy for harm that has occurred, without also taking moral or financial responsibility for that harm.[26]

A final question that emerges is whether the promise to change something in the future is an essential element of an effective apology. The promised change might relate to the offender's own behavior or it could involve promises to repair the harm done. Is an apology complete without this attempt to restore the status quo where possible? For lawyer negotiators, the precise wording, timing, and delivery of the apology will depend upon client preferences, the legal context, and the needs of the opposing party.

III. IMPLICATIONS

The existing literature on apology challenges us to think further about this important moment in conflict. In many legal disputes, the moments for apology come and go without notice or action, either because lawyers do not think to advise their clients on this point, or because aversion to vulnerability (emotional or legal) makes people overly cautious about pursuing this avenue toward resolution. If apology becomes a more accepted point of client counseling and subsequent negotiation, there will be many interesting lines for further inquiry. I will mention two.

First, what responsibilities does an apology create in the receiver? Lee Taft conceives of apology as a necessary link between "an inner urging to repent" and "forgiveness as a moral option for the offended," the "centerpiece in a moral dialectic between sorrow and forgiveness." Does the outcome of the apology matter? Having delivered a heartfelt apology, is the offender entitled in any way to expect a positive

---

[25] Jonathan Cohen, Advising Clients to Apologize, 72 S. Cal. L. Rev. 1009, 1048 (1999).
[26] Id. at 1067.

response from the other party? To what extent can an offender expect that a moral victim will accept the apology and even forgive? If such acceptance and forgiveness are not forthcoming, can the apologizing person somehow be converted into a victim of a new harmful event?

Second, from a policy perspective, what sort(s) of apologies should we be trying to encourage, and how might the law play a role in creating the conditions that will facilitate desired apologies? When we create incentives for people to apologize, do we rob the resulting apologies of their potential power?

This takes us back to the debate concerning "protected apologies." Lee Taft may be correct in finding stronger moral force when an offender apologizes against self-interest, incurring greater vulnerability or exposure. For apologies designed primarily to restore the offender's moral integrity, perhaps such action against self-interest is essential.

But as I explained above, not all apologies are formulated for this purpose. When the primary audience is the victim or a third party, even a "protected" apology can achieve laudable ends. After all, bringing true comfort to a suffering victim is no small matter.

IV.   CONCLUSION

For some victims words will not be enough. Actions must accompany and give effect to the words if the apology is to have any meaning at all. Sometimes, the follow-on activity will be subject to negotiation. In many cases, an apology will be necessary to make that negotiation possible. The better we understand the potential purposes and formulations of effective apologies, therefore, the richer our understanding of negotiation will be.

Jonathan R. Cohen, ADVISING CLIENTS TO APOLOGIZE

72 S. Cal. L. Rev. 1009, 1013-1015, 1018-1025, 1028-1029, 1031-1034, 1036-1045, 1047, 1053 (1999)

Should lawyers discuss the possibility of apology with clients more often? . . . [I]n civil cases, lawyers should discuss with clients the possibility of apology more often than they now do. Not only is apology morally right and socially beneficial, but in many cases making an apology is in the client's (defendant's) best interest. This is not to say that there are no risks associated with apology, not the least of which is the fear that an apology can be used against one's client in court as an admission of fault. However, when attention is paid to the context in which an apology is offered and how it is made, often "safe" apologies posing relatively little risk of increased liability can be offered. Further, the possible benefits of apology to the client (defendant) are under-recognized. . . .

BENEFITS AND COSTS OF APOLOGY

Benefits to the Client

[An] apology and forgiveness can be value-creating. If I apologize for having injured you, and you accept this apology, both of us are likely to be better off. This does not

---

Apologies Save Money

Professor Jonathan Cohen writes about the Veteran Affairs Hospital in Lexington, Kentucky, which adopted a new policy in 1987 requiring all staff to inform patients about any errors:

From the financial viewpoint, the new approach of assuming responsibility, including apology, passed the Hippocratic test: it appears to have done the hospital no financial harm and may have done some financial good. Recall that in 1985 and 1986 the hospital paid two malpractice verdicts that together totaled $1.5 million. From 1990 through 1996, the hospital paid an average of only $190,113 per year in malpractice claims, with an average (mean) payment of $15,622 per claim. This placed the Lexington VA in the lowest quartile of thirty-six comparable VA hospitals for malpractice payments and in the bottom sixth in terms of average liability payment per claim....

Many lawyers see only the obvious economic risks to apology but overlook the possible economic benefits. Stepping back for a moment from the example of the Lexington VA, two reasons apology can be economically beneficial to the apologizer are as follows. First, in some cases injured parties may refrain from suing if they receive an apology.... Second, an apology can greatly facilitate the settlement process and thereby reduce settlement costs. An apology often cannot substitute for compensation for the injury but can be a way of avoiding compounding insult upon the injury — insult that can prevent settlement.... As VA hospital lawyer Ginny Hamm described, "The attorneys around here in Lexington used to think we were crazy [when we initiated our new policy]." As one who studies the possible benefits and risks of apology, I can attest that many attorneys and legal academics greet the idea that apology can financially benefit the apologizer with much skepticism. The Lexington VA's experience helps refute the skeptic's view that apology necessarily entails financial suicide. Rather, it indicates the opposite: apology can be to the apologizer's financial benefit.

Jonathan R. Cohen, Apology and Organizations: Exploring an Example from Medical Practice, 27 Fordham Urb. L.J. 1447 (2000).

---

mean that when an apology occurs distributive elements disappear. After an apology, the parties still may need to settle on a level of compensation for the injury....

For an apology to be most effective, it must also be *voluntary* — made of a party's own free will. Apologies are sometimes brought about from external pressures rather than internal remorse, as when a child is forced by a parent to apologize. However, in general, the more an apology is coerced, the less meaning it carries, for the less sincere is the regret it expresses....

With these comments in mind, let me now address more specifically some of the value-creating benefits of apology.

1. Subtract Insult from Injury

An apology many help prevent piling insult onto injury, something both parties may want. An injured party usually wants to receive an apology, for absent an apology she may be angered to think that the offender was glad to have caused the injury. Moreover, failing to apologize following an injury can be a deeply disrespectful act and thus become a second injury....

2. Prevent Antagonistic Behavior

An apology can be an important step in preventing future antagonistic behavior, including litigation. When an injury has occurred, there is a root question to be resolved: Are you (the offender) my friend or my foe? An apology signals that the offender wishes to establish or re-establish a friendly relationship. . . .

3. Repair Damaged Relationship

An apology may also help restore a damaged relationship between parties. Many legal disputes arise in the context of a pre-existing relationship. . . . Often these relationships are very close ones. If a friend harms another friend, the injured friend may well ask, "If we were friends, why did you injure me?" Absent an apology, it may be impossible for parties to put a problem behind them and restore their normal functioning. One aspect of this is the need to construct an explanation for what has occurred. Paying monetary damages may help take care of the financial consequences of an injury, but it may take an apology to "wipe the moral ledger" clean and construct understandings of the injury and the relationship which both parties can accept. . . .

4. Permit Serious Settlement Negotiations

Indignity can be a large barrier to compromise, and in many cases, an apology is needed before other aspects of the dispute, such as monetary compensation, can be settled. . . .

5. Spiritual and Psychological Growth

Apology and forgiveness may also offer paths for spiritual and psychological growth. . . . Responsibility and respect, rather than denial and avoidance, lie at apology's core. Within many religious and ethical systems, offering an apology for one's wrongdoing is an important part of moral behavior, as is forgiving those who have caused offense. . . .

6. Strategic and Distributive Benefits

Making an apology can also benefit an offender in ways that are largely strategic or distributive, rather than value-creating.

One strategic benefit of an apology is that, if the injured party receives the apology early enough, she may decide not to sue. For a legal dispute to occur, injury alone is not sufficient. The injured party must also decide to bring a legal claim. Taking the step to make a legal claim is often triggered by the injured party's anger. An early apology can help diffuse that anger and thereby prevent a legal dispute. . . .

Risks to the Client

The risks of apology need to be weighed against its possible benefits. Below I discuss four such risks to the client to which I attach the labels psychological, strategic, void insurance coverage, and legal liability.

1. Psychological

Some clients may find making an apology to be demeaning, a psychic cost that they do not wish to pay. Apology requires humbling oneself before another and admitting a wrongdoing. . . .

2. Strategic

Strategic risks...may also inhibit apology. Though apology may help one develop "internal strength" and "character," others may see apology as a sign of weakness. For example, consider the position of President Clinton when he was first charged with sexually harassing Paula Jones. Even if, arguendo, President Clinton did sexually harass Paula Jones, and even if he wished to make full and sincere apologies for it, Clinton may have believed that the political cost of such admissions was prohibitive: His enemies could use such apologies to force his impeachment....

3. Void Insurance Coverage

In some cases, such as car accidents or medical malpractice, offenders possess insurance coverage. At first, one might think that such insured offenders should feel particularly free to apologize: If it is the insurance company, rather than the offender, that will pay for the damages, what does the offender risk by apologizing? There is much truth to this. However, the matter is not as simple as it might first appear, for a question arises: Will making an apology void the offender's insurance coverage?

4. Liability

Yet it is liability, or the fear of liability, that forms the central barrier to apology in most disputes. If one apologizes, isn't one admitting that one is liable? More specifically, can one's apology be used against oneself as an admission in court? The short answer to these questions is that much depends upon the context in which one offers the apology....

... [A]ny discussion of the interplay between apology and liability must recognize that unless care is taken to ensure otherwise, an apology *can* be used as evidence of liability. Although courts may be hesitant to find guilt upon an apology alone, an apology can be used as evidence against the defendant. Despite the fact an apology would normally be excluded as hearsay, in a case against the offender, the offender's apology falls under the exception for admissions by a party opponent....

"Safe" Apology

1. The Legal Tension

The central legal tension in seeking to apologize "safely" is an evidentiary one. The law has two competing goals. On the one hand, courts want to admit all probative evidence, and what could be more probative than a party's own admission of fault? On the other hand, courts want to encourage private settlement, and what could be a greater impediment to private settlement than the fear that if one offers words of apology they will be turned against one to prove one's guilt?...

2. Rules of Evidence

Rules of evidence that create evidentiary exclusions for statements made during settlement negotiations provide an important avenue for excluding an apology at trial. However, it is an avenue with many potholes. Such rules vary by jurisdiction, and for simplicity I will analyze here only Federal Rule of Evidence 408 ("F.R.E. 408")....

Instead of using the benchmark that statements made in settlement negotiations were admissible unless legal formalisms were invoked, F.R.E. 408 sought to set the benchmark that settlement negotiations were inadmissible, with or without such legal formalisms, and make the law follow human practice rather than the converse....

The purpose of F.R.E. 408 was straightforward: Create a protected space so as to encourage private settlements. As the F.R.E. 408 Advisory Committee explained, "The purpose of this rule is to encourage private settlements which would be discouraged if such evidence were admissible."...

3. In Mediation

Mediation offers a second possible avenue toward a "safe" apology, and here the protection is *much* stronger. As mediation confidentiality provisions are created by state statutes and court rules, they vary widely; however, where they do afford protection, often the protection they afford is quite strong....

Mediation is also a natural place for apology, for a main goal of mediation is to help the parties work out their differences. Apologies often do take place in mediation. Not only are many mediators experienced at fostering apologies, but making an apology during mediation may fit well with the expectations the parties bring to the mediation process. Further, many types of disputes (family, employment, neighborhood, and the like) are commonly mediated, making mediation a feasible option in many cases.

However, mediation is not without some drawbacks. First, not all jurisdictions have strong mediation confidentiality statutes, which makes mediation an avenue available to some, not all. Second, parties typically go to mediation only *after* the dispute has escalated, but, from a relational viewpoint, making an apology very soon after the injury may be most helpful.... Third, not all cases are well-suited to mediation, and for some disputes neither of the parties may see mediation as a plausible option.

4. By Contract

Confidentiality agreements, which are often used in conjunction with mediation, provide a third avenue for making a "safe" apology. This avenue has both strengths and weaknesses. A main strength is that, unlike the statutory protections for settlement negotiations and mediations which typically address whether statements will be admissible in court, confidentiality agreements allow parties to limit more broadly the uses of statements....

Yet confidentiality agreements have weaknesses, and for a party wishing to make a "safe" apology inadmissible in court, one weakness is particularly severe. Courts usually disregard clauses within confidentiality agreements that purport to preclude a court from hearing evidence as being contrary to public policy. What right, after all, do two private parties have to write a contract that precludes a court from hearing evidence? None, most courts reason....

5. By Judicial Order

Once litigation is well under way, judicial orders provide a fourth potential avenue for "safe" apology. Federal Rule of Civil Procedure 26(c) provides that a court may, "for good cause shown...make any order which justice requires to protect a party or person from annoyance, embarrassment, oppression, or undue burden or expense." Courts can order statements made in settlement negotiations, like an apology, to be kept confidential. Possible uses of such orders include preventing the disclosure of mediation proceedings or settlement negotiations, or the revelation of the settlement agreement reached. An advantage of such an order is the judge's ability to tailor it to parties' specific needs. Another advantage of an order is the weight of judicial force: A party who would not fear breaking a private confidentiality agreement may well fear violating a judicial order. . . .

First, obtaining a judicial order, if it comes at all, usually comes quite "late in the game," after litigation is well under way. Second, obtaining a judicial order can be difficult. . . . Third, courts have the power to modify their orders and allow disclosure in later proceedings, raising the specter that what one had hoped would be a confidential communication will not remain so. . . .

MAKING THE APOLOGY

Factors

When discussing apology with a client, a lawyer should be sensitive to . . . (1) the appropriateness of the case for apology, (2) the timing of the apology, (3) the scope of the apology, (4) the method of the apology, (5) nuance, and (6) interpersonal variation. . . .

Summary Advice

[T]he lawyer and the client-offender ought to think about whether the case is appropriate for apology and, if so, how an apology should be made. In particular, the lawyer might discuss with the client the legal ramifications of apology and, if the client is concerned that an apology will be used in court to show liability, how that risk may be minimized. The lawyer and client should bear in mind that an early apology soon after the injury, while it may be most promising relationally, may also have the least legal protection, and that the "safest" avenue for apology could come later. . . . [O]ne strategy is to make a statement early on which expresses sympathy only, and to wait until a later stage to make a full apology (one which also admits fault and expresses regret) if need be. If such a full apology is to be made, a mediation session preceded by a confidentiality agreement may often be the best place for it. Not only are the statutory protections afforded mediation proceedings generally strong, but mediation is a natural forum for apology. If maintaining insurance coverage is a concern, the possibility of admitting fault without assuming financial liability should also be kept in mind.

Notes and Questions

7.22 One pathbreaking study has experimentally studied the effects of apology in negotiation. See Jennifer Robbennolt, Apologies and Legal Settlement: An Empirical Examination, 102 Mich. L. Rev. 460 (2003) (finding that the type of apology offered affects the willingness of the other side to settle—a full apology is better than a partial apology, and a partial apology is often no different from no apology — and that differences in evidentiary rules about the legal effects of apology did not affect settlement rates). Additional studies have examined the impact of types of apologies. For example, one study found that rebuilding cooperation is feasible via apologies and simple explanations in short interactions. However, for longer-term interactions, substantive amends are more effective at restoring cooperation than just explanations or simple apologies. William P. Bottom, Kevin Gibson, Steven E. Daniels & J. Keith Murnighan, When Talk Is Not Cheap: Substantive Penance and Expressions of Intent in Rebuilding Cooperation, 13 Org. Sci. 497 (2002).

7.23 Public figures also use apology without admitting a wrong, such as when British Prime Minister Tony Blair apologized for the misinformation surrounding the invasion of Iraq but defended the invasion, see Patrick E. Tyler, Blair Offers an Apology, of Sorts, Over Iraq, N.Y. Times, Sept. 29, 2004, at A10, and New York Yankee Jason Giambi also issued a public apology for the steroid controversy that had surrounded him, without ever mentioning what he was sorry for and never using the word *steroid*, see Tyler Kepner, A Careful Apology from Giambi, N.Y. Times, Feb. 11, 2005, at D1.

7.24 Would you as the attorney suggest that your client apologize if he or she were involved in a car accident? Why or why not? What if your client was a doctor who made a medical error? Would it matter if the patient knew?

7.25 In 2003, Colorado changed its evidence code to state that "any and all statements, affirmations, gestures or conduct expressing apology, fault, sympathy, commiseration, condolences, compassion, or a general sense of benevolence . . . made by a health care provider . . . are inadmissible as evidence of an admission of liability" in civil actions. This change serves to provide a "safe harbor" for apologies made in this context. Jonathan R. Cohen, Toward Candor After Medical Error: The First Apology Law, 5 Harv. Health Poly. Rev. 21 (2004). Lee Taft argues against the use of safe harbor statutes that protect apologies given during the course of a case or dispute resolution. He argues that these statutes take away the essential purpose of an apology, to admit you were wrong. He argues that such statutes make apology a more strategic option than a sincere gesture, and, thus, apology lacks its important moral qualities. See Lee Taft, Apology Subverted: The Commodification of Apology, 109 Yale L.J. 1135 (2000). Do you agree that safe harbor statutes might make apology more strategic than sincere? For a good review of whether new laws would be necessary to facilitate apology, see Jonathan R. Cohen, Legislating Apology: The Pros and Cons, 70 U. Cinn. L. Rev. 819 (2002).

7.26 What about the morality of apology? What do you think about the disconnect between the law and moral beliefs?

> Somewhere between childhood and adulthood, our society, in part through our legal system, dismantles one of life's most basic moral lessons. If a child injures another, good parents will teach that child to take responsibility for what he has done. If an adult injures another and goes to a lawyer, the usual focus is on precisely the reverse: denial. The goal is to avoid responsibility or, if that is not possible, to minimize liability. To see how morally bizarre this common practice is, imagine instead that the adult injurer were to see a

minister or psychologist. It is nearly axiomatic that such professionals would try to help the injurer face what he has done and take responsibility for it. The benefits to the injured party notwithstanding, from the viewpoint of the *injurer*'s moral and psychological development, embracing responsibility for harms one has caused is critical. Indeed, it is hard to imagine a more basic ethical dictate or psychological prescription than voluntarily assuming responsibility when one has harmed another. Yet our legal system typically encourages denial. The immoral has become the normal. Although frequently, but not always, denial benefits injurers economically, this path of moral regression poses significant psychological and spiritual risks for injurers.

Jonathan R. Cohen, The Immorality of Denial, 79 Tul. L. Rev. 903, 904 (2005).

7.27 While much of the literature on apology focuses on civil cases, apology can also be valuable in criminal procedures. Some authors believe that criminal proceedings can involve more social, psychological, and moral elements for both the offender and the victim.

> Criminal punishment is one essential part of balancing the scales of justice, but it is not the only part. Offenders should also realize the wrongfulness of their acts, feel sorrow for their misdeeds, and accept responsibility.... If encouraged in the right way, remorse and apology can help offenders cleanse their consciences and return to the moral fold. It can also touch victims, allowing them to achieve catharsis, let go of their anger, and forgive....
>
> Remorse and apology are fundamentally moral, and the law cannot force them.... But the law can remove roadblocks to remorse, provide opportunities and venues, and encourage offenders and victims to speak face to face.

For an in-depth discussion of incorporating apology into criminal proceedings, see Stephanos Bibas & Richard A. Bierschbach, Integrating Remorse and Apology into Criminal Procedure, 114 Yale L.J. 85 (2004). Much of the "restorative justice" movement in criminal law is based on the importance of apology and acknowledgment of the effects of actions on others. See, e.g., John Braithwaite, Restorative Justice and Social Justice (2003).

 **Chapter 8** | Recognizing and
Responding to Barriers
in Negotiation

This chapter turns to some of the psychological and social factors that can inhibit building a relationship, exchanging offers, and progressing in the negotiation. Most of the articles in this chapter build on interdisciplinary and empirical work done by law professors, economists, psychologists, and others in order to understand how negotiators make choices in their negotiations. There is much disagreement about what is "rational" to do in making negotiation choices. The second part of this chapter focuses on particular barriers and concerns in negotiations in criminal law and plea bargaining. Finally, the last part of the chapter discusses strategies, tactics, and effective responses to some of these difficulties.

A. PSYCHOLOGICAL FACTORS IN NEGOTIATION

This first excerpt is an overview of the field of decision theory. Many of the particular issues discussed in the article are further clarified in the excerpts that follow.

 Russell Korobkin & Chris Guthrie, **HEURISTICS AND BIASES AT THE BARGAINING TABLE**

87 Marq. L. Rev. 795, 795–808 (2004)

I. INTRODUCTION

Negotiation is an inherently *interpersonal* activity that nonetheless requires each participant to make *individual* judgments and decisions. Each negotiator must evaluate a proposed agreement, assess its value and the value of alternative courses of action — such as continuing to negotiate or pursuing an alternative transaction — and ultimately choose whether to accept or reject the proposal.

The interdisciplinary field of "decision theory" offers both a normative account (how *should* individuals act) and descriptive accounts (how *do* individuals act) of decision making in the negotiation context. According to the normative model, negotiators should compare the subjective expected value of an agreement to the subjective expected value of non-agreement, taking into account such factors as risks, differential transaction costs, and reputational and relational consequences of each possible course of action. Once a negotiator has calculated the expected value of each course of action, the negotiator should then select the one that promises the greatest return.

There is less agreement about whether negotiators actually make decisions consistent with this approach. Proponents of descriptive or "positive" models based on "rational choice theory" assume that negotiators will invest optimally in the amount of information needed for decision making, draw accurate inferences from the information they acquire, and then select the option that maximizes their expected utility. In short, proponents of the rational choice-based models assume that negotiators will make choices consistent with the normative model.

Skeptics of rational choice-based models argue that negotiators rarely behave this "demonically." Instead, negotiators routinely employ more intuitive approaches to judgment and choice that rely on a variety of "heuristics" or mental shortcuts to reduce the complexity and effort involved in the reasoning process. While some researchers believe that negotiators intentionally employ such heuristics to economize on the time and effort required to make decisions, others believe that reliance on heuristics is unconscious. In all likelihood, there is truth in both perspectives; that is, negotiators rely on heuristics intuitively and unconsciously in some circumstances and consciously employ heuristics in others. Either way, negotiators should appreciate the important role that heuristics are likely to play in their decision making — and in the decision making of their counterparts — at the bargaining table.

II. UNDERSTANDING NEGOTIATOR JUDGMENT AND DECISION MAKING

When deciding whether to accept or reject an actual or anticipated set of deal terms, a negotiator must perform two cognitive tasks. First, the negotiator must evaluate the content of the available options, a task we can loosely call "judgment." For example, a negotiator contemplating the purchase of a particular business must try to evaluate the market value of the business's assets, determine what percentage of the business's current clients will be retained in case of a change of ownership, estimate how much profit the business will earn in the future, and evaluate the likelihood that the negotiator would find a similar business to purchase if the negotiator opted not to purchase this one. From this perspective, judgment tasks concern a search for facts about the world.

Second, the negotiator must determine which available option he prefers, a task we can call "choice." For example, would he rather purchase the business under consideration for a specific price or reject such a deal in favor of continuing his search, thus taking a chance that he will find an equally desirable business at a lower price or a more desirable business at the same price?

In performing both of these tasks — i.e., judgment and choice — the negotiator *should* evaluate options and make decisions consistent with the normative model of choice. However, both social science research and common experience suggest the negotiator's decision making processes will often depart from the normative model.

A. Judgment

Negotiators cannot know the objective values and probabilities of every option they might consider before reaching a negotiated outcome. Thus, to estimate the values and probabilities associated with each option, negotiators are likely to rely on heuristics. Heuristics often enable negotiators to make good judgments in a "fast and frugal" manner. On other occasions, heuristics prove to be poor substitutes for more complex reasoning and result in negotiator decisions that fail to best serve the negotiator's interests.

1. Anchoring and Adjustment

One heuristic approach to judgment tasks that can lead to suboptimal results is known as "anchoring and adjustment." To estimate the value of an option, negotiators are likely to start with the value of a known option, the "anchor," and then adjust to compensate for relevant differences in the character of the known and unknown item. . . .

2. Availability

When a negotiator's option could have a variety of consequences, each probabalistic, rather than a single certain outcome — for example, if the negotiator enters an agreement to buy the business under consideration, the business might make a large profit or, alternatively, it might go bankrupt — the negotiator will often evaluate the likelihood of the various possible outcomes based on the ease with which the possible outcomes come to mind. Because probabilistic judgments are based on how mentally *available* the possible results are, this method of judgment is known as the "availability" heuristic.

Like anchoring and adjustment, basing judgments on the availability of outcomes is a reasonable, time-saving device that will often yield acceptable outcomes because availability is often correlated with frequency. But when the available outcomes are not typical, or when there are important differences between the past and future circumstances, the heuristic can lead to flawed predictions. For example, a negotiator evaluating the prospects of entrusting his or her lawsuit to a jury for the purpose of deciding whether to accept a settlement offer might overestimate the likelihood of winning punitive damages at trial if he recalls a recent multi-million dollar verdict in a tobacco lawsuit publicized in the news, because the media exposure afforded to that verdict does not reflect its typicality.

3. Self-Serving Evaluations

Substantial evidence indicates that individuals are particularly likely to make judgments concerning existing facts and future probabilities in ways that confirm pre-existing belief structures, assume high degrees of personal agency in the world, and create a positive presentation of self. This tendency will often result in judgments compromised by what is called the "self-serving" or "egocentric" bias.

A plethora of studies demonstrate that individuals often judge uncertain options as more likely to produce outcomes that are beneficial to them than an objective analysis would yield. Depending on the specific context, the bias could cause negotiators to overestimate either the likely benefits that would result from reaching a negotiated agreement or the likely benefits that would result from rejecting the proposed agreement and pursuing an alternate course of action. In one study, for example, George Loewenstein and his colleagues assigned some experimental subjects to the role of plaintiff and others to the role of defendant and then asked each to judge the value of the lawsuit based on the very same information. Both plaintiff and defendant subjects believed that a judge would be more likely to rule for their side should the case go to trial, suggesting that, on average, subjects' judgments of the quality of their non-agreement option (i.e., adjudication) were inflated relative to the objective quality of that option.*

B. Choice

After judging the objective attributes of available options, negotiators must eventually make a choice between them. Normative models assume that negotiators will make choices based on a comparison of the expected values of each option; the decision theory literature suggests that choices often fail to reflect this reasoning process.

1. Framing

When choosing between an option with a known outcome and one with an uncertain outcome, research demonstrates that individuals often consider not only the expected value of each choice, but also whether the possible outcomes appear to be "gains" or "losses" relative to a reference point, typically the status quo. . . .

2. The Status Quo Bias

All other things being equal, individuals on average tend to prefer an option if it is consistent with the status quo than if it requires a change from the status quo. Often, we prefer the status quo because we receive more utility from the current state of affairs than we expect to receive from some other state of affairs, suggesting that the status quo bias is consistent with the normative model of choice. In other circumstances, however, reliance on this heuristic can lead decision makers to make choices that depart from the normative model. The status quo bias suggests that, all other things being equal, negotiators will prefer their initial endowments over endowments they might hope to receive through exchange, that they will favor deal terms that are consistent with legal default rules, and that they will prefer terms of trade that are conventional for the type of bargain that is at issue. . . .

3. Contrast Effects

Evidence also suggests that choice can depend on the full range of options available to the decision maker, even when the normative model suggests that the availability of certain options should be irrelevant. Researchers investigating such "contrast effects" have demonstrated, for example, that individuals are more likely to select an option in the presence of a similar, inferior option than in the absence of the inferior option. [See Chris Guthrie's article in Chapter 3.] In one illustrative experiment, Itamar Simonson and Amos Tversky found that 28% more subjects chose an elegant Cross pen when they were also offered the alternative choices of $6 in cash or an inferior pen than when subjects were offered only the choice between the Cross

---

* Linda Babcock & George Loewenstein, "Explaining Bargaining Impasse: The Role of Self-Serving Biases," 11 (1) J. of Econ. Perspectives 109 (1997).

pen and the $6 in cash. That is, the availability of the inferior pen substantially increased the likelihood that subjects would choose the Cross pen over the $6.[35] The implication is that a negotiator's preference for one agreement possibility over another, or for a proposed agreement over an outside alternative, might depend on whether other options that make the proposed agreement appear desirable in contrast are also considered as part of the calculus.[36]

In some contexts, the presence of a third option, C, could logically affect a decision maker's preference for A versus B, because C provides information about the quality of A or B. But if C sheds no new light on A or B, its effect on the A versus B decision would violate the normative model of choice. As Mark Kelman and his colleagues explain, an individual who prefers chicken over pasta might rationally change her preference from pasta to chicken upon learning that veal parmesan is on the menu because "the availability of veal parmesan on the menu might [indicate] that the restaurant specializes in Italian [food]." But "[a] person who prefers chicken over pasta should not change this preference on learning that fish is also available."

4. Reactive Devaluation

Finally, some evidence indicates that a negotiator's choice might depend on the source of one or more options, even when that source provides no information about the objective quality of the options. More simply stated, a proposal can look less desirable than it otherwise would merely because a counterpart offered it. This phenomenon is known as "reactive devaluation."

III. INFLUENCING NEGOTIATOR JUDGMENT AND DECISION MAKING

Negotiators who recognize that their counterparts are likely to rely on heuristics when making the types of judgments and choices commonly required in bargaining settings can use this knowledge to increase the likelihood of securing agreements and of securing agreements on highly favorable terms. This section briefly outlines some ways in which a negotiator can make use of heuristic reasoning to influence her counterpart's judgment and choice behavior. We use litigation bargaining anecdotes as examples, but the concepts can be employed just as effectively in other negotiation contexts.

A. Influence Through Anchoring

The anchoring and adjustment heuristic suggests that a negotiator can affect her counterpart's judgment of the quality of a proposed agreement if she can determine the content of the anchor. In commercial negotiations, where monetary values are usually the bargaining currency, a monetary figure that appears, even superficially, related to the subject of the negotiation can affect one's counterpart's judgments.

In litigation bargaining, the settlement versus adjudication decision rests in large part on the negotiator's judgment of what a court would award the plaintiff should

---

[35] Itamar Simonson & Amos Tversky, Choice in Contest: Tradeoff Contrast and Extremeness Aversion, 29 J. Marketing Res. 281, 287 (1992).
[36] See Chris Guthrie, Panacea or Pandora's Box?: The Costs of Options in Negotiation, 88 Iowa L. Rev. 601, 617-19 (2003).

settlement negotiations fail. Because adjudication results are notoriously difficult to predict, the plaintiff's lawyer has a clear opportunity to improve his chances of convincing the defendant to choose settlement at a favorable price over adjudication (and vice versa for the defendant's lawyer) by manipulating the defendant's judgment of the adjudication option. Of course, the plaintiff's lawyer might accomplish this by persuasive argumentation. He might also accomplish this, however, by exposing the defendant to a high anchor — perhaps by making a very high initial settlement demand. Even if the defendant immediately rejects the high demand out of hand, the demand could anchor the defendant's prediction of a jury verdict, making that judgment higher than it otherwise would be, and thus increasing the likelihood that the defendant would choose a somewhat lower settlement demand over the adjudication alternative.

Several pieces of experimental evidence support this contention. Researchers have found, for instance, that those who open with an extreme demand may be more likely to reach agreement; that those who open with extreme demands may be more likely to receive larger settlements; and that extreme demands are likely to influence mock jurors' assessments of the value of a plaintiff's case.

B.   Influence Through Availability

Recall that the availability heuristic causes probability estimates of outcomes to be effected by the mental availability of similar prior outcomes. That an outcome's availability is not always highly correlated with its frequency offers an opportunity for exploitation in bargaining. A negotiator can increase the chances that her counterpart will accept a proposed agreement favorable to the negotiator if the negotiator can increase the availability in the counterpart's mind of outcomes that are favorable to the negotiator and unfavorable to the counterpart.

As we identified in the context of the anchoring and adjustment heuristic, the best opportunity to exploit the availability heuristic is when negotiation decision making requires probabilistic judgments of highly uncertain events, such as outcomes of adjudication. By drawing the defendant's attention to large verdicts in recent cases that bear at least a surface similarity to the case at hand, for example, the plaintiff's lawyer might increase the defendant's prediction of the likelihood that a jury would return a large plaintiff's verdict. This might, in turn, induce the defendant to accept a particular settlement offer that he would otherwise reject.

C.   Influence Through Framing

The framing effect suggests that a negotiator's choice between a certain option, such as a litigation settlement agreement, and a probabilistic option, such as adjudication, will depend in part on the reference point from which she compares the two options. Assuming that the options have a similar perceived expected value, she is more likely to choose the certain choice if the options appear favorable (i.e., look like gains); if the options appear unfavorable (i.e., look like losses), she is more likely to prefer the risky choice. A negotiator can therefore increase the likelihood that her counterpart will accept a settlement agreement proposal if she can cause the counterpart to select a reference point that makes settlement look positive in contrast.

Relative to the reference point of the current state of affairs, a litigation settlement or a trial verdict would naturally appear to be gains from the perspective of the plaintiff, who will receive compensation in either event, and a loss for the defendant, who must pay in either event. From this perspective, we would predict that a defendant is more likely to reject rather than to accept a settlement proposal that is roughly equivalent to the expected value of trial. A plaintiff who wishes to maximize the likelihood that the defendant will accept such a proposal, or even one more favorable to the plaintiff, can do so by attempting to provide a different reference point by reframing the options.

Specifically, the plaintiff's lawyer might try to induce the defendant to compare his available options not to the status quo, but to a different reference point that will make those options seem more attractive. For example, she might try to persuade him to compare his options to a realistic worst-case outcome at trial. Relative to that reference point, the defendant's options are likely to look like gains, which should prompt him to find paying the certain settlement relatively more attractive.

D. Influence Through Contrast Effects

A negotiator familiar with contrast effects will recognize that her counterpart is likely to evaluate an option more favorably if a similar but inferior option is available. The negotiator may thus be able to increase the likelihood that her counterpart will select a particular agreement proposal if a similar but inferior proposal is offered in the alternative.

Suppose, for example, that a fired employee files suit against a company for which she used to work, asserting employment discrimination claims under Title VII. Suppose further that the defendant has offered to pay the plaintiff a $30,000 cash payment to settle the case but that the plaintiff is wavering because trial holds some appeal. Assuming that the defendant wants the plaintiff to accept the $30,000 settlement offer, what might defense counsel do to encourage her to accept it?

In lieu of the $30,000 lump sum payment, for example, defense counsel might offer to donate $30,000 to the charity of the plaintiff's choice, offer $30,000 in merchandise to the plaintiff, or offer to pay her $10,000 per year for three years. Research on contrast effects suggests that the presence of any of these alternative options should make the $30,000 cash offer seem more attractive by comparison than it would appear standing alone. This, in turn, should increase the likelihood that the plaintiff will choose to accept the settlement proposal and [forgo] trial.

IV. CONCLUSION

Negotiators often lack control over the identity of counterparts, the issues, and the bargaining environment, but they do enjoy control over how they make decisions. By understanding the decision making process, the negotiator can exercise that control effectively and even exercise some control over how her counterpart makes decisions as well.

1. Status Quo Barriers

These next excerpts further explain the framing and status quo bias outlined in the first article above. Status quo barriers refer to the mistakes or assumptions that negotiators make because they like their current situation or what they already have more. They like the items they have in their possession and fear losing them. Economics professor Daniel Kahneman and psychology professor Amos Tversky discuss a phenomenon called the "endowment effect," which occurs when negotiators value what they own more than what they do not. This effect also brings in the element of risk. What are we willing to risk to avoid losing something we have? In 2002, Kahneman won the Nobel Prize in economics for his work on the endowment effect.

 Daniel Kahneman & Amos Tversky, **CONFLICT RESOLUTION: A COGNITIVE PERSPECTIVE**

in Barriers to Conflict Resolution 54-55 (Kenneth Arrow et al. eds., 1995)

Loss aversion refers to the observation that losses generally loom larger than the corresponding gains. This notion may be captured by a value function that is steeper in the negative than in the positive domain. In decisions under risk, loss aversion entails a reluctance to accept even-chance gambles, unless the payoffs are very favorable. For example, many people will accept such a gamble only if the gain is at least twice as large as the loss. . . .

The following classroom demonstration illustrates the principle of loss aversion. An attractive object (e.g., a decorated mug) is distributed to one-third of the students. The students who have been given mugs are *sellers* — perhaps better described as owners. They are informed that there will be an opportunity to exchange the mug for a predetermined amount of money. The subjects state what their choice will be for different amounts, and thereby indicate the minimal amount for which they are willing to give up their mug. Another one-third of the students are *choosers*. They are told that they will have a choice between a mug like the one in the hands of their neighbor and an amount of cash; they indicate their choices for different amounts. The remaining students are *buyers*: they indicate whether they would pay each of the different amounts to acquire a mug. In a representative experiment, the median price set by sellers was $7.12, the median cash equivalent set by the choosers was $3.12, and the median buyer was willing to pay $2.88 for the mug.

The difference between the valuations of owners and choosers occurs in spite of the fact that both groups face the same choice: go home with a mug or with a prespecified sum of money. Subjectively, however, the choosers and owners are in different states: the former evaluate the mug as a gain, the latter as something to be given up. Because of loss aversion, more cash is required to persuade the owners to give up the mug than to match the attractiveness of the mug to the choosers. In the same vein, Thaler tells of a wine lover who will neither sell a bottle that has gained value in his cellar nor buy another bottle at the current price.* The experimental

---

* Richard Thaler, Toward a Positive Theory of Consumer Choice, 1 J. Econ. Behav. & Org. 1, 39-60 (1980).

studies of the discrepant valuation of owners, choosers, and buyers demonstrate that loss aversion can be induced instantaneously; it does not depend on a progressive attachment to objects in one's possession.

CONCESSION AVERSION

Loss aversion, we argue, could have a significant impact on conflict resolution. Imagine two countries negotiating the number of missiles that they will keep and aim at each other. Each country derives security from its own missiles and is threatened by those of the other side. Thus, missiles eliminated by the other side are evaluated as gains, and missiles one must give up are evaluated as losses, relative to the status quo. If losses have twice the impact of gains, then each side will require its opponent to eliminate twice as many missiles as it eliminates — not a promising start for the achievement of an agreement. The symmetry of the positions might help negotiators reframe the problem to trade missiles at par, but in most negotiations the sacrifices made by the two sides are not easily compared. In labor negotiations, for example, a union may be asked to give up a third pilot in the cockpit, and might be offered improved benefits or a more generous retirement plan in return. These are the circumstances under which we expect to find *concession aversion*, a systematically different evaluation of concessions made and of concessions received.

Notes and Questions

8.1 Why are negotiators willing to risk more to avoid a loss? Is this just denial?

8.2 What can the lawyer do to help the client deal with these tendencies (or the lawyer's own tendencies)? How does framing the offer from the other side matter?

 Russell Korobkin & Chris Guthrie, **PSYCHOLOGICAL BARRIERS TO LITIGATION SETTLEMENT: AN EXPERIMENTAL APPROACH**

93 Mich. L. Rev. 107, 130-135, 137-138 (1994)

Although researchers have studied the impact of framing on negotiation and bargaining in general, no studies have examined the framing effect in the litigation context. Yet litigation — which often requires parties to decide between a certain settlement offer and an uncertain trial verdict — presents an important, real-world example of decisionmaking under uncertainty. To begin to fill this void, we conducted a series of experiments in which we examined the impact of frames on parties to legal disputes. We hypothesized that the propensity to accept a settlement offer during a legal dispute would be dependent on whether the offeree viewed the settlement offer as a gain or a loss.

To test this hypothesis, we first asked two groups of subjects to consider a hypothetical lawsuit based on the most common of all torts: an automobile collision. All the subjects received a nearly identical set of facts. All had suffered $28,000 worth of damages in an automobile accident that was not their fault. The other party was insolvent and could pay nothing, but he did have insurance coverage. The subjects learned that they had filed suit against the insurance carrier; the carrier, in turn, had conceded liability and agreed that the plaintiff incurred $28,000 in damages but claimed that the policy covered a maximum of $10,000 for accidents involving rental cars. Because the negligent driver was driving a rental car at the time of the accident, the insurance company contended that its liability was limited to $10,000. The subjects' attorney advised them that the only legal issue was whether the policy language — which was unclear on the subject — limited the carrier's liability to $10,000. The attorney also told the subjects that if the case went to trial, a judge would render a decision based on the language of the insurance policy. Based on his research, the attorney informed the subjects that the case could go either way. Depending upon the judge's interpretation of the insurance policy, the subjects would recover either $28,000 or $10,000. Prior to trial, the insurance company offered the subjects a settlement of $21,000; the subjects could either accept the offer or reject it and proceed to trial.

In this scenario, all subjects found themselves in an identical legal situation. All faced a choice between a certain $21,000 settlement and a trial in which they would receive either $28,000 or $10,000, depending on the outcome. Subjects were randomly assigned to either Group A or Group B of the automobile accident scenario. The subjects in the two groups received versions of the scenario that had only a single difference: the frames were altered.

Subjects in Group A were told they had been driving a $14,000 Toyota Corolla, which was destroyed in the accident. In addition, they suffered injuries that resulted in $14,000 worth of medical bills. Their health insurance company had paid their medical bills, but they had no private insurance to cover the replacement cost of the car. In contrast, Group B subjects had been driving a $24,000 BMW. Their BMW was totaled, and they suffered injuries resulting in $4,000 worth of medical bills. This group's health insurance had also already paid the medical bills, but they had not been reimbursed for the car. Both groups had losses from the accident totaling $28,000, but Group A subjects had already been reimbursed for $14,000 of that total, while Group B subjects had been reimbursed for only $4,000 of their losses. This meant that accepting the $21,000 offer would leave Group A subjects better off financially than they were prior to the accident (− $28,000 + $14,000 + $21,000 = $7,000). The same offer would leave Group B subjects in a worse position than before the accident occurred (− $28,000 + $4,000 + $21,000 = − $3,000).

The survey asked the subjects to indicate their willingness to accept the settlement offer by selecting one of the following options:

Definitely accept the offer [5]
Probably accept the offer [4]
Undecided [3]
Probably reject the offer [2]
Definitely reject the offer [1]

Although the legal endowments of subjects in Groups A and B were identical, the framing of the settlement offer made a significant difference in the propensity of the subjects to accept the offer or to reject it and proceed to trial. Subjects in Group A (Toyota Drivers) responded very favorably to the offer, providing an average response of 4.43 (n = 42). Subjects in Group B (BMW Drivers) also tended to favor the offer, but with much less fervor. Their average response was 3.64 (n = 44). The difference between these two means is highly statistically significant. Ninety percent of Toyota Drivers said they would "probably accept" or "definitely accept" the offer, while only 64% of BMW Drivers would "probably" or "definitely" accept. Only 2% of Toyota Drivers — one subject out of forty-two — would "probably" or "definitely" reject the offer, but 20% of BMW Drivers would "probably" or "definitely" reject the offer. The Toyota Drivers were inclined to choose the certain gain offered by the settlement over the risk that they might receive less at trial. The BMW Drivers apparently coded the decision options differently than did the Toyota Drivers. They perceived the settlement offer as a loss relative to the preaccident position and were, as a result, much less likely than the Toyota Drivers to accept the settlement. Many were prepared to accept the risk of a large loss in return for an uncertain chance at a payout that would leave them $4,000 better off than they were prior to the accident.

We found similar results in a hypothetical scenario involving a property dispute between neighbors. Subjects assumed the role of homeowners in a densely populated section of Palo Alto, California. When they began construction of a swimming pool in their backyard, they discovered that their neighbor's wine cellar was built under their property. They discussed the matter with the neighbor and discovered that he had known for fifteen years that the cellar was built in the wrong location but had never mentioned it because it had never been in their way. The subjects were told that they agreed to allow their neighbor to keep the cellar where it was but they felt that he should compensate them for the past and future use of the land. The neighbor refused, so the subjects responded by filing suit against the neighbor. The subjects' lawyer advised them that if they prevailed at trial, the property values and length of use suggested that an award of $15,000 was in order. It was difficult to predict, however, whether the subjects would prevail. The neighbor's lawyer argued that fifteen years of uninterrupted use qualified the neighbor for free, perpetual use of the land, known as an easement by prescription. The subjects were told that their attorney advised them the case could go either way, as there was no recorded case quite like this in California. The subjects could recover $15,000 at trial, or nothing at all. In a final attempt to settle the case before trial, the neighbor offered a $6,750 cash settlement.

Again, we divided the subjects into two groups and, again, manipulated the frames. The instructions told the Group A subjects that, due to the location of the wine cellar, construction of the swimming pool cost $2,000 more than it otherwise would have. For members of this group, the $6,750 settlement offer appeared to represent a gain (− $2,000 + $6,750 = $4,750). Members of Group B learned that the placement of the wine cellar caused construction to cost $13,000 more than it otherwise would have. To this group, a $6,750 settlement offer appeared to be a loss (− $13,000 + $6,750 = − $6,250). Again, the scenario presented the case in a way that made it quite clear that the costs incurred by the subjects in no way affected their legal endowments.

As in the automobile collision scenario, subjects in the wine cellar scenario were more likely to settle out of court when the frame of reference made the settlement offer look like a gain, rather than a loss. Group A subjects (Gainers) were more likely than not to accept the settlement, giving a mean score of 3.77 on the five-point scale (n = 44). Group B subjects (Losers), on the other hand, were more likely to risk the uncertain outcome of a trial than to accept the settlement offer. They provided a mean score of 2.57 (n = 42). Again, the difference between the two groups is highly statistically significant. While 45% of Gainers said they would "definitely" accept the settlement offer, only 7% of Losers would "definitely" accept the offer. Fifty-seven percent of Losers "probably" or "definitely" preferred trial, as compared to 25% of Gainers. . . .

Our results make it clear that frames matter in legal dispute resolution. Disputants may reject a settlement offer economically sufficient to produce a negotiated settlement if they view it in relation to a reference point that suggests accepting the offer would mean accepting a net loss on the transaction. Conversely, an adverse party might perceive an offer framed in its best light as favorable, even if she would reject a frameless presentation of the same substance. To place the discussion in terms of negotiation theory, if an offer made by one party is either marginally within the other party's range of acceptable settlements or marginally outside the other party's range, the frame could affect whether the dispute settles out of court or goes to trial.

It is, of course, little more than common sense to suggest that an attorney involved in settlement negotiations should try to convince her adversary that the adversary will gain, rather than lose, by accepting the deal — that is, to suggest to one of our BMW Driver subjects that he consider the settlement offer in relation to his post-accident position as opposed to his preaccident position. Our studies indicate one reason why this is sound advice: a positive frame creates a psychological state that favors risk-averse behavior — that is, settlement — and disfavors risk-seeking behavior — that is, trial.

Notes and Questions

8.3 Can you think of an example where you lost something you had and expected to replace it exactly? One law student, for example, had a clerkship with a prestigious judge — a U.S. Second Circuit judge — when the judge died during the student's third year of law school. Rather than starting her clerkship search anew, she limited her search for replacement clerkships to similarly prestigious and well-located judges. What was her reasoning? How would you advise her?

8.4 How can you frame a settlement offer to your client to increase the odds the client will accept the offer?

2. Informational Barriers

Earlier chapters have already discussed the importance of gathering information to prepare for the negotiation and the key roles that listening and understanding play in seeking information from the client and the other side. This section examines problems with information gathering. What happens when negotiators do not share useful information? What happens when negotiators get too wedded to the information they already have?

The following excerpt examines the strategic barriers to negotiation and why negotiators do not share information. The problem that results is that it becomes much harder to work out integrative agreements without the information necessary to find them.

 Robert Mnookin, **WHY NEGOTIATIONS FAIL: AN EXPLORATION OF BARRIERS TO CONFLICT RESOLUTION**

8 Ohio St. J. on Disp. Resol. 235, 240-242 (1993)

In order to create value, it is critically important that options be created in light of both parties' underlying interests and preferences. This suggests the importance of openness and disclosure, so that a variety of options can be analyzed and compared from the perspectives of all concerned. However, when it comes to the distributive aspects of bargaining, full disclosure — particularly if unreciprocated by the other side — can often lead to outcomes in which the more open party receives a comparatively smaller slice. To put it another way, unreciprocated approaches to creating value leave their maker vulnerable to claiming tactics. On the other hand, focusing on the distributive aspects of bargaining can often lead to unnecessary deadlocks and, more fundamentally, a failure to discover options or alternatives that make both sides better off. A simple example can expose the dilemma. The first involves what game theorists call "information asymmetry." This simply means each side to a negotiation characteristically knows some relevant facts that the other side does not know.

Suppose I have ten apples and no oranges, and Nancy Rogers has ten oranges and no apples. (Assume apples and oranges are otherwise unavailable to either of us.) I love oranges and hate apples. Nancy likes them both equally well. I suggest to Nancy that we might both be made better off through a trade. If I disclose to Nancy that I love oranges and don't eat apples, and Nancy wishes to engage in strategic bargaining, she might simply suggest that her preferences are the same as mine, although, in truth, she likes both. She might propose that I give her nine apples (which she says have little value to her) in exchange for one of her very valuable oranges. Because it is often very difficult for one party to know the underlying preferences of the other party, parties in a negotiation may puff, bluff, or lie about their underlying interests and preferences. Indeed, in many negotiations, it may never be possible to know whether the other side has honestly disclosed its interests and preferences. I have to be open to create value, but my openness may work to my disadvantage with respect to the distributive aspect of the negotiation.

Even when both parties know all the relevant information, and the potential gains may result from a negotiated deal, strategic bargaining over how to divide the pie can still lead to deadlock (with no deal at all) or protracted and expensive bargaining, thus shrinking the pie. For example, suppose Nancy has a house for sale for which she has a reservation price of $245,000. I am willing to pay up to $295,000 for the house. Any deal within a bargaining range from $245,000 to $295,000 would make both of us better off than no sale at all. Suppose we each know the other's reservation price. Will there be a deal? Not necessarily. If we disagree about how the $50,000 "surplus" should be divided (each wanting all or most of it), our negotiation may end in a deadlock. We might engage in hardball negotiation tactics in which each tried to persuade the other that he or she was committed to walking away from a beneficial deal, rather than accept less than $40,000 of the surplus. Nancy might claim that she won't take a nickel less than $285,000, or even $294,999 for that matter. Indeed, she might go so far as to give a power of attorney to an agent to sell only at that price, and then leave town in order to make her commitment credible. Of course, I could play the same type of game and the result would then be that no deal is made and that we are both worse off. In this case, the obvious tension between the distribution of the $50,000 and the value creating possibilities inherent in any sale within the bargaining range may result in no deal.

Strategic behavior — which may be rational for a self-interested party concerned with maximizing the size of his or her own slice — can often lead to inefficient outcomes. Those subjected to claiming tactics often respond in kind, and the net result typically is to push up the cost of the dispute resolution process.... Parties may be tempted to engage in a strategic behavior, hoping to get more. Often all they do is shrink the size of the pie. Those experienced in the civil litigation process see this all the time. One or both sides often attempt to use pre-trial discovery as leverage to force the other side into agreeing to a more favorable settlement. Often the net result, however, is simply that both sides spend unnecessary money on the dispute resolution process.

Notes and Questions

8.5   How is the problem with strategic barriers linked to the Prisoner's Dilemma and Negotiator's Dilemma that we studied earlier?

8.6   What suggestions do you have for overcoming this barrier? How can lawyers help their clients deal with this barrier?

CALVIN AND HOBBES ©1993 Watterson. **Dist. by UNIVERSAL PRESS SYNDICATE. Reprinted with permission. All rights reserved.**

Business school professors Max Bazerman and Margaret Neale outline the informational barrier of anchoring. Anchoring occurs when negotiators rely too heavily on the information at hand. The following two excerpts then discuss optimistic overconfidence, which traps negotiators when they have more faith than they should in the accuracy of their positions, their evaluations of the other side, or other events occurring in the course of the negotiation. Often overconfidence stems from an inability to view information objectively.

 ***Max H. Bazerman & Margaret A. Neale*, NEGOTIATING RATIONALLY**

    26-28, 49, 54, 62-63 (1992)

LISTING OFFERS AS ANCHORS IN NEGOTIATION

With the cooperation of a real estate agent who had just put a house on the market, we asked a number of real estate brokers to evaluate the house. We also asked a separate group of brokers what information they used in valuing a piece of residential real estate and to give us an estimate of how accurately agents could appraise its value. This second group said that any deviation from the appraisal value of more than 5 percent would be highly unusual and easy to recognize.

To give each agent all the information they needed about the house, we created a ten-page packet of information that included (1) the standard Multiple Listing Service (MLS) listing sheet for the property, (2) a copy of the MLS summary of residential real estate sales for both the entire city and the immediate neighborhood of the house for the last six months, (3) information including listing price, square footage, and other characteristics of the property, and other property in the same neighborhood, divided into four categories: property currently for sale, property recently sold, property sold but the sale not complete, and property previously listed that did not sell, and (4) standard MLS listing information for the other property in the immediate neighborhood currently for sale.

We divided up the packets into four groups and changed two pieces of information in each. After having the property independently valued by appraisers, we took their average value and set the listing price 12 percent higher than the appraised value, 4 percent higher, 4 percent lower, or 12 percent lower. We changed the price per square foot so that it correctly reflected the listing price.

When the agents came to

> **How Hot Is It?**
>
> It is important to note that anchors do not even need to be reasonable in order for the effect to be felt. In a study on anchoring, researchers asked participants whether the average temperature in San Francisco was more or less than 558 degrees. They were then asked what they think the actual average temperature is. Those participants who were given the outrageously high number guessed that the temperature was higher than those participants who were given a reasonable number. Scott Plous, The Psychology of Judgment and Decision Making 146 (1993).

evaluate the house (in the normal course of their jobs), we gave them one of the four packets and asked them to estimate (1) the appraised value of the house, (2) an appropriate listing price for the house, (3) a reasonable price to pay for the house, and (4) the lowest offer they would accept if they were the seller. We also asked them to identify from a list the relevant considerations that had gone into their evaluation and briefly describe the process they used to arrive at the four figures.

When we analyzed the data from these real estate agents, we came up with some very interesting results. . . . The listing price had a major impact on their valuation process; they were more likely to have high estimates on all four prices when the listing price was high than when it was low.

When we tried to figure out what information they thought they were using, another interesting pattern emerged. Although it is clear that listing price had played a role in the agents' evaluations of the house, only 19 percent of the agents mentioned listing price as a factor they considered and only 8 percent indicated that listing price was one of their top three considerations. Interestingly, almost three quarters of the agents reported using a computational strategy to assess the value of the real estate. To determine the value of the property, 72 percent of the agents indicated that they took the average price per square foot of comparable houses that had recently sold, multiplied that number by the number of square feet in our property and then adjusted for the condition of the house. If they had, indeed, used such a strategy, then we couldn't have observed any anchoring effect of the listing price; it would have been irrelevant. Nevertheless, the anchoring effect is not only present, it is pronounced.

Research has shown that final agreements in any negotiation are more strongly influenced by initial offers than by the subsequent concessionary behavior of the opponent, particularly when issues under consideration are of uncertain or ambiguous value. Responding to an initial offer with suggested adjustments gives that anchor some measure of credibility. Thus, if an initial offer is too extreme, you need to re-anchor the process. Threatening to walk away from the table is better than agreeing to an unacceptable starting point. . . .

GOALS AS ANCHORS IN NEGOTIATION

Both negotiation and managerial literature emphasize the importance of setting and adhering to goals. Setting specific, challenging goals improves a manager's performance in a negotiation. Just as initial offers can affect your perception of what is possible, goals affect what you think is attainable or even acceptable. In fact, setting challenging goals in a negotiation can help limit the anchoring effect of the other side's initial offer. Goal setting only helps, however, if your goals are set appropriately. Goals themselves can also become anchors, which can either hamper or enhance how you negotiate.

When we set the goals in our studies, we had complete information about the negotiation. In most negotiations, however, managers face large, obvious gaps in what they know about their own priorities or expectations. For goal setting to work to your benefit, the goals you set must sufficiently stretch your performance expectations. Then, even when you adjust those expectations, your subsequent performance remains high.

It's difficult for executives to know just how high to set goals, particularly in a negotiation. Because it's sometimes in your interest to hide certain information, it may be impossible to judge what is or is not a challenging goal prior to the negotiation. Thus, goal setting shares many of the problems associated with the anchoring and adjustment bias.

In a study we conducted, we assigned negotiators one of three levels of goals based on the difficulty of a task. Easy goals were those that could be achieved by 99 percent of the negotiators; challenging goals, by approximately 75 percent of the negotiators; and difficult goals, by less than 5 percent of the negotiators. Once the negotiators had attempted the task, we asked them to assign their own, new goals for the same task. We found that those who were originally assigned harder goals chose easier new goals. In spite of the adjustments, however, the new goals chosen by the easy-goal participants were significantly easier than the new, easier goals chosen by the difficult-goal participants. Thus, the initial goal levels not only anchored current performance but also the setting of goals for future performance.

CONCLUSIONS

In a negotiation, potential anchors are ubiquitous. They can be as relevant as previous contracts or as irrelevant as a random number. Even factors normally associated with improved performance, such as goals, can reduce an executive's effectiveness in a negotiation if not carefully crafted. Don't let an initial anchor minimize the amount of information and the depth of thinking you use to evaluate a situation, and don't give too much weight to an opponent's initial offer too early in the negotiation.

To use anchoring to your advantage, you must decide what initial offer will attract the attention of the other party. It can't be so extreme that the opponent won't even consider it. You want your offer to be attractive enough to your opponent to serve as an anchor for subsequent offers.

You are most susceptible to anchors during the initial stages of a negotiation; don't legitimize an unacceptable initial offer by making a counteroffer. Know enough about the disputed issues to recognize unrealistic anchors. If you prepare before a negotiation and are flexible during that negotiation, you can reduce the adverse impact of anchoring.

Notes and Questions

8.7   If parties can get anchored by information, should you make the first offer in a negotiation? What are the risks? What are the benefits?

8.8   How does the concept of setting aspirations tie in with the concept of anchoring? How can you protect yourself from the anchoring phenomenon? How can lawyers assist their clients in this?

8.9   Researchers argue that a valuable strategy to avoid information barriers "may be to frame questions in a way that encourages disconfirming answers." Scott Plous uses the story of a top analyst at Kidder Peabody who asked questions *the* *opposite* of what he actually believed. "If Freedman thinks the disposable diaper business is becoming less price competitive, for example, he will ask executives a question that implies the opposite such as, 'Is it true that price competition is getting tougher in disposable diapers?' This kind of question makes him more likely than competing analysts to get the real story." Scott Plous, The Psychology of Judgment and Decision Making 239-240 (1993). How can you translate this advice into lawyering?

 Daniel Kahneman & Amos Tversky, **CONFLICT RESOLUTION: A COGNITIVE PERSPECTIVE**

in Barriers to Conflict Resolution 46-47 (Kenneth Arrow et al. eds., 1995)

OPTIMISTIC OVERCONFIDENCE

Overconfidence in human judgment is indicated by a cluster of related findings: uncalibrated assignments of probability that are more extreme than the judge's knowledge can justify, confidence intervals that are too narrow, and nonregressive predictions. Overconfidence is prevalent but not universal, and there are different views of the main psychological processes that produce it. One source of overconfidence is the common tendency to undervalue those aspects of the situation of which the judge is relatively ignorant.

Participants were presented with factual information about several court cases. In each case, the information was divided into three parts: background data, the plaintiff's argument, and the defendant's argument. Four groups of subjects participated in this study. One group received only the background data. Two other groups received the background data and the arguments for one of the two sides, selected at random. The arguments for the plaintiff or the defendant contained no new evidence; they merely elaborated the facts included in the background data. A fourth group was given all the information presented to the jury. The subjects were all asked to predict the percentage of people in the jury who would vote for the plaintiff. The responses of the people who received one-sided evidence were strongly biased in the direction of the information they had received. Although the participants knew that their evidence was one-sided, they were not able to make the proper adjustment. In most cases, those who received all the evidence were more accurate in predicting the jury vote than those who received only one side. However, the subjects in the one-sided condition were generally more confident in their prediction than those who received both sides. Thus, subjects predicted the jury's decision with greater confidence when they had only one-half, rather than all, of the evidence presented to it.

Conflicts and disputes are characterized by the presence of asymmetric information. In general, each side knows a great deal about the evidence and the arguments that support its position and much less about those that support the position of the other side. The difficulty of making proper allowance for missing information, demonstrated in the preceding experiment, entails a bias that is likely to hinder successful negotiation. Each side will tend to overestimate its chances of success, as well as its ability to impose a solution on the other side and to prevent such an attempt by an opponent.... Neale and Bazerman[*] illustrated this effect in the context of a final arbitration procedure, in which the parties submit final offers, one of which is selected by the arbitrator. Negotiators overestimated (by more than 15 percent, on the average) the chance that their offer would be chosen.

Notes and Questions

8.10 Often we worry in negotiation about the lack of information on the part of the negotiators. In a very interesting twist on the problem of information sharing, Ian Ayres and Barry Nalebuff explain the problems of *common knowledge* — both parties having the same information can actually create barriers to resolving the issue. In other words, when someone in the old joke says, "I could tell you, but then I'll kill you," it's actually unclear whether it is the additional information that is the problem or the fact that now both parties *know* that both parties know the information. Ian Ayres & Barry J. Nalebuff, Common Knowledge as a Barrier to Negotiation, 44 UCLA L. Rev. 1631 n.56 (1997).

8.11 For more explanation about how self-serving or egocentric biases can cause impasse, see Linda Babcock & George Loewenstein, Explaining Bargaining Impasses: The Role of Self-Serving Biases, 11 J. Econ. Persp. 109 (1997).

3. Gamesmanship Barriers

I hate to lose more than I like to win.

—Jimmy Connors[†]

This last section discusses the barriers that arise because negotiators are too concerned with winning the "game" of negotiation. Instead of concentrating on their own interests, negotiators become focused on how the other party is doing compared to themselves.

The first excerpt is from Bazerman and Neale's list of common negotiation mistakes begun in the last section. This mistake, the irrational escalation of commitment, occurs when negotiators can't back down — even though it makes rational sense — because they perceive it as "losing" the negotiation.

---

[*] Margaret A. Neale & Max H. Bazerman, The Role of Perspective-Taking Ability in Negotiating Under Different Forms of Arbitration, 36 Indus. & Lab. Rel. Rev. 378 (1983).
[†] Tony Kornheiser, Borg Ends Dominance by Connors, N.Y. Times, Jan. 24, 1977, at 34.

Max H. Bazerman & Margaret A. Neale, NEGOTIATING RATIONALLY

9-11 (1992)

IRRATIONAL ESCALATION OF COMMITMENT

People often behave in ways inconsistent with their own self-interests. One common mistake is to irrationally stay committed to an initial course of action. . . . The desire to "win" at any cost preempts developing a rational negotiation strategy. . . .

Maxwell House and Folgers have battled for over ten years to dominate the U.S. coffee market. In addition to using costly incentives, both companies spent $100 million on coffee advertising in 1990 alone, roughly four times what they spent only three years earlier. This escalation has depressed prices to a level that hurts the entire industry, and neither Maxwell House nor Folgers has significantly improved its market share.

CALVIN AND HOBBES © 1994 Watterson Dist. by UNIVERSAL PRESS SYNDICATE. Reprinted with permission. All rights reserved.

Competition of this type is common. The story of the coffee wars is also the story of the cola wars (Pepsi/Coke) and the camera wars (Polaroid/Kodak). Each side views its goal as beating the other firm as opposed to making the industry more profitable. While the information often exists to pursue a rational end to the conflict, each side sticks with its initial course of action, and catastrophe follows. . . . American coffee makers continue to lose millions of dollars in opportunity costs. Even when conflict is not leading to the desired outcome, decision makers are often obsessed by the small probability that escalating the conflict one step further could lead to victory.

We define *irrational escalation* as continuing a previously selected course of action beyond what rational analysis would recommend. Misdirected persistence can lead to wasting a great deal of time, energy, and money. Directed persistence can lead to commensurate payoffs. Rational analysis enables you to distinguish the two.

You must recognize that the time and money already invested are "sunk costs." They *cannot* be recovered and should *not* be considered when selecting future courses of action. Your reference point for action should be the present. Consider your alternative by evaluating only the *future* costs and benefits associated with each.

This is a hard concept to absorb. Once committed to a course of action, executives often allocate resources in ways that justify their previous choices, whether or not they now appear valid.

The $20 Bill Auction

Imagine you are in a room with thirty people. Someone at the front of the room takes a twenty dollar bill from his or her pocket and announces the following:

I am about to auction off this twenty dollar bill. You are free to participate in the bidding or just watch. People will be invited to call out bids in multiples of one dollar until no further bidding occurs at which point the highest bidder will pay the amount bid and win the twenty dollars. The only feature that distinguishes this auction from traditional auctions is a rule that the second highest bidder must also pay the amount he or she bid, but he or she will obviously not win the twenty. For example if Bill bid $3 and Jane bid $4, and bidding stopped I would pay Jane $16 ($20 less $4) and Bill the second highest bidder would pay me $3.

Would you be willing to bid $1 to start the auction? (Make this decision before reading further.)

We've run this auction with investment bankers, consultants, physicians, professors, partners in Big Six accounting firms, lawyers and assorted other executives. The pattern is always the same. The bidding starts out fast and furious until the bidding reaches the $12 to $16 range. At this point, everyone except the two highest bidders drops out. The two bidders left feel the trap. If one has bid $16 and the other $17 the $16 bidder must either bid $18 or suffer a $16 loss. Bidding further, a choice that might produce a gain if the other person quits, seems more attractive than certain loss, so he or she bids $18. When the bids are $19 and $20, surprisingly, the rationale to bid $21 is very similar to all the previous decisions — you can accept a $19 loss or continue and hope to reduce your loss. Of course, the rest of the group roars with laughter when the bidding goes over $20 — which it nearly always does. Obviously, the bidders are acting irrationally. But what are rational bids?

Skeptical readers should try out the auction on their friends, co-workers or students. Final bids in the $30 to $70 range are common and our most successful auction sold a $20 bill for $407 (the final bids were $204 and $203). We've earned over $10,000 running these auctions in classes over the last four years.

The dollar auction paradigm, first introduced by Martin Shubik, helps explain why people escalate their commitment to a previously selected course of action. Participants naively enter the auction not expecting the bidding to exceed the true value of the object ($20) — "After all, who would bid more than $20 for $20?" The potential gain, coupled with the possibility of "winning" the auction, is reason enough to enter. Once in the auction, it takes only a few extra dollars for the bidder to stay in rather than accept a sure loss. This "reasoning," along with a strong need to justify entering the auction in the first place, keeps most bidders bidding.

Clearly, once someone else bids it creates a problem. A bidder may feel that one more bid may get the other person to quit. If both bidders feel this way, the result can be catastrophic. Yet, without knowing what to expect from the other bidder, continued bidding is not clearly wrong. So what is the bidder's solution?

The key is to recognize the auction as a trap and never make even a very small bid. Successful managers must learn to identify traps. One strategy is to try to consider the decision from the perspective of the other decision maker(s). In the dollar auction, this strategy would quickly tell you that the auction looks just as attractive to other bidders as it does to you. With this knowledge, you can predict what will happen and stay out.

Similar traps exist in business, war and our personal lives. It could be argued that in the Gulf War, Iraq's leader Saddam Hussein had the information necessary to pursue a negotiated settlement rationally. The initial "investment" incurred by invading Kuwait trapped him into further escalating his commitment not to compromise.

The Mythical Fixed-Pie

The best negotiations end in a resolution that satisfies all parties. Such agreements are rare. More commonly, successful negotiations end in trade-offs . . . [w]here each party gives up something of lesser value to them in return for something of greater value to them. Because people often value the multiple issues in a negotiation differently, trade-offs can speed up and improve a conflict's resolution.

A *distributive* negotiation usually involves a single issue — a "fixed-pie" — in which one person gains at the expense of the other. . . . In most conflicts, however, more than one issue is at stake, and each party values the issue differently. The outcomes available are no longer a fixed-pie divided among all parties. An agreement can be found that is better for both parties than what they would have reached through distributive negotiation. This is an *integrative* negotiation.

However, parties in a negotiation often don't find these beneficial trade-offs because each *assumes* its interests *directly* conflict with those of the other party. "What is good for the other side must be bad for us" is a common and unfortunate perspective that most people have. This is the mind-set we call the *mythical* "fixed-pie." . . .

People often fail to solve problems because of the assumptions they place on them. . . . People make an *assumption* that frames the problem, but keeps them from finding a solution. *This is the most critical barrier to creative problem solving.* People tend to make false assumptions about problems to fit them into their previously established expectations. However, successful *creative* solutions often lie outside these self-imposed assumptions. . . .

People who assume mythical fixed-pies will not find mutually beneficial trade-offs. However, consider what can happen even when both parties have identical preferences on a specific issue. . . . Psychologist Leigh Thompson has found that even when the two sides want the same thing, they often settle for a different outcome because they assume that they must compromise to get agreement. "If I want more training, they must not want me to get more training." This leads to what Thompson calls the "incompatibility bias" — the assumption that one side's interests are incompatible with the other's.

The mythical fixed-pie also causes managers to "reactively devalue" any concession simply because it's offered by an adversary.

The Winner's Curse

The famous comedian Groucho Marx said that he didn't want to be a member of any club that would have him as a member. Why? A club's acceptance of his application told him something about its standards — if they were so low as to accept him, he didn't want to join! Most people don't have Groucho's insight, and often make offers in negotiating without realizing the implications of having those offers accepted. Consider the following story:

You are in a foreign country and meet a merchant who is selling a very attractive gem. You've purchased a few gems in your life, but are far from an expert. After some discussion, you make what you're fairly sure is a low offer. The merchant quickly accepts, and the gem is yours. How do you feel?

Most people would feel uneasy. This is known as the "winner's curse." Yet, why would you voluntarily make an offer that you would not want accepted? . . .

There are ways to avoid the winner's curse. Sellers of high quality or reliable goods (new or used) and services can take steps to reassure buyers about their quality. . . .

Obviously, an ongoing relationship between parties can also solve or reduce the winner's curse, since a seller may not want to harm the relationship by taking advantage of a buyer. . . .

Government intervention can also help solve the winner's curse. Some state and local governments have created "lemon laws" in the used-car market to protect buyers and promote trade.

People don't fully realize the true importance of getting accurate information when making transactions. There's great value in a mechanic's unbiased evaluation of a used car, a professional inspector's assessment of a house, or an independent jeweler's assessment of a coveted gem. To protect yourself, you need to develop, borrow, or buy professional expertise to make up for any information you don't have. Many people don't like paying for something (an appraisal) that will probably confirm what they already thought was true. They see this as money for nothing. They would be acting more rationally if they looked at independent appraisals as insurance against buying a lemon, whether it's a car, an overpriced house, or a piece of glass disguising itself as a ruby.

This last excerpt focuses on reactive devaluation, which occurs when we automatically discount an offer made by the other side *because it is an offer made by the other side.*

 ### Lee Ross, REACTIVE DEVALUATION IN NEGOTIATION AND CONFLICT RESOLUTION

in Barriers to Conflict Resolution 28-29, 33-35 (Kenneth Arrow et al. eds., 1995)

One need only pick up the morning newspaper . . . to see that negotiations frequently fail and deadlocks persist even in conflicts where preservation of the status quo clearly seems to be against the best interest of the relevant parties. To some extent, the problem can be traced to barriers — strategic, psychological, or situational — that make it difficult to formulate, and/or get on the table, a proposal that both parties, given their different interests and views and their conflicting strategic goals, deem preferable, at least temporarily, to perpetuation of the status quo. But even when such a "mutually-acceptable-in-principle" proposal *can* be formulated, there may be an additional barrier to be overcome, one that arises, at least in large part, from the dynamics of the negotiation process. This barrier has been termed *reactive devaluation*. It refers to the fact that the very offer of a particular proposal or concession — especially if the offer comes from an *adversary* — may diminish its apparent value or attractiveness in the eyes of the recipient....

Initial evidence for the reactive devaluation barrier was provided in a 1986 sidewalk survey of opinions regarding possible arms reduction by the U.S. and the U.S.S.R. Respondents were asked to evaluate the terms of a simple but sweeping nuclear disarmament proposal — one calling for immediate 50 percent reduction of long-range strategic weapons, to be followed over the next decade and a half by further reduction in both strategic and short-range tactical weapons until, very early in the next century, all such weapons would have disappeared from the two nations' arsenals. As a matter of history, this proposal had actually been made slightly earlier, with little fanfare or impact, by the Soviet leader Gorbachev. In the Stillinger et al. survey,* however, the proposal's putative source was *manipulated* — that is, depending on experimental condition, it was ascribed by the survey instrument either to the Soviet leader, to President Reagan, or to a group of unknown strategy analysts — and only the responses of subjects who claimed to be hearing of the proposal for the first time were included in subsequent analyses.

The results of this survey showed, as predicted, that the proposal's putative authorship determined its attractiveness. When the proposal was attributed to the U.S. leader, 90 percent of respondents thought it either favorable to the U.S. or evenhanded; and when it was attributed to the (presumably neutral) third party, 80 percent thought it either favorable to the U.S. or evenhanded; but when the same proposal was attributed to the Soviet leader, only 44 percent of respondents expressed a similarly positive reaction....

[In the] next set of reactive devaluation studies conducted by Stillinger et al.... the responses contrasted were not ones made to proposals from hostile versus non-hostile sources. In fact, the responses examined were made in reaction to compromise measures offered by a source who was perceived by most recipients as not opposed to their own interests, but merely acting in that source's interests. The context of this research was a campus-wide controversy at Stanford about the university's investment policy. Students generally favored a policy calling for total and immediate divestment by the university of all stock holdings in companies doing business in South Africa. The university, claiming to share the students' opposition to apartheid, but to be constrained by its responsibilities to maximize the value of its portfolio and earnings, set up a committee to study the problem and devise a divestment policy that would be both financially prudent and socially responsible....

In the first such study, students simply were asked to read a booklet describing the divestment controversy, then to evaluate two potential compromise proposals. One of these proposals, which was termed the "Specific Divestment" plan, entailed immediate divestment from corporations doing business with the South African

---

* C. Stillinger, M. Epelbaum, D. Keltner & L. Ross (1990). The "Reactive Devaluation" Barrier to Conflict Resolution. Unpublished manuscript. Stanford: Stanford University.

military or police. The other alternative, termed the "Deadline" plan, proposed to create a committee of students and trustees to monitor "investment responsibility," with the promise of total divestment two years down the road if the committee was not satisfied with the rate of progress shown in dismantling the apartheid system in South Africa. Subjects were randomly assigned to three experimental conditions, identical in all respects except for the particular program that the university was purported to be on the verge of enacting. One group read that the university planned to undertake Specific Divestment; another group read that the university planned to undertake the Deadline plan; and the remainder were given no reason to believe that the university was considering the immediate adoption of either alternative. The experimental hypothesis, of course, was simply that the "offered" concession plan would be devalued relative to the "non-offered" one.

The results obtained in this study seemed once again to offer straightforward evidence for the predicted reactive devaluation phenomenon. That is, students tended to rate whichever of the two proposals the trustees had ostensibly offered as a smaller less significant compromise than the alternative, non-offered, proposal. Thus, when Stanford purportedly was ready to implement the Deadline plan, 85 percent of the respondents ranked Specific Divestment as a bigger concession than the Deadline. By contrast, when the university purportedly was ready to pursue Specific Divestment, only 40 percent rated Specific Divestment as the more consequential of the two compromise plans. Not surprisingly, when neither concession plan was purported to be imminent, the percentage of students rating Specific Divestment as a bigger and more significant concession than the Deadline plan was between the extremes in the two experimental conditions — i.e., 69 percent. Clearly, the "offered" versus "non-offered" status of the relevant divestment plans influenced the student respondents' evaluation of their apparent significance and attractiveness.

To the extent that adversaries devalue the compromises and concessions put on the table by the other side, they exacerbate an already difficult dilemma: that of forging an agreement that the relevant parties, with their differing views of history and their differing perceptions of entitlement, will perceive to be better than the status quo and not offensive to their sense of equity. Beyond alerting us to this dilemma, the Stillinger et al. studies raise two important, ultimately related, questions. First, what processes or mechanisms might cause the offer of a concession or compromise proposal to decrease its attractiveness in the eyes of the recipient? Second, what steps might be taken, either by the adversaries themselves or by third-party mediators, to overcome this barrier? . . .

One set of underlying processes involves changes in *perception, interpretation*, or *inference*, either about individual elements in a proposal or about the overall valence of that proposal. To the extent that the other side's initiative seems inconsistent with our understanding of their interests and/or past negotiation behavior, we are apt, perhaps even logically obliged, to scrutinize their offer rather carefully. That is, we are inclined to look for ambiguities, omissions, or "fine print" that might render the terms of that proposal more advantageous to the other side, and perhaps less advantageous to our side, than we had assumed them to be (or would have assumed them to be, had the question been asked) prior to their being offered. The results of such skeptical scrutiny — especially if the terms in question are unclear, complex, or imperfectly specified, and especially if trust vis-à-vis implementation of these terms is called for—are apt to be a revised assessment of what we stand to gain, both in absolute terms and relative to what we believe the other side stands to gain, from acceptance of the relevant proposal.

This process of inference and deduction, as psychologists would be quick to note, could be even simpler and less cognitively demanding.... [N]o reinterpretation, in fact no consideration of content at all, need take place for devaluation to occur. One might simply reason if "they" are offering a proposal it must be good for them; and if it is good for them (especially if "they" are adversaries who wish us harm) it must be bad for "us."... One can be led to conclude that any proposal offered by the "other side"—especially if that other side has long been perceived as an enemy—*must* be to our side's disadvantage, or else it would not have been offered. Such an inferential process, however, assumes a perfect opposition of interests, or in other words, a true "zero-sum" game, when such is rarely the case in real world negotiations between parties whose needs, goals, and opportunities are inevitably complex and varied.

The second type of underlying process or mechanism, suggested by demonstrations of the devaluation phenomenon in the Stanford divestment studies in which the source of the devalued proposal was not really an enemy of the recipient, is very different. This mechanism involves neither mindful nor mindless changes in interpretation, but rather changes in underlying *preferences*. Human beings, at least in some circumstance, may be inclined to reject or devalue whatever is freely available to them, and to covet and strive for whatever is denied them. Moreover, they may be inclined to do so even when no hostility is perceived on the part of the individual or institution determining what will or will not be made available.... The familiar aphorism that "the grass is always greener on the other side of the fence" captures this source of human unhappiness and frustration very well, and it is easy to think of anecdotal examples in which children or adults, rather than "counting their blessings," seem to place inordinately high value on whatever commodity or opportunity is denied them....

Notes and Questions

8.12 A couple plans to buy a car for the husband's parents, who live in New York. They research the car cost very carefully, know there is a year-end sale, and even talk to a friend who is a dealer in Wisconsin about the best price they could negotiate. When they arrive in New York, they also talk to a friend who had just purchased the same model to confirm the price she paid. They again call their friend in Wisconsin to check the price. In fact, he says that he cannot match that price. (He wonders out loud whether the company bonuses for dealers in New York are more than in Wisconsin.) So the couple walks into a New York dealership and asks for $200 under the price paid by their friend in New York several weeks before. They say that they would buy the car today if the dealer meets their price. The dealer checks with the manager and then agrees. The wife is thrilled. The husband worries for weeks that if the dealer took their opening price, the dealer would have taken less. What has happened?

8.13 In one study on reactive devaluation, the authors examined whether face-to-face negotiations (versus the original work in reactive devaluation where students were just presented with a proposal) would change negotiator's evaluations of their own or their opponent's proposals. In these face-to-face negotiations between a financial aid loan officer and student, the loan officer devalued proposals made by students; however, contrary to reactive devaluation theory, students did not devalue the proposals made by the loan officers. The authors note that while more studies are needed, perhaps the discussion in advance of proposals and the face-to-face interactions mitigate the effects of reactive devaluation. Jared R. Curhan, Margaret A. Neale & Lee Ross, Dynamic Valuation: Preference Changes in the Context of Face-to-Face Negotiation, 40 J. Experimental Psychol. 142 (2004).

8.14 During the 1980s, South Carolina Congressman Floyd Spence stated, "I have had a philosophy for some time in regard to SALT [Strategic Arms Limitation Treaty], and it goes like this: the Russians will not accept a SALT . . . that is not in their best interest, and it seems to me that if it is in their best interest, it can't be in our best interest." Max H. Bazerman & Margaret A. Neale, Negotiating Rationally 19 (1992). Does this make sense?

8.15 How is reactive devaluation linked to the strategic barriers discussed above in the section on informational barriers?

8.16 How is reactive devaluation linked to the concept of role reversal discussed previously in Chapter 7 on understanding the other side?

8.17 Can you think of an instance where, in negotiating with a parent or other authority figure, you automatically dismissed an otherwise "good" offer?

8.18 A phenomenon related to reactive devaluation is an elevated willingness to accept proposals — regardless of their objective or rational value or cost — if the proposal comes from someone loved or admired. Are there some people to whom you say "yes" before hearing even what they propose? Knowing that negotiators can gain power from being liked and trusted, how would that influence your strategy as an attorney negotiator?

B. PLEA BARGAINING

This next section briefly examines the impact of "rational actor" negotiation theory and the psychological barriers we have just covered as applied to criminal law. Most importantly, the authors note below that plea bargaining differs in crucial ways from civil settlement done "in the shadow of the law" and that many of the psychological factors we have discussed actually do *not* seem to explain plea bargains.

Richard Birke discusses his own experience as a prosecutor who then became a negotiation scholar and discovered the disconnect between what he knew as a former prosecutor and what theory was supposed to "teach" him.

❖❖ *Richard Birke,* RECONCILING LOSS AVERSION AND GUILTY
PLEAS

1999 Utah L. Rev. 205, 207-209, 209-210

For nearly five years I worked as a state prosecutor. I negotiated thousands of pleas. I believe that my experience as a prosecutor was typical. From 1986 until 1991, I was an assistant district attorney in Middlesex County, Massachusetts. At its height, my active caseload exceeded 400 cases, and my supervisors assigned new cases to me on a daily basis. In a busy week, I might receive as many as 40 new cases.

In order to keep from being inundated to incapacity, I had to terminate or dispose of a great many cases. I disposed of the bulk of my large caseload by plea bargaining and making agreements with defendants (through their defense counsel) about both charges and punishment. I went to trial on a small percentage of my caseload — less than 10% — and trying this small percentage of my caseload accounted for more than 75% of my time at work. I dismissed a tiny handful of cases when circumstances warranted, but for the most part my cases terminated with plea-bargained agreements between the defendants and me. I think that my situation was (and remains) typical of the life of a prosecutor. I thought that my colleagues and I rarely offered to the defendants deals that were better than what the defendants could expect after trial. Nonetheless, defendants pled in great numbers.

I later had the pleasure to work for the late Professor of Psychology Amos Tversky. . . .

I asked Professor Tversky why, if criminals were loss averse, they would plead guilty and accept the certain loss attendant to punishment. Professor Tversky's response was that every decision maker is loss averse, and criminals must be getting "good deals" that make the plea bargain a sensible thing to do. With all due respect for Amos Tversky, I do not think this is the correct explanation.

I believe that my fellow prosecutors and I, by and large, offered the defendants mediocre deals and that we were skilled at making the deals look better than they were. Defendants accepted these deals despite loss aversion, not because they were good deals, but rather because they were led by their attorneys to believe that they were good deals.

Judges and prosecutors placed a constant and systematic pressure on defense attorneys to make their clients plead guilty. This pressure led defense attorneys to frame plea offers in ways that made the offers look better than they were — good enough to overcome loss aversion and culminate in pleas.

In the eight years since I stopped prosecuting and studied decision making under a variety of conditions, I have become increasingly convinced that the rate of pleas is a symptom of a breakdown in the criminal justice system. . . .

Decision makers tend to seek risk in the domain of losses. When confronted with the choice of accepting losses or taking risks that might avoid the losses, decision makers are more likely to gamble in order to avoid losses than they would be under normal circumstances. Moreover, decision makers demonstrate an even greater pre-disposition to choose risk when facing the prospect of sure losses.

Plea bargaining, however, appears to contradict this well-established principle of cognitive psychology. When apprehended and offered plea bargains, criminals face the choice of accepting a certain loss of liberty or property or taking a risk and going to trial. In the vast majority of cases, defendants accept the certain loss. More than ninety percent of criminal cases in America end not with verdicts, but when defendants make plea agreements with prosecutors, waive their right to trial, and plead guilty to a judge. This behavior violates the tendency to seek risk in the domain of losses. Given the overwhelming evidence that loss aversion operates in every facet of decision making, a reason or set of reasons must exist to explain why criminal defendants so readily accept sure losses and willingly waive gambles that might avoid these losses.

This Article proposes and examines four hypotheses that attempt to reconcile the rate of guilty pleas and the principle of loss aversion. All four theories present potential answers to the question of why, if criminals are as risk seeking in the domain of losses as the general population, they plead guilty and waive the right to trial. The first hypothesis suggests that the plea bargains that defendants are offered may reflect sufficient discounts from the expected post-trial punishment, such that even risk-seeking defendants are maximizing utility in accepting pleas; in other words, the expected value of the plea exceeds that of a trial — even when adjusted for risk preference. Simply put, the defendants are getting deals too good to refuse. The second hypothesis proposes that defendants are making mistakes, accepting plea bargains that produce equivalent or lower utility than would trials. Defendants accept these "bad deals" either because they lack accurate information about the values of the pleas and the trials and are unable to make good choices, or they lack the competence to make intelligent, utility-maximizing choices. The third hypothesis assumes that defendants do not perceive punishment as a loss, in which case principles of loss aversion would not apply to the plea bargaining scenario. If decision makers seek risk when facing losses, then in the absence of loss, the failure to seek risk is not surprising. The fourth and final hypothesis suggests that the class of criminal defendants may be uniformly risk averse, in which case the rate of plea bargains simply reflects their predisposition to favor sure losses to risky choices; in other words, criminal defendants may never seek risk — even in the domain of losses. . . .

I support the explanation of the second hypothesis, that defendants make mistakes in accepting plea agreements. Specifically, I argue that the most convincing basis for why defendants plead guilty despite loss aversion is that defendants *are* risk seeking in the domain of losses, that they *are not* offered sufficiently "good deals" to warrant their risk-averse behavior, but rather, that institutional pressures cause defense attorneys to induce pleas from their clients in two different ways. First, the attorneys provide information about the expected value of trial that is too rudimentary to present an accurate picture to the defendant of the value of trial. Second, the attorneys frame prosecutorial offers in ways that cause defendants to perceive the value of pleas to be much better than they really are — either as gains instead of losses, or as higher in expected value than they really are. In short, the criminal justice system coerces defense attorneys into providing information to their clients that leads their clients to make poor choices.

Notes and Questions

8.19   In an important article, Stephanos Bibas analyzes how the above barriers operate within the structure of the criminal justice system. Stephanos Bibas, Plea Bargaining Outside the Shadow of Trial, 117 Harv. L. Rev. 2463 (2004) (suggesting that the distortions away from rational decision making are even stronger in the criminal context with poor lawyering, agency costs, and lawyers' self-interest preventing decisions about whether to plead guilty from being rationally or "legally" based). William Stuntz, in his response to Bibas, agrees with Bibas's conclusion that despite what one may be inclined to believe, plea bargaining in criminal law does not operate in the shadow-of-law but rather the shadow of the prosecutor.

> [I]n a variety of ways and for a variety of reasons, criminal settlements do *not* efficiently internalize the law. . . . [Bibas's] basic claim — that there are serious impediments to efficient bargaining in criminal cases — is true and important. His article makes a substantial contribution to our understanding of how the strange and inefficient market for plea bargains works, or fails to.
>
> There is, though, a deeper problem with plea bargains, one that goes squarely to the relationship between those bargains and the bodies of law that define crimes and sentences. The problem is that law's effect on plea bargaining is much smaller than conventional wisdom would have it. For some crimes, the law may have *no* effect at the margin. That is quite different from the world of civil settlements. In employment discrimination or products liability cases, a change in the governing legal rules (either liability rules or remedies) is certain to have some effect on settlements, and the effects are, at least in rough measure, predictable. In criminal cases, by contrast, the definition of the relevant crime or the applicable sentence can change dramatically yet leave plea bargains unaffected.
>
> This difference between civil and criminal settlements stems from a difference between the bodies of law that govern civil and criminal cases. Civil laws define obligations; those obligations in turn define litigation outcomes. Parties bargain in the shadow of those outcomes, hence in the law's shadow. Some of criminal law works like that. But for the most part, criminal law and the law of sentencing define prosecutors' options, not litigation outcomes. They are not rules in the shadow of which litigants must bargain. Rather, they are items on a menu from which the prosecutor may order as she wishes. She has no incentive to order the biggest meal possible. Instead, her incentive is to get whatever meal she wants, as long as the menu offers it. The menu does not define the meal; the diner does. The law-on-the-street — the law that determines who goes to prison and for how long — is chiefly written by prosecutors, not by legislators or judges. . . .
>
> While civil settlements ordinarily internalize the governing law, there is no reason to assume that most plea bargains do. The shadow the law casts on plea

bargaining is different for different crimes and different at the federal and state levels. For many crimes, law's shadow may disappear altogether. For those crimes, plea bargains take place in the shadow of prosecutors' preferences, voters' preferences, budget constraints, and other forces — but not in the shadow of the law.

> William J. Stuntz, Plea Bargaining and Criminal Law's Disappearing Shadow, 117 Harv. L. Rev. 2548, 2548-2550 (2004).

8.20 How do the psychological barriers explained earlier in this chapter seem to impact plea bargaining? Do we think that accused criminals are more rational actors than other negotiators?

8.21 Are the structural reasons for why plea bargaining does not work like other civil negotiations sufficient to explain the differences? What else might explain the differences outlined above?

8.22 Do the arguments made above seem to argue in favor of changing the plea bargaining system? How could these changes occur?

8.23 As the above articles note, plea bargaining is highly problematic. One author has proposed mediating pleas as a way to improve the system. Brandon J. Lester, System Failure: The Case for Supplanting Negotiation with Mediation in Plea Bargaining, 20 Ohio St. J. on Disp. Resol. 563, 563-566 (2005).

C. STRATEGIES FOR RECOGNIZING AND RESPONDING TO NEGOTIATION BARRIERS AND DILEMMAS

This section focuses on how to deal with some of the more difficult situations that might occur in a negotiation. The fear of being taken advantage of is a salient one for young lawyers about to go out and practice on their own. Knowing how to deal with tactics will go a long way toward enabling attorneys to maintain a problem-solving focus when that makes sense and to know when it is necessary to leave problem solving behind. See Robert S. Adler, Flawed Thinking: Addressing Decision Biases in Negotiation, 20 Ohio St. J. on Disp. Resol. 683 (2005).

The first excerpt provides some advice for dealing with offensive comments whether or not they are used as a tactic in the negotiation.

 Andrea Kupfer Schneider, **EFFECTIVE RESPONSES TO OFFENSIVE COMMENTS**

10 Negot. J. 107, 110-113 (1994)

ASSESSING THE MOTIVATION

A useful tool for analyzing the motive of an offensive comment is a modified version of the decision tree analysis. . . . [This tool is explained in Chapter 2.] If the comment does not betray bias (i.e., we have found another satisfactory explanation for it) then we do not respond. In the first step, we tried to assess our own assumptions and adjust for them. In this second step, we look at the other side's understanding of the comment and analyze how they perceive it. The focus of the inquiry has thus turned to the speaker.

If you have determined that the comment was indeed one motivated by bias, the next question is to ask if it was made consciously or unconsciously. The distinction between a conscious comment and unconscious one is important. Many "tough" negotiators use derogatory comments regularly as a form of gamesmanship. Such comments may indeed stem from their usual strategy of belittling the other side. If the person is biased, then the comment may come from a conscious decision to denigrate you, with the intent of interfering with your effectiveness as a negotiator.

Your response to someone who is consciously using bias as a tactic should be different from that made to someone who made the comment out of a lack of awareness or even out of well-intentioned curiosity. An inappropriate response (e.g., aggressively confronting someone about their insensitivity and discrimination when they had no idea you would find the comment offensive) may not be useful either for their edification or your effectiveness in the negotiation. A common reaction in that situation is for the other side to become defensive and deny that anyone could ever find the comment offensive. This rarely moves the negotiation further.

Conscious use of derogatory commentary can be either tactical or malevolent. While the majority of negotiators use such comments or questions as tactics, there are those in the world who say nasty things to others because it brings them pleasure. If you believe you are dealing with this type of person, a different response might be warranted than one you would make to someone using commentary for tactical advantage who may or may not believe substantively in what they are saying.

If you determine that the comment was unconscious, you can then ask yourself whether it stems from prejudice or ignorance. Ignorance implies a situation that can be remedied through education ("Perhaps you did not realize I am very sensitive about my increasing baldness."). Prejudice, on the other hand, implies a long-standing predetermination against another group.

RESPONDING

There are four major responses a negotiator can make to an offensive comment — ignoring, confronting, deflecting, or engaging. The response you choose should be based on a number of factors, including an analysis of your own assumptions and the other side's motivation for making such a comment.

Other factors — such as whether there is an audience for the comment, whether it has been repeated over time, and how much the comment personally offends you — may also be important. But the question of most significance in these situations is: What is your purpose in responding and what do you hope to achieve?

The response of ignoring the comment needs little explanation — you choose not to respond in any way. Many people end up doing this automatically in response to a comment that makes them uncomfortable. Instead, ignoring a comment should be a conscious, affirmative decision by you that either the comment does not bother you that much or it is just not worth your time and effort to deal with it.

Similarly, the response of confronting the comment is also relatively simple theoretically. Confronting is a counterattack either on the person or the comment (e.g., "That's racist! How can you say that?" or "What a stupid thing to say!"). This response should also be a conscious one, a response made to achieve a purpose, not a response made just because you cannot think of anything else to say. At times, confronting is wholly appropriate and is often a highly useful response, particularly with bullies.

Deflecting means acknowledging the comment and moving on. For example, in response to someone who is bragging about his or her grandiose office space compared with yours (which could be interpreted as demeaning), you might respond, "Yes, your office is lovely and perhaps we might now move to the subject at hand." ... Deflecting, more than any other response, is a question of personal style and comfort level. It often demands a sense of humor and even quicker thinking than other responses.

Engaging is the fourth type of response one can make to an inflammatory remark. Engaging means having a conversation about the other side's purpose in making the remark and your feelings upon hearing it. First, you check your assumptions about their intentions by asking what their purpose was in making the comment. After they respond, you can gather additional data about their intentions and ask further questions. Finally, when you think that you understand their point of view and also have demonstrated the ability to listen to them, you share your perceptions. Explain your reaction and your reasoning (e.g., "when I hear that comment, I usually assume ... and it makes me feel, think, etc. ... "). ...

Engaging the other side with regard to the objectionable comment has several advantages over the other responses. Since engaging follows a pattern, it can be a learned skill. Having a practiced reaction to a comment that throws you off balance in a negotiation can be a great advantage. Engaging also gives you more time to think since you are asking questions — another advantage when you are surprised.

Engaging allows you the opportunity to check your perceptions and assumptions once again. ...

Since engaging is nonconfrontational, it is more appropriate for professional and long-term relationships. Engaging allows both you and the other side to rethink assumptions without escalating the conflict. The two of you can *agree* that there was a misunderstanding and move on to the substance of the negotiation rather than continue to *disagree* about the comment and each other's worth as a person. It is better for the relationship than confronting since it may provide each side with a way out of the conflict. It is also better than ignoring the comment if the comment will fester within you and color your future interactions.

Using the structure outlined above, this section will outline a variety of responses to tactics.

1. Deflect — Change the Subject

One way of dealing with tactics is to change the subject or ignore the tactic. There is no reason that you have to respond directly to the other side. For example, they could say: "It's $15,000 for the (used) car, take it or leave it." You can say: "Let's take a look at some creative options. Are you willing to guarantee its performance for the first year?" They might say: "You're incompetent" and you could say: "So, tell me about your client." They say: "What's the lowest you'll take?" You can say: "Very funny! Why don't we talk about the car first?"

You can also use silence as a powerful tool. If they use a tactic, don't respond at all. After sitting quietly for even 30 seconds (try this and see how uncomfortable it is!), the other side might come back with a better offer or a more appropriate approach. You should also use silence after asking questions to keep the subject where you want it. Once you have asked a question or made an offer, be quiet! A common mistake negotiators can make is to bid against themselves. Avoid this mistake by being sure that they answer your question or make a counteroffer before you speak again.

2. Confront — Play Their Game

The first response that many negotiators take when faced with a positional negotiator and someone engaged in tactics is to play their game. If you can play the game well and are in a strong position in the negotiation, this can work out well. This is similar to the bully on the playground who, once he sees that intimidation will not work, may decide to try another tack. Of course, the risk with responding in kind is the escalation that can occur. In the game of chicken, the other car might swerve to get out of your way, but you could end up crashing.

If you choose to play their game, you reciprocate their tactics. If they commit high, you commit low. If they threaten to sue (go to their BATNA), you respond that you are looking forward to court. If they insult you, you insult them. You could also respond positionally but in a different manner. For example, they make a high offer, and you respond, "After our long relationship, your offer is an insult!"

3. Confront — Name Their Game

A third very effective method of dealing with tactics is to "name their game" or talk explicitly about the impact of their tactics on the negotiation. For example, if they have opened with a very low bid, you could respond, "You've taken a very low figure. That's often an anchoring tactic." If they are yelling, you could respond, "When you raise your voice, it looks like you're trying to intimidate me." If they seem to be avoiding making a clear commitment, you could respond, "You keep changing the subject. Why?"

This is also an opportunity to use humor in recognizing their tactic. "Oh you guys aren't going to try the good-guy/bad-guy routine, are you?" In response to an insult, you could respond, "Is that all you've got? I've been called much worse!" The use of humor depends both on how fast you think on your feet and how comfortable you are in the situation. For many of us, our funniest responses only come to us after we've left the tense situation. For others, humor can be a very effective tool in dealing with the tactics.

Finally, you could also recognize their tactics and offer another way out of the situation. You could negotiate over the process of your negotiation. For example, you could say, "I think that just trading offers is unhelpful. . . . Why don't you first tell me what you want and why it is important to your client? Then I can do the same. After that, we can exchange numbers."

4. Ignore — Change Participants

If you find you cannot deal with this person or that he cannot make the decision you need, you may be able to find another decision maker. Go to another car dealership. Ask the other side to take this offer back to his client anyway. Find out if your senior partner would be willing to contact the senior partner on the other side. Often, businesspeople will kick out the lawyers in order to make a deal. While you never want to be the lawyer kicked out (!), you may need to suggest this to your client if you feel the lawyer on the other side is the barrier.

5. Change the Game to Problem Solving

A final way of handling tactics is to convince the other side to engage in problem solving. You can do this more explicitly by negotiating over the rules (as discussed above), and you can also do this by asking questions that steer the negotiation in a problem-solving way. Positional and tactical negotiating usually focus on commitment (what they will or will not take), *your* BATNA (they try to persuade you how bad it is), and one-way communication (me, me, me). To play a different game, you would try to get them to talk about

- Their real interests and your interests;
- What creative options you could come up with;
- What objective criteria there is in order to judge the fairness of a settlement;
- *Their* BATNA (why it makes sense for them to settle);
- The relationship between the parties and the two attorneys; and
- The communication between both of you.

In order to do this, you need to reframe their positions into the elements of problem-solving negotiations:

a. Listen for interests behind their positions. Ask why this is important. How will their proposal help them? Why couldn't they do X?
b. When they state a position, treat that position as one potential option among many others you can discuss. "You will not settle for less than $25,000? Well, let's write that down as one option. There are probably other things that would make your client happy?"

c. Listen for standards embedded within positions (i.e., "We could never accept less than market value."). Also turn the conversation to standards by asking why that is fair. You can also communicate what would persuade you: "If you could guarantee that this contract price is the market rate. . . ."

d. You can also remind them of the effect that positional bargaining might have on the relationship between the clients or between the two of you. "I am not sure how your 'take-it-or-leave-it' approach is going to help our clients operate under this contract for the next ten years."

Notes and Questions

8.24 Think back to an annoying comment someone once made to you. How did you judge whether the comment was intentional? What do you think was the motivation? How did you deal with it? What other ways could you have dealt with it?

8.25 When is it a good idea to play the other side's game? Why do we find this a satisfying response in many cases? What are the risks? In what contexts does this not make sense?

8.26 In what negotiation situations can you take advantage of changing participants? Or add or subtract a party? When is this strategy most useful?

8.27 At the beginning of a negotiation, the attorney on the other side says to you, "When I passed you out in the hallway earlier, I just assumed that you were a paralegal. I am surprised that your supervisors felt a new lawyer would be able to handle this difficult situation without becoming too nervous. Do you want to defer this negotiation and have someone come with you to help you negotiate?" What would you do?

8.28 In a medical malpractice suit where your client is being sued, the other side states that they will not settle for less than $50,000. How do you turn this statement into a conversation about interests? About options? About criteria?

The following excerpts deal with competitive tactics and give advice on how to transform those situations into problem-solving or collaborative negotiations.

Robert S. Adler & Elliot M. Silverstein, WHEN DAVID MEETS GOLIATH: DEALING WITH POWER DIFFERENTIALS IN NEGOTIATIONS

5 Harv. Negot. L. Rev. 1, 92-103 (2000)

I. IDENTIFY AND COUNTER POWER PLOYS

Perhaps the most commonly cited reason given by our students for taking a course about negotiation is to learn how to use and to counter bargaining "tricks" and "ploys." . . . The number of potential ploys is enormous, leading some, we fear, to conclude that those who learn the largest number of tricks will "win" the negotiation. We disagree. Although one should certainly be alert for power ploys and tricks, we remain skeptical that most can prove successful against negotiators who have planned carefully and who have thought out their strategies thoroughly.

Most power ploys and tricks aim to gain a psychological advantage. Some do so by tricking opponents into lowering their guards and revealing valuable information; others seek to intimidate or disorient adversaries so that they lose focus and open themselves to exploitation; still others attempt to maneuver other parties to negotiate against themselves, i.e., to engage in a series of unilateral offers that are not reciprocated. We briefly describe below several of the more commonly used ploys and then offer some suggestions for countering them.

1.   Intimidating Atmosphere

Because negotiation power arises from perceptions, those who effectively manage the image they present can substantially enhance their leverage when they bargain. . . . They dress in "power" clothing, they work in large, elegant offices, and they sprinkle their discussion with important names and events with which they have personal connections. Other more aggressive measures include: insisting that meetings be held on one's home turf, scheduling meetings for inconvenient times, seating opponents in uncomfortable chairs, seating opponents with the sun in their faces, making opponents wait for extended periods for meetings to start, interrupting meetings with "important" phone calls to impress or intimidate opponents, engaging in side conversations that demonstrate "toughness" while knowing that one's opponents are overhearing the conversations, or asserting that certain issues are "nonnegotiable."

Perhaps the most effective way to deal with these annoying ploys is to act confidently and ignore them. In some cases, however, it may be necessary to take specific steps to counter them. In most cases, merely identifying the tactic and asking that it cease will put an end to the ploy. For example, if one has been kept waiting for a meeting to start, one might pleasantly, but firmly, inform the other side that one does not appreciate being kept waiting and ask whether future meetings will start late.

2.   "Good Guy/Bad Guy"

One of the most widely recognizable power ploys, the so-called "good guy/bad guy" technique, appears to command a large following despite the fact that its use rarely surprises any of those subjected to it. . . .

Despite the popularity of the ploy, we know of no empirical research demonstrating that it produces anything other than annoyed or amused reactions among those subjected to it. . . .

3.   Anger, Threats and the Madman's Advantage

We can think of no greater deal breaker than runaway emotions. In fact, we suspect that as many negotiations terminate because of lost tempers and hurt feelings as from irreconcilable goals. . . .

Effective responses to anger vary widely. If an opponent's anger has disoriented a negotiator, it makes sense to call a break in the negotiation in order to give both sides an opportunity to regain their composure. In some cases, ignoring the temper tantrum can embarrass and quiet the angry opponent. In other instances, responding with a temper display of one's own can lead the angry opponent to abandon the approach. . . .

4. Boulwarism, or "Take-It-or-Leave-It"

The "take-it-or-leave-it" approach to bargaining undoubtedly goes back to antiquity, but seems to have been refined to an unprecedented degree by Lemuel R. Boulware, head of labor relations for General Electric from the late 1940s through the late 1960s. Prior to each labor negotiation, Boulware would meticulously research the company's productivity, the cost of living, and other financial factors and then would enter each negotiation with a fixed — and what he believed, fair — offer to the union. Thereafter, Boulware would invite the union to examine his analysis, but would not budge from this number unless his facts and figures were shown to be incorrect. This take-it-or-leave-it approach worked for nearly twenty years until G.E.'s thirteen unions joined forces and undertook a long and costly strike against the practice. Simultaneously, they filed a complaint with the National Labor Relations Board alleging that Boulware's approach constituted a failure to bargain in good faith and obtained a ruling that this approach violated the National Labor Relations Act.

What made Boulwarism unique compared to many other take-it-or-leave-it negotiations is that Boulware *opened* the bargaining with the "final" offer. Although the unions put up with this approach for many years, ultimately it led to intense labor strife. The reason, we suspect, was that the approach appeared to be arrogant and demeaning. Most people have a need to play a role in the final outcome of a deal. . . .

To counter a "take-it-or-leave-it" approach, one needs first to probe the underlying assumptions of the party who has made such a statement to see whether such assumptions can be disproved. . . . One should also assess the commitment that the other side has made to a take-it-or-leave-it approach. . . . If the other side seems emotionally committed to the approach at the moment, calling a halt to the proceedings may permit both sides to return at a later date and re-commence negotiations. Further, depending on the circumstances, one might appeal to the other side's sense of fairness, asking how a deal can ever be struck if one side becomes or remains intransigent. Finally, if the other side refuses to budge, one needs to consider in as calm a fashion as possible, whether accepting the offer is better than walking away. If this negotiation is the beginning of a long-term relationship, one needs to assess the precedential value of agreeing to this type of offer. . . .

5. Limited Authority

Those who bargain with "limited" authority present a power paradox. That is, the less authority they carry in bargaining, the greater their power actually may be. . . .

We recommend several responses to these "limited authority" ploys. In some cases, a useful reaction is to request a meeting with the individual who has been identified as having the authority to reach an agreement on the terms that one seeks. In cases where one suspects that the other side truly has adequate authority, one might simply continue negotiating as though the other person had adequate authority, all the while insisting that one retains the right to modify one's own offer so long as the other side has not committed to the deal. The key to most authority issues is to avoid becoming either legally or psychologically committed while the other side remains free to reject or modify the deal.

A final word of advice: negotiators who face bargaining with high power opponents should seriously consider entering the talks with some limits on their own authority. This will give them time to ponder offers made by the other side and may well moderate the heavy pressures exerted by the other side to reach an agreement.

6.   Artificial and Actual Deadlines

Time limits in negotiation can arise in a number of ways. The parties can set them or an outside authority can do so. Time limits may be explicit or implicit, and they may be flexible or rigid. A solid body of research confirms that deadlines often play a significant role in leading parties to agreements. Deadlines increase the likelihood of favorable deals because, as time grows short, "bargaining aspirations, demands, and the amount of bluffing that occurs" diminish substantially. . . .

Negotiating under a deadline requires skill, persistence, patience, and brinkmanship to be successful. Because deadlines can help as well as hurt weaker negotiators, we cannot offer a "one remedy fits all" suggestion. When facing deadlines, one needs constantly to weigh the benefits of agreeing versus not agreeing. One particularly needs to monitor the other side to see how much harm they will suffer, or how much benefit they will receive, from the deadline. Those who suspect that the other side is playing the deadline game, need to call the opponent on the tactic and indicate that one's flexibility will lessen as the time approaches. . . .

7.   Other Power Ploys and General Responses

It is not possible — nor is it necessary in our view — to devise specific counterploys to the entire multitude of tricks and tactics that an opponent might attempt to perpetrate in a negotiation. Instead, we offer several general thoughts to consider when powerful opponents use annoying or unethical tactics:

Negotiate about the negotiation: Try to agree on how the negotiation will be conducted. For example, the parties might agree that only one person at a time will be permitted to get angry or that no personal attacks will be permitted.

Ignore the ploy: Recognizing that an opponent is engaged in a negotiation "trick" is often sufficient to render it ineffective. One can then simply take quiet steps to deflect whatever the ploy is.

Call the ploy: Sometimes it is useful to call one's opponent on the ploy as a way of showing that one recognizes the trick and will not be either intimidated or taken in by it.

Halt the negotiation: Sometimes one should simply leave the room when a ploy is being attempted as a way of stopping it. . . .

Robert S. Adler, Benson Rosen & Elliot M. Silverstein, HOW TO
MANAGE FEAR AND ANGER

14 Negot J. 161, 168-174 (1998)

Two millennia ago, poet and satirist Horace wrote *Ira furor brevis est* — anger is a short
madness. When we become truly furious, we may act in an utterly irrational way for a
period of time. Although a temper tantrum may relieve pent-up feelings for a
moment, we often find regret and negative recriminations following such displays.
On this point, Queen Elizabeth I reportedly observed, "anger makes dull men witty,
but it also keeps them poor." . . .

   In the negotiation context, a host of factors can contribute to anger and aggression: . . . where bargainers are accountable to angry constituents; where bargainers
face time pressures; where they perceive the situation as win-lose with divergent
goals between the parties; or, generally, where the parties are otherwise unconcerned
with protecting a working relationship. In a study of anger in mergers and acquisitions, . . . other types of behavior [are] likely to trigger anger: misrepresentations;
making excessive demands; overstepping one's authority; showing personal animos-
ity; questioning a representative's authority to negotiate; seeking to undermine a
representative's authority by "going over his head"; and dwelling on unimportant
details. There are occasions when anger, legitimately expressed, can play a positive
role in producing agreement — for example, when it helps persuade others because it
demonstrates intensity and sincerity of a position. . . . On the other hand, this emotion often injects a sour note into the proceeding, impeding agreement. Anger does
this in at least three ways: it clouds our objectivity because we lose trust in the other
side; it narrows our focus from broad topics to the anger-producing behavior; and it
misdirects our goals from reaching agreement to retaliating against the offender. . . .

   [N]egotiators can take steps to control the excesses of anger and to manage it to
productive ends. What follows is a series of observations and recommendations for
doing so.

DEALING WITH YOUR ANGER

The critical need for self-awareness. Virtually all researchers and commentators on
emotions and negotiations insist that the first step necessary in controlling anger is
self-awareness. If we cannot sense when our anger has been aroused, we will miss any
opportunity to control it. Anger typically has physical manifestations, such as rapid
heartbeat, muscle tensing, increased sweating, or flushed face.

   In a quiet moment, one should reflect on the warning signs that indicate the
onset of one's anger. We need to know how quickly we anger and how soon we get
over it. . . . One also needs to determine how visibly one displays anger. Some people
lose their temper in extremely obvious ways. Others smolder but show few external
signs that they are angry. Showing anger is not always bad, but the trick is to do so
only when it serves strategic purpose.

   Determine situations that trigger inappropriate anger. In some cases, anger is an appropriate response to a provocative situation. At other times, we may instantly, and
inappropriately, ignite in circumstances that most other bargainers would not find

provocative.... Determining those things that trigger inappropriate anger may permit us to take steps to avoid them or to take preventative measures to control anger.

Decide whether to display anger. Recognizing how and why our anger arises does not mean that we should always avoid angry feelings or never display anger. But, if one can recognize the onset of anger, one can decide how best to deal with it.... This requires a careful assessment of the circumstances and of our opponent's reaction to our anger, and a measured approach to expressing our feelings.

Behavioral techniques to reduce anger. In some cases, one may feel anger but realize that it is inappropriate to the setting.... Experts suggest a variety of behavioral techniques that can work, including:

- Call a temporary halt to the negotiation to cool off;
- Count backwards from 10 to 1;
- Go to the restroom;
- Get a drink of water or soda;
- Tense and untense your leg muscles under the table;
- Begin writing points that you wish to discuss later in the negotiation (this will help you stay organized and will give you some time to cool off);
- Consciously try to take deep breaths in a silent manner;
- Think about a scene from your past in which you were relaxed;
- Imagine the source of your anger in a setting where he or she is getting his or her just desserts;
- Exercise vigorously prior to and after a challenging negotiation.

Express anger and disappointment effectively. In addition to behavioral techniques for dealing with the physical and emotional aspects of anger, we need ways to communicate our displeasure and convey our concerns.... [W]e need to be assertive without provoking or escalating deal-killing emotions in the other side. Among the approaches for doing so are the following:

- Explain the behavior that upsets you in specific and objective terms;
- Describe your feelings about what bothers you;
- Try to get your opponent to view the matter from your perspective;
- Do not accuse your opponent of misbehavior;
- Show respect for your opponent;
- Apologize for any misunderstandings that your own behavior might have caused if that will help move the discussion without making you appear weak.

Avoid "negotiator's bias." Most negotiators view themselves as fair and honest. Yet, we often fall into a perception trap in which we, without justification, view opponents whom we know nothing about as hostile.... To say the least, the tendency to jump to such negative, and often unwarranted, conclusions explains why emotions can become instantly heated. Avoiding hasty judgments about our opponent's intentions requires realistic, clear thinking.

Try to promote trust. Trust is a key underpinning of successful negotiations. If negotiators cannot trust each other, then every issue requires verification and each agreement necessitates ironclad guarantees. Anger, expressed inappropriately, can destroy trust. To promote good feelings and trust, various commentators recommend "positive framing." . . . In fact, research suggests that the most effective concessions that one can make are those that reduce or eliminate an opponent's losses; the least effective are those that somewhat improve gains already made by the other side.

DEALING WITH YOUR OPPONENT'S ANGER

Just as we need to develop a good instinct for determining when we become angry, we also need to be able to read our opponent's moods, particularly those involving frustration and anger. Here are some techniques that may be useful:

Defuse heated emotional buildups. . . . If one senses a rising temper on the other side, it may help to ask directly: "Mary, is something bothering you?" or "Tom, did my comment about the necessity of meeting deadlines disturb you?" or "Regina, you look angry. Are you?"

Assess the significance of angry displays. When an opponent erupts in anger, one should assess as carefully as possible the significance of the anger. Does it seem calculated? . . . Trying to placate someone who is using anger strategically to gain concessions may well lead us to make overly generous offers.

Address your opponent's anger. . . .

Respond to anger in strategic ways. . . . Responding in kind, however, is usually not effective. Instead, think strategically. . . . If you need a break to avoid losing your temper, take one. If not, you can wait silently for the angry person to become contrite and to make concessions. Sometimes a modest concession on your part immediately after an outburst by your opponent will elicit a much larger one from him or her.

Help an angry opponent save face. Perhaps the biggest deal breaker in negotiation is "face loss." Where parties feel they will lose face if they agree to an opponent's demands, they are likely to derail the negotiation even if it is not in their interest to do so. So critical is "face" to a negotiation that parties will hold to untenable positions that will cost them money or even provoke wars. . . . [O]ne should always try to help an angry opponent save face especially if lost face is what triggered the outburst in the first place. A friendly, reassuring (but not patronizing) approach may work wonders in these situations.

Involve a mediator when you anticipate anger. If you believe that a strong potential for destructive anger exists in a particular negotiation, enlist the aid of a mediator or someone whose presence will act as a calming influence to the process.

 Gary Goodpaster, A PRIMER ON COMPETITIVE BARGAINING

1996 J. Disp. Resol. 325, 370-375

DEFENDING AGAINST COMPETITORS: DEFENSIVE COOPERATIVENESS

The Innocent or Naïve Cooperator and the Cooperative Negotiator's Dilemma. The cooperator's desire to be a certain kind of person — noncompetitive, nonaggressive, fair, decent, honorable — may also result in turning the other cheek to the other party's hard-bargaining tactics. In fact, naïve cooperators may undercut getting what they want by assuming that they must make unilateral concessions or compromises without a return just to get an agreement. They sometimes fail to distinguish between their behavior toward others and their behavior toward the problem they are trying to resolve. In other words, they are "soft on the people" and "soft on the problem."

The cooperator faces a dilemma: the reasonable, compromising conduct in which he wishes to engage in order to obtain a fair and just agreement also puts him at risk. If the other party is also cooperative, all is well and good. The other party, however, may not be cooperative. Instead, the other party may either be overtly competitive or cooperative in demeanor and competitive in substance. If, for example, to be reasonable and attempt to have the union understand its point of view, management volunteers important information, such as planning a plant expansion, the union may simply take the information and use it to its advantage without volunteering information in return or reciprocating in any other way. Similarly, if Susan, being cooperative, makes a concession hoping to trigger a concession from Jerry, Jerry may simply take the concession and either give nothing in return or give a non-commensurate concession. Indeed, the cooperator's concession may encourage the other side to seek more or greater concessions. In this situation, the truly naïve cooperator may respond by conceding more in the hope of inducing a concession and movement toward an agreeable settlement rather than by noting the lack of reciprocity and adjusting his own behavior to protect himself.

The cooperator faces the dilemma that the way he wants to negotiate may put him at risk of being taken or exploited. Obviously, cooperative negotiators should not naïvely *assume* that the other party will also act cooperatively. Indeed, they must recognize that they cannot successfully bargain cooperatively unless the other party cooperates. They also need to devise ways to protect themselves from the other party's possible competitive moves that are often masked or hidden by a genial, reasonable, or cooperative demeanor.

Aware of the potential risks involved in their cooperative behavior, a negotiator could adopt a hard bargaining strategy. This strategy would certainly not be necessary in all cases. In fact, many negotiators might object to hard bargaining in principle. How does a wise and careful cooperative negotiator protect herself from competitive bargainers?

Defensive cooperativeness. During the initial stages of a negotiation the parties feel each other out, not only to gain information respecting positions, wants, and desires, but also to get a sense of whether, and how far, they can trust another. Since trust, or providing security that one can trust, is a key issue, cooperators should try to anticipate negotiations, develop information about the other party, and build a relationship with the other party prior to negotiation.

Because cooperative behavior promotes trust, it tends to induce reciprocal cooperative behavior. Once in a negotiation, the careful cooperator adopts a cooperative, yet wary, demeanor and indicates a general posture of flexibility on issues. This may signal or hint at a willingness to make concessions on certain issues. Nevertheless, the defensive or cautious cooperator adopts a cooperative, yet wary, demeanor and indicates a general posture of flexibility on issues.

Fractionating concessions. A careful negotiator can, in part, fashion a self-protective concession strategy by fractionating concessions. One fractionates concessions by dividing an issue into smaller issues and therefore, into smaller concessions where one gives on an issue. Using this method, the negotiator can make a small concession and wait to see how the other party responds. If the other party makes an equivalent concession, the negotiator can proceed.

Ambiguous or disownable signals. A negotiator makes a "disownable" concession move by making an ambiguous statement that suggests a willingness to make a concession but which can also be plausibly interpreted as not expressing such willingness. If the other party interprets the statement as offering a concession and reciprocates, then the negotiator confirms the other side's interpretation in some way. If the other party seeks to grab the assumed concession without offering a return, the negotiator denies making it. Suppose, for example, that one party has repeatedly argued that two conditions had to be met before he would consider changing his position. After a time, however, he begins to mention only one condition, thereby signaling a willingness to drop the unmentioned condition.

This sort of signaling is, in effect, a testing of the other party. This test, however, does not run the actual risk of making a concession or exposing weakness. At most, it is an unclear expression of a contingent willingness to concede. As another example, consider two parties negotiating over contract terms. The buyer wants the seller to give her the same discount on equipment that the seller gives some of its other, much larger customers. The seller says, "We can write something like a 'favored nations' clause into the contract." The buyer responds, "I'll take that, and I appreciate getting the same discount as your larger customers," but he makes no concession in return. The seller then responds, "Well, you can have the clause, but it doesn't apply to discounts." Alternatively, had the buyer shown a willingness to concede, the seller could let the buyer's first interpretation of the statement stand.

If there is little trust, this process of signaling can be quite subtle because the target of the signal may be uncertain whether to interpret a statement as expressing a willingness to concede. If the target is uncertain, he may fear responding in a way which clearly shows his willingness to reciprocate because that may put him at risk. Consequently, the parties sometimes engage in trading ambiguous statements until one party feels secure enough to make a clear proposal or until both parties simultaneously make a clear move.

"Directional" information. Sometimes a negotiator may encourage cooperative bargaining simply by indicating on which issues the other party should improve its proposals. This tactic provides the other party with some information about the negotiator's priorities but without clearly committing to anything.

Demanding reasoned justifications. A negotiator should make a practice of asking the other party to justify its positions in terms of some objective criteria. If the other party simply behaves competitively and attempts to extract whatever gains it can, it may have difficulty in stating satisfactory justifications for its positions.

Contingent cooperativeness and the reformed sinner strategy. There is good evidence that even those who wish to bargain cooperatively can succeed with competitive negotiators by adopting a shifting "competitive to cooperative" or "reformed sinner" strategy. This strategy involves making a high, initial demand, remaining firm initially, and then moving to a "contingently cooperative" strategy. Contingent cooperativeness involves behaving cooperatively if the other party reciprocates cooperative behavior and increasing cooperative behavior as the other party does so. Interestingly, the cooperator's initial firmness may signal to the other party that competitive behavior will not work. By making high demands, a bargainer avoids the pitfall of adopting a stance that may prove to be too "generous"; he is thus less likely to accept a smaller division of the resources than the other is willing to offer. Second, by making extreme initial demands, the bargainer often gives himself more time to assemble information about the other's preferences and intentions. Third, he communicates his expectations of how he should be treated by the other—namely that he should not be exploited. Finally, his extreme initial offers provide the other with valuable information about his subjective utilities.

The contingently competitive strategy appears to work by giving the other party evidence that its own cooperative behavior, but not its competitive behavior, has a desirable effect. In carrying out this general strategy, the cooperator may expressly negotiate over the negotiation ground rules and seek the other party's commitment to negotiate cooperatively as well, but, in any case, asserting a norm and expectation of cooperative behavior. The cooperator may then attempt to structure the negotiation to handle small issues first, where the risk of loss is not great. When ready to take some risks, the cooperator makes the contingent proposal. The proposal expressly offers a concession or adopts a position closer to the other party's demands yet contingent on some specific concession or change of position from the other party.

Strategy imitation or tit-for-tat. Response-in-kind or tit-for-tat is a form of contingent cooperation a negotiator can use to handle a competitor. If the cooperator observes competitive tactics, she can call attention to them and state that she knows how to bargain that way too and will respond in kind unless the other party bargains cooperatively. Alternatively, the cooperator can just respond in kind by using tit-for-tat to discipline the other party.

Tit-for-tat is a negotiation strategy designed to shape the other party's bargaining behavior. One dilemma negotiators face is figuring out whether to bargain cooperatively or competitively. If one wishes to be reasonable and bargain cooperatively, there is a risk that the other party will bargain competitively and gain an advantage. Using tit-for-tat, a negotiator solves that problem by competing just as the other party does and, in effect, sends the message that "I will bargain the way you bargain and will use the same tactics you use." This teaches the other party that it cannot get away with anything, and may lead to cooperative behavior.

In general, using a tit-for-tat or matching strategy appears to be an effective way to induce cooperation. The strategy makes it clear to the other party that it risks retaliation and increasing conflict if it continues to bargain competitively.

Time-outs. Negotiating parties deadlock when no party is willing to make a further concession to bring the parties closer together. When the parties are nearing a deadline and are deadlocked, they may realize that the negotiation will fail completely unless they cooperate. Declaring a time-out when a deadlock is apparent gives the parties time to assess the situation without continued conflict, reconsider their reading of the negotiation thus far, and determine more rationally whether to risk trusting the other party. Often enough, when the parties return to formal negotiation, each side signals a willingness to move towards an agreement or make concessions leading to an agreement.

 ### *William Ury*, GETTING PAST NO: NEGOTIATING WITH DIFFICULT PEOPLE

143-146 (1991)

THE FIVE STEPS OF BREAKTHROUGH NEGOTIATION

Whether you are negotiating with a hostage-taker, your boss, or your teenager, the basic principles remain the same. In summary, the five steps of breakthrough negotiation are:

1.   Go to the Balcony

The first step is to control your own behavior. When your opponent says no or launches an attack, you may be stunned into giving in or counterattacking. So, suspend your reaction by naming the game. Then buy yourself time to think. Use the time to figure out your interests and your BATNA. Throughout the negotiation, keep your eyes on the prize. Instead of getting mad or getting even, focus on getting what you want. In short, go to the balcony.

2.   Step to Their Side

Before you can negotiate, you must create a favorable climate. You need to defuse your opponent's anger, fear, and suspicions. He expects you to attack or to resist. So do the opposite: Listen to him, acknowledge his point, and agree with him wherever you can. Acknowledge his authority and competence, too. Disarm him by stepping to his side.

3.   Don't Reject . . . Reframe

The next step is to change the game. Instead of rejecting your opponent's position — which usually only reinforces it — direct his attention to the problem of meeting each side's interests. Take whatever he says and reframe it as an attempt to deal with the problem. Ask problem-solving questions, such as "Why is it that you want that?" or "What would you do if you were in my shoes?" or "What if we were to . . . ?" Rather than trying to teach him yourself, let the problem be his teacher. Reframe his tactics, too: Go around stone walls, deflect attacks, and expose tricks. To change the game, change the frame.

4.   Build Them a Golden Bridge

At last you're ready to negotiate. Your opponent, however, may stall, not yet convinced of the benefits of agreement. You may be tempted to push and insist, but this will probably lead him to harden and resist. Instead, do the opposite — draw him in the direction you would like him to go. Think of yourself as a mediator. Involve him in the process, incorporating his ideas. Try to identify and satisfy his unmet interests, particularly his basic human needs. Help him save face and make the outcome appear as a victory for him. Go slow to go fast. In sum, make it easy for him to say yes by building him a golden bridge.

5. Bring Them to Their Senses, Not Their Knees

If your opponent still resists and thinks he can win without negotiating, you must educate him to the contrary. You must make it hard for him to say no. You could use threats and force, but these often backfire; if you push him into a corner, he will likely lash out, throwing even more resources into the fight against you. Instead, educate him about the costs of not agreeing. Ask reality-testing questions, warn rather than threaten, and demonstrate your BATNA. Use it only if necessary and minimize his resistance by exercising restraint and reassuring him that your goal is mutual satisfaction, not victory. Make sure he knows the golden bridge is always open. In short, use power to bring him to his senses, not his knees.

The breakthrough strategy requires you to resist normal human temptations and do the opposite of what you usually feel like doing. It requires you to suspend your reaction when you feel like striking back, to listen when you feel like talking back, to ask questions when you feel like telling your opponent the answers, to bridge your differences when you feel like pushing for your way, and to educate when you feel like escalating.

At every turn the strategy calls on you to choose the path of indirection. You break through by going around your opponent's resistance, approaching him from the side, acting contrary to his expectations. The theme throughout the strategy is to treat your opponent with respect — not as an object to be pushed, but as a person to be persuaded. Rather than trying to change his mind by direct pressure, you change the environment in which he makes decisions. You let him draw his own conclusions and make his own choice. *Your goal is not to win over him but to win him over.*

It takes two to tangle, but it takes only one to begin the process of untangling a knotty situation. It is within your power to transform your most difficult negotiations. During the American Civil War, Abraham Lincoln made a speech in which he referred sympathetically to the Southern rebels. An elderly lady, a staunch Unionist, upbraided him for speaking kindly of his enemies when he ought to be thinking of destroying them. His reply was classic: "Why madam," Lincoln answered, "do I not destroy my enemies when I make them my friends?"

The breakthrough strategy is designed to do precisely that — to destroy your adversary by making him your partner in problem-solving negotiation.

Notes and Questions

8.29 Which step suggested by Adler do you think would be most helpful for you if you were angry?

8.30 How does Goodpaster suggest that cooperative negotiators protect themselves against competitive negotiators?

8.31 What do you think is the hardest step that Ury is suggesting? Why?

8.32 At the beginning of a negotiation, the other party's attorney says to you, "We could negotiate over this all day, but this is our best offer. Do you really want to waste your client's money and your time by discussing this all day?" How would you respond?

8.33 You are a ceramic artist and sell your artwork in galleries and various regional art fairs. At one of these art fairs, a young professional woman approaches your display and becomes very interested in a large bowl. It cost you a total of approximately $30 to make the bowl. You have sold similar bowls upwards of $200 in some galleries. Your reservation price is $50 — at this point you are indifferent between selling the bowl at this value and waiting for another interested art buyer (your BATNA). After a brief discussion about your artistic background and the method you used to create the bowl, you think you have this woman very interested. She then asks for the price. In response, you explain that you have read *Getting to YES*, and have no interest in haggling over prices. You then begin to discuss how much these bowls sell for in the market generally and how much you have received for other comparable bowls, but the potential customer interrupts. She tells you that you are wasting her time and she offers $55 for the bowl — take it or leave it. How do you respond?

8.34 You had been working for several weeks negotiating a custody agreement in a divorce case, working out all the details for joint custody, including such details as who will transport the children between visitations. In your last meeting to finalize the agreement, the other party's attorney demanded that her client now have the children on each of their birthdays and during spring break from school. You did not want to ruin all the progress that had been made, so you reluctantly agreed, pending that you would need to finalize it with your client. What should you have done differently?

8.35 How would you advise the French businessman in the following situation?

> The president of a small, successful French company meets with the CEO of a large U.S. corporation. Largely because of the strong relationship the two businessmen have developed, they agree to an arrangement where the U.S. corporation will acquire the French company. With a tentative agreement in place, the two arrange for a meeting to finalize the details of the acquisition. Because of their strong relationship, the two agree to a small, personal meeting where they will discuss all the details of the acquisition. Furthermore, they agree that although it will be held at the U.S. headquarters in Chicago, the meeting will be held in French to retain the culture of the acquired company. When the French businessman arrives at the American CEO's office for the meeting, he is greeted by the American CEO and several of his colleagues, all of whom speak only English and can manage to say only *bonjour* in French.

8.36 How would you advise the person in the following situation?

> Yesterday, my son fell and broke his leg and I had to rush him to the doctor to get his leg set. I called work and left a message with my supervisor explaining my absence. Later that day, she called me back, not out of concern for my son, but to complain how she had to cover all of my appointments and work. This was extremely upsetting to me given the stress I was already under because of my son's accident. Upon returning to the office the next day, I went to my supervisor's office to discuss the phone call with her. I explained my frustration over her statement that I was intentionally shirking my duties. She never even looked away from the e-mail on her computer screen. This just further angered me, but I didn't know how to respond.

Chapter 9 | Dealing with Differences: Culture, Gender, and Race

In every negotiation, differences exist between the negotiators — hometown, education, religion, politics, affiliations, sexual orientation, interests — any of which could exert more influence over negotiation behavior than any of the three factors of culture, gender, and race. This chapter discusses these differences in part because these are the differences negotiators perceive most easily. Yet, as some of the following articles point out, there is no reason to assume that any of these differences affect negotiation behaviors more than individual characteristics. In fact, to assume that gender, race, or culture will play a determining factor in the negotiation is to oversimplify dramatically, and potentially to your detriment. So this chapter discusses these differences as some salient ones, but not necessarily the most important ones, in any individual's negotiation behavior and asks you to think about how you might be perceived by others based on "obvious" demographic characteristics, as well as how you might perceive others. The chapter cautions you to be more sophisticated in your thinking and your behavior, rather than relying on often inaccurate stereotypes.

A. CULTURE

Advice on dealing with cultural differences in negotiation runs the risk of either being too simplistic (don't cross your legs in certain cultures) or being so general that it is not helpful (there may be different assumptions about how negotiations are conducted). This chapter steers through these alternatives by providing both some general and more specific advice. Obviously, if one were planning on conducting extensive negotiations in another country, this brief foray into cultural differences is insufficient. This chapter points out only some common cultural differences in negotiation while also reminding negotiators that cultural differences may or may not explain any one individual's approach to negotiations.

1. Culture and Negotiation

These excerpts discuss the concept of culture as applied to negotiation. First, Kevin Avruch outlines some of the common (mistaken) assumptions about culture and a more nuanced way of thinking about culture. Next Jayne Seminare Docherty outlines what we negotiators really need to understand about culture and building intercultural skills. Jeffrey Rubin and Frank Sander note how broad cultural assumptions are often too simplistic, especially where we might share other cultures like problem-solving negotiation culture or cosmopolitanism. Finally, James Sebenius presents empirical data demonstrating how we cannot assume that culture is a negotiation determinant for any given individual or negotiation team.

 Kevin Avruch, **CULTURE AND NEGOTIATION PEDAGOGY**
16 Negot. J. 339, 340-341, 343-345 (2000)

WHAT CULTURE IS NOT

The notion of culture that predominates in much work on negotiation typically relies on recycling remnants of what used to be "national character" studies in the 1950s and 1960s. This is perhaps exemplified nowadays in work dealing with "national negotiating styles." Such a notion of culture is based upon at least six mutually related ideas, ways of conceiving culture that are inadequate. Peter Black and I have discussed these ideas at length elsewhere.[*] Briefly, they are as follows:

1. *Culture is homogenous.* This presumes that cultures are free of dissensions, of internal contradictions or paradoxes such that culture provides unambiguous behavioral instructions for individuals.

2. *Culture is a thing.* Reified, culture is presumed to act independent of individual agency. As in Samuel Huntington's scheme,[†] cultures "clash" with one another across static geopolitical landscapes in Spenglerian epics.

3. *Culture is uniformly distributed among members of a group.* This inadequate idea is what makes nominalizing culture — turning it into a label — possible. Like "national character," it fits the requirements of work that stress the "national negotiating styles" approach. Intracultural variation, if ever noted, whether at the individual or group level is dismissed as "deviance."

4. *An individual possesses but a single culture.* Usually the "culture" here is national or ethnic. The individual is simply and monolithically Mexican, Moroccan, Moluccan. Once again, the effect is to make culture a synonym for group identity. When predominantly identified with national or ethnic groupings, moreover, this inadequacy makes it more difficult for researchers to think productively about other "vessels" filled by cultural content: professions or occupations, or organizations and institutions, for example. It also tends to "freeze" culture in a single sociological category, at the expense of recognizing situational or contextual factors — think of the important research on "boundary roles" or negotiating definitions of the situation, that could benefit from a nuanced cultural perspective.

---

[*] Kevin Avruch & Peter W. Black, The Culture Question and Conflict Resolution, 16 Peace & Change 22 (1991).
[†] Samuel Huntington, The Clash of Civilizations and the Remaking of World Order (1996).

5. *Culture is custom.* Here, culture is virtually synonymous with "tradition," customary ways of behaving. It is thus reduced to a sort of surface-level etiquette. Cultural variation becomes, as Peter Black once put it, merely a matter of "differential etiquette."

6. *Culture is timeless.* In this construct, a changeless quality is imputed to culture, especially to so-called traditional cultures. We speak here, for example, of the "Arab mind" as though a unitary cognizing element has come down to us from Muhammad's Mecca. Or, "Be careful," the neophyte heading off to Beijing on a mission is told: "The Chinese have been negotiating for a thousand years." (One wonders if the adviser has any particular Chinese in mind.) . . .

SOME THOUGHTS ON WHAT CULTURE IS

Thus far I have dwelt mostly on what culture, in my view, is not: an homogenous, essentialized, uniformly distributed, customary, timeless, and stable thing. I shall now say a few words about how, in contrast, I conceptualize culture, and then some words on how I approach teaching it to students of conflict resolution.

Following Schwartz,* I see culture as consisting of the "derivatives of experience, more or less organized, learned or created by the individuals of a population, including those images or encodements and their interpretations (meanings) transmitted from past generations, or contemporaries, or formed by individuals themselves." In the main, this is a symbolic (stressing interpretation and meaning) and cognitivist definition, stressing images or encodements that others have called schemas or cognitive representations.

But note that such schemas are not just handed down unchanged and authoritatively by generations past: some are created afresh by individuals, and all derive ultimately from experience in and of the world — from social practice. Moreover, the definition must be expanded to maintain that these images and encodements are not uniformly distributed in a population; they are differentially distributed both sociologically (i.e., in terms of class, gender, ethnicity, occupation, region, etc.) and psychologically (in terms of their differential psychodynamic internalization — their affective and motivational "loading" — by specific persons). . . .

SOME THOUGHTS ON TEACHING ABOUT CULTURE

Finally, with respect to negotiation, how do I teach students using this conceptualization of culture?

First, I do not teach that culture is another "variable" that can be arrayed alongside age, income, or passport nationality. Nor is culture another independent causal vector in schematic models of negotiation. Culture is context, not cause. It is, speaking metaphorically, the "lens" through which causes are refracted.

---

* Theodore Schwartz, Anthropology and Psychology: An Unrequited Relationship, in New Directions in Psychological Anthropology (Theodore Schwartz, Geoffrey M. White & Catherine A. Lutz eds., 1992).

Secondly, I am mistrustful of simulations wherein students are expected to "play" the roles of cultural others, particularly in negotiations involving so-called deep-rooted or protracted identity conflict. . . .

Third, although students expect to jump right into problems of "negotiating with other cultures," I never begin by teaching about intercultural negotiation. . . . Instead, I begin with two or three substantive ethnographies, or cultural accounts, of particular cultures, preferably those that also stress social conflict and conflict resolution. . . .

And fourth and finally, I have to remind some of my students that they — we — "have culture" as well. Culture is not just something possessed by the others — the ethnics, the third-worlders, the clients of the World Bank and the IMF, the objects of our humanitarian peacekeeping interventions. . . .

 Jayne Seminare Docherty, CULTURE AND NEGOTIATION: SYMMETRICAL ANTHROPOLOGY FOR NEGOTIATORS

87 Marq. L. Rev. 711, 712, 713, 714-715, 717, 718, 719 (2004)

One commonly used heuristic device for thinking about culture is the iceberg. This model begins with the empirical observation that cultures differ in terms of normative behaviors and other traits, but assumes that these are like the tip of an iceberg. There is much more to culture under the surface of what we can readily observe. Above the surface we find behaviors, artifacts and institutions. Just below the surface we find norms, beliefs, values and attitudes. A sensitive observer can "uncover" these and become more knowledgeable about a culture. The deepest level is all but invisible even to members of a cultural group. It contains the deepest assumptions about the world, the sense-making and meaning-making schemas and symbols, the beliefs about what is real in the world, and beliefs about how individuals experience the world. This is a useful model, but it is also misleading. It does not reflect the dynamic quality of cultures, which are far from frozen. It also implies that all of the individuals in a given iceberg (culture) share that culture evenly; this is never the case. . . .

Unfortunately, some negotiation texts — particularly but not exclusively popular books on negotiation — focus almost entirely on the part of the iceberg visible above the surface. In these texts, cultures are presented as lists of do's and don'ts. These lists are rooted in stereotypes and are of dubious value. Teaching negotiators about culture in this manner is of limited value and might actually be dangerous in some settings.

LEARNING PATTERNS OF CULTURE

A more sophisticated approach to culture in negotiation involves identifying patterns or types of cultures by studying a large group of cultures. Instead of getting inside of a specific culture to understand it, this approach stands outside of cultures and looks for patterns or cultural styles. These are often presented as a list of dichotomous characteristics including: high context/low context; individualism/collectivism; and egalitarian/hierarchical. A high-context culture often relies on indirect communication, because the participants are expected to understand the complex meaning of relatively small non-verbal gestures. A low-context culture will tend to rely on direct statements and formal, clear ratification of written negotiated agreements. Negotiators from individualist cultures may worry less about preserving relationships than negotiators from collectivist cultures. And, negotiators from egalitarian cultures are likely to be less concerned about issues of rank and privilege than negotiators from hierarchical cultures. . . .

At least this approach to culture alerts people to the fact that *they* have a culture too! The issue is not what is wrong with that person from another culture, but where the mismatches are between our cultures. On the other hand, describing cultures as a collection of styles or preferences that impact communication and therefore negotiation still does not get us to the deepest part of the iceberg. . . .

SYMMETRICAL ANTHROPOLOGY

The most complete and sophisticated way of thinking about culture and negotiation requires that we greatly enrich our definition of culture. Avruch offers the following definition: "For our purposes, culture refers to the socially transmitted values, beliefs and symbols that are more or less shared by members of a social group, and by means of which members interpret and make meaningful their experience and behavior (including the behavior of 'others')."[*] He also points out that this definition includes a number of assumptions. First, individuals belong to multiple groups and therefore carry multiple cultures. The implication is that an encounter between two individuals is likely to be a *multicultural* encounter since each participant can draw on more than one culture to make sense of the situation. This includes negotiation encounters. Second, it is important to understand the institutions and mechanisms that transmit culture. Third, culture is almost never perfectly shared by all members of a community or group. Individuals have the capacity to selectively adopt and adapt their multiple cultures, so you cannot assume that a person from culture X will do Y. Each party can draw from, adapt, and modify a multifaceted set of cultural norms and rules; therefore every intercultural encounter is a complex improvisational experience. . . .

 Jeffrey Z. Rubin & Frank E.A. Sander, **CULTURE, NEGOTIATION, AND THE EYE OF THE BEHOLDER**

7 Negot. J. 249, 251-253 (1991)

The purpose of this brief column is to draw attention to several considerations that should be borne in mind in any analysis of culture and negotiation. Our thesis is that, although differences in culture clearly *do* exist and have a bearing on the style of negotiation that emerges, some of the most important effects of culture are felt even before the negotiators sit down across from one another and begin to exchange

---

[*] See Kevin Avruch, Culture as Context, Culture as Communication: Considerations for Humanitarian Negotiators, 9 Harv. Negot. L. Rev. 391 (2004), portions of which are reprinted later in this chapter.

offers. Culture, we believe, is a profoundly powerful organizing prism, through which we tend to view and integrate all kinds of disparate interpersonal information. . . .

Robert Rosenthal and his colleagues have demonstrated the power of expectations and labels in an important series of experimental studies. In one of these experiments,[*] teachers were told that some of the children in their elementary school classes had been identified as "intellectual bloomers," children who were likely to grow and develop substantially in the coming year. About other children (who had been privately matched with the "bloomers" in terms of measured aptitude) nothing was said. When an achievement test was administered at the end of the academic year, a shocking and important discovery was made: those children who had been labeled as intellectual bloomers scored significantly higher than those with whom they had been matched. In explanation, the researchers hypothesized that children who were expected to do very, very well were given more attention by their teachers; this increased attention, organized by hypothesis that the child in question was a talented individual, created a self-fulfilling prophecy.

The label of culture may have an effect very similar to that of gender or intellectual aptitude; it is a "hook" that makes it easy for one negotiator (the perceiver) to organize what he or she sees emanating from that "different person" seated at the other side of the table. To understand how culture may function as a label, consider the following teaching exercise, used during a two week session on negotiation. . . . During one class session, the fifty or so participants were formed into rough national groups, and were asked to characterize their national negotiating style — as seen by others. That is, the task was not to describe true differences that may be attributable to culture or nationality, but to characterize the stereotypic perceptions that others typically carry around in their heads.

This exercise yielded a set of very powerful, albeit contradictory, stereotypic descriptions of different nationalities. To give a couple of examples, British participants characterized others' stereotypic characterization of the British as "reserved, arrogant, old-fashioned, eccentric, fair, and self-deprecating." . . . And a cluster of Central Americans listed others' stereotypes of them as negotiators as "idealistic, impractical, disorganized, unprepared, stubborn in arguments, and flowery in style."

Now imagine that you have begun to negotiate with someone from another culture, who at some point in the proceedings simply insists that he or she can go no further, and is prepared to conclude without an agreement if necessary; in effect, says this individual, his BATNA has been reached, and he can do just as well by walking away from the table. How should you interpret such an assertion? If you share the general cluster of stereotypes described by the students, your interpretation will probably depend on the other person's culture or nationality. Thus, if the other negotiator is British, and (among other things) you regard the British as "fair," you may interpret this person's refusal to concede further as an honest statement of principle. The same behavior issuing from a Central American, however (someone you suspect of being "stubborn in arguments"), may lead you to suspect your counterpart of being stubborn and perhaps deceitful. Wouldn't you therefore be

---

[*] Robert Rosenthal & Lenore Jacobson, Pygmalion in the Classroom: Teacher Expectation and Pupils' Intellectual Development (1968).

more likely to strike an agreement with a British than a Central American negotiator—despite the fact that each has behaved in the identical way?

If there is any truth to our surmise, you can see how powerful the effects of culture may prove to be, leading us (even before we have had a chance to gather information about our counterpart) to hold a set of expectations that guide and inform our judgments. Moreover, once our "hypotheses" about others are in place, it becomes very difficult to disprove them. We tend to gather interpersonal information in such a way that we pay attention only to the "facts" that support our preconceived ideas, ignoring or dismissing disconforming data. . . .

[P]robably the wisest thing any of us can do to prepare for such negotiations is to: be aware of our biases and predispositions; acquire as much information as possible about our counterpart as an individual; and learn as much as we can about the norms and customs (of all kinds) that are to be found in our counterpart's home country.

 James K. Sebenius, **CAVEATS FOR CROSS-BORDER NEGOTIATIONS**

18 Negot. J. 121, 122–128 (2002)

Starting with the obvious: All American negotiators are not like John Wayne and all Chinese negotiators are not like Charlie Chan. Or Bill Gates and Mao Zedong. Or Michael Jordan and Zhu Chen, the phenomenal women's world chess champion who recently also defeated the world men's champion. We also know that some negotiators in southeastern France may bear more resemblance to northern Italian negotiators than to their Parisian compatriots. Likewise, the culture of western Chinese Uighers is far more akin to neighbors in Pakistan than comrades in Beijing. . . . In the face of such internal variation, we wisely caution ourselves against mindless stereotyping by nationality (as well as by gender, religion, race, profession, or age). Even so, in many situations it remains all-too-common to hear offhand remarks such as "all Chinese negotiators . . ." (as well as generalizations about "women . . ." or "engineers"). To combat this, a strong version of the anti-stereotyping prescription calls for ignoring nationality altogether in preparing for negotiations.

That advice by itself is too strong. Nationality often does have a great deal to do with cultural characteristics, particularly in relatively homogeneous countries like Japan. . . . It would be foolish to throw away potentially valuable information. But what does information on a particular group's behavioral expectations or deeper cultural characteristics really convey? Typically, cultural descriptions are about central tendencies of populations that also exhibit considerable "within-group" variation. Suppose that a trait like "cooperativeness" (versus "competitiveness") is carefully measured by a psychological testing instrument for the citizens of Country X. The results will be *distribution* with a few citizens rating highly cooperative, a few rating highly uncooperative, and the majority clustered around a more middle range.

Suppose that this distribution was a normal or bell-shaped curve with the most likely value equal to the mean of the distribution. Extremely homogeneous cultures would be characterized by a "tight" distribution around the mean; the greater the heterogeneity on the cooperative-competitive dimension, the more "spread out" the distribution would be.

[K]nowing that someone is from Country X, one naturally assumes that this person is about as cooperative as the mean or most likely point in that distribution. Yet a bit of statistical reasoning exposes some of the dangers of this common-sense approach. Take a randomly chosen citizen of Country X whose distribution of cooperativeness is accurately portrayed by Figure 2. Question: How likely is it that this randomly chosen citizen displays a level of cooperativeness somewhere within the range of 20 percentile points above or below the mean, which is the most probable description? Answer: There is only a 40 percent chance that this person exhibits cooperativeness 20 percentile points above or below the most likely value for Country X. Equivalently, there is a 60 percent chance — more than even odds — that this person displays a level of cooperativeness *outside* this centrally representative, most likely, range.

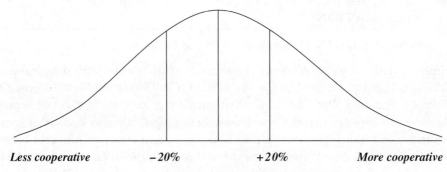

Less cooperative   − 20%   + 20%   More cooperative

Figure 2
The Individual Country X Citizen

This means that even the most likely trait for a population as described in Figure 2 will not likely apply to a given individual from that group. Remember, you negotiate with individuals, not averages. . . .

National culture clearly matters. But there is a tendency to see it as the Rosetta Stone, the indispensable key to describe, explain, and predict the behavior of the other side. Of course there are many possible "cultures" operating within a given individual. Beyond her French citizenship, an ABB executive may well be from Alsace, have a Danish parent, feel staunchly European, have studied electrical engineering, and have earned an MBA from the University of Chicago. . . . Nationality often matters when considering someone's bargaining characteristics but so too does gender, ethnicity, functional specialty, etc. Figure 4 reminds us that national culture is but one of many "cultures" that can influence bargaining behavior.

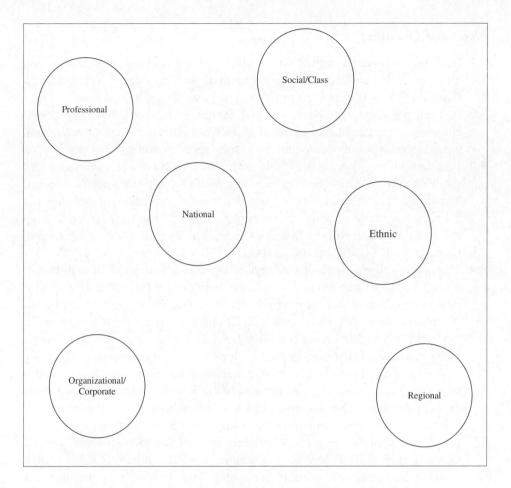

Figure 4
The Many "Cultures" That Influence Bargaining Behavior

Just as there are many cultures influencing bargaining behavior, there are many other potential contributing factors such as personality, finance, business, politics, and strategy. . . .

Psychologists have extensively documented this dynamic, a systematic tendency to focus on supposed characteristics of the person on the other side of the table, rather than on the economic or other powerful contextual factors. The antidotes? First, remember that "culture" doesn't just mean nationality; instead there are many potentially influential "cultures" at work. Second, beyond "culture" are many other factors that have potential to affect negotiation behavior. Nationality can carry important information, but with many other cultures and many other factors at work, you should be careful not to treat your counterpart's passport as the Rosetta Stone.

Notes and Questions

9.1 Each of the readings defines culture and outlines common assumptions and mistakes. Why is defining culture important to negotiators? What do you think are the most important mistakes, and how can we avoid them?

9.2 Perform the same exercise Rubin and Sander write about. Identify yourself culturally (or regionally or by other identifying characteristics). What are the typical stereotypes of your culture? Do they apply to you?

9.3 Pat Chew views culture as the "'lens' through which we define, experience, and resolve conflict." All negotiators have a cultural profile that frames the conflict. This influences the outcome of any negotiation, regardless of whether the frames are accurate or whether attempts are made by the legal system to keep culture out of the process. See Pat Chew, The Pervasiveness of Culture in Conflict, 54 J. Legal Educ. 60 (2004).

9.4 The authors above argue that cultural differences often appear in nonobvious ways. The 51-day standoff in Waco, Texas, between the FBI and Branch Davidians, in which there were neither ethnic nor nationality differences, resulted in the death of over 70 people, including 23 children. In her fascinating study of this conflict, conflict studies professor Jayne Docherty illustrates how worldviews can have a dramatic impact on how each party negotiates. Docherty argues that the clash and misunderstanding between the modern secular narrative of the FBI and the religious narrative of the Branch Davidians resulted in the final conflagration. She also argues that it is the complex mix of similarities and differences between worldviews that usually drives conflict escalation. Most people focus on the differences between the FBI and Branch Davidians and overlook their shared tendency to think in good/bad binary categories, their similar reliance on power-based negotiation, and their shared belief that it is morally acceptable to use lethal force in the defense of "good." The conflict might not have escalated to a deadly outcome if one party had held different worldview assumptions about the nature of truth and the legitimacy of using force to defend truth. Jayne Seminare Docherty, Learning Lessons from Waco: When the Parties Bring Their Gods to the Negotiation Table (2001).

9.5 Despite the surge in courses on alternative dispute resolution in U.S. law schools, and the importance of culture in dispute resolution and modern legal practice, exceedingly few law schools offer courses in "cross-cultural negotiation." Ilhyung Lee discusses this lack of adequate coursework and proposes what a cross-cultural negotiations course should entail. Ilhyung Lee, In re Culture: The Cross-Cultural Negotiations Course in the Law School Curriculum, 20 Ohio St. J. on Disp. Resol. 375 (2005).

2. Cultural Differences

As our earlier excerpts note, there have been studies of specific differences among cultures even when these differences do not apply to all members of a culture. The next several excerpts will outline particular areas of difference that people have found when studying cultures. As you read, think about where you would place your own culture and other cultures with which you are familiar on these cultural ranges.

 Jeswald W. Salacuse, **TEN WAYS THAT CULTURE AFFECTS NEGOTIATING STYLE: SOME SURVEY RESULTS**

14 Negot. J. 221, 223, 225-238 (1998)

A survey of 310 persons of different nationalities and occupations asked respondents to rate their negotiating style with respect to ten factors involved in the negotiation process. . . . Reporting on the responses of persons from 12 countries and eight different occupations, this study finds that, in many instances, persons from the same cultures and occupations tended to respond to these negotiating elements in a similar fashion. Survey responses were also examined with respect to the respondents' gender. The study would appear to support the proposition that culture, occupational background, and gender can influence negotiating style. . . .

The ten negotiating factors and the range of possible cultural responses to each are illustrated in Figure 1. . . .

Figure 1
The Impact of Culture on Negotiation

Negotiation Factors		**Range of Cultural Responses**	
Goal	Contract	←——————→	Relationship
Attitudes	Win/Lose	←—————→	Win/Win
Personal Styles	Informal	←—————→	Formal
Communications	Direct	←————————→	Indirect
Time Sensitivity	High	←——————→	Low
Emotionalism	High	←————→	Low
Agreement Form	Specific	←——————→	General
Agreement Building	Bottom Up	←———————→	Top Down
Team Organization	One Leader	←—————→	Consensus
Risk Taking	High	←————→	Low

In general, the survey revealed significant correlations between the respondents' assessment of certain traits of their negotiating styles on the one hand and their national cultures and professional backgrounds on the other. . . .

NEGOTIATING GOAL: CONTRACT OR RELATIONSHIP?

As a group, the respondents in this survey were fairly evenly divided on this question, with 54 percent viewing contract as a negotiating goal and 46 percent indicating that pursuing relationship was the goal. . . .

[T]he survey results revealed significant differences both among cultures and professionals on this question. Thus, with respect to national cultures only 26 percent of the Spanish respondents claimed that their primary goal in a negotiation was a relationship compared to 66 percent of the Indians....

An analysis of responses on the basis of occupational background also revealed significant variations. For example, while 71 percent of the lawyers favored contract as a negotiating goal, 61 percent of those with management or marketing experience preferred relationships....

Although for the group as a whole, the responses by males and females did not reveal significant differences, one did find substantial variations between genders within certain cultures....

NEGOTIATING ATTITUDE: WIN/LOSE OR WIN/WIN

[T]he survey revealed wide differences among the cultures represented in the survey on this question. Whereas 100 percent of the Japanese viewed negotiation as a win/win process, only 36.8 percent of the Spanish were so inclined....

An analysis of the responses by profession also found significant variations. Whereas only 14 percent of diplomats/public service personnel and 18 percent of management and marketing persons considered negotiations to be a win-lose process, 42 percent of the lawyers, 43 percent of the students, and 40 percent of the military held this view....

PERSONAL STYLE: INFORMAL OR FORMAL?

Except for the Nigerians, a majority of the respondents within each of the twelve groups surveyed claimed to have an informal negotiating style, however, the strength of this view varied considerably. While 83 percent of the Americans considered themselves to have an informal negotiating style, only 54 percent of the Chinese, 52 percent of the Spanish, and 58 percent of the Mexicans were similarly inclined. Among the four European national cultures surveyed, the French were the strongest in claiming an informal style....

COMMUNICATION: DIRECT OR INDIRECT?

In the survey, respondents in all cultural groups by a high margin claimed to have a direct form of communication.... Among occupational groups, 50 percent of those with public service or diplomatic backgrounds claimed to have a formal style, while in all other occupational groups this response was limited to no more than 20 percent.

SENSITIVITY TO TIME: HIGH OR LOW?

Among respondents as a whole, 80 percent asserted time sensitivity and 20 percent claimed a low time sensitivity. This same distribution was found among men, women, and the various occupational grouping represented in the survey.

However, a different pattern emerged among certain cultural groups.... The Indians, French and Germans included a substantial percentage of respondents asserting a low sensitivity to time.... Cultural discussions about time in negotiations often refer to two elements: promptness in meeting deadlines and the amount of time devoted to a negotiation. Germans, it has been observed, are highly time-sensitive with regard to promptness but less so with respect to their willingness to devote large amounts of time to a negotiation. Thus they are punctual (high time sensitivity) but slow to negotiate and make decisions (low time sensitivity).

EMOTIONALISM: HIGH OR LOW?

Accounts of negotiating behavior in other cultures almost always point to a particular group's tendency or lack thereof to display emotions....

Among all respondents, 65 percent claimed to tend toward high emotionalism while 35 percent indicated a tendency to low emotionalism. Roughly the same distribution was to be found among male and female respondents. Professional groups revealed a similar distribution, except for teachers, 90 percent of whom saw themselves tending toward high emotionalism.

The various cultures surveyed indicated greater variations. The Latin Americans and the Spanish were the cultural groups that ranked themselves highest with respect to emotionalism in a clearly statistically significant fashion. Among Europeans, the Germans and English ranked as least emotional, while among Asians the Japanese held that position, but to a lesser degree than the two European groups....

FORM OF AGREEMENT: GENERAL OR SPECIFIC?

Cultural factors may also influence the form of the written agreement that parties try to make....

Among all respondents in the survey, 78 percent preferred specific agreements while only 22 percent preferred general agreements.... The survey found that a majority of respondents in each cultural group preferred specific agreements over general agreements. This result may be attributable in part to the relatively large number of lawyers among the respondents, as well as to the fact that multinational corporate practice favors specific agreements and many respondents, regardless of nationality, had experience with such firms....

On the other hand, the degree of intensity of responses on the question varied considerably among cultural groups. While only 11 percent of the British favored general agreements, 45.5 percent of the Japanese and of the Germans claimed to do so....

Occupational groups demonstrated wider variations, a factor which supports the notion that professional culture may dominate national culture on this question. For example, while 100 percent of the respondents with military backgrounds preferred specific agreements, only 64 percent of management and marketing persons and of diplomats and civil servants had a similar inclination....

BUILDING AN AGREEMENT: BOTTOM UP OR TOP DOWN?

Related to the form of the agreement is the question of whether negotiating a business deal is an inductive or a deductive process.... Different cultures tend to emphasize one approach over the other....

The survey did not reveal significant cultural trends on this issue among Americans, Germans, and Nigerians, since the respondents from the three groups were relatively evenly divided on the question. On the other hand, the French, Argentineans, and Indians tended to view deal making as a top-down (deductive) process while Japanese, Mexicans, and Brazilians tended to see it as a bottom-up (inductive) process....

Responses among professional groups showed marked variation, with 71.4 percent of the diplomats and civil servants viewing the process as bottom-up while only 38 percent of accounting and financial respondents taking a similar position....

TEAM ORGANIZATION: ONE LEADER OR GROUP CONSENSUS?

In any international negotiation, it is important to know how the other side is organized and makes decisions.... One extreme is the negotiating team with a supreme leader who has complete authority to decide all matters. Many American teams tend to follow this approach, which has been labeled the "John Wayne-style of negotiations." Other cultures stress team negotiations....

The cultural group with the strongest preference for consensus organization was the French.... Despite the Japanese reputation for consensus arrangements, only 45 percent of Japanese respondents claimed to prefer a negotiating team based on consensus. The Brazilians, Chinese, and Mexicans, to a far greater degree than any other groups, preferred one-person leadership, a reflection perhaps of the political traditions in those countries....

The survey also revealed significant differences among occupational groups. For example, while 100 percent of the military respondents preferred a single leader for a negotiating team, only 43 percent of persons in finance expressed a similar view....

RISK TAKING: HIGH OR LOW?

Among all respondents, approximately 70 percent claimed a tendency toward risk taking while only 30 percent characterized themselves as low risk takers.... The Japanese are said to be highly risk-averse in negotiations, and this tendency was affirmed by the survey which found Japanese respondents to be the most risk-averse of the twelve cultures. Americans in the survey, by comparison, considered themselves to be risk takers, but an even percentage of French, British, and Indians claimed to be risk takers....

The survey also found significant differences among professional groups. For example, whereas 100 percent of the military respondents considered themselves to be high risk takers in negotiations, only 36 percent of diplomats and civil servants characterized themselves similarly.

CONCLUSION

[T]he survey suggests that professional and occupational culture may be as important as national culture in shaping a person's negotiation style and attitudes toward the negotiation process. If true, this finding has at least two important implications. First, both scholars and practitioners need to take into account professional culture, as well as national culture, in their studies and analysis of the impact of culture on negotiating behavior. Second, when faced with a cultural difference at the negotiating table, negotiators from different cultures but similar occupational or professional backgrounds might seek to rely on the elements of their professional culture in trying to bridge the cultural gap between them.

Notes and Questions

9.6 What type of advice does Salacuse provide for practitioners? How is this advice different from that offered by Rubin and Sander? How is it the same? How do Salacuse's findings compare to Rubin and Sander's advice that culture may not matter? For another study of national and ethnic differences in negotiation see Jeanne Brett, Negotiating Globally: How to Negotiate Deals, Resolve Disputes, and Make Decisions Across Cultural Boundaries (2001).

9.7 One example that shows creativity in manipulating cultural differences in negotiation is that in which Nigerian women successfully negotiated with Chevron Texaco for more jobs and better schools while Nigerian men had been unsuccessful, often using violent strikes. The Nigerian women successfully negotiated by occupying and striking against an export terminal. They also used a particularly persuasive threat that was unique to their culture. "When several days had passed without success in negotiations, they threatened to take off their clothes if their demands were not met. In the culture of the Niger Delta, women bring great shame upon men by stripping naked in front of them." Nigerian Women Show Their Power, at *http://www.news24.com* (July 19, 2002).

9.8 For a contextually rich discussion of a cross-cultural negotiation see Elsa Walsh, The Negotiator, The New Yorker, Mar. 18, 1996, at 86-97, describing the trade negotiations between U.S. trade representative Charlene Barshefsky and Chinese trade minister Wu Yi. The Chinese intended to turn these negotiations into an "endurance test" but "patience was one of Barshefsky's greatest strengths."

Wu Yi's reputation as a hard bargainer continued even in other contexts and in other countries. In May 2005, Wu Yi, in her role as vice premier of China, was in Japan to meet with the Japanese prime minister to improve strained relations with Japan. In response to ongoing tensions stemming from a World War II shrine honoring Japanese dead that included war criminals, Wu Yi canceled the meeting with the Japanese prime minister. The Japanese foreign minister stated that "there was not even a word of apology over the sudden cancellation. Such things go against human society." To U.S. students, cultural differences between two Asian countries may not seem all that vast, but clearly in this case, cultural conceptions of diplomacy were quite different. James Brooke, Relations Fray as Japan Criticizes Chinese Official's Snub, N.Y. Times, May 25, 2005, at A10.

In this next excerpt, Kevin Avruch writes about how culture can impact humanitarian workers who routinely engage in negotiations with individuals and parties with diverse cultural backgrounds.

Kevin Avruch, CULTURE AS CONTEXT, CULTURE AS COMMUNICATION: CONSIDERATIONS FOR HUMANITARIAN NEGOTIATORS

9 Harv. Negot. L. Rev. 391, 392-395, 396-399, 400, 404-405, 406, 407 (2004)

In this essay I consider some of the special problems that humanitarian workers in the field encounter when engaging in negotiations with parties whose cultural backgrounds differ substantially from their own. . . .

CULTURE

In his memoirs, former United Nations Under Secretary General Sir Brian Urquhart tells the story of the first night in 1957 that a contingent of the United Nations Emergency Force (UNEF) was deployed to Gaza. That evening, upon hearing from the minarets the muezzin's call to prayers, but not understanding Arabic or the meaning of the act, the U.N. troops believed it to be a call to civil disorder and fired in panic on the mosque.

Today, it is hard to imagine such a complete lack of fundamental and substantive knowledge about the "host" society and its culture by the majority of international participants in a complex humanitarian intervention. Yet the level of culture-specific pre-deployment training in most IOs [international organizations], NGOs [non-governmental organizations], and militaries is far from sufficient. Typically, humanitarian agents learn about their host society's culture by committing to memory a standardized list of "do's and don'ts" (e.g., "don't offer your left hand to an Arab"; "don't pat a Buddhist on the head"; "don't expect the Latin Americans to be on time for the meeting"). This practice conceives of cultures as collections of static traits and customs. What gets left out is the dynamism—the conflicts, change, and quality of emergence that characterize cultures. To try to learn about another culture from lists of traits and customs is akin to trying to learn English by memorizing the Oxford English Dictionary—all vocabulary, no grammar. This method is particularly ill-suited for those trying to master a dynamic process like negotiation in a foreign cultural context.

There are numerous definitions of culture and they continue to proliferate. For our purposes, culture refers to the socially transmitted values, beliefs and symbols that are more or less shared by members of a social group. These constitute the framework through which members interpret and attribute meaning to both their own and others' experiences and behavior. One key assumption implicit in this definition is that culture is a quality of social groups and perhaps communities, and that members may belong to multiple such groups. Therefore, an individual may "carry" several cultures, for example, ethnic or national, religious, and occupational affiliations. Thus, for any given individual, culture always comes "in the plural," and therefore every interaction (including negotiation) between individuals is likely to be multicultural on several levels. Another assumption is that culture is rarely, if ever, perfectly shared by all members of a group or community. Intracultural variation is likely to be present, perhaps considerable, and this should caution us against ascribing value, belief, or behavioral uniformity to members of a group—against stereotyping.

These assumptions suggest that socialization is the aggregate of numerous social interactions where culture is transmitted. It therefore becomes crucial to understand the different sources of culture and their different modes of transmission.

These assumptions militate against using lists of traits and do's and don'ts to learn about another culture. Rather, as specialists in intercultural communication put it, a more sophisticated approach is necessary to become "culturally competent." For humanitarian workers, who routinely find themselves working under difficult conditions in unfamiliar cultural settings, the attainment of such cultural competence is especially important — it might mean the difference between the success or failure of the mission. Certainly, it lies at the core of the broader concept of "communicational competence," which in turn is a prerequisite for social interaction generally, and in particular, for the kind of interaction called negotiation.

One popular model of culture is the "iceberg," commonly depicted as a triangle or pyramid. In this model, the top level visible above the surface is comprised of behavior, artifacts, and institutions. Underlying this level, just beneath the surface but fairly easily accessible to sensitive observers, are norms, beliefs, values and attitudes. At the deepest level, all but invisible even to members of a cultural group, lie the fundamental assumptions and presuppositions, the sense-and-meaning-making schemas and symbols, the ontology, about the world and individuals' experience in it. While a useful heuristic, the iceberg concept tends unhelpfully to assume a homogeneity of cultural sharing among individuals (this is never the case), and it lacks dynamism. Much more goes on "inside" the iceberg than the simple model implies; furthermore, icebergs frequently move about, often with disastrous results for shipping.

NEGOTIATION

Before leaving structural (and static) models like the iceberg to focus on cultural process, a word about what similar models may teach us regarding negotiation itself follows. Perhaps the most popular model of negotiation that is currently taught (indeed, prescribed) is the so-called Harvard model, exemplified in Fisher, Ury and Patton's *Getting to YES*. This model first instructs negotiators to get below the positions taken by the parties to try and identify the underlying interests. This is excellent advice, since while positions may clash or appear irreconcilable, some interests may be mutual and therefore amenable to bridging. This model has been demonstrably successful in intracultural commercial settings within the same nation or similar nations sharing a capitalist or free market context. The interest-based model of negotiation takes shared context for granted, as *given*. Yet such sharing is precisely what is problematic when negotiating cross-culturally. Moreover, the stratified iceberg implies that fundamental assumptions or presumptions about the world may lurk beneath even shared interests. I argue that it is far more difficult to reconcile or "bridge" conflicts of values or worldviews than interests. I am less confident of the success of interest-based negotiation in conflicts around deeply held values such as identity, or around religiously-inspired worldviews. While not all negotiations faced by humanitarians in the field will necessarily involve such fundamental parts of the cultural iceberg, some will, and in those cases the limitations of strictly interest-based bargaining ought to be considered. . . .

With respect to negotiation, to see culture as context is to understand that even before parties meet and converse for the first time, their most fundamental comprehensions of their respective positions, interests, and values have been set and circumscribed by the very language (i.e. culture) with which they bring them to expression.

UNICEF representative Daniel Toole provides two examples of the role of "deep" cultural context — the base parts of the iceberg — in humanitarian negotiations. While not addressing culture specifically, he first describes the deep divide between U.N. negotiators and the Taliban in Afghanistan over fundamental conceptions of human rights, such as treatment of girls and women. The lack of shared values and norms respecting gender equality made any discussion across the cultural divide on these issues next to impossible. "As a consequence," Toole writes, "negotiation of numerous issues was very difficult and made little headway." Many humanitarian programs in Afghanistan were subsequently suspended.

Toole's second example relates to the different principles of action that distinguish the U.N. from many humanitarian organizations. Such principles underlying action are sometimes called "strategic culture." In difficult cases, the U.N.'s strategic culture employs a principle of "conditionality" — using a combination of carrots and sticks to induce change in recalcitrant negotiation partners. For many humanitarians, however, who remain committed to providing aid to people in need regardless of political considerations, such conditionality appears ethically unsound and unacceptable.

The debate over conditionality raises concerns about the viability of traditional negotiation concepts when applied in humanitarian contexts. In classical negotiation theory, parties must always bear in mind their "reservation prices" (the point at which each will not "sell" or "buy"), and what Roger Fisher and his collaborators famously called the BATNA, or "best alternative to a negotiated agreement[.]" This is the imagined best-case scenario should negotiations break down, and correlates to "the point at which a negotiator is prepared to walk away from the negotiation table." If a party has not settled on a reservation price or thought through his BATNA, he is seriously disadvantaged in subsequent negotiation. Consider what the lack of conditionality implies for humanitarian negotiators — especially if the other party learns of that deficiency. The principle that one gives aid or renders protection to those in need, irrespective of identity, past actions, or "politics," means that there is no "reservation price" available to humanitarians, save in the field an operational withdrawal point if the situation becomes too dangerous. Also, in humanitarian negotiation there is no real BATNA for access or aid or protection — all the alternatives are bad ones, and inaction becomes unthinkable. Humanitarians thus face ethically precarious options of negotiating how many sacks of rice a warlord takes for allowing the convoy through, or (even more unsavory) of allowing militias or *genocidaires* to distribute the food in a refugee camp so that any is distributed at all.

In both cases described by Toole, any negotiations that take place will be framed from the start by the different cultural constructions of the world brought to the table by the parties. In this sense, the parties never wholly define the negotiating situation; it comes to them, as they come to it, partly predefined. Such predefinition may create an obstacle for negotiations. For instance, should one negotiating party's construction of the world be based upon a universal human rights discourse not shared by other parties, an impasse may result. Such is the power of cultural context. . . .

In a complex humanitarian operation, the number of such contexts can appear overwhelming. Not uncommonly, they include (1) the cultures of the host country populations (often comprised of several distinct subcultural groups); (2) those of international aid, development, humanitarian and relief organizations; (3) those of heavily bureaucratized institutions such as the U.N. (itself subculturally differentiated by nationality, and, more importantly, by functional divisions with geographically disparate headquarters); and (4) often by various militaries, with their own internal service divisions, inculcations of ethos, and national peacekeeping "doctrines." Add, perhaps, international media to the mix and humanitarian negotiators face an exceedingly complex operation in a multicultural arena of national, ethnic, institutional, and professional interactions.

For example, in a multicultural arena an American military officer and an American civilian aid worker may share many of the same understandings and perceptions of the world based upon their shared American culture, and easily communicate about many matters (though they may still have much to disagree about, of course). However, on matters relating to security, force protection, command-and-control, or rules of engagement, the American military officer may share more cultural commonality with an Indian, Pakistani, or Nigerian military colleague; the mutual premises of a transnational "military culture" will facilitate communication between them. This may be the case even when language differences necessitate the services of an interpreter. On the other hand, within the NGO community, even the English-speaking one, conflicts may arise in the field because of differences in the organizational or strategic cultures of relief or humanitarian workers focused on quick response, immediate access to populations in need, and crisis problem solving; those of workers representing sustainable development organizations who have longer term or infrastructural concerns; and those of a U.N. official focused on political or diplomatic issues.

One practical implication is that humanitarian negotiators, like all parties to a conflict, ought to begin with a process of "conflict mapping" that includes learning about the history, sources, and parties that define the conflict arena. In addition to this traditional mapping, I also suggest a preliminary cultural mapping including cultural knowledge about the host populations (e.g., Sunni and Shi'a Muslims in the following proportions . . .), and the various national and institutional cultures participating from the international community — NATO, U.N. peacekeepers, the ICRC, CARE, Oxfam, and Medecins Sans Frontieres (MSF). . . .

It is critical to underline the "preliminary" nature of such a culture mapping, for two reasons. First, the knowledge about these cultures must come from somewhere — most likely from the experiential base that those in the field bring from having worked in such operations with some or all of the same international parties before. For instance, what does it mean that the U.S. Marines, rather than U.K. or Italian forces, are responsible for security in this sector; that the U.N. Development Program (UNDP) rather than the U.N. High Commissioner for Refugees (UNHCR), is the "lead" U.N. organization, and so on. Experience is indispensable. . . .

Second, cultures are neither timeless nor changeless; they are always emerging within the larger framework of social action and social practice. This emergent quality means in effect that each operation will after a time generate its own cultural context, along with (as we have come [to learn]) its own political economy. For this reason, we must revisit the preliminary cultural mapping, both to sift out the difference between useful experience and costly prejudice, and to take account of the cultural emergence that occurs when individuals from different backgrounds work together, particularly under stress, in crisis, and in fitful communication with their respective headquarters and bureaucracies.

One brief example of an admittedly modest cultural emergence may be found in Chris Seiple's excellent monograph, *The U.S. Military/NGO Relationship in Humanitarian Interventions.* The setting is Operation Provide Comfort in Northern Iraq in 1991. During the first week, the NGO MSF-France doctors had wanted nothing whatsoever to do with U.S. Army Special Forces personnel working in their area. This aversion stemmed from several factors, including the rather thorny reputation that MSF enjoyed in those days even among other NGOs, coupled with their dislike of working with the military in general, and a pointedly French dislike of working with the American military. Even worse, these were not only American soldiers, but Special Forces — Green Berets — whose overwhelming image probably still conjures for most outsiders the persona of Rambo (just as the overall image of America still comes to many in the world courtesy of Hollywood and American television). However, Seiple relates, once the MSF physicians had witnessed Special Forces medics in the field, superbly trained and saving lives; once they had witnessed the Special Forces administering to basic health needs; and — my favorite — once they realized that many, undoubtedly because of language training, spoke French, the situation changed dramatically. By the end of the first week, Seiple writes, the MSF doctors had invited the Special Forces teams to dinner.

Notes and Questions

9.9 What are the different cultures that Avruch discusses? How do these organizational cultures help or hinder communication for humanitarian workers?

This last excerpt discusses what happens when gender and culture mix up some of our assumptions in both areas. It is a great cautionary tale exemplifying the advice provided by all of the authors — that in making assumptions about cultural differences, we should proceed with caution.

 Sharon Doerre, **NEGOTIATING GENDER AND AUTHORITY IN NORTHERN SYRIA**

6 Intl. Negot. J. 251, 252-253, 255-261 (2001)

The analysis centers on the experiences of American volunteers, both male and female, who participate in the archaeological excavation as the immediate "supervisors" of the local, all-male, Syrian work crews. These archaeological "tourists," distinct from the professional, academic archaeologists who direct and organize the excavation, pay for the opportunity to participate in the dig. Although the composition of the American crew changes from year to year, it is possible to sketch out a few generalizations. Younger volunteers, those between 18 and 40, are primarily community college and seminary students. Some of them are earning college credits in anthropology or Biblical archaeology while on the dig. This group can be divided into students continuing their education directly from high school and returning students who are resuming their education or changing careers. Many in this group express interest in the excavation primarily as an opportunity to travel to an unusual place and to break away from their everyday routine. Older volunteers, ranging in age from 40 to 68, frequently explain that they have wished to participate in an archaeological excavation all of their lives and have finally reached a point where they have the resources to do so. To varying degrees the chance to visit a land of Biblical significance also plays a role in the decision to join the excavation. Generally, these tourist-volunteers lack any familiarity with the local language or Middle Eastern Muslim societies. As middle-class Midwesterners, few have ever supervised manual laborers or engaged in heavy physical labor themselves. Attention is drawn to these features only to underscore the point that unlike the lone cultural anthropologist immersed in fieldwork, most archaeological volunteers are not prepared or inclined to reflexively examine their social position or personal practices in a foreign setting. They tend to see their own social behavior as universally natural and normal, not culturally specific.

In contrast, the men hired as site workers and the women hired as household help, although dismissed as hopelessly backward or *shaawi* by townspeople, have some practical experience dealing with foreign archaeologists. Since the mid-1980s the Khabur river valley has been the site of intensive archaeological excavation in advance of a new series of dams. Although different constellations of villages and settlements provided labor for each excavation, the majority of workers hired at Tell Tuneinir have some direct experience with or indirect knowledge of foreign archaeological projects. Furthermore, the workers, ranging in age from 15 to 35, possess a particular fluency in negotiating power relations, a product of their subordinate position as sharecroppers, agricultural laborers, clients, and sons (or in the case of household workers, daughters and wives) in the local economy. Most of the local workers at the site are first or second generation settled nomads from client sections of Bedouin tribes. After the Ba'th party revolution broke up the large landholdings of the tribal heads, their former clients became farmers, raising wheat and cotton along with small herds along the Khabur River. Working at foreign archaeological excavations enables families to supplement their earnings with cash wages. . . .

It quickly became evident that gender is a key pivot in the power relations at the site when, in sharp contrast to the commonsense notions of most Westerners, the workers excavate squares headed by female volunteers much more quickly and smoothly than squares run by male volunteers. This disparity is clearly visible to all observers through the amount of soil removed from an excavation square which thus becomes an approximate and readily measurable index of social competence and authority of the volunteer.

The following journal excerpt, written by an undergraduate volunteer in June 1998 after her first day of digging, illustrates this dynamic.

> I was so nervous before we started up to the tell that I could hardly speak or eat, but actually it went pretty well once I reached my square.... I just took a big breath; pointed to the area I had outlined with my trowel, looked the pickman in the eyes, smiled and said *men fadluk* (please). That's all I had to do.... By the time we stopped for second breakfast at nine o'clock my whole square was dug down ten centimeters below the surface. This drove Dick crazy. His workers had barely scratched the surface of his square; in fact none of the guys had gotten their squares dug deeper than mine.... The more Dick yells and screams the slower his workers seemed to go. I just try to be polite and not interfere too much. So far it seems to be working.

The greater success of the female volunteers, in terms of soil excavated from their squares, persisted throughout the eight-week digging season and has generally remained true for each succeeding season (1988-1996).

Anticipating a hostile response to their requests from the Arab-Muslim work-men, female volunteers generally approach their excavation squares with trepidation. This anxiety tends to emerge in particular physical displays—shifting weight from side to side, lowered eyes, closed smiles, hesitations, and raised pitch in speech, and fidgeting—characteristics of deferent, self-humbling behavior in many societies. This deference defuses the challenge of the verbal commands (i.e. shugal—work) by indicating an asymmetrical social ranking in which the volunteer is not in a position to coerce the worker's compliance in any way. Here, politeness itself forms a gendered tactic or "art of the weak" for "making do" in an unfamiliar situation that reflects a felt absence of power. Women volunteers tend to alternate these deferential practices with displays of positive attention—direct, lingering eye contact, open smiles, nodding of the head. Generally, workers respond to the implicit but usually unintended sexuality of these gestures by intensifying and exaggerating their work efforts; exhibitions of masculine strength and vigor oriented as much towards their audience of co-workers as to the female volunteers.

Male volunteers generally do not foresee any difficulties in directing a crew of Arab-Muslim workers. On the contrary, many of them express confidence that as men their position will be enhanced in a clearly patriarchal society. Mistaking simple male identity (the sexual difference) for the continually achieved and contested status of a man of honor and stature, male volunteers are ill-prepared to enter the open, public forum of the dig site. Unfamiliar with the verbal and physical repertoire employed in local performances of masculinity, male volunteers compound their difficulties by misreading the highly performative, status-laden arena of social inter-action created by this new workplace for a simple, task-orientated sphere. Their focus is archaeology—recovering artifacts—not interacting with workers.

Thus, male volunteers tend to view the workers as tools, the physical means to an archaeological end. Again, this approach emerges bodily. In addition to shouting, pointing fingers, crossing arms, and other expressions and gestures of frustration, male volunteers often physically interrupt the workers' actions; jumping into the dig square with loud cries of la, la, la (no, no, no), to mime a more "efficient," "productive" way of digging. Volunteers justify these disruptions of the flow of social interactions as expedient measures, mirroring [the] insight that "where the focus of interaction is task-orientated, face redress may be felt to be irrelevant." Indeed many male volunteers meet the suggestion that they need to monitor their self-presentation to workers with astonishment. They are unaware of how childish and undignified their outbursts appear to the local workers. . . .

Efforts by American male volunteers to re-organize their crews "more efficiently" threatens to disrupt the pre-existing social hierarchies among the local men who motivate and organize the work crews. When the men are hired, the Arab foreman arranges each five-man crew in accordance to his understanding (often imperfect) of local kinship and patronage ties as well as strength and ability. This principle of organization often remains invisible to American volunteers who are not familiar with local family and residence patterns. The volunteers tend to view each worker according to his function in the excavation, either as a pickman, shovel man, or wheelbarrow boy. A shovel man in one crew, however, is not necessarily replaceable by a shovel man from any other crew due to his particular village, family, and friendship ties. Certain people simply will not work together or will not work together well. Whether genuine or instrumental, the strategy of yielding employed by female volunteers allows the underlying local system of authority to operate freely. For example, the pickman whose wheelbarrow pusher is his wife's younger brother can more effectively demand better work performance from him than the American volunteer. Yielding by women seems "natural" to the workers as it puts the onus for a successful outcome on the most high status man in the crew. To maintain their position in the local systems of male authority and prestige, these men ensure that the work goes smoothly. Whether intentional or accidental, male volunteers' behavior is more likely to be perceived as contentious by their workers. Workers may interpret their interference as an affront to their dignity and skill as workmen, particularly if they are highly sought after pickmen who work with many excavations throughout the year, or as a challenge to their authority if they are prominent men in the community, or simply as a ridiculous demand by someone who is not strong (manly) enough to do the actual labor himself. Inevitably, less digging is done.

Even when American men attempt to exhibit yielding behavior, it is likely to be interpreted as contending, which produces corresponding contentious actions from their workers. For example, some men try to signal their disengagement from the politics of the crew by bringing a stool to their square. Instead of actively managing their crew, the male volunteer intends to signal his willingness to simply record and organize the finds by sitting on a stool alongside the square with his notebook. To the workers, however, sitting in this manner can be interpreted as a sign of superiority. . . .

Successful female volunteers may consciously and unconsciously employ many different tactics to manage their work crews. In addition to deference, American women can also choose a more confrontational approach. Surprisingly, this may succeed as well as yielding because their behavior is consistent with that of local women who have a reputation for hard work, toughness, and a brash approach towards men. *Shaawi* women regularly confront their husbands, sons, brothers or neighbors verbally, often ridiculing their attempts to "sit" like Bedouins. Thus, an

American volunteer who "gets tough" with her workers does not threaten their masculinity in the way that similar displays by American men might, in fact, she momentarily mirrors the public stance of *shaawi* women.

Notes and Questions

9.10 What advice would you provide to a male friend participating in the dig? To a female friend?

9.11 Note that in order to really learn from this experience, the writer had to have knowledge of the Syrian culture, knowledge about the particular business (archaeological digs), and knowledge of negotiation theory. What can we do if we do not possess such expertise and we are about to negotiate with someone from another culture?

B. GENDER

Building on the last example of U.S. crews in Syria, we now turn to gender as a factor in negotiation. Having read about the caveats in cultural differences, we encourage you to keep the same caveats in mind. While gender can be a salient difference between negotiators, oversimplification or overattribution of negotiation behavior should be avoided. This first excerpt is a classic in the field of gender psychology, which outlines the perceived differences between girls' and boys' conceptions of justice and fairness. We start here because this is where so much gender analysis starts in the related fields of psychology and communication. But this first article is not where the analysis of gender communication should end. The other articles in this section first place the concepts of justice in a legal context. The next articles show that even if the conclusions from Carol Gilligan's study do not apply to grown women (and we are not sure they do), perceptions and stereotypes affect negotiation behavior on both sides. The final articles in this section take a look at empirical studies of women negotiating in law and upper management.

 Carol Gilligan, **IN A DIFFERENT VOICE: PSYCHOLOGICAL THEORY AND WOMEN'S DEVELOPMENT**

> 25-28 (1982)

The two children were in the same sixth-grade class at school and were participants in the rights and responsibilities study, designed to explore different conceptions of morality and self. The sample selected for this study was chosen to focus the variables of gender and age while maximizing developmental potential by holding constant, at a high level, the factors of intelligence, education, and social class that have been associated with moral development, at least as measured by existing scales. The two children in question, Amy and Jake, were both bright and articulate and, at least in their eleven-year-old aspirations, resisted easy categories of sex-role stereotyping, since Amy aspired to become a scientist while Jake preferred English to math. Yet their moral judgments seem initially to confirm familiar notions about differences between the sexes, suggesting that the edge girls have on moral development during the early school years gives way at puberty with the ascendance of formal logical thought in boys.

The dilemma that these eleven-year-olds were asked to resolve was one in the series devised by [Lawrence] Kohlberg to measure moral development in adolescence by presenting a conflict between moral norms and exploring the logic of its resolution. In this particular dilemma, a man named Heinz considers whether or not to steal a drug which he cannot afford to buy in order to save the life of his wife. In the standard format of Kohlberg's interviewing procedure, the description of the dilemma itself — Heinz's predicament, the wife's disease, the druggist's refusal to lower his price — is followed by the question, "Should Heinz steal the drug?" The reasons for and against stealing are then explored through a series of questions that vary and extend the parameters of the dilemma in a way designed to reveal the underlying structure of moral thought.

Jake, at eleven, is clear from the outset that Heinz should steal the drug. Constructing the dilemma, as Kohlberg did, as a conflict between the values of property and life, he discerns the logical priority of life and uses that logic to justify his choice:

> For one thing, a human life is worth more than money, and if the druggist only makes $1,000, he is still going to live, but if Heinz doesn't steal the drug, his wife is going to die. (*Why is life worth more than money?*) Because the druggist can get a thousand dollars later from rich people with cancer, but Heinz can't get his wife again. (*Why not?*) Because people are all different and so you couldn't get Heinz's wife again.

Asked whether Heinz should steal the drug if he does not love his wife, Jake replies that he should, saying that not only is there "a difference between hating and killing," but also, if Heinz were caught, "the judge would probably think it was the right thing to do." Asked about the fact that, in stealing, Heinz would be breaking the law, he says that "the laws have mistakes, and you can't go writing up a law for everything that you can imagine."

Thus, while taking the law into account and recognizing its function in maintaining social order (the judge, Jake says, "should give Heinz the lightest possible sentence"), he also sees the law as man-made and therefore subject to error and change. Yet his judgment that Heinz should steal the drug, like his view of the law as having mistakes, rests on the assumption of agreement, a societal consensus around moral values that allows one to know and expect others to recognize what is "the right thing to do." . . .

Fascinated by the power of logic, this eleven-year-old boy locates truth in math, which he says is "the only thing that is totally logical." Considering the moral dilemma to be "sort of like a math problem with humans," he sets it up as an equation and proceeds to work out the solution. Since his solution is rationally derived, he assumes that anyone following reason would arrive at the same conclusion and thus that a judge would also consider stealing to be the right thing for Heinz to do. Yet he is also aware of the limits of logic. Asked whether there is a right answer to moral problems, Jake replies that "there can only be right and wrong in judgment," since the parameters of action are variable and complex. Illustrating how actions undertaken with the best of intentions can eventuate in the most disastrous of consequences, he says, "like if you give an old lady your seat on the trolley, if you are in a trolley crash and that trolley seat goes through the window, it might be that reason that the old lady dies." . . .

In contrast, Amy's response to the dilemma conveys a very different impression, an image of development stunted by a failure of logic, an inability to think for herself. Asked if Heinz should steal the drug, she replies in a way that seems evasive and unsure:

> Well, I don't think so. I think there might be other ways besides stealing it, like if he could borrow the money or make a loan or something, but he really shouldn't steal the drug — but his wife shouldn't die either.

Asked why he should not steal the drug, she considers neither property nor law but rather the effect that theft could have on the relationship between Heinz and his wife:

> If he stole the drug, he might save his wife then, but if he did, he might have to go to jail, and then his wife might get sicker again, and he couldn't get more of the drug, and it might not be good. So, they should really just talk it out and find some other way to make the money.

Seeing in the dilemma not a math problem with humans but a narrative of relationships that extends over time, Amy envisions the wife's continuing need for her husband and the husband's continuing concern for his wife and seeks to respond to the druggist's need in a way that would sustain rather than sever connection. Just as she ties the wife's survival to the preservation of relationships, so she considers the value of the wife's life in a context of relationships, saying that it would be wrong to let her die because, "if she died, it hurts a lot of people and it hurts her." Since Amy's moral judgment is grounded in the belief that, "if somebody has something that would keep somebody alive, then it's not right not to give it to them," she considers the problem in the dilemma to arise not from the druggist's assertion of rights but from his failure of response.

This next excerpt translates Gilligan's study into the legal system by assessing how each voice would actually work in establishing rules of problem solving.

 Carrie Menkel-Meadow, **FEMINIST DISCOURSE, MORAL VALUES AND THE LAW — A CONVERSATION**

34 Buff. L. Rev. 11, 50-54 (1985)

I would like to . . . use Carol [Gilligan's] example to tell you what Amy and Jake said to me about the legal system. I'd like to use the example to explore further how we might look at the legal system with that double lens or double vision Carol describes. . . . One of the interesting things about the Amy and Jake description is the different way in which they approach the problem. . . .

One of the things that Amy does that might be of interest to law students is typical of a "bad" law student: Amy "fought the hypo." When asked whether or not Heinz should steal the drug, Amy asked a lot of questions about the situation. At fifteen, she is still fighting the hypo. "Look," she says to the researchers, "you have given me a totally silly situation that I do not think really exists in the world. Or if it did, I would know a whole lot more about it." She asks for what has come to be known in academic circles as "a greater feeling for the context." Law students, when faced with hypotheticals that seem to be missing something (perhaps facts about the particular people in the situation, or about the political context in which the case is found, or — to use the legal realist phrase — about what the judge had for breakfast that morning), usually behave the same way Amy did. They feel that the problems are disembodied and disemboweled from the way in which they occur in the world.

When I thought about Amy's response, I thought that we in the legal system may be focusing our problems too narrowly. Through her use of a different voice, Amy tells us that we may need to know a great deal more about facts and about situations before we can make decisions about them. . . . Take that a step further. Amy not only fights the hypo, she approaches it in a different way. As Carol has pointed out in her book . . . Jake saw the problem as an algebraic equation with people; there is the druggist, and there is Heinz with Heinz's wife. How do we balance those equities? How do we decide between those two people? Jake "gets it right." He says: "Life is more important than property, so life wins." Amy says: "I see two people with a problem here: the druggist, whose goal in life is to make a profit; and Heinz, who would like to save his wife's life. Is there not some way of holding the needs of both of these parties constant, and trying to work out another solution?" . . . Have Heinz and the druggist talked about some other ways to solve this problem? How about an installment contract? How about payments over time? Has Heinz explored other ways to raise the money? Has the druggist thought about ways of providing a drug and perhaps getting payment in some other way?

Amy doesn't see the problem as presenting, by necessity, a bipolar choice. Amy's approach to the problem is in direct contradiction, I think, to the way we typically solve problems in the legal system: in a bipolar, win-lose way. The drug is either stolen or it is not, and it is either right or wrong to steal. . . . Amy tells us that if we learn more facts and we take the needs of the parties and hold them constant, perhaps we can come up with some other solutions — solutions, as Carol pointed out, which might not have been thought about if we looked at the problem from the perspective of only one party in the problem, either Heinz or the druggist. Amy is trying to remember everybody as she tries to solve the problem.

Amy then does another thing with the problem. She asks, as Carol reports in her book, whether Heinz and the druggist ever sit down and talk about this. She wants to know why *she* has to solve the problem. She uses "I" as a third person looking at this problem from the outside. Maybe, she muses, if they sat down and talked to each other, they would come up with yet a whole bunch of other solutions that I, sitting here as a third person, could not think about. . . . Amy thus suggests not only different kinds of substantive solutions, she also thinks of a whole different sort of process:

dialogue between the parties. Now, I think that has obvious implications for our adversary culture and our adversary system. Our Anglo-American culture and adversary system require, for the most part, that two parties talk to a judge. Amy and Jake are asked to play judge for Heinz and the druggist; they are asked to decide whether Heinz is right to steal the drug or not. Perhaps there are other forms that might encourage the parties to come up with other solutions.

I want to come back to yet another dimension of how Amy and Jake reform the way in which we might look at legal decision making and problem solving. This is something that is evident during both of Amy's interviews. She says: "Well, suppose Heinz steals the drug and then he goes to jail. That is not going to do his wife any good because in addition to the drug she also needs the relationship with her husband to get her through this difficult time of what may turn out to be terminal cancer." Amy is thus concerned with preserving the relationship of the parties and looking at the situation in which they are imbedded. She looks both at the past and at the future, considering the effect on the parties of a certain decision. . . .

[W]hat we see in Jake's description is pretty much how the Heinz dilemma would get solved if it wound up either in court or if the parties attempted to negotiate something between themselves. It was from that work, in looking at how to be a practicing lawyer — in a courtroom, as a negotiator, or as a legal problem solver — that I began to rethink the theory of legal structure. My re-examination could well have been inspired by how Amy looked at the problem.

I should add here that I have noticed, as did Carol in psychology, how many of our conceptions of what the legal system ought to be and ought to do were derived exclusively from male practitioners and male scholars. The law may thus represent an embodiment of Jake's voice, the male voice. As a double footnote, I, like Carol, want to say that although I am speaking of male and female voices, I am simply using those terms as a code for what she observed to exist empirically in those two genders. All of us have elements of both of those voices. Those men who see themselves fitting the description of the female voice should know that that is probably who they are, and vice versa for women. I use that as an easy way to talk about this material, but one that is not necessarily accurate for each of you individually.

What would the legal system look like if Amy had devised it, either alone or with Jake's help? As I said, Amy might use different forms or different processes. To do this, let's look at the way the Anglo-American court system is in fact structured. We have basically a one-way communication, adverse parties talking to a judge. . . . There is very little direct communication between the parties. Picking up on Amy's process notion that the parties might talk to each other, we can imagine a structure in which the parties might be asked to sit down and talk about whether the drug should be stolen or financed in some other way. One form that is beginning to emerge, which in some sense is a reaction to this adversary structure, is alternative dispute resolution or mediation. . . .

If the parties are not in accord, they will do what most parties do when they are in dispute — they will probably arrive at a solution by negotiation. Typically, a plaintiff and a defendant — Heinz and the druggist — will start arguing with each other. Heinz might say: "I can't pay you anything." The druggist would respond: "I want one hundred dollars." At some point, they will split the difference, settling on paying perhaps half of what the druggist wanted.

What's wrong with that? What's wrong, according to some people, is that it reflects one form of the female voice — it is compromise, it is a combination, it is meeting somewhere in the middle, and it may leave both parties unhappy. What Amy was trying to do was to hold both parties' needs constant and to meet both sets of needs at the same time. Having the parties meet each other's needs does not necessarily result in compromise or accommodation, which is the way in which the female voice is frequently and inaccurately seen — as conciliatory, accommodating, giving up. . . . A new synergistic solution might emerge simply from having them talk to each other directly about their needs. If we learn to listen to the "Amys" of the world, we might begin to imagine different kinds of constructions and different ways of looking at our legal system in solving our legal problems.

That is just a very brief introduction to the kinds of things that you can do with this. One thing I always like to tell my "Jake" students is to try to think of themselves as "Amys." Similarly, "Amys" ought to look at the world from a "Jake" perspective; there is, after all, great value in the current system. The key, as Carol has indicated, is to try to imagine a legal system that might include both.

Notes and Questions

9.12 What are Gilligan's conclusions about how Jake thinks? About how Amy thinks? Are there value judgments attached to these differences?

9.13 How much insight can we get from a study performed on 11-year-olds? Does our approach change with age?

9.14 Menkel-Meadow notes clearly that "Jake" and "Amy" are just codes for certain types of voices. Each person has elements of both voices in him or her. Which voice is stronger for you? What happens when you follow Menkel-Meadow's advice from the end of this excerpt to take on the other voice? Can you see the problem from that perspective? Menkel-Meadow writes that looking at the legal system through Amy's eyes might help us better problem-solve. Which of Amy's skills would be useful in a negotiation?

9.15 What implications do different voices of justice and fairness have for negotiation? Why do differences in approaches affect our ability to negotiate?

9.16 Is it good or bad to "fight the hypo"? Why do or why don't all law students do this? What does this tell us about the legal system?

It used to be commonly thought that women were more interested in getting along, in preserving relationships and compromising in negotiations. In this next article, Carol Rose discusses the implications of this stereotype for negotiations. Furthermore, she notes what can happen *even when this stereotype is not true* and women are wrongly assumed to be more interested in cooperation.

Carol Rose, **BARGAINING AND GENDER**

18 Harv. J. L. & Pub. Poly. 547, 549-552, 555-557 (1995)

I adopted as a hypothesis the idea that in the real world there is a "taste for coopera-tion" . . . but I further adopted the hypothesis that the taste is unevenly distributed between the genders — that women are likely to have this taste more intensely than men, or apply it to more kinds of people. As my article noted, this hypothesis leaves room for individually cooperative men and stiff-necked uncooperative women — any such distribution, if it were to exist, would only be a matter of statistical dis-tributions, somewhat like height or weight, and would say nothing about individuals. Moreover, I left the whole idea entirely as a hypothesis, and in fact would not vouch for it, even though the proposition is advanced (and disputed) in a variety of ways in feminist literature. For example, the much-cited Carol Gilligan discusses women's relationship-based morality; studies suggest that women are more likely than men to take care of the children, the elderly relatives, the sibling relationships, and the neighbors; and many kinds of pop books refer to "women who care too much," as if their caring attitudes got them into trouble.

Well, maybe they do. But as I worked through the subject, it seemed that women's actual taste for cooperation — if such a taste exists — is much less important than something else: people think women are likely to be cooperative types. It appeared that the strong assumption of women's greater taste for cooperation in thinking about gender differences in bargains is unnecessary. Much can be explained about women's lesser assets on the much weaker assumption that people simply believe women are more likely to be cooperators than men.

GENDER BARGAINS WITH DIFFERENT TASTES

Garden variety bargains are normally a positive-sum game. I have a candy bar, you have an extra notebook; I want your notebook and you want my candy bar; we trade; we are both happier and better off. "Win-win" is the current phrase for this happy result.

Consider another example: two people, Sam and Louise, have access to a com-mon field, and they decide to cooperate by restraining their cows, so that the grasses can regenerate. Suppose that they are collectively better off by some amount, which I will call "X." Their now-renewable grassy field has a capitalized value of X dollars more than it would have been if their respective Bossies and Sadies had just munched and tramped away until all the grass died out. That X amount is the surplus of their positive-sum, win-win deal.

But another question lurks here: how are Sam and Louise going to split that X gain? Sam and Louise have entered a positive sum game from their big decision to cooperate, but after that, they face a zero sum game about splitting gains made from cooperation. What Sam gets of X is at Louise's expense, and vice versa.

Suppose Louise has a greater taste for cooperation than Sam does. This char-acterization should make their bargaining develop along predictable lines, but those lines will not be to Louise's advantage. First, while it is predictable that she will indeed be better off when she and Sam decide to cooperate, it is also predictable that she will not be as much better off as Sam is. She will find herself getting less than Sam because of her greater taste for cooperation.

Louise has to offer Sam more incentives for him to cooperate, or even to notice that cooperation might be a good idea. He was not terribly interested in cooperating in the first place, so he will not cooperate at all unless he receives a disproportionate amount of the gain. Conversely, Louise is more interested in a cooperative relationship, more quickly sees its necessity, or feels more responsible for it; for those reasons, she is likely to agree to the deal even though, in a sense, she has to pay a somewhat higher price for it. In sum, Sam has a bargaining advantage, because of his relative indifference or even hostility to cooperation.

Moreover, this advantage continues. When the two of them later buy fertilizer or fenceposts to improve the field, Sam will be the more stringent enforcer of the deal. He can more credibly threaten to walk away from the whole arrangement unless she contributes a disproportionate amount of the upkeep costs.

Notice that Louise is still ahead of where she would have been without the deal. Without the deal, she and Sam would have been in a classic "prisoners' dilemma," where both parties have an incentive to overuse the resource, to the ultimate damage of the resource itself, and to their mutual loss thereby. She is better off with the deal, but not so much better off as Sam is, because the deal costs her more. He gets a larger portion of the X amount they jointly realize from dealing. His portion may not be a much bigger cut of X, but it is still more than the cut Louise gets. . . .

Next, we consider the labor market. We should note that a transaction for employment should be a win–win or positive-sum exchange, despite the way labor relations may sometimes appear to labor theorists and historians. The employer presumably values labor more than the dollars it costs to hire that labor, while the employee values the dollars more than the leisure he or she would otherwise enjoy. Some X gains result from this exchange, too.

The next question is, how will employer and employee split those gains? Generally, the employer might have to offer more to Sam than to Louise. Sam is not all that interested in a cooperative exchange or relationship at the outset, and he can more credibly threaten to bail out later, because he is more tolerant of confrontation. On the other hand, the employer might offer Louise somewhat less: she is more alert to cooperative gains, and more attracted to cooperative relationships, so it does not take as much to get her on board. . . .

GENDER BARGAINS WITH SEEMINGLY DIFFERENT TASTES

Social issues lead to the next point: we can considerably relax any assumption that women have a taste for cooperation, and still come to depressingly similar results with respect to Sam's and Louise's share of X. It is not as important that a gendered difference in tastes for cooperation actually exists, as that people simply think it exists.

Returning to the employment situation, when an employer offers Louise a job, let us suppose that he believes she has a taste for cooperation, so that he offers her a smaller percentage of the gains made from trading wages for labor. He may also think — again related to his views on her taste for cooperation — that she is the one doing the bulk of the housework and the child care at home, so she has little time to search for other employment. Consequently, he offers her less of the gains from trade. What if she refuses? Beliefs do not vanish instantly; the employer will continue to make low bids to women, and at least some will accept, making him think that he was right in the first place. Indeed, in a sense, perhaps he is right, if his beliefs are sufficiently widely shared. Louise knows what people think about her wage demands, and she knows that even if she refuses, she will continue to get low bids from other potential employers. Thus, it costs her something and avails her little to break the pattern, and so she may well accede to the very stereotype that disadvantages her. . . .

We may see the same pattern at home. Loutish husband Sam may assume that his wife Louise will cook, do the dishes and iron his shirts as well, and he will yell at her if she does not perform these chores. But when he is out hunting with the guys, he assumes that they will all split the chores. While he does not even raise the issue with his friends on vacation, at home, Louise would be lambasted if she were to refuse to do all the work. On occasion, Louise may well give in rather than face another scene, and when she does, she reinforces Sam's smug assumptions about her willingness to take on a disproportionate set of the household duties.

The upshot is that whether Louise really has a taste for cooperation or is just thought to have it, she receives a smaller share of any gains than Sam. She does get something from her various cooperative relationships — just not as much as Sam. And the perception that she is more cooperative — probably much more than any actual taste for cooperation — plays a large role in creating patterns that make her life more difficult, and puts her to more challenges than Sam has to face.

Notes and Questions

9.17 Do you think that these assumptions about cooperativeness are correct? Think about your family and friends — does this apply? How could you deal with or change this assumption of cooperativeness?

9.18 Two *New York Times* editorials tackled this issue directly. In the first, John Tierney wrote that women's tendency toward cooperation has its advantages in the corporate world.

> Suppose you could eliminate the factors often blamed for the shortage of women in high-paying jobs. Suppose that promotions and raises did not depend on pleasing sexist male bosses or putting in long nights and weekends away from home. Would women make as much as men? . . . [No.]
>
> It was due to different appetites for competition.
>
> "Even in tasks where they do well, women seem to shy away from competition, whereas men seem to enjoy it too much," Professor Niederle said. "The men who weren't good at this task lost a little money by choosing to compete, and the really good women passed up a lot of money by not entering tournaments they would have won."
>
> You can argue that this difference is due to social influences, although I suspect it's largely innate, a byproduct of evolution and testosterone. Whatever

the cause, it helps explain why men set up the traditional corporate ladder as one continual winner-take-all competition — and why that structure no longer makes sense.

Now that so many employees (and more than half of young college graduates) are women, running a business like a tournament alienates some of the most talented workers and potential executives. It also induces competition in situations where cooperation makes more sense.

The result is not good for the bottom line, as demonstrated by a study from the Catalyst research organization showing that large companies yield better returns to stockholders if they have more women in senior management. A friend of mine, a businessman who buys companies, told me one of the first things he looks at is the gender of the boss.

"The companies run by women are much more likely to survive," he said. "The typical guy who starts a company is a competitive, charismatic leader — he's always the firm's top salesman — but if he leaves he takes his loyal followers with him and the company goes downhill. Women C.E.O.'s know how to hire good salespeople and create a healthy culture within the company. Plus they don't spend 20 percent of their time in strip clubs. . . ."

Maybe women, like the ones who shunned the experimental tournament, know they could make more money in some jobs but also know they wouldn't enjoy competing for it as much as their male rivals. They realize, better than men, that in life there's a lot more at stake than money.

John Tierney, What Women Want, N.Y. Times, May 24, 2005, at A25.

After Tierney's first article, the author received a significant number of letters from women readers who argued that they were just as competitive as men. In response to these letters, the author wrote an additional article exploring the reasons there are not more highly competitive women in the corporate world. In this article, Tierney suggests that discrimination may be one culprit for keeping the number of competitive women low due to the fact that traditionally women have not been allowed access. Additionally, through a scrabble analogy, Tierney suggests that while men are competitive with others, more women are competitive with themselves. John Tierney, The Urge to Win, N.Y. Times, May 31, 2005, at A19. Have you experienced women as less competitive than men? Is this common sense or nonsense?

9.19 One could also imagine the same extortion for cooperation as described by Carol Rose in different contexts. Assume that Noah wants to play tic-tac-toe (or go to the movies). His brother Joshua knows that Noah loves to play this game. Even though Joshua would also like to play, by not sharing his preference, he can demand that he be "X's" and go first (or pick the movie) since Noah does not know Joshua also wants to play.

9.20 For an in-depth discussion of the differences in mood and well-being in negotiation between the genders, see Susan Nolen-Hoeksema & Cheryl L. Rusting, Gender Differences in Well-Being, in Well-Being: The Foundations of Hedonic Psychology 330 (Daniel Kahneman et al. eds., 1999).

This next excerpt discusses an empirical study of risk taking by law students in their negotiation class (a group very similar to those students reading this book!).

 Charles B. Craver & David W. Barnes, **GENDER, RISK TAKING, AND NEGOTIATION PERFORMANCE**

5 Mich. J. Gender & L. 299, 320-321, 346-347 (1999)

One might reasonably expect gender-based communication stereotypes to place women at a disadvantage when facing legal negotiation exercises in the classroom. They would be likely to be perceived as less dominant and less forceful, and they would be expected to be less logical and more emotional. Nonetheless, two significant factors counterbalance these stereotypes. First, the advanced education possessed by law students and the specific training received in a legal negotiation course would minimize gender-based communication differentials. Second, the female negotiators may benefit from the established fact that women are typically more sensitive to nonverbal messages than their male cohorts. Since a significant amount of critical communication during interpersonal transactions is nonverbal, the enhanced ability of female negotiators to decode such signals could offset any disadvantage associated with latent stereotyping. . . .

Both psychological theory and empirical research suggest that women have a lower preference for risk and competition than men. If this perception is correct, more women would be inclined to take a competitive legal negotiating course on a credit/no-credit basis than men. If the women taking the course on a credit/no-credit basis were more desirous of avoiding competition than of obtaining easy credit hours, the credit/no-credit women might be expected to work more diligently on both the negotiation exercises and course papers than males who may select the credit/no-credit alternative to enable them to slack off.

The Legal Negotiating course data do indicate that a greater percentage of women take the class on a credit/no-credit basis than men, lending support for the alternative hypothesis with respect to the competition avoidance issue. Nonetheless, the data do not support the theory that the difference between the performance of graded and credit/no-credit women would be less than that between graded and credit/no-credit men.

Sociological theory also suggests that males are more acculturated to overt competition during their formative years than females, providing men with an advantage when they encounter openly competitive situations as adults. If this theory were correct, male students might be expected to achieve more beneficial results on negotiation exercises than female students. Our data found no statistically significant differences between male and female performance with respect to negotiation exercise achievement. . . .

Read together, our findings suggest that while women and men may not perform identically in negotiation settings, there is no factual basis for assuming that women are weaker or less capable negotiators. Our results directly challenge beliefs about women suggesting that female negotiators are likely to perform less proficiently than their male peers. These stereotypical perceptions have undoubtedly disadvantaged women in numerous academic and professional settings, including those seeking entry level associate positions and female associates seeking entrance to firm partnerships. We hope that legal professionals who hold gender-based beliefs such as those we have discussed will reevaluate their expectations in a manner that will diminish — if not entirely eliminate — subtle biases against women attorneys.

Notes and Questions

9.21 Why do you think this study's results are different from Gilligan's study? Is it the issues being studied? The audience? The passage of time?

9.22 In an empirical analysis of gender differences in negotiation, there are few gender differences found. Most importantly, there is *no* statistically significant difference in *overall* effectiveness between the genders. This finding continued even when breaking down how the genders rated each other (that is, how men rated women, how women rated women, and so on). One interesting result to study further, however, is that men rated men higher than they rated women, and this "similarity" effect was statistically significant. Of the 89 adjectives in which negotiators could be rated, only 5 showed a statistically significant difference between men and women. While the overall number of similarities

Adjectives for Effective Negotiators		
ADJECTIVE	**WOMEN RANKING**	**MEN RANKING**
Ethical	1 (4.50)	1 (4.29)
Confident	2 (3.94)	5 (3.92)
Personable	2 (3.94)	3 (3.97)
Trustworthy	2 (3.94)	9 (3.77)
Experienced	5 (3.89)*	1 (4.29)
Rational	6 (3.80)	4 (3.96)
Realistic	7 (3.78)	6 (3.84)
Accommodating	8 (3.75)	12 (3.75)
Communicative	8 (3.75)	11 (3.76)
Fair-minded	10 (3.67)	16 (3.65)
Dignified	11 (3.66)	13 (3.74)
Perceptive	12 (3.64)	7 (3.83)
Adaptable	13 (3.61)	18 (3.57)[†]
Self-controlled	14 (3.58)	8 (3.81)
Agreeable	15 (3.56)	17 (3.63)
Astute about the law	16 (3.53)	9 (3.77)
Poised	17 (3.44)	15 (3.66)
Analytical	18 (3.42)	22 (3.45)
Careful	19 (3.41)	21 (3.47)
Sociable	20 (3.36)	14 (3.69)

* Statistically significant.
† Masculine was tied for 18 for the men.

is impressive (84 of 89), the different ones are also interesting. Women were rated significantly higher in being "assertive" and "firm" while men were rated significantly higher in being "an avoider," "creative," "experienced," and "wise." Finally, in describing effective men and effective women, the overall adjectives did not differ, although the order of them did, as the boxed table shows. We can hypothesize several conclusions about this data: (1) By the time men and women have significant client responsibility, childhood differences have mostly disappeared through maturity and experience; (2) men and women who self-select for law school and then are trained through law school have few differences; and/or (3) the differences found in the Gilligan study a generation ago no longer appear in our current society. (Data on file with authors and based on Andrea Kupfer Schneider, Shattering Negotiation Myths: Empirical Evidence on the Effectiveness of Negotiation Style, 7 Harv. Negot. L. Rev. 143 (2002).) What do you think? For other discussions of gender and negotiation, see Deborah Kolb & Gloria Coolidge, Her Place at the Table: A Consideration of Gender Issues in Negotiation, in Negotiation Theory and Practice (J. William Breslin & Jeffrey Z. Rubin eds., 1991); Deborah Kolb, More Than Just a Footnote: Constructing a Theoretical Framework for Teaching About Gender in Negotiation, 16 Negot. J. 347 (2000); Carrie Menkel-Meadow, Teaching About Gender and Negotiation: Sex, Truths and Video Tape, 16 Negot. J. 357 (2000).

9.23 The lack of differences between men and women in other fields has also been documented. In a review of studies of male and female managers, researchers have concluded that men and women do not differ in their managerial philosophy, personal values, or management of resources. "We've reviewed five studies involving almost 2,000 people compared on a total of 43 scales. We've studied matched pairs and controlled for level of managerial achievement. . . . [W]e are left with one conclusion: *Women, in general, do not differ from men, in general, in the ways in which they administer the management process.*" Susan M. Donnell & Jay Hall, Men and Women as Managers: A Significant Case of No Significant Difference, Organizational Dynamics, Spring 1980, at 76. See also Gary N. Powell, One More Time: Do Female and Male Managers Differ?, 4 Acad. Mgmt. Exec. 68 (1990).

This next excerpt argues that women, when asking for salaries on behalf of themselves, do not do as good a job as men. The impact of this willingness to negotiate can be quite dramatic — $500,000 over the course of a career. The following excerpt, from the book *Everyday Negotiation*, makes a slightly different point. Researchers Deborah Kolb and Judith Williams found that their first book, *The Shadow Negotiation: How Women Can Master the Hidden Agendas That Determine Bargaining Success* (2000), was quite popular and applicable to men as well. In fact, they argue, it was not that men and women negotiate differently from one another, but that women had insights into negotiation that had not been widely discussed. These insights, into hidden agendas and shadow negotiations, were useful regardless of gender.

Linda Babcock & Sara Laschever, **WOMEN DON'T ASK: NEGOTIATION AND THE GENDER DIVIDE**

1-2, 4-6, 8-10 (2003)

A few years ago, when Linda was serving as the director of the Ph.D. program at her school, a delegation of women graduate students came to her office. Many of the male graduate students were teaching courses of their own, the women explained, while most of the female graduate students had been assigned to work as teaching assistants to regular faculty. Linda agreed that this didn't sound fair, and that afternoon she asked the associate dean who handled teaching assignments about the women's complaint. She received a simple answer: "I try to find teaching opportunities for any student who approaches me with a good idea for a course, the ability to teach, and a reasonable offer about what it will cost," he explained. "More men ask. The women just don't ask."

The women just don't ask. This incident and the associate dean's explanation suggested to Linda the existence of a more pervasive problem. Could it be that women don't get more of the things they want in life in part because they don't think to ask for them? Are there external pressures that discourage women from asking as much as men do — and even keep them from realizing that they can ask? Are women really less likely than men to ask for what they want?

To explore this question, Linda conducted a study that looked at the starting salaries of students graduating from Carnegie Mellon University with their master's degrees. When Linda looked exclusively at gender, the difference was fairly large: The starting salaries of the men were 7.6 percent or almost $4,000 higher on average than those of the women. Trying to explain this difference, Linda looked next at who had negotiated his or her salary (who had asked for more money) and who had simply accepted the initial offer he or she had received. It turned out that only 7 percent of the female students had negotiated but 57 percent (eight times as many) of the men had asked for more money. Linda was particularly surprised to find such a dramatic difference between men and women at Carnegie Mellon because graduating students are strongly advised by the school's Career Services department to negotiate their job offers. Nonetheless, hardly any of the women had done so. The most striking finding, however, was that the students who had negotiated (most of them men) were able to increase their starting salaries by 7.4 percent on average, or $4,053 — almost exactly the difference between men's and women's average starting pay. This suggests that the salary differences between the men and the women might have been eliminated if the women had negotiated their offers.

Spurred on by this finding, Linda and two colleagues, Deborah Small and Michele Gelfand, designed another study to look at the propensity of men and women to ask for more than they are offered. They recruited students at Carnegie Mellon for an experiment and told them that they would be paid between three and ten dollars for playing *Boggle*™, a game by Milton Bradley. In *Boggle*, players shake a cube of tile letters until all the letters fall into a grid at the bottom of the cube. They must then identify words that can be formed from the letters vertically, horizontally, or diagonally. Each research subject was asked to play four rounds of the game, and then an experimenter handed him or her three dollars and said, "Here's three dollars.

Is three dollars okay?" If a subject asked for more money, the experimenters would pay that participant ten dollars, but they would not give anyone more money if he or she just complained about the compensation (an indirect method of asking). The results were striking—almost *nine times* as many male as female subjects asked for more money. Both male and female subjects rated how well they'd played the game about equally, meaning that women didn't feel they should be paid less or should accept less because they'd played poorly. There were also no gender differences in how much men and women complained about the compensation (there was plenty of complaining all around). The significant factor seemed to be that for men, unhappiness with what they were offered was more likely to make them try to fix their unhappiness—by asking for more. . . .

Ask . . . And Keep on Asking

Winning your career battles requires . . . devising strategies to get what you want and not taking no for an answer in critical matters. Yet, as Gail Evans points out in her book *Play Like a Man, Win Like a Woman*, "Men learn at an early age that 'no' has a range of meanings: no, maybe, or later. But the female definition of the word 'no' is often absolutely not, how could you even ask?"

Brianne Leary had a secure career as entertainment co-anchor of *Good Day New York*. . . . When the first plane hit the World Trade Center, Leary had a hunch that Osama bin Laden was behind the attack. Years earlier, she had worked in Afghanistan . . . and had plenty of sources there.

As the story unfolded, Leary's hunch proved to be correct. She . . . made contact with two of her connections. General Abdul Rahim Wardak, former chief of staff of the Afghan military, promised her an exclusive interview. And Mujahideen commander Abdul Haq pledged to give her any assistance she needed.

Immediately, she relayed all of this information to the news director at her station. "I told him about my previous experience inside Afghanistan and offered to help with this developing story," she says. "He politely took my e-mail printouts and said, 'We'll see.' " . . .

When days passed with no word from her boss, Leary decided to go over his head and meet with the general manager of Fox. . . . "He claimed to understand my desire to go to Afghanistan, but turned me down, citing money as the main reason," she says. Yet, soon after that, Fox hired Geraldo Rivera to go.

Not one to give up so easily, Leary contacted a friend who put her in touch with Eason Jordan, head of international news gathering for CNN. After . . . [an] interview with him, she was told that many of CNN's more experienced journalists were eager to go to Afghanistan. "But he didn't say no," she says.

Two weeks went by, however, with no word from Jordan. . . . Then, on November 13 . . . Leary realized she needed to be doing something more substantial with her life. So she booked a flight to Pakistan with plans to leave two days later. . . . The next morning, she called Jordan at the crack of dawn and talked nonstop for five minutes in an effort to convince him to say yes. Finally, he told Leary, "Okay, go."

Leary spent five weeks in Afghanistan filing "day-in-the-life" stories for CNN.

Connie Glaser & Barbara Smalley, What Queen Esther Knew: Business Strategies from a Biblical Sage 120-122 (2003).

THE ASKING ADVANTAGE

But just because women don't ask for things as often as men do, is that necessarily a problem? Perhaps directly negotiating for advantage — asking for what you want — is a male strategy and women simply employ other equally effective strategies to get what they want. This is an important point, but only partly accurate. Women often worry more than men about the impact their actions will have on their relationships. This can prompt them to change their behavior to protect personal connections, sometimes by asking for things indirectly, sometimes by asking for less than they really want, and sometimes simply by trying to be more deserving of what they want (say, by working harder) so they'll be given what they want without asking. Women also frequently take a more collaborative approach to problem-solving than men take, trying to find solutions that benefit both parties or trying to align their own requests with shared goals. In many situations, women's methods can be superior to those typically employed by men. . . . Unfortunately, however, in our largely male-defined work culture, women's strategies can often be misinterpreted and can leave them operating from a position of weakness. And in many cases, the only way to get something is to ask for it directly.

So let's look at the importance of asking.

First, consider the situation of the graduating students at Carnegie Mellon, in which eight times as many men as women negotiated their starting salaries. The women who did not negotiate started out not just behind their male peers, but behind where they could and should have been. With every future raise predicated on this starting point, they could be paying for this error for a long time — perhaps for the rest of their careers. . . .

Suppose that at age 22 an equally qualified man and woman receive job offers for $25,000 a year. The man negotiates and gets his offer raised to $30,000. The woman does not negotiate and accepts the job for $25,000. Even if each of them received identical 3 percent raises every year throughout their careers (which is unlikely, given their different propensity to negotiate and other research showing that women's achievements tend to be undervalued), by the time they reach age 60 the gap between their salaries will have widened to more than $15,000 a year, with the man earning $92,243 and the woman only $76,870. While that may not seem like an enormous spread, remember that the man will have been making more all along, with his extra earnings over the 38 years totaling $361,171. If the man had simply banked the difference every year in a savings account earning 3 percent interest, by age 60 he would have $568,834 more than the woman — enough to underwrite a comfortable retirement nest egg, purchase a second home, or pay for the college education of a few children. This is an enormous "return on investment" for a *one-time* negotiation. It can mean a higher standard of living throughout one's working years, financial security in old age, or a top-flight education for one's kids.

The impact of neglecting to negotiate in this one instance — when starting a new job — is so substantial and difficult to overcome that some researchers who study the persistence of the wage gap between men and women speculate that much of the disparity can be traced to differences in entering salaries rather than differences in raises. . . .

MORE THAN MONEY

The penalties for not negotiating extend far beyond the merely monetary, too. As Pinkley and Northcraft demonstrate,

> Applicants with identical experience and performance records but different salary histories are rated differently by employers. If your compensation record is better than others, employers will assume that your performance is better too. . . . Accepting less will imply that you have less value than other new hires.[*]

In many cases, employers actually respect candidates more for pushing to get paid what they're worth. This means that women don't merely sacrifice additional income when they don't push to be paid more, they may sacrifice some of their employers' regard too. The experience of Hope, a business school professor, tells this story clearly. When she completed graduate school, Hope was offered a job at a prestigious management consulting firm. Not wanting to "start off on the wrong foot," she accepted the firm's initial salary offer without asking for more. Although she feared that negotiating her salary would damage her new bosses' impression of her, the opposite occurred: She later learned that her failure to negotiate almost convinced the senior management team that they'd made a mistake in hiring her. . . .

These findings are momentous because until now research on negotiation has mostly ignored the issue of when and why people attempt to negotiate, focusing instead on tactics that are successful once a negotiation is underway — what kinds of offers to make, when to concede, and which strategies are most effective in different types of negotiations. With few exceptions, researchers have ignored the crucial fact that the most important step in any negotiation process must be deciding to negotiate in the first place. Asking for what you want is the essential first step that "kicks off" a negotiation. If you miss your chance to negotiate, the best negotiation advice in the world isn't going to help you much. And women simply aren't "asking" at the same rate as men.

 Deborah Kolb & Judith Williams, **EVERYDAY NEGOTIATION: NAVIGATING THE HIDDEN AGENDAS IN BARGAINING**

3-5, 8-13 (rev. ed. 2003)

Restricting negotiation to formal deal making skews our sense of what is possible through negotiation. Suspecting that we are neither sufficiently artful nor naturally persuasive, we let opportunities to negotiate slip by us, unclaimed or unnoticed. Cramped by circumstance, we

> **What Women Know**
>
> As Anita Roddick, the Founder of the Body Shop, once said, "Any woman who has dealt with two children and one piece of toffee can negotiate any contract in the world." Deborah Kolb & Judith Williams, Everyday Negotiation xvi-xvii (rev. ed. 2003).

---

[*] Robin L. Pinkley & Gregory B. Northcraft, Get Paid What You're Worth: The Expert Negotiator's Guide to Salary and Compensation 6 (2000).

don't consider negotiation a possibility. We just make do and move on, not realizing that we might have bargained. Often, from lack of training or experience, we fail to recognize that we are in the midst of a negotiation until it is too late to change the outcome. Even when we are well aware that we are negotiating and of the stakes involved, we may have trouble getting the person we're negotiating with to listen, much less cooperate with us.

For the last several years we have been talking to women about what happens in their everyday negotiations. As they experienced negotiation, the tried-and-true methods of deal making came up short. It's not always so easy to get to yes as it seems on the pages of popular negotiation books or in seminars. The women's accounts of actual negotiations alerted us to broader challenges than the deal-making approach suggests. They often faced an unwilling seller or buyer. Then the greatest obstacle was getting the other person to the table. Once there, they encountered barriers in communication. They had to do more than resist efforts to put them at a disadvantage; they also had to deepen the conversation if they hoped to achieve any dialogue on the problem. Collectively, their comments keyed on two major concerns:

- How to position themselves in the negotiation conversation so that the other person was willing to take them seriously
- How to position the other person so that he or she was willing to cooperate in reaching a mutual solution

As the women we interviewed talked about what happened in their everyday negotiations, the emphasis shifted from deal making to problem solving. Their commentary centered not so much on particular results, but on the process used in getting them. Occasionally they did have transactions to negotiate, but even these had relational issues where the common notions of deal making offered only partial help. Their insights have important messages for everyone who negotiates, which turns out to be all of us—male and female. Any negotiation can involve subtle or not-so-subtle differentials in status or skill, and men as well as women can find themselves in situations where the tide seems to be running against them for reasons that have little to do with the topic formally under consideration. . . .

Focus on the problem. Seldom do negotiators have the luxury of paying attention only to the problem. In real-life negotiations unspoken wants and expectations come into play that interfere with "getting to yes." Negotiators have histories—established ways of doing things and resolving conflict. They have accepted, if sometimes unarticulated, standards of conduct. They have complicated systems of relating as well as complex relationships with each other. These all bear on a negotiation. They frame its context.

Differences in influence can distort the balance at the table, affecting flexibility and candor on both sides. How can you convince the other person to accept a creative trade when he or she sees no need to trade at all? Conversely, those with power can have trouble persuading subordinates to be honest and forthright with them. How do people who lack bargaining power because of their position in an organization, their professions, their age, their gender, their race, their class, or their ethnicity make negotiations happen? How do those with influence create an atmosphere where those with less authority aren't afraid to communicate openly? . . .

Know what you want. You may know what you want, but being in a good position to get it can be an entirely different matter. Even when bargainers recognize that negotiation is a possibility, they can have trouble getting themselves into a good position to negotiate. Afraid of causing dissension or doubting their persuasive powers, they set their sights low and prepare to settle for less than they want or deserve. To counteract these tendencies, they need to do some careful stock taking, not just brainstorming.

Going into a negotiation, bargainers are not always clear about what they want. Nor do objectives always remain the same over the course of a negotiation. Attitudes and goals can shift on both sides of the table. Moreover, the main issue being negotiated may not be the whole story. Even bargainers adept at defining their objective do not always grasp its full scope or the implications of taking a certain path. Delighted at capturing a promotion or a high-visibility assignment, for example, they overlook the conditions — reduced workload or increased resources — necessary to make a success of that new job or assignment.

Willingness to negotiate. Mutual-gains approaches pretty much assume that self-interest is a sufficient motivator. Sometimes an attractive set of trade-offs does provide the necessary incentive. But not everyone is always ready to negotiate through a problem.

Something more, it seems, is required than an elegant solution. Before you can propose or weigh possible trades, you may have to do some serious strategizing to get the other party to the table, particularly someone who is perfectly content for things to remain as they are. Sure you can schedule a meeting with your boss; that does not mean that you can convince your boss to talk about your increased responsibilities or the compensation and recognition that should go along with them. A whole array of strategic moves, not creative ideas alone, are needed to make an unwilling bargainer see any personal advantage in negotiating with you. . . .

Bargainers operate out of enlightened self-interest. In the mutual-gains world, bargainers are essentially independent actors bent on realizing personal goals. Assertive, objective, and cool under pressure, they probe each other for information. They care about the other person's concerns more or less as a means to an end — to the extent that those concerns help or hinder their case.

This individualistic approach — which has been called the pursuit of "enlightened self-interest" — takes into account only half of the negotiation equation. Any negotiation is a form of social interaction; it involves a *you* and a *them*. Complex relationships can exist between bargainers, and those relationships have weight. They often determine whether good solutions will even be entertained.

Of course, personal agendas matter. You're negotiating because you want something, after all. If you're not going to be a forceful advocate for yourself, who is? But too narrow a focus on individual goals can get in the way of the communication needed to reach a good solution. Real skills and an attitude about the other person often essential to success can drop by the wayside or be co-opted when only self-interest is sought, however enlightened.

Creative ideas carry the day. The deal-making or mutual-gains orientation skews the negotiation process toward rational and objective analysis. It assumes you can pretty much figure out what motivates other people and trade on that....

Rationality and objectivity, however, do not always rule at the bargaining table. Dispositions toward conflict, biases, remembered slights or successes, and the feelings that the participants have about each other intrude on the process. Personal preoccupations encroach. Dirty dishes in the sink or an impending deadline can have more impact than frequent flyer miles on where a family decides to spend its vacation. A bargainer sure of losing ground at the office might feel obliged to take a strong stand. Worries about a valued colleague whose job is in jeopardy or about the extra time needed to care for a frail parent can shape a case. To get to yes, these hidden agendas must be brought out into the open....

A good idea alone rarely carries the day. Going after mutual gains is a worthy goal, but it is not enough. You have to know how to get there and have the tools at hand.

Negotiations, it turns out, are not purely rational exercises in the pursuit of self-interest or the development of creative trades. They are more akin to conversations that are carried out simultaneously on two levels. First there is the discussion of substance — what the bargainers have to say about the issues. But then there is the interpersonal communication that takes place — what the talk encodes about their relationship. Yes, people bargain over issues; but they also negotiate how they are going to negotiate. All the time they are bargaining over issues, they are conducting a parallel negotiation in which they work out the terms of their relationship and their expectations. Even though they seldom address the subject directly, they decide between them whose interests and needs command attention, whose opinions matter, and how cooperative they are going to be in reaching an agreement. This interchange, often nonverbal and masked in the stands taken on issues, has a momentum all its own quite apart from the substance of what is being discussed.

We call this parallel negotiation the *shadow negotiation*. The shadow negotiation takes place below the surface of any debate over the issues. As bargainers try to turn the discussion to their advantage or persuade the other side to cooperate in resolving the issues, they make assumptions about themselves — how much leverage they have and what they can legitimately demand. They make assumptions about the other person — about that person's wants, weaknesses, and probable behavior. They size each other up, poking here and there to find out where the give is. They test for flexibility, trying to gauge how strongly an individual feels about a certain point.

The shadow negotiation is no place to be a passive observer. You can maneuver to put yourself in a good position or let others create a position for you. Your action — or inaction — here determines what takes place in the negotiation over issues. If you don't move to direct the shadow negotiation to your advantage, you can find the agreement tipping against you.

Slight changes in positioning can cause a major shift in the dynamics within the shadow negotiation. To have a credible voice on the issues, you must create the conditions for that voice to be heard. At the same time, you must make room for the other person's voice.

Notes and Questions

9.24 Babcock and Laschever refer to statistics of negotiating starting salaries by business school graduates. Do you think the rates of negotiating starting salaries would be different for law school graduates? Why or why not?

9.25 Some researchers have hypothesized that power may actually be a better predictor of negotiator behavior than gender is. Consider the conclusion drawn by Carol Watson based on multiple studies done on gender and negotiation.

> Power generally leads to greater dominance, competitiveness, and success for both genders. On the one hand, this indicates that women are not softer or less effective negotiators than men are. . . . Given a reasonable degree of situational power, women are likely to be just as oriented toward beating their opponents as men are, and just as successful at doing so. . . .
>
> On the other hand, this finding also implies that women are not nicer negotiators than men are. Women are not necessarily any more fair-minded or compassionate, despite what earlier research and some current feminist writers would have us believe.

Carol Watson, Gender Versus Power as a Predictor of Negotiation Behavior and Outcomes, 10 Negot. J. 117 (1994).

C. RACE

This last section turns to racial differences, which, of course, can also be closely linked to cultural differences. Yet in the United States, as we know, the legacy of slavery and discrimination adds another element to negotiation. These next two excerpts from Ian Ayres discuss very troubling empirical studies examining the impact of discrimination on negotiation.

Ian Ayres, FAIR DRIVING: GENDER AND RACE DISCRIMINATION IN RETAIL CAR NEGOTIATIONS

104 Harv. L. Rev. 817, 818-819 (1991)

This Article examines whether the process of negotiating for a new car disadvantages women and minorities. More than 180 independent negotiations at ninety dealerships were conducted in the Chicago area to examine how dealerships bargain. Testers of different races and genders entered new car dealerships separately and bargained to buy a new car, using a uniform negotiation strategy. The study tests whether automobile retailers react differently to this uniform strategy when potential buyers differ only by gender or race.

The tests reveal that white males receive significantly better prices than blacks and women. . . . [W]hite women had to pay forty percent higher markups than white men; black men had to pay more than twice the markup, and black women had to pay more than three times the markup of white male testers. Moreover, the study reveals that testers of different race and gender are subjected to several forms of nonprice discrimination. Specifically, testers were systematically steered to salespeople of their own race and gender (who then gave them worse deals) and were asked different questions and told about different qualities of the car.

 ***Ian Ayres*, FURTHER EVIDENCE OF DISCRIMINATION IN NEW CAR NEGOTIATIONS AND ESTIMATES OF ITS CAUSE**

94 Mich. L. Rev. 109, 109-110, 124, 127-128, 142, 145 (1995)

This article extends the results of this initial test by presenting not only more authoritative evidence of discrimination but also a new *quantitative* method of identifying the causes of discrimination. . . .

This article presents the results of an expanded audit study. . . . In the expanded audits, 38 testers, including 5 black males, 7 black females, and 8 white females, negotiated for over 400 automobiles. The results are more authoritative than the prior test because there is a larger sample size and more testers in each race-gender category, and because the tests were conducted with enhanced controls to ensure further that testers were similar except for their race and gender.

The results of the expanded audit confirm the previous finding that dealers systematically offer lower prices to white males than to other tester types. But the more comprehensive data reveal a different ordering of discrimination than in the prior study: as in the original study, dealers offered all black testers significantly higher prices than white males, but unlike the original study, the black male testers were charged higher prices than the black female testers. This

> **STUDIES AS EVIDENCE**
>
> Professors Marc A. Cohen and Ian Ayres were recently hired as expert counsel for the plaintiffs in a class action law suit against General Motors Acceptance Corp. (GMAC). In this action, plaintiffs alleged that GMAC's automobile lending policies could harm black car buyers because the dealers "marked up" loans more frequently and aggressively with blacks than whites, in other words, charging higher interest rates to black buyers and adding to the total amount of the loan. In addition to the Ayres studies, Professor Cohen's study was also used as evidence in the case. He analyzed information on 1.5 million GMAC loans for the past four years where dealers had marked up loans. Cohen's main conclusion from this study was the blacks applying for loans paid markups of an average of $1,229, whereas whites with similar credit histories paid about $867 in markups. Amazingly, some of GM's own black employees are part of the class action suit! See Lee Hawkins, Jr., GM's Finance Arm Is Close to Setting Racial-Bias Lawsuit, Wall. St. J., Jan. 30, 2004, at A1.

article examines whether this different gender ordering of discrimination for black testers provides insights about the causes of discrimination or whether it suggests weaknesses in the audit design. . . .

CAUSAL THEORIES OF DISCRIMINATION IN BARGAINING

The bargaining model we derived can accommodate four competing explanations as to why dealers would offer higher prices to a disfavored group than to white males:

1. Sellers may have higher costs of bargaining with a disfavored group — "associational animus"...
2. Sellers may desire to disadvantage a disfavored group — "consequential animus"...
3. Sellers may believe that a disfavored group has higher costs of bargaining — "cost-based" discrimination... and
4. Sellers may believe that a disfavored group has higher reservation prices — "revenue-based" discrimination....

First, consider associational animus. In the employment context, Gary Becker showed that if a bigoted employer dislikes spending time with members of a particular group, the employer may offer members of that group a lower wage to compensate the employer for this associational animus.[57] In our model a seller's dislike of spending time with a particular group, associational animus, can be naturally captured by an increase in the seller's costs per period of associating, when negotiating with testers from the disfavored group.

In our bargaining model, "associational animus" yields a startlingly perverse result: black consumers can benefit from the presence of bigotry. One of the robust results of bargaining theory is that higher bargaining costs tend to reduce one's bargaining power. Thus, higher per period costs of negotiating with black consumers should lower sellers' bargaining power and induce them to make lower offers to black buyers. Thus, even before we formally estimate the model, theory suggests that associational animus against black customers will not be able to explain why, in a bargaining context, dealers offered black testers higher prices.

The perverse result that seller bigotry might benefit blacks suggests that allowing animus to take only the form of an associational tax does not account for all possible forms of bigotry. For example, bigoted sellers might alternatively enjoy extracting a high profit more from black or female customers than from white males.... We refer to this type of discriminatory motive as "consequential animus" because the seller dislikes the consequence of contracting with disfavored groups on equal terms. Sellers motivated by consequential animus act as if they had lower per period costs of bargaining; they are willing to bargain longer for a high price because they attach a higher value to extracting profits at the expense of a disfavored group. Unlike associational animus, consequential animus — by reducing the seller's effective costs of bargaining — enhances a seller's bargaining power and is compatible with blacks and/or women receiving higher offers than white males.

The model can also capture two types of "statistical discrimination" based on sellers' inferences about a group's cost of bargaining or its willingness to pay.

---

[57] Gary Becker, The Economics of Discrimination (2d ed. 1971).

Statistical discrimination is caused not by sellers' animus, but rather by their use of observable variables such as race or gender to maximize profits. "Cost-based" discrimination could occur, for example, if a seller believes that a disfavored group is on average more averse to bargaining. Bargaining aversion or impatience might cause buyers to act as if they had higher bargaining costs. The sellers' statistical inference about a group's cost of bargaining might cause profit-maximizing sellers to quote higher prices to all members of this group because sellers would believe that members of this group on average have less bargaining power. The model captures the possibility of "cost-based" discrimination by allowing sellers to form different beliefs about the bargaining costs of specific tester race-gender types.

Finally, we can use the model to examine "revenue-based" statistical inferences founded on perceived differences in the distribution of reservation prices among consumer groups. If sellers believe that blacks or women have different distributions of reservation prices than white males — for example, distributions with higher means or greater variances, this could lead dealers to offer higher prices to members of these groups.

The bargaining model used in the current study formalizes the assertion in the original article that revenue-based discrimination will often become a "search for suckers":

> Anecdotal evidence suggests that at some dealerships up to fifty percent of the profits can be earned on just ten percent of the sales. . . . From a dealer's perspective, bargaining for cars is a "search for suckers" — a search for consumers who are willing to pay a high markup. . . .
> . . . In their quest to locate high-markup buyers, dealers are not guided by the amount that the *average* black woman is willing to pay. Rather, they focus on the proportion of black women who are willing to pay close to the sticker price.

The model starkly replicates this result because profit-maximizing sellers do not care about a group's *average* willingness to pay; rather, revenue-based discrimination turns solely on the seller's belief about the *maximum* amount any given group member would be willing to pay. The dealers' exclusive interest in estimating the "upper tail" of the buyer's willingness-to-pay distribution is an artifact of the uniform distribution assumption. However, the intuition that dealers' behavior will be more attuned to their beliefs about high-markup buyers rather than the average buyer still holds true under less restrictive assumptions. Therefore, even if blacks have a lower average willingness to pay than whites, profit-maximizing sellers might nevertheless make higher offers to blacks — as long as a sufficient number of black consumers are willing to pay an especially high markup.

This section has shown that the traditional game-theoretic determinants of bargaining behavior — that is, the buyer's and seller's costs of bargaining and inferences about the buyer's willingness to pay — can capture four different explanations of discrimination. On theoretical grounds, we have been able to reject "associational animus" as a plausible explanation for higher prices encountered by minority and/or female testers [because the testers would have actually benefited — a car salesman would have given them a better deal in order to end the negotiation faster. All three other explanations are plausible.] . . .

CONCLUSION

The audits analyzed in this article further demonstrate a strong dealer tendency to offer white male testers lower prices than black testers. The task of combatting this disparate treatment may be particularly difficult because that discrimination may have diverse causes. While enhanced enforcement of section 1981's prohibitions against disparate racial treatment is a laudable goal, I continue to be pessimistic that private litigation will be sufficient to deter discrimination. This conclusion suggests instead that encouraging "no-haggle" selling might reduce dealers' discretion to discriminate. . . .

To be sure, shifting to no-haggle sales might not be a panacea, but more than efficiency is at stake. This article has further substantiated the possibility of systematic racial and gender discrimination in new car sales. Our tentative estimation of the bargaining model suggests that this discrimination has diverse causes. Instead of using traditional civil rights approaches to eliminate race and gender disparities within a larger system of haggling, it may be more appropriate to target haggling itself and the inequitable price dispersion that haggling induces.

Notes and Questions

9.26 What do you think explains the results of these two studies? Which of the theories offered by Ayres is most persuasive to you? How could Rose's theory of perceived cooperativeness also be used to explain the results? Is it persuasive?

9.27 What advice would you give to a female or black friend the next time he or she went to purchase a car?

9.28 In fact, making these kinds of snap judgments about people can often be as big a detriment to the salesperson as it is to the customer. Malcolm Gladwell tells the story of one of the most successful car salesmen in the country, Bob Golomb, and why he is so successful.

> He follows, he says, [a] very simple rule. He may make a million snap judgments about a customer's needs and state of mind, but he tries never to judge anyone on the basis of his or her appearance. He assumes that everyone who walks in the door has the exact same chance of buying a car. . . .
>
> [Other car salesmen] see someone, and somehow they let the first impression they have about that person's appearance drown out every other piece of information they manage to gather in that first instant. . . .
>
> Golomb tries to treat every customer exactly the same because he's aware of just how dangerous snap judgments are when it comes to race and sex and appearance. Sometimes the unprepossessing farmer with his filthy coveralls is actually an enormously rich man with a four-thousand-acre spread, and sometimes the teenager is coming back later with Mom and Dad. Sometimes the young black man has an MBA from Harvard. Sometimes the petite blonde makes the car decisions for her whole family. Sometimes the man with the silver hair and broad shoulders and lantern jaw is a lightweight. So Golomb doesn't try to spot the lay-down. He quotes everyone the same price, sacrificing high profit margins on an individual car for the benefits

of volume, and word of his fairness has spread to the point where he gets up to a third of his business referrals from satisfied customers.

Malcolm Gladwell, Blink: The Power of Thinking Without Thinking 90, 95–96 (2005).

When reading these studies about how women or minorities are treated differently, many tend to focus on the behavior of the stereotyper and how these stereotypes can be changed. This next excerpt points out the overlooked effect that stereotypes have on the target of the stereotype.

 Sharon Begley, THE STEREOTYPE TRAP

Newsweek, Nov. 6, 2000, at 66-68

The power of stereotypes, scientists had long figured, lay in their ability to change the behavior of the person holding the stereotype. If you think women are ninnies ruled by hormonal swings, you don't name them CEO; if you think gays are pedophiles, you don't tap them to lead your Boy Scout troop. But five years ago Stanford University psychologist Claude Steele showed something else: it is the *targets* of a stereotype whose behavior is most powerfully affected by it. A stereotype that pervades the culture the way "ditzy blondes" and "forgetful seniors" do makes people painfully aware of how society views them—so painfully aware, in fact, that knowledge of the stereotype can affect how well they do on intellectual and other tasks. . . .

Steele and Aronson gave 44 Stanford undergrads questions from the verbal part of the tough Graduate Record Exam. One group was asked, right before the test, to indicate their year in school, age, major and other information. The other group answered all that, as well as one final question: what is your race? The results were sobering. "Just listing their race undermined the black students' performance," says Steele, making them score significantly worse than blacks who did not note their race, and significantly worse than all whites. But the performance of the black Stanfordites who were not explicitly reminded of their race equaled that of whites, found the scientists.

You do not even have to believe the negative stereotype to be hurt by it, psychologists find. As long as you care about the ability you're being tested on, such as golfing or math, and are familiar with the stereotype ("girls can't do higher math"), it can sink you. What seems to happen is that as soon as you reach a tough par 3 or a difficult trig problem, the possibility of confirming, and being personally reduced to, a painful stereotype causes enough distress to impair performance. . . .

Stereotypes seem to most affect the best and the brightest. Only if you're black and care about academics, or female and care about math, will you also care if society thinks you're bad at those things. . . .

Can the pernicious effects of stereotypes be vanquished? If no one reminds you of a negative stereotype, your performance doesn't suffer. It can actually improve if instead you think of a positive stereotype—Steele recommends bellowing something like "You are Stanford students!" but clearly that has limited applicability. Deception helps, too: if women are told that a difficult math test reveals no gender differences, finds Stephen Spencer of Waterloo, they perform as well as men. Otherwise, women score much lower. While such manipulations may weaken the brutal power of stereotypes, at the end of the day they remain manipulations. But until stereotypes fade away, that may be the best we can hope for.

Notes and Questions

9.29 How can the results of the *Newsweek* article be translated into negotiation behavior?

9.30 What is the antidote for this? How can we avoid being trapped by these negotiation stereotypes?

9.31 A student came to see her professor about her trial advocacy class. She explained that there was a group of four students working together on the different projects for the class—the dismissal motion, the summary judgment motion, the brief, and so on. Each of them was responsible for a particular task. She noted that thus far in the semester, each person had written his or her motion after consulting with the group, but then drafted it and handed it directly to the professor. When it was her turn, the other students in the group asked her to circulate her draft to them first before handing it in. The student, who is black, is concerned and has come to you for advice. What suggestions do you have for how the professor should respond?

9.32 Researchers have begun manipulating gender stereotypes linked to effectiveness to see how stereotypes can affect mixed gender negotiations. For example, when stereotypically feminine traits were linked to effectiveness, women performed better, but they did not when gender-neutral traits were linked to success. Laura J. Kray, Adam D. Galinsky & Leigh Thompson, Reversing the Gender Gap in Negotiations: An Exploration of Stereotype Regeneration, 87 Org. Behav. & Hum. Decision Processes 386 (2002).

This last excerpt tries to provide some practical advice when you feel you are disadvantaged in a negotiation. Phyllis Beck Kritek writes about having less power than the other negotiators in her position as a nurse negotiating with doctors and a woman negotiating with men. She often felt that she faced an "uneven table" in a negotiation.

Phyllis Beck Kritek, NEGOTIATING AT AN UNEVEN TABLE: A PRACTICAL APPROACH TO WORKING WITH DIFFERENCE AND DIVERSITY

187, 200, 209-210, 224, 228, 244, 252-253, 261, 281, 292, 298, 314-315 (1994)

[The ten ways of being at an uneven table:]

1. *Find and inhabit the deepest and surest human space that your capabilities permit. . . .* I have a personal system of ethics and spirituality that is very deeply important to me. I share it on occasion with others, but I never assume anyone at a negotiation shares it or wants to hear about it. This is not a starting point for surer and deeper. The starting point is shared values, common commitments to surer and deeper that we have all at some point claimed as our own. It is the Constitution and the Bill of Rights; civil rights; the mission of our schools, universities, hospitals, and businesses; the promises we make to one another. These shared values can take both me and all those with me at a table back to some more compelling time and place where we made those commitments and knew that we shared those beliefs. The deeper and surer, the more creative the outcome. . . .

2. *Be a truth teller. . . .* Over the years, I have learned that when I am sitting at an uneven table, many other people at the table who know the same truths as I do elect to sit back and let me do the truth telling on their behalf. There just aren't enough truth tellers around, and when folks find one, they like to ask for a lot of overtime. These are the people who meet you in the hall after the negotiation and say, "I really appreciated what you said in there; you're absolutely right!" Beware of such people. They are not truth tellers. Real truth tellers say that at the table. . . .

3. *Honor your integrity, even at great cost. . . .* Most people, in my experience, actually welcome the opportunity to begin to focus on personal integrity as part of a negotiation. Most people like to have the best in themselves drawn forth, not the worst. Most people would really like to be more of who they are when they are a person they like a lot. Introducing moral choice gives them access to that person in themselves and changes the negotiation quite dramatically. While some people will persist in wanting to sacrifice their own or another's integrity, saying that they are more "realistic," coping with such people is a modest price to pay if all the other people at an uneven table are trying to reach for the best in themselves. It is a difficult way of being, but an intensely rewarding one. It can, of course, also dramatically alter outcomes in any negotiation, since it moves the process to a focus on more profound and compelling human issues and adds strength to truth telling. . . .

4. *Find a place for compassion at the table. . . .* Compassion at an uneven table changes everything. If I am compassionate with myself, I forgive myself, without self-indulgence, for my failures and my limits. I am then more able to give the same compassion to others, and therefore the same forgiveness, once more without indulgence. If I can make a commitment to trying to seat compassion at the table, I myself find the position I take changes. I enter the negotiation without demanding perfection of others or myself. I know before I start that I am going to forgive myself and others. This changes how I approach the entire process. In the end, it is liberating. . . .

5. *Draw a line in the sand without cruelty. . . .* I needed to know what would make me leave the table. I needed to know my "bottom line." That is how I discovered the

importance of drawing a line in the sand without cruelty. I learned that I needed to draw a line. I have put it in the sand, because I have learned over time that if I can draw others into a more positive agenda, I can move the line. Having it in the sand helps. If another person manifests compassion, or goes to a surer and deeper place, or becomes a truth teller, or explains components of personal integrity that clarify my understanding, I can adjust the line. . . .

What the claim-create research taught me is that I always have the option of leaving the table. If my line is unacceptable, I can choose to not be part of the negotiation. It has taken me many years to understand that because I come to the table with so much less, I have so much less to lose, and in that sense have greater freedom. I once thought that it was imperative that I stay at a table, that I was there to represent women or nursing or patients who desperately needed health care. It took me a long time to realize that if my presence deterred the outcomes I embraced, it was better that I not be there. Either way, the injustice would continue. If I stayed at the table, I risked becoming a party to it. Better leaving than co-optation. This has been a hard lesson for me to learn. . . .

6. *Expand and explicate the context.* . . . Perhaps nothing does more to clarify the actual nature of a conflict than expanding the context. It invariably introduces discomforting sources of variance that unveil unstated assumptions. For that reason, it is critical to become aware of people who want to deal with conflicts in a bounded, reductionistic fashion. They usually argue for a form of isolationism but present as a commitment to discriminating thought: no need to confuse the issue of racism by acknowledging the silent Hmong community, or to confuse the issue of air pollution from auto emissions by noting the committee is chaired by the president of a polluting factory.

This error to eliminate systematic sources of bias must be dealt with in a somewhat persistent fashion, since the silent voice will repeatedly be silenced. It helps to ask people to explain to you why these contextual factors are not germane, why they keep being ignored. It helps here to be clever and quick on your feet, since the silencing is often subtle and swift. . . .

7. *Innovate.* . . . When you're sitting at an uneven table, by its very nature, it includes people who have already told you by setting the uneven table that they like things just the way they are, that they do not want things to change. You need not be startled and amazed by this, nor does it help to become enraged or petulant. It is foolish to expect enthusiasm for change at an uneven table. If people wanted it, we all would have changed by now. Assume that, and you will have both the ease of mind and soul and the impetus necessary to move you to innovate. You will also have more fun. . . .

8. *Know what you do and do not know.* . . . Knowing what you do and do not know is more complex than it looks at first, and more demanding. For just that reason, it also has more capacity to make a difference. Neglecting it can make a difference you will rue, and attending to it actively, deliberately, will often make a difference you can celebrate. . . .

9. *Stay in the dialogue.* . . . The decision to stay in the dialogue is actually a question of principle. You do not stay because you are "winning" or leave because you are "losing." The dialogue itself is often the issue, and keeping conversation going may

do more to substantively enhance compassion and increase your capacity to be a truth teller than any gains or losses you may believe have occurred within the dialogue. If you make a commitment to a conversation, it is often a simple conviction about integrity that keeps you in the dialogue. . . .

10. *Know when and how to leave the table.* . . . Leaving tables is always difficult, but it is even more difficult to stay where you know you don't belong. When you are seated at an uneven table, you know that you started the process with participants who accepted the inequity. They may choose not to change. This is their right. Your unwillingness to accept this fact is your problem, not theirs. If you value your own worth enough, if you recognize the fact that you have something important to bring to conflict resolution, you will not waste your time and energy on people who have made a commitment to staying locked into ways of being that you do not embrace.

Hence, leaving the table can also prove to be an act of self-worth and self-affirmation. If you value your life, your energy, your very self, you want to only negotiate at the best of tables. They may still be uneven, but that will always be the case. If they must be uneven, it would be nice if they were at least the best of the lot. It is important to leave with pride and dignity, with graciousness. This helps you focus on the ways of being as you walk toward your next table with hope.

Notes and Questions

9.33 Much of Kritek's advice focuses on the negotiator rather than changing the situation. Why do you think this is so?

9.34 Which do you think is easier to change — the negotiator or the situation? Why?

PART III LAW AND ETHICS IN NEGOTIATION

Chapter 10 | Ethics in Negotiation

Negotiation is fraught with difficult ethical issues. How much can one "take" for oneself or one's client? How much can one deceive, dissemble, or deflect in order not to tell the other parties everything about your case? What do parties in negotiation owe each other? How much does the context of negotiation affect what we can do? Should we worry about the effects of our negotiations on others (both adversaries and those who might be affected by negotiations we undertake)?

Since you are learning about negotiation in a legal context, you must, at the very least, know the laws that affect negotiation, including the law of fraud and misrepresentation, from contract and tort principles, agency law, malpractice, and formal legal ethics rules, for which lawyers may be disciplined. These legal issues are explored in both this chapter and the next on the law of negotiation. But, in addition to the law, every negotiator needs to think about his or her ethical stance with respect to other parties, loyalties to clients, and duties to the self. These are larger philosophical, moral, and personal, as well as professional, ethical concerns. After we review the legal issues in the ethics of negotiation below, you will read several divergent accounts of what negotiators and commentators think are appropriate ethical stances — including instrumental approaches, aspirational hopes, and reactive justifications. We want you to think about how your own ethical limits have been or are being constructed by who you are, what kind of a negotiator and lawyer you want to be, and how the pulls and demands of negotiation and legal practice are affecting who you are becoming and what you will or won't be willing to do in a negotiation. In the end, although there are a lot of rules and standards, you will be the major determinant of your own behavior. Think about who you want to be in negotiation. You will begin to create your professional (and personal) reputation as a negotiator in this course and, as you know from the readings in Chapter 6, this reputation is critical.

A. HOW LAWYERS (SHOULD) BEHAVE IN NEGOTIATIONS

 Carrie Menkel-Meadow, **WHAT'S FAIR IN NEGOTIATION? WHAT IS ETHICS IN NEGOTIATION?**

in **What's Fair: Ethics for Negotiators xiii-xvi (Carrie Menkel-Meadow & Michael Wheeler eds., 2004)**

What do we owe other human beings when we negotiate for something that we or our clients want? How should we behave toward our "adversaries" — opponents, partners, clients, friends, family members, strangers, third parties and future genera- tions — when we know what we do affects them, beneficially, adversely or unpre- dictably? How do we think about the other people we interact with in negotiations? Are they just means to our ends or people like us, deserving of respect or aid (depending on whether they are our equals or more or less enabled than ourselves)? How do we conceive of our goals when we approach others to help us accomplish together what we cannot do alone?

Perhaps after the question "What should I do?" in negotiation (seeking strategic or behavioral advice), the next most frequently asked question is, "What may I do?" (seeking advice, permission, or approval for particular goals, strategies, and tactics that comprise both the conceptualizations and behaviors of the human strategic interaction that we call negotiation). . . .

"What's fair" in negotiation is a complex and multi-faceted question, asking us to consider negotiation ethics on many different levels simultaneously. First, there are the concerns of the individual negotiator: What do I aspire to? How do I judge my own goals and behavior? What may I do? How will others judge me (my counterpart in a two-party negotiation, others in a multi-lateral negotiation, those with whom I might do business in the future, those who will learn of and judge my behavior or results in any negotiation that might become more public than the involved parties)? How do I calibrate my actions to those of the others with whom I am dealing? (Should I have a "relative" ethic that is sensitive, responsive, or malleable to the context, circumstances, customs or personalities of the situation at hand?) What limits are there on my goals and behavior, set from within (the "mirror" test [how do I appear to myself at the end of the day?]) or without, either informally, (the "video-tape test" [what would my mother, teacher, spouse, child or clergy person think of me if they could watch this?]) or formally (rules, laws, ethics stan- dards, religious or moral principles to which I must or choose to adhere)? With what sensibility should I approach each negotiation I undertake?

For those who negotiate as agents, there is the added dimension of what duty is owed a client or principal. When do agent and principal goals properly align? When are they different . . . and how are differences to be reconciled? When do legal rules (like the creation of fiduciary relationships) define the limits and obligations of negotiator-principal interactions?

Third, there is the question of duty, responsibility or relationship to the Other (call him "counterpart," "opponent," "adversary," "partner," "boss" or "subordinate," spouse, lover, child or parent). . . . Do we follow some version of the Golden Rule and treat others as we would hope to be treated by them (a norm of aspirational reciprocity), or does the Golden Rule tarnish a bit on application in particular contexts? . . .

How do those outside of a negotiation judge its ethical "externalities" or social effects? Has a particular negotiation done more good than harm? For those inside the negotiation? Those affected by it (employees, shareholders, vendors and clients, consumers and the public)? And, to what extent must any negotiation be morally accountable for impacts on third parties (children in a divorce, customers in labor-management negotiation, similarly situated claimants in mass torts) and for its inter-generational effects (future generations in environmental disputes)?

B. ETHICAL RULES AND LEGAL OBLIGATIONS

In this chapter, we address some of these questions by examining formal rules, standards, case law, and other sources of ethical guidance on negotiation behavior. But, as you will learn, formal standards do not cover many situations so that, in the end, you will form your own ethical practice and reputation as a negotiator. What do you think will most influence your choices?

1. The Law of Misrepresentation and Fraud

There are numerous cases in which the law has regulated negotiation behavior. Whereas existing ethics rules regarding negotiation seem to leave plenty of room for strategic behavior and deception, the negotiation lawyer who relies solely on that interpretation clearly will be in trouble. The common law, as these cases outline, requires truthfulness in many elements of negotiation.

RESTATEMENT (SECOND) OF TORTS §525 (1977)

§525 Liability for Fraudulent Misrepresentation

One who fraudulently makes a misrepresentation of fact, opinion, intention or law for the purpose of inducing another to act or to refrain from action in reliance upon it, is subject to liability to the other in deceit for pecuniary loss caused to him by his justifiable reliance upon the misrepresentation.

RESTATEMENT (SECOND) OF CONTRACTS §§161, 164 (1981)

§161 When Non-Disclosure Is Equivalent to an Assertion

A person's non-disclosure of a fact known to him is equivalent to an assertion that the fact does not exist in the following cases only:

(a) where he knows that disclosure of the fact is necessary to prevent some previous assertion from being a misrepresentation or from being fraudulent or material.

(b) where he knows that disclosure of the fact would correct a mistake of the other party as to a basic assumption on which that party is making the contract and if non-disclosure of the fact amounts to a failure to act in good faith and in accordance with reasonable standards of fair dealing.

(c) where he knows that disclosure of the fact would correct a mistake of the other party as to the contents or effect of a writing, evidencing or embodying an agreement in whole or in part.

(d)   where the other person is entitled to know the fact because of a relation of trust and confidence between them.

§164 When a Misrepresentation Makes a Contract Voidable

(1)   If a party's manifestation of assent is induced by either a fraudulent or material misrepresentation by the other party upon which the recipient is justified in relying, the contract is voidable by the recipient. . . .

Building on the definition of a fraudulent statement, the cases below further define the elements of misrepresentation, material fact, reliance, and damages.

a. Misrepresentation

A misrepresentation clearly includes a deliberate lie. The law, however, goes further so that uncorrected mistakes are also included under knowing misrepresentation.

 **STARE v. TATE**

---

21 Cal. App. 3d 432, 98 Cal. Rptr. 264 (1971)

Justice KAUS delivered the Opinion of the Court. . . .

FACTS

The agreement in question was signed by both parties on February 21, 1968. . . .

In the negotiations both sides apparently agreed that the community property was to be evenly divided. They did not agree, however, on the value of certain items and on the community property status of certain stocks which stood in the husband's name alone.

These disagreements centered principally on items which, it was understood, were to be retained by the husband. . . .

In January, 1968, Joan's attorney prepared a document entitled "SECOND PROPOSAL FOR A BASIS OF SETTLEMENT — TATE v. TATE" which, among other things, arrived at a suggested figure of $70,081.85 for the value of Joan's share in the Holt property. This value was arrived at by a computation set forth in the proposal. It is copied in the footnote.[4]

---

[4] "888 East Holt Avenue, Pomona
(Note: value as per previous offer)

Total value	$550,000.00
Less encumbrance	− 308,362.99
Net value	$141,637.01
One-half community	$ 70,081.85"

It is obvious that Joan's attorney arrived at the figure of $70,081.85 for the community equity in the property only by making two substantial errors. First, the net value after deducting the encumbrances from the asserted gross value of $550,000 is $241,637.01, not $141,637.01; second, one-half of $241,637.01 is substantially more than $70,081.85. The correct figure for the equity should have been $120,818.50 or, roughly $50,000 more.

The mistake did not escape Tim's accountant who discovered it while helping Tim's attorney in preparing a counter-offer. He brought it to the attention of the attorney who, in his own words, reacted as follows:

"I told him that I had been arguing with [the wife's attorney] to use the value that was on the real property tax statement, but I knew that that was low and [he] would never go for it, that the appraisal had been $425,000.00 when the building had been purchased by said owners, and I thought that until we got it, that we would use something like a $450,000.00 value, and he said, 'Fine.' It is my recollection that I said to him, 'You know, you might as well use the figure that Walker has there because his mistake is a hundred thousand dollars and we value it at a hundred thousand dollars less, so it is basically the same thing, so give it a $70,000.00 equity.' And that is what he did and that is how it came about."

A counter-offer was then submitted to Joan and her lawyer. It lists all of the community assets, with the property in question being valued at $70,082.00, rounding up the erroneous figure in Joan's offer to the nearest dollar. There can be no reasonable doubt that the counter-offer was prepared in a way designed to minimize the danger that Joan or her attorney would discover the mistake....

On February 16, 1968, the parties and their attorneys had a settlement conference. The counter-offer was the basis for the discussion. There was no mention that the figure of $70,082 for the equity in the Holt property was based on an agreed value of $550,000 or any other figure....

The mistake might never have come to light had not Tim desired to have that exquisite last word. A few days after Joan had obtained the divorce he mailed her a copy of the offer which contained the errant computation. On top of the page he wrote with evident satisfaction: "PLEASE NOTE $100,000.00 MISTAKE IN YOUR FIGURES...." The present action was filed exactly one month later....

DISCUSSION

There is really no substantial conflict in the evidence and it is hard to understand how the trial court could do anything but grant Joan's prayer for relief.

Section 3399 of the Civil Code provides:

"When, through fraud or a mutual mistake of the parties, *or a mistake of one party, which the other at the time knew or suspected*, a written contract does not truly express the intention of the parties, it may be revised on the application of a party aggrieved, so as to express that intention, so far as it can be done without prejudice to rights acquired by third persons, in good faith and for value." (Emphasis added.)

Clearly there was a mistake, Joan and her attorney thinking that a $550,000 value resulted in a community equity of about $70,000.... Inasmuch as the error was discovered by Tim's attorney, it is, of course, no defense that it was negligently made by Joan's attorney....

The case was fully tried and, as we said at the outset of our discussion, the record supports nothing but a judgment for the plaintiff as prayed.

The judgment is reversed with directions to make findings and conclusions and to enter a judgment in conformity with this opinion.

Notes and Questions

10.1 Aside from the lesson of never gloating over seeming negotiation victories, what other lessons can we take from this case? How should the husband and his lawyer have handled the mistake?

10.2 What if the mistake had been a mistake of law rather than of math? Is there a duty to correct this?

10.3 What about a situation when one side intentionally shields itself from the truth so that it does not "know"?

10.4 Although the settlement agreement above was voided, most settlement agreements are enforced just like any other contract. Settlements, however, incorporated into a court decree (anti-trust violation settlements, class actions, and institutional reforms such as school desegregation, environmental regulation, and housing reform) often must receive judicial oversight of their enforcement. See Chapter 11.

b. Omissions

The law generally requires that a misrepresentation is a positive misstatement rather than an omission of information. The next excerpt, however, outlines the exceptions to this rule. Also, take a look at the earlier excerpt of the Restatement (Second) of Contracts §161.

 G. *Richard Shell*, BARGAINING FOR ADVANTAGE: NEGOTIATION STRATEGIES FOR REASONABLE PEOPLE

208-209 (1999)

Surprisingly, there are circumstances when it may be fraudulent to keep your peace about an issue *even if the other side does not ask about it.* When does a negotiator have a duty to voluntarily disclose matters that may hurt his bargaining position? American law imposes affirmative disclosure duties in the following four circumstances:

1. *When the negotiator makes a partial disclosure that is or becomes misleading in light of all the facts.* If you say your company is profitable, you may be under a duty to disclose whether you used questionable accounting techniques to arrive at that statement. You should also update your prior statement if you show a loss in the next quarter and negotiations are still ongoing.

2. *When the parties stand in a fiduciary relationship to each other.* In negotiations between trustees and beneficiaries, partners in a partnership, shareholders in a small corporation, or members of a family business, parties may have a duty of complete candor and cannot rely on the "be silent and be safe" approach.

3. *When the nondisclosing party has vital information about the transaction not accessible to the other side.* A recent case applying this exception held that an employer owed a duty of disclosure to a prospective employee to disclose contingency plans for shutting down the project for which the employee was hired. In general, sellers have a greater duty to disclose hidden defects about their property than buyers do to disclose "hidden treasure" that may be buried there. Thus, a home seller must disclose termite infestation in her home,[*] but an oil company need not voluntarily disclose that there is oil on a farmer's land when negotiating to purchase it.[†] This is a slippery exception; the best test is one of conscience and fairness.

4. *When special codified disclosure duties, such as those regarding contracts of insurance or public offerings of securities, apply.* Legislatures sometimes impose special disclosure duties for particular kinds of transactions. In the United States, for example, many states now require home sellers to disclose all known problems with their houses.

If none of these four exceptions applies, neither side is likely to be found liable for fraud based on a nondisclosure. Each party can remain silent, passively letting the other proceed under its own assumptions.

The third exception listed by Shell is when the nondisclosing party has "superior information" to the other side. The following case outlines how the law has developed in this area.

 WEINTRAUB v. KROBATSCH

64 N.J. 445, 317 A.2d 68 (1974)

Justice JACOBS delivered the Opinion of the Court....

Mrs. Weintraub owned and occupied a six-year-old Englishtown home which she placed in the hands of a real estate broker (The Serafin Agency, Inc.) for sale. The Krobatsches were interested in purchasing the home, examined it while it was illuminated and found it suitable. On June 30, 1971, Mrs. Weintraub, as seller, and the Krobatsches, as purchasers, entered into a contract for the sale of the property for $42,500. The contract provided that the purchasers had inspected the property and were fully satisfied with its physical condition, that no representations had been made and that no responsibility was assumed by the seller as to the present or future condition of the premises. A deposit of $4,250 was sent by the purchasers to the broker to be held in escrow pending the closing of the transaction. The purchasers requested that the seller have the house fumigated and that was done....

---

[*] See, e.g., Miles v. McSwegin, 388 N.E.2d 1367 (Ohio 1979).
[†] Zaschak v. Travers Corp., 333 N.W.2d 191 (Mich. App. 1983).

During the evening of August 25, 1971, prior to closing, the purchasers entered the house, then unoccupied, and as they turned the lights on they were, as described in their petition for certification, "astonished to see roaches literally running in all directions, up the walls, drapes, etc." On the following day their attorney wrote a letter to Mrs. Weintraub, care of her New York law firm, advising that on the previous day "it was discovered that the house is infested with vermin despite the fact that an exterminator has only recently serviced the house" and asserting that "the presence of vermin in such great quantities, particularly after the exterminator was done, rendered the house as unfit for human habitation at this time and therefore, the contract is rescinded." . . .

Mrs. Weintraub rejected the rescission by the purchasers and filed an action with the Law Division joining them and the broker as defendants. . . .

The Law Division denied the motion by the purchasers for summary judgment but granted Mrs. Weintraub's motion and directed that the purchasers pay her the sum of $4,250. It further directed that the deposit monies held in escrow by the broker be paid to Mrs. Weintraub in satisfaction of her judgment against the purchasers. . . .

Before us the purchasers contend that they were entitled to a trial on the issue of whether there was fraudulent concealment or nondisclosure entitling them to rescind: if there was, then clearly they were under no liability to either the seller or the broker and would be entitled to the return of their deposit held by the broker in escrow. . . .

Mrs. Weintraub asserts that she was unaware of the infestation and the Krobatsches acknowledge that, if that was so then there was not fraudulent concealment or nondisclosure on her part and their claim must fall. But the purchasers allege that she was in fact aware of the infestation and at this stage of the proceedings we must assume that to be true. She contends however, that even if she were fully aware she would have been under no duty to speak and that consequently no complaint by the purchasers may legally be grounded on her silence. She relies primarily on Swinton v. Whitinsville Sav. Bank, 42 N.E.2d 808 (Mass. 1942). . . .

In *Swinton* the plaintiff purchased a house from the defendant and after he occupied it he found it to be infested with termites. The defendant had made no verbal or written representations but the plaintiff, asserting the defendant knew of the termites and was under a duty to speak, filed a complaint for damages grounded on fraudulent concealment. The Supreme Judicial Court of Massachusetts sustained a demurrer to the complaint and entered judgment for the defendant. In the course of its opinion the court acknowledged that "the plaintiff possess a certain appeal to the moral sense" but concluded that the law has not "reached the point of imposing upon the frailties of human nature a standard so idealistic as this." 42 N.E.2d at 808-809. That was written several decades ago and we are far from certain that it represents views held by the current members of the Massachusetts court. . . . In any event we are certain that it does not represent our sense of justice or fair dealing and it has understandably been rejected in persuasive opinions elsewhere. . . .

In Obde v. Schlemeyer, 353 P.2d 672 [(Wash. 1960)], the defendants sold an apartment house to the plaintiff. The house was termite infested but that fact was not disclosed by the sellers to the purchasers who later sued for damages alleging fraudulent concealment. The sellers contended that they were under no obligation whatever to speak out and they relied heavily on the decision of the Massachusetts court in *Swinton*. The Supreme Court of Washington flatly rejected their contention, holding that though the parties had dealt at arms length the sellers were under "a duty to inform the plaintiffs of the termite condition" of which they were fully aware. . . .

In Loghry v. Capel, [132 N.W.2d 417 (Iowa 1965)], the plaintiffs purchased a duplex from the defendants. They examined the house briefly on two occasions and signed a document stating that they accepted the property in its "present condition." 132 N.W.2d at 419. They made no inquiry about the subsoil and were not told that the house had been constructed on filled ground. They filed an action for damages charging that the sellers had fraudulently failed to disclose that the duplex was constructed on improperly compacted filled ground. The jury found in their favor and the verdict was sustained on appeal in an opinion which pointed out that "fraud may consist of concealment of a material fact." 132 N.W.2d at 419. The purchasers' stipulation that they accepted the property in its present condition could not be invoked to bar their claim. See Wolvord v. Freeman, 35 N.W.2d 98 (Neb. 1948), where the court pointed out that the purchase of property "as is" does not bar rescission grounded on fraudulent conduct of the seller. 35 N.W.2d at 103. . . .

If the trial judge finds such deliberate concealment or nondisclosure of the latent infestation not observable by the purchasers on their inspection, he will still be called upon to determine whether, in the light of the full presentation before him, the concealment or nondisclosure was of such significant nature as to justify rescission. Minor conditions which ordinary sellers and purchasers would reasonably disregard as of little or no materiality in the transaction would clearly not call for judicial intervention. While the described condition may not have been quite as major as in the termite cases which were concerned with structural impairments, to the purchasers here it apparently was of such magnitude and was so repulsive as to cause them to rescind immediately though they had earlier indicated readiness that there be adjustment at closing for damage resulting from a fire which occurred after the contract was signed. We are not prepared at this time to say that on their showing they acted either unreasonably or without equitable justification.

Our courts have come a long way since the days when the judicial emphasis was on formal rules and ancient precedents rather than on modern concepts of justice and fair dealing. While admittedly our law has progressed more slowly in the real property field than in other fields, there have been notable stirrings even there. . . .

Notes and Questions

10.5 Home buyers are generally delighted by the *Weintraub* case and the evolution of the law in this way. What other elements of the home, besides termite infestation, should be covered under the "superior information" category?

10.6 If your neighbors are unpleasant, are you required to reveal this? If your neighbors belong to a rock band that practices late into the night, are you required to reveal this? If you are selling a home in which a murder occurred, are you required to reveal this? See Reed v. King, 193 Cal. Rptr. 130 (Cal. Ct. App. 1983) (seller of a house who represented it as fit for an elderly woman living alone had a duty to disclose that the house was the site of a multiple murder ten years ago).

10.7 The question of superior information can also arise in writing job recommendations. If you are recommending a school principal, how honest should you be? Should you reveal that this person is only mediocre? Shows up late? Has been accused of improper advances to students? Should you be liable if you do not share any of this information? See Randi W. v. Livingston Union Sch. Dist., 50 Cal. App. 4th 447 (1996).

---

c. Material Facts

The next question under fraud is whether the facts under discussion are material. In negotiations in which puffing and bluffing are seen as part of the game (at least under the poker model), could a lawyer get in trouble for stretching too far? The answer is that it depends on what you are talking about in the negotiation. When the parties are of equal bargaining power, courts have permitted a certain amount of puffing and predictions of quality. The following case highlights some traditional ways that courts have examined sales promises.

 VULCAN METALS CO. v. SIMMONS MANUFACTURING CO.

248 F. 853, 856-857 (2d Cir. 1918)

Judge Learned HAND delivered the Opinion of the Court.

The first question is of the misrepresentations touching the quality and powers of the patented machine. These were general commendations, or, insofar as they included any specific facts, were not disproved; e.g., that the cleaner would produce 18 inches of vacuum with 25 pounds of water pressure. They raise, therefore, the question of law how far general "puffing" or "dealers' talk" can be the basis of an action for deceit.

The conceded exception in such cases has generally rested upon the distinction between "opinion" and "fact"; but that distinction has not escaped the criticism it deserves. An opinion is a fact, and it may be a very relevant fact; the expression of an opinion is the assertion of a belief, and any rule which condones the expression of a consciously false opinion condones a consciously false statement of fact. When the parties are so situated that the buyer may reasonably rely upon the expression of the seller's opinion, it is no excuse to give a false one. And so it makes much difference whether the parties stand "on an equality." For example, we should treat very differently the expressed opinion of a chemist to a layman about the properties of a composition from the same opinion between chemist and chemist, when the buyer had full opportunity to examine. The reason of the rule lies, we think, in this: There are some kinds of talk which no sensible man takes seriously, and if he does he suffers from his credulity. If we were all scrupulously honest, it would not be so; but, as it is, neither party usually believes what the seller says about his own opinions, and each knows it. Such statements, like the claims of campaign managers before election, are rather designed to allay the suspicion which would attend their absence than to be understood as having any relation to objective truth. It is quite true that they induce a compliant temper in the buyer, but it is by a much more subtle process than through the acceptance of his claims for his wares. . . .

In the case at bar, since the buyer was allowed full opportunity to examine the cleaner and to test it out, we put the parties upon an equality. It seems to us that general statements as to what the cleaner would do, even though consciously false, were not of a kind to be taken literally by the buyer. As between manufacturer and customer, it may not be so; but this was the case of taking over a business, after ample chance to investigate. Such a buyer, who the seller rightly expects will undertake an independent and adequate inquiry into the actual merits of what he gets, has no right to treat as material in his determination statements like these. . . . We therefore think that the District Court was right in disregarding all these misrepresentations.

As respects the representation that the cleaners had never been put upon the market or offered for sale, the rule does not apply; nor can we agree that such representations could not have been material to Freeman's decision to accept the contract. The actual test of experience in their sale might well be of critical consequence in his decision to buy the business, and the jury would certainly have the right to accept his statement that his reliance upon these representations was determinative of his final decision. . . .

Notes and Questions

10.8 What type of lie was the lie about whether the vacuum cleaners had been marketed? Do you agree with the court that this type of lie should be illegal? What was the court's reasoning?

10.9 What type of lie was the lie about the *performance* of the vacuum cleaners? Do you agree with the court that this type of lie should be permitted (and expected)? What was the court's reasoning?

Courts have distinguished between opinion and fact as a way to determine when there is material misrepresentation of fact. This distinction also applies to your own views of the strength of your position. A demand — "my client will accept only X" — is not deemed to be material as a matter of law. This type of statement is seen as an opinion rather than fact. Similarly, the reservation price — "my client won't settle for less than X" — is also viewed as an opinion. The comments to Model Rule of Professional Conduct 4.1 also make this point. However, other types of tactics in a negotiation could be problematic if you start to inflate your own alternatives. The following cases are good examples of what can happen with too much bluffing.

BEAVERS v. LAMPLIGHTERS REALTY

556 P.2d 1328, 1329-1331 (Okla. Ct. App. 1976)

BRIGHTMIRE, Judge.

It was sometime in January 1974 [that] plaintiff saw a Lamplighters' for sale sign in front of an attractive Spanish style house at 4912 Larissa Lane. He liked the storybook looks of the abode, called the telephone number printed on the sign, and eventually was shown the house by agent Norma Ray. Shortly thereafter, on February 11, 1974, plaintiff's offer of $34,500 for the dwelling was rejected.

Plaintiff still wanted the place, however. He let a day or two pass and again called Lamplighters. This time a "Mr. Taylor came on the phone" and asked if plaintiff was still interested in the home. "Yes," said plaintiff, "but doggone it . . . they were asking too much."

"If you are going to do anything, you had better do it pretty quick, because I've got a buyer for it," said the realtor.

"You do?" responded plaintiff.

"Yes," said Taylor, "it [is] the original builder and he is coming in."

"Paul Good?" asked plaintiff.

"Yes," answered Taylor, adding that Good was coming in with a check right away.

"How much is it?" plaintiff asked concerning the check.

"Thirty-seven thousand dollars" was the answer.

"Well, he's bought it."

"No," retreated Taylor, "[i]f you want to put in a bid, he's going to be here within the hour. I just talked to him."

The high pressure tactic worked. Said plaintiff, "I [don't] know whether 'panicked' [is] the [right] word or not, but I figured . . . that [if] the original builder would pay thirty-seven thousand for the home, that maybe . . . it absolutely should be worth that much to me . . . and I just increased it [the fictitious offer] two hundred and fifty dollars. And the next thing I know I bought myself a home" for $37,250 by executing a contract dated February 15, 1974.

It was a while before plaintiff found out he had been a victim of a gross deception. One day, after he had moved into the house — and found, incidentally, that the agent Ray had made false representations about the condition of the house, requiring him to expend about $6,000 for repairs — he chanced to meet builder Paul Good at a neighbor's home, got to talking to him about plaintiff's house and came upon some interesting facts. Good said he had earlier looked at the house "but it was out of the ball park as far as he was concerned" and that he "would have given in the . . . lower thirties."

"Well," said plaintiff, "I'd offered thirty-four five to start."

"That should have bought it," said Good.

"Didn't you offer thirty-seven thousand?" plaintiff asked Good.

"No," he answered. . . .

In the instant case the evidence so far adduced establishes that realtor Taylor, upon becoming aware of plaintiff's desire for the Spanish villa, undertook to bring about a rather rapid resolution of the price problem by using, as it were, a dynamite sales technique to blast an immediate positive response out of plaintiff. The deliberate lie did indeed achieve the intended and expected effect and induced plaintiff to purchase the property for a figure higher than he would have had to pay absent the fraud. [The court held that this was fraudulent inducement.]

 KABATCHNICK v. HANOVER-ELM BUILDING CORP.

328 Mass. 341, 103 N.E.2d 692 (1952)

Justice SPALDING delivered the Opinion of the Court.

In this action of tort for deceit the material averments of the declaration are as follows: The plaintiff, who was engaged in selling novelties, toys, and games at retail, occupied as a tenant under a written lease the first floor and basement of certain premises on Bromfield Street, Boston. The annual rental reserved in the lease was $4,500. The lease was dated January 15, 1945, and ran to March 1, 1947. Upon acquiring title to the premises in November, 1946, the defendants represented to the plaintiff "that they had a bona fide offer from one Melvin Levine for the leasing of the said premises to him at the rate of $10,000 per year and that unless the plaintiff met that offer and signed a lease for twelve (12) years at $10,000 per year the defendants would evict the plaintiff at the end of his lease on March 1, 1947." Believing these representations and in reliance upon them the plaintiff on December 6, 1946, entered into a written lease with the defendant Hanover-Elm Building Corporation for the term of twelve years from January 1, 1947, at an annual rental of $10,000 payable in monthly installments of $833.33. At the time that this lease was executed the defendants demanded as a condition to its execution that the plaintiff pay the sum of $833.33 beginning with the month of December, 1946. The plaintiff complied with this demand and has thereafter paid this amount monthly. "In truth and in fact the representations made by the defendants to the plaintiff . . . [concerning the offer purporting to have been made by Melvin Levine] were false and known by the defendants to be false and were made by them with the intent that the plaintiff rely thereon and execute the said lease and make the aforesaid payments." These facts were recently discovered by the plaintiff and "if he had known of the true facts he would not have executed the said lease." "The rental value of the said premises," it is alleged, "was not worth $10,000 per year for twelve (12) years, but was worth only $4,500 per year; all to . . . [the plaintiff's] great damage." . . .

Most, if not all, courts hold that there are certain types of statements upon which a purchaser is not justified in placing reliance. . . .

But the statement in the case at bar was not of that class. The defendants represented to the plaintiff that they had received a bona fide offer from Levine to take a lease of the premises at an annual rental of $10,000. This was more than a statement of opinion; it was a representation of an existing fact. . . .

The time has come, we think, to depart from [an earlier] rule, in so far as it affords no remedy for representations of the sort here involved. Not only is it opposed to the weight of authority but it is difficult to justify on principles of ethics and justice. . . .

Notes and Questions

10.10 The court in Beavers v. Lamplighters Realty and Kabatchnick v. Hanover-Elm Building Corp. held that lying about another offer was fraudulent inducement. Do you think this holding is going too far?

10.11 If you were selling a home and wanted to make it look like it was very popular and likely to be sold soon, could you do this without violating the law? What can you say and what should you not say under the holdings in *Beavers* and *Kabatchnick*? How can you strengthen your BATNA without violating the law?

10.12 Another relevant law covering negotiation is confidentiality. As discussed further in Chapter 11, settlement discussions and settlements themselves can be kept confidential. Federal Rule of Evidence 408 states that settlement discussions cannot be revealed in litigation to demonstrate liability. However, courts have differed as to the extent of protection provided by Rule 408. Compare, e.g., Thomas v. Resort Health Related Facility, 539 F. Supp. 630 (E.D.N.Y. 1982) (an ex-employee's rejection of a reinstatement offer was admissible because it fell outside Rule 408), with Affiliated Mfrs. v. Alcoa, 56 F.3d 521 (3d Cir. 1995) (the court interpreted the scope of the term *dispute* to include less formal stages of a dispute that occurred before litigation keeping an earlier dispute confidential). See also Big O Tires, Dealers v. Goodyear Tire & Rubber Co., 561 F.2d 1365 (10th Cir. 1977); Alpex Computer Corp. v. Nintendo Co., 770 F. Supp. 161 (S.D.N.Y. 1991). Settlements themselves can also impose confidentiality as part of the agreement. In some cases such as consumer safety, sexual harassment, and similar situations in which others might face the same danger as a settling plaintiff, this confidentiality could be troubling for public policy reasons. For more information on the confidentiality of settlements, see Carrie Menkel-Meadow, Public Access to Private Settlements: Conflicting Legal Policies, 11 Alternatives 85 (1993).

This next case also demonstrates what can happen when there is reliance and damages based on false statements in the negotiation.

 MARKOV v. ABC TRANSFER & STORAGE CO.

76 Wash. 2d 388, 457 P.2d 535 (1969)

HALE, Judge.

In 1962, the plaintiffs organized a 15-man copartnership, under the name of Auburn Industrial Center, to purchase from the General Services Administration of the United States the land, storage, warehouses, railroad tracks and other facilities comprising a large commercial and industrial tract in Auburn, Washington. Successful in its bid, the partnership bought the property and took possession. On September 15, 1962, the partnership by written instrument leased two of the warehouse buildings to the ABC Transfer & Storage Company, a corporation, for a 3-year term to expire September 14, 1965. The lease agreement had no renewal provision. . . .

ABC, with Scott Paper Company — a large national corporation — as its principal customer and occupant, assumed possession. Indeed, so conspicuous and important was Scott Paper's relationship to ABC that both ABC and the partnership carried on subsequent negotiations largely on the basis that both lessor and lessee stood to benefit greatly from Scott Paper's continued business. Because of the continuous process of shipping its products into and out of the warehouse, Scott Paper Company's needs for space fluctuated. . . .

Apparently the lease agreement was under nearly constant negotiations for modification [based on Scott Paper's fluctuating needs].

By the time these modifications had been adopted, ABC faced the possibility that the lease would expire within about a year, for it contained no renewal clause and the partnership had placed itself under no legal duty to promise a renewal. ABC was painfully aware that the Scott Paper Company patronage depended in large measure on its capability of giving authentic assurances of continuous availability. The dire necessity of a firm commitment from the Auburn Industrial Center partnership of a lease renewal precipitated the very events which led to this case. . . .

Scott Paper Company too had a natural anxiety that the lease be renewed for it was concurrently negotiating with ABC for a new storage and warehousing contract to run from September 15, 1965, to September 15, 1968 — a period coextensive with the sought-after lease renewal term. Whether Scott Paper could continue doing business with ABC or had to seek another warehouse depended on the success of ABC's renewal negotiations. . . .

The trial court was convinced that the Auburn Industrial Center partnership made representations to ABC Storage and Scott Paper that it would renew the lease for 3 years. . . .

In the meanwhile, however, the partnership was parleying with others concerning the property. After defendant ABC Transfer & Storage Company had begun negotiations in February, 1965, for a lease renewal, a real-estate dealer representing an undisclosed principal informed the partnership in late May or June, 1965, that he had a probable buyer for the ABC Transfer & Storage Company warehouse but insisted that their communications concerning the sale be kept confidential. Thus, while the partnership was conferring with ABC for a renewal of the lease, it was at the same time quietly negotiating for a sale of the premises.

Negotiations between the partnership and the real-estate agent prior to July 1 resulted July 1, 1965, in an option agreement to an undisclosed buyer to sell the Auburn warehouse facility at a price of $4,000,000. Not long afterward, the Boeing Company, the undisclosed optionee, announced that it was exercising the option and, tendering the purchase price, demanded possession. ABC, having no knowledge of the negotiations leading to the pending sale or the sale itself, continued to operate the warehouse on the assumption that its lease would be renewed for a 3-year term. It continued operating on this assumption until it received a categorical notice from Boeing on August 25 to vacate by September 15, 1965.

The trial court found, too, that ABC suffered substantial damage not only from the loss of the leased premises but because of the misleading representations that the lease would be renewed. The court found that other storage space was then available at similar rates and had ABC known, during its negotiations for a renewal, that the lease would not be renewed, it could have leased another warehouse. ABC showed that, because of the rapid turnover of warehoused materials, it could have made an orderly and inexpensive vacation of the partnership's warehouse and removed the stored goods of Scott Paper Company to a newly leased warehouse at very little cost.

Thus, the court found it to be a fact that had ABC been timely advised that there would be no renewal of its lease, it could, during July, August and the first 2 weeks in September, readily have planned and carried out a removal of Scott Paper's stored materials at little more than the cost of regular operations. By shipping out outgoing materials from the old warehouse and shipping incoming materials to the new warehouse at the average rate of between 6 and 60 railroad cars a week, the court found that ABC could have completed an orderly removal and transfer at a cost of not more than $1,000 plus $18,281.25 rental on the new premises for the 2 1/2 month period. ABC proved to the court's satisfaction, too, that, because of the misrepresentations that the lease would be renewed, it reasonably incurred expenses of $45,598.99, lost the Scott Paper Company account which it would otherwise have retained, and suffered damages thereby in lost profits from the Scott Paper Company contract in the sum of $91,127.88.

The trial court awarded ABC Transfer & Storage Company judgment of $114,934.92 on its counterclaim as damages proximately resulting from the partnership's deceptive and misleading representations that it intended to and would renew the lease for 3 years. . . .

d. Recovery

The final element in fraudulent misrepresentation is realizing that defrauded parties can seek damages in addition to whatever they received under the negotiated agreement. As the following case outlines, the previous law used to require that parties to an agreement rescind the settlement (give back whatever they received in the agreement) and then sue to reopen the case. That law has been changed to make it easier for defrauded parties to bring a case.

 ## CRESSWELL v. SULLIVAN & CROMWELL

668 F. Supp. 166 (S.D.N.Y. 1987)

Judge SWEET delivered the Opinion of the Court. . . .

The plaintiffs in this case are seeking damages for an alleged fraud committed upon them in the earlier actions [by Sullivan & Cromwell], which they contend induced them to settle their claims for less than they otherwise would have been able to obtain. The issue raised on this motion is whether an action such as this is governed by Rule 60(b) of the Federal Rules of Civil Procedure. Rule 60(b) specifies the procedure for obtaining relief from a judgment when fraud or other misconduct has allegedly been committed in connection with obtaining the judgment. . . .

If plaintiffs' action fell under Rule 60, plaintiffs would essentially be suing for rescission and presumably would be required to tender back their part of the settlement to return to the status quo and possibly face preclusion from suing for damages. The plaintiffs here, however, are not seeking "relief" from a "judgment" within the terms of Rule 60(b). Instead, they seek to affirm the judgment of settlement, and sue for additional damages caused only by the fraud involving the failure to produce certain documents. Of course, in trying such a case, the merits of the prior actions will be relevant, but the issue will be different: whether the settlement value of the cases would have been higher absent the fraud, and if so, by how much.

Because Rule 60(b) by its terms does not control this situation, it is necessary to look to New York law governing what is essentially a common law fraud claim.

Neither party disputes that under New York law, a second action for damages rather than for rescission of the judgment or settlement may be brought when a *state court* judgment or settlement is allegedly procured by fraud. . . . This result arises from the common law rule that a defrauded party can elect between rescission on the one hand and ratification and suit for damages on the other.

In Slotkin v. Citizens Casualty Co., 614 F.2d 301 (2d Cir.), *cert. denied*, 449 U.S. 981 (1980), the Second Circuit noted that New York law is "clear that one who has been induced by fraudulent misrepresentation to settle a claim may recover damages without rescinding the settlement." Id. at 312 (citing cases). . . .

If all that will result from a misrepresentation is a new trial, then the party making it has everything to gain and nothing to lose. The plaintiffs would be placed at a disadvantage by a new trial; the defendants would not. If anything, defendants would benefit by having a preview of plaintiffs' case. As McCormick notes in the case of willful fraud:

> [I]f the defendant by willful falsehood has cozened the plaintiff into risking his property upon a bargain, which, upon the information given by the defendant, would have been profitable, a remedy which merely seeks to place the plaintiff back in the position he was in before seems hardly adequate. The plaintiff might well be given the value of the expected bargain. A willful fraud should cost as much as a broken promise. If the cheat can anticipate that the worst that can happen is that he shall be called upon to pay back his profit upon the trade, he may be encouraged to defraud.

C. McCormick, Handbook on the Law of Damages, §121, at 453 (1935). Thus the New York rule serves to deter fraud. 614 F.2d at 312. . . .

Most importantly, the reasoning behind the application of this rule to state court settlements is equally persuasive with respect to settlements in federal court. This rule will be much more likely to deter fraud than the rule the defendants advocate.

Therefore, the motion to dismiss the complaint for failure to allege compliance with the requirements of Rule 60(b) is denied. Because the relief sought falls outside the reach of Rule 60, that Rule cannot be said to require the plaintiffs to tender back their settlement and sue to reopen the earlier judgment. Plaintiffs may instead affirm the earlier settlement and seek damages for the alleged fraudulent inducement of the settlement.

Notes and Questions

10.13 What is the difference between the two procedures outlined in the case above? Why did the court hold that rescission was no longer required?

10.14 Sullivan & Cromwell is one of the most prestigious law firms in the country. When this case found against the firm (for some pretty unethical behavior) it sent quite a message to law firms around the country.

10.15 For a brief overview of how the law of bargaining generally constrains negotiator behavior, see Russell Korobkin, Michael Moffitt & Nancy Welsh, The Law of Bargaining, 87 Marq. L. Rev. 839 (2004).

2. Ethical Rules

In addition to case law on misrepresentation, ethical rules provide guidelines for how lawyers should behave in negotiations. In this excerpt, Carrie Menkel-Meadow reviews the most important of these rules and explains the impact of these ethical rules on negotiation conduct.

Carrie Menkel-Meadow, ETHICS, MORALITY AND PROFESSIONAL RESPONSIBILITY IN NEGOTIATION

in Dispute Resolution Ethics 131-139 (Phyllis Bernard & Bryant Garth eds., 2002)

Most discussions of negotiation ethics begin with Model Rule of Professional Conduct 4.1(a) and (b) which provides that a lawyer shall not, in the course of representing a client,

> Make a false statement of material fact or law to a third person; or fail to disclose a material fact to a third person when disclosure is necessary to avoid assisting a criminal or fraudulent act by a client, unless disclosure is prohibited by Model Rule 1.6 [client confidentiality rule].

What the black-letter rule appears to require (a fair amount of candor) is in fact greatly modified by the Comments. For example, Comment 2 states that this rule applies only to "statements of fact," and "whether a particular statement should be regarded as one of fact can depend on the circumstances." "Opinions" (of value, of interpretations of facts or of case law) are not considered "facts" under this rubric. Most significantly, the Comment goes on to exempt from the operation of the rule three particular kinds of statements made in negotiation. According to the Comment, there are "generally accepted conventions in negotiation" (a nod to the sociological phenomenology of negotiation) in which no one really expects the "truth" because these statements are not "material" statements of fact. These are (1) estimates of price or value placed on the subject of the transaction, (2) a party's intentions as to an acceptable settlement of a claim and (3) the existence of an undisclosed principal, except where non-disclosure of the principal would otherwise (by other law) constitute fraud.

Thus, the exception in the Comment defines away, as not material, several key notions of how negotiations are conducted, including inflated offers and demands (otherwise known as "puffing" and "exaggeration"), failure to disclose "bottom lines" or "reservation prices," and non-disclosure of a principal (say Donald Trump or Harvard University) where knowledge of who the principal is might raise a price or demand, on the assumption that the principal has deep pockets. In addition, as discussed more fully below, Comment 1 suggests that while a negotiating lawyer "is required to be truthful when dealing with others on a client's behalf," a lawyer does not have an *affirmative duty* to inform an opposing party of relevant facts (subject to some further qualifications that failure to act or to correct may sometimes constitute a misrepresentation and that substantive law may, in fact, sometimes require affirmative disclosure — see Comment 3).

A simple reading of these provisions demonstrates how indeterminate

---

MODEL RULE OF PROFESSIONAL CONDUCT

4.1 Truthfulness in Statements to Others

In the course of representing a client a lawyer shall not knowingly:

(a) make a false statement of material fact or law to a third person . . .

(b) fail to disclose a material fact to a third person when disclosure is necessary to avoid assisting a criminal or fraudulent act by a client, unless disclosure is prohibited by Rule 1.6.

COMMENT

Misrepresentation
[1] A lawyer is required to be truthful when dealing with others on a client's behalf, but generally has no affirmative duty to inform an opposing party of relevant facts. A misrepresentation can occur if the lawyer incorporates or affirms a statement of another person that the lawyer knows is false. Misrepresentations can also occur by failure to act.

Statements of Fact
[2] This Rule refers to statements of fact. Whether a particular statement should be regarded as one of fact can depend on the circumstances. Under generally accepted conventions in negotiation, certain types of statements ordinarily are not taken as statements of material fact. Estimates of price or value placed on the subject of a transaction and a party's intentions as to an acceptable settlement of a claim are in this category, and so is the existence of an undisclosed principal except where nondisclosure of the principal would constitute fraud.

Fraud by Client
[3] Paragraph (b) recognizes that substantive law may require a lawyer to disclose certain information to avoid being deemed to have assisted the client's crime or fraud. The requirement of disclosure created by this paragraph is, however, subject to the obligations created by Rule 1.6.

---

and unhelpful the formal rules of professional responsibility are. First, the claim that there are "generally accepted conventions" is an empirical one, without substantiation in the text of the Comments. Who, in fact, generally "accepts" these conventions? All lawyers? Lawyers who subscribe to the conventional, adversarial and distributive models of negotiation? Many lawyers would probably "accept" even more classes of "untruthful" or less-than-full disclosure statement in negotiations. . . .

In an important test of these "generally accepted conventions," Larry Lempert asked 15 legal and ethics experts how — under these rules — they would resolve several important disclosure dilemmas, including lying about authorized limits given by the client, lying about the extent of a personal injury as a plaintiff's lawyer during a litigation negotiation, exaggerating an emotional distress claim in a torts negotiation, and failing to correct the other side's misimpression about the extent of injuries. Not surprisingly, there was relatively little consensus among the experts about how far a

---

MODEL RULE OF PROFESSIONAL CONDUCT

1.6 Confidentiality of Information

(a) A lawyer shall not reveal information relating to representation of a client unless the client consents after consultation, except for disclosures that are impliedly authorized in order to carry out the representation, and except as stated in paragraph (b).

(b) A lawyer may reveal such information to the extent the lawyer reasonably believes necessary:

(1) to prevent the client from committing a criminal act that the lawyer believes is likely to result in imminent death or substantial bodily harm; or

(2) to establish a claim or defense on behalf of the lawyer in a controversy between the lawyer and the client, to establish a defense to a criminal charge or civil claim against the lawyer based upon conduct in which the client was involved, or to respond to allegations in any proceeding concerning the lawyer's representation of the client.

---

lawyer-negotiator could go in lying about, deceiving or misrepresenting these issues, all of which could be argued to be within the three "generally accepted conventions" excluded from the general non-misrepresentation rule.

Recently, I have added to this list the following negotiator's ethical dilemmas in a variety of lawyer-negotiator ethics CLE programs. Consider what you would do in the following situations, in addition to those four listed above.

1. Just before the closing of a sale of a closely held business, a major client of the business terminates a long-term commercial relationship, thereby lessening the value of the firm being purchased and you represent the seller. Do you disclose this information to the buyer?

2. On the morning of a scheduled negotiation about a litigation matter, you receive notice that your request for a summary judgment has been denied. The lawyer for the other side is coming to your office and clearly has no notice of the judge's ruling. Do you disclose it before negotiating or seek to "close the deal" quickly with an offer before the other side finds out about the summary judgment decision?

3. You receive, by mistake, a fax addressed to all of the counsel on the other side of a multi-party litigation. It contains important and damaging-to-the-other-side information that would enhance your bargaining position. What do you do? . . .

4. In a hotly contested contractual negotiation the other side demanded the inclusion of a particular clause that your client did not want to agree to but finally did when it was made a "deal-breaker." The final draft of the contract, prepared by the other side, arrives at your office without the disputed clause, which you know the other side really wants included in the final deal. What do you do? . . .

Remarkably, time after time, use of these hypotheticals reveals exactly the opposite of what Comment 2 to Model Rule 4.1 so baldly states. In my experience, there are virtually no "generally accepted conventions" with respect to what should be done in these situations. Different negotiators bring to the table different assumptions of what they are trying to do, and with those assumptions come different ethical orientations.

Thus, for those who are "tough negotiators" or who see legal negotiation as an individual maximization game, whether in the litigation or transactional context, most of the deceptions above can be justified by reference either to "expectations" about how the legal-negotiation game is played, or to the lawyer's obligation to be a zealous advocate and not to "do the work" of the other side. For those lawyers who are concerned about making a good agreement "stick" — the instrumentalists — some disclosure is considered desirable (for example, in the scenarios above that describe the omission of a contract provision or the failure to correct misimpressions) because of a concern that some failures to disclose might lead to a post-hoc attack on the agreement (fraud, negligent misrepresentation, unilateral mistake).

Still others regard negotiations as opportunities for problems to be solved and so are more likely to thoughtfully consider the later impact of doing some of the things suggested above. These lawyers ask questions such as these: What would be gained or lost by revealing to the landlord's lawyer that you know he is lying? How can you honestly return the helpful fax and honestly disclose what you now know, but perhaps shouldn't use? When should clients be consulted about these ethical choices, as Model Rule 1.2 suggests they should be, at least about some matters? And those who value their reputations and/or see negotiations as a method for achieving some modicum of justice outside of courtrooms or in deals would disclose (as some ethics opinions and fraud cases say they must) the omitted con-

> **MODEL RULE OF PROFESSIONAL CONDUCT**
>
> **1.2 Scope of Representation**
>
> (a) A lawyer shall abide by a client's decisions concerning the objectives of representation, . . . and shall consult with the client as to the means by which they are to be pursued. A lawyer shall abide by a client's decision whether to accept an offer of settlement of a matter. . . .
>
> (d) A lawyer shall not counsel a client to engage, or assist a client, in conduct that the lawyer knows is criminal or fraudulent, but a lawyer may discuss the legal consequences of any proposed course of conduct with a client and may counsel or assist a client to make a good faith effort to determine the validity, scope, meaning or application of the law. . . .

tract clause and the diminished value of the purchased company (is it a material matter?).

Thus, there are no "generally accepted conventions" in negotiation practice, especially as more and more lawyers and law students are trained in the newer canon of *Getting to YES*, collaborative, integrative and problem-solving negotiation models. Who decides what "generally accepted

> ## MODEL RULE OF PROFESSIONAL CONDUCT
>
> ### 1.4 Communication
>
> (a) A lawyer shall keep a client reasonably informed about the status of a matter and promptly comply with reasonable requests for information.
>
> (b) A lawyer shall explain a matter to the extent reasonably necessary to permit the client to make informed decisions regarding the representation.

conventions" are? The drafters of the ethics rules, without empirical verification? And, more importantly, why should "generally accepted conventions" prevail in an ethics code? Are we looking at "generally accepted conventions" in other areas of the Rules? ... The answer is usually "no" — we require lawyers appearing before tribunals to reveal adverse authority without regard to what "accepted conventions" of advocacy might suggest, e.g. that each side should do its own research and it is up to the judge or her clerk to find the cases.

After some discussion, the Ethics 2000 Commission of the ABA, tasked with amending the Model Rules of Professional Conduct, suggested virtually no "material" changes to Model Rule 4.1. Even though many commentators requested clarification of the candor obligations under Model Rule 4.1, the Ethics 2000 Commission declined to change any language in the black-letter rule. Some changes to the Comments make explicit that substantive fraud and "other applicable law" may, in fact "trump" the general language of Model Rule 4.1. Comment 2, for example, has been modified by the addition of the word "ordinarily" to the statement that estimates of price are not subject to the misrepresentation-of-fact requirement. This modification references the fact that in some contexts, under some other laws, some misstatements about the "generally accepted conventions" of price, value, and so forth

> ## MODEL RULE OF PROFESSIONAL CONDUCT
>
> ### 8.3 Reporting Professional Misconduct
>
> (a) A lawyer who knows that another lawyer has committed a violation of the Rules of Professional Conduct that raises a substantial question as to that lawyer's honesty, trustworthiness or fitness as a lawyer in other respects shall inform the appropriate professional authority.
>
> (b) A lawyer who knows that a judge has committed a violation of applicable rules of judicial conduct that raises a substantial question as to the judge's fitness for office shall inform the appropriate authority.
>
> (c) This Rule does not require disclosure of information otherwise protected by Rule 1.6 or information gained by a lawyer or judge while participating in an approved lawyers assistance program.

could constitute actionable misrepresentation, and "lawyers should be mindful of their obligations under applicable law to avoid criminal and tortuous misrepresentation."

In addition, changes to Comment 1 recognize that "partially true but misleading" statements, as well as failure to act, may also constitute a misrepresentation under some state or other laws if they are "the equivalent of affirmative false statements." Most significantly, Comment 3, which deals with the prohibition in Model Rule 4.1(b) against the lawyer's assistance in a client's criminal or fraudulent acts, has been modified to reflect a growing consensus that lawyers have an increasing duty to reveal client crimes and frauds when necessary to prevent physical and some economic harm, and to either withdraw from representation or rectify certain crimes and frauds, especially when required to rectify a fraud committed upon a tribunal. These proposed changes to the Model Rules have been adopted by the ABA House of Delegates, but do not become "law" with disciplinary consequences unless adopted by the appropriate body in each state, either court, legislature or disciplinary agency.

Model Rule 4.1, however, is not the only rule that might be seen to govern negotiation ethics. Model Rule 1.2, defining the scope of legal representation, has implications for negotiation behavior in several respects. First, Model Rule 1.2 provides for allocation of decision-making responsibility between lawyers and clients in any representation. Clients are to make decisions about the "objectives of representation," and lawyers, in consultation with clients, may make decisions about the "means" of representation. Some states now require, and others recommend, that this consultation about "means" should include counseling about and consideration of the forms of dispute resolution that should be considered in any representation, including negotiation, mediation, arbitration or other forms of "appropriate dispute resolution." Some might think that such consideration of "means" should extend to the different models of negotiation or different strategies now possible within the growing sophistication about different approaches to negotiation.

Second, and most importantly, Model Rule 1.2 requires the lawyer to "abide by a client's decision whether to settle a matter" and thus requires the lawyer to transmit settlement offers to the client, especially in conjunction with the requirements of Model Rule 1.4(a) that a lawyer "shall keep the client reasonably informed about the status

---

MODEL RULE OF PROFESSIONAL CONDUCT

8.4 Misconduct

It is professional misconduct for a lawyer to:

(a) violate or attempt to violate the rules of professional conduct, knowingly assist or induce another to do so, or do so through the acts of another; . . .

(c) engage in conduct involving dishonesty, fraud, deceit or misrepresentation;

(d) engage in conduct that is prejudicial to the administration of justice. . . .

---

of the matter" and Model Rule 1.4(b) that a lawyer "shall explain a matter to the extent reasonably necessary to permit the client to make informed decisions regarding the representation." Model Rule 1.2(d) also admonishes lawyers not to counsel a client to engage in and not to assist the client in conduct the lawyer knows is fraudulent or criminal, and thus, once again, the Rule implicates the substantive law of fraud and crimes. Lawyers may not assist clients in such activities, and thus, what constitutes a misrepresentation in a negotiation is dependent on tort and criminal law, outside the rules of professional responsibility. The lawyer may, then, be more restricted in 1.2(d) by what other laws prohibit clients from doing than by what the lawyer might be restricted from in 4.1.

Beyond these more specific requirements, Model Rules 8.3 and 8.4 can be and have been invoked with respect to the lawyer's duty to be honest and fair in negotiation. Model Rule 8.4 states that "it is professional misconduct for a lawyer to . . . (c) engage in

> ### MODEL RULE OF PROFESSIONAL CONDUCT
>
> #### 4.4 Respect for Rights of Third Persons
>
> In representing a client, a lawyer shall not use means that have no substantial purpose other than to embarrass, delay, or burden a third person, or use methods of obtaining evidence that violate the legal rights of such a person.

conduct involving dishonesty, fraud, deceit or misrepresentation," once again incorporating by reference not only substantive standards of legal fraud and misrepresentation, but also suggesting that certain forms of dishonesty or breach of trust or "serious interference with the administration of justice" (especially when a "pattern of repeated offenses" exists) may subject a lawyer to discipline for his deceptive or other fraudulent actions in negotiations. Model Rule 8.3 requires a lawyer who "knows that another lawyer has committed a violation of the Rules of Professional Conduct that raises a substantial question as to the lawyer's honesty, trustworthiness or fitness as a lawyer" to report such misconduct to the appropriate professional authority. Thus, lawyers who repeatedly deceive or play some versions of negotiation "hardball" or "hide and seek" may be subject to discipline for their professional misconduct, though such misconduct is rarely reported.

Several other ethics rules, seldom invoked, also have possible applicability to the conduct of negotiations. Model Rule 4.4 prohibits lawyers from using means that have "no substantial purpose other than to embarrass, delay, or burden a third person," and thus requires lawyers to exercise some degree of "care" toward third parties (such as opposing parties in a negotiation, whether in litigation or transactional settings).

Finally, Model Rule 5.6 prohibits any agreement "in which a restriction on the lawyer's right to practice is part of the settlement of a client controversy." This section is intended to prevent a common practice of defense counsel settling favorably with one plaintiff under the condition that the plaintiff's lawyer be barred from representing similarly situated plaintiffs, or alternatively, be prevented from using evidence or other information acquired in one representation in another, as a condition of the settlement. Despite this rule, many civil settlements, including those in class-action and mass-torts settings, have utilized such conditions. Despite this ethics rule, a variety of case rulings now place substantial restraints on what some lawyers can negotiate for in settlements of civil matters, such as statutory attorneys fees.

Regardless of, or perhaps because of, the general inefficacy of the lawyers' general rules of professional conduct to affect negotiation ethics, various groups have suggested more specialized rules or guidelines. Recently, the ABA Section of Litigation has proposed a set of Ethical Guidelines for Civil Settlement Negotiations (for lawyers who "represent private parties in non–mediated settlement negotiations in civil cases"), making suggestions about such matters as relations with clients, disputes with clients, fees, disclosures to third parties and other clients, but most specifically, authorizing a variety of conditions on settlement, including secrecy and con-

---

MODEL RULE OF PROFESSIONAL CONDUCT

5.6 Restrictions on Right to Practice

A lawyer shall not participate in offering or making:

(a) a partnership or employment agreement that restricts the right of a lawyer to practice after termination of the relationship, except an agreement concerning benefits upon retirement; or

(b) an agreement in which a restriction on the lawyer's right to practice is part of the settlement of a controversy between private parties.

---

fidentiality of agreements and information or evidence disclosed in the context of settlement negotiations and the return of documents or evidence discovered during litigation or settlement talks. These provisions, drafted with a litigator's (and mostly "defense") view toward settlement-agreement issues, are unlikely to have the force of law in any jurisdiction.

MODEL RULE OF PROFESSIONAL CONDUCT

3.3 Candor Toward the Tribunal

(a) A lawyer shall not knowingly:
  (1) make a false statement of fact or law to a tribunal or fail to correct a false statement of material fact or law previously made to the tribunal by the lawyer;
  (2) fail to disclose to the tribunal legal authority in the controlling jurisdiction known to the lawyer to be directly adverse to the position of the client and not disclosed by opposing counsel; or
  (3) offer evidence that the lawyer knows to be false. If a lawyer, the lawyer's client, or a witness called by the lawyer, has offered material evidence and the lawyer comes to know of its falsity, the lawyer shall take reasonable remedial measures, including, if necessary, disclosure to the tribunal. A lawyer may refuse to offer evidence, other than the testimony of a defendant in a criminal matter, that the lawyer reasonably believes is false.
(b) A lawyer who represents a client in an adjudicative proceeding and who knows that a person intends to engage, is engaging or has engaged in criminal or fraudulent conduct related to the proceeding shall take reasonable remedial measures, including, if necessary, disclosure to the tribunal.
(c) The duties stated in paragraphs (a) and (b) continue to the conclusion of the proceeding, and apply even if compliance requires disclosure of information otherwise protected by Rule 1.6.
(d) In an ex parte proceeding, a lawyer shall inform the tribunal of all material facts known to the lawyer that will enable the tribunal to make an informed decision, whether or not the facts are adverse.

Notes and Questions

10.16 Why did the Ethics 2000 Commission choose not to change the language of Rule 4.1? How would you redraft this rule? What about the comments?

10.17 How much guidance do the Model Rules provide in negotiation? Is there a need for more?

10.18 How does Rule 3.3 (reprinted above) differ in its requirements toward a court versus requirements during negotiation (see Rule 4.1)?

10.19 Scott Peppet proposes a change to Rule 4.1 that would specifically incorporate obligations for negotiation into the Model Rules.

Rule 4.1 Truthfulness in Statements to Others

[Rule 4.1(1) would contain the existing Rule 4.1, as follows:]

(1) In the course of representing a client a lawyer shall not knowingly:

(a) make a false statement of material fact or law to a third person; or

(b) fail to disclose a material fact to a third person when disclosure is necessary to avoid assisting a criminal or fraudulent act by a client, unless disclosure is prohibited by Rule 1.6.

[then add the following:]

(2) A lawyer may opt for a more collaborative engagement with third persons by so designating, by reference to this Rule provision, in a written agreement signed by all clients and attorneys involved in a matter, so long as all parties to the agreement provide informed consent. Lawyers practicing pursuant to this provision agree to:

(a) be truthful in all respects regarding the matter for which this section has been invoked;

(b) disclose all material information needed to allow the third person in question to make an informed decision regarding the matter;

(c) negotiate in good faith by, among other things, abstaining from causing unreasonable delay and from imposing avoidable hardships on another party for the purpose of securing a negotiation advantage.

(3) A lawyer may further opt for a more collaborative engagement with third persons by so designating, by reference to this Rule provision, in a written agreement signed by all clients and attorneys involved in a matter, so long as all parties to the agreement provide informed consent. Lawyers practicing pursuant to this provision agree to:

(a) refuse to assist in the negotiation of any settlement or agreement that works substantial injustice upon another party; [sic]

(4) (a) A lawyer obligated by designation under provision 4.1(2) or 4.1(3) may terminate such designation only by written notice, signed by the attorney and the client, to all relevant parties affected by the matter.

(b) A lawyer and client may also agree, by so designating by reference to this Rule provision in a written agreement, that a lawyer obligated by designation under provision 4.1(2) or 4.1(3) shall withdraw from representation if unable to comply with the requirements of that provision. Such agreement must be signed by both and all signatories must provide informed consent.

Scott R. Peppet, Lawyers' Bargaining Ethics, Contract, and Collaboration: The End of the Legal Profession and the Beginning of Professional Pluralism, 90 Iowa L. Rev. 475, 523-524 (2005).

How do you think Peppet's suggestions would improve negotiation and reputation? How do these suggestions deal with reputation?

As Carrie Menkel-Meadow writes, Rule 4.1 can be interpreted differently. The excerpts that follow take alternative approaches to negotiation both in terms of how they view negotiation and in terms of how they set out the lawyer's role in negotiation. The first excerpt from Richard Shell outlines three views of negotiation.

 ### G. *Richard Shell*, BARGAINING FOR ADVANTAGE: NEGOTIATION STRATEGIES FOR REASONABLE PEOPLE

215-220 (1999)

I want to challenge you to identify what *your* beliefs are. To help you decide how you feel about ethics, I will briefly describe the three most common approaches to bargaining ethics I have heard expressed in conversation with literally hundreds of students and executives. See which shoe fits — or take a bit from each approach and construct your own.

As we explore this territory, remember that nearly everyone is sincerely convinced that they are acting ethically most of the time, whereas they often think others are acting either naively or unethically, depending on their ethical perspective and the situation. Thus, a word of warning is in order. Your ethics are mainly your own business. They will help you increase your level of confidence and comfort at the bargaining table. But do not expect others to share your ethics in every detail. Prudence pays.

THREE SCHOOLS OF BARGAINING ETHICS

The three schools of bargaining ethics I want to introduce for your consideration are (1) the "It's a game" Poker School, (2) the "Do the right thing even if it hurts" Idealist School, and (3) the "What goes around, comes around" Pragmatist School.

Let's look at each one in turn. As I describe these schools, try to decide which aspects of them best reflect your attitudes. After you figure out where you stand today, take a moment and see if that is where you ought to be. My advice is to aim as high as you can, consistent with your genuinely held beliefs about bargaining. In the pressured world of practice, people tend to slide down rather than climb up when it comes to ethical standards.

The "It's a Game" Poker School

The Poker School of ethics sees negotiation as a "game" with certain "rules." The rules are defined by the law, such as the legal materials we covered above.... Conduct within the rules is ethical. Conduct outside the rules is unethical.

The modern founder of the Poker School was Albert Z. Carr, a former Special Consultant to President Harry Truman. Carr wrote a book in the 1960s called, appropriately enough, *Business as a Game*. In a related article that appeared in the *Harvard Business Review*, Carr argued that bluffing and other misleading but lawful negotiation tactics are "an integral part of the [bargaining] game, and the executive who does not master [these] techniques is not likely to accumulate much money or power."

People who adhere to the Poker School readily admit that bargaining and poker are not exactly the same. But they point out that deception is essential to effective play in both arenas. Moreover, skilled players in both poker and bargaining exhibit a robust and realistic distrust of the other fellow. Carr argues that good players should ignore the "claims of friendship" and engage in "cunning deception and conceal-ment" in fair, hard bargaining encounters. When the game is over, members of the Poker School do not think less of a fellow player just because that person successfully deceived them. In fact, assuming the tactic was legal, they may admire the deceiver and vow to be better prepared (and less trusting) next time.

We know how to play poker, but how exactly does one play the bargaining "game"? Stripped to its core, it looks like this: Someone opens, and then people take turns proposing terms to each other. Arguments supporting your preferred terms are allowed. You can play or pass in each round. The goal is to get the other side to agree to terms that are as close as possible to your last proposal.

In the bargaining game, it is understood that both sides might be bluffing. Bluffs disguise a weak bargaining hand, that is, the limited or unattractive alternatives you have away from the table, your inability to affect the other side's alternatives, and the arguments you have to support your demands. Unlike poker players, negotiators always attempt to disclose a good hand if they have one in a bargaining game. So the most effective bluffs are realistic, attractive, difficult-to-check (but false) alternatives or authoritative (but false) supporting standards. Experienced players know this, so one of the key skills in the bargaining game is judging when the other party's alternatives or arguments are really as good as he or she says. If the other side calls you on your bargaining bluff by walking away or giving you a credible ultimatum, you lose. Either there will be no deal when there should have been one, or the final price will be nearer to their last offer than to yours.

As mentioned above, the Poker School believes in the rule of law. In poker, you are not allowed to hide cards, collude with other players, or renege on your bets. But you are expected to deceive others about your hand. The best plays come when you win the pot with a weak hand or fool the other players into betting heavily when your hand is strong. In bargaining, you must not commit outright, actionable fraud, but negotiators must be on guard for anything short of fraud.

The Poker School has three main problems as I see it. First, the Poker School presumes that everyone treats bargaining as a game. Unfortunately, it is an empirical fact that people disagree on this. For a start, neither the idealists nor the pragmatists (more on these below) think bargaining is a game. This problem does not deter the Poker School, which holds that the rules permit its members to play even when the other party disagrees about this premise.

Second, everyone is supposed to know the rules cold. But this is impossible, given that legal rules are applied differently in different industries and regions of the world. Finally, as you now know (having read about the legal treatment of fraud), the law is far from certain even within a single jurisdiction. So you often need a sharp lawyer to help you decide what to do.

The "Do the Right Thing Even if It Hurts" Idealist School

The Idealist School says that bargaining is an aspect of social life, not a special activity with its own unique set of rules. The same ethics that apply in the home should carry over directly into the realm of negotiation. If it is wrong to lie or mislead in normal social encounters, it is wrong to do so in negotiations. If it is OK to lie in special situations (such as to protect another person's feelings), it is also OK to lie in negotiations when those special conditions apply.

Idealists do not entirely rule out deception in negotiation. For example, if the other party assumes you have a lot of leverage and never asks you directly about the situation as you see it, you do not necessarily have to volunteer the information weakening your position. And the idealist can decline to answer questions. But such exceptions are uncomfortable moments. Members of the Idealist School prefer to be candid and honest at the bargaining table even if it means giving up a certain amount of strategic advantage.

The Idealist School draws its strength from philosophy and religion. For example, Immanuel Kant said that we should all follow the ethical rules that we would wish others to follow. Kant argued that if everyone lied all the time, social life would be chaos. Hence, you should not lie. Kant also disapproved of treating other people merely as the means to achieve your own personal ends. Lies in negotiation are selfish acts designed to achieve personal gain. This form of conduct is therefore unethical. Period. Many religions also teach adherents not to lie for personal advantage.

Idealists admit that deception in negotiation rarely arouses moral indignation unless the lies breach a trust between friends, violate a fiduciary responsibility, or exploit people such as the sick or elderly, who lack the ability to protect themselves. And if the only way you can prevent some terrible harm like a murder is by lying, go ahead and lie. But the lack of moral outrage and the fact that sometimes lying can be defended does not make deception in negotiations right.

Idealists strongly reject the idea that negotiations should be viewed as "games." Negotiations, they feel, are serious, consequential communication acts. People negotiate to resolve their differences so social life will work for the benefit of all. People must be held responsible for all their actions, including the way they negotiate, under universal standards.

Idealists think that the members of the Poker School are predatory and selfish. For its part, the Poker School thinks that idealists are naïve and even a little silly. When members of the two schools meet at the bargaining table, tempers can flare.

Some members of the Idealist School have recently been trying to find a philosophical justification for bluffs about bottom lines. There is no agreement yet on whether these efforts have succeeded in ethical terms. But it is clear that outright lies such as fictitious other offers and better prices are unethical practices under idealist principles.

The big problem for the idealist is obvious: Their standards sometimes make it difficult to proceed in a realistic way at the bargaining table. Also, unless adherence to the Idealist School is coupled with a healthy skepticism about the way other people will negotiate, idealism leaves its members open to exploitation by people with standards other than their own. These limitations are especially troublesome when idealists must represent others' interests at the bargaining table.

Despite its limitations, I like the Idealist School. Perhaps because I am an academic, I genuinely believe that the different parts of my life are, in fact, whole. I aspire to ethical standards that I can apply consistently. I will admit that I sometimes fall short of idealism's strict code, but by aiming high I am leaving myself somewhere to fall that maintains my basic sense of personal integrity.

I confess my preference for the Idealist School so you will know where I am coming from in this discussion. But I realize that your experience and work environment may preclude idealism as an ethical option. That's OK. As I hope I am making clear, idealism is not the only way to think about negotiation in ethical terms.

The "What Goes Around Comes Around" Pragmatist School

The final school of bargaining ethics, the Pragmatist School, includes some original elements as well as some attributes of the previous two. In common with the Poker School, this approach views deception as a necessary part of the negotiation process. Unlike the Poker School, however, it prefers not to use misleading statements and overt lies if there is a serviceable, practical alternative. Uniquely, the Pragmatist School displays concern for the potential negative effects of deceptive conduct on present and future relationships. Thus, lying and other questionable tactics are bad not so much because they are "wrong" as because they cost the user more in the long run than they gain in the short run.

As my last comment suggests, people adhere to this school more for prudential than idealistic reasons. Lies and misleading conduct can cause serious injury to one's credibility. And credibility is an important asset for effective negotiators both to preserve working relationships and to protect one's reputation in the market or community. The latter concern is summed up in what I would call the pragmatist's credo: What goes around comes around. The Poker School is less concerned with reputation and more focused on winning each bargaining encounter within the rules of the "game."

What separates the Pragmatist School from the Idealist School? To put it bluntly, a pragmatist will lie a bit more often than will an idealist. For example, pragmatists sometimes will draw fine distinctions between lies about hard-core facts of a transaction, which are always imprudent (and often illegal), and misleading statements about such things as the rationales used to justify a position. A pragmatic car salesman considers it highly unethical to lie about anything large or small relating to the mechanical condition of a used car he is selling. But this same salesman might not have a problem saying "My manager won't let me sell this car for less than $10,000" even though he knows the manager would sell the car for $9,500. False justifications and rationales are marginally acceptable because they are usually less important to the transaction and much harder to detect as falsehoods than are core facts about the object being bought and sold.

Pragmatists are also somewhat looser within the truth when using so-called blocking techniques — tactics to avoid answering questions that threaten to expose a weak bargaining position. For example, can you ethically answer "I don't know" when asked about something you *do* know that hurts your position? An idealist would refuse to answer the question or try to change the subject, not lie by saying "I don't know." A pragmatist would go ahead and say "I don't know" if his actual state of knowledge is hard to trace and the lie poses little risk to his relationships.

Notes and Questions

10.20 Which of Shell's negotiation schools do you think most approaches your view of negotiation?

10.21 Do you think that each of these schools applies in different contexts? Give an example of a context in which each school would apply best.

10.22 How would each school answer the hypotheticals posed by Menkel-Meadow in the article that preceded this one?

10.23 Thinking back to the readings in the prior chapter on trust, consider the differences between the views expressed there and the approach taken by the Pragmatist School.

10.24 Much of the justification for deception in negotiation is explained by analogy to a poker game — the players understand the rules and consent to play. But some challenge this paradigm:

> Deception in poker ordinarily is morally permitted because the conditions necessary for genuine consent are ordinarily satisfied: a player who sits down at the felt enters into an actual (not hypothetical), informed (not manipulated), and voluntary (not coerced) agreement to play by the rules. And since he may leave the table at virtually no cost, his acceptance of each deal of the cards signals continued acceptance of the terms of play. The argument from consent straightforwardly gives moral permission to actions permitted by the rules of poker because we presume that the player has chosen to participate and that the choice is both in his own interests and his to make. There are no doubt limits to the authority of self-rule, even when the stringent condition of free and informed consent are met. Freedoms that destroy the worth of freedom — the classic and most extreme example being the conundrum of voluntary slavery — are deeply problematic. But choosing to play poker does not test the limits of the permission-generating property of consent.
>
> Unlike poker, consent to the rules of larger social games played by business managers, lawyers, and politicians may be absent or defective. First, most public and professional games profoundly affect those who are not players. Campaign mudslingers take aim at opposing candidates, but also cloud public discourse and deceive citizens; defense attorneys aim to defeat the prosecution, but also malign the reputations of reluctant

witnesses; a cigarette manufacturer's manipulative advertising aims to take market share away from a competitor, but also harms teenagers. Second, not all players are knowledgeable about the rules of the game. Marketers distract consumers from *caveat emptor*; real estate brokers, who have a fiduciary responsibility to sellers, cultivate trust and dependency in buyers, and in the end work for themselves, depend on ambiguity about their loyalties. Third, even when players are knowledgeable, they may face exit barriers or their alternatives may be so poor that their continued participation in an adversary game cannot be assumed fully voluntary.

Arthur Isak Applbaum, Rules of the Game, Permissible Harms, and the Principle of Fair Play, in Wise Choices: Decisions, Games, and Negotiations 301, 304-305 (Richard J. Zeckhauser, Ralph L. Keeney & James K. Sebenius eds., 1996).

The next excerpt from law professor James J. White is considered one of the classics on negotiation ethics and reviews five different examples of how to apply the Model Rules.

 ### *James J. White*, MACHIAVELLI AND THE BAR: ETHICAL LIMITATIONS ON LYING IN NEGOTIATION

1980 Am. B. Found. Resol. J. 926, 926-928, 931-935

[I]n negotiation, more than in other contexts, ethical norms can probably be violated with greater confidence that there will be no discovery and punishment. Whether one is likely to be caught for violating an ethical standard says nothing about the merit of the standard. However, if the low probability of punishment means that many lawyers will violate the standard, the standard becomes even more difficult for the honest lawyer to follow, for by doing so he may be forfeiting a significant advantage for his client to others who do not follow the rules....

On the one hand the negotiator must be fair and truthful; on the other he must mislead his opponent. Like the poker player, a negotiator hopes that his opponent will overestimate the value of his hand. Like the poker player, in a variety of ways he must facilitate his opponent's inaccurate assessment. The critical difference between those who are successful negotiators and those who are not lies in this capacity both to mislead and not to be misled.

Some experienced negotiators will deny the accuracy of this assertion, but they will be wrong. I submit that a careful examination of the behavior of even the most forthright, honest, and trustworthy negotiators will show them actively engaged in misleading their opponents about their true position.... To conceal one's true position, to mislead an opponent about one's true settling point, is the essence of negotiation.

Of course there are limits on acceptable deceptive behavior in negotiation, but there is the paradox. How can one be "fair" but also mislead? Can we ask the negotiator to mislead, but fairly, like the soldier who must kill, but humanely?...

FIVE CASES

To test these limits, consider five cases. Easiest is the question that arises when one misrepresents his true opinion about the meaning of a case or a statute. Presumably such a misrepresentation is accepted lawyer behavior both in and out of court and is not intended to be precluded by the requirement that the lawyer be "truthful." ...

A second form of distortion that the Comments [to the Model Rules of Professional Conduct] plainly envision as permissible is distortion concerning the value of one's case or of the other subject matter involved in the negotiation. Thus the Comments make explicit reference to "puffery." ... [T]his ... generally means that the seller of a product has the right to make general statements without having the law treat those statements as warranties and without having liability if they turn out to be inaccurate estimates of the value....

A third case is related to puffing but different from it. This is the use of the so-called false demand. It is a standard negotiating technique in collective bargaining negotiation and in some other multiple-issue negotiations for one side to include a series of demands about which it cares little or not at all. ... Such behavior is untruthful in the broadest sense; yet at least in collective bargaining negotiation its use is a standard part of the process and is not thought to be inappropriate by any experienced bargainer.

Two final examples may be more troublesome. The first involves the response of a lawyer to a question from the other side. Assume that the defendant has instructed his lawyer to accept any settlement offer under $100,000. Having received that instruction, how does the lawyer respond to the plaintiff's question, "I think $90,000 will settle this case. Will your client give $90,000?" Do you see the dilemma that question poses for the defense lawyer? ... A truthful answer to it concludes the negotiation and dashes any possibility of negotiating a lower settlement even in circumstances in which the plaintiff might be willing to accept half of $90,000. Even a moment's hesitation in response to the question may be a nonverbal communication to a clever plaintiff's lawyer that the defendant has given such authority. Yet a negative response is a lie....

[C]onsider a final example recently suggested to me by a lawyer in practice. There the lawyer represented three persons who had been charged with shoplifting. Having satisfied himself that there was no significant conflict of interest, the defense lawyer told the prosecutor that two of the three would plead guilty only if the case was dismissed against the third. Previously those two had told the defense counsel that they would plead guilty irrespective of what the third did, and the third said that he wished to go to trial unless the charges were dropped. Thus the defense lawyer lied to the prosecutor by stating that the two would plead only if the third were allowed to go free....

Taken together, the five foregoing cases show me that we do not and cannot intend that a negotiator be "truthful" in the broadest sense of that term. At the minimum we allow him some deviation from truthfulness in asserting his true opinion about cases, statutes, or the value of the subject of the negotiation in other respects. In addition some of us are likely to allow him to lie in response to certain questions that are regarded as out of bounds, and possibly to lie in circumstances where his interest is great and the injury seems small. It would be unfortunate, therefore, for the rule that requires "fairness" to be interpreted to require that a negotiator be truthful in every respect and in all of his dealings. It should be read to allow at least those kinds of untruthfulness that are implicitly and explicitly recognized as acceptable in this forum, a forum defined both by the subject matter and by the participants.

Notes and Questions

10.25 What type of negotiation school does White come from? What does this mean in terms of a lawyer's role in negotiation? How would you answer each of the five cases White examines?

10.26 Review the Model Rules of Professional Conduct at the beginning of this section. Do you agree with White's analysis about what the rules permit?

10.27 How would White have ruled in the Vulcan Metals Co. v. Simmons Manufacturing Co. case (distinguishing puffing about the quality of the vacuum cleaner versus material representations of prior marketing)? Why?

10.28 In a Colorado case, a district attorney was sanctioned by the state disciplinary board for deception. During a hostage negotiation, when the murder suspect asked for an attorney, the district attorney pretended that he was a public defender and acting on behalf of the murder suspect to encourage him to surrender. In affirming the sanctions, the Colorado Supreme Court held that "Purposeful deception by an attorney licensed in our state is intolerable. . . ." In the Matter of Pautler, 47 P.3d 1175, 1176 (Colo. 2002). If the Colorado Supreme Court would not condone deceiving a murder suspect during a hostage negotiation, do you think there is any lying of which it might approve?

This next excerpt is from a comprehensive effort to categorize all of the different types of lying that can occur in a negotiation. Note that the author, Gerald Wetlaufer, refers to a variety of different types of deception as lying. See whether you agree with his approach.

 ### Gerald B. Wetlaufer, THE ETHICS OF LYING IN NEGOTIATIONS

75 Iowa L. Rev. 1219, 1236-1239, 1241-1243, 1245, 1248, 1250-1251, 1254-1255, 1265, 1270-1271 (1990)

There are a great number of arguments that are offered in support of the claim that the lies we tell are not ethically reprehensible. First, we sometimes argue that what we did was not a lie because, for instance, we did not mean to mislead or because we were merely putting matters in their best light. Second, we may admit that we have lied but then assert that the lie we told was of a kind that is ethically permissible. Here, for instance, we may claim that the lie was permissible because it was legal, because it was on some subject as to which it is permissible to lie, or because it had little or no harmful effect. We may also admit lying but then claim that the lie was permissible because of the circumstances in which it was told. These claims include, among others, arguments concerning the nature of negotiations, the rules of the game, the adversary system, and the bad conduct or incompetence of our adversary. Next, there are a series of arguments purporting to justify lies on the basis of some duty — usually loyalty, zeal, or the protection of confidences — that we owe to our client. Finally, we will sometimes claim that the lies we tell in negotiations are warranted by the good consequences, justice sometimes among them, that the lies are said to produce.

These are the kinds of distinctions, excuses and justifications that I mean to identify and to examine. The list is long but finite. . . .

A. "I DIDN'T LIE."

In this section, we will take up a series of statements by which lawyers sometimes assert that whatever they did was not a lie. These claims are of at least five kinds. . . .

1. *"I Didn't Engage in the Requisite Act or Omission."* . . . I was careful to define lying to include all acts or omissions taken in the expectation that they might create or maintain a belief at variance with our own. I was equally careful to separate our definition of lying from our specification of those lies that might be ethically permissible. Within this analytical structure, the first version of this claim, "I didn't do anything," constitutes the statement that the speaker has not lied and, if the denial is warranted, that what he has done shall be taken not to violate the ethical rule against lying. . . .

2. *"I Didn't Have the Requisite Intent. . . ."*

3. *"My Statement Was Literally True."* . . . These arguments seem reasonably persuasive, but only when the qualifiers are in plain view and the speaker makes no effort to suppress them or to promote the situation's potential for deception. If the qualifiers are hidden or suppressed, then the statement is meant to deceive and the argument about its "literal" meaning is insufficient to remove the statement from the category of lies.

4. *"I Was Speaking on a Subject About Which There Is No Truth."* . . . The problem with this assertion is that our definition of lying has been drawn not in terms of saying things that are not true, but rather in terms of saying things that are contrary to our belief. As this term has been defined, it is a lie when, contrary to our own belief, we assert that a car we have driven for five years is "swell" or that a particular price is "unacceptable." . . .

5. *"I Was Merely Putting Matters in the Best Light."* . . .

B. "I LIED, IF YOU INSIST ON CALLING IT THAT, BUT IT WAS AN OMISSION OF A KIND THAT IS PRESUMED TO BE ETHICALLY PERMISSIBLE."

Here the question is whether there is certain conduct that may fall within our definition of lying, but that is not, as may be the case with other "lies," presumed to be ethically impermissible. If the speaker is right, then the conduct in question is permissible simply on the basis of the showing that it falls within this category and it does not require further excuse or justification.

At least as to one small category of conduct, this argument seems persuasive. That category is comprised of certain omissions as to which it is undeniably true that the speaker is leaving out information for the purpose of maintaining a belief at variance with his own and that he is doing it in the usually accurate expectation that he will be enriched by his advantage. What distinguishes the omissions in this category as ethically permissible is found in the speaker's relationship to the information being withheld. If that information has been properly obtained and if it is not the subject of some ethical duty of disclosure, then it may be ethically permissible to withhold it. . . .

C. "I LIED BUT IT WAS LEGAL."

This is the claim that "I may have lied but it was ethically permissible because it was not legally forbidden." But the logic of this claim fails if, as has previously been argued, ethics is different from, and more demanding than, law. I have already argued that such differences exist and that they arise from the fact that law must deal with certain problems of knowledge, implementation, transaction costs and the social stability that ethics need not take into account. Further, I have argued that for these purposes the lawyer's code of professional responsibility is a code of law not ethics. If this is so, it is no more persuasive to say that something is ethically permissible because it is not forbidden by that code than to say that it is ethically permissible because it is not forbidden by law.

D. "I LIED BUT IT WAS ON AN ETHICALLY PERMISSIBLE SUBJECT."

Those who make this argument admit that they were seeking to create a belief at variance with their own. They claim, however, that there are certain subjects as to which, simply by virtue of the subject, it is ethically permissible to lie. Some will assert, for instance, that it is permissible to lie about the value of a property which is the subject of a transaction. Others will say that it is permissible to lie about the law or about the strength of a cause of action. More generally, some will say that it is ethically permissible to lie about those subjects about which their adversary could have or should have known the truth. Finally, some will assert that it is permissible to lie about such "soft" subjects as their opinions or about those matters that are "internal" to the negotiation, these being subjects like their interests and priorities, authority, intentions, and, ultimately, their reservation price.

The difficulty with all these excuses is that they rely upon distinctions that make no difference. A lie about a negotiator's authority is told with the same purpose and with the same effect as a lie about the true mileage of a used car. The speaker's hope is that, by creating some belief at variance with her own, she will get a better deal than she could have gotten without having created that belief. The advantages she may hope to secure through these lies are every bit as tangible, every bit as great, and every bit as illegitimate as those she might hope to secure through lies on other subjects. So is the damage that will be caused. . . .

E. "I LIED BUT IT HAD LITTLE OR NO EFFECT."

Next, there are three categories of lies that might be said to be permissible because they are likely to have, or in retrospect appear to have had, little or no effect. These include white lies, puffing and other small lies and lies that failed. . . .

F. "I LIED BUT IT WAS JUSTIFIED BY THE VERY NATURE OF NEGOTIATIONS."

This section deals with two related claims, both of which assert that lying is permissible because of the particular nature of negotiations. The first is the argument that lying is ethically permissible because it is either necessary or useful in negotiations. The second is the argument that lying in negotiations is ethically permissible because it is within "the rules of the game." . . .

It is often asserted that lying in negotiations is within "the rules of the game" and therefore ethically permissible. . . .

G. "I LIED BUT IT WAS JUSTIFIED BY THE NATURE OF MY RELATIONSHIP TO THE VICTIM." — THE ADVERSARY'S AND COMPETITOR'S EXCUSES

This section deals with the justification for partisanship, and perhaps for lying, that may arise from the fact that, in one degree or another, persons who are negotiating with each other are adversaries. The next section will take up the justifications for partisanship, and potentially for lying, that may arise from the lawyers' relationships with their clients. Taken together, these comprise what is surely the lawyer's favorite bit of moral discourse: the justification by reference to the adversary system. This first of these two sections, then, deals with the justifications that may arise by virtue of the relationship between the parties to the negotiation. The next deals with the justifications that may arise by virtue of the relationship that exists between one of those parties and her lawyer.

The adversary's excuse can be invoked in two distinctly different circumstances: one a three-party form involving two contestants and a judge who may be asked to decide their case, the other involving the more common two-party form in which no judge or other third party plays a part. . . .

H. "I LIED BUT IT WAS JUSTIFIED UNDER THE SPECIAL ETHICS OF LAWYERING."

In addition to claiming that their lies are permissible because of the adversarial excuse, lawyers also offer a range of other justifications for conduct that is legal but otherwise unethical. Many of these justifications arise from what are said to be the special ethics of lawyering. Specifically, lawyers will argue that they owe special duties to their clients and that those duties render ethically permissible, even mandatory, acts that we would otherwise regard as ethically impermissible. These arguments are said to rest on the duties of loyalty and zealous representation and the duty to preserve a client's confidences. Additionally, lawyers will sometimes argue that, by virtue of their position in the profession, those otherwise impermissible acts in which they may engage are permissible for the lawyer because they are somehow attributable not to the lawyer's own ethical "account" but instead to that of the client or the state. . . .

I. "I LIED BUT IT WAS ETHICALLY PERMISSIBLE BECAUSE OF THE BAD CONDUCT OR THE INCOMPETENCE OF MY ADVERSARY."

Lying in negotiation is sometimes justified by reference to the bad conduct of the person with whom the liar is negotiating. The bad conduct that is said to justify lying may have occurred outside of the negotiation (e.g., in a prior negotiation or in the events leading to the lawsuit which the parties may settle through the negotiation) or it may have occurred in the course of the negotiation itself. The bad conduct may or may not have involved lying. . . .

J. "I LIED BUT IT WAS JUSTIFIED BY THE GOOD CONSEQUENCES IT PRODUCED."

The final claim to be considered is that lying in negotiations may be justified because of the good consequences that it may produce. This argument comes in at least three forms.

The strongest of these three forms involves such fact patterns as lying to Genghis Khan in order to save the city, lying in negotiations with terrorists, or lying to the wheat-hording monopolist in order to get a lower price so that one can buy more grain for the starving children. The argument is that these lies are ethically permissible because they work to prevent a greater immorality. In this strong form of the claim, we assume, first, that there is a broad, perhaps authoritative, consensus that the intended victim of our lies is trying to do bad things, and second, that the lies we tell are specifically calculated to block the greater evil.

The same argument could be made, though less compellingly, if we were to weaken either of those two conditions. This weaker form of this argument is as strong as it normally gets. "That guy hurt my client and I'm going to make him pay." "She calls herself an industrialist! She's a criminal and I'm going to see that money ends up where it belongs." "I can't believe that my tax dollars are being spent to bring cases like this." In these situations there is less of a consensus that our cause is totally right and that our adversary's is wrong. And the lie that will be told is less likely to block an egregious act than simply to disadvantage our adversary. Not only is the consensus much weaker, but there is a strong possibility that statements of this kind may be, at some level, motivated by self-interest. The problem of immoral means and of taking the law into one's own hands are compounded by the lack of consensus and the probability of bias.

That is not to say, however, that this weaker form of the argument may not provide justification for lying. It seems clear, for instance, that our system of civil litigation is strongly biased in favor of those people who have resources and against those who do not. I am not satisfied that those who represent people who lack resources are obliged to conduct themselves in their negotiations as if that bias did not exist. But this slope is as slippery as they get, for others will find "the right" in places that I do not, and the possibility of bias is ever-present.

Notes and Questions

10.29 What do you think about all of the different actions that Wetlaufer calls lies? Which ones do you agree are lies? Which actions would you say are something different? What would you call them?

This next excerpt takes quite a different view of ethics and how to practice as an ethical lawyer. Former big firm partner and now professor Patrick J. Schiltz wrote this article as both advice and guidance to law students about to enter the profession.

 Patrick J. Schiltz, **ON BEING A HAPPY, HEALTHY, AND ETHICAL MEMBER OF AN UNHAPPY, UNHEALTHY, AND UNETHICAL PROFESSION**

52 Vand. L. Rev. 871, 906-912, 915-918 (1999)

THE ETHICS OF LAWYERS

[T]he legal profession is widely perceived — even by lawyers — as being unethical. Only one American in five considers lawyers to be "honest and ethical," and "the more a person knows about the legal profession and the more he or she is in direct personal contact with lawyers, the lower [his or her] opinion of them." This should concern you.

There are many reasons why ethics courses are so unpopular, but the most important is probably that law students do not think that they will become unethical lawyers. Students think of unethical lawyers as the sleazeballs who chase ambulances (think Danny DeVito in *The Rainmaker*) or run insurance scams (think Bill Murray in *Wild Things*) or destroy evidence (think Al Pacino's crew in *The Devil's Advocate*). Students have a hard time identifying with these lawyers. When students think of life after graduation, they see themselves sitting on the 27th floor of some skyscraper in a freshly pressed dark suit (blue, black, or gray) with a starched blouse or shirt (white or light blue) doing sophisticated legal work for sophisticated clients. Students imagine — wrongly — that such lawyers do not have to worry much about ethics, except, perhaps, when the occasional conflict of interest question arises.

If you think this — if you think that you will not have any trouble practicing law ethically — you are wrong. Dead wrong. In fact, particularly if you go to work for a big firm, you will probably begin to practice law unethically in at least some respects within your first year or two in practice. This happens to most young lawyers in big firms. It happened to me, and it will happen to you, unless you do something about it.

A.   Practicing Law Ethically

Let's first be clear on what I mean by practicing law ethically. I mean three things. First, you generally have to comply with the formal disciplinary rules — either the Model Rules of Professional Conduct, the Model Code of Professional Responsibility, or some state variant of one or the other. As a law student, and then as a young lawyer, you will often be encouraged to distinguish ethical from unethical conduct solely by reference to the formal rules. Most likely, you will devote the majority of the time in your professional responsibility class to studying the rules, and you will, of course, learn the rules cold so that you can pass the Multi-State Professional Responsibility Exam ("MPRE"). In many other ways, subtle and blatant, you will be encouraged to think that conduct that does not violate the rules is "ethical," while conduct that does violate the rules is "unethical." . . .

I don't have anything against the formal rules. Often, they are all that stands between an unethical lawyer and a vulnerable client. You should learn them and follow them. But you should also understand that the formal rules represent nothing more than "the lowest common denominator of conduct that a highly self-interested group will tolerate." For many lawyers, "[e]thics is a matter of steering, if necessary, just clear of the few unambiguous prohibitions found in rules governing lawyers." But complying with the formal rules will not make you an ethical lawyer, any more than complying with the criminal law will make you an ethical person. Many of the sleaziest lawyers you will encounter will be absolutely scrupulous in their compliance with the formal rules. In fact, they will be only too happy to tell you just that. . . .

The second thing you must do to be an ethical lawyer is to act ethically in your work, even when you aren't required to do so by any rule. To a substantial extent, "bar ethical rules have lost touch with ordinary moral intuitions." To practice law ethically you must practice law consistently with those intuitions. . . .

The third thing you must do to be an ethical lawyer is to live an ethical life. Many big firm lawyers — who can be remarkably "smug[ ] about the superiority of the ethical standards of large firms" — ignore this point. So do many law professors who, when writing about legal ethics, tend to focus solely on the lawyer at work. But being admitted to the bar does not absolve you of your responsibilities outside of work — to your family, to your friends, to your community, and, if you're a person of faith, to your God. To practice law ethically, you must meet those responsibilities, which means that you must live a balanced life. If you become a workaholic lawyer, you will be unhealthy, probably unhappy, and, I would argue, unethical.

Now I recognize that we live in an age of moral relativism — an age in which "behavior is neither right nor wrong but a matter of personal choice." Your reaction to my claim that an unbalanced life is an unethical life may very well be, "That's just your opinion." It is my opinion, but it is surely not *just* my opinion. I would be surprised if the belief system to which you subscribe — whether it be religiously or secularly based — regards a life dominated by the pursuit of wealth to the exclusion of all else as an ethical life, or an attorney who meets only his responsibilities to his clients and law partners as an ethical person.

B. Big Firm Culture

It is hard to practice law ethically. Complying with the formal rules is the easy part. The rules are not very specific, and they don't demand very much. You may, on rare occasions, confront an extremely difficult conflict of interest problem that will require you to parse the rules carefully. You may even confront a situation in which some ethical or moral imperative compels you to violate the rules. But by and large, you will have no trouble complying with the rules; indeed, you are unlikely to give the rules much thought....

But even practicing law ethically in the sense of being honest and fair and compassionate is difficult. To understand why, you need to understand what it is that you will do every day as a lawyer. Most of a lawyer's working life is filled with the mundane. It is unlikely that one of your clients will drop a smoking gun on your desk or ask you to deliver a briefcase full of unmarked bills or invite you to have wild, passionate sex (or even un-wild, un-passionate sex). These things happen to lawyers only in John Grisham novels. Your life as a lawyer will be filled with the kind of things that drove John Grisham to write novels: dictating letters and talking on the phone and drafting memoranda and performing "due diligence" and proofreading contracts and negotiating settlements and filling out time sheets. And because your life as a lawyer will be filled with the mundane, whether you practice law ethically will depend not upon how you resolve the one or two dramatic ethical dilemmas that you will confront during your entire career, but upon the hundreds of little things that you will do, almost unthinkingly, each and every day.

Work Out the Rules of Engagement....

Balancing life and work is possible but you have to negotiate. For example:

A promotion thrust Diana, a marketing executive in the fashion industry, not only into a pivotal role at her company but also into daily contact with a demanding CEO. Before their first official meeting, he sent her a list of topics he wanted to cover and told her to set aside at least two hours the next evening. He'd have dinner delivered.

Diana, a working mother, prized efficient time management — even with her bosses. She did not want to launch her new reporting relationship with a bad precedent. She responded to the peremptory summons with a memo — along with backup data organized by product line and market segment. The memo systematically addressed the CEO's topics. She also told him that she had to leave at six o'clock to pick up her kids.

Colleagues were surprised that Diana would push back right after a promotion. But, as it turned out, the information she had forwarded answered the CEO's questions. Their eventual meeting lasted ten minutes. This interaction, however brief, told him that Diana had information at the ready and would not hesitate to share good news and bad in accessible form. It also signaled that she had boundaries.

Deborah M. Kolb, Judith Williams & Carol Frohlinger, Her Place at the Table: A Woman's Guide to Negotiating Five Key Challenges to Leadership Success 81-82 (2004).

Because practicing law ethically will depend primarily upon the hundreds of little things that you will do almost unthinkingly every day, it will not depend much upon your thinking. You are going to be busy. The days will fly by. When you are on the phone negotiating a deal or when you are at your computer drafting a brief or when you are filling out your time sheet at the end of the day, you are not going to have time to reflect on each of your actions. You are going to have to act almost instinctively.

What this means, then, is that you will not practice law ethically — you *cannot* practice law ethically — unless acting ethically is *habitual* for you. You have to be in the habit of being honest. You have to be in the habit of being fair. You have to be in the habit of being compassionate. These qualities have to be deeply ingrained in you, so that you can't turn them on and off — so that acting honorably is not something you have to *decide* to do — so that when you are at work, making the thousands of phone calls you will make and writing the thousands of letters you will write and dealing with the thousands of people with whom you will deal, you will *automatically* apply the same values in the workplace that you apply outside of work, when you are with family and friends.

Here is the problem, though: After you start practicing law, nothing is likely to influence you more than "the culture or house norms of the agency, department, or firm" in which you work. If you are going into private practice — particularly private practice in a big firm — you are going to be immersed in a culture that is hostile to the values you now have. The system does not *want* you to apply the same values in the workplace that you do outside of work (unless you're rapaciously greedy outside of work); it wants you to replace those values with the system's values. The system is obsessed with money, and it wants you to be, too. The system wants you — it *needs* you — to play the game.

Now, no one is going to say this to you. No one is going to take you aside and say, "Jane, we here at Smith & Jones are obsessed with money. From this point forward the most important thing in your life has to be billing hours and generating business. Family and friends and honesty and fairness are okay in moderation, but don't let them interfere with making money." No one will tell you, as one lawyer told another in a Charles Addams cartoon, "I admire your honesty and integrity, Wilson, but I have no room for them in my firm." Instead, the culture will pressure you in more subtle ways to replace your values with the system's. . . .

C. Becoming Unethical

As the values of an attorney change, so, too, does her ability to practice law ethically. . . .

Unethical lawyers do not start out being unethical; they start out just like you — as perfectly decent young men or women who have every intention of practicing law ethically. They do not become unethical overnight; they become unethical just as you will (if you become unethical) — a little bit at a time. And they do not become unethical by shredding incriminating documents or bribing jurors; they become unethical just as you are likely to — by cutting a corner here, by stretching the truth a bit there.

Let me tell you how you will start acting unethically: It will start with your time sheets. One day, not too long after you start practicing law, you will sit down at the end of a long, tiring day, and you just won't have much to show for your efforts in terms of billable hours. It will be near the end of the month. You will know that all of the partners will be looking at your monthly time report in a few days, so what you'll do is pad your time sheet just a bit. Maybe you will bill a client for ninety minutes for a task that really took you only sixty minutes to perform. However, you will promise yourself that you will repay the client at the first opportunity by doing thirty minutes of work for the client for "free." In this way, you will be "borrowing," not "stealing."

And then what will happen is that it will become easier and easier to take these little loans against future work. And then, after a while, you will stop paying back these little loans. You will convince yourself that, although you billed for ninety minutes and spent only sixty minutes on the project, you did such good work that your client should pay a bit more for it. After all, your billing rate is awfully low, and your client is awfully rich.

And then you will pad more and more — every two minute telephone conversation will go down on the sheet as ten minutes, every three hour research project will go down with an extra quarter hour or so. You will continue to rationalize your dishonesty to yourself in various ways until one day you stop doing even that. And, before long — it won't take you much more than three or four years — you will be stealing from your clients almost every day, and you won't even notice it.

You know what? You will also likely become a liar. A deadline will come up one day, and, for reasons that are entirely your fault, you will not be able to meet it. So you will call your senior partner or your client and make up a white lie for why you missed the deadline. And then you will get busy and a partner will ask whether you proofread a lengthy prospectus and you will say yes, even though you didn't. And then you will be drafting a brief and you will quote language from a Supreme Court opinion even though you will know that, when read in context, the language does not remotely suggest what you are implying it suggests. And then, in preparing a client for a deposition, you will help the client to formulate an answer to a difficult question that will likely be asked — an answer that will be "legally accurate" but that will mislead your opponent. And then you will be reading through a big box of your client's documents — a box that has not been opened in twenty years — and you will find a document that would hurt your client's case, but that no one except you knows exists, and you will simply "forget" to produce it in response to your opponent's discovery requests.

Do you see what will happen? After a couple years of this, you won't even notice that you are lying and cheating and stealing every day that you practice law. None of these things will seem like a big deal in itself — an extra fifteen minutes added to a time sheet here, a little white lie to cover a missed deadline there. But, after a while, your entire frame of reference will change. You will still be making dozens of quick, instinctive decisions every day, but those decisions, instead of reflecting the notions of right and wrong by which you conduct your personal life, will instead reflect the set of values by which you will conduct your professional life — a set of values that embodies not what is right or wrong, but what is profitable, and what you can get away with. The system will have succeeded in replacing your values with the system's values, and the system will be profiting as a result.

Notes and Questions

10.30 Which of Richard Shell's negotiation schools does Schiltz most closely resemble? Why?

10.31 How exactly does Schiltz define *ethical*? What do you think about his definition?

10.32 What do you think of Schiltz's view of lawyers? Of big firms? How do you think Schiltz assumes these lawyers negotiate?

10.33 Schiltz probably would tell you to sit down now and make a list of things you will *not* do when you practice law. Make that list somewhere you can check five years from now.

10.34 A wise master once wanted to test his students. The temple where they studied was run down, and students normally begged for food in the nearby town. One day the master told the students that each of them was to go into the town and steal something they could sell to raise money. "In order not to defile our excellent reputation by committing illegal and immoral acts, please be certain to steal when no one is looking. I do not want anyone to be caught." After some hesitation, the group of students set out except for one young boy. When the master asked him why he did not go, the boy responded, "I cannot follow your instructions to steal where no one will see me. Wherever I go, *I* am always there watching. My *own* eyes will see me steal." The boy was the only one who passed the test. Adapted from Heather Forest, The Wise Master, Wisdom Tales from Around the World 15-16 (1996). How is this folktale similar to Schiltz's advice?

10.35 For more on the "unhealthy" part of Schiltz's article, see Susan Daicoff, Lawyer, Know Thyself: A Review of Empirical Research on Attorney Attributes Bearing on Professionalism, 46 Am. U. L. Rev. 1337 (1997).

3. Civility

One of the most striking things about being a lawyer in the twenty-first century is how the reputation and appearance of lawyers in the popular culture have declined over U.S. history. Where once lawyers were hailed as the saviors of the Constitution (Clarence Darrow), the weak (*To Kill a Mockingbird*), or falsely accused (*Perry Mason*), movies and television now portray lawyers with few morals and large egos (*Devil's*

Advocate; The Practice; Liar, Liar; The Firm). See Carrie Menkel-Meadow, Legal Negotiation in Popular Culture: What Are We Bargaining For?, in Law and Popular Culture (Michael Freeman ed., 2005); Carrie Menkel-Meadow, Can They Do That? Legal Ethics in Popular Culture: Of Character and Acts, 48 UCLA L. Rev. 1305 (2001). In the nineteenth century, Alexis de Toqueville argued that lawyers were the aristocracy of this new nation. That is clearly no longer the case, at least in how lawyers are viewed by the public. A reason often cited for this decline is how the practice of law has changed — in the size of firms, amounts of money, types of cases. Connected with the change in the practice of law is the lack of civility in the profession. Civility is often connected to ethics and so the book includes it here. We believe it is appropriate to extend the conversation over negotiation behavior past the limited guidelines that ethics provide. The civility movement has made headway in many jurisdictions, and we include some of that work here. The end of this section also includes a call to negotiate based on respect for the other side as a person.

This first brief excerpt is from Chief Justice Warren Burger in 1971 — already recognizing the decline in civility — talking about the necessity of civility in the practice of law.

 Warren Burger, **THE NECESSITY FOR CIVILITY**

52 F.R.D. 211, 212-215 (1971)

I recall a statement — probably something I read in the memoirs of a diplomat — that if the secret files of all nations could be opened we would find that the politeness, the good manners, the civility of diplomats and statesmen avoided more wars than all the generals ever won. Unprovable or not, I am prepared to believe that.

It is surely important for a gathering of lawyers, judges and law professors to focus our thoughts, for the few minutes I will detain you, on the conduct of members of our profession. Lawyers are granted monopoly to perform essential services for hire, and it has long been almost an article of faith to us that monopolies are subject to strict regulation and public accountability for adherence to standards. Today more and more new and vexing problems reach the courts and they call for the highest order of thoughtful exploration and careful study. Yet all too often, overzealous advocates seem to think the zeal and effectiveness of a lawyer depends on how thoroughly he can disrupt the proceedings or how loud he can shout or how close he can come to insulting all those he encounters — including the judges. . . .

I suggest this is relevant to law teachers because you have the first and best chance to inculcate in young students of the Law the realization that in a very hard sense the hackneyed phrase "order in the court" articulates something very basic to the mechanisms of justice. Someone must teach that good manners, disciplined behavior and civility — by whatever name — are the lubricants that prevent lawsuits from turning into combat. More than that it is really the very glue that keeps an organized society from flying apart.

Many teachers of law have thought teaching these fundamentals was not the function of law schools and law teachers. Many good friends of mine in the law schools, over the past 20 years or so, have said to me, "We are teaching students to *think*—we are not running a trade school." But civility is to the courtroom and adversary process what antisepsis is to a hospital and operating room. The best medical brains cannot outwit soiled linen or dirty scalpels—and the best legal skills cannot either justify or offset bad manners.

With all deference, I submit that lawyers who know how to think but have not learned how to behave are a menace and a liability, not an asset, to the administration of justice. And without undue deference, I say in all frankness that when insolence and arrogance are confused with zealous advocacy, we are in . . . trouble.

Notes and Questions

10.36   Where did you get your ideas about how lawyers should behave?
10.37   What are your favorite lawyer books or movies? Why? How do the lawyers negotiate?

The next excerpts are from the Seventh Circuit interim and final reports on civility in the early 1990s. The excerpts include first comments about the lack of civility and then the specific recommendations for behavior in the Seventh Circuit. Most of these recommendations apply to litigation and particularly discovery. However, since negotiation is often part of the litigation process, these rules would apply.

 INTERIM REPORT OF THE COMMITTEE ON CIVILITY OF THE SEVENTH FEDERAL JUDICIAL CIRCUIT

143 F.R.D 371, 385-386 (1991)

The judicial perspective of lawyer relations is further revealed in these comments:

- There must be a way to continue the spirit of the adversarial profession of law without the mentality of warfare and bitterness. We have lost sight of the fact that we are all brothers and sisters of a truly noble profession. We should be showing the best of the rule of law, not showing how to conduct a brawl. . . .
- Rudeness that is characterized by a refusal to extend common courtesy and an inability to concentrate on representing a client because egocentricity gets in the way.
- Overly adversarial—nearly combatant—failure to cooperate—act as though a trial is a personal contest between the counsel rather than a search for truth.

- A growing number of attorneys seem unwilling to extend common courtesy (let alone professional courtesy) to each other. . . .
- Too many litigators think "winning" every point is the name of the game. They often seem to have a compulsive, and childish, need to fight over everything.
- Certain lawyers have always been uncivil. They have made their reputations based upon discourtesy and unwillingness to compromise on even the smallest trivial detail. Their clients pay in the end. Attorney Roy Cohn of the McCarthy hearings is an example. He was hated and eventually disbarred. Little can be done to cope with such evil, I suspect, except through a state bar's licensing authority. I believe it is the uncivil lawyer's client who often suffers the most. An attorney who has no respect for his profession, his colleagues, the courts, no doubt has no respect for his client.

 FINAL REPORT OF THE COMMITTEE ON CIVILITY OF THE SEVENTH FEDERAL JUDICIAL CIRCUIT

143 F.R.D 441, 448–449 (1992)

PROPOSED STANDARDS FOR PROFESSIONAL CONDUCT WITHIN THE SEVENTH FEDERAL JUDICIAL CIRCUIT

Preamble

A lawyers' conduct should be characterized at all times by personal courtesy and professional integrity in the fullest sense of those terms. In fulfilling our duty to represent a client vigorously as lawyers, we will be mindful of our obligations to the administration of justice, which is a truth-seeking process designed to resolve human and societal problems in a rational, peaceful, and efficient manner. . . .

Lawyers' Duties to Other Counsel

1. We will practice our profession with a continuing awareness that our role is to advance the legitimate interests of our clients. In our dealings with others we will not reflect the ill feelings of our clients. We will treat all other counsel, parties, and witnesses in a civil and courteous manner, not only in court, but also in all other written and oral communications.

2. We will not, even when called upon by a client to do so, abuse or indulge in offensive conduct directed to other counsel, parties, or witnesses. We will abstain from disparaging personal remarks or acrimony toward other counsel, parties, or witnesses. . . .

4. We will not, absent good cause, attribute bad motives or improper conduct to other counsel or bring the profession into disrepute by unfounded accusations of impropriety.

5. We will adhere to all express promises and to agreements with other counsel, whether oral or in writing, and will adhere in good faith to all agreements implied by the circumstances or local customs.

Notes and Questions

10.38 A study was done in the Eighth Circuit to determine the severity of incivility in the federal courts and its connection, if any, to gender. The study included examples of general incivility such as being disrespectful or dishonest but also included forms of gender-related incivility such as gender disparagement, unprofessional forms of address such as *honey* or *dear*, comments on appearance, and exclusion during "male bonding" situations.

> [A]lmost two-thirds of attorneys have experienced general incivility, gendered incivility, and/or unwanted sexual attention while in litigation in the Eighth Circuit federal courts — with women encountering such mistreatment more frequently than men. Nearly all of these experiences involve general incivility and — for most *male* targets — general incivility alone. According to our narrative results, generally uncivil behavior takes many forms — from mildly annoying to harmfully abusive to blatantly unethical. For *women* targets, by contrast, these generalized forms of mistreatment typically go hand-in-hand with incivility explicitly tied to their gender. Overall, women are overwhelmingly more likely than men to encounter gender-related incivility.

Lilia M. Cortina et al., What's Gender Got to Do with It? Incivility in the Federal Courts, 27 Law & Soc. Inquiry 235, 253 (2002).

10.39 A more specific attempt to make negotiation rules was proposed in Wisconsin in 1999. See Wisconsin Standards for Negotiation (1999), which are intended to encourage "considerations of ethics, efficiency, civility and professionalism, including expectations of confidentiality, civility and courtesy, preparation, and communication with clients." These standards, like many of their kind, attempted to ensure more particularized ethics rules but were not adopted. Why do you think this happened?

In the next excerpt, Professor Jonathan Cohen suggests that ethics (and perhaps the civility movement too) are missing the point.

 Jonathan Cohen, **WHEN PEOPLE ARE THE MEANS: NEGOTIATING WITH RESPECT**

14 Geo. J. Legal Ethics 739, 741-743, 760-763, 766-767 (2001)

To introduce this domain, consider the following question: What distinguishes negotiation from interpersonal interactions generally? A basic difference is that in negotiation, each party attempts to get the other party to do something, or at least explores that possibility. Put differently, in negotiation the other party is a potential means towards one's ends. If two people are chatting about the weather, rarely will their conversation end with an exchange of promises. If they are negotiating the sale of a car, it very well may.

This basic difference between negotiation and most social interactions points to a core question, or tension, lying within the domain of orientation ethics. Usually we think of other people as, well, people. Yet negotiation may pull us towards seeing others as mere instruments for achieving our purposes. To borrow from the language of Martin Buber, in negotiation we are drawn towards reducing the other person from a "Thou" to an "It." Negotiation thus presents an apparent ethical tension that I call the object-subject tension: *when negotiating, how is one to reconcile the impulse to treat the other person as a mere means towards one's ends with general ethical requirements for treating people*? In response, I argue that in negotiation one should see the other party both as a means towards one's ends *and* as a person deserving respect. More specifically, the act of negotiation does not relieve one of the moral duty to respect others. This duty of respect implicates both the traditional negotiation ethics topics of deception, disclosure and fairness and also topics such as manipulation, coercion, listening, and autonomy. . . .

Respect, in its deepest form, is a choice of how one wants to see other people. It is the process of striving to recognize the fundamental dignity of the other person and to act in accordance with that orientation. Though we often think of respect as a noun signifying certain actions (e.g., "Did he treat me with respect?") or feelings (e.g., "She felt respect for her parents"), the core of respect is best understood as a verb. As the word itself suggests, *respect is the process we undertake when we "look again"—when we challenge ourselves about how we want to see, and thus treat, others.* This is not to negate the nominal aspects of respect when that process instantiates into particular external signs (e.g., courtesies) or internal feelings (e.g., esteem), but rather to identify its core. . . .

If in a negotiation I see you as no more than a means, then I have not only defined you as an object, but I have also defined myself as a manipulator. How one negotiates helps define one's identity. . . .

PROFILE: SUCCESS OF SOUTHWEST AIRLINES

Treating the other side well was much of the explanation given for Southwest Airlines' success in dealing with its union. While other airlines face bankruptcy from high labor costs, labor slowdowns, and strikes, Southwest Airlines continues to be successful. In an interview on National Public Radio with Southwest President Colleen Barrett, reporter Wade Goodwyn noted that: "It surprises many to learn that Southwest is among the most unionized airlines in the industry. But Barrett and other top management have avoided the bloody battles that have crippled other carriers. Barrett sees to it that the unions understand they're not considered the enemy."

Barrett explained: "When I came up here, one of the first things that I did, any time that we had an event, a company event—a Christmas party, a chili cook-off, whatever—I always assured that the union folks were invited. I mean, to me, we are one family. It's an extended family member, perhaps, but nevertheless, I wanted them to say 'we' when they talked about Southwest. That really was my thinking." NPR, Morning Edition, Profile: Southwest Airlines Soars Above Industry's Turbulence, Dec. 4, 2002.

Where one party to a negotiation does not treat the other party with respect, we can draw a negative inference. Either the first party does not view the second party as an equal — a position to which few would admit, though many implicitly harbor these views — or the first party has a very low assessment of the dignity of all people. . . .

How I see and treat you in a negotiation also helps to define who *we* are. People are not just individuals. They are also members of groups. If I deceive you to get what I want, then *we* do not have an honest relationship. If I intimidate you to get what I want, *we* lack mutual respect. Irrespective of whether our interests are largely convergent or divergent (and divergent interests can result in beneficial exchanges too), how we negotiate with one another is critical to [how] we define ourselves and how others perceive us (e.g., how the public perceives lawyers). . . .

I recently gave a guest lecture in a colleague's professional responsibility class. At one point I asked the students, "How many of you think it's wrong to manipulate other people?" Most of the hands shot up. I then asked, "How many of you think that manipulating other people is a significant part of lawyering?" Most of the hands again shot up. "What do you make of this?" I asked. There was dead silence. . . .

Given both the moral responsibility to respect others in negotiation and (what I take as) the fact that many of us commonly fall short of this goal, objectifying the other person and simultaneously, though unwittingly, diminishing ourselves, one may at first see a dismal, pessimistic picture. If we had no capacity for change, then pessimism might be warranted. However, if one accepts a capacity for human change, then a more optimistic image of human existence can emerge.

Notes and Questions

10.40 What questions would you ask Cohen about his proposal to respect the other in a negotiation? What concerns you most? What ideas make the most sense to you?

10.41 In which ethics rules and civility recommendations do you think Cohen's ideas are already being carried out? Do these rules go far enough? Why or why not?

Chapter 11   The Law of Negotiation

Individuals in a wide variety of contexts bargain in the shadow of the law.
— Robert H. Mnookin and Lewis Kornhauser

As Robert Mnookin and Lewis Kornhauser have famously declared, bargaining occurs in "the shadow of the law."* By this they mean that what negotiators agree to away from courts is often affected by, indeed almost dictated by, what would happen if a case were fully litigated. The law, they argue, provides "bargaining endowments" (along with power, negotiating skill, facts, and client desires) that affect what can be accomplished consensually, away from court. The role of law in negotiation in this sense is the substantive law of whatever the subject matter of the negotiation is about — family law, corporate law, real estate law, civil rights law — all of which (whether statutory, case-based, or regulatory law) attempt to provide clear boundaries of liabilities, duties, and responsibilities of the parties or regulated entities. A party who can successfully point to a case or statute that "favors" his position is likely to have additional "power" in the negotiation (emanating from the threat to go to court if they don't get what they want in the negotiation). Of course, in legal negotiations, the lawyer negotiator will also have to persuade the other side that particular facts are actually covered by a particular law or regulation.

But as you know from your learning in this course so far, parties often will negotiate precisely because they seek to craft their own solutions to problems (and not use those solutions provided by legislatures that are writing laws for the whole polity or the "general public" or by administrative agencies that are dealing with repeat players in particular contexts) and may want to "depart" from the legally prescribed solution. Thus, one question presented by any negotiation concluded away from a court decision (this would include both dispute/litigation negotiations and transactional negotiations) is how much can a consensual agreement ignore or supplement existing regulations with respect to any particular matter? For the most part, parties may agree to anything that is not otherwise unlawful, as long as the settlement agreement itself meets the requirements of formal contract law.

As you saw in the last chapter, however, misrepresentation, fraud, mistaken communication, and other unlawful or unethical conduct, before, during, or

---

*Robert H. Mnookin & Lewis Kornhauser, Bargaining in the Shadow of the Law: The Case of Divorce, 88 Yale L.J. 950 (1979).

even after the negotiation is completed may make a negotiated agreement unenforceable or may even lead to damages and penalties for breaches of contract or violations of law.* In some settings, an agreement can be rescinded, or reformed by a court, under contract law principles, sometimes changing the original intention of the parties.

In many settings, statutes or regulations may fill in "default terms" if the parties don't specify what they want (as in corporate bylaws or commercial sales agreements), so the parties may be governed by laws they do not officially include in their negotiated agreements. In some other settings, particular clauses that might be agreed to will turn out later to be unlawful (e.g., clauses or contracts that are unconscionable or adhesive, liquidated damages, certain penalties, interest rates, or attorneys' fees provisions). There may be a question of contract interpretation as to whether the invalidation of one or more clauses will invalidate a whole agreement (the contract issue of "integration" or "severability" or the effects of adhesive or unconscionable clauses within a larger agreement).

In many transactional settings, lawyers will need to know the substantive law of the subject area in order to craft a fully enforceable and legal agreement (such as in real estate, commercial sales agreements, corporate mergers and acquisitions, some employment contracts, divorce and child custody). And every legal negotiation is likely to have tax issues. If the primary negotiating lawyer is not a tax expert, there is likely to be a need for a specialist to review any negotiated agreement for its tax consequences.

In addition to these obvious questions of the substantive law of negotiated agreements or transactions, there are many legal issues and much regulation that affects what can be accomplished and how it can be accomplished when parties seek to give their agreements legal effect. There is also a growing body of law that regulates when an agreement is enforceable or valid under particular legal rules (e.g., class action settlements, agreements made by legal "incompetents," secret agreements, etc.). This chapter, then, reviews some of these important enforcement, legality, and process issues in determining the legal limits of negotiated outcomes. We first remind you that the requirements for making an enforceable negotiated agreement are the requirements for a legally enforceable contract (and avoiding *post hoc* attacks on agreements for fraud or other contract defenses or counterclaims). Then we explore some of the issues implicated in the use of lawyers as agents to conduct negotiations legally on behalf of clients, their principals. Next we briefly examine some of the requirements of the scope and strength of the duty to bargain or negotiate and what specific approvals or legal forms might be necessary in particular settings, such as with multiple parties and class actions. We examine when courts may or must review negotiated settlements, and when negotiated agreements must be made public, even if privately negotiated. And finally, we review briefly some recent case law on the taxation of settlements and fees for negotiating settlements. Although we cannot treat all of the legal issues pertaining to negotiation here, all legal negotiators must remember that when they "bargain in the shadow of the law," they have

---

* See also Carrie Menkel-Meadow, Ethics, Morality and Professional Responsibility in Negotiation, in Dispute Resolution (Phyllis Bernard & Bryant Garth eds., 2002).

a continuing obligation to know what the law is that governs both the substantive area they are dealing with and the process of the negotiation itself.

A. NEGOTIATED SETTLEMENTS AS CONTRACTS

As you saw in the previous chapter, negotiation agreements are enforced as contracts and, therefore, must meet the formal requirements of contract law — offer, acceptance, and consideration (usually dismissal of a lawsuit in a dispute or mutual promises in a transaction). Negotiations are often challenged by *post hoc* complaints about those contracts, usual standard contract concepts like failure of consideration, fraud, misrepresentation, nondisclosure of information that must be disclosed by law, and unconscionability. For a good summary, see Russell Korobkin, The Role of Law in Settlements, in Handbook of Dispute Resolution 254 (Michael L. Moffitt & Robert C. Bordone eds., 2005).

One of the great difficulties with determining whether deceit, fraud, or lack of disclosure has occurred when seeking to enforce or challenge a negotiated agreement is that negotiations most often occur in secret or private settings and can easily turn into a "he said/she said" factual dispute with no clear or corroborating evidence. It was for this reason that Professor White argued (see Chapter 10) that it is virtually impossible to ethically regulate what lawyers say to each other in negotiations. Only in the rarest of cases (see, for instance, Stare v. Tate in Chapter 10) when someone discloses what was or was not said in a negotiation can courts scrutinize what actually was said to create the contract or negotiated agreement. The issue of how to determine if a contract (whether negotiated or assisted by a third-party mediator) is a "good" (enforceable) contract becomes even more complicated when, through agreements in mediation, for example, the parties promise each other (and the mediator) to keep their negotiations private, whether according to mediation contract, privilege, court rules, or evidence rules (such as Federal Rule of Evidence 408, which generally protects statements made in negotiation from disclosure in litigation). See Ellen E. Deason, Enforcing Mediated Settlement Agreements: Contract Law Collides with Confidentiality, 35 U.C. Davis L. Rev. 33 (2001).

Notes and Questions

11.1 To what extent do you think the private process of negotiating should be subject to "public" controls, such as court review, ethical standards, or other forms of legal scrutiny?

11.2 How practical or likely is it that we can effectively regulate or police what gets said or done in a private negotiation? Do you agree with Professor White that to have rules, whether formal contract enforcement rules or ethical rules, that cannot be enforced easily hurts the legitimacy of the rules themselves? Is it better to have no rules at all?

11.3 Should negotiated agreements be treated the same as "ordinary" contracts, or are they different in some way? Should there be special rules for the enforcement of negotiated agreements? Should there be different rules for negotiations of disputes already filed in courts (settlements of lawsuits) and transactional negotiations?

11.4 Do you think the enforcement of a negotiated agreement is any different if a third party, such as a mediator, participates in the drafting or negotiation of the agreement?

11.5 How do you feel about suggestions (as made by Ellen Deason in the article cited above) that all mediated (or negotiated) agreements be reduced to writing? Does that take care of all the enforcement problems that might occur? How would you balance the competing concerns of supporting confidentiality in mediation or negotiation with being sure that the parties are really agreeing to an enforceable contract?

11.6 Can you think of any other laws or principles that should control whether a negotiated agreement should be enforced?

11.7 At least one commentator (from practice) has recently argued that we need to give more latitude to negotiators and that lawyers should not be disciplined or otherwise penalized (by withdrawing enforcement of a negotiated agreement) for "omissions" of certain information in negotiation. He argues for a "safe harbor" of misrepresentation, given the continuing culture of client expectations of "zealous advocacy." See Barry Temkin, Misrepresentation by Omission in Settlement Negotiations: Should There Be a Silent Safe Harbor?, 18 Geo. J. Legal Ethics 179 (2004). Do you think distinctions can or should be made between affirmative misrepresentations, silence, or omissions, "half- or incomplete truths," and failures to correct misinformation in negotiations for purposes of contract enforcement? See ABA Section of Litigation, Ethical Guidelines for Settlement Negotiations (2002); David Aaron, Ethics, Law Enforcement and Fair Dealing: A Prosecutor's Duty to Disclose Nonevidentiary Information, 67 Fordham L. Rev. 3005 (1999); Nathan Crystal, The Lawyer's Duty to Disclose Material Facts in Contract or Settlement Negotiations, 87 Ky. L.J. 1055 (1999); Donald Langevoort, Half-Truths: Protecting Mistaken Inferences by Investors and Others, 52 Stan. L. Rev. 88 (1999).

11.8 Is "contracting" the best legal framework for analyzing when a negotiated agreement should be enforced? See Louis Kaplow & Steven Shavell, Contracting (2004). What other legal or social frameworks might be applied? Trust? Fairness? Finality? Can you think of other ways to conceptualize what the negotiation process is about legally?

B. LEGAL AUTHORITY TO NEGOTIATE: LAWYER-CLIENT/AGENT-PRINCIPAL

One of the major legal issues in any negotiation in which someone other than the principal does the negotiating is what authority the agent-negotiator has to commit the principal to particular agreements. In addition to considering what authority is available for the ultimate agreement, modern conceptions of negotiation also ask whether the agent should consult with the principal about what process she is going to use (a competitive or collaborative approach) and whether every particular offer or statement made in a negotiation should be cleared with the client. These issues are also dealt with in many different areas of law, including the law of agency, fiduciary relationships (to the extent lawyers or certain special-purpose negotiators are considered fiduciaries), and legal ethics and professional responsibility. As you saw in Chapter 5, "Working with Your Client," there are also many strategic, as well as moral, issues implicated in the use of agents (lawyers) in legal negotiations.

RESTATEMENT (THIRD) OF AGENCY §§1.01, 2.02 (TENTATIVE DRAFT NO. 2, 2001)

§1.01 Agency Defined

Agency is the fiduciary relationship that arises when one person (a "principal") manifests assent to another person (an "agent") that the agent shall act on the principal's behalf and subject to the principal's control, and that the agent manifests assent or otherwise consents so to act.

§2.02 SCOPE OF ACTUAL AUTHORITY

(1) An agent has actual authority to take action designated or implied in the principal's manifestations and acts necessary or incidental to achieving the principal's objectives, as the agent reasonably understands them when the agent determines how to act.

(2) An agent's interpretation of the principal's manifestation is reasonable if it reflects any meaning known by the agent to be ascribed by the principal and, in the absence of any meaning known to the agent, as a reasonable person in the agent's position would interpret the manifestation in light of the context, including circumstances of which the agent has notice and the agent's fiduciary duty to the principal.

(3) An agent's understanding of the principal's objectives is reasonable if it accords with the principal's manifestations and the inferences that a reasonable person in the agent position would draw from the circumstances creating the agency.

RESTATEMENT (SECOND) OF AGENCY §348 (1958)

§348 Fraud and Duress

An agent who fraudulently makes representations, uses duress, or knowingly assists in the commission of tortuous fraud or duress by his principal or by others is subject to liability in tort to the injured person although the fraud or duress occurs in a transaction on behalf of the principal.

As Professor Deborah A. DeMott, currently the Reporter for the Restatement (Third) on Agency (American Law Institute), has said:

> Agency's intellectual distinctiveness is its focus on relationships in which one person, as a representative of another, has derivative authority and a duty as a fiduciary to account for the use made of the representative position. Agency doctrine is

two-fold, governing rights and duties between the principal and the agent as well as legal consequences stemming from the agent's interaction with third parties. . . . As defined by section 1 of Restatement (Second), any agent is a fiduciary subject to the principal's right of control. . . .

More generally, agency doctrine defines the legal consequences of choosing to act through another person in lieu of oneself. The relationship between a principal and the agent is interactive, and the principal's capacity to control the agent is heavily dependent on the principal's use of language and other signaling devices that the agent must interpret. For the principal, the legal consequences of the agent's conduct stem from the principal's decision to create or participate in an agency relationship in anticipation of certain benefits. The principal has the right to define the terms of the agency relationship, including the incentives created for the agent, and has the right of control over the agent and the ability to terminate the relationship. The principal establishes for the agent which of the agent's acts will be treated as the agent's own. The principal's ability to define the agency relationship and structure its meaning for the agent justifies the link between the agent's conduct and its legal consequences for the principal.

A Revised Prospectus for a Third Restatement of Agency, 31 U.C. Davis L. Rev. 1035, 1037-1040 (1998).

Agency law itself is a hybrid body of doctrines, including contract, tort, and business enterprise law. Whether an agent has real or "apparent" authority to act for someone else — whether an individual, or increasingly, an organizational body — is one of the many questions that may arise when lawyers are used as negotiating representatives for their clients. Lawyers, as agents of their clients in negotiation, may be held liable in tort or contract for what they do as agents (and their principals, the clients, occasionally may be held liable or responsible for the acts of their agents). Responsibility, care, duty, and liability run in complex ways, for both agents and principals.

As lawyers, acting on behalf of clients, legal negotiators have additional duties under the profession's professional codes of conduct:

MODEL RULE OF PROFESSIONAL CONDUCT 1.2 (2004)

Scope of Representation and Allocation of Authority Between Client and Lawyer

(a) Subject to paragraphs (c) and (d), a lawyer shall abide by a client's decisions concerning the objectives of representation and, as required by Rule 1.4 [Communication], shall consult with the client as to the means by which they are to be pursued. A lawyer may take such action on behalf of a client as is impliedly authorized to carry out the representation. A lawyer shall abide by a client's decision whether to settle a matter. In a criminal case, the lawyer shall abide by the client's decision, after consultation with the lawyer, as to a plea to be entered, whether to waive jury trial and whether the client will testify.

(b) A lawyer's representation of a client, including representation by appointment, does not constitute an endorsement of the client's political, economic, social or moral views or activities.

(c)   A lawyer may limit the scope of the representation if the limitation is reasonable under the circumstances and the client gives informed consent.

(d)   A lawyer shall not counsel a client to engage, or assist a client, in conduct that the lawyer knows is criminal or fraudulent, but a lawyer may discuss the legal consequences of any proposed course of conduct with a client and may counsel or assist a client to make a good faith effort to determine the validity, scope, meaning or application of the law.

In the following case, the question of how much authority an attorney-agent has to settle a case was treated under state law, in a federal diversity case. In the case, a group of plaintiffs involved in an accident sued a tire manufacturer for their accident. When their lawyer settled the case with the manufacturer based on an adverse expert's report, the plaintiffs refused to be bound by the settlement, claiming that they did not expressly assent to it.

 COVINGTON v. CONTINENTAL GENERAL TIRE, INC.

381 F.3d 216, 216-219, 221 (3d Cir. 2004)

FACTS AND PROCEDURAL BACKGROUND

Plaintiffs Emma Jean Williams, Jamie Williams, Mary Lou Covington, Richard Abrams, and Sheila Abrams were passengers in a car that was involved in an accident allegedly caused by a defective tire manufactured by Continental General Tire, Inc. Plaintiffs subsequently retained Carl R. Schiffman, Esq. to bring suit against Continental as well as Sears and Roebuck. As part of the retainer agreement, plaintiffs executed a power of attorney in favor of Schiffman, that stated in relevant part that: Schiffman, "shall not make any settlements without [clients'] consent."

During the ensuing discovery, Schiffman engaged tire expert Gary A. Derian who prepared a report and provided deposition testimony. However, Derian's testimony turned out to be problematic for plaintiffs. Schiffman concluded that Derian's testimony seriously weakened his case against Continental, and he decided to enter into settlement discussions with Clem Trischler, counsel for Continental. Plaintiffs and Schiffman disagree about whether Schiffman ever informed them of those negotiations. However, it is undisputed that Schiffman eventually represented to Trischler that plaintiffs were willing to settle their case against Continental and proceed only against Sears. Schiffman and Trischler then reached an agreement whereby plaintiffs would dismiss their action against Continental and pursue only Sears in return for Continental's agreement to provide its expert for plaintiffs to use against Sears. Upon learning of the purported settlement, plaintiffs told Schiffman they would not sign the agreement and stipulated dismissal.

When Schiffman informed Trischler that plaintiffs would not execute the settlement documents, Continental filed the instant motion to enforce the agreement. The District Court granted the motion based upon the Magistrate Judge's Report and Recommendation. This appeal followed. . . .

Plaintiffs contend that they are not bound by Schiffman's representation of settlement authority because they never expressly agreed to settle their claims, which they argue is required under Pennsylvania law before an attorney can settle his/her client's case. Defendants, on the other hand, argue that Pennsylvania recognizes an attorney's apparent authority to bind a client to a settlement, and that Schiffman's apparent authority to act on behalf of his clients in this instance was sufficient to compel enforcement of the settlement agreement.

Although the Pennsylvania Supreme Court has not recently addressed this issue, our analysis is informed by our own decision in Farris v. JC Penney Co., Inc., 176 F.3d 706 (3d Cir. 1999), as well as early decisions of the Pennsylvania Supreme Court, which we examined in reaching our decision in *Farris*.

In *Farris*, plaintiffs' attorney represented in open court that plaintiffs had agreed to a settlement with defendant. However, plaintiffs never actually agreed to settle the case and, in fact, had told their attorney that they would not settle until medical treatment was completed. Although plaintiffs were in court when the agreement was read into the record, they did not understand what was happening until after the proceeding was over. Upon realizing the nature of the settlement, plaintiffs expressed their displeasure to their attorney and told opposing counsel they had not authorized the settlement that had just been presented to the court. Nevertheless, the District Court entered an order dismissing the suit under Federal Rule of Civil Procedure 41(b). Plaintiffs subsequently obtained new counsel and filed a motion for relief from the dismissal pursuant to Federal Rule of Civil Procedure 60(b). The District Court denied the motion and plaintiffs appealed.

We reversed the District Court's decision based largely upon the Pennsylvania Supreme Court's decision in Starling v. West Erie Bldg. & Loan Ass'n, 3 A.2d 387 (Pa. 1939). In *Starling*, the court had stated that "[w]ithout express authority [an attorney] cannot compromise or settle his client's claim. . . ." Id. at 388. Although the court recognized that the authority granted an attorney by virtue of his/her office is broad and includes the authority to "bind [his/her] clients by admissions and acts in the course of suit or in the management of the regular course of litigation," it cautioned that "such apparent or implied authority does not extend to unauthorized acts which will result in the surrender of any substantial right of the client, or the imposition of new liabilities or burdens upon him." [The court then distinguished some alternative authority to conclude]:

[W]e rule that an attorney has to have an express authority to settle a client's claims.

Notes and Questions

11.9 Where a client hires a lawyer-agent to conduct his negotiations, what must the client-principal communicate to the lawyer about how he wants the negotiation to be conducted, what he hopes to achieve, and what the lawyer must tell him during the negotiation?

11.10   What subjects must a lawyer-agent discuss with her client before, during, or after a negotiation?

11.11   Under what circumstances can a lawyer settle a case on behalf of a client?

C. DUTY TO BARGAIN

There is very little regulation of what lawyers must actually do when they come together to negotiate, either in dispute negotiations or transactions. If they don't settle where there is litigation pending, the lawyers (and clients) will simply have to go to trial to resolve the matters between them. If they don't successfully conclude a transactional negotiation, the parties will go their separate ways, perhaps to negotiate another deal with someone else. There are, however, a few specialized areas in which the law does either command or constrain lawyer negotiation behavior. In labor law, as indicated in the case below, there is a "duty to bargain" about certain particular topics in collective bargaining and some legal nudge about how far the parties have to go before they can declare a legal "impasse" (which, in labor law, allows them certain other rights, like the right to strike, in some cases). There is also increasing scrutiny of how much (or how little) lawyers and clients are actually negotiating when they are "ordered" to some litigation-related negotiation settings, like mandatory settlement conferences or court-sponsored mediation sessions. A growing body of case law, at both the federal and state levels, is deciding such questions as who must attend such proceedings, how much "authority" they must bring to the table, and whether they can be sanctioned, by the court, if they refuse to negotiate. In addition, procedural and other rules now include both incentives and disincentives to negotiate. The Federal Rules of Civil Procedure, for example, provides that if a party receives an offer to settle and does worse at trial than the offer, that party may have to pay costs of litigation for the other side. See Fed. R. Civ. Proc. 68. Many states have similar rules.

As you read the material below, consider what effects formal law or rules about requiring negotiations do for or to the parties, what standards courts can or should use to assess if bargaining is being conducted "in good faith," and whether you think parties and lawyers should be sanctioned when they don't negotiate "enough." You should also think about how courts enforcing procedural or substantive duties to bargain can learn what actually transpired in a negotiation session (especially one that is denominated "confidential") and by what standards they should judge whether there has, in fact, been good-faith bargaining.

1. Duty to Bargain — Labor Law

The National Labor Relations Act (NLRA) requires both management and labor unions to bargain "in good faith." 29 U.S.C. §§151 *et seq*. What this requires has been the subject of much litigation in the labor field and also much commentary. The policy issues implicated in the labor law debates have their analogues in general civil (and even criminal) legal bargaining. How much should the state enter into scrutiny of what parties do in private negotiations? In the labor field, Congress passed a major piece of federal legislation to regularize and "pacify" violent labor confrontations by providing collective rights for workers to organize and bargain together. At the same time, the courts (and Congress) have been reluctant to closely examine what the parties actually do in those collective bargaining negotiations. In a series of cases, both the National Labor Relations Board (NLRB) and the courts have specified some parameters for "required" bargaining activities. In NLRB v. General Electric Co., 418 F.2d 736 (2d Cir. 1969), *cert. denied*, 397 U.S. 965 (1970), the Second Circuit held that the practice now known as "Boulwarism" (named for Lemuel R. Boulware, a GE vice president in the 1940s, and discussed in Chapter 8) or "take it or leave it" offers, coupled with a refusal to negotiate, was, "in the totality of the circumstances," an unfair labor practice and violative of the act:

> We hold that an employer may not so combine "take it or leave it" bargaining methods with a widely published stance of unbending firmness that he is himself unable to alter a position once taken. . . . Such conduct we find, constitutes a refusal to bargain "in fact." . . . It also constitutes, as the facts of this action demonstrate, an absence of subjective good faith, for it implies that the Company can deliberately bargain and communicate as though the Union did not exist, in clear derogation of the Union's status as exclusive representative of its members under §9(a).

418 F.2d at 763.

In NLRB v. Katz, 369 U.S. 736 (1962), the Supreme Court held that employers could not engage in unilateral actions (such as wage or substantial conditions of employment changes) during collective bargaining (providing some formal judicial recognition of the problematic nature of unequal bargaining power in some settings). To change wages or other major working conditions during bargaining was, in essence, to remove certain issues from the bargaining table altogether, in violation of the intent of the statute.

Despite these cases, employers are not prohibited under the NLRA or the case law from what is called "hard bargaining" and certain forms of intransigence. During his presidency, Ronald Reagan essentially broke the air traffic controller's union by announcing he would not bargain with it and ordering the union members back to work during a strike. (As public employees, the labor laws affecting these employees were different from those under the NLRA.) Nevertheless, from time to time the NLRB and the courts do actually scrutinize the particular substantive proposals made during bargaining to see if unfair labor practices have been committed (practices such as, for example, insistence on an "open" (nonmandatory union dues) shop, employers' total control over wages, uncompromising management prerogatives, or total rejection of union proposals that are protected by the Act). Employers can defend hard bargaining by presenting "legitimate business reasons" for their proposals. And although the NLRB and courts have not required employers to make specific "counterproposals," long delays have, in some instances, been held "in the totality of the circumstances" to indicate "bad faith" in bargaining. Section 8(d) of the Act requires the parties to "meet and confer at reasonable times and in good faith with respect to wages, hours and other terms and conditions of employment." These subjects are now considered "mandatory" subjects of bargaining; case law permits certain nonmandatory subjects to be treated differently. More complicated issues (not specifically dealt with by the statute) are implicated when employees bargain with multiple employers, such as in construction, trucking, longshore, and some wholesale and retail industries. See generally Douglas Ray, Calvin William Sharpe & Robert Strassfeld, Understanding Labor Law 189-235 (1999); Theodore J. St. Antoine, Charles C. Craver & Marion Crain, Labor Relations Law (10th ed. 1999); Archibald Cox, The Duty to Bargain in Good Faith, 71 Harv. L. Rev. 1401 (1958); R.P. Duvin, The Duty to Bargain: Law in Search of Policy, 64 Colum. L. Rev. 248 (1964); B.J. Fick, Negotiation Theory and the Law of Collective Bargaining, 38 Kan. L. Rev. 426 (1989).

Notes and Questions

11.12 Without reviewing all of the complexities of labor law here, can you think of other places in the law where some scrutiny of whether the parties are bargaining in good faith would be appropriate? All contracting? All lawsuit settlements? Large mergers and acquisitions? Sales of particular goods (e.g., health care, real estate)?

11.13 Because the law of collective bargaining is one of the first places courts and legislatures have had to deal with both the forms and content of negotiations, the doctrines developed there have been significant for other areas of law (see below), such as whether to scrutinize "unfair contracts" (unconscionability in both its substantive and procedural dimensions), class action settlements, and bargaining in and around the courthouse (court-annexed ADR programs).

2. Duty to Participate and Bargain — Court-Directed Negotiation

As part of the growth and institutionalization of alternative dispute resolution processes, many courts are now requiring parties and their lawyers to engage in various forms of court-sponsored or supervised negotiation or settlement efforts. The Federal Rules of Civil Procedure require pretrial conferences that may entail "facilitated" negotiations with a judge or magistrate, or a judge may strongly urge, and in some cases "order," the parties to negotiate on their own or to use either a court-appointed or private mediator. See Fed. R. Civ. Proc. 16. Some courts now require the use of some form of ADR — whether negotiation, settlement conferences, mediation, or arbitration — before the parties can go on to trial. Many states have similar rules or practices. One of the key issues that has arisen with these requirements is whether parties must participate in good faith in these court programs, which often use court, as well as private, resources. Some courts and rules permit judges to assess sanctions in the form of costs, fees, or dismissal of claims if parties do not participate. The question of what constitutes "good-faith participation" has become as difficult as good-faith bargaining in labor law, with different courts taking different positions on this issue. In some cases, the question is whether it is merely enough to show up with the right people (parties with authority to negotiate and settle) or whether lawyers and parties must actually do something (negotiate with real movement, participate fully in mediation or arbitration, and so on). Do you think it is a good idea to mandate "good-faith participation" in these processes? How can such a rule or standard be measured and enforced?

G. HEILEMAN BREWING CO., INC. v. JOSEPH OAT CORP.

871 F.2d 648 (7th Cir. 1989)

May a federal district court order litigants — even those represented by counsel — to appear before it in person at a pretrial conference for the purpose of discussing the posture and settlement of the litigants' case? After reviewing the Federal Rules of Civil Procedure and federal district courts' inherent authority to manage and control the litigation before them, we answer this question in the affirmative and conclude that a district court may sanction a litigant for failing to comply with such an order.

A federal magistrate ordered Joseph Oat Corporation to send a "corporate representative with authority to settle" to a pretrial conference to discuss disputed factual and legal issues and the possibility of settlement. Although counsel for Oat Corporation appeared, accompanied by another attorney who was authorized to speak on behalf of the principals of the corporation, no principal or corporate representative personally attended the conference. The court determined that the failure of Oat Corporation to send a principal of the corporation to the pretrial conference violated its order. Consequently, the district court imposed a sanction of $5,860.01 upon Oat Corporation pursuant to Federal Rule of Civil Procedure 16(f). This amount represented the costs and attorneys' fees of the opposing parties attending the conference. . . .

Oat Corporation appeals, claiming that the district court did not have the authority to order litigants represented by counsel to appear at the pretrial settlement conference. Specifically, Oat Corporation contends that, by negative implication, the language of Rule 16(a)(5) prohibits a district court from directing represented litigants to attend pretrial conferences. That is, because Rule 16 expressly refers to "attorneys for the parties and any unrepresented parties" in introductory paragraph (a), a district court may not go beyond that language to devise procedures which direct the pretrial appearance of parties represented by counsel. . . .

Rule 16 addresses the use of pretrial conferences to formulate and narrow issues for trial as well as to discuss means for dispensing with the need for costly and unnecessary litigation. As we stated in Link v. Wabash R.R., 291 F.2d 542, 547 (7th Cir. 1961), *aff'd*, 370 U.S. 626 (1962):

> Pre-trial procedure has become an integrated part of the judicial process on the trial level. Courts must be free to use it and to control and enforce its operation. Otherwise, the orderly administration of justice will be removed from control of the trial court and placed in the hands of counsel. We do not believe such a course is within the contemplation of the law.

The pretrial settlement of litigation has been advocated and used as a means to alleviate overcrowded dockets, and courts have practiced numerous and varied types of pretrial settlement techniques for many years. See, e.g., Manual for Complex Litigation 2d, §§21.1-21.4 (1985); Federal Judicial Center, Settlement Strategies for Federal District Judges (1988); Federal Judicial Center, The Judge's Role in the Settlement of Civil Suits (1977) (presented at a seminar for newly-appointed judges); Federal Judicial Center, The Role of the Judge in the Settlement Process (1977). Since 1983, Rule 16 has expressly provided that settlement of a case is one of several subjects which should be pursued and discussed vigorously during pretrial conferences. . . .

We agree with this interpretation of Rule 16. The wording of the rule and the accompanying commentary make plain that the entire thrust of the amendment to Rule 16 was to urge judges to make wider use of their powers and to manage actively their dockets from an early stage. We therefore conclude that our interpretation of Rule 16 to allow district courts to order represented parties to appear at pretrial settlement conferences merely represents another application of a district judge's inherent authority to preserve the efficiency, and more importantly the integrity, of the judicial process. . . .

At the outset, it is important to note that a district court cannot coerce settlement. Kothe v. Smith, 771 F.2d 667, 669 (2d Cir. 1985). In this case, considerable concern has been generated because the court ordered "corporate representatives with authority to settle" to attend the conference. In our view, "authority to settle," when used in the context of this case, means that the corporate representative attending the pretrial conference was required to hold a position within the corporate entity allowing him to speak definitively and to commit the corporation to a particular position in the litigation. We do not view "authority to settle" as a requirement that corporate representatives must come to court willing to settle on someone else's terms, but only that they come to court in order to consider the possibility of settlement. As Chief Judge Crabb set forth in her decision which we now review:

> There is no indication . . . that the magistrate's order contemplated requiring Joseph Oat . . . to agree to any particular form of settlement or even to agree to settlement at all. The only requirement imposed by the magistrate was that the representative [of Oat Corporation] be present with full authority to settle, should terms for settlement be proposed that were acceptable to [Oat Corporation]. . . .

The Advisory Committee Notes to Rule 16 state that "[a]lthough it is not the purpose of Rule 16(b)(7) to impose settlement negotiations on unwilling litigants, it is believed that providing a neutral forum for discussing [settlement] might foster it." Fed. R. Civ. P. 16 advisory committee's note, subdivision (c) (1983). These Notes clearly draw a distinction between being required to attend a settlement conference and being required to participate in settlement negotiations. Thus, under the scheme of pretrial settlement conferences, the corporate representative remains free, on behalf of the corporate entity, to propose terms of settlement independently — but he may be required to state those terms in a pretrial conference before a judge or magistrate. . . .

We hold that Rule 16 does not limit, but rather is enhanced by, the inherent authority of federal courts to order litigants represented by counsel to attend pretrial conferences for the purpose of discussing settlement. Oat Corporation violated the district court's order requiring it to have a corporate representative attend the pretrial settlement conference on December 19, 1984. Under these circumstances, the district court did not abuse its discretion by imposing sanctions for Oat Corporation's failure to comply with the pretrial order.

EASTERBROOK, Circuit Judge, with whom POSNER, COFFEY and MANION, Circuit Judges, join, dissenting.

Our case has three logically separate issues. First, whether a district court may demand the attendance of someone other than the party's counsel of record. Second, whether the court may insist that this additional person be an employee rather than an agent selected for the occasion. Third, whether the court may insist that the representative have "full settlement authority" — meaning the authority to agree to pay cash in settlement (maybe authority without cap, although that was not clear). Even if one resolves the first issue as the majority does, it does not follow that district courts have the second or third powers, or that their exercise here was prudent.

The proposition that a magistrate may require a firm to send an employee rather than a representative is puzzling. Corporate "employees" are simply agents of the firm. Corporations choose their agents and decide what powers to give them. Which agents have which powers is a matter of internal corporate affairs. Joseph Oat Corp. sent to the conference not only its counsel of record but also John Fitzpatrick, who had authority to speak for Oat. Now Mr. Fitzpatrick is an attorney, which raised the magistrate's hackles, but why should this count against him? . . . Why can't the corporation make its own decision about how much of the agent's time to hire? . . .

At all events, the use of outside attorneys as negotiators is common. Many a firm sends its labor lawyer to the bargaining table when a collective bargaining agreement is about to expire, there to dicker with the union (or with labor's lawyer). Each side has a statutory right to choose its representatives. 29 U.S.C. §158(b)(1)(B). Many a firm sends its corporate counsel to the bargaining table when a merger is under discussion. See Ronald J. Gilson, Value Creation by Business Lawyers: Legal Skills and Asset Pricing, 94 Yale L.J. 239 (1984). Oat did the same thing to explore settlement of litigation. A lawyer is no less suited to this task than to negotiating the terms of collective bargaining or merger agreements. Firms prefer to send skilled negotiators to negotiating sessions (lawyers are especially useful when the value of a claim depends on the resolution of legal questions) while reserving the time of executives for business. Oat understandably wanted its management team to conduct its construction business. . . .

Magistrate Groh exercised a power unknown even in labor law, where there is a duty to bargain in good faith. 29 U.S.C. §158(d). Labor and management commonly negotiate through persons with the authority to discuss but not agree. The negotiators report back to management and the union, each of which reserves power to reject or approve the position of its agent. . . .

Settling litigation is valuable, and courts should promote it. Is settlement of litigation more valuable than settlement of labor disputes, so that courts may do what the NLRB may not? The statutory framework — bona fide negotiations required in labor law but not in litigation — suggests the opposite. Does the desirability of settlement imply that rules of state law allocating authority within a corporation must yield? We have held in other cases that settlements must be negotiated within the framework of existing rules; the desire to get a case over and done with does not justify modifying generally applicable norms. E.g., Dunn v. Carey, 808 F.2d 555, 560 (7th Cir. 1986) (consent decrees, and hence settlement, may be more attractive if parties may agree not to follow state law, but the value of settlement does not authorize that).

D. RULES WITH INCENTIVES TO BARGAIN: FEES AND COSTS OF NEGOTIATING

While courts decide whether by rule or case law to require various forms of participation in negotiation and court-annexed forms of dispute resolution, most modern Rules of Civil Procedure provide strong incentives to negotiate and settle cases by assessing various forms of fees or "penalties" if subsequent trials produce "lower" results than what was offered in negotiation.

FEDERAL RULE OF CIVIL PROCEDURE 68 (2004)

Offer of Judgment

At any time more than 10 days before the trial begins, a party defending against a claim may serve upon the adverse party an offer to allow judgment to be taken against the defending party for the money or property or to the effect specified in the offer, with costs then accrued. If within 10 days after the service of the offer the adverse party serves written notice that the offer is accepted, either party may then file the offer and notice of acceptance together with proof of service thereof and thereupon the clerk shall enter judgment. An offer not accepted shall be deemed withdrawn and evidence thereof is not admissible except in a proceeding to determine costs. If the judgment finally obtained by the offeree is not more favorable than the offer, the offeree must pay the costs incurred after the making of the offer. The fact that an offer is made but not accepted does not preclude a subsequent offer. When the liability of one party to another has been determined by verdict or order or judgment, but the amount or extent of the liability remains to be determined by further proceedings, the party adjudged liable may make an offer of judgment, which shall have the same effect as an offer made before trial if it is served within a reasonable time not less than 10 days prior to the commencement of hearings to determine the amount or extent of liability.

Notes and Questions

11.14 Why does this rule provide only for defendants to make offers of settlement (judgment) to plaintiffs, but not the other way around?

11.15 What incentives to negotiate or bargain in the context of litigation does this rule provide? Any disincentives? Do you think it is a good idea? Other legal systems provide similar incentives, but offer them to both sides. A state court in Georgia recently struck down a Georgia statute as unconstitutional, modeled on Rule 68, which punished tort plaintiffs (but not defendants) for rejecting certain settlement offers. See Muenster v. Suh, No. 03-A-0183-4 (Sup. Ct. Gwinnett Co., Ga. Sept. 22, 2005).

11.16 Do you think the collective bargaining context and its case law provide a useful analogy for requiring good-faith participation in negotiation? Why or why not?

11.17 Do you think there is a difference in "requiring" good-faith participation in private negotiations (even if within the "shadow" of litigation) and in court-annexed dispute resolution programs such as court-mandated mediation?

11.18 Do you think there is a difference between requiring the parties and/or lawyers to (1) show up; (2) produce relevant information; (3) bargain in good faith; or (4) come with "settlement authority"? Would you draw distinctions between these behaviors in negotiation or settlement-seeking activities? Can you think of other kinds of negotiation behaviors that might be subject to a "good-faith" requirement? (Negotiation ethics? See Chapter 10.)

11.19 Can good-faith participation in private negotiations ever be enforced? (Who will see the activity and judge it? See James J. White's argument in Machiavelli and the Bar in Chapter 10.) Is court-annexed negotiation different? Does it matter if the negotiation is being conducted pursuant to some court rule or requirement to engage in negotiation or settlement activity?

11.20 In Marek v. Chesney, 473 U.S. 1 (1985), the Supreme Court interpreted part of Rule 68 by holding that plaintiffs in a civil rights case had to achieve, in their trial judgment, an amount larger than that offered by the defendants for settlement of the case, pursuant to the Rule and could not include the attorneys' fees (authorized by civil rights statutes) earned as part of the "judgment" used in calculating whether the Rule 68 offer was higher or lower than the judgment amount. In the case, the defendants offered to settle the case for $100,000, including attorneys' fees and costs, which offer was turned down. At the trial, the plaintiffs won a verdict of $60,000, plus costs and fees. Since their costs and fees were ultimately greater than $40,000, the plaintiffs argued that their "judgment" was for more than the $100,000 offered, under Rule 68, and they were not responsible for the costs and fees of the defendant. The defendants argued that costs and fees had to be assessed at the time of the offer (which they argued in this case was about $32,000, so that the final judgment was actually only $92,000), and the court ruled on behalf of the defendants, holding that post-offer costs and fees could not be included in the Rule 68 calculations.

11.21 Rule 68 is somewhat of a departure for American procedure in which the usual rule, the "American Rule," is that each party pays its own costs and fees, as contrasted to the "English Rule," which provides that the loser pays costs and fees for both sides. There is vast literature on both sides of the Atlantic arguing about which of these rules is better, from a policy perspective, for encouraging meritorious litigation and discouraging frivolous or unfounded litigation. See, e.g., John J. Donahue, Opting for the British Rule, or if

Posner and Shavell Can't Remember the Coase Theorem Who Will?, 104
Harv. L. Rev. 1093 (1991); James W. Hughes & Edward A. Snyder, Litiga-
tion and Settlement Under the English and American Rules: Theory and
Evidence, 38 J. L. & Econ. 225 (1995); Herbert Kritzer, The English Rule, 78
A.B.A. J. 54 (1992); George Priest & Benjamin Klein, The Selection of
Disputes for Litigation, 13 J. Leg. Stud. 1 (1984); Steven Shavell, Suit, Set-
tlement and Trial: A Theoretical Analysis Under Alternative Methods for the
Allocation of Legal Costs, 11 J. Leg. Stud. 55 (1982). What impact do you
think these different attorneys' fees and costs rules have on negotiations in the
litigation context? See Edward F. Sherman, From "Loser Pays" to Modified
Offer of Judgment Rules: Reconciling Incentives to Settle with Access to
Justice, 76 Tex. L. Rev. 1863 (1998).

EVANS v. JEFF D.

475 U.S. 717 (1986)

Justice STEVENS delivered the opinion of the Court.

The Civil Rights Attorney's Fees Awards Act of 1976 (Fees Act) provides that
"the court, in its discretion, may allow the prevailing party . . . a reasonable attorney's
fee" in enumerated civil rights actions. 42 U.S.C. §1988. In Maher v. Gagne, 448
U.S. 122 (1980), we held that fees may be assessed against state officials after a case has
been settled by the entry of a consent decree. In this case, we consider the question
whether attorney's fees must be assessed when the case has been settled by a consent
decree granting prospective relief to the plaintiff class but providing that the defendants shall not pay any part of the prevailing party's fees or costs. We hold that the
District Court has the power, in its sound discretion, to refuse to award fees.

The petitioners are the Governor and other public officials of the State of Idaho
responsible for the education and treatment of children who suffer from emotional
and mental handicaps. Respondents are a class of such children who have been or will
be placed in petitioners' care. On August 4, 1980, respondents commenced this
action by filing a complaint against petitioners in the United States District Court
for the District of Idaho. The factual allegations in the complaint described deficiencies in both the educational programs and the health care services provided respondents. These deficiencies allegedly violated the United States Constitution, the Idaho
Constitution, four federal statutes, and certain provisions of the Idaho Code. The
complaint prayed for injunctive relief and for an award of costs and attorney's fees,
but it did not seek damages. . . .

Shortly after petitioners filed their answer, and before substantial work had been
done on the case, the parties entered into settlement negotiations. They were able to
reach agreement concerning that part of the complaint relating to educational services with relative ease and, on October 14, 1981, entered into a stipulation disposing
of that part of the case. The stipulation provided that each party would bear its "own
attorney's fees and costs thus far incurred." . . . The District Court promptly entered
an order approving the partial settlement.

Negotiations concerning the treatment claims broke down, however, and the parties filed cross-motions for summary judgment. Although the District Court dismissed several of respondents' claims, it held that the federal constitutional claims raised genuine issues of fact to be resolved at trial. Thereafter, the parties stipulated to the entry of a class certification order, engaged in discovery, and otherwise prepared to try the case in the spring of 1983.

In March 1983, one week before trial, petitioners presented respondents with a new settlement proposal. As respondents themselves characterize it, the proposal "offered virtually all of the injunctive relief [they] had sought in their complaint." . . . The Court of Appeals agreed with this characterization, and further noted that the proposed relief was "more than the district court in earlier hearings had indicated it was willing to grant." . . . As was true of the earlier partial settlement, however, petitioners' offer included a provision for a waiver by respondents of any claim to fees or costs. Originally, this waiver was unacceptable to the Idaho Legal Aid Society, which had instructed Johnson to reject any settlement offer conditioned upon a waiver of fees, but Johnson ultimately determined that his ethical obligation to his clients mandated acceptance of the proposal. The parties conditioned the waiver on approval by the District Court.

After the stipulation was signed, Johnson filed a written motion requesting the District Court to approve the settlement "except for the provision on costs and attorney's fees," and to allow respondents to present a bill of costs and fees for consideration by the court. . . . At the oral argument on that motion, Johnson contended that petitioners' offer had exploited his ethical duty to his clients — that he was "forced," by an offer giving his clients "the best result [they] could have gotten in this court or any other court," to waive his attorney's fees. The District Court, however, evaluated the waiver in the context of the entire settlement and rejected the ethical underpinnings of Johnson's argument. Explaining that although petitioners were "not willing to concede that they were obligated to [make the changes in their practices required by the stipulation], . . . they were willing to do them as long as their costs were outlined and they didn't face additional costs," it concluded that "it doesn't violate any ethical considerations for an attorney to give up his attorney fees in the interest of getting a better bargain for his client[s]." . . . Accordingly, the District Court approved the settlement and denied the motion to submit a costs bill. . . .

The question we must decide, therefore, is whether the District Court had a duty to reject the proposed settlement because it included a waiver of statutorily authorized attorney's fees.

That duty, whether it takes the form of a general prophylactic rule or arises out of the special circumstances of this case, derives ultimately from the Fees Act rather than from the strictures of professional ethics. Although respondents contend that Johnson, as counsel for the class, was faced with an "ethical dilemma" when petitioners offered him relief greater than that which he could reasonably have expected to obtain for his clients at trial (if only he would stipulate to a waiver of the statutory fee award), and although we recognize Johnson's conflicting interests between pursuing relief for the class and a fee for the Idaho Legal Aid Society, we do not believe that the "dilemma" was an "ethical" one in the sense that Johnson had to choose between conflicting duties under the prevailing norms of professional conduct. Plainly, Johnson had no ethical obligation to seek a statutory fee award. His ethical duty was to serve his clients loyally and competently. Since the proposal to settle the merits was more favorable than the probable outcome of the trial, Johnson's decision to recommend acceptance was consistent with the highest standards of our profession. The District Court, therefore, correctly concluded that approval of the settlement involved no breach of ethics in this case.

The defect, if any, in the negotiated fee waiver must be traced not to the rules of ethics but to the Fees Act. Following this tack, respondents argue that the statute must be construed to forbid a fee waiver that is the product of "coercion." They submit that a "coercive waiver" results when the defendant in a civil rights action (1) offers a settlement on the merits of equal or greater value than that which plaintiffs could reasonably expect to achieve at trial but (2) conditions the offer on a waiver of plaintiffs' statutory eligibility for attorney's fees. Such an offer, they claim, exploits the ethical obligation of plaintiffs' counsel to recommend settlement in order to avoid defendant's statutory liability for its opponents' fees and costs. . . .

The text of the Fees Act provides no support for the proposition that Congress intended to ban all fee waivers offered in connection with substantial relief on the merits. On the contrary, the language of the Act, as well as its legislative history, indicates that Congress bestowed on the "prevailing *party*" (generally plaintiffs) a statutory eligibility for a discretionary award of attorney's fees in specified civil rights actions. It did not prevent the party from waiving this eligibility any more than it legislated against assignment of this right to an attorney, such as effectively occurred here. . . . The statute and its legislative history nowhere suggest that Congress intended to forbid *all* waivers of attorney's fees — even those insisted upon by a civil rights plaintiff in exchange for some other relief to which he is indisputably not entitled any more than it intended to bar a concession on damages to secure broader injunctive relief. . . .

In fact, we believe that a general proscription against negotiated waiver of attorney's fees in exchange for a settlement on the merits would itself impede vindication of civil rights, at least in some cases, by reducing the attractiveness of settlement. . . .

In approving the package offer in Marek v. Chesny we recognized that a rule prohibiting the comprehensive negotiation of all outstanding issues in a pending case might well preclude the settlement of a substantial number of cases:

> If defendants are not allowed to make lump-sum offers that would, if accepted, represent their total liability, they would understandably be reluctant to make settlement offers. As the Court of Appeals observed, "many a defendant would be unwilling to make a binding settlement offer on terms that left it exposed to liability for attorney's fees in whatever amount the court might fix on motion of the plaintiff." 720 F.2d [474], at 477. . . .
>
> In considering whether to enter a negotiated settlement, a defendant may have good reason to demand to know his total liability from both damages and fees.

Most defendants are unlikely to settle unless the cost of the predicted judgment, discounted by its probability, plus the transaction costs of further litigation, are greater than the cost of the settlement package. If fee waivers cannot be negotiated, the settlement package must either contain an attorney's fee component of potentially large and typically uncertain magnitude, or else the parties must agree to have the fee fixed by the court. Although either of these alternatives may well be acceptable in many cases, there surely is a significant number in which neither alternative will be as satisfactory as a decision to try the entire case. . . .

What the outcome of this settlement illustrates is that the Fees Act has given the victims of civil rights violations a powerful weapon that improves their ability to employ counsel, to obtain access to the courts, and thereafter to vindicate their rights by means of settlement or trial. For aught that appears, it was the "coercive" effect of respondents' statutory right to seek a fee award that motivated petitioners' exceptionally generous offer. Whether this weapon might be even more powerful if fee waivers were prohibited in cases like this is another question, but it is in any event a question that Congress is best equipped to answer. Thus far, the Legislature has not commanded that fees be paid whenever a case is settled. Unless it issues such a command, we shall rely primarily on the sound discretion of the district courts to appraise the reasonableness of particular class-action settlements on a case-by-case basis, in the light of all the relevant circumstances. In this case, the District Court did not abuse its discretion in upholding a fee waiver which secured broad injunctive relief, relief greater than that which plaintiffs could reasonably have expected to achieve at trial.

Notes and Questions

11.22 What does this ruling do to the negotiating power of civil rights lawyers? Does it give them more power by allowing claims for large attorneys' fees to be bargained away for "greater relief" for their clients, or does it disadvantage certain classes of lawyers, like those Legal Aid civil rights lawyers in the case, by allowing defendants to "hold them up" for fee waivers in order to get relief for their clients?

11.23 Does this case put all civil rights or other statutory-fee-entitled lawyers (authorized by many different kinds of statutes) in conflict with their clients? Isn't it an ethical issue of a conflict of interest if the attorney is asked to waive his fees in order to negotiate relief for his client? Is this fee conflict any different from the fee conflicts that exist in any agent-principal/lawyer-client relationship? Doesn't the hourly fee or the contingent fee lawyer also have a conflict of interest with respect to how the fee structure provides incentives or disincentives for certain kinds of negotiation behavior? Can negotiation with an agent who is getting paid ever be without a conflict of interest? Will fee structures always provide both incentives and disincentives for particular kinds of negotiating actions?

11.24 Following the holding in this case, many civil rights and legal aid lawyers tried to get states to ban certain negotiated fee waivers (such as in cases of statutory "entitlements" to fees) as a matter of ethics or professional responsibility,

mostly to no avail. Do you see that whether the statutory fees are characterized as "entitlements" or "eligibilities" by the courts or legislatures construing
these statutes affects whether these are "bargainable" items?

E. MULTIPLE-PARTY SETTLEMENTS

The most ordinary way for legal negotiations to occur is when two lawyers negotiate
for two parties engaged in a transaction or lawsuit. The lawyers and/or parties will
make agreements about various issues in dispute and how responsibility will be
allocated among multiple parties. In many legal settings, there will be more than
one party on at least one side of the negotiation (consider even the simple personal
injury case, which will have an insurer lurking behind and usually representing the
defendant). In cases of multiple tortfeasors, joint actors, and class action plaintiffs
seeking group relief for torts, discrimination, consumer, or securities fraud, how
settlements are allocated can become more complicated. Within the law of subrogation, indemnification, and joint and several liability, there will be complex questions
about who is actually governed or bound by or "released" by a settlement agreement.

   While we cannot treat all of these legal issues here, it is useful for any legal
negotiator to know that there are important bodies of law that will affect what
can be accomplished during negotiations, such as releases, joint liability, taxes,
fees, allocations of responsibilities, and, at least in the case of class actions, the
need for judicial approval of some settlements. We introduce you to at least some
of these issues below.

1. Lawyers' Duties with Multiple Clients

   When lawyers represent more than one client at the same time, they may have
conflicts of interests. Whether the joint representation of multiple clients is a conflict
of interest is usually a question of legal ethics and state law. See Model Rules of Profl.
Conduct 1.7-1.13 (2005). Because these are often quite complex issues, we don't
treat all of them here, but there are particular issues when a single lawyer or group of
lawyers seeks to negotiate on behalf of multiple clients. Whether a lawyer can act for
multiple clients in a transaction (whether all on the "same" side or on "both" sides of
a transaction, such as a sale of property or business) is governed, in part, by Rules 1.7
and 1.8 (conflicts of current clients). See also Geoffrey Hazard, Jr., Lawyer for the
Situation, Ethics in the Practice of Law 58-68 (1978); Clyde Spillenger, Elusive
Advocate: Reconsidering Brandeis as People's Lawyer, 105 Yale L.J. 1445 (1996)
(describing Justice Louis Brandeis's activities as a practicing lawyer who often represented several "sides" of a transaction, lobbying event, or piece of litigation (such as
bankruptcy) in order to perform the role of mediator or "deal manager" as a "counsel
to the situation"). In more modern times, it is often suggested that having one lawyer
for many parties may create value, not only by saving legal fees, but by having a
lawyer who can reduce adversarial negotiation behavior and help the parties reach

creative and good solutions. Modern divorce lawyers, for example, include some who call themselves "collaborative lawyers" who seek to achieve good solutions for divorcing clients, sometimes representing both parties. (Some states, whether by statute or case law, have prohibited this practice.)

Where lawyers seek to negotiate settlements of lawsuits on behalf of multiple clients, there are ethical rules, statutes, and case law (and in some cases, like class actions, judicial review of settlements) that govern what the lawyer may or may not do.

MODEL RULE OF PROFESSIONAL CONDUCT 1.8(g) (2005)

CONFLICT OF INTEREST: Current Clients: Specific Rules

A lawyer who represents two or more clients shall not participate in making aggregate settlement of the claims of or against the clients, or in a criminal case an aggregated agreement as to guilty or nolo contendere pleas, unless each client gives informed consent, in a writing signed by the client. The lawyer's disclosure shall include the existence and nature of all the claims or pleas involved and of the participation of each person in the settlement.

When there are multiple parties in cases (on both plaintiff and defendant sides of the case), there may be questions of who can bind the groups of litigants. This legal issue affects not only the lawyers, but also the parties who litigate or negotiate together. The following case involved what was then the biggest negotiated settlement in legal history, through the class action device, a settlement of a national class of asbestos injured claimants. Analyzing the requirements of Rule 23 of the Federal Rules of Civil Procedure, the court found that because there were so many different and disparate interests of the claimants (past, present, and potentially future injured individuals), no one class of claimants could "adequately represent" all of them in the national class settlement, which contemplated the use of a national claims facility administered jointly by plaintiffs' lawyers (who would have been bound by Model Rule of Professional Conduct 1.8(g), reprinted above) and a consortium of defendants. Since class action settlements must be reviewed by the court under Federal Rule of Civil Procedure 23(e), there is greater scrutiny of settlements of class actions than other individual or group settlements.

2. Class Actions

 AMCHEM PRODUCTS, INC. v. WINDSOR

521 U.S. 591 (1997)

Justice GINSBURG delivered the opinion of the Court.

This case concerns the legitimacy under Rule 23 of the Federal Rules of Civil Procedure of a class-action certification sought to achieve global settlement of current and future asbestos-related claims. The class proposed for certification potentially encompasses hundreds of thousands, perhaps millions, of individuals tied together by this commonality: Each was, or some day may be, adversely affected by past exposure to asbestos products manufactured by one or more of 20 companies. Those companies, defendants in the lower courts, are petitioners here.

The United States District Court for the Eastern District of Pennsylvania certified the class for settlement only, finding that the proposed settlement was fair and that representation and notice had been adequate. That court enjoined class members from separately pursuing asbestos-related personal-injury suits in any court, federal or state, pending the issuance of a final order. The Court of Appeals for the Third Circuit vacated the District Court's orders, holding that the class certification failed to satisfy Rule 23's requirements in several critical respects. We affirm the Court of Appeals' judgment.

The settlement-class certification we confront evolved in response to an asbestos-litigation crisis. See Georgine v. Amchem Products, Inc., 83 F.3d 610, 618, and n.2 (C.A.3 1996) (citing commentary). A United States Judicial Conference Ad Hoc Committee on Asbestos Litigation, appointed by THE CHIEF JUSTICE in September 1990, described facets of the problem in a 1991 report:

> [This] is a tale of danger known in the 1930s, exposure inflicted upon millions of Americans in the 1940s and 1950s, injuries that began to take their toll in the 1960s, and a flood of lawsuits beginning in the 1970s. On the basis of past and current filing data, and because of a latency period that may last as long as 40 years for some asbestos related diseases, a continuing stream of claims can be expected. The final toll of asbestos related injuries is unknown. Predictions have been made of 200,000 asbestos disease deaths before the year 2000 and as many as 265,000 by the year 2015.
>
> The most objectionable aspects of asbestos litigation can be briefly summarized: dockets in both federal and state courts continue to grow; long delays are routine; trials are too long; the same issues are litigated over and over; transaction costs exceed the victims' recovery by nearly two to one; exhaustion of assets threatens and distorts the process; and future claimants may lose altogether.

Report of The Judicial Conference Ad Hoc Committee on Asbestos Litigation 2-3 (Mar. 1991). . . .

In the face of legislative inaction, the federal courts—lacking authority to replace state tort systems with a national toxic tort compensation regime—endeavored to work with the procedural tools available to improve management of federal asbestos litigation. Eight federal judges, experienced in the superintendence of asbestos cases, urged the Judicial Panel on Multidistrict Litigation (MDL Panel), to consolidate in a single district all asbestos complaints then pending in federal courts. Accepting the recommendation, the MDL Panel transferred all asbestos cases then filed, but not yet on trial in federal courts, to a single district, the United States District Court for the Eastern District of Pennsylvania; pursuant to the transfer order, the collected cases were consolidated for pretrial proceedings before Judge Weiner. See In re Asbestos Products Liability Litigation (No. VI), 771 F. Supp. 415, 422-424 (Jud. Pan. Mult. Lit. 1991). The order aggregated pending cases only; no authority resides in the MDL Panel to license for consolidated proceedings claims not yet filed.

After the consolidation, attorneys for plaintiffs and defendants formed separate steering committees and began settlement negotiations. Ronald L. Motley and Gene

Locks — later appointed, along with Motley's law partner Joseph F. Rice, to represent the plaintiff class in this action — cochaired the Plaintiffs' Steering Committee. Counsel for the Center for Claims Resolution (CCR), the consortium of 20 former asbestos manufacturers now before us as petitioners, participated in the Defendants' Steering Committee. Although the MDL Panel order collected, transferred, and consolidated only cases already commenced in federal courts, settlement negotiations included efforts to find a "means of resolving . . . future cases." Record, Doc. 3, p. 2 (Memorandum in Support of Joint Motion for Conditional Class Certification); see also Georgine v. Amchem Products, Inc., 157 F.R.D. 246, 266 (E.D. Pa. 1994) ("primary purpose of the settlement talks in the consolidated MDL litigation was to craft a national settlement that would provide an alternative resolution mechanism for asbestos claims," including claims that might be filed in the future). . . .

CCR counsel approached the lawyers who had headed the Plaintiffs' Steering Committee in the unsuccessful negotiations, and a new round of negotiations began; that round yielded the mass settlement agreement now in controversy. At the time, the former heads of the Plaintiffs' Steering Committee represented thousands of plaintiffs with then-pending asbestos-related claims — claimants the parties to this suit call "inventory" plaintiffs. CCR indicated in these discussions that it would resist settlement of inventory cases absent "some kind of protection for the future" . . . (CCR communicated to the inventory plaintiffs' attorneys that once the CCR defendants saw a rational way to deal with claims expected to be filed in the future, those defendants would be prepared to address the settlement of pending cases).

Settlement talks thus concentrated on devising an administrative scheme for disposition of asbestos claims not yet in litigation. In these negotiations, counsel for masses of inventory plaintiffs endeavored to represent the interests of the anticipated future claimants, although those lawyers then had no attorney-client relationship with such claimants.

Once negotiations seemed likely to produce an agreement purporting to bind potential plaintiffs, CCR agreed to settle, through separate agreements, the claims of plaintiffs who had already filed asbestos-related lawsuits. In one such agreement, CCR defendants promised to pay more than $200 million to gain release of the claims of numerous inventory plaintiffs. After settling the inventory claims, CCR, together with the plaintiffs' lawyers CCR had approached, launched this case, exclusively involving persons outside the MDL Panel's province — plaintiffs without already pending lawsuits.

The class action thus instituted was not intended to be litigated. Rather, within the space of a single day, January 15, 1993, the settling parties — CCR defendants and the representatives of the plaintiff class described below — presented to the District Court a complaint, an answer, a proposed settlement agreement, and a joint motion for conditional class certification. . . .

A stipulation of settlement accompanied the pleadings; it proposed to settle, and to preclude nearly all class members from litigating against CCR companies, all claims not filed before January 15, 1993, involving compensation for present and future asbestos-related personal injury or death. An exhaustive document exceeding 100 pages, the stipulation presents in detail an administrative mechanism and a schedule of payments to compensate class members who meet defined asbestos-exposure and medical requirements. The stipulation describes four categories of compensable disease: mesothelioma; lung cancer; certain "other cancers" (colon-rectal, laryngeal, esophageal, and stomach cancer); and "non-malignant conditions" (asbestosis and bilateral pleural thickening). Persons with "exceptional" medical claims — claims that do not fall within the four described diagnostic categories — may in some instances qualify for compensation, but the settlement caps the number of "exceptional" claims CCR must cover. . . .

Objectors raised numerous challenges to the settlement. They urged that the settlement unfairly disadvantaged those without currently compensable conditions in that it failed to adjust for inflation or to account for changes, over time, in medical understanding. They maintained that compensation levels were intolerably low in comparison to awards available in tort litigation or payments received by the inventory plaintiffs. And they objected to the absence of any compensation for certain claims, for example, medical monitoring, compensable under the tort law of several States. Rejecting these and all other objections, Judge Reed concluded that the settlement terms were fair and had been negotiated without collusion. See 157 F.R.D., at 325, 331-332. He also found that adequate notice had been given to class members, see id., at 332-334, and that final class certification under Rule 23(b)(3) was appropriate, see id., at 315. . . .

We granted review to decide the role settlement may play, under existing Rule 23, in determining the propriety of class certification. . . .

Rule 23(e), on settlement of class actions, reads in its entirety: "A class action shall not be dismissed or compromised without the approval of the court, and notice of the proposed dismissal or compromise shall be given to all members of the class in such manner as the court directs." This prescription was designed to function as an additional requirement, not a superseding direction, for the "class action" to which Rule 23(e) refers is one qualified for certification under Rule 23(a) and (b) . . . (adequate representation does not eliminate additional requirement to provide notice). Subdivisions (a) and (b) focus court attention on whether a proposed class has sufficient unity so that absent members can fairly be bound by decisions of class representatives. That dominant concern persists when settlement, rather than trial, is proposed. . . .

Nor can the class approved by the District Court satisfy Rule 23(a)(4)'s requirement that the named parties "will fairly and adequately protect the interests of the class." The adequacy inquiry under Rule 23(a)(4) serves to uncover conflicts of interest between named parties and the class they seek to represent. [Citations omitted.] "[A] class representative must be part of the class and 'possess the same interest and suffer the same injury' as the class members." [Citations omitted.]

As the Third Circuit pointed out, named parties with diverse medical conditions sought to act on behalf of a single giant class rather than on behalf of discrete subclasses. In significant respects, the interests of those within the single class are not aligned. Most saliently, for the currently injured, the critical goal is generous immediate payments. That goal tugs against the interest of exposure-only plaintiffs in ensuring an ample, inflation-protected fund for the future. ("In employment discrimination litigation, conflicts might arise, for example, between employees and applicants who were denied employment and who will, if granted relief, compete with employees for fringe benefits or seniority. Under Rule 23, the same plaintiff could not represent these classes.") [Citation omitted.] . . .

The settling parties, in sum, achieved a global compromise with no structural assurance of fair and adequate representation for the diverse groups and individuals affected. Although the named parties alleged a range of complaints, each served generally as representative for the whole, not for a separate constituency. In another asbestos class action, the Second Circuit spoke precisely to this point:

> [W]here differences among members of a class are such that subclasses must be established, we know of no authority that permits a court to approve a settlement without creating subclasses on the basis of consents by members of a unitary class, some of whom happen to be members of the distinct subgroups. The class representatives may well have thought that the Settlement serves the aggregate interests of the entire class. But the adversity among subgroups requires that the members of each subgroup cannot be bound to a settlement except by consents given by those who understand that their role is to represent solely the members of their respective subgroups.

In re Joint Eastern and Southern Dist. Asbestos Litigation, 982 F.2d 721, 742-743 (1992), *modified on reh'g sub nom.* In re Findley, 993 F.2d 7 ([2d Cir.] 1993).

Because we have concluded that the class in this case cannot satisfy the requirements of common issue predominance and adequacy of representation, we need not rule, definitively, on the notice given here. . . .

The argument is sensibly made that a nationwide administrative claims processing regime would provide the most secure, fair, and efficient means of compensating victims of asbestos exposure. Congress, however, has not adopted such a solution. And Rule 23, which must be interpreted with fidelity to the Rules Enabling Act and applied with the interests of absent class members in close view, cannot carry the large load CCR, class counsel, and the District Court heaped upon it. . . .

Notes and Questions

11.25 Can you think of any way a national class action with so many different kinds of claimants could be settled, with proper "representation," by both lawyers and appropriate class representatives? Does this decision suggest any solutions or alternatives? See Carrie Menkel-Meadow, Ethics and the Settlement of Mass Torts: When the Rules Meet the Road, 80 Cornell L. Rev. 1159 (1995); cf. Susan Koniak, Feasting While the Widow Weeps: *Georgine v. Amchem Products*, 80 Cornell L. Rev. 1045 (1995).

11.26 Class actions represent a special case where judicial approval is required of all settlements. See Fed. R. Civ. Proc. 23(e). Do you think there should be court supervision or review of all settlements that involve many people whose legal rights are being represented by one lawyer or set of lawyers? Under what other circumstances do you think it would be beneficial to have court review of settlements? (See Section G below.)

11.27 Given the purposes of class action litigation, when would it be appropriate, in your view, for lawyers to settle a case on behalf of class members who may not actually know they are part of a lawsuit?

11.28 As the opinion above makes clear, in so-called limited fund cases, where class members are competing for recompense from a dedicated fund or particular settlement amount, there must be court approval (at least in the class action context). What happens in nonclass actions when a group of claimants may be competing in settlements for what may turn out to be, in effect, a limited sum, if, for example, there are limited assets or insurance coverage? If the claimants are represented by a single lawyer, Rule 1.8(g) clearly applies; but what happens if there is a limited fund and claimants have their own or many lawyers? Should "first come" be "first served"? What laws exist to allocate funds of settlements in such contexts? What happens in litigation? Is it different from what happens in negotiation?

3. Joint and Several Liability for and Contributions to Settlements: Mary Carter Agreements

Under standard tort principles, all defendants who have contributed to the injuries of a plaintiff or set of plaintiffs are liable for the entire damages caused under the doctrine of joint and severable liability. Thus, while a plaintiff may sue all possible defendants who caused her injury, she might pursue the richest one (or "deepest pocket") for negotiating a settlement. Since defendants may also have rights of contribution from each other for claims of liability among them for causing plaintiff injuries, there are a host of legal issues that arise when a plaintiff seeks to negotiate a settlement with one or more (but not all) of the defendants. Such questions include these: (1) If a plaintiff settles with one defendant and "releases" that defendant, can she continue to sue or pursue negotiations with the other defendants? (2) Can a defendant who settles a matter with a plaintiff pursue the remaining defendants for contribution to that settlement? (3) Can defendants who continue to pursue litigation (and perhaps lose it and have to pay the plaintiff) seek contribution from the defendant(s) who have previously settled with plaintiff? Add the likely fact of insurance coverages that may vary for these defendants, both in terms of liability and defense (insurance company pays litigation costs) policies, and you can see that there are a host of complicated relationships of parties and lawyers on both sides of the "v." for purposes of both litigation and negotiation. Insurance companies who settle with plaintiffs will then have subrogation rights to seek contribution from other joint tortfeasors. Parties who pay settlements may also seek money or other relief from other parties who have agreed to indemnify particular parties, by contract or by law. Most of these legal issues depend on state law, though in a few areas there have been attempts to provide some uniformity of treatment (such as in the Uniform Contribution Among Tortfeasors Act, which has been adopted in some, but not all, states and which describes what legal effect a "release" will have when there are multiple defendants). Whether joint tortfeasors will be liable *pro tanto* or under comparative negligence rules will depend on state law.

Here it is crucial for releases and settlement documents to be as clear as possible about parties' intent and to be written with understanding of what the governing law of the governing jurisdiction is on these issues. While we don't include much about it in this book, drafting good settlement agreements is an important part of being a good negotiator. To be a valid and enforceable agreement, as discussed in Section A above, a negotiated agreement must be a legally enforceable contract, but to properly allocate all of the duties and various responsibilities of multiple parties, a settlement agreement and release must be well crafted and clearly written. See, e.g., Eugene F. Lynch, Negotiation and Settlement (2d ed. 2005).

In a variation on the full settlement with one defendant, sometimes a defendant will seek to limit liability by making an agreement with the plaintiff to help the plaintiff (e.g., by testifying in a way that helps that defendant and places blame on other defendants) in return for some limit on its liability, or makes that defendant's liability dependent on what is recovered from other defendants. Agreements of this sort, which almost always have a secrecy clause in them, are called Mary Carter agreements, from the case Booth v. Mary Carter Paint Co., 202 So. 2d 8 (Fla. Dist. Ct. App. 1967) (guaranty agreements), or Gallagher agreements, after the case City of Tucson v. Gallagher, 383 P.2d 798 (Ariz. Ct. App. 1971), *vacated*, 493 P.2d 1197 (Ariz. 1972).

Because these kinds of agreements can lead to what amounts to collusion between a plaintiff and a selected defendant to throw blame onto other defendants (perhaps those with the deepest pockets!), many jurisdictions have prohibited these agreements as against public policy or as impeding the trial process, either by statute or by case law. See, e.g., Dosdourian v. Garsten, 624 So. 2d 241 (Fla. 1993); Elbaor v. Smith, 845 S.W.2d 240 (Tex. 1992). Other jurisdictions see these agreements as allowing defendants and plaintiffs to agree to "sliding scale" liability and do not absolutely prohibit them, but review them on a case-by-case basis for unethical or other prohibited conduct. See Note, It's a Mistake to Tolerate the Mary Carter Agreement, 87 Colum. L. Rev. 368 (1987). Some jurisdictions require disclosure of such agreements, either through the discovery process to all parties or to the jury at trial. From a judicial policy perspective, Mary Carter agreements are seen alternatively as promoting settlements, providing appropriate additional resources to plaintiffs to try worthy cases, or seriously disturbing the adversary system, which continues trials (and doesn't aid settlement) and may distort how the facts are presented. Over the years, clever lawyers have also developed other variations on these themes (e.g., "loan-receipt" agreements in which defendants may invest in or help finance litigation against other defendants, in return for releases or limited liability). Courts that review these kinds of agreements are balancing policies that promote settlement but that may undermine the rules and understandings of the American litigation system.

Notes and Questions

11.29 Do you think it is a good idea to prohibit Mary Carter-like agreements *per se*, or would you prefer a case-by-case review of what the parties are doing in a particular case? What policies do such prohibitions, whether *per se* or case-by-case, serve?

11.30 Can you think of any other agreements that multiple litigants, whether plaintiffs or defendants, might make that you think should be declared unlawful?

11.31 In recent years, there have been efforts by third-party investors of various sorts to "purchase" a plaintiff's claims in return for immediate payment to the plaintiff, with the plaintiff promising full cooperation at trial against defendants. Do you think these kinds of agreements or investments in claims are like Mary Carter agreements or different? Should they be prohibited? What if the purchaser of the claim is aggregating claims and is able to negotiate higher amounts than the individual could negotiate on her own? Should we allow investments in lawsuits and settlements? Under what legal theories might these practices be prohibited? Consider how the plaintiffs' lawyer (Jan Schlictmann) in the case described in *A Civil Action* (Jonathan Harr, 1996) had to seek bank financing and loans to pursue his claims on behalf of a group of water pollution victims against several major corporations.

F. CONFIDENTIALITY, SECRECY, AND TRANSPARENCY OF NEGOTIATIONS

Most legal negotiations are conducted in private sessions. Legal policy has been to encourage settlements, both on the grounds of allowing parties to consensually resolve matters between themselves in a system that is based on party initiatives (bringing lawsuits, presenting evidence) and to control the caseload of public adjudication. The formal expression of this policy is found in the federal and in most states' evidence codes (see Federal Rule of Evidence 408 below). Some negotiations may be more public (as when in labor or diplomatic negotiations there are press conferences and reports about offers, progress, deadlines, and impasses), and a few are required to be reviewed in public settings, like courts, as in the class action settlement review we have studied above (Federal Rule of Civil Procedure 23(e)).

Recently, some have argued that certain matters should be negotiated in public and that certain agreements to settle lawsuits or other matters should be disclosed, especially when they affect public health and safety. Some jurisdictions have begun to approve laws that ban "secret" settlements in some cases, that prohibit confidentiality and nondisclosure of settlement clauses, or that require a court to review whether a particular settlement should be made public. These arguments (represented below in the article by David Luban) suggest that resolution of legal conflicts is for the general public (in creating and generating precedent and laws to guide everyone) and not for the private parties who bring them.

The line between encouraging confidentiality in negotiation (and mediation, which is protected by separate mediation confidentiality and privilege rules) in order to have parties declare candidly what they want in negotiation and the policy of having public information about what is being negotiated is a difficult one to draw. As you read the excerpts that follow, consider where you think the line between confidentiality and open disclosure should be drawn. Are all negotiations the same, or should there be legal or policy differences in different substantive areas?

FEDERAL RULE OF EVIDENCE 408 (2005)

Compromise and Offers to Compromise

Evidence of (1) furnishing or offering or promising to furnish, or (2) accepting or offering or promising to accept, a valuable consideration in compromising or attempting to compromise a claim which was disputed as to either validity or amount, is not admissible to prove liability for or invalidity of the claim or its amount. Evidence of conduct or statements made in compromise negotiations is likewise not admissible. This rule does not require the exclusion of any evidence otherwise discoverable merely because it is presented in the course of compromise negotiations. This rule also does not require exclusion when the evidence is offered for another purpose, such as proving bias or prejudice of a witness, negativing a contention of undue delay, or proving an effort to obstruct a criminal investigation or prosecution.

This is the general rule that excludes from admissible evidence settlement offers and discussions, the settlement offer itself, and any information about settlement negotiations (unless admissible for other reasons). In addition to this rule, under Federal Rule of Civil Procedure 26(c), parties may apply for protective orders to make certain information (such as trade secrets or negotiated settlements) nondisclosable, either to the other party or more generally. (Indeed, some of the states that are limiting the secrecy of information about settlements have altered their versions of the procedural rules about judicial protective orders, prohibiting the granting of protective orders if they "shield" important information about public health or safety. See Menkel-Meadow below.)

Scholars and consumer activists have suggested that agreed-to confidentiality of negotiated settlements limits the public from knowing about dangerous things. (Consider the "secret" settlements of many product liability cases, such as the recent Explorer-Firestone Tire cases.) David Luban makes this claim and a more general one about the importance of the public knowing about and being engaged in all the negotiations that occur in conflicts that are so important they are brought to a court of law.

 David Luban, **SETTLEMENTS AND THE EROSION OF THE PUBLIC REALM**

83 Geo. L.J. 2619, 2619-2662 (1995)

THE NORMATIVE VALUE OF ADJUDICATION

Learned Hand once wrote, "I must say that as a litigant I should dread a lawsuit beyond almost anything short of sickness and death." This is conventional wisdom. Lawsuits are expensive, terrifying, frustrating, infuriating, humiliating, time-consuming, perhaps all-consuming. Small wonder, then, that both judges and litigants prefer settlements, which are cheaper, quicker, less public, and less all-or-nothing than adjudications. In an aphorism recently cited by Samuel Gross and Kent Syverud, a trial is a failed settlement.[9] Though trials and judgments may sometimes be necessary, they are like surgeries: painful last resorts for otherwise incurable ailments, which are likely to place the patient in a weakened condition at least temporarily and almost certain to leave lasting scars. Pursuing this metaphor, settlements provide the noninvasive alternate therapy that, if successful, is invariably better than surgery.

[Owen] Fiss's opposition to settlements[*] arises because of his unexpected dissent from the conventional wisdom that trials signal pathologies — his belief that adjudication may be a sign of health rather than a drastic cure for disease. This view is counterintuitive and wildly unpopular in a culture in which lawyer-bashing has become a national hobby, lawsuits a lightning rod for talk show resentniks, and the civil justice system a cherished target of rage and demagoguery. Yet the arguments for adjudication are neither eccentric nor frivolous. The first group of arguments, which is less controversial and more familiar, is instrumental in nature. These arguments do not commend adjudication as a good in itself, but rather as a necessary condition for fulfilling other values that our culture accepts. The second argument, at once less familiar and more controversial, considers adjudication an intrinsic good, a process that is as much a sign of a healthy society as free elections.

1. Adjudication as a Public Good

Some years ago, University of Chicago economist William M. Landes and then-law-professor Richard A. Posner wrote an article entitled Adjudication as a Private Good[10] in which they consider our courts as though they were private vendors of a service — dispute resolution — in competition with other purveyors of the same service, such as commercial arbitrators. Landes and Posner argue that treating adjudication as a private good is perfectly coherent, and that economic competition could increase the efficiency of the judicial system. After all, litigants hiring their own judges would create an incentive for quick and cheap dispute resolution as well as for judicial fairness, because litigants would refuse to hire an inefficient or biased judge. If public courts couldn't compete, litigants would switch to alternative providers.

However, Landes and Posner continue, our court system not only resolves disputes, but also produces rules and precedents. Though private judges may well be efficient purveyors of dispute resolution, they are terribly inefficient producers of rules. Why would litigants who engage the services of a rent-a-judge want to pay extra for a reasoned opinion enunciating a rule that benefits only future litigants? Future litigants, after all, would receive the benefits of the rule for free. Landes and Posner thus conclude that because the private market would systematically under-

---

[9] Samuel Gross & Kent D. Syverud, Getting to No: A Study of Settlement Negotiations and the Selection of Cases for Trial, 90 Mich. L. Rev. 319 (1991).

[*] Owen Fiss's now classic objection to settlements generally is found in Against Settlement, 93 Yale L.J. 1073 (1984).

[10] 8 J. Leg. Stud. 235 (1978).

produce rules and precedents, the state should control the provision of judicial services.

The Landes-Posner objection to private adjudication is an objection to settlements as well, a point that Jules Coleman and Charles Silver have elaborated: settlements, like private adjudications, produce no rules or precedents binding on nonparties.[11] Rules and precedents, in turn, have obvious importance for guiding future behavior and imposing order and certainty on a transactional world that would otherwise be in flux and chaos. Even those who favor settlement over adjudication generally rank order and certainty very high on the scale of legal values. Indeed, one of Fiss's criticisms of the alternative dispute resolution (ADR) movement is that its proponents value peace over justice. Settlements bring peace whereas adjudication, though perhaps more just, creates disruption. Regardless of whether Fiss is right that to be prosettlement is to value peace over justice, the present argument yields a surprising result: adjudication may often prove superior to settlement for securing peace because the former, unlike the latter, creates rules and precedents. . . .

2. Settlements and Public Bads

. . . Let us first consider two "pure" accounts of the legitimacy of government and of the judicial role. The first . . . is the familiar view that human freedom is best realized in settings free from governmental interference — the "private realm," which ambiguously includes both intimate relationships (the private as the personal) and market transactions (the private as "the private sector"). On this view, because of government's inevitable tendency to invade and to interfere with privacy, the public sector is bound to prove an impediment to human freedom. Government is nevertheless necessary to solve certain otherwise intractable problems. It defends against external enemies and keeps the internal peace by punishing wrongdoers, protecting rights, and resolving disputes. In addition, government provides some public goods, such as highways or legal precedents.

Let us call this account the "problem-solving conception." Its essential features are three: (1) it identifies "public" with "governmental" and "private" with "intimate or market relationships"; (2) it locates human freedom in the private sphere, and hence mistrusts governmental intervention; and (3) it understands the functions of government in wholly pragmatic terms, as interventions meant to solve problems within civil society that civil society cannot solve on its own. Thus, one can invoke this conception to defend the activist state, but that defense will be couched entirely in instrumental terms. The problem-solving conception is, I think it is safe to say, the dominant version of state legitimacy in contemporary America. Political discussion in today's Congress and mass media revolves largely around the question of whether government or private initiative is better able to solve our national problems. The idea that government might have some purpose other than competing with the private sector to build better mousetraps seems entirely absent

---

[11] Jules Coleman & Charles Silver, Justice in Settlements, 4 Soc. Phil. & Poly. 102, 114-119 (1986).

from contemporary debates between liberals and conservatives, Democrats and Republicans.

At the other extreme lies what I shall call the "public-life conception," which derives from the political thought of the ancient world and has enjoyed a periodic revival from Machiavelli to Rousseau to contemporary civic republicans. The best known modern defender of the public-life conception is Hannah Arendt.[*] For the ancient Greeks, Arendt tells us, active participation in political life constituted the highest human good, the kind of fulfillment that distinguishes us from the beasts. Only political action in the "public space" can redeem our lives from the futility born of the knowledge that we will soon be gone from the world. Far from "the private sector" providing a temple of individual liberty, dwelling in it amounted in the ancient view to a kind of slavery. Freedom lies in the public realm. Thus, although the public-life conception agrees with the problem-solving conception that "public" has to do with public affairs, the public-life conception locates freedom in the public sphere, not in market relationships or personal intimacy. Moreover, though adherents of the public-life conception do not deny that political action aims to solve problems, they insist that at bottom we engage in action for the sake of exercising our freedom. . . .

On the public-life conception, by contrast, the values realized in laws are a kind of public morality — objective spirit — and even ostensibly private disputes between apolitical citizens may have a public dimension engaging these values. Because the law is the visible residue of public action . . . , the law elevates private disputes into the public realm. Fiss defines adjudication as "the process by which the values embodied in an authoritative legal text, such as the Constitution, are given concrete meaning and expression," and he adds that these "public values" are "the values that define a society and give it its identity and inner coherence." . . .

At this point, we can see why Fiss finds nothing to celebrate in settlements. When a case settles, it does so on terms agreeable to its parties, but those terms are not necessarily illuminating to the law or to the public. Indeed, those terms may be harmful to the public. Instead of reasoned reconsideration of the law, we often find little more than a bare announcement of how much money changed hands (often accompanied by a disclaimer of actual liability) — unless the settlement is sealed, in which case we don't even find that out. It is true that settlement information has some precedential value: both plaintiffs' lawyers and defense lawyers share information about settlements to evaluate cases for future settlements. However, settlement information offers no reasons or reasoning, nothing to feed or provoke further argument. The relationship between settlements and judgments is like the relationship between a signal (such as a cry of unhappiness) and an explanation (such as a description of why I am unhappy). Both reveal information, but only the latter provides a basis for further conversation. A world without adjudication would be a world without public conversation about the strains of commitment that the law imposes. . . .

---

[*] Hannah Arendt, The Human Condition 22-78 (1958).

SETTLEMENTS AND THE PUBLIC REALM

Secret Settlements

The opacity of settlements is particularly troubling when their terms are secret. Kant once wrote: "All actions relating to the right of other human beings are wrong if their maxim is incompatible with publicity." This publicity principle lies at the core of democratic political morality. Although the principle has exceptions because political morality cannot dispense with all forms of secrecy and confidentiality, these exceptions are themselves governed by the publicity principle. That is, awarding officials the discretion to keep secrets or grant confidentiality is itself a policy that should be able to withstand public scrutiny. This section proposes that the widespread practice of secret settlements carves out an unacceptable area of exceptions to democratic publicity.

The basic scenario underlying sealed settlements arises in the field of products liability. Typically, a plaintiff sues a manufacturer and undertakes discovery. The manufacturer, concerned about the prospect of additional lawsuits by others, offers the original plaintiff a generous settlement in return for a promise of secrecy and the return of the discovery materials. Without the secrecy stipulations, there is no settlement. The parties submit the settlement agreement to the court, and ask the court for an order sealing the terms of the settlement. The court, eager to close the case, mindful that "facilitating the settlement of the case" is a stated objective of pretrial conferences under Rule 16 of the Federal Rules of Civil Procedure or its state equivalents, and understanding that the secrecy stipulations are the sine qua non for the plaintiff achieving a generous settlement, or perhaps any settlement at all, seals the records of the case.

Variations on this basic scenario can arise without this level of cooperation from the court. The parties can draft a contract exchanging money for confidentiality even before anyone files a lawsuit. In such a case, the court plays no role unless one of the parties breaches the contract. Alternatively, the parties can write a secret settlement contract before discovery. In that case, the court will be asked to seal nothing except the settlement contract itself. . . .

In 1989, the American Trial Lawyers Association began intensive political activity to curtail secret settlements and protective orders. Numerous state courts and legislatures also began deliberating over "open records" or "sunshine in litigation" rules. Two pioneering rules were adopted in Texas[12] and Florida,[13] and federal sunshine legislation has been introduced as well. Moreover, in three recent decisions, the Third Circuit created what amounts to a common-law open records rule for nondiscovery material.[14]

The Texas rule is paradigmatic of the sunshine laws. It creates a "presumption of openness" of court records to the general public. The rule permits sealing records

---

[12] Tex. R. Civ. P. Ann. R. 76a (West 1995) (stating that court records are open to the public and sealed only upon specific showing).

[13] Fla. Stat. §69.081 (1990) (sunshine in litigation statute prohibiting concealment of public hazards).

[14] United States v. A.D. PG Publishing Co. 28 F.3d 1353 (3d Cir. 1994); Pansy v. Borough of Stroudsburg, 23 F.3d 772 (3d Cir. 1994); Leucadia, Inc. v. Applied Extrusion Technologies, Inc. 998 F.2d 157 (3d Cir. 1993).

only when the case involves "a specific, serious and substantial interest which clearly outweighs: (1) this presumption of openness; (2) any probable adverse effect that sealing will have upon the general public health or safety" and when no less restrictive means will suffice to protect the interest. Significantly, court records include not only officially filed records, but also "settlement agreements not filed of record" and "discovery, not filed of record" if either concerns "matters that have a probable adverse effect upon the general public health or safety, or the administration of public office, or the operation of government, except discovery in cases originally initiated to preserve bona fide trade secrets or other intangible property rights." Hearings on any motion to seal court records are public, require public notice, and nonparties have a right to intervene. . . .

The biggest worry about sunshine regimes is that secret settlements may be the only way that a weak plaintiff who has suffered serious harm can obtain compensation. If judges make secrecy agreements unenforceable, a weak plaintiff may not receive a serious settlement offer and the case goes to trial. Since plaintiffs can demand a generous settlement in return for secrecy, and trials are expensive, banning secret settlements may cost plaintiffs money.

 Carrie Menkel-Meadow, **PUBLIC ACCESS TO PRIVATE SETTLEMENTS: CONFLICTING LEGAL POLICIES**

11 Alternatives to the High Cost of Litigation 85, 85-87 (1993)

Legal policy has long protected the confidentiality of negotiations designed to produce settlements. Yet a growing number of legal jurisdictions have been moving in the opposite direction — permitting, and in some cases mandating, disclosure of settlements. The context is an ever-expanding movement to require the disclosure of settlements dealing with public health and safety, hazards, public officials, public bodies or most broadly, "public issues." To that end, more and more states are passing new laws requiring disclosure of settlements, or revising their rules of procedure to modify common practices involving confidentiality of discovery, protective orders and sealing of litigation records. Inevitably, policies allowing public access to settlements where there is a "public interest" will clash with long-standing policies that encourage settlement by providing both an atmosphere for candid discussion and the protection of a confidential or sealed settlement.

WHO WANTS ACCESS?

A number of different interest groups, each with its own rationale, favor public disclosure of settlements. Public interest organizations seek both information about and disclosure of "public harms," ranging from environmental problems, to products liability to discrimination cases. Plaintiffs' lawyers want to share information in cases involving multiple injuries or potential harms and prevent the "first" plaintiff from securing a large settlement (in return for secrecy promises) at the expense of other injured victims. Elected and other public officials (including some judges and regulatory officials) believe that certain issues should almost always be aired in the public eye. The media seek to report disputes with "public implications," ranging from alleged corruption of public or private officials to public health and safety, products liability, antitrust, patent infringements and individual injuries. Press attempts to intervene as interested third parties and gain access to discovery or settlement proceedings pose starkly the question of what is public and what is private (see e.g. Cincinnati Gas & Elect. Co. v. General Electric, 854 F.2d 900 (6th Cir. 1988)). Do disputes between private individuals or organizations become public at a particular stage in the litigation process such as: the time of filing a lawsuit, conducting discovery, arguing a motion, participating in a summary jury trial or mandatory settlement conference? Of what relevance is the location of the proceeding: if the parties attend an early neutral evaluation conference at the court's request, for example, is that proceeding public even if it is held in a private law office (as is the case in the Northern District of California and a growing number of other federal jurisdictions)? Or, as some argue, is it the nature or subject matter of the dispute (public health and safety, hazards or "injuries" to the public, disputes involving public officials or agencies) that renders it ripe for public disclosure regardless of the timing or location of the proceeding?

HOW AND WHY IS PUBLIC ACCESS MANDATED?

Both the media and public interest groups have argued that a constitutional "right to know," derived from the First Amendment and other common law principles, provides a public right of access to any dispute that uses public institutions or fora, such as the courts. Another rationale is that there should be exceptions to the usual presumptions in favor of confidentiality when the public may be affected. Such exceptions must apply, for example, in cases involving utility rate setting, hazardous waste sites, products liability; and class actions in securities or discrimination matters. The claims here are that the public has the right to know if products are defective and likely to hurt them or that they live near hazardous waste sites or that the cost of consuming resources may rise. Although styled as individual lawsuits, the claims go, these are issues that affect us all. Some people who favor access perceive the courts as another instrument of public legal regulation, even if the parties to a given case are simply seeking to resolve their private dispute.

Efforts to make public the conduct of litigation and negotiations have been applied to discovery (challenging protective orders) and settlements (challenging the sealing of specific settlements or whole court files). For the most part, courts have continued to protect some secrecy and confidentiality interests in both the discovery and settlement contexts. They also have preferred to retain a case-by-case approach to protecting the broad scope of discovery and encouraging cooperation in both information disclosure and the settlement of cases (see Seattle Times v. Rhinehart, 467 U.S. 20 (1984); Wayne D. Brazil, Protecting the Confidentiality of Settlement Negotiations, 39 Hastings L.J. 955 (1988)). When considering challenges to confidentiality, courts look to such factors as whether the common law treats a particular event as public (a trial is, a negotiation discussion isn't) or whether particular documents are public records (discovery documents are rarely filed with the courts anymore), or whether there is some important public function (like monitoring of the judicial process) being served. But there are a variety of "hybrid" situations just waiting for litigation on issues of confidentiality. These may include early neutral evaluation procedures held in private law offices under the court's aegis, or mandatory settlement conferences held in courtrooms or judges' chambers.

Case law favoring confidentiality is being challenged in a variety of ways. Some state legislatures have passed statutes mandating disclosure of information and settlements, such as Florida's Sunshine in Litigation Law. In other states, procedural rules have been modified to shift the burdens of presumption away from confidentiality in the seeking of protective orders or sealing of records. Texas, for example, in Rule 76a creates a presumption of openness applied to unfiled discovery documents and settlement agreements that "have a probable adverse effect on public health and safety."

Challenges to settlement agreements can come from disgruntled third parties, renegade parties, the media and even sua sponte from the courts themselves. Some courts have allowed non-parties to an agreement to force disclosure of terms or to force disclosure of private side-agreements to publicly entered court orders (see e.g. Bank of America v. Hotel Rittenhouse Assoc., 800 F.2d 339 (3d Cir. 1986), *cert. denied*, 107 S. Ct. 921 (1987); Janus Films, Inc. v. Miller, 801 F.2d 578 (2d Cir. 1986)). Courts differ greatly in the scrutiny applied to private settlements in our party-initiated litigation system. With class action settlements and desires to make a private settlement an order of the court for enforcement purposes, the imprimatur of the court is clear. In other cases the role the court plays in facilitating a settlement in pre-trial conferences or elsewhere is less clear.

As the movement for openness in litigation expands, we are likely to see legal challenges at every level of the system — legislative, judicial and administrative — with all of the complexity and conflicting commands that such issues inevitably entail. . . .

WHAT'S NEXT?

The challenge facing legislatures and courts is how to balance the competing concerns. How can they make some matters accessible to the public when, for instance, there are significant public health, safety and accountability issues at stake, without at the same time destroying our system's ability to serve parties who seek to resolve their disputes amicably and privately? To the extent that privacy remains one of the reasons lawsuits are settled, some disputants will depart the public courts altogether rather than have their settlement made public. That prospect, already evident in the use of private judging and other private ADR mechanisms, raises questions about the legitimacy of the judicial process. In other cases, settlements will be pushed forward in time, before litigation is instituted. That strategy would preserve secrecy, but with the possible effect of rushing a settlement before an optimal exchange of information.

Those who seek full and open disclosure must also consider what harm is done to "innocent" third parties in the course of discovery or settlement negotiations, and even the occasional harm done to those who benefit from settlements. At a jurisprudential level, those who seek full openness in all cases must justify the transformation of our civil system from a voluntary (at least for plaintiffs), party-initiated system to one that will become literally just another arm of state regulation.

Some assurances of confidentiality and secrecy are often needed to insure the candor that is required to settle cases on the basis of party needs and interests that go beyond the legally relevant facts in cases and that might be damaging to the parties and others if released. These concerns motivate the many efforts to grant mediators and other third party intervenors confidentiality, privilege and immunity. It is ironic that in states like California competing bills are currently pending to increase confidentiality protections for some mediators, while other proposals seek to open up to greater public scrutiny a wide variety of alternative dispute resolution mechanisms.

Out of these competing concerns, one thing is clear: it is unlikely that one simple rule can govern all situations. Some parties may prefer to leave decisions about confidentiality up to judicial discretion and let the common law system do what it does best — make judgments on a case-by-case basis. Others may aim to legislate with greater precision — where real public harm is demonstrated and revelations of litigation information or settlement is the only or best way to prevent harm.

To improve both the quality and quantity of satisfactory settlements to legal problems, many interests need to be considered and balanced. Complete openness will likely thwart the legal process as much as facilitate it, and bright-line rules about public fora and public issues will not always be easily drawn. We are likely to see a volatile period of legislative and judicial activity in this area. During this confusing period of conflicting legal mandates, consumers and providers of dispute resolution services should continue to draft individualized contract terms to meet the needs of their dispute. They also should be fully cognizant of the legal conditions and restrictions of the jurisdictions in which dispute resolution is being conducted.

Notes and Questions

11.32 What are your views on whether settlements should be confidential? Does it matter what the case is about? Who the parties are? Do you favor procedural rules, legislation, or a case-by-case approach to deciding the competing issues here? See The Sedona Guidelines: Best Practices, Addressing Protective Orders, Confidentiality and Public Access in Civil Cases (Working Group on Protective Orders, Confidentiality and Public Access, WG2, Apr. 2005) (a working group of judges and lawyers exploring best practices for maintaining party confidentiality and public access to litigation).

11.33 Which conception of litigation or dispute resolution resonates more for you — the "problem-solving" conception or the "public-life" conception as described by Luban? Are disputes and cases either-or, or could they be both at the same time? In a response to Luban, Carrie Menkel-Meadow suggests that it is hard to answer this question because it is not always clear who "owns" the dispute — the disputants (in our party-initiated litigation system) or the public realm in which the disputing institutions are situated. See Carrie Menkel-Meadow, Whose Dispute Is It Anyway? A Philosophical and Democratic Defense of Settlements (in Some Cases), 83 Geo. L.J. 2663 (1995).

G. JUDICIAL REVIEW OF NEGOTIATED SETTLEMENTS

As discussed above, in general a negotiated settlement of litigation is not reviewed by the court, except in special circumstances. A negotiated settlement of a lawsuit, usually culminating in a release of claims and liability, with duties to be performed (such as the payment of money), is a contract and usually will be looked at by a court only if there is a claim of breach of that agreement. In a few specialized situations, by law, however, courts will scrutinize settlement agreements. You saw one example above in the mandatory court review of a class action settlement. Consent decrees after large institutional litigation, whether class actions or not, are often monitored by courts or special masters for compliance. Most divorce settlements are entered into court records (in order to have a judicial judgment and decree of divorce), but there is little substantive scrutiny of the agreement itself. Probate settlements are also entered into court records, which are subject to probate rules. And there are a few other specialized areas where courts review agreements at the time they are made (as contrasted to after the fact, if one party claims a contract breach or infirmity and challenges the settlement).

The case below is a classic for negotiators. Because the court was required to review the negotiated settlement of a personal injury claim of a minor, the court learned about some of the internal behavior in the negotiation and ruled on an important ethical lapse. In the case, a minor's father sued defendants for an automobile accident in which his son was injured. The boy was examined by plaintiff's own physician and by the defendant's physician. The defendant's physician discovered an aortic aneurysm, which was disclosed to the defendant's lawyer, who did not disclose it to the plaintiff's lawyer. Without knowing about the aneurysm, the plaintiff settled for $6,500. Subsequently, the plaintiff learned about his son's condition, which required further surgery, and he then sued for additional damages since it appeared that the condition had been caused by the accident. The legal issue presented was whether the settlement agreement should be vacated because of the condition that defendant knew about but did not disclose at the time of the settlement. The court vacated the settlement and, in so doing, laid down some now famous rules about what lawyers in negotiation might have to disclose to the other side. Consider, however, the specific facts of the case below and whether such failures to disclose would come to light (or to court!) in most ordinary lawsuit settlement negotiations.

❖ **SPAULDING v. ZIMMERMAN**

263 Minn. 346, 116 N.W.2d 704 (1962)

... The principles applicable to the court's authority to vacate settlements made on behalf of minors and approved by it appear well established. With reference thereto, we have held that the court in its discretion may vacate such a settlement, even though it is not induced by fraud or bad faith, where it is shown that in the accident the minor sustained separate and distinct injuries which were not known or considered by the court at the time settlement was approved and even though the releases furnished therein purported to cover both known and unknown injuries resulting from the accident. The court may vacate such a settlement for mistake even though the mistake was not mutual in the sense that both parties were similarly mistaken as to the nature and extent of the minor's injuries, but where it is shown that one of the parties had additional knowledge with respect thereto and was aware that neither the court nor the adversary party possessed such knowledge when the settlement was approved. . . .

From the foregoing it is clear that in the instant case the court did not abuse its discretion in setting aside the settlement which it had approved on plaintiff's behalf while he was still a minor. It is undisputed that neither he nor his counsel nor his medical attendants were aware that at the time settlement was made he was suffering from an aorta aneurysm which may have resulted from the accident. The seriousness of this disability is indicated by Dr. Hannah's report indicating the imminent danger of death there from. This was known by counsel for both defendants but was not disclosed to the court at the time it was petitioned to approve the settlement. While no canon of ethics or legal obligation may have required them to inform plaintiff or his counsel with respect thereto, or to advise the court therein, it did become obvious to them at the time, that the settlement then made did not contemplate or take into consideration the disability described. This fact opened the way for the court to later exercise its discretion in vacating the settlement and under the circumstances described we cannot say that there was any abuse of discretion on the part of the court in so doing under Rule 60.02(6) of Rules of Civil Procedure. . . .

Notes and Questions

11.34 You saw in Chapter 10 how a wife discovered her representative's arithmetic error of property value in Stare v. Tate, 98 Cal. Rptr. 264 (Cal. Ct. App. 1971), when her husband wrote gleefully to claim "victory" in the divorce negotiation by taking advantage of the (known) error. Because the husband opened his mouth to have the last laugh, the court did more than "review" the agreement, following the wife's claim for rescission after fraud or mistake; the court reformed the contract and gave the wife the benefit of the bargain — in large measure to "punish" the husband's professionals for not informing the wife of the error in calculations.

11.35 Under ethics rules and other regulations, there are now certain clear rules (in some areas) about what must be disclosed in negotiations (such as the death of a client, arithmetic errors, or some unilateral mistakes known to one party, such as in Stare v. Tate). See Nathan Crystal, The Lawyer's Duty to Disclose Material Facts in Contract or Settlement Negotiation, 87 Ky. L.J. 1055 (1998); Patrick Emery Longan, Ethics in Settlement Negotiations, Foreword, 52 Mercer L. Rev. 807 (2001). The tricky enforcement question here is, under what circumstances will "the other party" or a court ever know whether someone is not disclosing something if negotiations are conducted privately and without substantive court review?

11.36 Do you think all settlement agreements should be reviewed for fairness or full disclosures by courts? What would happen to negotiation (and litigation) if that happened? Some have argued that negotiated settlements should "track" the legal results of reported precedents. See, e.g., Robert Condlin, Bargaining in the Dark: The Normative Incoherence of Lawyer Dispute Bargaining Role, 51 Md. L. Rev. 1 (1992); Judith Maute, Public Values and Private Justice: A Case for Mediator Accountability, 4 Geo. Legal Ethics 503 (1991). Do you think negotiated settlements should be reviewed for whether they are consistent with or "follow" the relevant precedent?

11.37 Courts, and juries also, get to examine settlement agreements and the negotiation behaviors that produced them on the rare occasion when lawyers are sued for malpractice, though suits for negotiation malpractice are rare precisely because what a lawyer does in a legal negotiation is not visible to anyone but his opponent, who has a strong interest in having the settlement stick (usually!). Clients will seldom learn, as did the wife in Stare v. Tate, that their lawyers made a mistake, failed to disclose something, or negotiated badly and just made a bad deal. See Lynn Epstein, Post-Settlement Malpractice, Undoing the Done Deal, 46 Cath. U. L. Rev. 453 (1997); Rex Perschbacher, Regulating Lawyer's Negotiations, 27 Ariz. L. Rev. 75 (1985).

H. TAXATION OF NEGOTIATED SETTLEMENTS AND ATTORNEYS' FEES

The final legal issue in negotiation we take up here is to remind you that the Internal Revenue Service is always sitting at the bargaining table in both dispute and transactional negotiations. No good legal negotiator should ever conclude a negotiation without examining the tax consequences of the terms of the deal or agreement. In many cases, particularly in complex business deals, the tax consequences may very well dictate what terms are acceptable or preferable for the parties. So, if you are not a tax expert, be sure to consult a specialist in the subject matter of your negotiation before you agree to anything.

The settlement of lawsuits raises a host of important tax issues. Spousal support in divorce is treated as income to the ex-spouse receiving it, but child support is not; however, the person paying support can deduct spousal support, but not child support, so family dissolution negotiations often have issues of "characterization" of payments. Internal Revenue Code §104(a)(2) excludes from income damages received for "personal injuries or physical sickness," and so lawyers negotiating personal injury cases (and a variety of other kind of cases) try to have as much as possible of the damages paid characterized as personal injury. Punitive damages are taxable. So are strictly "emotional" damages not attributable to physical injuries. Structured settlements, or annuities paid over time and not in a lump sum, may also reduce tax liability for the recipient or at least spread the tax liability out over some years.

Recently, some important tax issues have affected an important area of legal negotiation — the settlement of employment discrimination and other civil rights lawsuits. The Supreme Court held in Commissioner v. Banks and Commissioner v. Banaitis, 125 S. Ct. 826 (2005), that attorneys' fees, granted to plaintiffs after prevailing in certain civil rights matters (such as employment discrimination), pursuant to the statutes like those at issue in Evans v. Jeff D. above, or contingent fees (portions of the total settlement paid to the attorney pursuant to agreement for payment for services of the attorney), are "income" to the plaintiff and taxable as such. The Court reached this conclusion by holding that the plaintiff's claim or cause of action was an income-generating asset that the plaintiff "controls." Consider that, in some cases, the attorneys' fee award could be larger than the monetary amount of settlement for damages, back pay, or other relief for the claim. In such cases, plaintiffs could actually experience net losses or debts after settling their cases by having to pay more in taxes than they actually receive in settlement of their cases. Fortunately, at about the same time the Supreme Court was considering these cases, Congress passed a statute that makes certain classes of attorneys' fees deductible for plaintiffs in some civil rights and employment cases (but does not affect all fee-shifting statutes, such as in some environmental, torts, and other government-related litigation), prospectively only. See Jobs Creation Act of 2004, Pub. L. No. 108-357, 118 Stat. 1418 (2004). For a comprehensive discussion of these issues, arguing that the Court's (and IRS's) treatment of this issue undermines the purposes of the fee-shifting statutes (granting attorneys' fees to prevailing plaintiffs in certain classes of cases), see Stephen B. Cohen, Misassigning Income: The Supreme Court and Attorneys' Fees, forthcoming (arguing that the attorney fee is economically earned by the lawyer for his labor and thus, is taxable income to the attorney, but not to the plaintiff); Stephen Cohen & Laura Sager, Discrimination Against Discrimination Damages, 35 Harv. J. Legis. 447 (1998); Stephen B. Cohen & Laura Sager, How the Income Tax Undermines Civil Rights Law, 73 So. Cal. L. Rev. 1075 (2000).

By now, you should realize why you went to law school. Negotiating legal claims and transactions is far more complicated than the everyday negotiations for consumer goods, jobs, cars, and personal favors. Negotiations that implicate the law are complicated. To be a good legal negotiator, you must master all the concepts and skills in this book, as well as at least know about the potential legal consequences of each negotiated agreement, so that you can research what relevant laws may affect your negotiation. As Mnookin and Kornhauser tell us, "bargaining does occur in the shadows" of many different kinds of laws. As you conduct negotiations in this course, you should always be asking these questions: What is the role of law in this negotiation? What laws do I need to know or learn about? How will certain legal endowments, requirements, duties, or liabilities affect what I can and cannot accomplish here?

PART IV | COMPLEX NEGOTIATION PROCESSES

Chapter 12   Multiparty Negotiation

If two heads are better than one, are three heads better than two?

— Anonymous

Most modern conflicts and disputes involve more than just two parties (a plaintiff and a defendant) and many more than one or two issues. Even a simple personal injury case involves multiple parties — the injured party, his or her family members, insurance companies, employers, manufacturers, or retailers. Complex cases or disputes such as class actions, mass torts, civil rights cases, environmental matters, corporate cases, and regulatory matters always involve more than two parties.

Much of what is studied in negotiation assumes two parties in dyadic negotiation (or two disputants with their third-party "neutral," an arbitrator, mediator, or judge). Increasingly, those who study dispute resolution have been interested in analyzing how what we know about negotiation might have to be adapted when there are more than two or three parties. Many new forms of conflict resolution are specially designed to deal with multiparty processes, both in public and governmental settings and in private disputes. Indeed, the use of conflict and dispute resolution theory and practice has created not just new processes, but whole new institutions in which negotiation and other forms of consensual decision making now take place. These include negotiated rule making ("reg-neg"), consensus-building fora in the setting of public policy or in the resolution of particularly intractable disputes (such as in environmental siting or community disputes). International disputes also must focus on multiple parties and new fora for negotiation and other forms of dispute resolution, such as multitrack diplomatic negotiations.

As you learn in this chapter about some of these new processes and institutions, consider what propositions about negotiation are applicable in multiparty contexts and what new concepts, principles, or propositions are needed with multiple parties and multiple issues. Obviously, with more than two players, the dynamics change: Two may align against one, and coalitions can radically change the interactions. "Defections" and new alliances introduce another form of instability to what is already a dynamic process. In addition, processes with multiple parties are more complex and difficult to coordinate, and, for that reason, may need more formal management than other processes. Conflict is always dynamic, but with the addition of more than two, three, or five parties, these changes become even more complex, harder to predict, and more difficult to manage.

In this chapter, we explore some of the theoretical and empirical underpinnings of multiparty processes (such as coalitions and alliances), some of the new ways of conceptualizing and organizing multiparty processes, and some of the new institutions that are developing to formally provide assistance in multiparty negotiations. We also look at some of the practice and skill sets that improve these processes (meeting management, group process, and facilitation skills). And we assess the "appropriateness" of these processes, both in terms of functionality — how well they meet particular objectives and needs — and their moral and ethical integrity. For example, conflict resolution, dispute settlement, and policy formation, through multiparty negotiation processes, always raise issues about participation of the relevant stakeholders (interested parties) and who decides who should participate in and make decisions about a negotiation.

When multiple-party processes are used to settle legal disputes, make public policy, and resolve complex social issues, they raise important jurisprudential and philosophical issues about the separation of powers in our constitutional government, the kinds of "discourse" that are permitted in these "proceedings," and their relation to democracy and formal rules of governance.

A. THEORIES AND APPROACHES TO MULTIPARTY DISPUTE PROCESSES: HOW ARE THEY DIFFERENT?

The readings in this section suggest some of the ways in which multiparty negotiation may be different from dyadic (negotiation) or triadic (mediation or arbitration) processes. See if you can think of particular ways in which adding more parties changes some of the basic principles you have learned already about negotiation. For a good review of some of these issues, see Lawrence Susskind, Robert Mnookin, Lukasz Rozdeiczer & Boyd Fuller, What We Have Learned About Teaching Multiparty Negotiation, 21 Negot. J. 395 (2005).

 Robert H. Mnookin, **STRATEGIC BARRIERS TO DISPUTE RESOLUTION: A COMPARISON OF BILATERAL AND MULTILATERAL NEGOTIATIONS**

159(1) J. Institutional & Theoretical Econ. 199, 200, 201, 219 (2003)

Why do negotiations so often fail even when there are possible resolutions that would better serve disputants than protracted struggle? And why, when resolutions are achieved, are they so often sub-optimal for the parties, or are achieved only after heavy and avoidable costs?...[I have begun] to think through and compare the barriers to the negotiated resolution of conflict in bilateral and multilateral negotiations. For this initial foray, I will primarily focus on what I have previously called *strategic barriers* — those which arise from the efforts of "rational" bargainers to maximize individual returns, but may preclude the achievement of the greatest possible "gains in trade" at the lowest cost. In other words, strategic barriers are those that can cause rational-self-interested disputants to act in a manner that proves to be both individually and collectively disadvantageous.

I enter the multiparty world of strategic interaction with some trepidation. For one thing, the most conspicuous body of relevant theoretical scholarship is game theory, which explores issues of strategic interaction between rational self-interested actors. While suggestive, it is also limiting. The axiomatic approach of game theoretical work on "n-person games" is mathematically daunting, has restricted descriptive power, and makes no claims at offering powerful prescriptive advice for negotiators. . . .

Nor is there very much theoretical work outside of game theory to build on. . . .

I suggest that Pareto-criterion may not provide an appropriate standard to evaluate issues of efficiency in multiparty bargaining. In a two party case, any negotiated deal presumably better serves the parties than the *status quo*. The same could be said in a multiparty negotiation only if the consent of *every party* were necessary. A requirement of unanimity in multilateral negotiation, however, creates potential holdout problems that may pose severe strategic barriers to resolution. This problem can be mitigated if the consent of less than all the parties can permit action. But other problems may arise. If conditions of less than all are able to change the *status quo*, this necessarily means that a party left out of a coalition may potentially be made worse off.

A variety of procedural rules may permit decision-making without unanimity in multiparty negotiations. Majority voting is but one of many possible mechanisms to allocate decision-making authority. The outcome of any multilateral negotiation can be profoundly affected by these procedural rules and various decisions about agenda. [Elsewhere I explore] the application of an unusual procedural rule — the "sufficient consensus" standard — that was employed in the multiparty "constitutional" negotiations in South Africa and in Northern Ireland. . . .

[M]y own belief is that no theoretical perspective, and no single discipline, has a monopoly on useful insights concerning the barriers to the fair and efficient resolution of conflict. Indeed, I suspect that progress will turn very fundamentally on the ability of people from different disciplines to learn from one another and to work together to improve theory and practice. Our goal should ultimately be to go beyond simply understanding why negotiations sometimes fail and sometimes succeed — it should be to help us overcome the barriers and achieve more consistent success in the negotiated resolution of conflict.

Leigh Thompson, THE MIND AND HEART OF THE NEGOTIATOR

208-214, 217-222 (3d ed. 2005)

MULTIPARTY NEGOTIATIONS

A **multiparty negotiation** is a group of three or more individuals, each representing their own interests, who attempt to resolve perceived differences of interest. For example, a group of individuals who must collectively prepare and present a group project for a course grade is involved in a multiparty negotiation, as is a group of specialists in an architectural firm who must design a house for a client. The parties to a negotiation may be individuals, teams, or groups. The involvement of more than two principals at the negotiation table complicates the situation enormously: Social interactions become more complex, information-processing demands increase exponentially, and coalitions can form. In the dyadic case, parties cannot reach settlement without the consent of the opponent; however, in multiparty negotiations, parties can exclude individuals from an agreement. . . .

KEY CHALLENGES OF MULTIPARTY NEGOTIATIONS

There are several challenges at both the cognitive (mind) and the emotional (heart) level that crop up in multiparty negotiations. We present four key challenges of multiparty negotiations [dealing with coalitions, formulating trade-offs, voting and majority rule, and communication breakdowns] and follow with some practical advice.

Dealing with Coalitions

A key difference between two-party and group negotiations is the potential for two or more parties within a group to form a coalition to pool their resources and have a greater influence on outcomes. A **coalition** is a (sub)group of two of more individuals who join together in using their resources to affect the outcome of a decision in a mixed-motive situation involving at least three parties. For example, parties may seek to maximize control over other members, maximize their status in the group, maximize similarity of attitudes and values, or minimize conflict among members. Coalition formation is one way that otherwise weak group members may marshal a greater share of resources. Coalitions involve both cooperation and competition. Members of coalitions cooperate with one another in competition against other coalitions, but compete against one another regarding the allocation of rewards the coalition obtains. . . .

Formulating Trade-Offs

Integrative agreements are more difficult to fashion in multiparty negotiations because the trade-offs are more complex. The issues may be linked, making trade-offs across issues difficult to construct. Moreover, in a multiparty negotiation, integrative trade-offs may be achieved either through circular or reciprocal logrolling. **Circular logrolling** involves trade-offs that require each group member to offer another member a concession on one issue while receiving a concession from yet another group member on a different issue. A circular trade-off is typified by the tradition of drawing names from a hat to give holiday gifts to people. People receive a gift from one person and give a gift to yet another person. Ideally, we give gifts that are more appreciated by the recipient than by the giver. In contrast, **reciprocal trade-offs** are fashioned between two members of a larger group. Reciprocal trade-offs are typified in the more traditional form of exchanging presents. Circular trade-offs are more risky than reciprocal trade-offs because they involve the cooperation of more than two group members.

Voting and Majority Rule

Groups often simplify the negotiation of multiple issues among multiple parties through voting and decision rules. However, if not used wisely, decision rules can thwart effective negotiation, both in terms of pie expansion and pie slicing. There are a number of problems associated with voting and majority rule that we will now describe.

Problems with Voting and Majority Rule

Voting is the procedure of collecting individuals' preferences for alternatives on issues and selecting the most popular alternative as the group choice. The most common procedure used to aggregate preferences of team members is **majority rule**. However, majority rule presents several problems in the attainment of efficient negotiation settlements. Despite its democratic appeal, majority rule fails to recognize the strength of individual preferences. One person in a group may feel very strongly about an issue, but his or her vote counts the same as the vote of someone who does not have a strong opinion about the issue. Consequently, majority rule does not promote integrative trade-offs among issues. In fact, groups negotiating under unanimous rule reach more efficient outcomes than groups operating under majority rule.

Although unanimity rule is time consuming, it encourages group members to consider creative alternatives to expand the size of the pie and satisfy the interests of all group members. Because strength of preference is a key component in the fashioning of integrative agreements, majority rule hinders the development of mutually beneficial trade-offs. Voting in combination with other decision aids, such as agendas, may be especially detrimental to the attainment of efficient outcomes because it prevents logrolling.

Other problems arise with voting. Within groups that demonstrate "egoistic" motives (as opposed to pro-social), majority rule leads to more distributive and less integrative behaviour. Group members may not agree upon a method for voting; for example, some members may insist upon unanimity, others may argue for a simple majority rule, and still others may advocate a weighted majority rule. Even if a voting method is agreed upon, it may not yield a choice. For example, a group may not find a majority if the group is evenly split. Voting does not eliminate conflicts of interest, but instead, provides a way for group members to live with conflicts of interest; for this reason, majority rule decisions may not be stable. In this sense, voting hides disagreement within groups, which threatens long-term group and organizational effectiveness.

Voting Paradoxes

Consider a three-person (Raines, Warner, and Lassiter) product development team. The three are in conflict over which design to use — A, B, or C.

The preference ordering is depicted in Table 9-1. Everyone is frustrated, and the group has argued for hours. As a way of resolving the conflict, Warner suggests voting between designs A and B. In that vote A wins, and B is tossed in the trash. Warner then proposes that the group vote between A and C. In that vote, C wins. Warner then declares that design C be implemented. Lassiter concludes that the group vote was fair and agrees to develop design C. However, Raines is perplexed and suggests taking another vote. Warner laughs and says, "We just took a vote and you lost — so just accept the outcome!" Raines glares at Warner and says, "Let's do

Table 9-1
Managers' Preferences for Product Designs

MANAGER	DESIGN A	DESIGN B	DESIGN C
Raines	1	2	3
Warner	2	3	1
Lassiter	3	1	2

the vote again, and I will agree to accept the outcome. However, this time I want us to vote between B and C first." Warner has no choice but to go along. In this vote B is the clear winner, and C is eliminated. Next, the vote is between A and B, and A beats B. Raines happily declares A the winner. Lassiter then jumps up and declares that the whole voting process was fraudulent, but cannot explain why.

Raines, Warner, and Lassiter are victims of the **Condorcet paradox**. The Condorcet paradox demonstrates that the winners of majority rule elections will change as a function of the order in which alternatives are proposed. Alternatives that are proposed later, as opposed to earlier, are more likely to survive sequential voting. Thus, clever negotiators arrange to have their preferred alternatives entered at later stages of a sequential voting process.

The unstable voting outcomes of the product development team point to a larger concern, known as the **impossibility theorem**. This theorem states that the derivation of group preference from individual preference is indeterminate. Simply put, no method can combine group member's preferences that guarantees that group preference is maximized when groups have three or more members and are facing three or more options. In other words, even though each manager's preferences are transitive, the group-level preference is intransitive.

Strategic Voting

The problem of indeterminate group choice is further compounded by the temptation for members to **strategically misrepresent** their true preferences so that a preferred option is more likely to be favored by the group. For example, a group member may vote for his least-preferred option to ensure that the second choice option is killed. Raines could have voted strategically in the first election to ensure that his preferred strategy was not eliminated in the first round.

Consensus Decisions

Consensus agreements require the consent of all parties to the negotiation before an agreement is binding. However, consensus agreements do not imply unanimity. For an agreement to be unanimous, parties must agree inwardly as well as outwardly. Consensus agreements imply that parties agree publicly to a particular settlement, even though their private views about the situation may be in conflict.

Although consensus agreements are desirable, they precipitate several problems. They are time consuming because they require the consent of all members, who are often not in agreement. Second, they often lead to compromise, in which parties identify a lowest common denominator acceptable to all. Compromise agreements are an extremely easy method of reaching agreement and are compelling because they appear to be fair, but they are usually inefficient because they fail to exploit potential Pareto-improving trade-offs.

Communication Breakdowns

Most people take communication for granted in their interactions with multiple parties. In a perfect communication system, a sender transmits or sends a message that is accurately received by a recipient. There are at least three points of possible error: The sender may fail to send a message; the message may be sent, but is inaccurate or distorted; or an accurate message is sent, but is distorted or not received by the recipient. In a multiparty environment, the complexity grows when several people are simultaneously sending and receiving messages.

Private Caucusing

When groups grow large, communication among all parties is difficult. One way of simplifying negotiations is for negotiators to communicate in smaller groups, thereby avoiding full-group communication. Group members often form private caucuses for strategic purposes. However, private caucusing may cause problems. Full-group communication is more time consuming but enhances equality of group members' outcomes, increases joint profitability, and minimizes perceptions of competition. However, there is a caveat to the benefits of full communication. When the task structure requires group members to logroll in a reciprocal fashion (as opposed to a circular fashion), restricted communication leads to higher joint outcomes than full communication. . . .

Perspective-Taking Failures

People are remarkably poor at taking the perspective of others. For example, people who are privy to information and knowledge that they know others are not aware of nevertheless act as if others are aware of it, even though it would be impossible for the receiver to have this knowledge. This problem is known as the **curse of knowledge**. For example, in a simulation, traders who possessed privileged information that could have been used to their advantage behaved as if their trading partners also had access to the privileged information. Perspective-taking deficiencies also explain why some instructors who understand an idea perfectly are unable to teach students the same idea. They are unable to put themselves in their students' shoes to explain the idea in a way the students can understand. . . .

Multiple Audience Problem

In some negotiation situations, negotiators need to communicate with another person in the presence of someone who should not understand the message. For example, consider a couple selling a house having a face-to-face discussion with a potential buyer. Ideally, the couple wants to communicate information to one another in a way that the spouse understands but the buyer does not — better yet, in such a way that the buyer is not even aware that a surreptitious communication is taking place. [This is called] the **multiple audience problem**. . . .

COALITIONS

Coalitions face three sets of challenges: (1) the formation of the coalition, (2) coalition maintenance, and (3) the distribution of resources among coalition members. Next, we take up these challenges and provide strategies for maximizing coalition effectiveness.

KEY CHALLENGES OF COALITIONS

Optimal Coalition Size

Ideally, coalitions should contain the minimum number of people sufficient to achieve a desired goal. Coalitions are difficult to maintain because members are tempted by other members to join other coalitions, and agreements are not enforceable.

Trust and Temptation in Coalitions

Coalitional integrity is a function of the costs and rewards of coalitional membership; when coalitions are no longer rewarding, people will leave them. Nevertheless, there is a strong pull for members of coalitions to remain intact even when it is not rational to do so. According to the **status quo bias** even when a new coalition structure that offers greater gain is possible, members are influenced by a norm of **coalitional integrity**, such that they stick with their current coalition. The implication is that negotiators should form coalitions early so as to not be left without coalitional partners.

Dividing the Pie

The distribution of resources among members of coalitions is complex because a normative method of fair allocation does not exist (Raiffa 1982).[*] To illustrate this consider the following example. Lindholm, Tepe, and Clauson are three small firms producing specialized products, equipment, and research for the rehabilitation medicine community. This area has become a critical, high-growth industry, and each firm is exploring ways to expand and improve its technologies through innovations in the research and development (R&D) divisions. Each firm has recently applied for R&D funding from the National Rehabilitation Medicine Research Council (NRMR).

The NRMR is a government agency dedicated to funding research in rehabilitation medicine and treatment. The NRMR is willing to provide funds for the proposed research, but because the firms' requests are so similar, they will fund only a **consortium** of two or three firms. The NRMR will not grant funding to Lindholm, Tepe, or Clauson alone.

The largest of the three firms is Lindholm, followed by Tepe, and then Clauson. The NRMR took a variety of factors into consideration when [it] set caps on funding, as shown in Table 9-3.

---

[*] Howard Raiffa, The Art and Science of Negotiation (1982).

Table 9-3
Maximum Funding Caps as a Function of Parties in Consortium

ORGANIZATION IN CONSORTIUM	CAP FOR R&D FUNDING
Lindholm alone	0
Tepe alone	0
Clauson alone	0
Lindholm and Tepe	$220,000
Lindholm and Clauson	$190,000
Tepe and Clauson	$150,000
Lindholm, Tepe, and Clauson	$240,000

The NRMR has strictly stipulated that for a consortium of firms to receive funding, the parties in the consortium (either two or three firms) must be in complete agreement concerning the allocation of resources among firms.

If you are Lindholm, what consortium would you consider to be the best for you? Obviously, you want to be in on some consortium, with either Tepe or Clauson or both, to avoid being left out in the cold. But what is the best division of resources within each of those consortiums? Suppose that you approach Tepe about a two-way venture, and Tepe proposes that she receive half of the $220,000 or $110,000 for herself. You argue that because you are bigger, and bring more synergy to the agreement, you should earn more. You demand $200,000 for yourself, leaving $20,000 for Tepe. At this point, Tepe threatens to leave you and approach Clauson. Tepe argues that she and Clauson can command $150,000 as a consortium without you, and each can receive $75,000. At this point, you argue that you can outbid her offer to Clauson with $80,000 and keep $110,000 for yourself. Just as Tepe is threatening to overbid you for Clauson, Clauson steps in and tells Tepe that she would want at least $100,000 of the $150,000 pie that she and Tepe could command. Tepe is frustrated, but relents.

You get nervous in your role as Lindholm. You certainly do not want to be left out. You could attempt to get Clauson or Tepe in a consortium. But, then, a thought occurs to you: Maybe all three of you can be in a consortium. After all, all three firms command the greatest amount of funding ($240,000). But how should the $240,000 be divided between the three of you? You are the biggest firm, so you propose that you keep half of the $240,000 (or $120,000), that Tepe get $80,000, and that Clauson get $40,000. This strikes you as fair. At this point, Clauson gets upset and tells you that she and Tepe can go it alone and get $150,000. She thinks that your share is unfair and should be reduced to something less than $90,000. You then remind Clauson that you and Tepe can get $190,000 together, of which you certainly deserve at least half, which is better than the $90,000 offer. Then the three of you are at it again in a vicious circle of coalition formation and demolition.

The negotiation between Lindholm, Tepe, and Clauson illustrates the unstable nature of coalitions. In this example, the left-out party is always able to approach one of the two parties in the coalition and offer him or her a better deal, which can then be beaten by the remaining party, ad infinitum. Furthermore, splitting the pie three ways seems to offer no obvious solution. So, what should the three parties do? Is there a solution? Or are the parties destined to go around in circles forever?

Getting Out of the Vicious Circle

As a way out of the vicious circle, let's conceptualize the problem as a system of simultaneous equations to solve. Namely,

$$L + T \quad\quad = \$220{,}000$$
$$L + C \quad\quad = \$190{,}000$$
$$T + C \quad\quad = \$150{,}000$$
$$L + T + C \quad = \$240{,}000$$
$$L + T + C \quad = (\$220{,}000 + \$190{,}000 + \$150{,}000)/2$$
$$\quad\quad\quad\quad = \$560{,}000/2$$
$$\quad\quad\quad\quad = \$280{,}000 \text{ total funds needed}$$

However, it is impossible to solve all simultaneous equations. We are $40,000 short of satisfying each party's minimum needs. What should we do? Consider the following three solutions: the core solution, the Shapley solution, and a hybrid model.[*]

The Core Solution

The core solution is a set of alternatives that are undominated. An alternative is in the core if no coalition has both the power and desire to overthrow it.

The first step in computing the core solution is to determine what would be each party's share if there were no shortage of funds. Thus, we solve for L, T, and C shares as follows:

$$(L + T) - (L + C) \quad = \$220{,}000 - 190{,}000$$
$$\quad\quad\quad\quad\quad = (T - C) = \$30{,}000$$
$$(L + T) - (T + C) \quad = \$220{,}000 - \$150{,}000$$
$$\quad\quad\quad\quad\quad = (L - C) = \$70{,}000$$
$$(T + C) + (T - C) \quad = \$150{,}000 + \$30{,}000$$
$$\quad\quad\quad\quad\quad 2T = \$180{,}000$$
$$\quad\quad\quad\quad\quad T = \$90{,}000$$

---

[*] Howard Raiffa, The Art and Science of Negotiation (1982).

$$L + T = \$220,000$$
$$L + \$90,000 = \$220,000$$
$$L = \$220,000 - \$90,000$$
$$L = \$130,000$$
$$L + C = \$190,000$$
$$\$130,000 + C = \$190,000$$
$$C = \$190,000 - \$130,000$$
$$C = \$60,000$$

check:

$$L = \$130,000$$
$$T = \$90,000$$
$$C = \$60,000$$
$$\text{Total} = \$280,000$$

Thus, if we had a total of $280,000, we could solve each equation. But, the harsh reality is that we do not. So, the second step is to get the total down to $240,000 by deducting $40,000 from somewhere. In the absence of any particular argument as to why one party's share should be cut, we deduct an equal amount, $13,333, from each party's share. In the final step, we compute the "core" shares as follows:

Lindholm:	$116,670
Tepe:	$ 76,670
Clauson:	$ 46,670

As Lindholm, you are delighted. Tepe agrees, but Clauson is not happy. She thinks that $46,670 is too little. She hires an outside consultant to evaluate the situation. The consultant proposes a different method, called the Shapley model.

The Shapley Model

Consider a coalition formation in which one player starts out alone and then is joined by a second and third player. The Shapley model determines the overall payoff a player can expect on the basis of his or her **pivotal power**, or the ability to change a losing coalition into a winning coalition. The consultant considers all possible permutations of players joining coalitions one at a time. The marginal value added to each coalition's outcome is attributed to the pivotal player. The Shapley value is the mean of a player's added value (see Table 9-4). When all players bring equal resources, the Shapley value is the total amount of resources divided by the total number of people. This, of course, is the "equal division" principle, as well as the "equity principle."

Table 9-4
Analysis of Pivotal Power in Shapley Model

ORDER OF JOINING	LINDHOLM ADDED VALUE	TEPE ADDED VALUE	CLAUSON ADDED VALUE
LTC	0	$220,000	$20,000
LCT	0	50,000	190,000
TLC	$220,000	0	20,000
TCL	90,000	0	150,000
CLT	190,000	50,000	0
CTL	90,000	150,000	0
Shapley (average)[2]	98,333	78,333	63,333

[2]These figures are rounded slightly.

When Clauson's consultant presents this report, Clauson is delighted—her share has increased by almost $20,000. Lindholm is nonplussed because her share has decreased. Tepe is tired of all the bickering and proposes that they settle for something in between the two proposed solutions.

Raiffa's Hybrid Model

We have presented two models to solve for shares in coalition situations. The medium-power player's share in both models is identical, but the high- and low-power player's shares fluctuate quite dramatically. It is possible that an egocentric argument could ensue between Lindholm and Clauson as to which model to employ. One solution is a hybrid model in which the mean of the Shapley and core values is computed. This model yields the following shares:

Lindholm: $107,500

Tepe: $ 77,500

Clauson: $ 55,000

Tips for Low-Power Players

We presented three different models of fair solutions. Each is compelling and defensible because each makes explicit the logic underlying the division of resources. It is easy to be a high-power player in coalition situations. However, the real trick is to know how to be an effective low-power player. Weakness can be power if you can recognize and disrupt unstable coalitions.

Power is intimately involved in the formation of coalitions and the allocation of resources among coalition members. Power imbalance among coalition members can be detrimental for the group. Compared to egalitarian power relationships, unbalanced power relationships produce more coalitions defecting from the larger group, fewer integrative agreements, greater likelihood of bargaining impasse, and more competitive behavior. Power imbalance makes power issues salient to group members, whose primary concern is to protect their own interests. What is best for the coalition is often not what is best for the organization.

Can an optimal way be found for multiple parties to allocate resources so that group members are not tempted to form coalitions that may hinder group welfare?

Usually not. Whereas there are several defensible ways to allocate resources among coalition members, there is no *single* best way. . . .

STRATEGIES FOR MAXIMIZING COALITIONAL EFFECTIVENESS

Make Your Contacts Early

Because of the commitment process, people tend to feel obligated to others with whom they have made explicit or implicit agreements. For this reason, it is important to make contact with key parties early in the process of multiparty negotiation before they become psychologically committed to others. . . .

Seek Verbal Commitments

One of the most effective strategies for enhancing coalitional effectiveness is to obtain verbal commitments from people with whom you want to develop trust and follow-through. Most people feel obligated to follow through with promises they make to others, even when verbal commitments are not legally binding in any sense. . . .

Use Unbiased-Appearing Rationale to Divide the Pie

Remember that "fairness" is a psychological construct and is the strongest determinant of negotiators' satisfaction with the outcome and consequently, their willingness to follow through on their verbal commitments. If one or more members of the coalition regard the proposed allocation of resources to be unfair, the coalition will be less stable and [members] will be likely to renege. To the extent to which coalitional members feel that the distribution of the coalition pie is fair, they are more likely to resist persuasion from others to break away from the coalition.

The question of how people behave in groups, whether forming coalitions or seeking to achieve something as a group, has long been the subject of study by sociologists and social psychologists. Not surprisingly, scholars have differed on whether people within a group become more solidified in their views (Irving Janis, Groupthink (2d ed. 1982); Robert B. Cialdini, Influence: The Psychology of Persuasion (rev. ed. 1993)), especially as "against" other groups, or whether individuals within groups resist collective thinking. This has important implications for forming coalitions among individuals and is even more complex when one tries to bring groups, organizations, or nations together for multiple-party negotiations in the political, commercial, policy, or international arenas. Legal scholar Cass Sunstein explores some of the implications of this research next.

 Cass R. Sunstein, **DELIBERATIVE TROUBLE? WHY GROUPS GO TO EXTREMES**

110 Yale L.J. 71, 73-78, 82, 85-86, 88-90, 105-106, 113-116 (2000)

Every society contains innumerable deliberating groups. Church groups, political parties, women's organizations, juries, legislative bodies, regulatory commissions, multimember courts, faculties, student organizations, those participating in talk radio programs, Internet discussion groups, and others engage in deliberation. It is a simple social fact that sometimes people enter discussions with one view and leave with another, even on moral and political questions. Emphasizing this fact, many recent observers have embraced the traditional American aspiration to "deliberative democracy," an ideal that is designed to combine popular responsiveness with a high degree of reflection and exchange among people with competing views. But for the most part, the resulting literature has not been empirically informed. It has not dealt much with the real-world consequences of deliberation, and with what generalizations hold in actual deliberative settings, with groups of different predispositions and compositions.

The standard view of deliberation is that of Hamilton and Rawls.* . . . Group discussion is likely to lead to better outcomes, if only because competing views are stated and exchanged. Aristotle spoke in similar terms, suggesting that when diverse people all come together . . . they may surpass — collectively and as a body, although not individually — the quality of the few best. . . . [W]hen there are many [who contribute to the process of deliberation], each has his share of goodness and practical wisdom. . . . [S]ome appreciate one part, some another, and all together appreciate all. But an important empirical question is whether and under what circumstances it is really true that "some appreciate one part, some another, and all together appreciate all."

My principal purpose in this Essay is to investigate a striking but largely neglected statistical regularity — that of group polarization — and to relate this phenomenon to underlying questions about the role of deliberation in the "public sphere" of a heterogeneous democracy. In brief, group polarization means that members of a deliberating group predictably move toward a more extreme point in the direction indicated by the members' predeliberation tendencies. "[L]ike polarized molecules, group members become even more aligned in the direction they were already tending." . . . Notably, groups consisting of individuals with extremist tendencies are more likely to shift, and likely to shift more; the same is true for groups with some kind of salient shared identity (like Republicans, Democrats, and lawyers, but unlike jurors and experimental subjects). When like-minded people are participating in "iterated polarization games" — when they meet regularly, without sustained exposure to competing views — extreme movements are all the more likely.

Two principal mechanisms underlie group polarization. The first points to social influences on behavior and in particular to people's desire to maintain their reputation and their self-conception. The second emphasizes the limited "argument pools" within any group, and the directions in which those limited pools lead group members. An understanding of the two mechanisms provides many insights into deliberating bodies. Such an understanding illuminates a great deal, for example, about likely processes within multimember courts, juries, political parties, and legislatures — not to mention ethnic groups, extremist organizations, criminal conspiracies, student associations, faculties, institutions engaged in feuds or "turf battles,"

---

* See Alexander Hamilton, The Federalist No. 70, at 426-427 in the Federalist Papers (Clinton Rossiter ed., 1961); John Rawls, A Theory of Justice 358-359 (1971).

workplaces, and families. At the same time, these mechanisms raise serious questions about deliberation from the normative point of view. If deliberation predictably pushes groups toward a more extreme point in the direction of their original tendency, whatever that tendency may be, is there any reason to think that deliberation is producing improvements?

One of my largest purposes is to cast light on enclave deliberation as simultaneously a potential danger to social stability, a source of social fragmentation, and a safeguard against social injustice and unreasonableness. Group polarization helps explain an old point, with clear constitutional resonances, to the effect that social homogeneity can be quite damaging to good deliberation. When people are hearing echoes of their own voices, the consequence may be far more than support and reinforcement. An understanding of group polarization thus illuminates social practices designed to reduce the risks of deliberation limited to like-minded people. Consider the ban on single-party domination of independent regulatory agencies, the requirement of legislative bicameralism, and debates, within the United States and internationally, about the value of proportional or group representation. Group polarization is naturally taken as a reason for skepticism about enclave deliberation and for seeking to ensure deliberation among a wide group of diverse people.

But there is a point more supportive of enclave deliberation: Participants in heterogeneous groups tend to give least weight to the views of low-status members — in some times and places, women, African Americans, less-educated people. Hence enclave deliberation might be the only way to ensure that those views are developed and eventually heard. Without a place for enclave deliberation, citizens in the broader public sphere may move in certain directions, even extreme directions, precisely because opposing voices are not heard at all. The ambivalent lesson is that deliberating enclaves can be breeding grounds both for the development of unjustly suppressed views and for unjustified extremism, indeed fanaticism. . . .

SOCIAL INFLUENCES AND CASCADES

A great deal of attention has recently been devoted to the topic of social influences on individual behavior. Because many of these influences are analogous to what happens in group polarization, and because they have a bearing on democratic deliberation as well, it is worthwhile to offer some brief notations here.

Social influences can lead groups to go quite rapidly in identifiable directions, often as a result of "cascade" effects involving either the spread of information (whether true or false) or growing reputational pressure. Sometimes cascade effects are highly localized, and lead members of particular groups, quite rationally, to believe or to do something that members of other groups, also quite rationally, find to be baseless or worse. Local cascades can ensure that different groups end up with very different, but equally entrenched, views about the same issues and events.

People frequently think and do what they think and do because of what they think relevant others think and do. Thus, for example, employees are more likely to file suit if members of the same work group have also done so; littering and non-littering behavior appear to be contagious; a good way to increase the incidence of tax compliance is to inform people of high levels of voluntary tax compliance; television networks tend to follow one another; and students are less likely to engage in binge drinking if they think that most of their fellow students do not engage in binge drinking, so much so that disclosure of low numbers of binge drinkers is one of the few successful methods of reducing binge drinking on college campuses.

HOW AND WHY GROUPS POLARIZE

How do small groups of like-minded people differ from large groups of heterogeneous people? What is likely to happen within isolated deliberating enclaves? How does all this bear on deliberative democracy? To answer these questions, and to understand the relationship between social processes within groups and democratic theory, it is necessary to have an understanding of group polarization.

Group polarization is among the most robust patterns found in deliberating bodies, and it has been found in many diverse tasks. Polarization "is said to occur when an initial tendency of individual group members toward a given direction is enhanced following group discussion." The result is that groups often make more extreme decisions than would the typical or average individual in the group (where "extreme" is defined solely internally, by reference to the group's initial dispositions). There is a clear relationship between group polarization and cascade effects: Both have a great deal to do with informational and reputational influences. An important difference is that group polarization, unlike cascade effects, involves deliberation. In addition, polarization may or may not involve a cascade-like process; polarization can result simply from simultaneous independent decisions to move toward the group extreme.

Though standard, the term "group polarization" is somewhat misleading. It is not meant to suggest that group members will shift to two poles, nor does it refer to an increase in variance among groups, though this may be the ultimate result. Instead the term refers to a predictable shift within a group discussing a case or problem. As the shift occurs, groups and group members move and coalesce, not toward the middle of antecedent dispositions, but toward a more extreme position in the direction indicated by those dispositions. The effect of deliberation is both to decrease variance among group members, as individual differences diminish, and also to produce convergence on a relatively more extreme point among predeliberation judgments. . . .

There have been two main explanations for group polarization. Both of these have been extensively investigated and supported. The first explanation of group polarization — social comparison — begins with the claim that people want to be perceived favorably by other group members and also to perceive themselves favorably. . . .

The second explanation is based on the commonsense intuition that any individual's position on an issue is partly a function of which arguments presented within the group seem convincing. The choice therefore moves in the direction of the most persuasive position defended by the group, taken as a whole. Because a group whose members are already inclined in a certain direction will have a disproportionate number of arguments going in that same direction, the result of discussion will be to move people further in the direction of their initial inclinations. The key is the existence of a limited argument pool, one that is skewed (speaking purely descriptively) in a particular direction. Hence there will be a shift in the direction of the original tilt.

There is a related possibility, not quite reducible to either of the two standard arguments, but incorporating elements of each. In their individual judgments, people are averse to extremes; they tend to seek the middle of the relevant poles. It is possible that when people are making judgments individually, they err on the side of caution, expressing a view in the direction that they really hold, but stating that view cautiously, for fear of seeming extreme. Once other people express supportive views, the relevant inhibition disappears, and people feel free to say what, in a sense, they really believe. There appears to be no direct test of this hypothesis, but it is reasonable to believe that the phenomenon plays a role in group polarization and choice shifts. . . .

DELIBERATIVE TROUBLE?

The central problem is that widespread error and social fragmentation are likely to result when like-minded people, insulated from others, move in extreme directions simply because of limited argument pools and parochial influences. As an extreme example, consider a system of one-party domination, which stifles dissent in part because it refuses to establish space for the emergence of divergent positions; in this way, it intensifies polarization within the party while also disabling external criticism.

In terms of institutional design, the most natural response is to ensure that members of deliberating groups, whether small or large, will not isolate themselves from competing views — a point with implications for multimember courts, open primaries, freedom of association, and the architecture of the Internet. Here, then, is a plea for ensuring that deliberation occurs within a large and heterogeneous public sphere, and for guarding against a situation in which like-minded people wall themselves off from alternative perspectives. . . .

It is important to ensure social spaces for deliberation by like-minded persons, but it is equally important to ensure that members of the relevant groups are not isolated from conversation with people having quite different views. The goal of that conversation is to promote the interests of those inside and outside the relevant enclaves, by subjecting group members to competing positions, by allowing them to exchange views with others and to see things from their point of view, and by ensuring that the wider society does not marginalize, and thus insulate itself from, views that may turn out to be right or at least informative. . . .

THE PUBLIC SPHERE AND APPROPRIATE HETEROGENEITY

For a designer or leader of any institution, it makes sense to promote ample social space both for enclave deliberation and for discussions involving a broad array of views, including views of those who have been within diverse enclaves. The idea of a "public sphere," developed most prominently by Jürgen Habermas,* can be understood as an effort to ensure a domain in which multiple views can be heard

---

* See Jürgen Habermas, The Structural Transformation of the Public Sphere: An Inquiry into a Category of Bourgeois Society 231-250 (Thomas Burger trans.,1989).

by people with multiple perspectives. This understanding strongly supports current initiatives designed to ensure deliberation among dissimilar people on the Internet. The fact of group polarization suggests that it could be desirable to take steps to reduce the likelihood that panels on federal courts of appeals consist solely of appointees of presidents of any single political party.

Of course, any argument pool will be limited. No one has time to listen to every point of view. But an understanding of group polarization helps show that heterogeneous groups are often a far better source of good judgments, simply because more arguments will be made available.

For a deliberative democracy, a central question is how to ensure appropriate heterogeneity. For example, it would not make sense to say that in a deliberating group attempting to think through issues of affirmative action, it is important to allow exposure to people who think that slavery was good and should be restored. The constraints of time and attention call for limits to heterogeneity; and — a separate point — for good deliberation to take place, some views are properly placed off the table, simply because time is limited and they are so invidious, or implausible, or both. This point might seem to create a final conundrum: To know what points of view should be represented in any group deliberation, it is important to have a good sense of the substantive issues involved, indeed a sense sufficient to generate judgments about what points of view must be included and excluded. But if we already know that, does deliberation have any point at all?

The answer is that we often do know enough to see which views count as reasonable, without knowing which view counts as right, and this point is sufficient to allow people to construct deliberative processes that should correct for the most serious problems potentially created by group polarization. What is necessary is not to allow every view to be heard, but to ensure that no single view is so widely heard, and reinforced, that people are unable to engage in critical evaluation of the reasonable competitors.

Of course, the provision of diverse views does not guarantee good deliberation. Among other things, most people are subject to "confirmation bias," in accordance with which exposure to a competing position will not dislodge and may even strengthen the antecedently held position. On questions of morality and fairness, and undoubtedly other questions as well, those who listen to diverse opinions may well emerge from the experience with an enhanced belief in the soundness of their original commitment. But this is not a universal phenomenon, and at least an understanding of competing views is likely to weaken the forms of fragmentation and misunderstanding that come from deliberation among the like-minded.

Notes and Questions

12.1 From these descriptions of the complexities of multiparty decision-making processes, including negotiation for consensual agreements or voting to resolve conflicts, can you begin to imagine how you might structure processes to facilitate the following:

a. The best possible process for a "good" decision

b. The best possible process for "maximum stakeholder participation"

c. The best possible process to avoid bad "group polarization" and promote optimal heterogeneity in participation?

Are these all the same thing, or do different end values suggest different process designs?

12.2 From these readings, what do you think about the stability of coalitions (multiple parties forming a group), groups, or even individuals within policy- or decision-making settings? How can policy be formed or conflicts or disputes "resolved" when there is instability? When there is too much stability (rigid adherence to a particular view, such as within an "enclave" as Sunstein describes it)?

12.3 What goals do you think are important to achieve in multiparty processes? Are those goals different from those in two- or three-party disputes or conflicts?

12.4 Can you think of a multiparty dispute you have been involved in? What issues were being resolved? What process was used? What would you have changed about the process?

12.5 Think about a major multiparty dispute in the public arena now (domestic or international). How would you structure a process to deal effectively with the issues and parties?

12.6 Consider whether there are or ought to be differences in process design for multiparty disputes that are public (governmental, international) or private. For a further discussion on activities that can precede or supplement large public policy disputes, see Jennifer Gerarda Brown et al., Negotiation as One Among Many Tools, 87 Marq. L. Rev. 853 (2004).

12.7 For an interesting application of these theories to a multiparty and multinational negotiation involving explicit efforts to "unify" or "disunify" the parties within and across coalitions, see Larry Crump, For the Sake of the Team: Unity and Disunity in a Multiparty Major League Baseball Negotiation, 21 Negot. J. 317 (2005). See also Andrew F. Daughety & Jennifer F. Reingamum, Economic Theories of Settlement Bargaining, 1 Ann. Rev. L. & Soc. Sci. 35 (2005) (exploring the economic externalities of multilateral bargaining in litigation settings).

Different kinds of problems (subject matter disputes) call up different kinds of participants (ad hoc interest groups, permanent organizations, or governmental institutions) who may speak in different languages (appeals to principles, reasons, logic, emotions, utilitarian interests or preferences, or moral, ethical, or religious norms). If negotiation is used in a wide variety of public and private settings to resolve conflicts, it will have to adapt to these different modes of discourse and to different institutional structures. Negotiation and conflict resolution theory have begun to affect political theory and political decision making in practice. Variously called *deliberative democracy* or *collaborative governance*, negotiation theorists and practitioners are studying how multiple groups in a society create the rules with which they govern themselves in constitutive or permanent situations (like constitutionmaking) and ad hoc policy decisions or law making. See, e.g., The Deliberative Democracy Handbook (John Gastil & Peter Levine eds., 2005); Archon Fong & Erik Olin Wright, Deepening Democracy: Institutional Innovations in Empowered Participatory Governance (2003); Carrie Menkel-Meadow, The Lawyer's Role(s) in Deliberative Democracy, 5 UNLV L. Rev. 347 (2004/2005).

The political scientist Jon Elster has compared the constitution-making processes of public, open, and plenary negotiation, which employed highly principled and politicized rhetoric in the French constitutional process to the more "secret," committee-based and "pragmatic bargaining" rhetoric of the American constitutional process. He suggests that sometimes "second best processes" (less transparent, more compromising, and less "principled") may make for better, more robust outcomes. (The American Constitution, even with its Civil War and many other amendments, has lasted far longer than the French.) See Jon Elster, The Strategic Uses of Argument, in Barriers to Conflict Resolution (Kenneth J. Arrow et al. eds., 1995). From this work of Elster's, Carrie Menkel-Meadow has elaborated a taxonomy of different modes of negotiation processes, to be used in different settings. Different kinds of processes may be structured with different goals, elaborating different modes of discourse (principled-reasons/bargaining-preference trading/appeals to emotion, passions, morality) with different structures of process (open-closed/plenary-committee/facilitated-led-naturalistic-leaderless) and different kinds of parties (ad hoc-temporary/permanent/constitutive), providing some illustrative examples of different kinds of group processes and decision making.

Carrie Menkel-Meadow, **INTRODUCTION: FROM LEGAL DISPUTES TO CONFLICT RESOLUTION AND HUMAN PROBLEM SOLVING**

in Dispute Processing and Conflict Resolution xxxi (2003)

MODES OF CONFLICT RESOLUTION*

MODE OF DISCOURSE	PRINCIPLED (REASONS)	BARGAINING (INTERESTS)	PASSIONS (NEEDS/ EMOTIONS/RELIGION)
FORMS OF PROCESS:			
Closed	Some court pro-ceedings; arbitration	Negotiation-U.S. Constitution; diplomacy	Mediation (e.g., divorce)
Open	French Constitution; courts; arbitration	Public negotiations; some labor	Dialogue movement
Plenary	French Constitution	Reg-Neg	Town meetings
Committees	Faculty committees; task groups	U.S. Constitution/ U.S. Congress	Caucuses-interest groups
Expert/Facilitator	Consensus building	Mini-trial	Public conversations
Naturalistic (Leaderless)			Grassroots organizing/ WTO protests
Permanent	Government; institutions	Business organizations; unions	Religious organizations; Alcoholics Anonymous; Weight Watchers
Constitutive	UN, national constitution	National constitu-tions/professional associations	Civil justice movements; peace
Temporary/Ad Hoc	Issue organizations/ social justice	Interest groups	Yippies; New Age; vigilantes

Principles = reasons, appeals to universalism, law
Bargaining = interests, preferences, trading, compromises

Open = public or transparent meetings or proceedings
Closed = confidential, secret process or even outcomes (settlements)

Plenary = full group participation, joint meetings
Committees = task groups, caucuses, parts of the whole

Expert-facilitator = led by expertise (process or substantive or both)
Naturalistic = leaderless, grassroots, ad hoc

Permanent = organizational, institutional
Constitutive = constitutional
Temporary = ad hoc groups or disputants

Some predicted effects of process on outcome:

Closed (confidential) proceedings allow more expression of interests, needs and passions = more "honest" and "candid," allow more "trades," less posturing, open to vulnerability

Open (transparent) proceedings require more principled/reasons justifications, produce more rigidity

---

* Partially derived from categories specified by Jon Elster, Strategic Uses of Argument, in Barriers to Conflict Resolution (Kenneth Arrow et al. eds., 1995).

Notes and Questions

12.8 How does private negotiated decision making (such as in commercial development or environmental waste siting) interact with public law requirements (zoning, regulation, and so on)? Must there be formal legal authority (the Constitution, zoning laws) to use these processes, antecedent to their use, or can the outcomes be legitimized or ratified *post hoc*, after "good" decisions are reached?

12.9 Who should convene these processes? Skilled process experts? Interested stakeholders? The government? How should these processes be evaluated? Who should participate? All the citizens? Interested stakeholders? Who decides?

12.10 Is it a good thing to "let a thousand flowers bloom" (Chairman Mao) in permitting many forms of decentralized decision making and processes ("devolution of power" to some)? Or should our government require equality (as in sameness) of process for decisions that it makes that affect many people in many different regions of the country? What is the relationship of informal or private dispute resolution processes to formal governmental federalism and separation of powers?

Perhaps the first effort to combine the insights of problem-solving negotiation theory with formal governmental processes in multiparty disputes and public policy setting was Philip Harter's development of the concept of negotiated rule making, otherwise known as *reg-neg*. His was really the first effort to actualize or operationalize the theory of formally recognizing negotiation theory in multiparty processes and granting governmental legitimacy to "alternative" processes based on negotiation and party participation. Following the publication of the article below, Congress enacted the Negotiated Rulemaking Act of 1990 (permitting these processes), 5 U.S.C. §§561-570 (2000), and multiparty negotiations in the form of reg-neg were employed in a variety of regulatory settings (occupational health and safety, food and drug administration, and environmental, to name a few). In 1996, these processes were more formally legitimated in the Administrative Dispute Resolution Act, 5 U.S.C. §§571-584 (2000). Though Harter's pathbreaking work has been influential primarily in federal policy making, many states have employed these processes (see Consensus Building Institute, at *http://www.cbuilding.org*, and Policy Consensus Institute, at *http://www.policyconsensus.org*, for many examples of state-level uses of these reg-neg or collaborative governance processes). Variations on this multiparty participation in negotiation have also been used in private disputes, such as those over land use and development, community issues, and racial and ethnic conflicts.

Philip J. Harter, NEGOTIATING REGULATIONS: A CURE FOR MALAISE

71 Geo. L.J. 1 (1982)

This article proposes that a form of negotiation among representatives of the interested parties, including administrative agencies, would be an effective alternative procedure to the current rulemaking process. Although virtually every rulemaking includes some negotiation, it is almost never the group consensus envisioned here. Negotiations among directly affected groups conducted within both the existing policies of the statute authorizing the regulation and the existing policies of the agency, would enable the parties to participate directly in the establishment of the rule. The significant concerns of each could be considered frontally. . . .

THE ADVANTAGES OF RULEMAKING BY NEGOTIATION

The idea of developing rules through negotiation among interested parties received brief attention when John Dunlop proposed it during his tenure as Secretary of Labor. Interest in the idea largely died before being translated into legal requirements or practice. Recently, however, a number of studies and articles have renewed the interest in using a form of negotiation to establish rules.

Negotiating has many advantages over the adversarial process. The parties participate directly and immediately in the decision. They share in its development and concur with it, rather than "participate" by submitting information that the decision maker considers in reaching the decision. Frequently, those who participate in the negotiation are closer to the ultimate decision making authority of the interest they represent than traditional intermediaries that represent the interest in an adversarial proceeding. Thus, participants in negotiations can make substantive decisions, rather than acting as experts in the decision making process. In addition, negotiation can be a less expensive means of decision making because it reduces the need to engage in defensive research in anticipation of arguments made by adversaries.

Undoubtedly the prime benefit of direct negotiation is that it enables the participants to focus squarely on their respective interests. They need not advocate and maintain extreme positions before a decision maker. Therefore, the parties can develop a feel for the true issues that lie within the advocated extremes and attempt to accommodate fully the competing interests. An example of this benefit occurred when a group of environmentalists opposed the construction of a dam because they feared it would lead to the development of a nearby valley. The proponents of the dam were farmers in the valley who were adversely affected by periodic floods. Negotiations between the two groups, which were begun at the behest of the governor, revealed a common interest in preserving the valley. Without the negotiations the environmentalists would have undoubtedly sued to block construction, and necessarily would have employed adversarial tactics. Negotiations, however, demonstrated the true interests of the parties and permitted them to work toward accommodation. . . .

Rulemaking by negotiation can reduce the time and cost of developing regulations by emphasizing practical and empirical concerns rather than theoretical predictions. In developing a regulation under the current system, an agency must prove a factual case, at least preliminarily, and anticipate the factual information that will be submitted in the record. Because the agency lacks direct access to empirical data, the information used is often of a theoretical nature derived from models. In negotiations, the parties in interest decide together what information is necessary to make a reasonably informed decision. Therefore, the data used in negotiations may not have to be as theoretical or as extensive as it is in an adversary process. For example, one agency proposed a regulation based on highly technical, theoretical data. The parties argued that the theoretical data was unnecessary because it simply did not reflect the practical experiences of the parties and of another agency. The agency determined the validity of the assertion and modified its regulation accordingly. The lesson of this example is that the data can emphasize practical and empirical concerns rather than theoretical predictions. In turn, this emphasis on practical experience can reduce the time and cost of developing regulations by reducing the need for developing extensive theoretical data.

Negotiation also can enable the participants to focus on the details of a regulation. In the adversary process, the big points must be hit and hit hard, while the subtleties and details frequently are overlooked. Or, even if the details are not overlooked, the decision maker may not appreciate their consequences. In negotiations, however, interested parties can directly address all aspects of a problem in attempting to formulate workable solutions.

Overarching all the other benefits of negotiations is the added legitimacy a rule would acquire if all parties viewed the rule as reasonable and endorsed it without a fight. Affected parties would participate in the development of a rule by sharing in the decisions, ranking their own concerns and needs, and trading them with other parties. Regardless of whether the horse under design turns out to be a five-legged camel or a Kentucky Derby winner, the resulting rule would have a validity beyond those developed under the current procedures. Moreover, nothing indicates that the results would be of any lesser quality than those developed currently. Surely the Code of Federal Regulations stable has as many camels as Derby winners. . . .

Genuine negotiation could be implemented under current law. Agencies could empanel representatives of the interests who have a stake in a rule and have them negotiate a proposed rule among themselves; the agency would then use the negotiated rule as the basis for a notice of proposed rulemaking. Agencies are understandably hesitant to do so, however. First, they would have to qualify the group as an advisory committee under the Federal Advisory Committee Act (FACA), which imposes various requirements not fully conducive to negotiations. Second, the full reach and applicability of judicially imposed ex parte rules is unclear. An agency may fear that a court would find it inappropriate to permit the parties to participate in a negotiated rulemaking when the avowed purpose of the negotiation is to develop a proposed rule for the agency. Several judicial decisions are sometimes read as casting doubt on the legality of all ex parte communications. Those decisions, however, probably can be limited to their facts because in each case the agency was importuned by and struck agreements with only a few parties; the agency did not develop a consensus among the range of affected interests. Thus, properly constituted committees and ex parte rules should not be insurmountable obstacles to the institution of negotiations in the rulemaking process. . . .

CONSENSUS STANDARDS . . .

Consensus standards are developed through a structured decision making process among representatives of interests materially affected by the standard. The parties frequently confront difficult value choices, such as trade offs between cost and safety.

Development of standards is, therefore, a form of regulatory negotiation, and their very existence demonstrates that complex, value-laden rules can be negotiated. Indeed, virtually every person in the United States daily entrusts his life to such negotiated rules, in the form of electrical and building codes, product safety standards, and workplace safety and health standards. Standards developed through a consensus process are available, however, only in situations in which a standards-writing organization can address adequately the issues raised by a proposed rule. . . .

NEGOTIATING REGULATIONS

What follows is a proposal designed to make negotiating rules attractive to agencies and to the affected private interests. It is derived from the accumulated experience in and analysis of areas in which policy has been negotiated. The proposal is also designed to provide appropriate legal safeguards to protect the rights of those affected by a regulation and to prevent abuse. Although these safeguards are based on traditional notions of administrative law, they are adapted to the negotiation situation. . . .

THE NEGOTIATIONS

1. Establishing the Ground Rules

Because the parties are unlikely to have previously engaged in negotiations among themselves, they need to establish the ground rules that will govern, or at least guide, the negotiations. . . . Therefore, defining the rules of acceptable conduct and the procedures under which negotiations will be conducted is important if the benefits of negotiation are to be realized. Although creative problem-solving can develop only with time, the rules can foster that process.

2. Rule of Reason

Milton R. Wessel has developed a set of dispute resolution principles that he calls the "Rule of Reason." Perhaps the fundamental application of the guidelines to negotiations is to remind the participants periodically that their purpose is to reach a mutually acceptable agreement when possible, not to seek victory for their positions. The parties should keep in mind that they must sort out, weigh, and accommodate conflicting interests. Thus, they need to be reminded of the give and take and good faith of the negotiation process.

The National Coal Policy Project used Wessel's Rule of Reason to develop its set of negotiating principles:

> Data should not be withheld from the other side. Delaying tactics should not be used. Tactics should not be used to mislead. Motives should not be impugned lightly. Dogmatism should be avoided. Extremism should be countered forcefully . . . but not in kind. Integrity should be given first priority.

The National Coal Policy Project found that "agreement to use these principles helped convince participants that [they] could resolve some of their differences constructively, and as it turned out, conducting project meetings in the spirit of the Rule of Reason did facilitate the search for workable solutions to the difficult issues being addressed." In essence, these principles establish a code of conduct designed to guide, to the extent possible, the participants in good faith negotiations.

3. Confidentiality

One significant issue the participants must face at the outset of negotiations is the extent to which the process will be open to public inspection. Under current theories agencies are accountable for reaching rational results based on the neutral exercise of their discretion. Thus, the rulemaking process is subject to public scrutiny at virtually every stage. For example, ex parte rules prohibit discussions and transmittal of data unavailable to others; advisory committees are open to public attendance; the Sunshine Act requires that meetings of collegial agencies be open to the public; and the Freedom of Information Act requires agencies to provide the public with many of their internal documents. In short, the current political climate distrusts meetings and other communications between agency officials and members of the private sector unless they are open to all. Therefore, confidential exchanges are frowned upon, if not banned outright. In keeping with this theory, the parties to a regulatory negotiation may agree to conduct their affairs in public.

Several experts, however, believe that negotiation is a process best carried on in private. Several examples demonstrate the benefits of privacy. First, the negotiators must make concessions on different issues to permit maximization of their own goals. Moreover, negotiators must be able to explain the results of their negotiations to their constituents and the reasons for conceding a particular issue that the negotiator believes is not of central importance. Second, a party may be reluctant to yield confidential data that can be useful to negotiations, if doing so will destroy its confidentiality. Third, a party reasonably could be reluctant to engage in the give and take of the negotiation process if it thought that a tentative position it raised in the negotiations subsequently would be held against it in another forum, such as litigation or an ensuing rulemaking process. Finally, and perhaps most significantly, a public forum may cause some of the parties to continue to posture and to take a hard, unyielding position. In short, public scrutiny could mean that the detrimental aspects of the adversarial process result without the correlative benefits of a neutral decision maker.

The negotiators therefore should be able to close their meetings in appropriate circumstances. The procedures of the negotiation process itself provide the safeguards that accrue from public meetings. The political legitimacy of the resulting rule derives from the acceptance of the rule by the parties in interest, and not on the public procedures by which it was developed. Further, the parties should feel no inhibition from meeting on a confidential basis with the mediator or other parties to the negotiation.

Under current law an agency likely would be inhibited from participating in a closed regulatory negotiation session. FACA would require that the negotiation group be established as an advisory committee. Thus, FACA also would require that notice of advisory committee meetings be published in the Federal Register and that such meetings be open to the public. On the other hand, agencies regularly meet on a confidential basis to settle lawsuits challenging rules. Arguably, one of the main advantages of working out rules in settlement rather than in negotiations before the final rule is issued is precisely the absence of ex parte rules which prohibit a confidential, sleeves-up working session in which the parties work out the details of a good rule. This is not to say that all meetings should be closed; rather, the committee should be able to close the meeting in appropriate circumstances.

If the committee decides to close the meeting, additional issues must be confronted. One is an agreement on how the group will release statements to the public. A basic requirement that no one may publicly characterize a position taken by another in a public statement could prevent pressure from being applied on parties through press releases. Or, the committee could agree that no public statement be made without review by all the parties.

A procedure should also be established whereby the parties' positions and the information exchanged cannot be held against them if negotiations are unsuccessful. This procedure would be similar to the traditional rule of evidence that prohibits the subsequent use of settlement offers and the customary practice of developing a protective order that preserves privileges and confidences for documents exchanged during discovery or in settlement negotiations. . . .

In addition, the parties need assurance that the information generated in negotiations will not be available under the Freedom of Information Act (FOIA). In most cases, the negotiation group would receive the same treatment as an advisory committee, which would make FOIA applicable. That status might preclude the withholding of confidential information. If the negotiation information is not protected from disclosure, the parties may feel inhibited from writing issues and taking tentative positions for fear that they would be released and held against them if negotiations fall apart. Therefore, it should be made clear, perhaps through legislation, that the FOIA would not apply to a regulatory negotiation committee and that confidentiality could be maintained. . . .

CONCLUSION: WORTH A TRY

Regulatory negotiation holds promise for success when the issues are relatively well defined, when there are a limited number of parties with sufficient power to prevent the others from emerging victorious, and when it is inevitable that some decision is imminent.

Thus, regulatory negotiations could best be conducted pursuant to a statute authorizing agencies to use the proposed process, at least on an experimental basis. There would be little to lose from such an experiment because there is ample opportunity in the process to protect against abuse or unforeseen problems. Moreover, the potential theoretical benefits of negotiation are attractive. Experience with negotiating solutions to complex policy questions indicates that, at least in some circumstances, many of those benefits can indeed be realized. The malaise of administrative law, which has marched steadily toward reliance on the judiciary to settle disputes and away from direct participation of affected parties, could be countered with a participatory negotiation process. Regulatory negotiations would provide the legitimacy currently lacking in the regulatory process.

Notes and Questions

12.11 Harter's suggestion was fully authorized by law in the Administrative Dispute
Resolution Act of 1996, 5 U.S.C. §§551 *et seq.* (fully authorizing negotiated
rule making as originally "permitted" in the Negotiated Rulemaking Act of
1990). Since his original suggestion, many negotiated rule makings have
occurred and become the subject of heated academic and evaluative debates
about their effectiveness and ability to accomplish the goals that Professor
Harter and others have set for them. See, e.g., Cary Coglianese, Assessing
Consensus: The Promise and Performance of Negotiated Rulemaking, 46
Duke L.J. 1255 (1997); Jody Freeman, Collaborative Governance in the
Administrative State, 45 UCLA L. Rev. 1 (1997); Jody Freeman & Laura
Langbein, Regulatory Negotiation and the Legitimacy Benefit, 9 NYU
Envtl. L. Rev. 60 (2000); Philip Harter, Assessing the Assessors: The Actual
Performance of Negotiated Rulemaking, 9 NYU Envtl. L. Rev. 32 (2000).

12.12 Professor Harter uses the Fisher and Ury model of principled negotiation as
his suggested form of negotiation in rule making. Do the more general theories of negotiation, such as "principled negotiation" or "integrative bargaining," work the same way in dyadic negotiation as in multiple-party
negotiation? Are public governmental negotiations the same as dyadic private
ones? (Consider Harter's discussions about confidentiality in government or
public-issues negotiations.)

12.13 What evaluative criteria would you use to assess whether stakeholder negotiations, held before formal rule making, have been more or less successful
than the more conventional draft, publish notice and comments, promulga-
tion of regulation and litigation model of administrative law? How can we
evaluate different kinds of processes when the subject matter of each process
may be different, and, unlike experimental evaluation, we cannot assign the
same "issue" to several different treatments simultaneously for evaluation?

12.14 Is "negotiation" a proper process in formal governmental processes about
public matters? Isn't this how laws are made in Congress, as well as in the
administrative process? Which processes are more transparent? Is transparency
the only goal? Must negotiations be "principled" to be legitimate?

12.15 How does government decision making about regulatory matters deal with
requirements for democracy? What is democracy here—a majority vote?
Plurality? Supermajority? Unanimity? What is consensus in these contexts?
Must all policy making be "democratic"? What about dispute resolution in
the public sphere? Does democracy mean only those "affected by a decision"
should participate? Or that all citizens should have some input into governmental decision making? How do we evaluate whether democracy has been
part of a decision-making process?

12.16 Is it undemocratic to use "experts" as process facilitators or substantive experts
in such processes? Is mediation or facilitated dialogue more or less democratic
than other decision-making processes? More or less participatory? Is participation synonymous with democracy?

B. STRUCTURES, FORMS, PROCEDURES, AND SKILLS IN MANAGING OR PARTICIPATING IN MULTIPARTY PROCESSES

Because multiparty negotiation processes occur in so many different subject areas and formats, it is much harder to specify in advance what a multiparty process does or should do. As a cutting edge issue in negotiation, scholars of conflict and dispute processes have begun to develop hypotheses for testing and some propositional learning about what happens when there are more than two or three actors in a conflict or transactional setting, trying to influence others to make something happen. Professionals, ranging from social psychologists to economists to lawyers, all offer important insights into what happens when the already highly dynamic process of negotiation is "opened out" to include many interested parties. Problems of intragroup or constituency behavior compound these processes when the parties are not single human beings but groupings of people, either based on function (economic groupings) or values or interests (political, religious, ethnic, identity groups). And, where there are representatives of parties or groups, the agent-principal problems may be even more complex. Preferences, values, and interests of individuals may change during a negotiation, but when groups align to get things accomplished, coalition behavior makes negotiated or facilitated processes even more unstable. In addition, while all negotiations raise the question of whether they are "one-shot" occurrences or will create the possibilities of more negotiations or longer-term relationships, multiple-party negotiations have another layer of complexity. There can be "repeat play" negotiations between and among some of the parties and not others; some multiple-party negotiations are between more or less "permanent" organizations or institutions; and others are with more transient parties or are convened to deal with *sui generis* or *ad hoc* issues, so there are variations in the temporal relationships between and among parties.

Because there is so much complexity to multiparty and multi-issue negotiations, those who engage in such processes, whether as representative-negotiators or neutral or expert facilitators, have begun to develop some organizing principles for the conduct of multiparty negotiations. Whether in very formal multistate diplomatic negotiations or in stakeholder negotiations in negotiated rule making, formal protocols and rules of process have been developed to attempt to structure multiple-party negotiations, focusing both on *rules of process* or *procedures* and *rules of decision* (voting procedures, definitions of consensus, majorities, or other decision rules). A whole new field of dispute resolution, variously called *consensus building, public policy fora, collaborative decision-making processes, facilitated decision making, collaboratives,* and *public conversations,* has been developing structures, formats, procedures, training models, and rules and protocols for the conduct of both formal and informal multiple-party negotiations.

One of the founders of this new field, Lawrence Susskind, Professor of Urban Planning at MIT and founder of the Consensus Building Institute, has pioneered the development of these facilitated processes in complex public policy matters and disputes. Professor Susskind and his colleagues have developed guidelines for conducting such facilitated processes in both formal (permanent) and *ad hoc* (more transient or "one-off" settings). See Lawrence Susskind, An Alternative to Robert's Rules of Order for Groups, Organizations, and Ad Hoc Assemblies That Want to Operate by Consensus, in The Consensus Building Handbook, ch. 2 (Lawrence Susskind, Sarah McKearnan & Jennifer Thomas-Larmer eds., 1999). The protocols and processes described there are intended to replace the more complex Robert's Rules of Order for parliamentary and other organized meetings. You might consider whether more simplified rules of engagement could replace the Federal Rules of Civil Procedure as well.

Notes and Questions

12.17 Susskind's Rules of Order provide an alternative to the more formal Robert's Rules of Order. Consider whether rules should be set by the participants or by the facilitators. Should rules be "laid down" or themselves be negotiated?

12.18 What might be the consequences (both on the process and on ultimate outcomes) of ground-rule setting by the parties versus the facilitators?

In addition to protocols for managing a formal consensus-building event with negotiations, modern lawyers need to know how to manage meetings that precede formal group or organizational negotiations or later become part of such negotiations. Here are a few suggested guidelines for effectively managing such meetings.

 David A. Straus, **MANAGING MEETINGS TO BUILD CONSENSUS**

> **in The Consensus Building Handbook 287-289, 302-304, 310-311, 313-314, 321-322 (Lawrence Susskind, Sarah McKearnan & Jennifer Thomas-Larmer eds., 1999)**

THE VALUE OF FACE-TO-FACE MEETINGS

Some models of mediation call for keeping opposing parties separate, minimizing their interactions, and engaging in *shuttle diplomacy*. In consensus building, on the other hand, most of the work of building agreements is accomplished in face-to-face, facilitated meetings. In these meetings, participants' interests are articulated and acknowledged so they can be discussed, understood, and used as the basis for seeking mutually agreeable solutions. The commitments that parties make to each other in meetings are built on a wide base of shared effort and learning — a base that brokered agreements developed through shuttle diplomacy often lack.

Participants sometimes find that effective meetings, in which opposing parties begin with strongly entrenched, opposing positions and then build consensus step-by-step, can actually be a transforming experience. They learn constructive ways of working together and communicating. They become empowered by the experience of being understood by, and understanding, their adversaries. They are often surprised at what they all have in common, and this realization can help them to see ways to meet everyone's needs. Indeed, in well-facilitated meetings, participants can develop agreements that they can enthusiastically support and help implement, for which they have not compromised their basic values, and that they can present to their constituents (those they represent) as worthy of support. Even when consensus is not achieved, the process of respectful, face-to-face exploration helps people to better understand each other's points of view and makes future attempts at consensus building more likely to succeed.

THE IMPORTANCE OF WELL-RUN MEETINGS...

Meetings can be evaluated in terms of three dimensions of success.

- *The results achieved.* Was the meeting productive? Did the group reach its goals? Did the participants produce a high-quality product?
- *The process used.* Were participants satisfied with the way the meeting was run? Did they feel in control of the meeting and not manipulated in any way? Did the facilitator employ effective and efficient consensus building techniques?
- *The relationships built.* Are participants able to communicate with each other more constructively as a result of the meeting? Do they feel that their viewpoints and concerns were acknowledged and understood by their fellow participants?

Effective meetings achieve positive results in all three dimensions. They are conducted according to proven principles of collaboration, include clear roles and responsibilities for participants and organizers, and offer carefully managed opportunities for discussion and decision making. In effective meetings, facilitators and participants are well prepared. Facilitators use effective problem-solving skills and tools, plan workable agendas, and model appropriate conflict resolution behaviors. They clearly delineate between content (*what* is to be discussed) and process (*how* to proceed with discussions). Participants recognize that the meeting's success depends on their positive, productive input; they do not rely on a facilitator to do it all for them. The atmosphere is safe and stimulating. Time is used well. There is little repetitious arguing, "speechifying," or personal gossip or attacks. Often, agreements are reached. People leave such meetings energized to implement decisions and, in fact, are eager to meet again to report on their efforts and take up new assignments. . . .

BEFORE A MEETING: SETTING UP FOR SUCCESS

Effective meetings do not just happen; they require considerable preparation and planning. To set up a meeting to succeed, the meeting planner(s) must consider and make conscious choices about every factor that could influence the outcome of the meeting. In particular, they must think through and make decisions about

- The purpose of the meeting,
- Who should be involved and how,

- The desired outcomes,
- The agenda,
- The roles and responsibilities of participants and organizers,
- What ground rules will guide discussions,
- How group decisions will be made, and
- Where the meeting will be held. . . .

Drafting Proposed Ground Rules

Meeting planners must develop a list of proposed ground rules. Ground rules, in a single-meeting setting, typically set forth behavioral norms that participants are expected to follow. In multimeeting consensus building processes, by contrast, ground rules are often quite detailed. They may describe, for example, the issues to be discussed in the process, the range of interests represented, the decision rule to be used, the goals of the process, and so forth. . . .

For ground rules governing a single meeting, we suggest guidelines such as the following.

- One person speaks at a time.
- No side conversations.
- No personal attacks (i.e., criticize ideas, not people).
- Listen as an ally.
- Respect agreements about time (e.g., return from breaks promptly).
- Turn off beepers and cell phones.

Draft ground rules should be presented to a group at the outset of a meeting and revised according to participants' suggestions. When process problems arise during a meeting that are not covered by the ground rules, participants should be asked to suggest additional ground rules to prevent the problems from recurring.

DETERMINING THE DECISION RULE

Meeting planners must be prepared to suggest a decision rule for the meeting, that is, to recommend how a group will make decisions (e.g., by consensus, by majority vote). Their recommendation should be discussed with group members at the beginning of the meeting. When people have had a role in determining how decisions are to be made, they are more likely to support the outcomes of a process. When consensus building is the prevailing method of decision making, a group must agree on a definition of *consensus*. Participants in one meeting may want it to mean that everyone in the group must actively support a decision, for example. Those in another meeting might agree to move forward with an agreement even if there are one or two holdouts.

Meeting planners and participants should also clarify what will happen if consensus can't be reached, that is, who the fallback decision makers will be. In a hierarchical organization, the fallback is usually an individual; in a horizontal organization, a majority vote; and in public sector consensus building efforts, the fallback is often a formal decision-making body (such as a public agency or a court). It is often the threat of having to rely on the fallback method of decision making that keeps participants engaged in the search for mutually agreeable solutions.

FACILITATIVE TOOLS: PREVENTIONS AND INTERVENTIONS

The most useful set of tools a facilitator possesses is what we call *preventions* and *interventions*. Preventions are the actions a facilitator takes before and during meetings to head off potential obstacles to success. Interventions are actions a facilitator can take to help a group get back on track during a meeting, after difficulties have occurred. The most skillful facilitators rely primarily on preventions; in a way, this makes their facilitation "invisible." After a meeting in which a facilitator was very skillful, participants will often leave saying, "That was a great meeting. I'm not sure we needed a facilitator." When a facilitator does not prepare well or makes mistakes, and then uses interventions to get back on track, participants are more aware of the role of facilitation and may compliment the facilitator on a job well done. Thus, a facilitator's best work may go unrecognized.

Preventions...

Up-Front Agreements

Facilitators have no formal power to control a group. It is only by building agreements among participants on various process decisions and then holding them to those agreements (at least until they choose to change them) that facilitators develop a measure of control — and even then always as a servant to the group. So, at the outset of a meeting, a facilitator must seek agreement on

- Who is playing which roles in the meeting,
- The basic "contract" between the group and the facilitator and recorder,
- The desired outcomes for the meeting,
- The agenda (i.e., the flow or sequence of agenda items),
- The decision-making rule to be used, and
- The ground rules to govern the meeting....

Notes and Questions

12.19 Can the processes described by Straus be used in settings where the parties do not formally commit to them in advance?

12.20 For what kind of issue or dispute would you advise a client, an organization, or a community group to use a formal negotiation or consensus-building process? Does it make a difference if the issue involves only parties internal to the organization? Why and how?

12.21 Can you think of particular ground rules you would want to have in any process you were a part of? As a participant? As a facilitator? Why?

12.22 Does it matter if the protocols, guidelines, or rules are "laid down" or suggested by the process expert or facilitator or arrived at by the parties themselves? Why and how might it matter who suggested particular ground rules?

What might happen to "enforcement" of the ground rules, depending on who proposed them?

12.23 These excerpts contemplate a very particular kind of process, a relatively formal multiparty negotiation or policy-setting consensus-building environment. There are many other ways to organize multiparty negotiations, including ad hoc/no rules at all to very formal rules of speaking and participation. Similarly, there are now many schools of thought about how to be an effective third-party neutral in facilitating such meetings, depending on whether a decision or action is required at the end or whether a group is being convened for different purposes, such as to foster understanding across divisive value differences. For some other sources on how to participate, facilitate, or lead such negotiations or group discussions, see, e.g., Center for Conflict Resolution, A Manual for Group Facilitators (1978); Donald Hackett & Charles Martin, Facilitation Skills for Team Leaders (1993); Tim Hindle, Managing Meetings (1998); Public Conversations Project, Constructive Conversations About Challenging Times: A Guide to Community Dialogue (2002); Roger Schwarz, The Skilled Facilitator (2003).

The preceding excerpts are addressed principally to those who lead or facilitate multiparty negotiations or decision-making fora. But we must also be concerned with how the parties inside these processes conceive of their roles as negotiators or representatives of particular needs or interests. Preceding chapters address many of the issues that arise for parties or representatives in dyadic negotiations. Participants in multiparty settings, however, confront some different issues, such as coalition formation, trust, sequencing, and ordering of interactions, alliance creation, and so on. The excerpt below is one of the classics in the emerging field of multiparty negotiation analysis. Its author is a scholar as well as a skilled participant in many complex international and commercial multiparty negotiations.

 James K. Sebenius, **SEQUENCING TO BUILD COALITIONS: WITH WHOM SHOULD I TALK FIRST?**

in Wise Choices: Decisions, Games and Negotiations 324-329, 332-333, 335, 337-338, 344-345 (Richard J. Zeckhauser, Ralph L. Keeney & James K. Sebenius eds., 1996)

Surprisingly little systematic consideration has been given to the processes by which negotiators build coalitions, the logic behind their tactical choices, and how these actions matter to outcomes. This essay explores one part of the issue: what David Lax and I have called "strategic sequencing," or the choice of which parties are approached, in what order, openly or secretly, separately or together. Sequencing choices can be a prominent feature of coalition building, an implicit logic governs the tactics employed, and these tactics may significantly affect the results.

For example, the 1985 Plaza accords represent a virtuoso example of sequencing. When James Baker became U.S. Treasury Secretary in 1985, the strong dollar was taking a severe toll on American industry and generating powerful protectionist reactions. The United States, under former Treasury Secretary Donald Regan, then Chief of Staff at the Reagan White House, had for some time spurned international economic cooperation to bring the dollar down. Baker's efforts to build a domestic and international coalition committed to a coordinated effort to accomplish this goal initially relied on secrecy. According to one insider's account:

"Reagan knew of the [Plaza Hotel ministerial] meeting in advance, of course, but was apprised of the full scope of Baker's plan only two days beforehand. Devaluation was sold to the President as necessary to stem the protectionist tide in Congress," says a Baker intimate. "It was sold to Don Regan as being consistent with an earlier call he had made for an international conference to discuss exchange rates. To this day, I don't think Don understood what we were about to do. We managed, [Federal Reserve Chairman Paul] Volcker . . . because he had carefully split his board. Paul had no alternative but to go along."

Armed with this domestic "mandate," Baker used the Plaza Hotel meeting to build the necessary international coalition both to act and to make it very difficult for his domestic rivals to later reverse the resulting policy course. As one finance minister said, "At first he split us just like he split the Fed. He began by using the U.S. and Japan against West Germany. Then he combined those three to bring along the whole Group of Five [including Britain and France]."

Baker carefully sequenced his actions to build the coalition of finance ministers committed to implementing his preferred agreement. The de facto coalition was larger, encompassing both domestic and international players. Secrecy and ambiguity, divide-and-conquer tactics, and a tight deadline were used domestically to gain Baker the right to move into the actual Plaza process. There, with the initial concurrence of the Japanese — whose economic interests and bargaining position on the dollar were firmly allied with that of the United States — it was possible to get German agreement. Then this powerful three-way coalition could press the others into the final agreement. To see the potential importance of sequencing here, imagine other possible orders of approach; for example, suppose that the Germans had in advance forged an ironclad coalition with the British, French, and others against the likely American proposal. Baker's coalitional machinations are fairly typical of one broad class of sequencing actions intended to create an irreversible commitment to a preferred agreement. They suggest a number of analytic and prescriptive issues. For example, under what conditions does sequencing matter? Why are some potential sequences preferred to others? When are natural allies likely to be approached first and when is the process most likely to commence among potentially blocking interests? How and why does the openness or secrecy of the process matter? Are there characteristic negotiation sequences when both internal and external actors are involved?

The most powerful advances in negotiation theory have been mainly inspired by the bilateral or two-party case — where issues of sequence inherently cannot arise. While multilateral bargaining has been the subject of considerable investigation, the additional complexities posed by coalitional possibilities render the analytic task much more formidable. As Howard Raiffa observed, "There is a vast difference between conflicts involving two disputants and those involving more than two disputants. Once three or more conflicting parties are involved, coalitions of disputants may form and may act in concert against the other disputants."

Yet while a rich array of sequential tactics pervades studies of multiparty bargaining, these actions are rarely the object of analysis, almost as if their range and variety preclude useful generalization, or as if they were intriguing details, merely epiphenomena. Indeed, the predominant emphasis of coalition theories developed thus far has been on the *outcomes* of coalitional actions rather than on the *processes* and *tactics* involved in reaching those outcomes. The founders of classical game theory, von Neumann and Morgenstern, characterized their work as "thoroughly static." Anatol Rapoport's later assessment of the contributions of N-person game theory noted that "If the behavioral scientist thinks about decision making in conflict systems in the mode suggested by N-Person Game Theory, he will focus on two fundamental questions: (1) Which coalitions are likely to form? (2) How will the members of a coalition apportion their joint payoff?" Note that both of these canonical questions are outcome-focused. As Rapoport went on to note, game theory still "lacks almost entirely the dynamic component, i.e., a model of the conflict *process*." . . .

While game theory has neglected sequencing issues, folk wisdom has not. For example, one standard admonition is to "get your allies on board first." Obviously, this sensible approach is the product of much experience and makes eminent sense in many situations; for example, Baker did just this with the Japanese in the international phase of the Plaza accord process. However, there are striking counterexamples to "allies on board first." For example, as the United States sought to build a global anti-Iraq coalition following the Kuwait invasion, many observers would have argued that Israel was its strongest regional ally. Yet the Israelis were pointedly excluded from the growing coalition: Israel's formal membership would have greatly complicated, if not precluded, numerous Arab states' joining.

A related bit of folk wisdom and standard diplomatic practice when preparing "your side" to negotiate with an "external" party is to "get your own house in order first," or "hammer out a common internal position." Ambassadors and bargaining agents often see a required first step for eventual external dealings as thrashing out a consensus internally on negotiating instructions. Evidently, this represents time-honored and often good advice. Yet in preparing for the Gulf War, President George Bush [Senior] did anything but get the U.S. house in order first and then negotiate externally. Instead, he committed U.S. troops to the region, and then exhaustively built up — in part by virtuoso sequential diplomacy — an external international U.N. coalition behind a Security Council Resolution authorizing "all necessary means" to eject Iraq from Kuwait. Only then did the Bush administration begin negotiating seriously for Congressional authorization to use force in the Gulf. Of course, the prior commitment of U.S. troops along with hard-won international backing for the use of force made it vastly harder for Congress to withhold approval. Had Bush started by seeking the approval of a deeply skeptical U.S. Congress, agreement would have been unlikely at best and, given Congressional refusal, any subsequent American-led international coalition-building enterprise would have been hobbled.

Exceptions to maxims — such as "allies first" or "internal consensus before external negotiation" — only raise more basic questions: when are they right and when are they wrong and why? This essay explores such questions, proposes a more general model for sequencing choices, and concludes with a few observations. In contrast with the "structure implies outcome" tradition, the "path effects" of different sequences will play a central role in the analysis.

PATH EFFECTS I: SEQUENCING TO EXPLOIT "PATTERNS OF DEFERENCE"

A common problem for the would-be coalition builder is that approaching the most difficult—and perhaps most critical—party offers slim chances for a deal. One approach is to discern what we will define as the "patterns of deference" involving the "target player." An illustration comes from observing the successful sequencing tactic of Bill Daley, President Clinton's key strategist for securing Congressional approval of the controversial North American Free Trade Agreement (NAFTA).

News might arrive that a representative who had been leaning toward yes had come out as a no. "Weenie," [Daley would] say. When he heard the bad news, he did not take it personally. He'd take more calls. "Can we find the guy who can deliver the guy? We have to call the guy who calls the guy who calls the guy."

More formally, suppose that the subjective probability of Party A saying yes if asked independently is less than the conditional probability of Party A saying yes given that A is informed that Party B has already said yes. In symbols, P(A says Yes/B says Yes) > P(A says Yes). A's deference to B might be due to several factors: B's perceived greater expertise, status, or reputation for having the same values as A; B may have done A a favor and A might feel the tug of reciprocity; or B's yes may "cover" A's choice and lessen the risk for A of agreement. In all these cases, we could say that "A tends to defer to B," or that a pattern of deference exists. Deference may be weak, strong, or absolute, depending on the situation and the magnitudes of the probabilities.

With such a pattern of deference, sequence matters; there is an optimal sequence that maximizes the probability of the desired winning coalition, and the coalitional outcome can be said to be path dependent. If B is the "easier" party in the sense that P (B says Yes) > P(A says Yes), then we might call the B-then-A sequence a "bootstrapping" approach to coalition building. The process of working out the sequence from this structure could be called "backward mapping" or reasoning from the hardest ultimate target to the easiest: "Can we find the guy who can deliver the [most difficult] guy? Call the guy who calls the guy who calls the guy who can deliver the [most difficult] guy.". . .

Does this mean that the most-likely-to-agree party should always be approached first? Not at all. Suppose A is the "harder" party in that P(A says Yes) = .4, while P(B says Yes) = .5, but that B defers to A, or P(B says Yes/A says Yes) = .9, while A shows no deference to B. Approaching the easy party (B) first yields a success probability of (.5)(.4) = .2, while the reverse order yields a higher value (.4)(.9) = .36. This "harder first" result is driven by the extent of B's deference to A. The path effect of sequence A-B over B-A equals the probability increment, .16, of successful coalition building. . . .

Prescriptive advice for would-be coalition builders in such cases suggests first, enumerating actual and potential parties relevant to the target coalition; second, assessing their interests, their likely position on joining the target coalition, and their likely alternatives to agreement; third, evaluating potential patterns of deference among the players; and fourth, constructing an optimal sequence by mapping backward from the target coalition to exploit deference patterns.

Thus far we have been investigating the effects of path dependence on sequencing choices that are driven by one important but particular mechanism: patterns of deference. Yet deference patterns comprise only one of several classes of factors that can influence the expected value of subsequent bargaining for a proposed path and given a bargaining history. For example, if the no-agreement alternatives (disagreement values) for subsequent parties worsen or improve as a function of the path so far taken, the chances of their agreement as well as the likely terms of such agreement may change. Further, suppose that an earlier phase of the bargaining changes the expectations of the outcome on the part of later players. Or, suppose that prior negotiations serve to conceal or reveal information that changes the expected value of subsequent bargaining. The next sections of this paper move beyond the path effects of exploiting deference patterns on sequencing choice to explore and illustrate several other such classes of factors that can change the expected value of subsequent bargaining. Then it becomes possible to propose a more general model.

PATH EFFECTS II: SEQUENCING TO CHANGE NO-AGREEMENT ALTERNATIVES

Considerable evidence suggests that a party is more likely to agree to a proposal, and on less attractive terms, the worse his or her no-agreement alternatives (disagreement utility) appear. An extreme version of this observation would be the Godfather's "offer you can't refuse" with its implied "or else." Popular negotiation accounts have enshrined the acronym BATNA (Best Alternative to Negotiated Agreement) as a standard part of prescriptive advice. In a multiparty negotiation aimed at securing the ultimate agreement of several parties, earlier agreement among some of the players may worsen the no-agreement alternatives of later players. Rather than face the status quo ante, later players may face the prospect of a growing coalition. Often the risk of being left out of such a coalition is quite undesirable, thus increasing the chances of the later players joining the growing coalition. Sequencing actions, therefore, may lead to higher agreement probabilities and more attractive terms from the point of view of the coalition builder. . . .

Worsening No-Agreement Alternatives of Internal Blocking Coalitions in Two-Level Games

Despite the conventional wisdom of negotiating "internally" first in order to present a united front in later "external" negotiations, the reverse sequence is often employed when internal would-be blockers are too strong. For example, of the Bush Administration decision to negotiate internationally first for the right to use force against Iraq, National Security Advisor General Brent Scowcroft observed:

"There has been some criticism of us for, in effect, pressuring Congress by building an international coalition and then making the argument, 'You mean, Congressman, you're not going to support the President, but the president of Ethiopia is supporting him?' But I don't think we should be apologetic about it. You build consensus in whatever way you can, and when this thing first started, we didn't have support from Congress, and we didn't have support from the American people. We couldn't have gotten Congress earlier, I don't think, and if there had been no coalition and no UN vote, we would never have gotten Congress." . . .

In each of these two-level examples — the Gulf War coalition, ABB, and arms control — an internal faction may well have functioned as a successful blocking coalition to the initiative favored by the protagonist. By choosing to negotiate with outsiders first, the protagonists in these cases hoped to generate an irreversible commitment to a preferred deal. The path effects could overcome the internal blockers and improve the terms of the deal. By examining a number of such instances, the likelihood and effects of an "outside-in" (or, more accurately, a "small inside, then outside, then larger inside") approach may be better assessed in situations with this structure.

PATH EFFECTS III: SHAPING OUTCOME EXPECTATIONS

Beyond patterns of deference and worsening no-agreement alternatives, a bootstrapper may seek to progressively shape the expectations of later players through the actions taken with earlier ones. Social psychological research points up the potent effects that parties' expectations of the outcome can have on bargaining results. An extraordinary story illustrating this class of path effects on the expected value of subsequent bargaining is how labor organizer Ray Rogers broke the anti-union board coalition at J.P. Stevens, a textile firm.

Although organized labor had sought to gain recognition from Stevens for almost 20 years, frontal bargaining assaults, consumer boycotts, demonizing publicity, and legal action had failed to achieve the union's goals. The first step of Rogers's bootstrapping approach was a highly publicized demonstration at Stevens's annual meeting, which raised the salience of the new campaign. Rogers's second step was to use labor's clout and sizable business in New York with Manufacturer's Hanover bank to oust Stevens's chairman and another Stevens board member from the Manufacturer's Hanover Board. The surprise success of this effort greatly enhanced the credibility of Rogers's approach both internally at the union, where there was considerable hesitancy about the approach, and with subsequent targets.

The next target was the New York Life Insurance Company, a Stevens creditor that also wrote many union life and health insurance contracts and managed sizable union pension funds. A New York state insurance law permits a sufficient number of policy holders to contest board elections. Rogers threatened New York Life with such an election and that inherently risk averse institution agreed to eject Stevens's chairman from its board.

Next, Rogers targeted Metropolitan Life, a much larger insurance company that, like New York Life, was a major Stevens creditor, wrote many union life and health policies, and managed substantial union pension funds. Rogers's threat to contest the board election at MetLife, combined with the credibility that his campaign had amassed with victories over both Manufacturer's Hanover and New York Life, predisposed MetLife to exert great pressure on J.P. Stevens to make a deal with the union. The anti-union coalition including the Stevens board and management was broken, the union recognized, and a new contract negotiated.

As with deference patterns and worsened no-agreement alternatives, this sequencing strategy depended on early moves to boost Rogers's credibility and share expectations of the outcome for later targets. By starting with the easiest target, Manufacturer's Hanover, raising credibility both internally and externally, and favorably shaping subsequent outcome expectations, Rogers's bootstrapping approach succeeded.

An oft-noted coalitional dynamic, the "bandwagon," normally operates by a combination of worsened no-agreement alternatives and reshaped expectations of the outcome. In getting classic bandwagons rolling, one seeks to get the easy parties on board first and to create the impression of inevitability of the desired final coalition—ideally facing later parties with the choice of (profitably) saying yes to joining or of saying no and being isolated in an undesirable, no-agreement alternative....

CONCLUSIONS

Although sequential tactics have been the focus of the essay, a prior question has been lurking in the background: when should one avoid sequencing and attempt a fully open, collective route to consensus? After all, many sequential moves appear to be — and often are — sneaky, manipulative, deceptive, coercive, and even plainly unethical. It is thus important to think them through both for their ethical *and* their prudential implications. In principle, the choice of a simultaneous or sequential process can be unraveled by specifying and weighing the relevant path effects. Such effects associated with a simultaneous process might include a greater sense of legitimacy and "ownership" of agreement, the possibility of new options generated by brainstorming, as well as altered roles of deference patterns and different possibilities for blocking coalitions to form or to be thwarted.

While sequencing has played a starring role in this essay, supporting roles have been played by other tactical choices — whether to act openly or secretly, whether to meet in subgroups or the full group, how commitments and other actions can be made credibly, how to set the negotiating agenda, which issues to link or separate, whether to bring in a third party or not, etc. A fuller account of coalitional process would obviously devote attention to these actions and their interactions with sequencing. Yet the key notion in this essay is coalitional "process" understood as the link between the structure of a situation and its outcome.

A more basic question is: Under what conditions do sequencing tactics affect outcomes? If a sequential action were costlessly reversible with no net path or outcome effects, sequencing would not matter and should be relegated to the "frictional." Thus, sequencing can matter only when its effects are costly or impossible to reverse. For example, such cost or irreversibility may occur where some commitments of resources or reputation are made in the process, where information is irretrievably conveyed, where an approach, once made, becomes less feasible or more expensive, where an ironclad blocking coalition is forged, or where a real deadline intervenes.

This essay has focused on such sequential processes ranging from exploiting patterns of deference, to progressively worsening no-agreement alternatives, to preventing private knowledge from becoming common knowledge, to shaping outcome expectations, and the like. It has analyzed common classes of tactical choice such as bootstrapping, pyramiding, and setting bandwagons in motion. It has ultimately urged a new step in coalitional negotiation analyses: Beyond characterizations of individual players (in terms of interests, beliefs, etc.) and coalitional possibilities (e.g., joint payoffs for different coalitions), the would-be coalition builder or negotiation analyst should map the relationships among the different players in terms of deference, influence, antagonism, and the like. Given this map, one can assess the relationship between given tactical actions — such as worsening no-deal alternatives, shaping outcome expectations, or revealing information — and the prospects for and terms of subsequent agreements.

Notes and Questions

12.24 Can you think of particular situations in which you would "get your allies on board first"? Situations in which you would go "outside" before inside?

12.25 Think of a current multiparty dispute (either domestic or international) and see if you can draw a "backward map" of the "deference patterns" of the parties.

C. LEGAL ISSUES IN MULTIPARTY NEGOTIATION SETTINGS

The use of class action settlements in the areas of mass torts, consumer actions, securities law, and similar cases has now raised a host of complex legal, procedural, and ethical issues involving both private and court-assisted settlements in major, multiparty litigation. See, e.g., Ortiz v. Fibreboard Corp., 527 U.S. 815 (1999) (disapproving the use of Rule 23 class action settlements of mass torts claims on both procedural and ethical grounds); Amchem v. Windsor, 521 U.S. 591 (1997); Robert H. Klonoff & Edward K.M. Bilich, Class Actions and Other Multi-Party Litigation ch. 8 (2000); John C. Coffee, Jr., Class Wars: The Dilemma of the Mass Tort Class Action, 95 Colum. L. Rev. 1343 (1995); Carrie Menkel-Meadow, Ethics and the Settlement of Mass Torts: When the Rules Meet the Road, 80 Cornell L. Rev. 1159 (1995); Nancy Morawetz, Bargaining, Class Representation, and Fairness, 54 Ohio St. L.J. 1 (1993).

The last chapter looked at some of the legal issues implicated in who can bind parties to negotiated settlements when there are multiple parties (on both sides of a litigated matter) and when courts must approve settlements in complex, multiparty cases like class actions. Federal Rule of Civil Procedure 24 also allows parties to "intervene" in the middle of cases if the parties can meet the requirements of the rule for being interested parties who were not brought into the original litigation, so which parties are involved in a litigation matter may change during the course of litigation and negotiation. Similarly, in transactional negotiations, new parties can come in later and questions may arise about who is bound by particular agreements. Once again, we cannot review all of the legal issues here, but when engaged in negotiation on behalf of multiple parties or when multiple parties are involved, it is always a good idea to be clear about who is agreeing to what and who has "authority" to bind others. "Get it in writing," while always a good rule for legal negotiations, may be particularly important in multiparty settings (even while parties will often want to make confidential "side agreements" without formal commitments).

We close this chapter with a recent article taking the controversial position that even the most complex litigated cases in modern jurisprudence (involving many parties in important legal and policy disputes) might have been productively handled through negotiation, rather than litigation.

Jeffrey R. Seul, SETTLING SIGNIFICANT CASES

79 Wash. L. Rev. 881, 887, 889 (2005)

I believe negotiation should be viewed as a credible alternative to litigation for resolving disputes that raise important public policy questions. As explained more fully below, I use the term "negotiation" in two senses. The first is "strategic settlement": pure, self-interested bargaining in which each party is willing to satisfy others' interests solely as a strategy for satisfying its own interests. The second is collective moral deliberation, in which parties explicitly seek mutually recognizable moral grounds on which to justify the terms of their agreement. When moral deliberation produces a formal or informal agreement among the parties, the agreement necessarily results from some degree of change regarding one's own perspective, others' perspectives, or both. Although I do not suggest that we should actively encourage crass bargaining as the best approach for resolving disputes involving deeply held values, I argue that both types of negotiation can play a legitimate role in the management and the eventual, just resolution of these disputes in various circumstances and make valuable contributions to democracy....

[M]ost difficult legal problems involve not only complicated empirical problems, but also problematic judgments concerning questions of moral value, and (often as a direct consequence of these other difficulties) various conceptually incommensurable definitions of what sorts of facts are said to constitute legal meaning. These latter types of disputes will tend not to be amenable to resolution through the procurement of more evidence via the workings of the dispute processing system, either because they involve conceptual disagreements about what should even count as evidence, or because they can't usefully be thought of as involving evidentiary questions at all.

One might say that ordinary cases involve questions of justice with a small "j," whereas significant cases involve questions of Justice writ large. In significant cases, the parties are trying to establish or buttress background legal norms, either by creating a new legal norm where none presently exists, or by subverting or reaffirming an existing legal norm that mirrors a favored social norm. Each party is pursuing justice in the larger sense of a legal order that affirms a social order one considers normative. The parties are pursuing their respective universalizing projects by attempting, through adjudication, to establish, alter or defend a legal rule. . . .

LETTING OTHERS NEGOTIATE FOR US

Although negotiation among the justices of the U.S. Supreme Court is highly stylized, there is no question that they negotiate. They do not engage in the type of coarse horse-trading that sometimes occurs within the other branches of government; rather, they "accommodate" their own ideological perspectives to others' perspectives as necessary to substantially achieve their own objectives. The author of an opinion may circulate many drafts in an effort to produce a majority, sometimes engaging in strategic behavior such as exposing less than the full court to a particular draft in an interim effort to address the requirements of a particular justice or group of justices. Because a single justice cannot dictate the Court's decision, most decisions are the product of some degree of compromise among those in the majority. Through discussion and successive draft opinions, justices tinker their way toward a conclusion that produces an outcome and supporting rationale with which each member of the majority is, by definition, at least minimally satisfied.

As a result of these efforts to accommodate the perspectives of other members of the Court, many judicially created norms represent an amalgam of reasons and values. The U.S. Supreme Court's holding in Roe v. Wade is one notable example of such a compromise result. The litigants themselves might have reached this compromise if they had attempted to author a draft bill on the issue and lobbied for its passage. Pro-life activists surely do not consider the Court's holding to be a "win-win" outcome, but at least some of them would admit that the Court attempted to balance respect for a pregnant woman's autonomy and respect for the developing human fetus.

Unanimous decisions frequently involve a high degree of mutual accommodation. . . .

EXPLAINING THE IRONIES: AN IMPLICIT REASON WE LITIGATE

If the explicit reason disputants litigate is to advance or defend some cherished value that conflicts with a value held by one's adversary, why do they submit their dispute to a process in which others will negotiate a resolution that may leave them wholly or partially disappointed?

I believe that a significant, implicit reason we litigate must be that we also value the relatively pacific resolution — or at least processing — of disputes. Litigation provides a forum in which we can safely confront our adversaries and be heard — by the court itself, if not by the other party or parties. The parties' choice among available means for addressing their dispute suggests they implicitly recognize that they, and the court before which they have brought their dispute, are participants in a larger social system that, overall, is worth maintaining and attempting to enhance. The disputants, like the rest of us, inhabit a social context in which many of their other cherished values are aligned, even though those that are the subject of their current dispute are not.... It seems little acknowledged, however, that litigation essentially permits us to negotiate what we allege is non-negotiable, effectively creating a market through which seemingly incommensurable values can be traded. In the realm of significant cases, litigation prevents — or at least buffers us against the worst potential effects of — failures in the market for social norms. The parties' competing values may be incommensurable in the abstract, but their actual disputing behavior seems to demonstrate that they are willing to compromise their values to some extent because they wish to inhabit a social system that is capable of containing and processing their dispute in a reasonably pacific manner.

Litigation also plays a significant role in the construction and maintenance of individual and group identities....

Despite the many barriers to settlement of the types of disputes that give rise to significant cases, two types of settlements, though rare, can and do occur. One type can be thought of as strategic settlement. Strategic settlement occurs when at least one of the parties is motivated primarily by a desire to avoid the risk of an adverse decision. This party hopes that progress can be made politically, without the burden of a recently affirmed, adverse legal norm. Perhaps this party also hopes to bring "better facts" before the court at a later date. The other type of settlement results from some degree of true perspective change that produces an informal understanding or a formal agreement regarding action the parties will (or will not) take regarding matters of common concern.

Strategic settlements result from bargaining, in which the goal is maximal satisfaction of one's own interests through compromise. Perspective change results from collective moral deliberation.... [T]he goal of moral deliberation is the complete or partial transformation of interests, rather than their mere aggregation.

A.   Strategic Settlement

The agreement reached shortly before the case of Piscataway Township Board of Education v. Taxman[1] was to be heard by the U.S. Supreme Court is an example of strategic settlement. Sharon Taxman, a white public high school teacher in Piscataway, New Jersey, lost her job when the school district decided to eliminate a position in her department. An African-American teacher in her department, Debra Williams, who started her job on the same day as Taxman and was equally qualified, was retained. Under New Jersey law, school workforce reductions are to be made on the basis of seniority, with less senior employees being laid off first. Because both teachers had received favorable performance reviews, the school needed another basis for making its decision about whom to release from Taxman's department. The board had broken all past seniority ties by drawing lots. In this instance, however, it made the decision on racial grounds, releasing Taxman and retaining Williams because the School Board believed its decision would promote diversity and support the goals of affirmative action.

---

[1] United States v. Bd. of Ed. 832 F. Supp. 836, 840 (D.N.J. 1993), *aff'd en banc sub nom.* Taxman v. Bd. of Educ. 91 F.3d 1547 (3rd Cir. 1996), *cert. granted sub nom.*, Piscataway Township Bd. of Educ. v. Taxman, 521 U.S. 1117 (1997), *cert. dismissed*, 522 U.S. 1010 (1997).

Taxman sued, claiming reverse discrimination. The trial and appellate courts ruled in her favor, and the U.S. Supreme Court granted certiorari. Fearing a precedent with a negative effect on affirmative action programs throughout the country, a coalition of civil rights groups persuaded the school board to settle. The Reverend Jesse Jackson, one of the leaders of the coalition, prevailed upon the board's president to make Ms. Taxman a generous offer of settlement, $300,000 of which would be supplied by the coalition.

Supporters and opponents of affirmative action alike decried the Piscataway settlement. Many accused both sides of selling out — of "placing the route to the Supreme Court on the open market." Nonetheless, the Piscataway settlement demonstrates that significant cases can be, and sometimes are, settled on strategic grounds. . . .

B. Moral Deliberation

When parties to a significant case are willing to engage in a process through which they examine their own values and commitments or explore the potential for cooperation on practical matters despite their conflicting values, a settlement born of perspective change may emerge. As Lon Fuller observed long ago with respect to mediation, its central quality . . . [is] . . . "its capacity to reorient the parties toward each other, not by imposing rules on them, but by helping them to achieve a new and shared perception of their relationship, a perception that will redirect their attitudes and dispositions toward one another." Fuller's view of mediation is highly idealized, and not all mediators and facilitators strive for the "new and shared perceptions" that Fuller sees as the principal byproduct of mediation or have the knowledge and skill to craft processes likely to produce perspective change when it is an explicit or implicit goal. Nonetheless, skilled neutrals are capable of structuring processes that increase the likelihood that perspective change will occur, typically over multiple sessions spanning a significant length of time. When perspective change does occur, any potential settlement discussed by the parties, will, like a strategic settlement, have both benefits and costs for the parties and society. . . .

As with strategic settlements, the principal costs of settlements resulting from genuine moral deliberation are opportunity costs and signaling costs, though each takes on a somewhat different character in this context. When parties settle a significant case primarily for strategic reasons, they do not intend the terms of their agreement to be a partial or complete substitute for the legal norm they hoped to establish or reaffirm through litigation. There is no mutual acknowledgement of others' perspectives, however incomplete or imperfect that acknowledgement may be, when a significant case is settled. The parties merely call a truce in what they assume will be an ongoing social struggle.

In contrast, settlements resulting from collective moral deliberation are intended to resolve the underlying dispute or some aspect of it, or to achieve incremental progress toward the dispute's ultimate resolution. One forgoes or postpones the chance to establish or reinforce a legal norm aligned with one's values, and the ancillary benefits that one hopes would flow from it, in return for an agreement that represents a partial advancement or preservation of the substantive values one had hoped could be advanced or preserved more completely through litigation. One also may forgo the opportunity for more complete retribution for, or public vindication of, past harms. . . .

Social psychologist Herbert Kelman[2] argues that the development of coalitions across conflict lines is critical to the resolution of deep-seated social conflict. Peaceful social change ultimately requires the progressive transformation of relationships within identity groups, as well as relations between them. As Kelman explains, conciliatory interactions between members of opposing groups help promote intra-group change as well as inter-group change, provided those who participate in the interactions maintain sufficient credibility within their own groups. It seems reasonable to assume, for example, that moderate white citizens' experiences interacting with blacks during the civil rights era played a role in transforming other white citizens' perspectives on racial issues. Conflict resolution practitioners often employ informal, nonbinding dialog processes in an effort to develop coalitions between members of opposing groups, in the hope that these interactions might eventually promote such intra-group change, creating the conditions from which informal cooperation and formal agreements between groups can emerge. Indeed, it is in all groups' interests to produce an agreement that their more extreme members can minimally support; otherwise, the agreement is unlikely to prove durable.

Public settlements — formal or informal agreements that involve some level of coordinated action or inaction — impose signaling costs on those who participate in them. As with opportunity costs, however, participants in settlements accept them because they believe the cumulative costs of foregoing litigation are outweighed by the cumulative benefits of cooperation. Those who incur these costs alter the social environment in a way that may decrease the signaling costs for those who later elect to cooperate with members of opposing groups. In other words, a settlement may sometimes provide social "cover" in the same way that a U.S. Supreme Court ruling can. By affirming the equal rights and dignity of black citizens, the Supreme Court's landmark civil rights decisions no doubt lowered the potential reputational costs incurred by whites inclined to express non-racist perspectives among whites who continued to hold racist views, or whose views were undisclosed. As Robinson and his colleagues observe,[3] when one sees other members of one's group expressing perspectives widely thought to be taboo, it becomes easier to express those perspectives oneself. . . .

To the extent deliberative forms of social and political engagement succeed in reorienting understandings and relationships among citizens divided by deep value differences, they may often contribute as much or more to the evolution of social norms than would a U.S. Supreme Court decision. While much of the discussion among political theorists regarding deliberative democracy focuses on promoting and enhancing moral deliberation among elected officials, some proponents of deliberative democracy also hope to increase the quantity and quality of deliberation between representatives and citizens, as well as directly among citizens. Deliberative democ-

---

[2] Herbert C. Kelman, Coalitions Across Conflict Lines: The Interplay of Conflicts Within and Between the Israeli and Palestinian Communities, in Conflicts Between People and Groups 236 (S. Worchel & J.A. Simpson eds., 1993).

[3] Robert Robinson, et al., Actual Versus Assumed Differences in Construal: "Naïve Realism in Intergroup Perception and Conflict, 68 J. Personality & Soc. Psychol. 404 (1995).

racy is practiced both when public officials deliberate and when deliberations among citizens are purposefully structured and managed to provide inputs into broader political processes. In order to maximize the potential for settlements of significant cases to contribute to the evolution of social norms and public policy, we must look for ways to connect deliberation among citizen-disputants to broader political processes and to encourage open (i.e., non-secret) settlements. . . .

Negotiation should be viewed as a legitimate alternative to litigation for processing and resolving disputes involving deep moral disagreements. People accept the compromise inherent in adjudication of ideological disputes because they value not only the substantive moral perspectives they seek to defend, but also the pacific resolution of the dispute itself. Settlements achieved through deliberative dispute resolution processes may benefit both the parties and society in ways that litigation cannot. From the public's perspective, deliberative dispute resolution processes can multiply opportunities for democratic participation and help citizens build social capacity to resolve tough problems. Even where parties are incapable of engaging in genuine moral deliberation, however, settlement for strategic reasons sometimes may be a sensible alternative for parties to a significant case, and one that should not invite scorn. Litigation and negotiation each have a legitimate role to play in our nation's moral discourse and the evolution of social norms. Litigation and negotiation are complementary, mutually reinforcing social processes, even in the realm of disputes involving deep moral disagreement. Settlement has an important and constructive role to play in the pursuit of justice, the development of social norms, and the strengthening of social bonds. Interactions between law and social norms, and between the processes and institutions that produce them, are complex and unpredictable. We should not assume that one institution or process always is superior to others for righting wrongs or producing social change.

Notes and Questions

12.26 Can you think of "significant cases" (Roe v. Wade, Brown v. Board of Education, others?) that you think could have been negotiated, rather than litigated? With what costs and benefits?

12.27 Seul describes two different kinds of negotiated settlements in significant cases — strategic settlements and those involving moral deliberation and transformation. What factors are likely to produce these different kinds of settlements? (Who the parties are? Resources? Substantive issues? Assessments of litigation risks?)

12.28 Can you think of other categories of negotiated settlements in significant cases? What would you call a "significant case"?

12.29 Seul seems to endorse Luban's arguments (see Chapter 11) that secret settlements are bad, especially in "significant" cases. Can you think of any circumstances in which even a significant case might require confidentiality or secrecy? If a significant case settles privately or confidentially, is the cost too great in Seul's terms? In other words, is Seul endorsing only "public negotiation" of significant cases?

Chapter 13 International Negotiation

There never was a good war or a bad peace.

—Benjamin Franklin

The importance of international conflict resolution has become increasingly urgent in recent years. The twentieth century's deadly wars led to the formation of the United Nations and many other multinational and nongovernmental organizations, which are now seeking to preserve peace as the twenty-first century explodes in new forms of concerted and randomized violence and terrorism. As life in an ever-shrinking world has become both more prosperous (for some) and more dangerous for most, new forms of international conflict resolution are being invented. We are trying to deal with economic and legal aspects of "globalization" or "internationalization," and are employing negotiation techniques to seek peace, ensure stability, and promote reconciliation and coexistence in a diverse world with conflicting values and national, group, and individual objectives. This chapter explores various forms of international negotiation, including formal international diplomatic relations, nongovernmental peace and development efforts, international trade, and economic and commercial relations.

A. CAUSES OF INTERNATIONAL CONFLICT

What is culture? Much of the literature on international conflict resolution assumes that culture is "out there"—something for the lawyer or party in a dispute to consider, adapt to, and be sensitive to when dealing with someone from a different culture. The premise here is that the person from the other culture might behave differently because her culture has different expectations and goals about negotiation or because individual behaviors are culturally structured. The individual may not even know that her behavior is culturally influenced. In our view, this is a wooden and imperialist notion of culture. All of us are in cultures, but most of us are like fish that live in water but don't know they are wet. Culture surrounds and is "in" all of us. At the same time, culture is not uniformly or universally distributed. You may be an American; come from a certain state; are male or female; have an ethnic/racial heritage, a family, a religion, and an age; and are now entering a profession. Is your culture American, Texan, or Californian, southern or midwestern, Catholic or Jewish, white or black, progressive or conservative, or lawyer-like or student-like? People hold several social statuses or roles at any one time, and nationality or ethnic identification is only one aspect of a multifaceted cultural identity. Indeed, as the U.S. Census now finally recognizes, individuals may consider themselves to be part white, black, Latino, and Native American. Different situations bring out different parts of demographically and behaviorally salient characteristics.

Whether the dispute resolution profession itself has become an international culture is a hotly debated question. This book asks you to think about your cultures, whatever those might be, as you think about others' cultures in the creation and use of international negotiation processes. Since Chapter 9 discusses the impact of national culture, this chapter examines broader concepts of conflict among cultures and what that means for resolving these conflicts.

The following excerpt is from a controversial article published long before September 11, 2001. In it, Samuel Huntington argues that the world was on track toward a series of clashes of several basic and virtually immutable and conflicting cultures. Huntington's article received a lot of criticism at the time and spawned many debates about the descriptions of the particular cultures, the immutability in cultural identifications, and the inevitability of the clashes he describes.

Many scholars, especially those who support the postmodern theories of the 1980s and 1990s, argue that differences in cultures are more socially constructed than given and unchangeable. The meanings attached to particular cultural identifications also change. It used to matter a great deal if one was Scottish American or Irish American, but now these are not very salient distinctions in the United States (even while they still might have some significance in the United Kingdom). Among those whose perspectives on cultural differences differ from Huntington's are Francis Fukuyama, The End of History and the Last Man (1993) (suggesting more global convergence through capitalism and democracy), and Vamik Voltan, Blood Lines: From Ethnic Pride to Ethnic Terrorism (2000) (a more psychological exploration of ethnic violence).

After September 11, 2001, Huntington's approach gained some ascendancy again. As you read the following excerpt, consider how persuasive you find it.

 Samuel P. Huntington, **THE CLASH OF CIVILIZATIONS?**

in The International System After the Collapse of the East-West Order 7, 8-11 (Armand Clesse et al. eds., 1994)

THE NATURE OF CIVILIZATIONS

What do we mean when we talk of a civilization? A civilization is a cultural entity. Villages, regions, ethnic groups, nationalities, religious groups, all have distinct cultures at different levels of cultural heterogeneity. The culture of a village in southern Italy may be different from that of a village in northern Italy but both will share in a common Italian culture, which distinguishes them from German villages. European communities, in turn, will share cultural features, which distinguish them from Arab or Chinese communities. Arabs, Chinese, and Westerners, however, are not part of any broader cultural entity. They constitute civilizations. A civilization, thus, is the highest cultural grouping of people and the broadest level of cultural identity people have short of that which distinguishes humans from other species.

Civilizations may involve a large number of people, as in the case of China, or a very small number of people, such as, for instance, the Anglophone Caribbean. A civilization may include several nation states, as is the case with European, Latin American, and Arab civilizations, or only one, as is the case with Japanese civilization. Civilizations obviously blend and overlap, and at least one civilization, the West, has two major variants: European and North American. Civilizations are nonetheless meaningful entities, and while the lines between them are seldom sharp, they are real. Civilizations are also dynamic; they rise and fall; they merge and divide; and, as any student of history knows, they also disappear and are buried in the sands of time.

WHY CIVILIZATIONS WILL CLASH

Civilization identity will be increasingly important in the future and the world will be shaped in large measure by the interactions among eight or nine major civilizations. These include the two variants of Western civilization, Confucian, Japanese, Islamic, Hindu, Slavic-Orthodox, Latin American civilizations, and possibly African civilization. The most important conflicts of the future will occur along the cultural fault lines separating these civilizations from one another.

Why May This Be the Case?

First, differences among civilizations are not only real; they are basic. Civilizations are differentiated from each other by history, language, culture, tradition, and, most importantly, religion. The people of different civilizations have different views on the relations between God and man, the individual and the group, the citizen and the state, parents and children, husband and wife, as well as differing views of the relative importance of rights and responsibilities, liberty and authority, equality and hierarchy. These differences are the product of centuries. They will not soon disappear. They are far more fundamental than differences among political ideologies and political regimes. . . .

Second, the world is becoming a smaller place: the interactions between peoples of different civilizations are increasing; these increasing interactions intensify civilization consciousness and awareness of differences between civilizations and commonalities within civilizations. . . . Americans react far more negatively to Japanese investment than to larger investments from Canada and European countries. Similarly as Donald Horowitz has pointed out, "An Ibo may be an Owerri Ibo or an Onitsba Ibo in what was the Eastern region of Nigeria. In Lagos, he is simply an Ibo. In London, he is a Nigerian. In New York, he is an African." The interactions among peoples of different civilizations enhance the civilization-consciousness of people which, in turn, reinvigorate traditional differences and animosities stretching back deep into history.

Third, the processes of economic modernization and social change throughout the world are separating people from traditional local identities. They also weaken the nation state as a source of identity. In almost every part of the world, religion has moved in to fill this gap, often in the form of movements which are labeled "fundamentalist." Such movements are found in Western Christianity, Judaism, Orthodox Christianity, and Hinduism, as well as in Islam. In most countries the leaders of and people most active in fundamentalist movements are young, college-educated, middle-class technicians, professionals, and business persons. . . . The revival of religion, "la revanche de Dieu," as Gilles Kepel labeled it, provides a basis for identity and commitment that transcends national boundaries and unites civilizations.

Fourth, the growth of civilization consciousness is enhanced by the dual role of the West. On the one hand, the West is at a peak of power. At the same time, however, and perhaps as a result, a return to the roots phenomenon is occurring among non-Western civilizations. Increasingly one hears references to trends towards a turning inward and "Asianization" in Japan, the end of the Nehru legacy and the "Hinduization" of India, the failure of Western ideas of socialism and nationalism and hence "re-Islamization" of the Middle East, and now a debate over Westernization versus Russianization in Mr. Yeltsin's country. A West at the peak of its power confronts non-Wests that increasingly have the desire, the will, and the resources to shape the world in non-Western ways. . . .

Fifth, cultural characteristics and differences are less mutable and hence less easily compromised and resolved than political and economic ones. In the former Soviet Union, communists can become democrats, the rich can become poor and the poor rich, but Russians cannot become Estonians and Azeris cannot become Armenians. In class and ideological conflicts, the key question was "Which side are you on?" and people could and did choose sides and change sides. In conflicts between civilizations, the question is "What are you?" That is a given that cannot be changed. And as we know, from Bosnia to the Caucasus to the Sudan, the wrong answer to that question can mean a bullet in the head. Even more than ethnicity, religion discriminates sharply and exclusively among people. A person can be half-French and half-Arab and simultaneously even a citizen of two countries. It is more difficult to be half-Catholic and half-Muslim.

Finally, economic regionalism is increasing. The proportions of total trade that were intraregional rose between 1980 and 1989 from 50.6% to 58.9% in Europe, 32.8% to 37.4% in East Asia, and 32.3% to 36.3% in North America. The importance of regional economic blocs is likely to continue to increase in the future. On the one hand, successful economic regionalism will reinforce civilization-consciousness. On the other hand, however, economic regionalism may succeed only when it is rooted in a common civilization. The European Community rests on the shared foundation of European culture and Western Christianity. The North American Free Trade Area is developing a comparable common cultural basis. Japan, in contrast, faces difficulties in creating a comparable economic entity in East Asia because Japan is a society and civilization unique to itself. . . .

Common culture, in contrast, is clearly facilitating the rapid expansion of the economic relations between the People's Republic of China and Hong Kong, Taiwan, Singapore, and the overseas Chinese communities in other Asian countries. If cultural commonality is a prerequisite for economic integration, the principal East Asian economic bloc of the future is likely to be centered on China. Culture and religion also form the basis of the Economic Cooperation Organization which brings together ten non-Arab Muslim countries: Iran, Pakistan, Turkey, Azerbaijan, Kazakhstan, Kyrgyzstan, Turkmenistan, Tajikistan, Uzbekistan, and Afghanistan. One impetus to the revival and expansion of this organization, founded originally in the 1960s by Turkey, Pakistan, and Iran, is the realization by the leaders of several of these countries that they had no chance of admission to the European Community.

As people define their identity in ethnic and religious terms, they are likely to see an "us" versus "them" relation existing between themselves and people of different ethnicity or religion. The end of ideologically defined states in Eastern Europe and the former Soviet Union permits traditional ethnic identities and animosities to come to the fore. Differences in culture and religion create differences over policy issues, ranging from human rights to immigration to trade and commerce to the environment. Geographical propinquity gives rise to conflicting territorial claims from Bosnia to Kashmir. Most importantly, the efforts of the West to promote its values of democracy and liberalism as universal values, to maintain its military predominance, and to advance its economic interests engender countering responses from groups in other civilizations. Decreasingly able to mobilize support and form coalitions on the basis of ideology, governments and groups will increasingly attempt to mobilize support by appealing to common religion and civilization identity.

The clash of civilizations thus occurs at two levels. At the micro-level, adjacent groups along the fault lines between civilizations struggle, often violently, over the control of territory and each other. At the macro-level, states from different civilizations [that] compete for relative military and economic power struggle over the control of international institutions and third parties, and competitively promote their particular political and religious values.

Notes and Questions

13.1 Do you agree with Huntington's characterization of the "monolithic" nature of some of the cultures he describes? Is it impossible to be "half-Catholic and half-Muslim"?

13.2 What relationship is there between regional economic trade groupings and culture? Is economic trade likely to accentuate differences or blur them in particular geographic regions?

13.3 Do you agree with Huntington that recognition of ethnic identity is more likely to lead to "us" versus "them" perspectives on the world that necessarily will lead to more conflict and violence?

13.4 Can you identify any historical, demographic, cultural, religious, or economic trends that counter Huntington's thesis?

13.5 What do you make of Huntington's "clash of civilizations" thesis for purposes of negotiating across cultural "divides"? Note that this excerpt was written before September 11, 2001. Did those events (and subsequent developments) change any of your own views about global cultural (and political) conflict?

This next excerpt by political science professor Ted Robert Gurr attempts to explain the increase of ethnic conflicts in the early 1990s.

 Ted Robert Gurr, PEOPLES AGAINST STATES:
ETHNOPOLITICAL CONFLICT AND THE CHANGING
WORLD SYSTEM: 1994 PRESIDENTIAL ADDRESS

38 Intl. Stud. Q. 347, 347–377 (1994)

The resurgence of conflicts centered on ethnic claims in the Balkans and the Caucasus, Africa and South Asia, has provoked renewed debate among social scientists about the nature and significance of ethnicity in contemporary societies. From the 1950s through the 1970s it was widely thought that economic development, the migration of rural people to cities, and growing literacy would lead to the creation of complex and integrated societies throughout the world. Modernization theory, which most political scientists accepted more or less on faith, made a specific prediction about ethnic identities: greater political and economic interaction among people and the growth of communication networks would break down peoples' "parochial" identities with ethnic kindred and replace them with loyalties to larger communities like Canada or the European Community or an emerging Pan-Africa.

   Of course it has not worked out that way, and the apparent explosion of conflicts centered on ethnicity has led to a scramble for theoretical explanations. One view is that ethnic identities are "primordial," perhaps even genetically based, and therefore more fundamental and persistent than loyalties to larger social units. A contrary view is that ethnic identities are no more salient than any other kind of identity; they become significant when they are invoked by entrepreneurial political leaders in the instrumental pursuit of material and political benefits for a group or region. The primordial view is held mainly by sociologists, especially those influenced by sociobiology. The instrumental interpretation is most common among social scientists who have succumbed to the lures of rational actor theory. Neither interpretation offers a wholly convincing explanation for the increase in ethnic claims during the 1980s and early 1990s, however. If ethnic identities are "primordial," one needs an accounting of why they are so much more in evidence now than at mid-century. If ethnic identities and claims are a matter of choice, then an explanation is needed of how the political opportunity structures of the world have changed so that appeals to interests defined in ethnic terms are instrumentally more effective now than they were several decades ago.

   I do not propose to resolve this theoretical debate, but to examine the issue in the larger contexts of global change. My particular concern is not the nature of ethnic identification per se but *ethnopolitical conflicts* in which groups that define themselves using ethnic criteria make claims on behalf of their collective interests against the state, or against other political actors. An analysis of ethnopolitical conflict nonetheless needs to proceed from a plausible set of assumptions about the nature of ethnicity and the circumstances under which it disposes to conflict. I assume that *culture* is the core of the identity of most groups that define themselves by ethnic criteria. Ethnic identity and continuity are maintained by the transmission of basic norms and customs across generations. [One researcher] characterizes ethnic identities in Western societies as "part-time"; much the same can be said of most other societies. The boundaries of ethnic groups and the content of their cultures both vary over time; individuals can adopt or reject a culture; and cultural identity becomes more or less salient for members of the collectivity as circumstances change. *Structures* established and maintained by dominant groups in stratified societies, and by historical circumstance and mutual consent among groups in unranked societies, contribute to the perpetuation of cultural distinctions. The greater the *competition* and *inequalities* among groups in heterogenous societies, the greater the salience of ethnic identities and the greater the likelihood of open conflict. When open conflict does occur it is likely to intensify, or reify, both perceptions of difference among contending groups and perceptions of common interest within each group. And the longer open conflict persists, and the more intense it becomes, the stronger and more exclusive are group identities.

Journalist and historian Michael Ignatieff discusses the impact of the clash of civilizations in a book written in the aftermath of the Bosnian civil war.

 Michael Ignatieff, BLOOD AND BELONGING: JOURNEYS INTO THE NEW NATIONALISM

11, 13 (1994)

For many years, I believed that the tide was running in favor of cosmopolitans like me. There seemed so many of us, for one thing. There were at least a dozen world cities — gigantic, multi-ethnic melting pots that provided a home for expatriates, exiles, migrants and transients of all kinds. For the urban professional populations of these major cities, a post-national state of mind was simply taken for granted. People in these places did not bother about the passports of the people they worked or lived with; they did not care about the country-of-origin label on the goods they bought; they simply assumed that in constructing their own way of life they would borrow from the customs of every nation they happened to admire. Cosmopolitans made a positive ethic out of cultural borrowing; in culture, exogamy was better then endogamy, and promiscuity was better than provincialism.

There was nothing new in itself about this cosmopolitan ethic. We have lived in a global economy since 1700, and many of the world's major cities have been global entrepôts for centuries. A global market has been limiting the sovereignty and freedom of maneuver of nation-states at least since Adam Smith first constructed a theory of the phenomenon at the outset of the age of nationalism in 1776. A global market in ideas and cultural forms has existed at least since the Enlightenment republic of letters. . . .

The Americans may be the last remaining superpower, but they are not an imperial power; their authority is exercised in the defense of exclusively national interests, not in the maintenance of an imperial system of global order. As a result, large sections of Africa, Eastern Europe, Soviet Asia, Latin America and the Near East no longer come within any clearly defined sphere of imperial or great power influence. This means that huge sections of the world's population have won the "right of self-determination" on the crudest terms; they have been simply left to fend for themselves. . . . Small wonder, then, that unrestrained by stronger hands, they have set upon each other for that final settling of scores so long deferred by the presence of empire.

Globalism in a post-imperial age permits a post-nationalist consciousness only for those cosmopolitans who are lucky enough to live in the wealthy West. It has brought chaos and violence for the many small peoples too weak to establish defensible states of their own. The Bosnian Muslims are perhaps the most dramatic example of a people who turned in vain to more powerful neighbors to protect them. The people of Sarajevo were true cosmopolitans, fierce believers in ethnic heterogeneity. But they lacked either a reliable imperial protector or a state of their own to guarantee peace among contending ethnicities.

. . . It is only too apparent that cosmopolitanism is the privilege of those who can take a secure nation state for granted. Though we have passed into a post-imperialist age, we have not moved to a post-nationalist age, and I cannot see how we will ever do so. The cosmopolitan order of the great cities — London, Los Angeles, New York, Paris — depends critically on the rule-enforcing capacities of the nation-state. When this order broke down, as it did during the Los Angeles riots of 1992, it becomes apparent that civilized, cosmopolitan multi-ethnic cities have as great a propensity for ethnic warfare as any Eastern European country.

In this sense, therefore, cosmopolitans like myself are not beyond the nation; and a cosmopolitan, post-nationalist spirit will always depend, in the end, on the capacity of nation-states to provide security and civility for their citizens.

Notes and Questions

13.6   By 2000, Gurr actually argued that the ethnic conflict he described above was on the wane. Measured by the number of conflicts as well as by whether these conflicts are escalating or de-escalating, the ethnic violence of the 1990s is not as prevalent. He argues that the global push toward better recognizing minority rights, granting autonomy to minorities and/or regions, and focusing on negotiation and accommodation have led to this reduction. Ted Robert Gurr, Ethnic Warfare on the Wane, 79 Foreign Aff. 52 (2000).

13.7   Does Ignatieff's argument that a strong nation-state is necessary to ensure security resemble the arguments made by some that the rule of law and justice should be present in negotiation and other forms of informal dispute resolution in the domestic context? Does international law or custom play a similar or different role than "the rule of law" in domestic conflict resolution?

13.8 Is Ignatieff's "cosmopolitan" class comprised, at least in part, of those who take negotiation training at the leading world universities, studying the same kinds of principles as you are learning in this course? What impediments might there be to creating a "world culture" of problem-solving negotiation?

13.9 Note the expressions in Huntington's and Ignatieff's articles of tensions between individual experiences of "culture," nationhood, and racial and ethnic identities and how these things are experienced in groups, institutional structures, and the wider society. Culture is thus a product of both psychology and sociology (not to mention geography and economy). Consider how culture is made salient in international negotiations.

B. INTERNATIONAL NEGOTIATION

As in all human relations, negotiation is the foundational process in international dealings — direct party-to-party communications that attempt to create or repair relationships, whether diplomatic, strategic, or commercial. Like the domestic negotiation processes already studied, international negotiations can be bilateral or multiparty, occur with or without representatives or agents, and result in mutual gain or distributive stalemate. As you read the materials below, consider whether the core or foundational principles of negotiation in the international context are different from those in domestic situations.

Perhaps one of the first practical negotiation theorists to take note of is Niccolo Machiavelli, who is often characterized as a theorist of diabolical self-interested leadership and manipulation. In his advice to potential princes or leaders of Renaissance Italian city-states, Machiavelli, in fact, might offer useful advice for modern-day negotiators who must both preserve internal legitimacy and acceptability from constituents and achieve respect, security, and advantage from others. In the international context, Machiavelli's caution to pay attention to what *is* rather than what *might be* is particularly apt. As you read the following excerpt, ask yourself if Machiavelli has anything to offer modern-day international negotiators beyond self-interest and manipulation.

 Niccolo Machiavelli, **THE PRINCE**

61, 68-70, 98-100 (Harvey Mansfield trans., 2d ed. 1998)

OF THOSE THINGS FOR WHICH MEN AND ESPECIALLY PRINCES ARE PRAISED OR BLAMED

[S]ince my intent is to write something useful to whoever understands it, it has appeared to me more fitting to go directly to the effectual truth of the thing than to the imagination of it. . . . For a man who wants to make a profession of good in all regards must come to ruin among so many who are not good. Hence it is necessary to a prince, if he wants to maintain himself, to learn to be able not to be good, and to use this and not use it according to necessity. . . .

IN WHAT MODE FAITH SHOULD BE KEPT BY PRINCES

How praiseworthy it is for a prince to keep his faith, and to live with honesty and not by astuteness, everyone understands. Nonetheless one sees by experience in our times that the princes who have done great things are those who have taken little account of faith and have known how to get around men's brains with their astuteness; and in the end they have overcome those who have founded themselves on loyalty.

    Thus, you must know that there are two kinds of combat: one with laws, the other with force. The first is proper to man, the second to beasts; but because the first is often not enough, one must have recourse to the second. Therefore it is necessary for a prince to know well how to use the beast and the man. . . .

    [S]ince a prince is compelled of necessity to know well how to use the beast, he should pick the fox and the lion, because the lion does not defend itself from snares and the fox does not defend itself from wolves. So one needs to be a fox to recognize snares and a lion to frighten the wolves. Those who stay simply with the lion do not understand this. A prudent lord, therefore, cannot observe faith, nor should he, when such observance turns against him, and the causes that made him promise have been eliminated. . . .

    Thus, it is not necessary for a prince to have all the above-mentioned qualities in fact, but it is indeed necessary to appear to have them. Nay, I dare say this, that by having them and always observing them, they are harmful; and by appearing to have them, they are useful, as it is to appear merciful, faithful, humane, honest, and religious, and to be so; but to remain with a spirit built so that, if you need not to be those things, you are able and know how to change to the contrary. This has to be understood: that a prince, and especially a new prince, cannot observe all those things for which men are held good, since he is often under a necessity, to maintain his state, of acting against faith, against charity, against humanity, against religion. And so he needs to have a spirit disposed to change as the winds of fortune and variations of things command him, and as I said above, not depart from good, when possible, but know how to enter into evil, when forced by necessity. . . .

HOW MUCH FORTUNE CAN DO IN HUMAN AFFAIRS, AND IN WHAT MODE IT MAY BE OPPOSED

I believe, further, that he is happy who adapts his mode of proceeding to the qualities of the times; and similarly, he is unhappy whose procedure is in disaccord with the times. For one sees that in the things that lead men to the end that each has before him, that is, glories and riches, they proceed variously: one with caution, the other with impetuosity; one by violence, the other with art; one with patience, the other with its contrary — and with these different modes each can attain it. One also sees two cautious persons, one attaining his plan, the other not; and similarly two persons are equally happy with two different methods, one being cautious, the other impetuous. This arises from nothing other than from the quality of the times that they conform to or not in their procedure. From this follows what I said, that two persons working differently come out with the same effect; and of two persons working identically, one is led to his end, the other not. On this also depends the variability of the good: for if one governs himself with caution and patience, and the times and affairs turn in such a way that his government is good, he comes out happy; but if the times and affairs change, he is ruined because he does not change his mode of proceeding. Nor may a man be found so prudent as to know how to accommodate himself to this, whether because he cannot deviate from what nature inclines him to or also because, when one has always flourished by walking on one path, he cannot be persuaded to depart from it. And so the cautious man, when it is time to come to impetuosity, does not know how to do it, hence comes to ruin: for if he would change his nature with the times and with affairs, his fortune would not change.

Notes and Questions

13.10 Is Machiavelli telling princes (negotiators) to be all things to all people? To take advantage of them? Or is he suggesting, in what has given him his maligned reputation, that a good leader must change with the times, be flexible, be willing to do that which might be considered bad or evil by others — to do what is necessary in the circumstances rather than act out of universal good principles?

13.11 Is Machiavelli's advice more apt in the international than in the domestic context? Why or why not?

13.12 For some, Machiavelli's *The Prince* is the first work of modern political science due to its use of case studies (ancient and, for him, modern European history) to extract general principles of pragmatic success in ruling and to use these case studies to offer some prescriptive advice for how to proceed in different kinds of present and future situations, against and with different kinds of adversaries and allies. Compare this to Howard Raiffa's distinctions between "descriptive" and "prescriptive" advice for negotiators in The Art and Science of Negotiation (1982). Note the differences in voice when one writes or strategizes from outside of the problem (as an advisor) or from inside as an actor (as one who must make decisions and negotiation moves).

13.13 Does Machiavelli suggest that all statesmen or international negotiators must be guarded adversarialists or competitive negotiators? Or that they must be flexible, with multiple repertoires of behaviors? Is problem solving or principled negotiation possible in international negotiation? Remember that Roger Fisher's ideas for *Getting to YES* came out of his experience as an international negotiator. See Roger Fisher, International Conflict for Beginners (1969); see also Roger Fisher, Elizabeth Kopelman & Andrea Kupfer Schneider, Beyond Machiavelli: Tools for Coping with Conflict (1994); Roger Fisher, Andrea Kupfer Schneider, Elizabeth Borgwardt & Brian

Ganson, Coping with International Conflict: A Systematic Approach to Influence in International Negotiation (1997); F.C. Iklé, How Nations Negotiate (1964).

13.14 Do models of prescription for negotiation change in different times (Machiavelli's notion of fortune)? Did we think differently about what was possible in international negotiation models after the Dayton Accords (ending violence in Bosnia in 1995), the Good Friday Accords (ending violence in Northern Ireland in 1998), and the Oslo Accords (between Yitzhak Rabin and Yasser Arafat, laying out a peace plan for Israel and Palestine in 1993) than we did after September 11 and the ongoing violence between Israelis and Palestinians? What makes the times or fortunes change? Events, circumstances, or negotiation models themselves? See Dennis Ross, The Missing Peace: The Inside Story of the Fight for Middle East Peace (2004).

These next two excerpts discuss how negotiators must deal with both their negotiation counterpart and their internal constituency. The first, by political science professor Robert Putnam, examines the impact of domestic politics. The second excerpt, by international relations professor Eileen Babbit, examines in particular the principal-agent problems in negotiation.

 Robert D. Putnam, **DIPLOMACY AND DOMESTIC POLITICS: THE LOGIC OF TWO-LEVEL GAMES**

in Double-Edge Diplomacy: International Bargaining and Domestic Politics 436-442, 459-460 (1993)

TWO-LEVEL GAMES: A METAPHOR FOR DOMESTIC-INTERNATIONAL INTERACTIONS

The politics of many international negotiations can usefully be conceived as a two-level game. At the national level, domestic groups pursue their interests by pressuring the government to adopt favorable policies, and politicians seek power by constructing coalitions among those groups. At the international level, national governments seek to maximize their own ability to satisfy domestic pressures, while minimizing the adverse consequences of foreign developments. Neither of the two games can be ignored by central decision-makers, so long as their countries remain interdependent, yet sovereign.

Each national political leader appears at both game boards. Across the international table sit his foreign counterparts, and at his elbows sit diplomats and other international advisors. Around the domestic table behind him sit party and parliamentary figures, spokesmen for domestic agencies, representatives of key interest groups, and the leader's own political advisors. The unusual complexity of this two-level game is that moves that are rational for a player at one board (such as raising energy prices, conceding territory, or limiting auto imports) may be impolitic for that same player at the other board. Nevertheless, there are powerful incentives for consistency between the two games. Players (and kibitzers) will tolerate some differences in rhetoric between the two games, but in the end either prices rise or they don't.

The political complexities for the players in this two-level game are staggering. Any key player at the international table who is dissatisfied with the outcome may upset the game board; and conversely, any leader who fails to satisfy his fellow players at the domestic table risks being evicted from his seat. . . .

TOWARD A THEORY OF RATIFICATION: THE IMPORTANCE OF "WIN-SETS"

Consider the following stylized scenario that might apply to any two-level game. Negotiators representing two organizations meet to reach an agreement between them, subject to the constraint that any tentative agreement must be ratified by their respective organizations. The negotiators might be heads of government representing nations, for example, or labor and management representatives, or party leaders in a multi-party coalition, or a finance minister negotiating with an IMF team, or leaders of a House-Senate conference committee, or ethnic-group leaders in a consociational democracy. For the moment, we shall presume that each side is represented by a single leader or "chief negotiator," and that this individual has no independent policy preferences, but seeks simply to achieve an agreement that will be attractive to his constituents.

It is convenient analytically to decompose the process into two stages:

1. Bargaining between the negotiators, leading to a tentative agreement; call that Level I.
2. Separate discussions within each group of constituents about whether to ratify the agreement; call that Level II.

This sequential decomposition into a negotiation phase and a ratification phase is useful for purposes of exposition, although it is not descriptively accurate. In practice, expectational effects will be quite important. There are likely to be prior consultations and bargaining at Level II to hammer out an initial position for the Level I negotiations. Conversely, the need for Level II ratification is certain to affect the Level I bargaining. In fact, expectations of rejection at Level II may abort negotiations at Level I without any formal action at Level II. For example, even though both the American and Iranian governments seem to have favored an arms-for-hostages deal, negotiations collapsed as soon as they became public and thus liable to de facto "ratification." In many negotiations, the two-level process may be iterative, as the negotiators try out possible agreements and probe their constituents' views. In more complicated cases . . . the constituents' views may themselves evolve in the course of the negotiations. Nevertheless, the requirement that any Level I agreement must, in the end, be ratified at Level II imposes a crucial theoretical link between the two levels. . . .

For two quite different reasons, the contours of the Level II win-sets are very important for understanding Level I agreements.

First, *larger win-sets make Level I agreement more likely*, ceteris paribus. By definition, any successful agreement must fall within the Level II win-sets of each of the parties to the accord. Thus, agreement is possible only if those win-sets overlap; and the larger each win-set, the more likely they are to overlap. Conversely, the smaller the win-sets, the greater the risk that the negotiations will break down. For example, during the prolonged prewar Anglo-Argentine negotiations over the Falklands/Malvinas, several tentative agreements were rejected in one capital or the other for domestic political reasons; when it became clear that the initial British and Argentine win-sets did not overlap at all, war became virtually inevitable. . . .

The second reason why win-set size is important is that *the relative size of the respective Level II win-sets will affect the distribution of the joint gains from the international bargain.* The larger the perceived win-set of a negotiator, the more he can be "pushed around" by the other Level I negotiators. Conversely, a small domestic win-set can be a bargaining advantage: "I'd like to accept your proposal, but I could never get it accepted at home." Lamenting the domestic constraints under which one must operate is (in the words of one experienced British diplomat) "the natural thing to say at the beginning of a tough negotiation." . . .

A Third World leader whose domestic position is relatively weak (Argentina's Alfonsin?) should be able to drive a better bargain with his international creditors, other things being equal, than one whose domestic standing is more solid (Mexico's de la Madrid?). The difficulties of winning Congressional ratification are often exploited by American negotiators. During the negotiation of the Panama Canal Treaty, for example, "the Secretary of State warned the Panamanians several times . . . that the new treaty would have to be acceptable to at least sixty-seven senators," and "Carter, in a personal letter to Torrijos, warned that further concessions by the United States would seriously threaten chances for Senate ratification." Precisely to forestall such tactics, opponents may demand that a negotiator ensure himself "negotiating room" at Level II before opening the Level I negotiations. . . .

CONCLUSION

The most portentous development in the fields of comparative politics and international relations in recent years is the dawning recognition among practitioners in each field of the need to take into account entanglements between the two. Empirical illustrations of reciprocal influence between domestic and international affairs abound. What we need now are concepts and theories that will help us organize and extend our empirical observations.

Analysis in terms of two-level games offers a promising response to this challenge. Unlike state-centric theories, the two-level approach recognizes the inevitability of domestic conflict about what the "national interest" requires. . . .

This theoretical approach highlights several significant features of the links between diplomacy and domestic politics, including:

- The important distinction between voluntary and involuntary defection from international agreements;
- The contrast between issues on which domestic interests are homogeneous, simply pitting hawks against doves, and issues on which domestic interests are

more heterogeneous, so that domestic cleavage may actually foster international cooperation;

- The possibility of synergistic issue linkage, in which strategic moves at one
  game-table facilitate unexpected coalitions at the second table;
- The paradoxical fact that institutional arrangements which strengthen decision-makers at home may weaken their international bargaining position, and
  vice versa;
- The importance of targeting international threats, offers, and side-payments
  with an eye toward their domestic incidence at home and abroad;
- The strategic uses of uncertainty about domestic politics, and the special utility
  of "kinky win-sets";
- The potential reverberation of international pressures within the domestic
  arena;
- The divergences of interest between a national leader and those on whose
  behalf he is negotiating — and in particular, the international implications of
  his fixed investments in domestic politics.

 Eileen F. Babbitt, **CHALLENGES FOR INTERNATIONAL
DIPLOMATIC AGENTS**

> **in Negotiating on Behalf of Others: Advice to Lawyers, Business Executives, Sports
> Agents, Diplomats, Politicians, and Everybody Else 136-137, 139, 141, 143, 145-146
> (Robert H. Mnookin & Lawrence E. Susskind eds., 1999)**

The traditional principal-agent issues . . . include structuring a mandate for the agent,
determining the authority an agent will have to make commitments, creating incentives that align the agent's interests with those of the principal, and determining the
extent of information that will be passed between the principal and the agent. The
basic model from which these concerns are drawn is that of a single principal operating with a single agent. In the international context, these issues are complicated by
several additional factors: multiple principals, shifting mandates, multiple agents, and
role conflicts for the agent. . . .

MULTIPLE PRINCIPALS

The most notable feature of international diplomatic negotiation is that it is carried
out by agents who are working for a multiplicity of principals in a complicated web of
relationships. This makes traditional principal-agent analysis quite problematic. In
the classic principal-agent analysis, there is one person in each role. . . .

There is no single point of reference for the agent, in terms of receiving instructions, gaining authority, or procuring information. For example, in the United
States, the secretary of state (agent) may give instructions to an assistant secretary
(agent), based on the instructions that the secretary has received from the president
(principal). Those instructions may be superseded at any point by the president
himself, especially if he is pressured by Congress (principal) or by adverse reactions
from the American public (principal). Thus, the assistant secretary, who is at the end
of this particular agent-principal chain, must pay attention to direct instructions

being given by the secretary but also be ready to respond to political intervention from Congress or a backlash in public opinion. . . .

The principal-agent dynamic becomes still more complicated when the agent is acting on behalf of the "international community." This quite often means receiving a mandate from the United Nations Security Council (UNSC), a consortium of permanent and rotating members who do not always agree. . . .

SHIFTING MANDATES

Many of the principals in an international negotiation are elected (e.g., in the United States, the president and Congress are prime examples). Agents are not. Instructions may therefore change on short notice, depending on events on the ground that stir public opinion or shift the political winds. "Elected" principals are very susceptible to such influences, and they can, in turn, put pressure on "appointed" and "career" agents. Mandates therefore can be a moving target, and agents may get caught in the shifting currents and then become scapegoats for failed foreign policies. . . .

Another related issue is the effect of technology on diplomacy. In previous eras, ambassadors and other foreign service staff were the only source[s] of information available to their principals. This gave them enormous power over their own mandates (and authority), as these were shaped by the perceptions of the world that they themselves formulated. With telephones, instantaneous news coverage, and now Internet access, the principals themselves have much more direct access to their counterparts abroad and to breaking news in other countries. This has diminished the role of diplomats to some degree (depending, of course, on the accessibility of a particular country via these technologies) and has certainly constrained their dominance over the information flow back home. . . .

MULTIPLE AGENTS

In addition to multiple principals manifesting multiple and mutable interests, there are often multiple agents working on the same issue as representatives of the same principal. Sometimes they are functioning as a designated team or delegation, but often they are using different points of entry from different parts of the coalition of principals. The U.S. delegations in post-Dayton Bosnia were an example, in which different messages were being conveyed by different agency representatives (i.e., State Department, Treasury, Commerce, Defense) to the European allies and to the Bosnian parties. Coordination among the agents was very difficult, and often impossible, to achieve, because coordination in their headquarters on both policy and implementation was not agreed upon. . . . The result was that others on the ground, particularly local organizations and officials, did not know who really spoke for the U.S. government. This type of situation obviously can undermine any authority or call into question the credibility of any or all of the agents, which in turn weakens the position of the principals for whom they work. . . .

ROLE CONFLICTS

If agents develop a relationship with the other side in which a "working trust" is established and negotiations can proceed, they may be seen as traitors to their own side. If they do not develop such trust, negotiations may break down and war will ensue. The problem is how to transfer their experience of the other side in such a way that the working trust (if it is built) can be brought back to one's constituency. This is not about relationships only as a means to achieving one's tangible goals; it is about a relationship as a goal in itself. How does an agent translate the trust and confidence that he or she has built back to a very scared and untrusting home community? It is the community that has to be convinced, not just the leaders (i.e., the multiple principal problem). In the international arena, this role conflict may be a difference in degree rather than in kind from other contexts. The difference in degree is striking: Yitzhak Rabin and Anwar Sadat were assassinated because they could not bring their constituencies along in supporting the relationship they had built with the other side.

These examples also bring up another form of role conflict: that of being both a mediator and a negotiator. As the negotiator, an agent must represent the interests of his or her principal. Often, the agent is spanning two very different cultures, defined in the traditional sense as cutting across national boundaries but often cutting across class or professional lines as well. In doing so, the agent must mediate between the two groups, representing not only the interests of each but also the understandings and perceptions of each to the other. . . .

A third form that such role conflict may take is that of representing one's principal versus being a cooperative member of the diplomatic community. . . . A tension could develop, especially in negotiations that take place over long periods of time, between being perceived as a "good" member of the guild versus being tough for one's own side.

Notes and Questions

13.15 Think of a recent international negotiation. Who were the Level II players? Who were the Level I players? Which negotiation was more difficult?

13.16 What are domestic examples of two-level bargaining games?

13.17 For more on principal-agent issues in negotiation, see Roger Fisher, Negotiating Inside Out: What Are the Best Ways to Relate Internal Negotiations with External Ones?, 5 Negot. J. 33 (1989).

13.18 William Canby, senior circuit judge for the U.S. Court of Appeals for the Ninth Circuit, embarked with several other past Peace Corps members on an attempted international mediation in the Eritrea and Ethiopian border conflict. As past Peace Corps members who had volunteered in either Eritrea or Ethiopia, Canby and his fellow negotiators were very well treated and were able to obtain meetings with important government officials, including both President Issais and Prime Minister Meles. William C. Canby, Jr., A Senior Judge's Foray into Diplomacy, 10 Experience 20 (2000). How does the involvement of interested outsiders change the principal-agent dynamic? Who is the agent here?

This section's final excerpt discusses the question of whether negotiation is always appropriate. Are there some people with whom we should *never* negotiate?

 Robert H. Mnookin, WHEN NOT TO NEGOTIATE: A NEGOTIATION IMPERIALIST REFLECTS ON APPROPRIATE LIMITS

74 U. Colo. L. Rev. 1077, 1078, 1081-1083, 1085, 1088-1090, 1095-1096, 1106-1107 (2003)

In this [article] I would like to share my thinking on some interrelated questions that came to my mind in light of the September 11, 2001, terrorist attacks on the U.S.: What are the limits of negotiation? How should one decide whether it makes sense to explore the possibility of resolving conflict through negotiation? And when should one refuse to negotiate? There is surprisingly little scholarship addressing these questions. . . .

In the present discussion, I narrow my interest to the strategic decision of not entering into the negotiation. The implicit assumption of many negotiation imperialists — that everything is or should be negotiable — certainly doesn't describe the world. In the family, at the workplace, and in the market, many matters are said to be "non-negotiable." A department store won't haggle over the price of its ties and a restaurant won't negotiate the price of an entrée. A political leader may refuse to negotiate with a terrorist kidnapper. Sometimes the refusal to negotiate may be unwise. But sometimes *it is better not to negotiate.* What considerations are and should be taken into account in deciding whether to negotiate at all? In various contexts, where a party refuses to negotiate, what reasons are typically used to justify that decision? How should a party think about and decide whether to enter into or begin a negotiation at all? . . .

My framework poses six questions that should be addressed, four of which draw from negotiation analysis. Negotiation imperialists — myself included — suggest that in preparing for a negotiation a party should identify its own interests and those of the other parties; think about each side's BATNA (best alternative to negotiated agreement); try to imagine options that might better serve the negotiators' interests than their BATNAs; and ensure that commitments made in any negotiated deal have a reasonable prospect of actually being implemented. These same considerations are equally valid in informing an individual's decision whether one should enter into a negotiation. In addition, one must also consider the expected costs — both direct and indirect — of engaging in the negotiation process, as well as issues of legitimacy and morality. . . .

What considerations of legitimacy and morality should be taken into account? In considering the benefits and costs of the decision whether to negotiate, there is no avoiding questions of legitimacy and morality. One aspect was mentioned earlier: when thinking about alternatives to negotiation, one must consider the legitimacy of those alternatives. A bigger child may have the power to grab the toy of a younger and smaller sibling, but most parents would prefer that the child not exercise that alternative but instead ask to use the toy. A self-help alternative to negotiation may not be considered legitimate, at least without some institutional approval. Few doubted the capacity of the U.S. to bring about a regime change in Iraq, but many have questioned the legitimacy of the American resort to force in the absence of U.N. Security Council authorization.

The mere process of negotiation with a counterpart is perceived as conferring some *recognition* and *legitimacy* on them. Providing a counterpart with "a place at the table" acknowledges their existence, actions, (and to some degree) the validity of their interests. To avoid validation of interests or claims, countries have often refused to negotiate with rebels or insurgent groups, denying them any recognition or legitimacy. Thus, for decades, Israel refused to negotiate with the Palestinian Liberation Organization, Britain denied any status from the Irish Revolutionary Army, the Spanish would not negotiate with the Basque separatist rebels, Peru would not engage in a dialogue with the Tupac Amaru, and Russia announced an absolute policy of not negotiating with the Chechen rebels. . . .

The policy of refusing to negotiate with terrorists derives not only from the fear of conferring legitimacy or recognition, but also from aversion to *rewarding past bad behavior.* When previous interactions have failed to satisfy the claims of a party, satisfying its claims under the pressure of violence implies that violence was indeed worthwhile. This consideration, of course, is problematic. Although most of the national liberation movements around the world have employed violence in their struggle to gain independence or self-determination (among very few Gandhi-like exceptions), once violence is employed it usually entrenches political rivals, at least in the short term following violence.

Perhaps the most renowned example of a refusal to negotiate for moral considerations is Sir Winston Churchill's refusal to negotiate directly or indirectly with Adolph Hitler in May of 1940. For Churchill, the refusal derived not only from the questionable effectiveness of such negotiations, given the dismal history of Hitler's negotiations with Chamberlain, or the potential effects of failed negotiations on his fellow citizens, but also from a strong moral aversion to *"doing business with the devil."* Churchill truly believed that Britain had a deep moral obligation, on behalf of itself as well as the rest of the world, to fight Nazi Germany. In relation to British advocates of appeasement, he said: "An appeaser is one who feeds a crocodile — hoping it will eat him last." . . .

The members of the Taliban were not innocent bystanders. They had been given advance warning by the U.S. government: according to a State Department official who had testified before Congress in the summer of 2000, the U.S. had let the Taliban "know, in no uncertain terms, that we will hold [the Taliban] responsible for any terrorist acts undertaken by bin Laden." There could be little doubt that the Taliban harbored thousands of Islamic terrorists from around the world and allowed its territory to serve as a training ground for armed secret agents capable of terrorist acts in the U.S. and elsewhere.

Under these circumstances, there would be moral costs associated with negotiating with the Taliban. Negotiating a deal that would save the Taliban regime would be tantamount to rewarding it for its flagrant defiance of the U.S. and the international community regarding its responsibility for al Qaeda's operations in Afghanistan. Moreover, it would have required the U.S. to negotiate with an intolerant and repressive regime that the U.S. had been unwilling officially to recognize heretofore and which the U.S. had already declared it would hold directly responsible for any future al Qaeda attack. Finally, although negotiation with the Taliban did take place after the 1998 bombing of the U.S. embassies, the nature, magnitude, and horror of the September 11th attacks brought many to feel that there would be something repulsive in negotiating the fate of the chief perpetrator of the attacks with the regime that was complicit.

To conclude, analyzed through the framework offered here, and specifically, by weighing the interests, the probability of a good negotiated outcome, the available BATNAs, and the costs associated with negotiating, I believe President Bush's decision not to negotiate with the Taliban, and instead, to use force to achieve U.S. goals, was correct. To negotiate with the Taliban would have imposed substantial costs:

1. In deterring future terrorists and those who might harbor them;
2. In maintaining credibility and self-respect;
3. In legitimizing a regime that the U.S. had not previously recognized;
4. In building and sustaining a broad international coalition and maintaining domestic political support; and
5. In allowing heinous acts to be the occasion for dialogue with a party that the U.S. believes is at least partially responsible for such acts.

Because of the combined weight of these costs, the lack of Taliban credibility, and improbability of a negotiated outcome that would serve American interests, the U.S. refusal to negotiate with the Taliban was justified. However, taken individually these costs should not be considered determinative of the decision whether to negotiate. For example, there may be cases where the costs of negotiating with a regime that the U.S. has not previously recognized would be outweighed by substantial benefits. . . .

My basic preference in favor of negotiation remains. For any number of reasons, disputants may tend to exaggerate the potential costs of entering into negotiations and may underestimate the possible benefits in comparison with more coercive alternatives. Indeed, it would be useful to explore both theoretically and empirically this possibility, which if true, might go some distance in justifying the preference of negotiation imperialists. But even if true this would do no more than justify a presumption in favor of using negotiation to resolve conflict. This presumption must be rebuttable.

For too long, negotiation imperialists have implicitly assumed that negotiation always makes sense. This is, of course, nonsense. Such a conclusion would require that the expected net benefits of negotiation are always greater than the expected net benefits of any alternative form of dispute resolution. Negotiation is not without costs, and my primary purpose in writing this article is to suggest a framework for the analysis of not only the expected benefits but also the expected costs of entering into negotiation.

Notes and Questions

13.19 What do you think about Mnookin's conclusion? To whom else would "no negotiation" apply? Who should decide this?

13.20 How does Mnookin define *negotiation* here? Is his definition broader or narrower than your own?

13.21 Are attorneys who refuse to negotiate with the other side simply making strategic judgments? Strategic errors? Is their behavior ever justifiable in the framework Mnookin offers? In other ways?

13.22 How do Mnookin's conclusions apply to other dispute resolution processes?

C. FACILITATED NEGOTIATION: INTERNATIONAL MEDIATION

As in domestic negotiations, when the parties themselves fail to accomplish their goals, they may call on a third-party intervenor for help. In the international arena, the disputants can seek an informal mediator, an institutionally appointed mediator, or they can appeal to a number of formal international institutions established to help resolve particular kinds of disputes or issues between citizens of different nations (as in commercial trade disputes), between governments and private parties (as in international investments), and between and among nations and other international groups (formal institutions such as the U.N. or nongovernmental organizations such as Search for Common Ground). A number of international and national organizations, both governmental and nongovernmental, provide technical assistance and training in dispute resolution processes both for internal "rule of law" and justice system development and for international development activities. These programs — from organizations such as the World Bank, USAID, the U.S. State Department, and the Consensus Building Institute — are often challenged as being ethnocentric (American or Anglo-American in origin) or culturally imperialistic in suggesting that other nations should follow "our" approaches to conflict resolution. (Of course, this criticism could also apply to our efforts to promote constitutionalism, rule of law, democracy, and separation of powers.)

Just as this chapter has asked with respect to international negotiation, it is useful to ask whether mediation in the international context is different from domestic

mediation. It seems fairly obvious that here the answer is yes. Third parties have attempted interventions in nation-to-nation, intranational, and multinational conflicts for thousands of years, with many very different role conceptions in mind. Often such intervenors did not think of themselves as mediators in the sense this book uses that term. Third-party intervenors in the international context often are not neutral but quite interested in the relations between other parties, such as in peacekeeping efforts, trade disputes, boundary disputes, and economic or political alliances. The phrase "muscle mediation" was probably first used in international contexts where mediators with strong political or economic power are able to control, persuade, or cajole disputing parties to agree by using implicit or explicit threats, promises of aid and benefits, or threats of sanctions and withholding of benefits. The phrase "shuttle diplomacy," too, usually refers to disputes of international origin. Used by such mediators as Secretary of State Kissinger and President Jimmy Carter at Camp David, shuttle diplomacy involves moving from party to party, using nothing but caucuses and confidential meetings to broker a settlement. In this form of mediation, the parties are almost never together, and the solutions or agreements are much more likely to be suggested by the mediators than developed in direct negotiations between the parties. (Contrast the mediation efforts at President Carter's and President Clinton's respective Camp David peace talks on the Mideast (1978 and 2000, respectively) with the Oslo peace accords.)

At present, mediation is much more common in diplomatic and peace-seeking efforts while arbitration is the more common process in international commercial dealings. But the use of mediation is increasing in commercial and private dealings with multinational actors. Why might the two different processes be used differently in these two spheres of international activity? Are there other forms of international interaction that might lead to other forms of dispute resolution?

Fortunately for dispute resolution students and analysts, many of those who have participated in international mediations, both successful and unsuccessful, have written *post hoc* case studies or memoirs of their activities, and third-party scholars have reported on conflict interventions, so it is possible to analyze what interventions or techniques have been successful or not in particular settings. See, e.g., Jacob Bercovitch, Resolving International Conflicts: The Theory and Practice of Mediation (1996); Jimmy Carter, Keeping Faith: Memoirs of a President (1982); Chester Crocker, Fen Osler Hampson & Pamela Aall, Herding Cats: Multi-Party Mediation in a Complex World (1999); Henry Kissinger, The White House Years (1979); Hugh Miall, The Peacemakers: Peaceful Settlement of Disputes Since 1945 (1992); George Mitchell, Making Peace (1999); Turbulent Peace: The Challenges of Managing International Conflict (Chester A. Crocker et al. eds., 2001); Words over War: Mediation and Arbitration to Prevent Deadly Conflict (Melanie Greenberg et al. eds., 2000).

The next excerpt starts by outlining broad roles third parties can take in a conflict and concludes by discussing a type of mediation strategy called the "One-Text Process."

Roger Fisher, Elizabeth Kopelman & Andrea Kupfer Schneider, **BEYOND MACHIAVELLI: TOOLS FOR COPING WITH CONFLICT**

123-132 (1994)

Players who are not principals in a conflict can play a wide range of constructive roles. Third-party interventions can contribute to problem-solving by making sure that disputants attack the problem rather than each other, and by keeping the focus on interests rather than on positions. Some roles are purely administrative, such as the functions associated with hosting a Devising Session or a conference. Other roles engage the third party in the substance of the dispute.

In a world filled with ready-made dispute-resolution procedures, it is important to look beyond the labels of "alternative dispute resolution," "negotiation," "mediation," and "arbitration" when considering useful roles for third parties. [Table] 31 illustrates a variety of roles that third parties can play, ranging from primarily process-oriented ones, such as hosting a diplomatic conference, to primarily substance-oriented ones, such as monitoring compliance after an agreement. In any action plan involving the participation of a third party, what is most important is to design a role for the third party that addresses the particular diagnosis of why a given conflict has not been settled. . . .

31. Some Third-Party Roles for Coping with a Conflict		
RANGE OF ROLES	**EXAMPLES**	**WHO MIGHT PLAY THEM**
Primarily process-oriented roles	Hosting a diplomatic conference	Another government
	Developing tools for the parties to use in diagnosing their conflict	Academic institutions
	Facilitating a brainstorming session	A trained facilitator
Mixed process and substantive roles	Holding a devising session to develop a range of options for the parties' consideration	A nonprofit foundation
	Facilitating a one-text procedure	A prominent international figure
	Providing peace-keeping forces to maintain a ceasefire while negotiations continue	The U.N. or a regional group such as the OAS
Primarily substance-oriented roles	Providing neutral evaluation of the merits of parties' claims	A professional association or specialized arbitration organization
	Providing a binding decision for outstanding issues in a dispute	The World Court

One way in which third parties often try to assist the parties is in mediating between them. The mediation technique perhaps most commonly used by third parties — concession hunting — often fails because it does not address the underlying interests of the disputants that have impeded a settlement. Focusing on positions rather than interests, this strategy tries to persuade the parties to give up bits of their opposing positions piece by piece. The goal is to edge the parties' positions toward each other until they eventually converge. . . .

Most players, in anticipation of this common strategy, adopt extreme positions from which they will later be able to make concessions without giving up anything important. Unfortunately, the "fat" that was originally included in order to pad a position is likely, through the process of public debate and commitment to one's constituents, to harden into "bone" that is now difficult to cut away. . . .

It is easy to see how this process encourages foot-dragging and haggling. This concession-hunting process tends to foreclose the possibility of generating creative options — the possibility that the pie can be enlarged through joint problem-solving.

A better process can change the choice. Rather than talking about two plans that reflect extreme partisan perceptions, it is usually better to talk about one plan that reflects some third party's judgment of what options might be acceptable to both sides. Consider how a lawyer might help two business professionals work out an agreement to become partners. One approach would be to ask each of them to draw up a separate plan, and then to ask each for concessions until a common plan could be reached. A better way would be for the lawyer to listen to the two parties discuss their individual and joint interests, and then to produce a rough draft of points that might be included in a partnership agreement. This draft would not be "the lawyer's proposal" but rather an open draft for all to discuss. . . .

Parties engaged in a conflict also need such a "business plan" of how they are going to deal with each other. Presenting disputants with a single draft that has been generated by the mediator and asking, "What would be wrong with doing it this way?" is more likely to garner a constructive response than asking for a concession. It is typically difficult to give something away and to make commitments, especially when we are uncertain about what we will receive in return. It is always easy to criticize. . . . Over the ensuing days and weeks, the mediator refines the draft by circulating among the parties, learning of concerns they may still have, and drafting new language designed to meet them as best he can. When the mediator feels that they cannot improve the draft any further — that it is fair, workable, and reconciles their conflicting interests as well as possible — he polishes the text and presents a final document to the parties for their approval. . . .

The One-Text Process was used by President Carter and Secretary of State Cyrus Vance at the 1978 Camp David negotiations between President Anwar Sadat of Egypt and Prime Minister Menachem Begin of Israel. The U.S. negotiating team prepared some twenty-three consecutive drafts or redrafts of parts of a text over ten days, each responding to some point raised by a party. On the last day, President Carter decided that this was the best he could do and asked each party to agree. A few hours later, the Camp David Accords were signed.

Some differences between the widely used strategy of hunting for concessions and the One-Text procedure are summarized [below] in [Table] 35. In some cases a mediator might want to employ a variation on the One-Text Process by producing two alternative drafts. These would not reflect partisan positions but, starting from different assumptions, would seek to meet as well as possible the interests of both parties. An architect, for example, might develop in parallel two alternative plans for his client, one a single-story house, the other a two-story house. Or a mediator working on a long-term settlement of the Palestinian-Israeli conflict might similarly develop in parallel drafts of two possible treaties. One would seek to meet Palestinian interests in acceptance, equality, self-government, and so forth without establishing a wholly independent sovereign Palestinian state. The other might start with such a state and then consider how best to meet Israeli interests, particularly in security, through provisions about neutrality, mutual inspection, restrictions on weapons, and so on. If the parties became unable to choose between the two texts, they might go to the Security Council for its recommendation or decision. . . .

35. Two Ways of Generating a Draft Proposal

CONCESSION-HUNTING	ONE-TEXT
Ask the parties for their positions and proposals.	Ask the parties about their interests and concerns.
Focus discussion on each party's position.	Focus discussion on a single text aimed at reconciling conflicting interests and developing joint gains.
In turn, ask each party for a concession.	Ask each party to criticize the text wherever it fails to meet a legitimate interest.
Communicate the concessions obtained.	Prepare a revised single text in light of criticism and suggestions.
Repeat the process of pressing first one and then the other party for more concessions.	Repeat the process of revision until [you] have the best draft you can prepare.
Press one party or the other for a final concession to produce an agreement between the original positions of the parties.	Ask each party to accept the final draft if the other will. The final agreement may bear no relationship to the parties' original positions.

Notes and Questions

13.23 Why isn't this One-Text Process used more widely in domestic negotiation? Should it be? What disadvantages does this procedure embody?

13.24 Who should play the role of drafter in a One-Text Process? Is it only relevant in a mediation? If not, how would this procedure work in the absence of third parties?

13.25 What other third-party roles do the authors of *Beyond Machiavelli* suggest? Can you think of examples of these roles in action?

13.26 In an effort to develop variations on the themes of mediation, many international peace workers and theorists have developed "hybrid" forms of proceedings, including "problem-solving workshops," John Burton, Resolving Deep-Rooted Conflicts: A Handbook (1987); Herbert C. Kelman, The Problem-Solving Workshop in Conflict Resolution, in Communication in International Politics (R.L. Merritt ed., 1972), and "public peace processes" that are intended to bring second-tier diplomats, policy makers, and some NGO participants together for limited periods of time to work together and learn from each other, without necessarily formally signing particular peace agreements. Much of this work is based in communication and group process theory. Advocates hope that strong ties and bonds, formed by activities, workshops, and interpersonal interactions, will build trust and longer-term relationships across disputing boundaries, relationships that can then be drawn from in times of acute crisis as well as for longer-term peace planning.

These next two excerpts, first, from international relations professor I. William Zartman and second, from conflict resolution professor Jean-Paul Lederach, are a point-counterpoint debate on the importance of timing and "ripeness" in helping parties settle a dispute. Some suggest that there are special opportunities for settling cases and they come, in the international context, from the potential of a "hurting stalemate" in Zartman's terms or the danger of violent conflict. The case study of Northern Ireland, which we will read later, is often cited as an example of "ripeness." See which argument seems more persuasive to you.

 ***I. William Zartman*, THE TIMING OF PEACE INITIATIVES: HURTING STALEMATES AND RIPE MOMENTS**

---

in Contemporary Peacemaking: Conflict, Violence and Peace Processes 19-20, 24, 26 (John Darby & Roger MacGinty eds., 2003)

While most studies on peaceful settlement of disputes see the substance of the proposals for a solution as the key to a successful resolution of conflict, a growing focus of attention shows that a second and equally necessary key lies in the timing of efforts for resolution. Parties resolve their conflict only when they are ready to do so — when alternative, usually unilateral, means of achieving a satisfactory result are blocked and the parties feel that they are in an uncomfortable and costly predicament. At that ripe moment, they grab onto proposals that usually have been in the air for a long time and that only now appear attractive. . . .

The concept of a ripe moment centers on the parties' perception of a mutually hurting stalemate (MHS), optimally associated with an impending, past or recently avoided catastrophe. The concept is based on the notion that when the parties find themselves locked in a conflict from which they cannot escalate to victory and this deadlock is painful to both of them (although not necessarily in equal degree or for the same reasons), they seek an alternative policy or way out. The catastrophe provides a deadline or a lesson indicating that pain can be sharply increased if something is not done about it now; catastrophe is a useful extension of MHS but is not necessary either to its definition or to its existence. Using different images, the stalemate has been termed the plateau, a flat and unending terrain without relief, and the catastrophe the precipice, the point where things suddenly and predictably get worse. If the notion of mutual blockage is too static to be realistic, the concept may be stated dynamically as a moment when the upper hand slips and the lower hand rises, both parties moving towards equality, with both movements carrying pain for the parties. . . .

Ripeness is necessarily a perceptual event, and as with any subjective perception, there are likely to be objective referents to be perceived. These can be highlighted by a mediator or an opposing party when they are not immediately recognized by the party itself, and resisted so long as the conflicting party refuses or is otherwise able to block out their perception. But it is the perception of the objective condition, not the condition itself, that makes for an MHS. If the parties do not recognize "clear evidence" (in someone else's view) that they are in an impasse, an MHS has not (yet) occurred, and if they do perceive themselves to be in such a situation, no matter how flimsy the "evidence," the MHS is present.

The other element necessary for a ripe moment is less complex and also perceptional: a way out. Parties do not have to be able to identify a specific solution, only a sense that a negotiated solution is possible and that the other party shares that sense and the willingness to search too. Without a sense of a way out, the push associated with the MHS would leave the parties with nowhere to go. Spokespersons often indicate whether they do or do not feel that a deal can be made with the other side and that requirement — i.e. the sense that concessions will be reciprocated, not just banked — exists, particularly when there is a change in that judgment.

Ripeness is only a condition, necessary but not sufficient, for the initiation of negotiations. It is not self-fulfilling or self-implementing. It must be seized, either directly by the parties or, if not, through the persuasion of a mediator. Thus, it is not identical to its results, which are not part of its definition, and is therefore not tautological. Not all ripe moments are so seized and turned into negotiations, hence the importance of specifying the meaning and evidence of ripeness so as to indicate when conflicting or third parties can fruitfully initiate negotiations. . . .

IMPLICATIONS

In itself, the concept explains the difficulty of achieving pre-emptive conflict resolution and preventive diplomacy, even though nothing in the definition of the MHS requires it to take place at the height of the conflict or at a high level of violence. The internal (and unmediated) negotiations in South Africa between 1990 and 1994 stand out as a striking case of negotiations opened (and pursued) on the basis of an MHS perceived by both sides on the basis of impending catastrophe, not of present casualties. However, the greater the objective evidence, the greater the subjective perception of the stalemate and its pain is likely to be, and this evidence is more likely to come late, when all other courses of action and possibilities of escalation have been exhausted. In notable cases, a long period of conflict is required before the MHS sinks in. Yet given the infinite number of potential conflicts which have not reached "the heights," evidence would suggest that perception of an MHS occurs either (and optimally) at a low level of conflict, where it is relatively easy to begin problem-solving in most cases, or, in salient cases, at rather high levels of conflict. . . .

Unripeness should not constitute an excuse for second or third parties' inaction, even if one or both of the conflicting parties are mired in their hopes of escalation and victory. Crocker states very forcefully (in boldface in the original) that "the absence of 'ripeness' does not tell us to walk away and do nothing. Rather, it helps us to identify obstacles and suggests ways of handling them and managing the problem until resolution becomes possible."

 John Paul Lederach, **CULTIVATING PEACE: A PRACTITIONER'S VIEW OF DEADLY CONFLICT AND NEGOTIATION**

in Contemporary Peacemaking: Conflict, Violence and Peace Processes 33-35, 37 (John Darby & Roger MacGinty eds., 2003)

RIPENESS SEES MEDIATOR ACTION AS CHERRY PICKING

When I played basketball many years ago our coach had a phrase with which he provoked us whenever we missed an easy shot, "I can't believe you missed that cherry picker." Essentially it meant that a lot of work had gone into place and then just when everything was right and a giveaway opportunity was presented, the basket was missed.

There are times when I have the impression that the metaphor of ripeness leads towards an emphasis on mediator action as if it were "cherry picking." The impression emerges from two understandings about mediation that I believe have significant limitations and implications. . . .

What the ripeness metaphor does not provide is a sense of the long-term nature of the process, the building and sustaining of the relationships, nor the multiplicity of roles, activities and functions that may be necessary to make a sustained dialogue and change in the relationships possible. . . .

It is not a metaphor that provides a vision of cultivating the soil, planting the seeds or nourishing the seedling in the face of winds, burning sun or icy storms, all of which speak to process, relationship and sustainability rather than a momentary action. . . .

ALTERNATIVE METAPHORS TO RIPENESS . . . CULTIVATION: THE BUILDING OF LONG-TERM AUTHENTIC RELATIONSHIPS

The cultivation metaphor suggests that a deep respect for, and connection to, the context is critical for sustaining a change process that is moving from deadly expressions of conflict to increased justice and peace in relationships. The context of protracted deadly conflict, like soil, is the people, commonly shared geographies but often sharply differing views of history, rights and responsibilities, and the formation of perception and understandings based on cultural meaning structures. Cultivation is recognizing that ultimately the change process must be taken up, embraced and sustained by people in these contexts. The cultivator, as a connected but outside element in the system, approaches this soil with a great deal of respect, the suspension of quick judgment in favour of the wisdom of adaptation, and an orientation towards supporting the change process through highs and lows, ebbs and flows of violence and thawing of tensions, whether or not the situation appears ripe. The cultivator gives attention to the well-being of the ecosystem, not just the quick production of a given fruit. . . .

EPILOGUE

So what do I say when the journalist asks, "And do you really believe it is possible to talk about negotiation and peace when war is raging?" I say hope is not negotiated. It is kept alive by people who understand the depth of suffering and know the cost of keeping a horizon of change as a possibility for their children and grandchildren. Quick fixes to long-standing violent conflict are like growing a garden with no understanding of seeds, soils and sweat. This conflict traces back across decades, even generations. It will take that long to sort out.

Journalists generally do not quote me in their papers. Sound bites about ripeness, people coming to their senses, and the need for realism and pressure seem to find their way into print more often. But I believe in cultivation. Cultivation as a metaphor suggests that the core of the peacebuilding work — fostering and sustaining committed, authentic relationships across the lines of conflict over time — does not rise and fall with the temporal ups and downs of the conflict cycles. It answers the question — is it possible to pursue peace when things are bad — with a resounding "Yes!" just as it also suggests that when things are suddenly headed towards an agreement the work is hardly over. It has only begun.

Notes and Questions

13.27 Are these two visions of ripeness at odds with one another? Can they be reconciled?

13.28 Can you think of examples that fit under these theories?

13.29 How does the idea of ripeness work (or not work) in domestic negotiation?

13.30 Consider this exhortation to learn from different models:

> If "third party intervention" and "deadline" setting or "ripeness" look
> different in different contexts we will have learned something. Lawsuits,
> even the longest ones, usually settle more quickly than centuries of inter-
> racial or inter-ethnic conflict. The threat of an authoritative decision
> maker may hasten voluntary settlement over situations where there is
> no enforcing authority, but agreements reached consensually when
> there is no outside threat of decision may be longer-lasting and more easily
> complied with. Learning to live with differences within national bound-
> aries or regional trade zones may provide a variety of "exemplars" for
> different modes of co-existence. If we are truly looking for "solutions"
> to domestic and international conflicts, disputes and problems, then we
> should be open to as many different and contextually specific ideas as it will
> take. Though I doubt there is a single theory to fit all human problems for
> decision, I think we can get better at it by "comparing and contrasting"
> specifics, rather than assuming uniformity or generality. I urge you to find
> your favorite conflict resolution idea, model or concept and try it out in a
> few different places. Our theory and our practice will be all the richer and
> deeper for it.

Carrie Menkel-Meadow, Correspondences and Contradictions in International and Domestic Conflict Resolution: Lessons from General Theory
and Varied Contexts, 2003 J. Disp. Resol. 319, 352. Can you think of
other conflict resolution models that have been tried for specific situations?

This next excerpt compares two mediators in action using some of the tools
described previously.

 Daniel Curran, James K. Sebenius & Michael Watkins, **TWO PATHS TO PEACE: CONTRASTING GEORGE MITCHELL IN NORTHERN IRELAND WITH RICHARD HOLBROOKE IN BOSNIA-HERZEGOVINA**

20 Negot. J. 513, 514-525, 530-531 (2004)

At least superficially, the efforts of George Mitchell in Northern Ireland and Richard
Holbrooke in Bosnia offer strong similarities. Two white, male, Democratic, U.S.
citizens assumed third-party roles in ethnic and religious conflicts in Europe in the
latter half of the 1990s. Each man took actions leading to what most observers would
regard as a provisional success — at least over the short to medium term, and certainly
relative to violent alternatives. . . . Yet, the personalities of these two men could
hardly be more different nor could they have taken more divergent approaches to
their roles.

Closer examination reveals two very different people facing very different challenges and following very different strategies to help resolve bitter and protracted disputes. This article contrasts their approaches across a number of dimensions to help build an understanding of a range of third-party actions that may be appropriate and effective under certain circumstances. The differences between the settlements obtained and questions about their long-term sustainability are large and, while relevant, beyond the scope of our comparison. The present article is not a structured focused comparison of the two situations but, rather, a presentation of contrasts between very different situations. As such, each case nicely highlights key aspects of the other and, by extension, a broader class of similar cases. . . .

COMPARISONS OF FUNDAMENTAL CHOICES

Basic Objectives

Richard Holbrooke's evident objective was to stop the violent and bloody war in Bosnia — and he needed to do it quickly. He wanted an immediate and comprehensive deal that would end the killing and create a new Bosnia. . . .

George Mitchell's objective in Northern Ireland was also to end the conflict. He found party leaders from both sides who were articulate in their understanding that unemployment and violence were inextricably linked and that a durable peace rested on a foundation of trust and prosperity. Yet, their hatred for one another remained and they were unable to act to realize shared interests. Mitchell was amazed to find that, although the party leaders had lived together in the same community all of their lives, many of them literally did not talk with each other. . . .

Fundamental Role

The roles of Mitchell and Holbrooke were well aligned with their objectives. Holbrooke assumed the role of an advocate with substantial potential clout from both the U.S. and NATO. . . .

By contrast, George Mitchell assumed the role of a neutral mediator on behalf of an agreement among the parties. The situation in Northern Ireland was of relatively peripheral concern to U.S. policy makers, although it had entangled a key ally (Britain) and served as something of a test bed for U.S. influence on post-Cold War ethnic conflicts. . . .

Means of Influence

In Bosnia, Holbrooke arguably adopted an approach of "whatever it takes to force a deal." In the language of negotiation, it was a best alternative to a negotiated agreement (BATNA)-focused approach of lowering the value of no-agreement alternatives and influencing the dynamics to impose ever-higher costs on the various parties who refused to play. . . .

By contrast to this BATNA-lowering approach, George Mitchell followed a strategy that focused on joint gains, continually alluding to the political and economic value of a deal. Mitchell has no formal power and only had a few carrots and sticks with which to influence negotiators and their constituents. . . .

COMPARISON OF STRATEGIES: COALITIONAL, PROCESS, ISSUE, AND TIMING

Coalition Strategy: Minimum Necessary Versus Maximum Feasible

Holbrooke's strategy in Bosnia, with respect to the various parties, consisted of four basic steps. First, he sought to simplify the overall decision making within the U.S., NATO, and the European Union (EU). . . .

Second, Holbrooke acted to take advantage of, and foster, the simplification of the hitherto fragmented Balkan parties. . . .

Third, he sought to apply considerable pressure on the Serbs to weaken their thus-far dominant position. . . .

By contrast with Holbrooke's sequential, divide–conquer–and–force approach and desire to limit participation, George Mitchell carefully built an outwardly rippling, relatively inclusive, coalition of the center against the extremes. . . .

He sought a wide participation of parties by first recommending the election to a negotiating forum and later allowing all parties to remain involved as long as they adhered to the "Mitchell Principles" of democracy and nonviolence. . . .

Process Strategy: Control Versus Consensus

Holbrooke essentially imposed a negotiation process by fiat. He engineered and manipulated representation in the talks and undertook his shuttles and summits to meet what he saw as the requirements of rapid closure. . . .

As part of the process, Holbrooke used the press to further the idea of an "abyss" in the event of no-deal and he consistently sought to lower expectations for the results he sought at each stage. . . .

Holbrooke also used the press and the process as tools to build perceptions in the minds of the players of his personal credibility and power. . . .

By contrast, Mitchell acted as the steward of a deliberate process of principled inclusion. The delegates were formally elected to a comprehensive forum and had to endorse the "Mitchell Principles" of democracy and nonviolence in order to enter the talks and continue participating. . . .

To gain acceptance, Mitchell agreed to dispense with the process and agenda created in advance by the Irish and British government[s]. Instead, he agreed to negotiate his role, the rules, the agenda, and the procedures of the talks[,] including the principle of "sufficient consensus," which gave veto power to all of the largest players and ensured the reality of power sharing. For months, he and his team sought proposals from parties, provided comparative tables to guide discussion, and used bilateral meetings to ease things forward. . . .

Throughout the talks, Mitchell kept the process going at all costs—however threadbare it seemed at any given time. He and the other chairmen were routinely called upon to speak to the press. Mitchell used the press to hold out a "pot of gold" waiting at the end of a negotiated settlement. He felt a need to optimistically assess the state of the talks. . . .

Issue Strategy: Substance Versus Procedure

Richard Holbrooke placed more emphasis on substance than procedure in the Bosnian negotiations. His agenda for discussion changed frequently and always revolved around substantive issues. It was highly sequential, using shuttles and late-night diplomatic pressure to explore concessions and then hold summits to lock in gains and build momentum towards a larger package. At these summits, Holbrooke consistently sought a series of agreed-upon *principles* followed by *specifics on the issues*. . . .

By contrast, George Mitchell deferred the difficult substantive issues until the very end of his involvement in favor of focusing on negotiations over the procedures and agenda themselves. . . .

When Mitchell did deal with substantive issues, he methodically separated them into three strands for the parties to discuss the nuances of each issue. His team shared information widely in an effort to avoid surprises or misunderstandings. The parties canvassed their various proposals, concepts, and models but, more importantly, they explored each other's ideas, seeking further explanations or offering explanations for their own reservations or objections. . . .

Mitchell later repackaged the issues in the final agreement for mutual gain. Mitchell progressively isolated and deferred the hardest issue, decommissioning of IRA weapons, in the hope that enough of a relationship would be built among the parties to tackle it later in a more productive way.

Timing Strategy: Forcing Versus Fostering

Holbrooke's timing strategy called for building momentum by gaining early wins through agreements on principles. He then accelerated the pace with a series of partial agreements and forcible actions to prevent backsliding on promises. He used several imposed deadlines — backed with the threat of bombing — to forge agreements. He also made well-timed persuasive arguments — backed by intelligence data — to force parties to back down. . . .

By contrast, Mitchell's patient strategy used time, not only to begin to foster a more constructive relationship among the parties, but to increase their sense of respect, obligation, liking, and credibility toward him. . . .

Mitchell deployed his hard-earned credibility on the final deadline, which he carefully negotiated with the parties and governments at the talks. . . .

CONCLUDING THOUGHTS

To sharpen the contrasts between these two men and the episodes in which they played central roles, consider the following thought experiment: Imagine the likely process and outcome in each case if Holbrooke had been assigned to Northern Ireland and Mitchell to Bosnia. While each man might have flexibly adapted to radically different situations, it is clear that simply juxtaposing the two approaches would sharply lower the chances of success in each case. . . .

Perhaps the most important contribution of this comparison of the sharply divergent approaches taken in Northern Ireland and Bosnia is the challenge it poses to easy generalizations about effective mediation. Holbrooke's results may confound those who see the essence of successful mediation as scrupulous neutrality buttressed by patient, interest-based, empathetic joint problem solving to find mutually beneficial solutions. For others who may see the coercive diplomacy of Holbrooke as the essential ingredient to cutting though intractable and violent situations, the success of Mitchell's low key, even-handed, endlessly persistent style may seem almost magical. Yet, in the course of their respective efforts, both men helped forge peace agreements in two immensely challenging situations that had defeated many prior attempts.

D. INTERNATIONAL NEGOTIATION AS AN ALTERNATIVE

International negotiation, like domestic negotiation, can be conducted in the shadow of the law and legal processes. The next excerpt outlines the difference between negotiation versus other structural options in resolving international disputes. The second excerpt discusses how the rulings of the International Court of Justice communicate the law to nations.

 Andrea Kupfer Schneider, GETTING ALONG: THE EVOLUTION OF DISPUTE RESOLUTION REGIMES IN THE INTERNATIONAL TRADE ORGANIZATIONS

20 Mich. J. Intl. L. 697, 712-725 (1999)

NEGOTIATION REGIME
Individual Rights & Standing

The first type of regime of an international dispute resolution system is the Negotiation Regime. The Negotiation Regime is exemplified by the dispute settlement system of the General Agreement on Trade and Tariffs ("GATT") as it existed prior to the creation of the WTO as well as the current form of Chapter 20 of the NAFTA [North American Free Trade Agreement]. In this regime, most of the factors we have discussed are on the lower end of the range. Typically, individuals are not granted rights under the organizations that use negotiation as their regime nor are individuals involved in the negotiation process. Disputes under this system are resolved informally using diplomacy between states. For example, in a disagreement over alleged dumping, two states might make an ad hoc agreement to change the particular system discussed. Historically, most disputes regarding trade, or anything else, have been resolved in this way.

Supremacy

Disputes under this regime are resolved by a negotiated agreement between states. This dispute resolution may result in changes to some law or practice in one or both states. More often, however, this type of dispute resolution agreement will not result in an amendment to an existing treaty or a new treaty itself, but rather will be a lesser type of commitment from the governments. . . .

Enforcement

Enforcement under a negotiation regime of dispute resolution is left to the respective states. There is no oversight institution. Any noncompliance with the underlying trade agreement would put the parties back at the negotiation table in order to work out the dispute. In other words, a negotiation regime relies on "first-order" compliance at all times. States either follow the agreement or renegotiate a new agreement.

REGIMES/ FACTORS	DIRECT EFFECT	STANDING FOR PRIVATE ACTORS	SUPREMACY	TRANS- PARENCY	ENFORCE- MENT
Negotiation	No	No	None	Optional	Negotiation
Investment Arbitration	Yes	Yes	Only as to that award	Optional	Likely
International Adjudication	No	No	Supreme, but not integrated into domestic law	Yes	Varying—none (NAFTA) to retaliation (WTO)
Supranational Court	Yes	Yes, directly and indirectly	Supreme and integrated	Yes	Fines & damages; domestic remedies also

INVESTOR ARBITRATION REGIME

The Investor Arbitration Regime was specifically created to give private actors both rights and remedies under the relevant international treaty. The move toward investment arbitration began with the creation of the International Centre for the Settlement of Investment Disputes ("ICSID") under the aegis of the World Bank. A decade later, the UN Commission for International Trade Law ("UNCITRAL") drafted rules for ad hoc arbitration. This concept of permitting individuals to bring cases against states has since been copied in bilateral investment treaties in order to encourage foreign direct investment and outlined in NAFTA for investor disputes under Chapter 11B.

Individual Rights

Under the treaties that establish investment arbitration, private actors are granted such rights as national treatment or a minimum standard of treatment in the host state. These rights are directly effective. In other cases, domestic implementing of legislation will provide for the rights to become directly effective. This makes sense because these types of treaties are specifically designed to encourage individual investment.

While an Investment Arbitration regime provides rights against the host government, none of these underlying treaties provide direct effect of rights against another individual. In other words, a private actor has no recourse against another private actor under this regime. Investment arbitration is established solely as a right and remedy between a private investor and the host state. Further, because investment arbitration is only available against a host state, nationals have no recourse against their own government. Finally, rights under this regime have limited scope. Investment Arbitration is provided for only the narrow right of national treatment in most regimes. Any state action falling outside those parameters is unreachable.

Individual Standing

In investment arbitration, private actors have the ability to bring cases directly against a state. This is quite an historic development in this century. . . .

[I]nternational commercial arbitration had become a popular method for resolving commercial disputes between private disputants because it provided a more neutral, fairer, and potentially faster way of resolving disputes. This regime appealed to investors who were concerned with the potential bias, inefficiency, or unfamiliarity of foreign courts. By creating an international arbitration option between individuals and states, creators of this regime hoped that investors would be more willing to bring their business to these states because disputes could be resolved through this international neutral body. . . .

Supremacy & Transparency

Arbitration decisions generally provide for damages and not a change in domestic laws. Therefore, the issue of supremacy does not really arise because there is no new law created. An arbitration decision can also be kept confidential if requested by the parties. This means that the decision cannot provide precedent or predictability in the system because outside lawyers cannot analyze the panel's thinking.

Enforcement

In terms of enforcement, an investment arbitration system does provide for relatively effective enforcement. The Convention on the Recognition and Enforcement of Arbitral Awards ("New York Convention") provides that all signatory states shall enforce arbitral awards in their domestic courts. As a result, if a state refuses to pay the arbitral award, the investor can go to the domestic court in that state or in any state where there are commercial assets in order to enforce the judgment. Although the investor still must go to the domestic court, the New York Convention provides for straightforward enforcement. In fact, many states that once ignored court orders from other states now willingly comply with arbitral awards. This method of enforcement, however, is limited to those states that have signed the New York Convention. While most developed states have signed it, there are a significant number of developing states that have not.

INTERNATIONAL ADJUDICATION REGIME

The regime of international adjudication is the one that we are most familiar with under international law as the structure for resolving disputes between states. Evolving from the Permanent Court of Arbitration, and the Permanent Court of International Justice, the International Court of Justice ("ICJ") is the most recognized international court. In the trade arena, the WTO Dispute Settlement Understanding is closest to international adjudication.

Individual Rights & Standing

Under the International Adjudication Regime, private actors are neither granted rights directly by the treaty establishing the international court nor have any right of standing to bring cases before the court. This regime exists to resolve disputes between states—international disputes—and therefore individuals have not had recourse to this regime. In some states, private actors may have the ability to petition their government to take action on their behalf. In the United States, the US Trade Representative makes the final decision whether or not to bring the case and there is no judicial review of this action.

Supremacy & Transparency

Under international law, the decisions of the international court are supreme to the domestic law and the relevant state must change its behavior or laws to comply. But the court's decision is not integrated into domestic law.

The decision is published and, thus, can provide persuasive precedent for similar disputes. The procedure of an international court is usually transparent and well understood by international lawyers in the field as well as by national governments. The transparency of the system provides the opportunity for both practitioners and academics to analyze, improve, and comprehend this particular international dispute resolution system.

Enforcement

Perhaps the most controversial part of international adjudication is the question of compliance and enforcement. Because international courts have not thus far had armies to forcibly carry out their decisions, many critics of the international system focus on those cases where states have chosen to ignore the international court. . . .

Without arguing as to whether an international court can ever truly "work," it is important to assess the level of enforcement a court can have.

Both GATT and the ICJ are examples of court systems that provide for no enforcement beyond censure of the international community. These systems stop at second-order compliance — states should obey the law and, if held to be violating the law, should pay the fine (or change their law). The WTO outlines more stringent enforcement measures by providing a menu of enforcement options. First, a state has the opportunity to follow the ruling and, usually, change the offending practice. Second, the state can continue the practice and pay damages to the harmed state. If neither of these options are taken, the harmed state can retaliate. The WTO provides that the harmed state must first retaliate in the same sector of trade. However, if this is not effective, the WTO provides that cross-sector retaliation is permitted. This newer evolution of the international adjudication regime has more teeth than its predecessors and attempts to correct some of the problems of the past.

SUPRANATIONAL COURT REGIME

Individual Rights & Standing

A Supranational Court Regime of international dispute resolution is different from the International Adjudication Regime in a number of ways. First, private actors are granted rights under the constituent treaty and have the ability to bring their complaints to the supranational court. The clearest example of this type of individual involvement occurs in the European Union. . . .

The EU also provides private actors the opportunity to bring cases before the ECJ — directly to the ECJ or indirectly through their domestic courts. The impact of individual involvement in international dispute resolution cannot be underestimated. . . . States may feel reluctant to bring cases against other states for somewhat minor infractions. Furthermore, it may be in many states' interests not to follow the letter of the law exactly or delay compliance with the numerous laws set out under the EU. If states permit this behavior between themselves, it becomes collusion to ignore the law at the expense of their citizens.

While the oversight body is more likely to bring cases than a state, it, too, has the problem of a vast number of potential cases while maintaining its political agenda. . . . Individuals do not have the political baggage of bringing a case against another state. Further, individuals can make a direct economic assessment about whether it is worth it to them to spend the time and money on litigation. For these reasons, where individuals are granted rights and where the benefits of the treaty are supposed to accrue directly to individuals, it makes sense to give individuals a remedy for violation of those rights.

Supremacy

The name "supranational" in this regime comes from the fact that the court and its rulings are clearly supreme in all ways to domestic law. The rulings from the supranational court must be followed by domestic courts, legislatures, and the executive branch. That is in contrast, for example, to rulings under the International Adjudication Regime above, which are usually only directed to the executive branch.

 Tom Ginsburg & Richard H. McAdams, **ADJUDICATING IN ANARCHY: AN EXPRESSIVE THEORY OF INTERNATIONAL DISPUTE RESOLUTION**

45 Wm. & Mary L. Rev. 1229, 1263-1275 (2004)

1. How Third-Party "Cheap Talk" Influences Behavior in Coordination Games: The Focal Point Theory

a. An Introduction to Cheap Talk and Focal Points

The easiest context for illustrating the focal point concept is the pure coordination game. Suppose you have plans to meet a friend in New York City on a particular day, but you failed to agree on a specific time or place. If you and your friend merely select the time and place at random among all of the possibilities, the chances of meeting will be vanishingly small. Yet when [Thomas] Schelling surveyed some of his Yale colleagues and students, he found that over half selected the same place, Grand Central Station, and almost everyone selected the same time, noon.[93] In Schelling's terminology, the equilibrium that emerges, Grand Central Station at noon, is a focal point. There is something about the nonpayoff features of this equilibrium that his subjects expected others to find salient. Experiments confirm that, in games of multiple equilibria, salient non-payoff features (focal points) significantly facilitate coordination.

b. Using Third-Party Cheap Talk to Construct a Focal Point

For our purposes, Schelling's most interesting insight combines cheap talk and focal points. He discusses the ability of a *third party*, someone who is not a player in the coordination game, to influence the players in the game merely by communicating in favor of a particular outcome. By endorsing a particular outcome in the common view or hearing of the players, the third party makes that equilibrium *stand out* from the rest, which may then create [a] self-fulfilling expectation that others will play the strategy associated with that equilibrium. In this way, third-party cheap talk *constructs* a focal point. . . .

c. Using Cheap Talk to Clarify Conventions: Resolving Conventional Ambiguity

To connect the cheap talk discussion to [an] analysis of conventions, [note that] the ambiguities that plague conventions are fuzziness and potential incompleteness. . . .

First, cheap talk can clarify a convention by eliminating the fuzziness of the underlying asymmetry. [To use an example:] Four countries might each believe they were the first possessor of an island territory because one was the first to observe the island, another the first to plant a flag on it, another the first to settle it, and another the first to exercise legal jurisdiction over it. Now imagine a dispute between

---

[93] Thomas C. Schelling, The Strategy of Conflict 55-56 (1963).

two of these nations, *B* and *C*, where *B* is the first to plant a flag on the island and *C* is the first to have citizens occupy it. Just like the bystander in the road signaling one car to stop and the other to proceed, a third party who proclaims that one of the nations is entitled to the island is likely to influence how the players behave. Specifically, suppose that only one third party speaks on the issue, or, more likely, only one whom the nations designated in advance as the coordinator. If the third party states "the territory belongs to *C*," then she makes salient the outcome where *C* plays Hawk to *B*'s Dove, which tends to create self-fulfilling expectations that that particular outcome will occur.

2. How Third-Party Signaling Influences Behavior in Iterated Coordination Games: The Informational Theory

Sometimes a third party may issue messages that are not cheap talk, but signals. In this section, we argue that signaling provides third parties with a second expressive means of influencing the behavior of individuals in a coordination game. Given imperfect information, third parties can influence behavior by expressions that signal their private information about the state of the world. . . .

In sum, in iterated coordination games, third-party expression can influence the behavior of nations in at least two ways. First, cheap talk can clarify ambiguities in the convention, due to fuzziness and potential incompleteness. Second, signals can clarify ambiguities in the facts. In the former situation, nations select strategies based in part on what they expect other nations to do, and cheap talk construction of a focal point can directly influence those expectations. In the latter situation, nations select strategies based on their beliefs about the state of the world and signaling can influence those beliefs. Neither effect requires that the third party be able to impose sanctions on a noncomplying nation, nor that national leaders recognize the moral authority of legitimate adjudication. . . .

The ICJ as Coordinator: Evidence of Compliance

This Article's theory engages this selection bias, and explains why it operates by focusing on not what cases are *filed* before the ICJ, but what cases are *resolved* by the ICJ. Although there may be multiple reasons that countries file cases, many of these cases will be incapable of resolution by a court lacking the power of sanctions. This theory predicts not just that *easy* cases will be resolved, but that the *only* cases effectively resolved by the ICJ will be coordination problems. In this subset of cases, each party can anticipate that the other party will comply with an adverse decision in the absence of centralized enforcement, thereby making signaling and cheap talk effective. . . .

CONCLUSION

The game theory concept of coordination explains compliance with international tribunals. Even in a state of anarchy, when nations face repeated games of coordination, conventions emerge. The coordinated expectations underlying a convention allow nations to avoid conflict. Ambiguity inevitably prevents the convention from perfectly coordinating expectations, however, and in this situation adjudication can work expressively, without sanctions, by clarifying the convention and the state of the world to which it applies. Adjudication can both construct a focal point and provide a signal that causes national leaders to update their beliefs, both of which can influence their behavior.

International adjudication should therefore be understood for what it is. Rather than serving as a utopian institution that can end all international conflict, international adjudication such as that provided by the ICJ can only provide solutions to parties faced with coordination problems. Compliance with ICJ decisions can occur, even absent centralized enforcement mechanisms, because the decisions make one outcome focal or provide an important signal of the state of the world, either of which facilitates the parties in ordering their own affairs. The law as declared by the ICJ and other international institutions is *merely* expressive, but expressive law often works to resolve or avoid disputes. In arguing that coordination problems deserve more attention in international relations and international legal scholarship, we have used realist/rational choice assumptions of optimizing behavior and self-interest to expand the understanding of the functions law can play. But our approach is clearly institutionalist in character, seeking to understand how institutions can resolve conflicts and what purposes they serve.

Notes and Questions

13.31 How does the shadow of the law impact international negotiations?

13.32 Compare Ginsburg and McAdams's expressive theory as a way of dealing with Prisoner's Dilemma at the international level with explanations for cooperation in the Prisoner's Dilemma from Chapter 4.

Dispute resolution within one legal system, even with all the layers and differences of purpose as the American legal system with its federalism and different kinds of conflicts and disputes, still, at least in theory, shares a particular legal culture. Disputing across legal and cultural boundaries raises different issues about whether there are processes that can be used across systems, cultures, and nations. Some have argued that because there are complex differences across cultures, legal systems, and nation-states, that alternative forms of dispute resolution are particularly appropriate for development across those boundaries and differences, allowing processes to be developed to meet the needs of the parties or the particular situations.

As you study dispute processes and institutions and examine different kinds of conflicts, consider whether there are any propositions or principles of conflict resolution that apply across both the domestic or international domains. Or do you think different contexts require different kinds of propositional knowledge and system design? Broader questions include, for example, the neutrality of a third party, the benefits of negotiation or diplomacy vs. mandatory arbitration, and economic support for disadvantaged parties on both the domestic and international level.

Chapter 14 — Facilitated Negotiation: Mediation for Negotiators

There is no intractable problem.

—Desmond Tutu

Conflicts are created and sustained by human beings. They can be ended by human beings.

—George Mitchell

Now that you have learned a great deal about negotiation, as a representative or party in negotiation, and as an advisor to clients who must negotiate with others, we close this book by introducing you to another process: facilitated negotiation or mediation. When some of the barriers described in earlier chapters prevent parties and their lawyers from reaching agreements directly with each other, people often turn to third parties for assistance in reaching agreements, seeking solutions, and helping with communication. One of the more common ways to seek assistance is to use mediation. Here a third party, who is usually, but not always, "neutral," or at least impartial to the matter, helps the parties reach their own solution. It is important to note that mediators assist parties in reaching their own solution; they do not "decide" anything—that would be arbitration or a more controversial form of mediation, evaluative mediation or med-arb.

In this chapter we introduce you to some of the key concepts, skills, and issues in mediation so that as skilled negotiators you can participate in and advise about mediation as another form of negotiation. Having an appropriate mind-set of seeking solutions to problems, disputes, and conflicts is essential in mediation, whether you are acting as a representative or as a mediator, so we think of mediation as a problem-solving, not an adversarial, process, even though some people may still regard it as an opportunity to argue for their own positions or try to claim value only for themselves, rather than focusing on possible joint gains. If you are interested in learning more about mediation, consider taking a separate course in it or consult one of the companion volumes to this book, Mediation: Practice, Policy, and Ethics (Menkel-Meadow, Love & Schneider, 2006) or Dispute Resolution: Beyond the Adversarial Model (Menkel-Meadow, Love, Schneider & Sternlight, 2006).

A. INTRODUCTION TO MEDIATION

1. What Is Mediation?

Mediation is a process in which an impartial third party acts as a catalyst to help others constructively address and perhaps resolve a dispute, plan a transaction, or define the contours of a relationship. A mediator facilitates negotiation between the parties to enable better communication, encourage problem solving, and develop an agreement or resolution by consensus among the parties. The process of mediation can best be understood by examining the many roles of the mediator.

A variety of metaphors describe the mediator's roles. The mediator acts as *host* and *chair*: convening the parties for discussions; making arrangements for adequate, safe, and comfortable facilities; attending to special needs of disputants (for example, disabilities or language differences); and ensuring that the agenda is constructive, that any obstacles that develop are addressed, and that agreements are memorialized. The mediator is a *guide*, *coach*, and *educator*, steering the parties toward effective negotiation behavior and away from destructive, self-defeating maneuvers. The mediator is a *referee*, offering each party an equal place at the bargaining table, allowing each voice to be heard, and encouraging parties to get additional resources or to withdraw from mediation if it is no longer constructive. The mediator is a master *communicator* and *translator*, gleaning insights from conversations rife with extreme positions, threats, and blame to help parties hear one another's interests, issues, proposals, feelings, principles, and values. In one sense, this function of translating is akin to that of an alchemist, turning the danger inherent in conflict into the "gold" of possibility and opportunity for disputants. The mediator serves as an *agent of reality*, urging evaluation and reevaluation of positions and assumptions and encouraging assessment and reassessment of what others are saying. The mediator is a *watchdog*, protecting the process itself and prohibiting parties from using a session merely to obtain an advantage in litigation or to abuse one another.

Mediators intervene in a wide array of disputes — from family and community to commercial and international. Mediation is useful for parties facing an actual dispute, trying to reconcile competing interests, or planning for the possibility of conflict. For example, a mediator can help divorcing couples determine parenting arrangements and asset division or help people who are contemplating marriage negotiate a prenuptial agreement. A mediator can help settle a controversy over liability and damages related to an environmental disaster such as an oil spill or can help a community determine the route for a highway or the site of a garbage facility.

In mediation, the parties retain control over the dispute and its outcome. This central feature of mediation — self-determination by the parties — is a facet of the democratic process — that the voice and wisdom of people can shape outcomes responsive to particular situations. In this respect, mediation is fundamentally different from adjudication, where power to determine the outcome is ceded to a judge, jury, or arbiter.

Adjudication and the rule of law can clarify and develop public norms. Adjudication supports the stability and predictability inherent in law and an evenhanded application of rules. Litigation — at least when decisions are made and published — gives society precedents that promote order by guiding similarly situated actors. Mediation, on the other hand, enhances communication, fosters collaboration, and encourages problem solving. These goals are also important to achieving individual and community well-being. If, for example, landlords and tenants, minority groups and school boards, or employers and employees can resolve existing controversies through mediation, they not only achieve a resolution tailored to their specific situation but also can bank their success in problem solving to help resolve future disputes.

In comparing these two very different approaches to addressing disputes, it is important to note that they serve different masters and have distinct logic and integrity. In adjudication, with ideals embedded in concepts of evolving law and precepts for ordering society, an arbiter determines facts and applies rules to determine rights and liabilities with respect to past acts. In mediation, a structuring of the future is possible: to avoid past pitfalls and to build new opportunities. The spotlight moves from evidence of past conduct and historic facts to parties' interests and finally to possibilities for optimal balancing of those interests. Where, for example, a supplier and a customer have taken a matter to court to determine damages for a shipment that was nonconforming under a contract, those same parties in mediation might adjust their differences by arrangements in future contracts, making allowances for past wrongs.

This chapter explores the foundations of mediation, the historical context for current perspectives, and the place mediation holds in the array of dispute resolution processes. As mediation has developed, different orientations, goals, and strategies have been propounded. A sampling of major approaches and varying descriptions of the mediation process follow. Some practice advice for attorney negotiators in mediation concludes the chapter.

2. The Advantages of Mediation

To understand the rationales for mediation, one need only examine the many shortcomings of adjudication: prohibitive expense, heart-breaking delay, a lack of party participation and control of the process, unsatisfactory outcomes, and an adversarial orientation that alienates parties from one another. Mediation can address each of these shortcomings.

a. Settlement: Avoiding the Expense, Delay, and Risk of Adjudication

The success and efficiency of mediated resolutions lead many lawyers to advise clients to mediate. Compared to the risky undertaking of adjudication — whether litigation or arbitration — mediation offers parties the possibility of acceptable conclusions, ones they have crafted themselves. In litigation, a judge or jury decides the matter, checked only by the appeal process. In binding arbitration, an individual decision maker (or a panel of decision makers), chosen by the parties, renders a final decision. Whenever a party gives another person the power to decide a controversy, the outcome is inherently unpredictable and may produce an unhappy surprise.

Litigation tends to be slow and expensive. Centuries ago William Shakespeare's Hamlet complained about "the law's delay." While the arbitration

> *Justice delayed is justice denied.*
> —attributed to William E. Gladstone

process, created by the parties in their agreement to arbitrate, can be fast, arbitration can also resemble litigation, in which case it too becomes slow and costly. The benefits of speedy closure are financial, practical, and psychological. Many disputes need prompt address. A patent dispute, for example, must be resolved before the patent expires. An allegation of discrimination in the workplace should be addressed before the employee becomes embittered and affects others in the office or before a similar act of discrimination occurs. Businesses embroiled in conflict are diverted from the pursuit of business goals. A mediation can be scheduled quickly, and sessions, for certain cases, can take as little as a few hours. Mediation can temper unrealistic positions, unwarranted assumptions, and demonization of another party. Overconfident views of a case and the dynamics of adversarial behavior can box parties into unproductive assertions and claims. Face-to-face interaction forces each side to hear each other and to take into account the other's perspective. The mediation process offers parties a chance to shift expectations and temper self-serving attitudes, while working to reach an acceptable accord; this, in turn, avoids the risk of an adverse judgment in adjudication.

Finally, settlement benefits the court system. In offering a variety of methods to resolve disputes, courts can serve the various interests of disputing parties and relieve court dockets as well.

b. Participation and Self-Determination: Giving Parties Voice and Choice

A central value of mediation is self-determination. Self-determination means that parties retain control over both the process and the outcome.

Parties in adjudicative processes must fit their story within the narrow frame of a legal "cause of action" or an allowable arbitral claim, confine themselves to evidence that the decision maker will consider relevant and persuasive, and give control over the outcome to a judge, jury, or arbiter. Because of these constraints, parties often do not feel they have had a chance to be heard. A fundamental lack of control — or self-determination — can be the price of obtaining a third-party decision. Similarly, remedies in adjudicative processes are those prescribed by the particular forum, rather than remedies tailored by the parties.

Mediators promote party empowerment and self-determination by carving out space and time for each side to tell its story and be heard in a meaningful way. This feature alone can be important to clients. Mediators also seek party involvement in crafting proposals that are responsive to each side's needs. Participation in finding and power in choosing the solution means the parties are invested in the outcome, and the resolution is more durable. Apologies and other benefits that will "satisfy the heart" can be both more valuable and less costly than outcomes dictated by third parties.

c. Better Outcomes: Generating Creative Problem Solving

Many proponents of mediation emphasize its ability to engage participants in a forward-looking exercise of developing options and optimal outcomes. Mediators try to get parties out of an adversarial contest and into creating better futures. Custom-tailored outcomes, developed to maximize benefits for all sides, can create more value for parties than standardized remedies provided in adjudicative forums. Agreements can be finely calibrated to balance out equities arising from past (mis)conduct and thus be reparative from a justice perspective. At the same time, the outcome must be better than the litigation (or other) alternatives of each party, since either party can "veto" the agreement. Such "quality" solutions will likely be perceived as fairer by the parties. From a societal perspective, community value flows from maximizing individual benefits and from reducing the disaffection costs of conflict.

Mediation can produce outcomes that litigation or arbitration cannot. For example, in commercial settings, parties can agree to enter into future contracts that take into account past wrongs and offer profit for all, instead of the more conventional monetary damages. Apologies can allow parties to have closure and move on with their lives. Agreements to communicate in a certain way, to write letters of reference, to refrain from contact or conduct can be valuable. Such results are not generally part of the remedies available to an arbitrator or judge.

Additionally, party-crafted agreements that are responsive to the interests parties articulate (as evidenced by the voluntary adoption of the agreement) are more durable than judgments that the "losing" party may find unfair and attempt to avoid through using an appeals process or simply by making it difficult to collect the judgment.

d. Relationship, Community, and Harmony: Building Bridges Between People

Many societies see conflict as a potential threat to the social fabric. These cultures value processes that rebuild connections between parties and bring both individual well-being and community harmony. Navajo peace-making tribunals and mediation in China and Japan are examples. Any process such as mediation that allows parties to recognize each other's perspectives and interests — even when these parties are strangers to one another — has a significant value in a world where strife and conflict threaten to tear families, communities, and nations apart. Society's interest in promoting healing relationships is measured, in part, by the costs of disaffection evident in depression, crime, productivity loss, and, ultimately, war.

The benefit of using mediation radiates beyond a single dispute to the larger system. In the context of a family, a school, an agency, a workplace, or an industry, mediation is used not only to resolve specific disputes but also to promote understanding and collaboration, for example, among parents and children, students from different ethnic groups, supervisors and employees, or customers and suppliers. As parties listen to each other, stereotypes can be shattered and more responsible, responsive, and profitable citizens, communities, and governments can emerge.

Notes and Questions

14.1 Are some types of cases or disputes more likely to produce the beneficial results discussed above? For example, are relationship and community as important in a construction case as they might be in a probate matter? Can you make an argument that all of these advantages are useful targets in most case types?

14.2 Are there some types of cases for which mediation should always be the preferred process? For which mediation should be prohibited? What criteria should be used in making the determination? Note the benefits and costs of litigation that Dickens highlights (see box).

"A Contempt for His Own Kind"

The receiver in the cause has acquired a goodly sum of money by it, but has acquired too a distrust of his own mother, and a contempt for his own kind.

Charles Dickens, Bleak House

14.3 In the context of civil litigation, some commentators believe that disputes are "all about money." Do you agree? Can mediation be effective even when a case appears to be "all about money"?

3. The History of Mediation in the United States

a. Roots

The resolution of conflict by both adversarial contests and peace-making activities has ancient origins. History chronicles parallel movements, as well as tensions, between justice as embodied in the imposition of law backed by force and justice inherent in voluntary agreement and reconciliation. Jesus Christ is referred to as a "mediator between God and men" (Tim. 2:5-6). The Talmud reports that "the Temple was destroyed because they judged only in accordance with law" (Babylonian Talmud, Bava Mezia 30b). In the Muslim tradition, the Hadith of Abi al Darda reports that Mohammed said, "Shall I inform you of merit greater than fasting, charity, and prayer? It is in the conciliation of people." Various religious groups have long traditions of mediation, from Jewish rabbinical courts to mediative mechanisms used by Puritans, Quakers, and other religious groups.

Professor David Luban describes an early reported settlement of a case that could have become an adversarial contest among the gods:

> The first trial in Greek literature occurs in the Homeric *Hymn to Hermes*. The infant Hermes, on the night of his birth, steals the cattle of Apollo, who eventually tracks him down. Hermes in the meantime has climbed back into his crib and donned his swaddling clothes. He indignantly denies the deed and swears mighty oaths of innocence: "I will swear the great oath on my father's head. I vow that I myself am not the culprit and that I have seen no one else stealing your cows — whatever these cows are." . . . Apollo takes Hermes before Zeus for judgment. Zeus is more amused than angered at Hermes' prodigious theft; he commands the two gods "to

come to an accord and search for the cattle." Hermes shows Apollo where he has hidden them, then he placates Apollo with the gift of a splendid tortoise shell lyre, together with the secret of playing it. The delighted Apollo reciprocates by granting Hermes "a beautiful staff of wealth and prosperity"; and the two gods become eternal allies. This delightful comic poem inaugurates a theme of profound importance. It is noteworthy that Zeus is concerned above all with harmony and friendship among the Olympians, and not with punishment for Hermes' crime or for his violation of a sacred oath. The dispute between Apollo and Hermes is resolved by an amicable settlement and not a judgment.

David Luban, Some Greek Trials: Order and Justice in Homer, Hediod, Aeschylus and Plato, 54 Tenn. L. Rev. 279, 280 (1986). Mediation is not a new approach to dispute resolution! Various forms of it have been used in many of the historical antecedents to our own legal system. See Carrie Menkel-Meadow, Is the Adversary System Really Dead? Dilemmas of Legal Ethics as Legal Institutions and Roles Evolve, in Current Legal Problems (Jane Holder, Colm O'Cinneide & Michael Freeman eds., 2004). What follows is an examination of some recent developments in the United States.

b. Labor

Formal institutionalization of mediation in the United States first occurred in the labor field. The U.S. Department of Labor created a panel in 1913 to handle labor-management conflicts. In 1947, this panel evolved into the Federal Mediation and Conciliation Service, which is charged with maintaining stability in industries through mediation.

Two types of mediation characterize labor and employment disputes: collective bargaining mediation and the mediation of individual employee grievances. In collective bargaining mediation, where the terms and conditions of employment are negotiated, participants are generally experienced professionals representing large constituencies. Mediators must be knowledgeable about workplace issues and special bargaining dynamics. Where mediators help to address individual employee grievances — including claims of discrimination — the parties describe the issues that have affected them personally. The discussion can be therapeutic insofar as parties feel heard, and indirectly the workplace may be improved by individuals getting responsive treatment to their concerns and reparations for their injuries.

c. Community

The Civil Rights Act of 1964 created the Community Relations Service (CRS) of the U.S. Department of Justice to help resolve discrimination disputes through negotiation and mediation. The CRS has intervened in a variety of controversies, including disruptions around desegregation orders and marches of the Ku Klux Klan. Today mediation programs in state and federal agencies still respond to disputes concerning discrimination.

Neighborhood justice centers (also called community dispute resolution centers), where volunteers mediate community cases or "minor disputes," have been funded by state and federal budgets since the 1960s. Community centers receive case referrals both from the courts and from agencies and institutions. These centers typically address disputes between landlords and tenants, neighbors, family members, persons involved in love triangles or workplace situations, and a variety of other matters. Developed to be responsive to disputes that the litigation system cannot handle effectively, community mediation centers have thrived on the simple premise that parties can solve their problems with the help of trained interveners and, in so doing, achieve better outcomes and alleviate the tensions that conflict brings to neighborhoods and communities.

d. Family

A major growth area for mediation has been family disputes. The acrimony and expense surrounding divorce and the breakup of families have had such an adverse impact on parents, children, extended families, and society generally that courts, clients, and practitioners have sought a better way than litigation. Many states now mandate mediation in child custody and visitation cases before litigation is permitted. Private practitioners, as well as court programs, provide mediation services to families. Success in divorce mediation has encouraged the development of mediation programs in other family situations such as probate disputes and mediation between parents and children in PINS (persons in need of supervision) proceedings.

Family mediators come to the field from a variety of backgrounds, including psychology, mental health, and social work, as well as law. It is not uncommon for co-mediation teams to work with divorcing parties. One mediator may be an expert in psychology and the other in law and financial issues. Such teams are often gender-balanced as well. See Gary Friedman, A Guide to Divorce Mediation (1993).

e. Civil Cases

In 1976 many eminent jurists and scholars gathered at the Pound Conference to address public dissatisfaction with the justice system. At the Conference, Professor Frank Sander described a different vision of a justice system in which courts "have many doors," some leading to litigation and others leading to alternative processes. Many legal scholars trace the modern U.S. alternative dispute resolution (ADR) movement to this event.

Overloaded judges and a purported "litigation boom" in the late 1970s and 1980s created the need to find ways to reduce court dockets. Insofar as relieving court congestion was the motivating factor for instituting mediation, methods that encouraged party understanding and creative problem solving were replaced, in some instances, by mediation techniques aimed more at case evaluation and settlement. Consequently, the lines defining mediation, case evaluation, and judicial settlement conferences in the context of court-annexed mediation blurred.

By 1988, Florida authorized civil trial court judges to refer almost any civil case to mediation. Other states and some federal courts followed suit, and today mediation is a predictable step in the prelitigation process in many venues.

f. Cybermediation

Mediation and other ADR processes have moved into the twenty-first century with the development of dispute resolution mechanisms on the Internet. Online dispute resolution involves a whole array of dispute resolution mechanisms offered by different providers. Cyberspace offers speed and the convenience of operating from your home computer. Such efficiencies are particularly appealing to parties residing in different countries. However, in the case of mediation services, the lack of face-to-face communication has been criticized as compromising one of mediation's key hallmarks of promoting better understanding between disputants.

g. Other Arenas

It is hard to find an area where mediation is not used for resolving disputes. Mediation is an important resolution tool today in organizations, in schools, for environmental disputes, in government agencies, in the criminal justice system, in construction disputes, in matters between the police and civilians, for international disputes, and for intellectual property disputes.

In business matters, CPR, the International Institute for Conflict Prevention and Resolution, has obtained commitments from many Fortune 500 companies to use mediation and other ADR processes rather than (or at least before) litigation. Mediation, with its forward-looking aspect, appeals to businesspeople who want to avoid the costs and risks of litigation and have an interest in preserving relationships.

4. Two Perspectives on Mediation

The following two excerpts capture critical features of the essence and origins of mediation.

 Carrie Menkel-Meadow, **INTRODUCTION**

in Mediation: Theory, Policy and Practice xiii-xviii, xxix (2001)

Mediation is both a legal process and more than a legal process, used for thousands of years by all sorts of communities, families and formal governmental units. . . . [It] has become a sort of aspirational ideology for those who see its promise in promoting more productive ways of expressing and dealing with human conflict. . . . Mediation, in this larger sense, represents a political theory about the role of conflict in society, the importance of equality, participation, self-determination and a form of leaderless leadership in problem-solving and decision-making. Mediation, as a theory, is aspirational and utopian. In its most grandiose forms, mediation theorists and proponents expect mediation, as a process, to achieve the transformation of warring nation-states, differing ethnic groups, diverse communities, and disputatious workplaces, families and individuals and to develop new and creative human solutions to otherwise difficult or intractable problems. For some, it is a process for achieving interpersonal, intrapersonal and intrapsychic knowledge and understanding. . . .

Mediation, as a structured form of conflict resolution, challenges the Anglo-American idea of adversarial dispute resolution, which presumes that two sides must argue their case to a third-party neutral who will make rule-based, often binary, decisions about who is right and wrong. Instead, it offers the possibility of party-crafted solutions to problems, disputes, conflicts, transactions and relationships, which are facilitated by a third party with no authority to decide anything or to impose any rules. Parties to mediation may engage in other legalistic processes, developing party-specific rules or understandings, even legislating or creating constitutions for their relationships in the future, all on a voluntary and consensual, rather than coercive, basis. Thus mediation's authority is derived from the voluntary commitment of the parties and their facilitator, rather than the coercion of rules, a judge or the state (with some modern exceptions . . . as when courts sometimes "mandate" mediation). . . .

For some critics of mediation this raises questions about how justice can be measured or achieved in settings where the law is not the final arbiter. For some, legal standards should be the measure of justice, for others, real justice may lie outside or beside the law. Mediation theory thus replicates classic jurisprudential debates about legal positivism, the morality of law, natural law and whether justice or fairness exist[s] outside of law. Mediation theory adds to the jurisprudential debate by questioning who dispute resolution institutions and justice are supposed to serve — the parties in dispute or the larger society?

The culture created by mediation theorists and practitioners has been called "harmony" culture and criticized when compared to alternative political and jurisprudential theories of individual and group justice. Critics are concerned that, in mediation, important social and legal conflict is muted, significant public matters are privatized, power imbalances skew results and disempower the already subordinated and that the mediation process encourages unjust compromises of principles or rights that require sharp demarcations and enforcement. . . .

. . . Mediation permits, indeed often requires, consideration of underlying interests, causes or values that produce conflict and thus permits the management, handling or resolution of broader concerns than just those "disputes" which crystallize at the tip of the iceberg. . . .

The forms that mediation takes are themselves subject to debate. While most definitions of mediation conclude that a third-party *neutral* should facilitate the negotiation among parties, many mediation processes — historically and with cultural variations — in fact involve a third party who is quite enmeshed in the community as a "wise elder" or, in more recent times, as a substantive expert who may promise *impartiality* to the parties but who may know quite a bit about the disputants or the subject matter of the dispute. Mediation's forms, then, are variable across cultures, times and different political systems. . . . To the extent that mediation privileges certain forms of communication ("talking cures") its use and its forms may be varied in different settings by culture, nationality, ethnicity, gender, race and class. . . . As anthropologists and other scholars have discovered, there is no cultural uniformity to the practice or form of mediation, and different social groupings and political configurations may re-form or deform the mediation mode to respond to their particular interests. Some have suggested that mediation, with its focus on words, communications and interpersonal competence, may be ethnocentrically based in cultures that privilege such forms of problem-solving. . . .

THE FUTURE HOPE AND PROMISE OF MEDIATION

Theorists and practitioners of mediation claim a central core of functions for mediation:

- That it is a consensual process, both in participation and in agreements reached;
- That it is, at its core, voluntarily engaged in (subject to recent efforts to mandate mediation in some contractual or court settings);
- That it is participatory by the principals engaged in whatever problem or issue is presented at the mediation (who may have representatives who appear as well);
- That it is "facilitated" by a third party "outside" the immediate dispute or conflict (the "neutrality" principle reframed to reflect some of the recent developments in use of expert facilitators);
- That it seeks to develop solutions to problems or resolutions of conflicts or disputes on terms of mutual agreement and fairness to the parties;
- That it seeks to facilitate mutual understanding and apprehension of the other parties' needs, interests and situations.

These core functions are located within an ideology or belief system, held by most theorists and practitioners of mediation, that such a process will reduce unnecessary conflict or acrimony among and between people in conflict, will lead to increased learning and knowledge about others and, where possible, will facilitate the creation of mutually satisfactory solutions to problems or resolutions of conflict that are better than what the parties might have achieved in other fora.

Notes and Questions

14.4 What, according to Menkel-Meadow, are the aspirational goals of mediation?
14.5 As you consider the story of Zeus' intervention in the dispute between Hermes and Apollo, what values were served by the approach Zeus took? What arguments could you make that judgment and punishment of Hermes would be a more prudent approach?

The excerpt that follows also analyzes the central values of mediation. The writings of Lon Fuller (legal philosopher and former Harvard law professor) explore core values in different processes. Themes raised here by Fuller — how mediation builds a different relationship among parties and hence affects the resolution of future controversies — emphasizes the potential of mediation beyond settlement of specific controversies.

❖❖ *Lon L. Fuller*, MEDIATION—ITS FORMS AND FUNCTIONS

44 S. Cal. L. Rev. 305, 307–309, 325–327 (1971)

Casual treatments of the subject in the literature of sociology tend to assume that the object of mediation is to make the parties aware of the "social norms" applicable to their relationship and to persuade them to accommodate themselves to the "structure" imposed by these norms. From this point of view the difference between a judge and a mediator is simply that the judge orders the parties to conform themselves to the rules, while the mediator persuades them to do so. But mediation is commonly directed, not toward achieving conformity to norms, but toward the creation of the relevant norms themselves. This is true, for example, in the very common case where the mediator assists the parties in working out the terms of a contract defining their rights and duties toward one another. In such a case there is no pre-existing structure that can guide mediation; it is the mediational process that produces the structure.

It may be suggested that mediation is always, in any event, directed toward bringing about a more harmonious relationship between the parties, whether this be achieved through explicit agreement, through a reciprocal acceptance of the "social norms" relevant to their relationship, or simply because the parties have been helped to a new and more perceptive understanding of one another's problems. The fact that in ordinary usage the terms "mediation" and "conciliation" are largely interchangeable tends to reinforce this view of the matter.

But at this point we encounter the inconvenient fact that mediation can be directed, not toward cementing a relationship, but toward terminating it. In a form of mediation that is coming to be called "marriage therapy," mediative efforts between husband and wife may be undertaken by a psychoanalyst, a psychiatrist, a social worker, a marriage counselor, or even a friendly neighbor. In this situation it will not infrequently turn out that the most effective use of mediation will be in assisting the parties to accept the inevitability of divorce. In a radically different context one of the most dramatically successful uses of mediation I ever witnessed involved a case in which an astute mediator helped the parties rescind a business contract. Two corporations were entrapped by a long-term supply contract that had become burdensome and disadvantageous to both. Canceling it, however, was a complicated matter, requiring a period of "phasing out" and various financial adjustments back and forth. For some time the parties had been chiefly engaged in reciprocal threats of a law suit. On the advice of an attorney for one of the parties, a mediator (whose previous experience had been almost entirely in the field of labor relations) was brought in. Within no time at all a severance of relations was accomplished and the two firms parted company happily.

Thus we find that mediation may be directed toward, and result in discrepant and even diametrically opposed results. This circumstance argues against our being able to derive any general structure of the mediational process from some identifiable goal shared by all mediational efforts. We may, of course, indulge in observations to the effect that the mere presence of a third person tends to put the parties on their good behavior, that the mediator can direct their verbal exchanges away from recrimination and toward the issues that need to be faced, that by receiving separate and confidential communication from the parties he can gradually bring into the open issues so deep-cutting that the parties themselves had shared a tacit taboo against any discussion of them and that, finally, he can by his management of the interchange demonstrate to the parties that it is possible to discuss divisive issues without either rancor or evasion. . . . [This] analysis . . . has dealt only inferentially and indirectly with what may be said to be the central quality of mediation, namely, its capacity to reorient the parties toward each other, not by imposing rules on them, but by helping them to achieve a new and shared perception of their relationship, a perception that will redirect their attitudes and dispositions toward one another.

This quality of mediation becomes most visible when the proper function of the mediator turns out to be, not that of inducing the parties to accept formal rules for the governance of their future relations, but that of helping them to free themselves from the encumbrance of rules and of accepting, instead, a relationship of mutual respect, trust and understanding that will enable them to meet shared contingencies without the aid of formal prescriptions laid down in advance. Such a mediational effort might well come into play in any of the various forms of mediation between husband and wife associated with "family counseling" and "marriage therapy." In the task of reestablishing the marriage as a going concern the mediator might find it essential to break up formalized conceptions of "duty" and to substitute a more fluid sense of mutual trust and shared responsibility. In effect, instead of working toward achieving a rule-oriented relationship he might devote his efforts, to some degree at least, in exactly the opposite direction.

. . . The negotiation of an elaborate written contract, such as that embodied in a collective bargaining agreement between an employer and a labor union, does indeed present a special set of problems for the mediator. . . . [I]t should be remembered that the primary function of the mediator in the collective bargaining situation is not to propose rules to the parties and to secure their acceptance of them, but to induce the mutual trust and understanding that will enable the parties to work out their own rules. The creation of rules is a process that cannot itself be rule-bound; it must be guided by a sense of shared responsibility and a realization that the adversary aspects of the operation are part of a larger collaborative undertaking. The primary task of the arbitrator [sic] is to induce this attitude of mind and spirit, though to be sure, he does this primarily by helping the parties to perceive the concrete ways in which this shared attitude can redound to their mutual benefit.

It should also be noted that the benefits of a collective bargaining agreement do not lie simply in the aptness of the numbered paragraphs that appear over the parties' signatures, but derive also from the mutual understanding produced by the process of negotiation itself. I once heard an experienced and perceptive lawyer observe, speaking of complex business agreements, "If you negotiate the contract thoroughly, explore carefully the problems that can arise in the course of its administration, work out the proper language to cover the various contingencies that may develop, you can then put the contract in a drawer and forget it." What he meant was that in the exchange that accompanied the negotiation and drafting of the contract the parties would come to understand each other's problems sufficiently so that when difficulties arose they would, as fair and reasonable men, be able to make the appropriate adjustments without referring to the contract itself.

Notes and Questions

14.6 After studying Fuller's excerpt, what are the prime benefits of mediation? Is it more important that the process can settle a given dispute or that it can realign relationships so that parties can resolve disputes themselves?

14.7 In light of the benefits that Fuller articulates, consider some reported case you have studied. In what ways might mediation have served the parties better than litigation?

B. APPROACHES TO MEDIATION

Mediation takes various forms, depending on variables such as culture, context, mediator goals and strategies, and party participation and preferences. This section explores different approaches that arguably fall within the family group of mediation. A lively debate about the proper boundaries of the mediation process itself exists. Where does "mediation" — a process where the neutral is in the middle helping parties to understand and resolve their own conflict with their own solutions — stop? And where does adjudication — processes where the neutral provides the answer to the question raised by the dispute — begin? As you read about various approaches to mediation below, keep those questions in mind. Also consider that the variety and flexibility of mediator approaches is cited as among the strengths of the mediation process. See generally, Carrie Menkel-Meadow, The Many Ways of Mediation: The Transfomation of Traditions, Ideologies, Paradigms, and Practices 11 (3) Negot. J. 217 (1995).

As an attorney representing a client in mediation, you will need to help your client think through what type of mediator and mediation process is wanted. Questions that must be answered include: Should your mediator stick with the legal cause of action presented by the dispute or address all concerns of the parties? What is the role of the parties and of the attorneys in the mediation process? How will (or will) caucuses be used? Will the mediator provide evaluations and proposals? This next section examines different variants of the mediation process.

1. Narrow or Broad Problem Definition, Evaluative or Facilitative

The various mediator orientations described by Len Riskin on his grid below are often-cited descriptors of key mediator orientations.

 Leonard L. Riskin, **MEDIATOR ORIENTATIONS, STRATEGIES AND TECHNIQUES**

12 Alternatives 111, 111-114 (1994)

Almost every conversation about "mediation" suffers from ambiguity. People have disparate visions of what mediation is or should be. Yet we lack a comprehensive system for describing these visions. This causes confusion when people try to choose between mediation and another process or grapple with how to train, evaluate, regulate, or select mediators.

I propose a system for classifying mediator orientations. Such a system can help parties select a mediator and deal with the thorny issue of whether the mediator should have subject-matter expertise. The classification system starts with two principal questions: (1) Does the mediator tend to define problems *narrowly* or *broadly*? (2) Does the mediator think she should *evaluate* — make assessments or predictions or proposals for agreements — or *facilitate* the parties' negotiation without evaluating?

The answers reflect the mediator's beliefs about the nature and scope of mediation and her assumptions about the parties' expectations.

PROBLEM DEFINITION

Mediators with a *narrow* focus assume that the parties have come to them for help in solving a technical problem. The parties have defined this problem in advance through the *positions* they have asserted in negotiations or pleadings. Often it involves a question such as, "Who pays how much to whom?" or "Who can use such-and-such property?" As framed, these questions rest on "win-lose" (or "distributive") assumptions. In other words, the participants must divide a limited resource; whatever one gains, the other must lose.

The likely court outcome — along with uncertainty, delay and expense — drives much of the mediation process. Parties, seeking a compromise, will bargain adversarially, emphasizing positions over interests.

A mediator who starts with a *broad* orientation, on the other hand, assumes that the parties can benefit if the mediation goes beyond the narrow issues that normally define legal disputes. Important interests often lie beneath the positions that the participants assert. Accordingly, the mediator should help the participants understand and fulfill those interests — at least if they wish to do so.

THE MEDIATOR'S ROLE

The *evaluative* mediator assumes that the participants want and need the mediator to provide some direction as to the appropriate grounds for settlement — based on law, industry practice or technology. She also assumes that the mediator is qualified to give such direction by virtue of her experience, training and objectivity.

The *facilitative* mediator assumes the parties are intelligent, able to work with their counterparts, and capable of understanding their situations better than either their lawyers or the mediator. So the parties may develop better solutions than any that the mediator might create. For these reasons, the facilitative mediator assumes that his principal mission is to enhance and clarify communications between the parties in order to help them decide what to do.

The facilitative mediator believes it is inappropriate for the mediator to give his opinion, for at least two reasons. First, such opinions might impair the appearance of impartiality and thereby interfere with the mediator's ability to function. Second, the mediator might not know enough — about the details of the case or the relevant law, practices or technology — to give an informed opinion.

Each of the two principal questions — Does the mediator tend toward a narrow or broad focus? and Does the mediator favor an evaluative or facilitative role? — yield responses that fall along a continuum. Thus, a mediator's orientation will be more or less broad and more or less evaluative.

STRATEGIES AND TECHNIQUES OF EACH ORIENTATION

Each *orientation* derives from assumptions or beliefs about the mediator's role and about the appropriate focus of a mediation. A mediator employs *strategies* — plans — to conduct the mediation. And he uses *techniques* — particular moves or behaviors — to effectuate those strategies. Here are selected strategies and techniques that typify each mediation orientation.

The following grid shows the principal techniques associated with each mediator orientation, arranged vertically with the most evaluative at the top and the most facilitative at the bottom. The horizontal axis shows the scope of problems to be addressed, from the narrowest issues to the broadest interests.

EVALUATIVE

• Urges/pushes parties to accept narrow (position-based) settlement • Develops and proposes narrow (position-based) settlement • Predicts court outcomes • Assesses strengths and weaknesses of legal claims	• Urges/pushes parties to accept broad (interest-based) settlement • Develops and proposes broad (interest-based) settlement • Predicts impact (on interests) of not settling • Probes parties' interests
NARROW Problem Definition Litigation Issues Others Distributive Issues	Business (Substantive) Issues Business Interests Personal Interests Societal Interests **BROAD** Problem Definition
• Helps parties evaluate proposals • Helps parties develop narrow (position-based) proposals • Asks parties about consequences of not settling • Asks about likely court outcomes • Asks about strengths and weaknesses of legal claims	• Helps parties evaluate proposals • Helps parties develop broad (interest-based) proposals • Helps parties develop options • Helps parties understand issues and interests • Focuses discussion on underlying interests (business, personal, societal)

FACILITATIVE

EVALUATIVE-NARROW

The principal strategy of the evaluative-narrow mediator is to help the parties understand the strengths and weaknesses of their positions and the likely outcome at trial. To accomplish this, the evaluative-narrow mediator typically will first carefully study relevant documents, such as pleadings, depositions, reports and mediation briefs. Then, in the mediation, she employs evaluative techniques.... [Representative techniques are described on the grid.]

FACILITATIVE-NARROW

Like the evaluative-narrow, the facilitative-narrow mediator plans to help the participants become "realistic" about their litigation situations. But he employs different techniques. He does not use his own assessments, predictions or proposals. Nor does he apply pressure. Moreover, he probably will not request or study relevant documents, such as pleadings, depositions, reports, or mediation briefs. Instead, because he believes that the burden of decision should rest with the parties, the facilitative-narrow mediator might ask questions — generally in private caucuses — to help the participants understand both sides' legal positions and the consequences of non-settlement. Also in private caucuses, he helps each side assess proposals in light of the alternatives....

EVALUATIVE-BROAD

The evaluative-broad mediator also helps the parties understand their circumstances and options. However, she has a different notion of what this requires. So she emphasizes the parties' interests over their positions and proposes solutions designed to accommodate these interests. In addition, because the evaluative-broad mediator constructs the agreement, she emphasizes her own understanding of the circumstances at least as much as the parties.'...

The evaluative-broad mediator also provides predictions, assessments and recommendations. But she emphasizes options that address underlying interests, rather than those that propose only compromise on narrow issues. In the mediation of a contract dispute between two corporations, for instance, while the evaluative-narrow mediator might propose a strictly monetary settlement, the evaluative-broad mediator might suggest new ways for the firms to collaborate (perhaps in addition to a monetary settlement).

FACILITATIVE-BROAD

The facilitative-broad mediator seeks to help the parties define, understand and resolve the problems they wish to address. She encourages them to consider underlying interests rather than positions and helps them generate and assess proposals designed to accommodate those interests....

The facilitative-broad mediator does not provide assessments, predictions or proposals. However, to help the participants better understand their legal situations, she will likely allow the parties to present and discuss their legal arguments. In addition, she might ask questions ... and focus discussion on underlying interests.

In a broad mediation, however, legal argument generally occupies a lesser position than it does in a narrow one. And because he emphasizes the participants' role in defining the problems and in developing and evaluating proposals, the facilitative-broad mediator does not need to fully understand the legal posture of the case. Accordingly, he is less likely to request or study litigation documents, technical reports or mediation briefs.

However, the facilitative-broad mediator must be able to quickly grasp the legal and substantive issues and to respond to the dynamics of the situation. He needs to help the parties realistically evaluate proposals to determine whether they address the parties' underlying interests. . . .

SUBJECT-MATTER EXPERTISE

In selecting a mediator, what is the relevance of "subject-matter expertise"? The term could mean substantial understanding of . . . the law, customary practices, or technology associated with the dispute. In a patent infringement lawsuit, for instance, a mediator with subject-matter expertise could be familiar with the patent law or litigation, practices in the industry, or the relevant technology — or with all three of these areas.

The need for subject-matter expertise typically increases to the extent that the parties seek evaluations — assessments, predictions or proposals — from the mediator. The kind of subject-matter expertise needed depends on the kind of evaluation or direction the parties seek. If they want a prediction about what would happen in court, they need a mediator with a strong background in related litigation. If they want suggestions about how to structure future business relations, perhaps the mediator should understand the relevant industries. If they want to propose new government regulations (as in a regulatory negotiation), they might wish to retain a mediator who understands administrative law and procedure.

In contrast, to the extent that the parties feel capable of understanding their circumstances and developing potential solutions — singly, jointly or with assistance from outside experts — they might prefer a mediator with great skill in the mediation process, even if she lacks subject-matter expertise. In such circumstances, the mediator need only have a rough understanding of the relevant law, customs and technology. In fact, too much subject-matter expertise could incline some mediators toward a more evaluative role, and could thereby interfere with developing creative solutions.

Notes and Questions

14.8 Facilitative mediation is also known as "pure" or classic mediation. Most of the training programs for mediators are based on a facilitative-broad approach to mediation. Despite this, there is a proliferation of evaluative mediation in legalized cases, that is, cases that are court-annexed or have attorney representatives. How do you explain this? For one interesting analysis of this question, see Robert A. Baruch Bush, Substituting Mediation for Arbitration: The Growing Market for Evaluative Mediation, and What It Means for the ADR Field, 3 Pepp. Disp. Resol. L.J. 111 (2002).

14.9 While the terminology of the original Riskin grid has been widely used and debated, in a more recent article, Riskin replaces the "facilitative-evaluative" dichotomy with "elicitive-directive." Leonard L. Riskin, Decisionmaking in Mediation: The New Old Grid and the New New Grid System, 79 Notre Dame L. Rev. 1 (2003). The new terminology may prove more helpful and less controversial, though Riskin expresses reservations about the static quality of the grid and its oversimplification as an accurate "map" of the mediation process. His "New New Grid" is a far more complex system that maps not only the predispositions, intentions, and influences of the mediator, but also those of parties and their attorneys.

2. Bargaining or Therapy

Scholars from the disciplines of anthropology and sociology, observing community, family, and small claims cases, describe two types of mediator styles: bargaining and therapy.

 Susan S. Silbey & Sally E. Merry, **MEDIATOR SETTLEMENT STRATEGIES**

8 Law & Poly. Q. 7, 19-20 (1986)

In the bargaining mode, mediators claim authority as professionals with expertise in process, law, and the court system, which is described as costly, slow and inaccessible. The purpose of mediation is to reach settlement. The bargaining style tends toward more structured process, and toward more overt control of the proceedings. In the bargaining style, mediators use more private caucuses with disputants, direct discussion more, and encourage less direct disputant communication than in the therapeutic style. Moreover, in the bargaining style the mediators tend to write agreements without the parties present, summarizing and synthesizing what they have heard from the parties. The job of the mediator is to look for bottom lines, to narrow the issues, to promote exchanges, and to side-step intractable differences of interest. Typically disputants will be asked directly "What do you want?," ignoring emotional demands and concentrating on demands that can be traded off. Following this bargaining mode, mediators seem to assume that conflict is caused by differences of interest and that the parties can reach settlement by exchanging benefits. When parties resist, the role of the mediator is to become an "agent of reality" and to point to the inadequacy of the alternatives, the difficulty of the present situation and the benefits of a settlement of any kind.

By contrast, the therapeutic style of mediation is a form of communication in which the parties are encouraged to engage in a full expression of their feelings and attitudes. Here, mediators claim authority based on expertise in managing personal relationships and describe the purpose of mediation as an effort to help people reach mutual understanding through collective agreements. Like the bargaining style, the therapeutic mode also takes a negative view of the legal system; but, instead of emphasizing institutional values and inadequacies, the therapeutic style emphasizes emotional concerns, faulting the legal system for worsening personal relationships. In this mode, agreement writing becomes a collective activity, with mediators generally maximizing direct contact between the parties wherever it may lead. Following the therapeutic style, mediators will typically ask, "How did this situation start?," or, "What was your relationship beforehand?" They rely more heavily upon expanding the discussion, situation, complaint, or charge. There is less discussion of legal norms than within the bargaining mode, and statements about alternatives tend to focus upon appropriateness of process rather than particular outcomes. In addition, the therapeutic mode tends to emphasize the mutuality, reciprocity, and self-enforcement of the agreement in contrast to court or program monitoring.

Notes and Questions

14.10 Is Riskin's categorization scheme related to that of Silbey and Merry's, or are they focusing on entirely different variables? Is the "therapeutic style" on Riskin's grid at all?

14.11 Silbey and Merry characterize mediation as "a bargaining process conducted in the shadow of the court" and "a communication process which resembles therapy." Can it be both? Each of Riskin's quadrants arguably focuses on bargaining. Do you think the professional orientation of the scholars — law versus anthropology and sociology — affects what they see when they examine mediation?

3. Problem-Solving, Understanding-Based or Transformative

The problem-solving approach to mediation, most clearly aligned with what has been called facilitative mediation by Riskin above, seeks to assist parties to understand both the issues and each other more fully and to generate options and ultimately solutions or agreements.

The following two excerpts describe two different models that take a facilitative orientation in different directions. First, the Understanding-Based Model incorporates knowledge of law with an emphasis on parties working together to find a resolution ideal for them. The second excerpt describes Transformative Mediation, which aims not at solving the problem or finding a resolution, but rather at changing the parties — making the parties stronger themselves ("empowerment") and also more open to and understanding of each other ("recognition").

 Gary Friedman & Jack Himmelstein, **THE UNDERSTANDING-BASED MODEL OF MEDIATION**

The Center for Mediation in Law (2004)

The overarching goal of this approach to mediation is to resolve conflict through understanding. Deeper understanding by the parties of their own and each other's perspectives, priorities and concerns enables them to work through their conflict together. With an enhanced understanding of the whole situation, the parties are able to shape creative and mutually rewarding solutions that reflect their personal, business and economic interests. To these ends, the mediator meets directly and simultaneously (rather than separately) with both sides and, if the parties desire, with their lawyers present as well.

The Center's model shares much in common with a number of other approaches to mediation. For example, we stress the importance of articulating interests that underlie the parties' conflicting positions and developing solutions that will serve those interests. There is also much that distinguishes this approach.

PARTIES' RESPONSIBILITY AND NON-CAUCUS APPROACH

In the Understanding-Based Model, the emphasis is on the parties' responsibility for the decisions they will make. Many models of mediation assume that the mediator should take a strong role in crafting a solution to the parties' dispute and persuading them to adopt it. In this approach, the assumption is that it is the parties, not the professionals, who have the best understanding of what underlies the dispute and are in the best position to find the solution. It is *their* conflict, and *they* hold the key to reaching a solution that best serves them both.

Meeting together with the parties (and counsel) follows from these assumptions about parties' responsibility. Many other approaches to mediation recommend that the mediator shuttle back and forth between the parties (caucusing), gaining information that he or she holds confidential. Our central problem with caucusing is that the mediator ends up with the fullest picture of the problem and is therefore in the best position to solve it. The mediator, armed with that fuller view, can readily urge or manipulate the parties to the end he or she shapes. The emphasis here, in contrast, is on understanding and voluntariness as the basis for resolving the conflict rather than persuasion or coercion.

We view the mediator's role in the Understanding-Based approach as assisting the parties to gain sufficient understanding of their own and each other's perspective so as to be able to decide together how to resolve their dispute. The parties not only know firsthand everything that transpires, they have control over fashioning an outcome that will work for both. And they also participate with the mediator (and counsel) in designing a process by which they can honor what they each value and help them reach a result that reflects what is important to both of them. As mediators, our goal is to support the parties in working through their conflict together — in ways that respect their differing perspectives, needs and interests as well as their common goals.

To work in this way is challenging for both the mediator and the parties. The parties' motivation and willingness to work together is critical to the success of this approach. Mediators often assume that the parties (and their counsel) simply do not want to work together, and therefore keep the parties apart. In our experience, many parties (and counsel) simply accept that they will not work together and that the mediator will be responsible for crafting the solution. But once educated how staying in the same room might be valuable, many are motivated to do so. If the parties (and the mediator) are willing, working together throughout can be as rewarding as it is demanding.

ROLE OF LAW AND LAWYERS

Mediators tend to be divided in how they approach the role of law in mediation. Some rely heavily on what a court would decide if the case were to go to trial, authoritatively suggesting or implying that law should be the controlling standard used to end the conflict. Other mediators, concerned that the parties might simply defer too readily to the law and miss the opportunity to find more creative decisions, try to keep the law out of mediation altogether.

In this model, we welcome lawyers' participation and we include the law. But we do not assume that the parties will or should rely solely or primarily on the law. Rather, the importance the parties give to the law is up to them. Our goals are (1) to educate the parties about the law and possible legal outcomes and (2) to support their freedom to fashion their own creative solutions that may differ from what a court might decide. In this way, the parties learn that they can together reach agreements that respond to both their individual interests and their common goals while also being well informed about their legal rights and the judicial alternatives to a mediated settlement. . . .

Friedman and Himmelstein include creative problem solving, along with enriched understanding, as a goal of mediation. Robert Baruch Bush and Joseph Folger, in their Transformative Mediation Model, reject problem solving as a goal of mediation and add party empowerment to that of enhanced understanding between parties.

 Robert A. Baruch Bush & Joseph P. Folger, **THE PROMISE OF MEDIATION: THE TRANSFORMATIVE APPROACH TO CONFLICT**

45, 49, 51-53, 65-66 (rev. ed. 2005)

The transformative theory of conflict starts by offering its own answer to the foundational question of what conflict means to the people involved. According to transformative theory, what people find most significant about conflict is not that it frustrates their satisfaction of some right, interest, or pursuit, no matter how important, but that it leads and forces them to behave toward themselves and others in ways that they find uncomfortable and even repellent. More specifically, it alienates them from their sense of their own strength and their sense of connection to others, thereby disrupting and undermining the interaction between them as human beings. This crisis of deterioration in human interaction is what parties find most affecting, significant — and disturbing — about the experience of conflict. . . .

Conflict, along with whatever else it does, affects people's experience of both self and other. First, conflict generates, for almost anyone it touches, a sense of their own *weakness* and incapacity . . . : a sense of lost control over their situation, accompanied by confusion, doubt, uncertainty, and indecisiveness. The overall sense of weakening is something that occurs as a very natural human response to conflict; almost no one is immune to it, regardless of his or her initial "power position." At the very same time, conflict generates a sense of *self-absorption*: compared with before, each party becomes more focused on self alone — more protective of self and more suspicious, hostile, closed, and impervious to the perspective of the other person. In sum, no matter how strong people are, conflict propels them into relative weakness. No matter how considerate of others people are, conflict propels them into self-absorption and self-centeredness. . . .

Taking the transformative view of what conflict entails and means to parties, one is led to a different assumption, compared with other theories of conflict, about what parties want, need, and expect from a mediator. If what bothers parties most about conflict is the interactional degeneration itself, then what they will most want from an intervenor is help in reversing the downward spiral and restoring constructive interacting. Parties may not express this in so many words when they first come to a mediator. More commonly, they explain that what they want is not just agreement but "closure," to get past their bitter conflict experience and "move on" with their lives. However, it should be clear that in order to help parties achieve closure and move on, the mediator's intervention must directly address the interactional crisis itself. . . .

From the perspective of transformative theory, reversing the downward spiral is the primary value that mediation offers to parties in conflict. That value goes beyond the dimension of helping parties reach agreement on disputed issues. With or without the achievement of agreement, the help parties most want, in all types of conflict, involves helping them end the vicious circle of disempowerment, disconnection, and demonization — alienation from both self and other. Because, without ending or changing that cycle, the parties cannot move beyond the negative interaction that has entrapped them and cannot escape its crippling effects.

This is transformative theory's answer to the question posed previously: What kind of help do people want from a mediator? As transformative theory sees it, with solid support from research on conflict, parties who come to mediators are looking for — and valuing — more than an efficient way to reach agreements on specific issues. They are looking for a way to change and transform their destructive conflict interaction into a more positive one, to the greatest degree possible, so that they can move on with their lives constructively, whether together or apart. . . .

[T]ransformative mediation can best be understood as a process of *conflict trans-formation* — that is, changing the quality of conflict interaction. In the transformative mediation process, parties can recapture their sense[s] of competence and connec-tion, reverse the negative conflict cycle, reestablish a constructive (or at least neutral) interaction, and move forward on a positive footing, with the mediator's help. . . .

[This] brings us to the definition of mediation itself, and the mediator's role, in the transformative model. Both of these definitions differ markedly from the normal definitions found in training materials and practice literature — in which mediation is usually defined as a process in which a neutral third party helps the parties to reach a mutually acceptable resolution of some or all of the issues in dispute, and the mediator's role is defined as establishing ground rules, defining issues, establishing an agenda, generating options, and ultimately persuading the parties to accept terms of agreement. . . .

By contrast, in the transformative model

- Mediation is defined as a process in which a third party works with parties in conflict to help change the quality of their conflict interaction from negative and destructive to positive and constructive, as they explore and discuss issues and possibilities for resolution.
- The mediator's role is to help the parties make positive interactional shifts (empowerment and recognition shifts) by supporting the exercise of their capacities for strength and responsiveness, through their deliberation, decision making, communication, perspective taking, and other party activities.
- The mediator's primary goals are (1) to support empowerment shifts, by supporting—but never supplanting—each party's deliberation and decision making, at every point in the session where choices arise (regarding either process or outcome) and (2) to support recognition shifts, by encouraging and supporting—but never forcing—each party's freely chosen efforts to achieve new understandings of the other's perspective.

Notes and Questions

14.12 Are the goals of a transformative mediator—empowerment and recognition—at odds with the goals of a problem-solving mediator? Of an understanding-based mediator? To understand a situation or solve a problem, it is helpful to have the parties both strong individually ("empowered") and responsive to each other ("recognition"). Consequently, the purposes, strategies, and techniques of transformative, understanding-based, and facilitative mediators may overlap. For an analysis of transformative mediation's comparative advantage in attaining empowerment and recognition, see Jeffrey R. Seul, How Transformative Is Transformative Mediation? A Constructive-Developmental Assessment, 15 Ohio St. J. on Disp. Resol. 135, 171 (1999).

14.13 Providing a laboratory for a particular mediation model, the U.S. Postal Service, one of the largest employers in the United States, adopted a transformative model for workplace disputes involving allegations of discrimination. The program, which is probably the largest employment mediation program in the world, uses outside mediators who have specialized training in transformative mediation. It provides a forum for supervisors and employees to mediate during their working hours. Noted scholar Lisa Bingham has collected data since the project's inception in 1994. Her findings include high levels of participant satisfaction with both the mediation process (91 percent) and the mediators (96 percent), high levels of satisfaction with the mediation outcome (from 64 percent for complainants to 72 percent for management), a significant drop in the number of formal discrimination complaints at the

Postal Service, and evidence of improved communication between employers and supervisors during mediation. See Lisa B. Bingham, Mediation at Work: Transforming Workplace Conflict at the United States Postal Service, IBM Center for the Bus. of Govt. (2003), available at *http://www.businessof government.org/pdfs/Bingham_Report.pdf.* Perhaps most significantly, these findings suggest there is a positive impact on the workplace itself as a result of the transformative mediation program.

4. Trashing, Bashing, or Hashing

Studying mediator approaches in civil court cases, including personal injury, construction, commercial, contract, and real estate, James Alfini finds three dominant approaches. He labels them "trashing, bashing, and hashing." As you read the accounts of these approaches (particularly "trashing" and "bashing"), note how far they are from transformative, understanding-based, or problem-solving mediation.

 James J. Alfini, TRASHING, BASHING, AND HASHING IT OUT: IS THIS THE END OF "GOOD MEDIATION"?

19 Fla. St. U. L. Rev. 47, 66-71, 73 (1991)

MEDIATOR STYLES AND STRATEGIES

Does circuit court mediation — because it is mandatory and conducted by legal professionals — anticipate a deviation from traditional mediation styles and strategies? Our interviews with the circuit mediators and lawyers revealed three distinct styles. These three approaches to the mediation process are characterized as (1) trashing, (2) bashing, and (3) hashing it out.

I. Trashing

The mediators who employ a trashing methodology spend much of the time "tearing apart" the cases of the parties . . . "to get them to a point where they will put realistic settlement figures on the table."

To facilitate uninhibited trashing of the parties' cases, the overall strategy employed by these mediators discourages direct party communication. Following the mediator's orientation and short (five to ten minutes) opening statements by each party's attorney, the mediator puts the parties in different rooms. . . .

Once the trasher has achieved the goal of getting both sides to put what she believes to be more realistic settlement figures on the table, she will shuttle back and forth trying to forge an agreement. If this is accomplished, the mediator may or may not bring the parties back together to work out the details of the agreement. One trasher explained that, once separated, he never brings the parties back together even at the final agreement stage. . . .

II. Bashing

Unlike the trashers, the mediators who use a bashing technique tend to spend little or no time engaging in the kind of case evaluation that is aimed at getting the parties to put "realistic" settlement figures on the table. Rather, they tend to focus initially on the settlement offers that the parties bring to mediation and spend most of the session bashing away at those initial offers in an attempt to get the parties to agree to a figure somewhere in between. Their mediation sessions thus tend to be shorter than those of the trashers, and they tend to prefer a longer initial joint session, permitting direct communication between the parties. . . .

As soon as the basher has gotten the parties to place settlement offers on the table, as one attorney explained, "there is a mad dash for the middle." One of the retired judges described a case he had mediated that morning:

> [T]he plaintiff wanted $75,000. The defendant told me he would pay $40,000. I went to the plaintiff and said to him, "They're not going to pay $75,000. What will you take?" He said, "I'll take $60,000." I told him I wasn't sure I could get $60,000 and asked if he would take $50,000 if I could get it. He agreed. I then went back to the defendant and told him I couldn't settle for $40,000, but "you might get the plaintiff to take $50,000" and asked if he would pay it. The answer was yes. Neither of them were bidding against themselves. I was the guy who was doing it, and that's the role of the mediator. . . .

III. Hashing It Out

The third circuit mediation style can best be described as one involving a hashing out of a settlement agreement because it places greater reliance on direct communication between the opposing attorneys and their clients. The hashers tend to take a much more flexible approach to the mediation process, varying their styles and using techniques such as caucusing selectively, depending on their assessment of the individual case and the needs and interests of the parties. When asked to describe the mediator's role in one sentence, a hasher responded, "Facilitator, orchestrator, referee, sounding board, scapegoat."

The hasher generally adopts a much less directive posture than the trashers and bashers, preferring that the parties speak directly with one another and hash out an agreement. However, if direct communication appears counterproductive, the hasher acts as a communication link. . . .

Flexibility apparently is the hallmark of the hasher style of mediation. Although hashers prefer to adopt a style that encourages direct party communication to hash out an agreement, they are willing to employ trasher or basher methodologies if they believe it to be appropriate in a particular case.

Notes and Questions

14.14 In ancient China, litigants came in to court on their knees, shamed because they could not work out their own conflict. Should "trashing" and "bashing" be a part of our justice system? Why or why not?

14.15 Elsewhere in the article, Alfini suggests that experienced trial lawyers tend to use trashing; retired judges tend to use bashing. Why do you think that is?

14.16 Alfini concludes that the growth of the three approaches for civil cases does not signal the end of "good mediation." What is "good mediation"? If his observations are correct regarding the prevalent styles, do you agree with his conclusion? Would you choose a trasher, a basher, or a hasher as your mediator?

5. Dispute Settlement or Transaction and Relationship Formation

In addition to settling disputes, mediation can facilitate deals and help form new relationships or organizations. Facilitating transactions, sometimes called transactional dispute resolution, are perhaps the newest, most informal, and undeveloped use of mediation.

Lawyers can bring creative perspectives to deal formation by employing problem-solving concepts, exploring underlying needs and interests, creating value, encouraging participation, and expanding and allocating resources. A mediator, however, can enhance all of these lawyer contributions by creating value, preventing waste, and removing strategic barriers to information asymmetries. Mediators also help deal with emotional, cognitive, and other barriers to agreement to facilitate Pareto-efficient and satisfying arrangements. Mediators, for example, may be better than attorneys at helping parties overcome self-serving assessments and reactive devaluation — phenomena that attorneys can fall prey to as well. Deal makers may require assistance in solving problems, allocating risk, deflecting future problems, and keeping the social climate positive. For certain matters, bringing in a mediator to develop the deal offers valuable potential benefits: speed, quality, and sustainable agreements. In the following excerpt, Scott Peppet examines the economic justifications of adding third-party mediators to deal creation. If transactional mediators can facilitate more efficient, durable deals and relationships, it follows that they may have a role as significant as that of dispute resolving mediators.

 Scott R. Peppet, **CONTRACT FORMATION IN IMPERFECT MARKETS: SHOULD WE USE MEDIATORS IN DEALS?**

38 Ohio St. J. on Disp. Resol. 283, 298-301 (2004)

ECONOMIC JUSTIFICATIONS FOR TRANSACTIONAL MEDIATION
Discovering and Optimizing Gains from Trade

Transactional negotiators theoretically face similar adverse selection problems to those faced by disputing parties. First, the parties may not discover that trade is possible. Just as a litigating defendant may posture and bluff to try to low-ball a plaintiff, a buyer in a transaction may be tempted to try to get a better deal by "looking cheap." In other words, even if a buyer is willing to pay a high price, she may do better by looking as if she will only pay a low one. The opposite is true of sellers. One common example from the transactional context illustrates the problem. Because a high-value buyer does not want to signal his type to the seller, and because a seller is likely to equate having deep pockets with a willingness to spend, a deep-pocketed buyer may seek to hide its identity to prevent giving away too much to the seller. In this case an agent—such as an attorney—can be used to present an anonymous offer, thereby eliminating any signal about reservation price that might be inferred from the buyer's identity. An agent cannot, however, overcome the more basic adverse selection problem caused by the simple fact that making *any* offer sends information about the offeror's previously private reservation price. Information asymmetries may thus lead parties to exaggerate offers and demands in order to get a better deal.

In one experiment, for example, small teams of experienced executives were given detailed information about two simulated companies. They were then assigned to represent one company or the other and asked to evaluate the companies and negotiate a merger. Although agreement was possible, only nine of the twenty-one pairings reached agreement. In addition, the executives disagreed wildly about the relevant valuations—selling prices ranged from $3.3 million to $16.5 million. This suggests that occasionally transacting parties fail to "close the deal" because of strategic posturing.

Second, as in litigation, transacting parties may fail to find Pareto-efficient agreements. In an idealized situation with full information and zero transaction costs, the parties should trade until they find an economically efficient contract. It is notoriously unclear, however, whether contracting parties reach Pareto-efficient agreements in practice. Information asymmetries and strategic posturing may again lead to inefficiencies. Two parties may not discover an efficient agreement if one or the other is reluctant to discuss it (or agreements of its type) for fear that doing so will reveal private information about the party's reservation price.

An executive negotiating her employment agreement, for example, might shy away from discussing certain packages that involve accepting a lower salary in exchange for better benefits or greater stock options, if the executive fears that doing so would send an unwise signal about her worth. Similarly, an experiment in the corporate acquisitions context suggests that even when experienced negotiators reach agreement, they do not necessarily reach Pareto-efficient contracts. Even subjects trained in decision analysis and finance succumbed to the strategic difficulties inherent in bargaining and, because of a failure to share information, sometimes concluded inefficient deals.

As in litigation, a mediator should be able to help. Interestingly, the researcher in this corporate acquisitions experiment re-ran the simulation offering each negotiating pair the service of a trained mediator, but not requiring that they use the mediator. Those executives [who] made use of the mediator reached more efficient contracts than those [who] did not. Similarly, Max Bazerman et al. found that a mediator intermediary—as opposed to an agent—can lower impasse rates in transactional bargaining. Although experimental economics regarding the role of mediators and intermediaries is in its infancy, and some research suggests that intermediaries merely add costs and thus preclude agreement in some bargaining, there is at least preliminary evidence that a transactional mediator can add value.

Notes and Questions

14.17   What kinds of transactions lend themselves to "deal mediators" (third-party neutrals who help put together the transaction)? What qualities would you look for in a deal mediator? What differences do you see in the roles of a "deal-facilitating" third party and a "dispute-resolving" third party? Can the same people be mediators in both of these contexts? In the same deal, if, after facilitating its making, it then falls apart? Should lawyers or businesspeople take the lead in mediating deals?

14.18   Consider what prenuptial and antenuptial agreements have done to make some marriages possible. See, e.g., Howard Raiffa, Post-Settlement Settlements, 1 Negot. J. 9, 9-12 (1985), in which the author analyzes how a third-party neutral such as a mediator can be a repository of information that parties might not want to reveal to each other without some assurance that the deal will go through or that the information will not be shared inappropriately, as in sharing trade secrets in merger discussions. Consider also the use of escrow accounts for monetary and documentary deposits while parties contingently perform on parts of contracts.

C. EXAMPLES OF MEDIATIONS

The following accounts of actual mediations illustrate the variety of practices and outcomes possible in the mediation of real cases. The first case is an appeal by shareholders against a large corporation, which was ordered into the mediation program of the U.S. Court of Appeals for the Second Circuit. The second case is a personal injury, medical malpractice matter involving the settlement of a damage claim. The final case involves a minority group, a town, and a litigation that raised constitutional questions.

These provide only a small window into the universe of cases that benefit from mediation. Nonetheless, you will find here examples of (1) outcomes that are more custom-tailored than litigation can provide and a process that leads parties to a deeper appreciation of the other side's perspective (the *Sisters v. Bristol* case); (2) outcomes that provide the closure and cost savings of a settlement and the personal connection and healing available from direct interaction between the parties (the medical malpractice case); and (3) outcomes that address a far broader range of issues than litigation and achieve a higher level of cooperation and community among the parties (the *Glen Cove* case). As you read about these situations, imagine how the stories would have come out differently if mediation had not been used.

Frank J. Scardilli, SISTERS OF THE PRECIOUS BLOOD v.
BRISTOL-MYERS CO.: A SHAREHOLDER-MANAGEMENT
DISPUTE[*]

**reprinted in Leonard Riskin & James Westbrook, Dispute Resolution and Lawyers
362-367 (2d ed. 1997)**

This case was on appeal to the U.S. Court of Appeals for the Second Circuit from a
grant of summary judgment in favor of Bristol-Myers Co., defendant-appellee (hereinafter "Bristol") and against the Sisters of the Precious Blood, plaintiff-appellant
(hereinafter "Sisters"). The latter, who owned 500 shares of Bristol stock, started a
lawsuit against Bristol under the proxy solicitation section of the Securities Exchange
Act of 1934 alleging that a shareholder resolution they proposed was defeated
because Bristol's stated opposition to the resolution in the proxy materials distributed
to the shareholders was based on serious misrepresentations of fact.

The Sisters were concerned that the company's sales practices in the third world
of its infant baby formula were contributing to serious illness, malnutrition and death
of infants because of the unsanitary conditions often prevailing there. Frequently the
formula is mixed with contaminated water, there is no refrigeration and its use
discourages breastfeeding which is clearly healthier in most instances than is the
formula.

The Sisters' proposed resolution requested that management report to the shareholders the full extent of its marketing practices of the infant formula in the third
world to alert other shareholders to what they perceived was irresponsible business
behavior. Their lawsuit was aimed at getting the company to come up with a
corrected proxy solicitation to be submitted to a special meeting of the shareholders
to be called specifically for that purpose rather than await the next annual meeting of
shareholders.

The court declined to grant the relief sought by the Sisters. . . .

MEDIATION EFFORTS ON APPEAL

The first of four conferences seeking to mediate this dispute was held on July 19,
1977. . . . Apparently because they believed no amicable resolution was possible,
counsel who appeared for the parties were very able but had virtually no settlement
authority. . . .

As is customary, I first explored the arguments of counsel relative to the strengths
and weaknesses of their legal positions on appeal. The parties seemed genuinely far
apart in their assessment of the likely outcome in our court. The issue on appeal
involved some complexity because of the rather technical requirements for suits
under Section 14 of the Securities Exchange Act of 1934. While generally appellees
have a distinct advantage, if for no other reason than that only about one out of eight
cases is reversed on appeal in our court, the outcome of this particular case was hard
to predict. Even if the district court decision were deemed technically correct, this
could have disturbing policy implications because the decision appeared to create a

---

[*] Presented at a Harvard faculty seminar on negotiation on April 13, 1982.

license for management to lie with impunity whenever it sought to defeat a proposed shareholder resolution. . . . The SEC was apparently disturbed by this implication and advised me it was seriously considering filing a brief amicus curiae urging our court to reverse the decision below. . . .

Predictably, the parties' respective positions on what might constitute a satisfactory settlement were far apart. The Sisters were adamant on the principle that no settlement terms could be discussed unless Bristol openly admitted that it had lied in its earlier proxy solicitation and that this fact had to be communicated through new proxy solicitations at a special meeting of the shareholders to be convened solely for that purpose. Bristol, of course, insisted it had been truthful all along. It offered, however, to permit the Sisters to make any written statement they wished at the next annual shareholders' meeting, and Bristol would simply state its opposition to the proposal without elaboration. This was unacceptable to the Sisters. Because it was clear I needed parties with more authority and flexibility, I set up a second conference requiring senior counsel to come in with their clients.

The second conference held in the middle of August, 1977, was attended by senior counsel for both sides, the inside General Counsel of Bristol, and a representative of the Advisory Committee of the Interfaith Group for Corporate Responsibility, which was the real moving force behind the Sisters' litigation.

It soon became apparent that there was very deep hostility and profound distrust between the parties. Each was convinced the other was acting in bad faith. The Sisters were outraged by Bristol's insistence that it had not lied. Its distrust of Bristol was total and uncompromising. At this conference, the Sisters, for the first time, insisted that they would have to be reimbursed for their litigation expenses of approximately $15,000 before any settlement could be effected. After checking with top management, counsel for management flatly refused to pay anything at all to the Sisters. . . .

It became clear that the respective parties' self-image was significantly at variance with the image each had of the other.

Bristol regarded itself as by far the most responsible marketer of infant formula in the third world, far more so than its three major American competitors and the giant Swiss company Nestle. It claimed it put out a quality nutritional product that was very useful when mothers either could not or chose not to breast feed their infants; that it did not advertise its infant formulas directly to consumers in the third world; that the company policy already sought to minimize the danger of improper use by its labeling. In short, it was convinced that its business practices were both prudent and responsible. Therefore, they were furious that they had been singled out as "baby killers" by the Sisters who had so testified before a Congressional committee and who had lost few opportunities to criticize them in the media. It was clear they viewed the Sisters as wild-eyed, misguided religious fanatics who were themselves engaging in a distortion of the facts and reckless character assassination.

The Sisters, on the other hand, had spent years accumulating data in affidavits taken throughout the world regarding the enormous peril to infants created by the indiscriminate use of infant formula in the third world. They had witnessed suffering and death and were suffused with the self-righteousness of avenging angels. To them,

Bristol was a monster who cared only about profits and not at all about the lives and health of infants. . . .

As negotiations proceeded, it became apparent that no meaningful communication could take place until each of the parties realized that its view of the other was a grossly distorted caricature and counter-productive.

I struck often at the theme that it was dangerous to assume that one with whom you disagree violently is necessarily acting in bad faith. Moreover, I stressed to both that I had become fully and firmly convinced that each of the parties was acting in complete good faith, albeit from a different perspective. I strove to get each to view the matter through the eyes of the other. . . .

It was necessary to convince each that its interests were not nearly as incompatible as they perceived them and that the interest of each would be best served by a cooperative problem-solving attitude rather than a litigious one.

I stressed that neither party's true interest would be served by "winning" the appeal. A "win" by Bristol would not be likely to stop the public attacks in the media which so angered and disturbed them. Likewise, a "win" by the Sisters could mean a remand for an expensive trial with no assurance whatever thereafter that Bristol's marketing practices would be altered in any way.

The point was made forcibly to the Sisters that their insistence that Bristol admit that it had lied was totally unrealistic and that progress was impossible so long as they insisted on humiliating the company's management. They were reminded that their real interest lay in effecting marketing changes in the third world and they could best achieve this in a climate of cooperative good will with management. So long as management perceived them as vindictive it was likely to simply dig in its heels and refuse to budge. I urged that a softening of their attitude would in turn create a more flexible attitude in management.

Bristol in turn was forced to concede that notwithstanding what they viewed as the distasteful stridency of the Sisters there was indeed a real moral issue to be faced and they had a real interest in being perceived as highly ethical, responsible businessmen who were not insensitive to the human tragedy which could result from the improper use of their product in the third world. . . .

After considerable negotiation in four face-to-face conferences supplemented by numerous telephone conferences over a period of nearly six months, in the course of which Bristol voluntarily changed some of its marketing practices, the parties finally agreed to resolve their differences as follows:

- The Sisters were satisfied that Bristol had already changed some of its marketing practices which the Sisters had regarded as particularly offensive.
- The Sisters would be given direct access to Bristol's Board of Directors and other representatives of the company at various times for the purpose of maintaining a first-hand continuing dialogue on the problems of marketing infant formula in the third world.
- Bristol and the Sisters would each prepare a separate written statement of its views not to exceed 1500 words to be presented to the shareholders in the next quarterly report of the Company. This would be preceded by an agreed-upon joint preamble which would recite the background of the litigation, its

resolution by the parties and that the Sisters and Bristol planned to continue to exchange views in an atmosphere of mutual respect for each other's good faith.

To insure that the statements would not be inflammatory each side was given the right to veto the statement of the other. Agreeing on the principle, however, was easier than its implementation. Numerous drafts were exchanged and when appropriate I mediated between their respective versions. The final agreement on language was arrived at as a result of a four-and-one-half-hour drafting session involving eight people sitting around a conference table in the court in the afternoon of Christmas Eve of 1977. In a sense of relief and elation, the Chairperson of the Interfaith Group for Corporate Responsibility stated: "It is fitting and perhaps prophetic that we have finally resolved our differences on how best to protect tender infants on this [Christmas] eve. . . ."

Notes and Questions

14.19 Using this example to reflect on the potential advantages and benefits of the mediation process described earlier in this chapter — settlement, participation and self-determination, better outcomes, relationship, and community — how was the mediation reflective (or not reflective) of those advantages? Is there public benefit from these private parties settling their case?

14.20 On the basis of this description, how would you characterize the mediator of this case? Is he facilitative, evaluative, or both? Is he a trasher, basher, or hasher? Is he broad or narrow? Transformative or problem-solving?

The next case illustrates a settlement-oriented approach that allows the parties to have meaningful closure to their conflict. Note how the recognition and personal closure generated by mediation was nearly undermined by the lawyers involved.

 Eric Galton, **MEDIATION OF MEDICAL NEGLIGENCE CLAIMS**

28 Cap. U. L. Rev. 321, 324-325 (2000)

During the joint session, it became apparent that both the physician and the parents had been instructed by counsel not to speak during joint session, despite my repeated attempts to engage the parties. Only the lawyers spoke during the joint session.

The case involved the following general facts. The wife was pregnant with the couple's third child. The couple's first two children were born with no complications. The physician caring for the mother delivered the couple's first two children.

The third pregnancy was unremarkable with appropriate prenatal care. The mother goes into labor and is instructed to go to the hospital. She arrives at 6:00 A.M. Although it is the physician's day off, the physician is called when the fetal monitor strips show some signs of distress. The physician arrives and during the fifteen minutes he is attending to the mother, the strips seem to return to normal. The physician leaves.

Thirty minutes later, the strips begin to show even greater evidence of distress. Attempts to locate the physician are initially futile, although the parents hear a nurse say, "Try the golf course." The physician is located on the golf course fifty minutes later, arrives at the hospital, and orders an emergency C-section. The baby is born, barely alive, and dies twenty minutes later.

Counsel for both sides agree to mediation after paper discovery is exchanged, but before depositions are taken. During the joint session, the lawyers make benign, constructive opening presentations. When engaged by the mediator during the joint session, neither the physician nor the husband and wife elect to speak.

The parties are split into different rooms and the mediator begins to caucus, privately, with each side. Negotiations commence and are productive. Five hours later the matter resolves with a written agreement, signed by all parties and counsel, in which the family is to receive $400,000.

As I walk into the physician's room with copies of the executed memorandum of agreement, I sense that the physician has something on his mind. I ask the physician if he wants an opportunity to meet with the family before he leaves. Immediately, the physician's lawyers state that such a meeting is unnecessary, would be awkward, and is something the physician is not required to do. The physician states (and these are *his* words almost verbatim), "I would like to meet with the family. I need some closure."

I next ask the mother and father whether they wish to meet with the physician. Similarly, the lawyers tell the parents they do not have to meet and that such a meeting would be awkward. The mother declares, "Yes, I would very much like to meet with *my* doctor."

The physician is escorted to the parents' room. As the physician enters the room, he stops just outside the door. The mother is seated ten feet away.

For several minutes, no words are exchanged. No one even moves. Suddenly, the mother gets up, tears begin to flow, and she holds out her arms. The physician goes over to the mother. As they embrace, the physician says, "I'm sorry. I'm so sorry." The mother, patting the physician's back responds, "It's okay, we forgive you." The husband comes over and joins the embrace. The lawyers, standing on the opposite end of the room, appear mystified. The physician, father, and mother sit together and talk for ten minutes.

No doubt, the economic settlement was important and a legitimate goal of the mediation process. But, for the parties, the opportunity for conciliation and closure was at least equally important. In cases where the parties desire such closure, the process must provide such an opportunity. In the case described above, the parties, without such opportunity, would have received neither the full benefits of the process nor what they needed or wanted.

It is equally clear in this, and in other instances, that the needs and goals of the parties in mediation are not necessarily the same as their lawyers. In fact, lawyers, because they often fail to either value or recognize or understand such needs, may even discourage a process that attempts to meet their clients' needs.

Notes and Questions

14.21 Think about the important moments in your life. Can you put a monetary value on those moments? Obviously, there are a host of critically important events — an apology, a handshake, a smile — that cannot be financially valued but have an immense impact. Should lawyers be in tune with the whole range of interests of their clients and capable of furthering interests in respect, recognition, healing, connection, and communication?

14.22 The lawyers in this example do not encourage their clients to participate but rather try to protect their clients from contact with the other side. Is this a mistake?

The case that follows, like the case of the Sisters and Bristol, has the potential for broad societal impact on groups of relatively weak and disenfranchised parties. As you read the case, reflect on the benefits of mediation to the parties in the case and in comparable situations.

 Lela P. Love, **GLEN COVE: MEDIATION ACHIEVES WHAT LITIGATION CANNOT**

20 Consensus 1, 1-2 (1993)

The city of Glen Cove, Long Island, and Central American refugees who sought day labor at a "shaping point" (a locale in the city where employers go to find day workers) experienced a bitter and protracted controversy with no end in sight — despite nearly two years of litigation — when the parties decided to attempt to work out their differences in mediation. Mediation resolved not only the issues which were being litigated, but also many other issues that, although not causes for legal action, were nonetheless extremely important to the individuals and groups involved in the controversy. I had the privilege of mediating the case and report on its success in order to encourage other communities facing difficult disputes to try the mediation process.

BACKGROUND: TENSIONS BUILD

In 1988 tensions began to build between Glen Cove officials and the Central American immigrants (some of whom were undocumented aliens) who congregated in front of Carmen's Deli to find employment. More than 100 men, many from other towns, would gather on a given day to seek odd jobs from landscapers and other contractors.

Local merchants and neighbors expressed concerns about disorderly and noisy behavior at the shaping point, including cat-calling to women, and littering and urinating in public. City officials were also concerned about traffic safety, since employers would stop on a major road to negotiate with and pick up day workers.

There also was a sentiment that it was illegal for those who were undocumented to seek employment.

Salvadoran workers, on the other hand, were interested in their survival, since the day labor was their means of livelihood, and a "shaping point" was essential for finding work. Many who gathered were political refugees from El Salvador, to whom a return home might mean a death sentence. There were those who felt that, since the laborers serviced the lawns and country clubs of the wealthy, the effort to remove them from gathering in public was unfair.

In addition to issues about the shaping point itself, the perception among the Hispanic community that the City — particularly the police — were hostile, created problems for both sides: poor channels of communication to cope with the host of problems; and a lack of resources for Central Americans when they were preyed upon by criminal elements in the community (a pressing problem).

ORDINANCES PROPOSED TO DEAL WITH PROBLEM

Tensions heightened in 1989 when the city, in an effort to curb the size of the gatherings, successfully urged the Immigration and Naturalization Service to round up and detain illegal aliens gathering in front of Carmen's Deli. This was followed by the city's proposing first an ordinance making it illegal for groups of five or more persons to assemble publicly to seek employment and later an ordinance which prohibited any "illegal undocumented alien" from soliciting work in a public or private place. These ordinances engendered a strident debate, although neither was adopted. In 1990, the City Council did adopt an ordinance which prohibited standing on a street or highway and soliciting employment from anyone in a motor vehicle and also prohibited occupants of a stopped or parked motor vehicle from hiring or attempting to hire workers.

The Hispanic community and civil libertarians saw the ordinance(s) as specifically targeted against Hispanics, as well as unconstitutional. Several months after the ordinance was adopted, advocacy groups for Central American refugees filed a three million dollar class action suit against Glen Cove, alleging violation of Hispanic persons' First Amendment right of freedom of speech and 14th Amendment right of equal protection.

WHAT MEDIATION ACHIEVED

Two full days of mediation, spaced a week apart to give the parties time to come up with innovative proposals to address the concerns raised the first day, were sufficient to achieve consensus on an outline of an acceptable accord. This agreement was refined over several months and adopted in late 1992, providing for the dismissal of the lawsuit and the enforcement of the terms of the agreement by the federal court.

The significant achievements of the mediation process in this case were:

- The parties recognized their mutual interest in improving communications with each other.
- Greater accessibility to the city soccer field for the Salvadoran community was arranged.

- The City agreed to help find alternative sites for a shaping point (including possible use of Industrial Development Agency funds) or to support alternatives to meet the Hispanic community's employment needs. The Central American Refugee Center (CARECEN) agreed to educate day laborers who congregate in public places about their responsibilities to the community.
- Relations between the police and the Salvadoran community were addressed by CARECEN's agreement to host community meetings giving the police a platform to educate Salvadorans about community interests and concerns and undertaking such education themselves. The police in turn agreed to: cultural awareness training for all city police officers; appointing a liaison to the Salvadoran community who would attend CARECEN-organized community meetings; training two officers in conversational Spanish; taking ability in Spanish into account in hiring officers; adopting a policy barring officers from inquiring about immigration status under certain circumstances; and instituting a written protocol (in consultation with CARECEN) for the police handling of situations where a party does not speak English.
- The Ordinance was amended to a form acceptable to all parties and designed to promote the City's interest in traffic safety without singling out the Salvadoran Community or infringing upon Constitutional rights.

Perhaps most importantly, the mediation created a respectful dialogue between the parties, which should result in an enhanced ability to confront new problems as they arise. . . . Alan Levine, the Director of the Hofstra Constitution Law Clinic, which represented CARECEN, was quoted as saying, "If everyone lives up to their obligations under this agreement, it promises to establish the kinds of relationships between a municipal government and a minority population that one would hope for."

Notes and Questions

14.23 Glen Cove has enjoyed improved relations between town officials and the Salvadoran community in part, arguably, as a byproduct of the mediation. A shaping point, with toilet facilities provided by the city and a variety of supportive services for day laborers, was ultimately put into place. See Lela P. Love & Cheryl B. McDonald, A Tale of Two Cities: Day Labor and Conflict Resolution for Communities in Crisis, Disp. Resol. Mag., Fall 1997, at 8-10. If mediation can set new precedents with respect to community interaction and constructive problem solving, do those results counterbalance the loss of a legal precedent in a case with important constitutional issues?

14.24 Compare the issues addressed in the litigation and mediation of the Glen Cove case:

LITIGATION	MEDIATION
• the *ordinance*: is it constitutional? • discrete incidents of *alleged police misconduct* at the shaping point	• *communication* between town officials and Salvadorans • *a shaping point* • *police interactions with non-English-speaking individuals and groups* (protocols when language barriers are present, cultural awareness and sensitivity, opportunities for communication) • concerns regarding *public conduct of Salvadorans* ("cat-calling," public urination, blocking entryways) • use of *the city soccer field* • *the ordinance*

Litigation entails an intensive inquiry into facts and evidence pertinent to the causes of action presented and the meaning of the norms and rules as they intersect with the facts. If, for example, the case had been litigated and the court had found the ordinance unconstitutional, the ordinance would be struck down. The town, however, could enact a new ordinance sensitive to the court's prohibition of certain language but not responsive to other issues that the mediation addressed.

Mediation, on the other hand, involved an intensive inquiry into information, interests, values, feelings, rules, and norms pertinent to the ordinance, the shaping point, interactions between the police and non-English-speaking civilians, interactions between the town and Salvadoran residents and workers, civic responsibilities of Salvadorans, and the use of the soccer field. Mediation engages participants in a forward-looking, problem-solving exercise, aimed as much at creating relationships conducive to addressing future problems as at solving the problems at hand.

As an attorney considering whether to advise your client to pursue mediation, understanding all the issues (legal and nonlegal) faced by your client is crucial.

D. ADVICE FOR ATTORNEY REPRESENTATIVES IN MEDIATION

The following excerpt is a primer on what not to do as a representative in mediation. The essence of the advice is to leave your adversarial approach outside and to become a problem solver. Note how many of the errors that Arnold describes come from an attorney mistaking mediation for an adjudicatory process.

Tom Arnold, **20 COMMON ERRORS IN MEDIATION ADVOCACY**

13 Alternatives to High Cost Litig. 69, 69-71 (1995)

Trial lawyers who are unaccustomed to being mediation advocates often miss important arguments. Here are . . . common errors, and ways to correct them.

WRONG CLIENT IN THE ROOM

CEOs settle more cases than vice presidents, house counsel or other agents. Why? For one thing, they don't need to worry about criticism back at the office. Any lesser agent, even with explicit "authority," typically must please a constituency which was not a participant in the give and take of the mediation. That makes it hard to settle cases.

A client's personality also can be a factor. A "Rambo," who is aggressive, critical, unforgiving, or self-righteous doesn't tend to be conciliatory. The best peace-makers show creativity, and tolerance for the mistakes of others. Of course, it also helps to know the subject. . . .

WRONG MEDIATOR IN THE ROOM

Some mediators are generous about lending their conference rooms but bring nothing to the table. Some of them determine their view of the case and urge the parties to accept that view without exploring likely win-win alternatives.

The best mediators can work within a range of styles . . . on a continuum, from being totally facilitative, to offering an evaluation of the case. Ideally, mediators should fit the mediation style to the case and the parties before them, often moving from style to style as a mediation progresses. . . . It may not always be possible to know and evaluate a mediator and fit the choice of mediator to your case. But the wrong mediator may fail to get a settlement another mediator might have finessed.

OMITTING CLIENT PREPARATION

Lawyers should educate their clients about the process. Clients need to know the answers to the types of questions the mediator is likely to ask. At the same time, they need to understand that the other party (rather than the mediator) should be the focus of each side's presentation.

In addition, lawyers should interview clients about the client's and the adversary's "best alternative to negotiated agreement," and "worst alternative to negotiated agreement." . . . A party should accept any offer better than his perceived BATNA and reject any offer seen as worse than his perceived WATNA. So the BATNAs and WATNAs are critical frames of reference for accepting offers and for determining what offers to propose to the other parties. A weak or false understanding of either party's BATNA or WATNA obstructs settlements and begets bad settlements. Other topics to cover with the client: the difference between their interests and their legal positions; the variety of options that might settle the case; the strengths and weaknesses of their case; objective independent standards of evaluation; the importance of apology and empathy.

NOT LETTING A CLIENT OPEN FOR HERSELF

At least as often as not, letting the properly coached client do most, or even all, of the opening and tell the story in her own words works much better than lengthy openings by the lawyer.

ADDRESSING THE MEDIATOR INSTEAD OF THE OTHER SIDE

Most lawyers open the mediation with a statement directed at the mediator, comparable to opening statements to a judge or jury. Highly adversarial in tone, it overlooks the interests of the other side that gave rise to the dispute.

Why is this strategy a mistake? The "judge or jury" you should be trying to persuade in a mediation is not the mediator, but the adversary. If you want to make the other party sympathetic to your cause, don't hurt him. . . .

MAKING THE LAWYER THE CENTER OF THE PROCESS

Unless the client is highly unappealing or inarticulate, the client should be the center of the process. The company representative for the other side may not have attended depositions, so is unaware of the impact your client could have on a judge or jury if the mediation fails. People pay more attention to appealing plaintiffs, so show them off.

Prepare the client to speak and be spoken to by the mediator and the adversary. He should be able to explain why he feels the way he does, why he is or is not responsible, and why any damages he caused are great or only peanuts. But he should also extend empathy to the other party.

FAILURE TO USE ADVOCACY TOOLS EFFECTIVELY

You'll want to prepare your materials for maximum persuasive impact. Exhibits, charts, and copies of relevant cases or contracts with key phrases highlighted can be valuable visual aids. A 90-second video showing key witnesses in depositions making important admissions, followed by a readable size copy of an important document with some relevant language underlined, can pack a punch.

TIMING MISTAKES

Get and give critical discovery, but don't spend exorbitant time or sums in discovery and trial prep before seeking mediation.

Mediation can identify what's truly necessary discovery and avoid unnecessary discovery. One of my own war stories: With a mediation under way and both parties relying on their perception of the views of a certain vice president, I leaned over, picked up the phone, called the vice president, introduced myself as the mediator, and asked whether he could give us a deposition the following morning. "No," said he, "I've got a Board meeting at 10:00." "How about 7:30 A.M., with a one-hour limit?" I asked. "It really is pretty important that this decision not be delayed." The parties took the deposition and settled the case before the 10:00 board meeting.

FAILURE TO LISTEN TO THE OTHER SIDE

Many lawyers and clients seem incapable of giving open-minded attention to what the other side is saying. That could cost a settlement.

FAILURE TO IDENTIFY PERCEPTIONS AND MOTIVATIONS

Seek first to understand, only then to be understood. . . .

HURTING, HUMILIATING, THREATENING, OR COMMANDING

Don't poison the well from which you must drink to get a settlement. That means you don't hurt, humiliate or ridicule the other folks. Avoid pejoratives like "malingerer," "fraud," "cheat," "crook," or "liar." You can be strong on what your evidence will be and still be a decent human being.

All settlements are based upon trust to some degree. If you anger the other side, they won't trust you. This inhibits settlement.

The same can be said for threats, like a threat to get the other lawyer's license revoked for pursuing such a frivolous cause, or for his grossly inaccurate pleadings.

Ultimatums destroy the process, and destroy credibility. Yes, there is a time in mediation to walk out — whether or not you plan to return. But a series of ultimatums, or even one ultimatum, most often is very counterproductive.

FAILURE TO TRULY CLOSE

Unless parties have strong reasons to "sleep on" their agreement, to further evaluate the deal, or to check on possibly forgotten details, it is better to get some sort of enforceable contract written and signed before the parties separate. Too often, when left to think overnight and draft tomorrow, the parties think of new ideas that delay or prevent closing.

LACK OF PATIENCE AND PERSEVERANCE

The mediation "dance" takes time. Good mediation advocates have patience and perseverance.

MISUNDERSTANDING CONFLICT

A dispute is a problem to be solved together, not a combat to be won. To prepare for mediation, rehearse answers to the following questions, which the mediator is likely to ask:

- How do you feel about this dispute? Or about the other party?
- What do you really want in the resolution of this dispute?
- What are your expectations from a trial? Are they realistic?
- What are the weaknesses in your case?
- What law or fact in your case would you like to change?
- What scares you most?
- What would it feel like to be in your adversary's shoes?

- What specific evidence do you have to support each element of your case?
- What will the jury charge and interrogatories probably be?
- What is the probability of a verdict your way on liability?
- What is the range of damages you think a jury would return in this case if it found liability?
- What are the likely settlement structures, from among the following possibilities: terms, dollars, injunction, services, performance, product, rescission, apology, costs, attorney fees, releases?
- What constituency pressures burden the other party? Which ones burden you?

We hope you have learned through this course how to negotiate, creatively solve problems, create value for your clients, and improve human relationships, whether in handling disputes and conflicts or crafting new relationships, entities, and transactions.

Good luck negotiating!

MODEL RULES OF PROFESSIONAL CONDUCT FOR ATTORNEYS

American Bar Association

MODEL RULES OF PROFESSIONAL CONDUCT

PREAMBLE: A Lawyer's Responsibilities

[1] A lawyer, as a member of the legal profession, is a representative of clients, an officer of the legal system and a public citizen having special responsibility for the quality of justice.

[2] As a representative of clients, a lawyer performs various functions. As advisor, a lawyer provides a client with an informed understanding of the client's legal rights and obligations and explains their practical implications. As advocate, a lawyer zealously asserts the client's position under the rules of the adversary system. As negotiator, a lawyer seeks a result advantageous to the client but consistent with requirements of honest dealings with others. As an evaluator, a lawyer acts by examining a client's legal affairs and reporting about them to the client or to others.

[3] In addition to these representational functions, a lawyer may serve as a third-party neutral, a nonrepresentational role helping the parties to resolve a dispute or other matter. Some of these Rules apply directly to lawyers who are or have served as third-party neutrals. See, e.g., Rules 1.12 and 2.4. In addition, there are Rules that apply to lawyers who are not active in the practice of law or to practicing lawyers even when they are acting in a nonprofessional capacity. For example, a lawyer who commits fraud in the conduct of a business is subject to discipline for engaging in conduct involving dishonesty, fraud, deceit or misrepresentation. See Rule 8.4.

[4] In all professional functions a lawyer should be competent, prompt and diligent. A lawyer should maintain communication with a client concerning the representation. A lawyer should keep in confidence information relating to representation of a client except so far as disclosure is required or permitted by the Rules of Professional Conduct or other law.

[5] A lawyer's conduct should conform to the requirements of the law, both in professional service to clients and in the lawyer's business and personal affairs. A lawyer should use the law's procedures only for legitimate purposes and not to harass or intimidate others. A lawyer should demonstrate respect for the legal system and for those who serve it, including judges, other lawyers and public officials. While it is a lawyer's duty, when necessary, to challenge the rectitude of official action, it is also a lawyer's duty to uphold legal process.

[6] As a public citizen, a lawyer should seek improvement of the law, access to the legal system, the administration of justice and the quality of service rendered by the legal profession. As a member of a learned profession, a lawyer should cultivate knowledge of the law beyond its use for clients, employ that knowledge in reform of the law and work to strengthen legal education. In addition, a lawyer should further the public's understanding of and confidence in the rule of law and the justice system because legal institutions in a constitutional democracy depend on popular participation and support to maintain their authority. A lawyer should be mindful of deficiencies in the administration of justice and of the fact that the poor, and sometimes persons who are not poor, cannot afford adequate legal assistance. Therefore, all lawyers should devote professional time and resources and use civic influence to ensure equal access to our system of justice for all those who because of economic or social barriers cannot afford or secure adequate legal counsel. A lawyer should aid the legal profession in pursuing these objectives and should help the bar regulate itself in the public interest.

[7] Many of a lawyer's professional responsibilities are prescribed in the Rules of Professional Conduct, as well as substantive and procedural law. However, a lawyer is also guided by personal conscience and the approbation of professional peers. A lawyer should strive to attain the highest level of skill, to improve the law and the legal profession and to exemplify the legal profession's ideals of public service.

[8] A lawyer's responsibilities as a representative of clients, an officer of the legal system and a public citizen are usually harmonious. Thus, when an opposing party is well represented, a lawyer can be a zealous advocate on behalf of a client and at the same time assume that justice is being done. So also, a lawyer can be sure that preserving client confidences ordinarily serves the public interest because people are more likely to seek legal advice, and thereby heed their legal obligations, when they know their communications will be private.

[9] In the nature of law practice, however, conflicting responsibilities are encountered. Virtually all difficult ethical problems arise from conflict between a lawyer's responsibilities to clients, to the legal system and to the lawyer's own interest in remaining an ethical person while earning a satisfactory living. The Rules of Professional Conduct often prescribe terms for resolving such conflicts. Within the framework of these Rules, however, many difficult issues of professional discretion can arise. Such issues must be resolved through the exercise of sensitive professional and moral judgment guided by the basic principles underlying the Rules. These principles include the lawyer's obligation zealously to protect and pursue a client's legitimate interests, within the bounds of the law, while maintaining a professional, courteous and civil attitude toward all persons involved in the legal system.

[10] The legal profession is largely self-governing. Although other professions also have been granted powers of self-government, the legal profession is unique in this respect because of the close relationship between the profession and the processes of government and law enforcement. This connection is manifested in the fact that ultimate authority over the legal profession is vested largely in the courts.

[11] To the extent that lawyers meet the obligations of their professional calling, the occasion for government regulation is obviated. Self-regulation also helps maintain the legal profession's independence from government domination. An independent legal profession is an important force in preserving government under law, for abuse of legal

authority is more readily challenged by a profession whose members are not dependent on government for the right to practice.

[12] The legal profession's relative autonomy carries with it special responsibilities of self-government. The profession has a responsibility to assure that its regulations are conceived in the public interest and not in furtherance of parochial or self-interested concerns of the bar. Every lawyer is responsible for observance of the Rules of Professional Conduct. A lawyer should also aid in securing their observance by other lawyers. Neglect of these responsibilities compromises the independence of the profession and the public interest which it serves.

[13] Lawyers play a vital role in the preservation of society. The fulfillment of this role requires an understanding by lawyers of their relationship to our legal system. The Rules of Professional Conduct, when properly applied, serve to define that relationship.

SCOPE

[14] The Rules of Professional Conduct are rules of reason. They should be interpreted with reference to the purposes of legal representation and of the law itself. Some of the Rules are imperatives, cast in the terms "shall" or "shall not." These define proper conduct for purposes of professional discipline. Others, generally cast in the term "may," are permissive and define areas under the Rules in which the lawyer has discretion to exercise professional judgment. No disciplinary action should be taken when the lawyer chooses not to act or acts within the bounds of such discretion. Other Rules define the nature of relationships between the lawyer and others. The Rules are thus partly obligatory and disciplinary and partly constitutive and descriptive in that they define a lawyer's professional role. Many of the Comments use the term "should." Comments do not add obligations to the Rules but provide guidance for practicing in compliance with the Rules.

[15] The Rules presuppose a larger legal context shaping the lawyer's role. That context includes court rules and statutes relating to matters of licensure, laws defining specific obligations of lawyers and substantive and procedural law in general. The Comments are sometimes used to alert lawyers to their responsibilities under such other law.

[16] Compliance with the Rules, as with all law in an open society, depends primarily upon understanding and voluntary compliance, secondarily upon reinforcement by peer and public opinion and finally, when necessary, upon enforcement through disciplinary proceedings. The Rules do not, however, exhaust the moral and ethical considerations that should inform a lawyer, for no worthwhile human activity can be completely defined by legal rules. The Rules simply provide a framework for the ethical practice of law.

[17] Furthermore, for purposes of determining the lawyer's authority and responsibility, principles of substantive law external to these Rules determine whether a client-lawyer relationship exists. Most of the duties flowing from the client-lawyer relationship attach only after the client has requested the lawyer to render legal services and the lawyer has agreed to do so. But there are some duties, such as that of confidentiality under Rule 1.6, that attach when the lawyer agrees to consider whether a client-lawyer relationship shall be established. See Rule 1.18. Whether a client-lawyer relationship exists for any specific purpose can depend on the circumstances and may be a question of fact.

[18] Under various legal provisions, including constitutional, statutory and common law, the responsibilities of government lawyers may include authority concerning legal matters that ordinarily reposes in the client in private client-lawyer relationships. For

example, a lawyer for a government agency may have authority on behalf of the government to decide upon settlement or whether to appeal from an adverse judgment. Such authority in various respects is generally vested in the attorney general and the state's attorney in state government, and their federal counterparts, and the same may be true of other government law officers. Also, lawyers under the supervision of these officers may be authorized to represent several government agencies in intragovernmental legal controversies in circumstances where a private lawyer could not represent multiple private clients. These Rules do not abrogate any such authority.

[19] Failure to comply with an obligation or prohibition imposed by a Rule is a basis for invoking the disciplinary process. The Rules presuppose that disciplinary assessment of a lawyer's conduct will be made on the basis of the facts and circumstances as they existed at the time of the conduct in question and in recognition of the fact that a lawyer often has to act upon uncertain or incomplete evidence of the situation. Moreover, the Rules presuppose that whether or not discipline should be imposed for a violation, and the severity of a sanction, depend on all the circumstances, such as the willfulness and seriousness of the violation, extenuating factors and whether there have been previous violations.

[20] Violation of a Rule should not itself give rise to a cause of action against a lawyer nor should it create any presumption in such a case that a legal duty has been breached. In addition, violation of a Rule does not necessarily warrant any other nondisciplinary remedy, such as disqualification of a lawyer in pending litigation. The Rules are designed to provide guidance to lawyers and to provide a structure for regulating conduct through disciplinary agencies. They are not designed to be a basis for civil liability. Furthermore, the purpose of the Rules can be subverted when they are invoked by opposing parties as procedural weapons. The fact that a Rule is a just basis for a lawyer's self-assessment, or for sanctioning a lawyer under the administration of a disciplinary authority, does not imply that an antagonist in a collateral proceeding or transaction has standing to seek enforcement of the Rule. Nevertheless, since the Rules do establish standards of conduct by lawyers, a lawyer's violation of a Rule may be evidence of breach of the applicable standard of conduct.

[21] The Comment accompanying each Rule explains and illustrates the meaning and purpose of the Rule. The Preamble and this note on Scope provide general orientation. The Comments are intended as guides to interpretation, but the text of each Rule is authoritative.

CLIENT-LAWYER RELATIONSHIP

RULE 1.2 Scope of Representation and Allocation of Authority Between Client and Lawyer

(a) Subject to paragraphs (c) and (d), a lawyer shall abide by a client's decisions concerning the objectives of representation and, as required by Rule 1.4, shall consult with the client as to the means by which they are to be pursued. A lawyer may take such action on behalf of the client as is impliedly authorized to carry out the representation. A lawyer shall abide by a client's decision whether to settle a matter. In a criminal case, the lawyer shall abide by the client's decision, after consultation with the lawyer, as to a plea to be entered, whether to waive jury trial and whether the client will testify.

(b) A lawyer's representation of a client, including representation by appointment, does not constitute an endorsement of the client's political, economic, social or moral views or activities.

(c) A lawyer may limit the scope of the representation if the limitation is reasonable under the circumstances and the client gives informed consent.

(d) A lawyer shall not counsel a client to engage, or assist a client, in conduct that the lawyer knows is criminal or fraudulent, but a lawyer may discuss the legal consequences of any proposed course of conduct with a client and may counsel or assist a client to make a good faith effort to determine the validity, scope, meaning or application of the law.

COMMENT

Allocation of Authority between Client and Lawyer

[1] Paragraph (a) confers upon the client the ultimate authority to determine the purposes to be served by legal representation, within the limits imposed by law and the lawyer's professional obligations. The decisions specified in paragraph (a), such as whether to settle a civil matter, must also be made by the client. See Rule 1.4(a)(1) for the lawyer's duty to communicate with the client about such decisions. With respect to the means by which the client's objectives are to be pursued, the lawyer shall consult with the client as required by Rule 1.4(a)(2) and may take such action as is impliedly authorized to carry out the representation.

[2] On occasion, however, a lawyer and a client may disagree about the means to be used to accomplish the client's objectives. Clients normally defer to the special knowledge and skill of their lawyer with respect to the means to be used to accomplish their objectives, particularly with respect to technical, legal and tactical matters. Conversely, lawyers usually defer to the client regarding such questions as the expense to be incurred and concern for third persons who might be adversely affected. Because of the varied nature of the matters about which a lawyer and client might disagree and because the actions in question may implicate the interests of a tribunal or other persons, this Rule does not prescribe how such disagreements are to be resolved. Other law, however, may be applicable and should be consulted by the lawyer. The lawyer should also consult with the client and seek a mutually acceptable resolution of the disagreement. If such efforts are unavailing and the lawyer has a fundamental disagreement with the client, the lawyer may withdraw from the representation. See Rule 1.16(b)(4). Conversely, the client may resolve the disagreement by discharging the lawyer. See Rule 1.16(a)(3).

[3] At the outset of a representation, the client may authorize the lawyer to take specific action on the client's behalf without further consultation. Absent a material change in circumstances and subject to Rule 1.4, a lawyer may rely on such an advance authorization. The client may, however, revoke such authority at any time.

[4] In a case in which the client appears to be suffering diminished capacity, the lawyer's duty to abide by the client's decisions is to be guided by reference to Rule

1.14. Independence from Client's Views or Activities

[5] Legal representation should not be denied to people who are unable to afford legal services, or whose cause is controversial or the subject of popular disapproval. By the same token, representing a client does not constitute approval of the client's views or activities.

Agreements Limiting Scope of Representation

[6] The scope of services to be provided by a lawyer may be limited by agreement with the client or by the terms under which the lawyer's services are made available to the client. When a lawyer has been retained by an insurer to represent an insured, for example, the representation may be limited to matters related to the insurance coverage. A limited representation may be appropriate because the client has limited objectives for the

representation. In addition, the terms upon which representation is undertaken may exclude specific means that might otherwise be used to accomplish the client's objectives. Such limitations may exclude actions that the client thinks are too costly or that the lawyer regards as repugnant or imprudent.

[7] Although this Rule affords the lawyer and client substantial latitude to limit the representation, the limitation must be reasonable under the circumstances. If, for example, a client's objective is limited to securing general information about the law the client needs in order to handle a common and typically uncomplicated legal problem, the lawyer and client may agree that the lawyer's services will be limited to a brief telephone consultation. Such a limitation, however, would not be reasonable if the time allotted was not sufficient to yield advice upon which the client could rely. Although an agreement for a limited representation does not exempt a lawyer from the duty to provide competent representation, the limitation is a factor to be considered when determining the legal knowledge, skill, thoroughness and preparation reasonably necessary for the representation. See Rule 1.1.

[8] All agreements concerning a lawyer's representation of a client must accord with the Rules of Professional Conduct and other law. See, e.g., Rules 1.1, 1.8 and 5.6.

Criminal, Fraudulent and Prohibited Transactions

[9] Paragraph (d) prohibits a lawyer from knowingly counseling or assisting a client to commit a crime or fraud. This prohibition, however, does not preclude the lawyer from giving an honest opinion about the actual consequences that appear likely to result from a client's conduct. Nor does the fact that a client uses advice in a course of action that is criminal or fraudulent of itself make a lawyer a party to the course of action. There is a critical distinction between presenting an analysis of legal aspects of questionable conduct and recommending the means by which a crime or fraud might be committed with impunity.

[10] When the client's course of action has already begun and is continuing, the lawyer's responsibility is especially delicate. The lawyer is required to avoid assisting the client, for example, by drafting or delivering documents that the lawyer knows are fraudulent or by suggesting how the wrongdoing might be concealed. A lawyer may not continue assisting a client in conduct that the lawyer originally supposed was legally proper but then discovers is criminal or fraudulent. The lawyer must, therefore, withdraw from the representation of the client in the matter. See Rule 1.16(a). In some cases, withdrawal alone might be insufficient. It may be necessary for the lawyer to give notice of the fact of withdrawal and to disaffirm any opinion, document, affirmation or the like. See Rule 4.1.

[11] Where the client is a fiduciary, the lawyer may be charged with special obligations in dealings with a beneficiary.

[12] Paragraph (d) applies whether or not the defrauded party is a party to the transaction. Hence, a lawyer must not participate in a transaction to effectuate criminal or fraudulent avoidance of tax liability. Paragraph (d) does not preclude undertaking a criminal defense incident to a general retainer for legal services to a lawful enterprise. The last clause of paragraph (d) recognizes that determining the validity or interpretation of a statute or regulation may require a course of action involving disobedience of the statute or regulation or of the interpretation placed upon it by governmental authorities.

[13] If a lawyer comes to know or reasonably should know that a client expects assistance not permitted by the Rules of Professional Conduct or other law or if the lawyer intends to act contrary to the client's instructions, the lawyer must consult with the client regarding the limitations on the lawyer's conduct. See Rule 1.4(a)(5).

CLIENT-LAWYER RELATIONSHIP

RULE 1.4 Communication

(a) A lawyer shall:

(1) promptly inform the client of any decision or circumstance with respect to which the client's informed consent, as defined in Rule 1.0(e), is required by these Rules;

(2) reasonably consult with the client about the means by which the client's objectives are to be accomplished;

(3) keep the client reasonably informed about the status of the matter;

(4) promptly comply with reasonable requests for information; and

(5) consult with the client about any relevant limitation on the lawyer's conduct when the lawyer knows that the client expects assistance not permitted by the Rules of Professional Conduct or other law.

(b) A lawyer shall explain a matter to the extent reasonably necessary to permit the client to make informed decisions regarding the representation.

COMMENT

[1] Reasonable communication between the lawyer and the client is necessary for the client effectively to participate in the representation.

Communicating with Client

[2] If these Rules require that a particular decision about the representation be made by the client, paragraph (a)(1) requires that the lawyer promptly consult with and secure the client's consent prior to taking action unless prior discussions with the client have resolved what action the client wants the lawyer to take. For example, a lawyer who receives from opposing counsel an offer of settlement in a civil controversy or a proffered plea bargain in a criminal case must promptly inform the client of its substance unless the client has previously indicated that the proposal will be acceptable or unacceptable or has authorized the lawyer to accept or to reject the offer. See Rule 1.2(a).

[3] Paragraph (a)(2) requires the lawyer to reasonably consult with the client about the means to be used to accomplish the client's objectives. In some situations — depending on both the importance of the action under consideration and the feasibility of consulting with the client — this duty will require consultation prior to taking action. In other circumstances, such as during a trial when an immediate decision must be made, the exigency of the situation may require the lawyer to act without prior consultation. In such cases the lawyer must nonetheless act reasonably to inform the client of actions the lawyer has taken on the client's behalf. Additionally, paragraph (a)(3) requires that the lawyer keep the client reasonably informed about the status of the matter, such as significant developments affecting the timing or the substance of the representation.

[4] A lawyer's regular communication with clients will minimize the occasions on which a client will need to request information concerning the representation. When a client makes a reasonable request for information, however, paragraph (a)(4) requires prompt compliance with the request, or if a prompt response is not feasible, that the lawyer, or a member of the lawyer's staff, acknowledge receipt of the request and advise the client when a response may be expected. Client telephone calls should be promptly returned or acknowledged.

Explaining Matters

[5] The client should have sufficient information to participate intelligently in decisions concerning the objectives of the representation and the means by which they are to be

pursued, to the extent the client is willing and able to do so. Adequacy of communication depends in part on the kind of advice or assistance that is involved. For example, when there is time to explain a proposal made in a negotiation, the lawyer should review all important provisions with the client before proceeding to an agreement. In litigation a lawyer should explain the general strategy and prospects of success and ordinarily should consult the client on tactics that are likely to result in significant expense or to injure or coerce others. On the other hand, a lawyer ordinarily will not be expected to describe trial or negotiation strategy in detail. The guiding principle is that the lawyer should fulfill reasonable client expectations for information consistent with the duty to act in the client's best interests, and the client's overall requirements as to the character of representation. In certain circumstances, such as when a lawyer asks a client to consent to a representation affected by a conflict of interest, the client must give informed consent, as defined in Rule 1.0(e).

[6] Ordinarily, the information to be provided is that appropriate for a client who is a comprehending and responsible adult. However, fully informing the client according to this standard may be impracticable, for example, where the client is a child or suffers from diminished capacity. See Rule 1.14. When the client is an organization or group, it is often impossible or inappropriate to inform every one of its members about its legal affairs; ordinarily, the lawyer should address communications to the appropriate officials of the organization. See Rule 1.13. Where many routine matters are involved, a system of limited or occasional reporting may be arranged with the client.

Withholding Information

[7] In some circumstances, a lawyer may be justified in delaying transmission of information when the client would be likely to react imprudently to an immediate communication. Thus, a lawyer might withhold a psychiatric diagnosis of a client when the examining psychiatrist indicates that disclosure would harm the client. A lawyer may not withhold information to serve the lawyer's own interest or convenience or the interests or convenience of another person. Rules or court orders governing litigation may provide that information supplied to a lawyer may not be disclosed to the client. Rule 3.4(c) directs compliance with such rules or orders.

CLIENT-LAWYER RELATIONSHIP
RULE 1.6 Confidentiality of Information

(a) A lawyer shall not reveal information relating to the representation of a client unless the client gives informed consent, the disclosure is impliedly authorized in order to carry out the representation or the disclosure is permitted by paragraph (b).

(b) A lawyer may reveal information relating to the representation of a client to the extent the lawyer reasonably believes necessary:

(1) to prevent reasonably certain death or substantial bodily harm;

(2) to prevent the client from committing a crime or fraud that is reasonably certain to result in substantial injury to the financial interests or property of another and in furtherance of which the client has used or is using the lawyer's services;

(3) to prevent, mitigate or rectify substantial injury to the financial interests or property of another that is reasonably certain to result or has resulted from the client's commission of a crime or fraud in furtherance of which the client has used the lawyer's services;

(4) to secure legal advice about the lawyer's compliance with these Rules;

(5) to establish a claim or defense on behalf of the lawyer in a controversy between the lawyer and the client, to establish a defense to a criminal charge or

civil claim against the lawyer based upon conduct in which the client was involved, or to respond to allegations in any proceeding concerning the lawyer's representation of the client; or

(6) to comply with other law or a court order.

COMMENT

[1] This Rule governs the disclosure, by a lawyer of information relating to the representation of a client during the lawyers representation of the client. See Rule 1.18 for the lawyer's duties with respect to information provided to the lawyer by a prospective client, Rule 1.9(c)(2) for the lawyer's duty not to reveal information relating to the lawyer's prior representation of a former client and Rules 1.8(b) and 1.9(c)(1) for the lawyer's duties with respect to the use of such information to the disadvantage of clients and former clients.

[2] A fundamental principle in the client-lawyer relationship is that, in the absence of the client's informed consent, the lawyer must not reveal information relating to the representation. See Rule 1.0(e) for the definition of informed consent. This contributes to the trust that is the hallmark of the client-lawyer relationship. The client is thereby encouraged to seek legal assistance and to communicate fully and frankly with the lawyer even as to embarrassing or legally damaging subject matter. The lawyer needs this information to represent the client effectively and, if necessary, to advise the client to refrain from wrongful conduct. Almost without exception, clients come to lawyers in order to determine their rights and what is, in the complex of laws and regulations, deemed to be legal and correct. Based upon experience, lawyers know that almost all clients follow the advice given, and the law is upheld.

[3] The principle of client-lawyer confidentiality is given effect by related bodies of law: the attorney-client privilege, the work product doctrine and the rule of confidentiality established in professional ethics. The attorney-client privilege and work product doctrine apply in judicial and other proceedings in which a lawyer may be called as a witness or otherwise required to produce evidence concerning a client. The rule of client-lawyer confidentiality applies in situations other than those where evidence is sought from the lawyer through compulsion of law. The confidentiality rule, for example, applies not only to matters communicated in confidence by the client but also to all information relating to the representation, whatever its source. A lawyer may not disclose such information except as authorized or required by the Rules of Professional Conduct or other law. See also Scope.

[4] Paragraph (a) prohibits a lawyer from revealing information relating to the representation of a client. This prohibition also applies to disclosures by a lawyer that do not in themselves reveal protected information but could reasonably lead to the discovery of such information by a third person. A Lawyer's use of a hypothetical to discuss issues relating to the representation is permissible so long as there is no reasonable likelihood that the listener will be able to ascertain the identity of the client or the situation involved.

Authorized Disclosure

[5] Except to the extent that the client's instructions or special circumstances limit that authority, a lawyer is impliedly authorized to make disclosures about a client when appropriate in carrying out the representation. In some situations, for example, a lawyer may be impliedly authorized to admit a fact that cannot properly be disputed or to make a disclosure that facilitates a satisfactory conclusion to a matter. Lawyers in a firm may, in the course of the firm's practice, disclose to each other information relating to a client of the firm, unless the client has instructed that particular information be confined to specified lawyers.

Disclosure Adverse to Client

[6] Although the public interest is usually best served by a strict rule requiring lawyers to preserve the confidentiality of information relating to the representation of their clients, the confidentiality rule is subject to limited exceptions. Paragraph (b)(1) recognizes the overriding value of life and physical integrity and permits disclosure reasonably necessary to prevent reasonably certain death or substantial bodily harm. Such harm is reasonably certain to occur if it will be suffered imminently or if there is a present and substantial threat that a person will suffer such harm at a later date if the lawyer fails to take action necessary to eliminate the threat. Thus, a lawyer who knows that a client has accidentally discharged toxic waste into a town's water supply may reveal this information to the authorities if there is a present and substantial risk that a person who drinks the water will contract a life-threatening or debilitating disease and the lawyer's disclosure is necessary to eliminate the threat or reduce the number of victims.

[7] Paragraph (b)(2) is a limited exception to the rule of confidentiality that permits the lawyer to reveal information to the extent necessary to enable affected persons or appropriate authorities to prevent the client from committing a crime or fraud, as defined in Rule 1.0(d), that is reasonably certain to result in substantial injury to the financial or property interests of another and in furtherance of which the client has used or is using the lawyer's services. Such a serious abuse of the client-lawyer relationship by the client forfeits the protection of this Rule. The client can, of course, prevent such disclosure by refraining from the wrongful conduct. Although paragraph (b)(2) does not require the lawyer to reveal the client's misconduct, the lawyer may not counsel or assist the client in conduct the lawyer knows is criminal or fraudulent. See Rule 1.2(d). See also Rule 1.16 with respect to the lawyer's obligation or right to withdraw from the representation of the client in such circumstances, and Rule 1.13(c), which permits the lawyer, where the client is an organization, to reveal information relating to the representation in limited circumstances.

[8] Paragraph (b)(3) addresses the situation in which the lawyer does not learn of the client's crime or fraud until after it has been consummated. Although the client no longer has the option of preventing disclosure by refraining from the wrongful conduct, there will be situations in which the loss suffered by the affected person can be prevented, rectified or mitigated. In such situations, the lawyer may disclose information relating to the representation to the extent necessary to enable the affected persons to prevent or mitigate reasonably certain losses or to attempt to recoup their losses. Paragraph (b)(3) does not apply when a person who has committed a crime or fraud thereafter employs a lawyer for representation concerning that offense.

[9] A lawyer's confidentiality obligations do not preclude a lawyer from securing confidential legal advice about the lawyer's personal responsibility to comply with these Rules. In most situations, disclosing information to secure such advice will be impliedly authorized for the lawyer to carry out the representation. Even when the disclosure is not impliedly authorized, paragraph (b)(4) permits such disclosure because of the importance of a lawyer's compliance with the Rules of Professional Conduct.

[10] Where a legal claim or disciplinary charge alleges complicity of the lawyer in a client's conduct or other misconduct of the lawyer involving representation of the client, the lawyer may respond to the extent the lawyer reasonably believes necessary to establish a defense. The same is true with respect to a claim involving the conduct or representation of a former client. Such a charge can arise in a civil, criminal, disciplinary or other proceeding and can be based on a wrong allegedly committed by the lawyer against the client or on a wrong alleged by a third person, for example, a person claiming to have been defrauded by the lawyer and client acting together. The lawyer's right to respond arises when an assertion of such complicity has been made. Paragraph (b)(5) does not

require the lawyer to await the commencement of an action or proceeding that charges such complicity, so that the defense may be established by responding directly to a third party who has made such an assertion. The right to defend also applies, of course, where a proceeding has been commenced.

[11] A lawyer entitled to a fee is permitted by paragraph (b)(5) to prove the services rendered in an action to collect it. This aspect of the rule expresses the principle that the beneficiary of a fiduciary relationship may not exploit it to the detriment of the fiduciary.

[12] Other law may require that a lawyer disclose information about a client. Whether such a law supersedes Rule 1.6 is a question of law beyond the scope of these Rules. When disclosure of information relating to the representation appears to be required by other law, the lawyer must discuss the matter with the client to the extent required by Rule 1.4. If, however, the other law supersedes this Rule and requires disclosure, paragraph (b)(6) permits the lawyer to make such disclosures as are necessary to comply with the law.

[13] A lawyer may be ordered to reveal information relating to the representation of a client by a court or by another tribunal or governmental entity claiming authority pursuant to other law to compel the disclosure. Absent informed consent of the client to do otherwise, the lawyer should assert on behalf of the client all nonfrivolous claims that the order is not authorized by other law or that the information sought is protected against disclosure by the attorney-client privilege or other applicable law. In the event of an adverse ruling, the lawyer must consult with the client about the possibility of appeal to the extent required by Rule 1.4. Unless review is sought, however, paragraph (b)(6) permits the lawyer to comply with the court's order.

[14] Paragraph (b) permits disclosure only to the extent the lawyer reasonably believes the disclosure is necessary to accomplish one of the purposes specified. Where practicable, the lawyer should first seek to persuade the client to take suitable action to obviate the need for disclosure. In any case, a disclosure adverse to the client's interest should be no greater than the lawyer reasonably believes necessary to accomplish the purpose. If the disclosure will be made in connection with a judicial proceeding, the disclosure should be made in a manner that limits access to the information to the tribunal or other persons having a need to know it and appropriate protective orders or other arrangements should be sought by the lawyer to the fullest extent practicable.

[15] Paragraph (b) permits but does not require the disclosure of information relating to a client's representation to accomplish the purposes specified in paragraphs (b)(1) through (b)(6). In exercising the discretion conferred by this Rule, the lawyer may consider such factors as the nature of the lawyer's relationship with the client and with those who might be injured by the client, the lawyer's own involvement in the transaction and factors that may extenuate the conduct in question. A lawyer's decision not to disclose as permitted by paragraph (b) does not violate this Rule. Disclosure may be required, however, by other Rules. Some Rules require disclosure only if such disclosure would be permitted by paragraph (b). See Rules 1.2(d), 4.1(b), 8.1 and 8.3. Rule 3.3, on the other hand, requires disclosure in some circumstances regardless of whether such disclosure is permitted by this Rule. See Rule 3.3(c).

Acting Competently to Preserve Confidentiality

[16] A lawyer must act competently to safeguard information relating to the representation of a client against inadvertent or unauthorized disclosure by the lawyer or other persons who are participating in the representation of the client or who are subject to the lawyer's supervision. See Rules 1.1, 5.1 and 5.3.

[17] When transmitting a communication that includes information relating to the representation of a client, the lawyer must take reasonable precautions to prevent the information from coming into the hands of unintended recipients. This duty, however,

does not require that the lawyer use special security measures if the method of communication affords a reasonable expectation of privacy. Special circumstances, however, may warrant special precautions. Factors to be considered in determining the reasonableness of the lawyer's expectation of confidentiality include the sensitivity of the information and the extent to which the privacy of the communication is protected by law or by a confidentiality agreement. A client may require the lawyer to implement special security measures not required by this Rule or may give informed consent to the use of a means of communication that would otherwise be prohibited by this Rule.

Former Client

[18] The duty of confidentiality continues after the client-lawyer relationship has terminated. See Rule 1.9(c)(2). See Rule 1.9(c)(1) for the prohibition against using such information to the disadvantage of the former client.

COUNSELOR

RULE 2.4 Lawyer Serving as Third-Party Neutral

(a) A lawyer serves as a third-party neutral when the lawyer assists two or more persons who are not clients of the lawyer to reach a resolution of a dispute or other matter that has arisen between them. Service as a third-party neutral may include service as an arbitrator, a mediator or in such other capacity as will enable the lawyer to assist the parties to resolve the matter.

(b) A lawyer serving as a third-party neutral shall inform unrepresented parties that the lawyer is not representing them. When the lawyer knows or reasonably should know that a party does not understand the lawyer's role in the matter, the lawyer shall explain the difference between the lawyer's role as a third-party neutral and a lawyer's role as one who represents a client.

COMMENT

[1] Alternative dispute resolution has become a substantial part of the civil justice system. Aside from representing clients in dispute-resolution processes, lawyers often serve as third-party neutrals. A third-party neutral is a person, such as a mediator, arbitrator, conciliator or evaluator, who assists the parties, represented or unrepresented, in the resolution of a dispute or in the arrangement of a transaction. Whether a third-party neutral serves primarily as a facilitator, evaluator or decisionmaker depends on the particular process that is either selected by the parties or mandated by a court.

[2] The role of a third-party neutral is not unique to lawyers, although, in some court-connected contexts, only lawyers are allowed to serve in this role or to handle certain types of cases. In performing this role, the lawyer may be subject to court rules or other law that apply either to third-party neutrals generally or to lawyers serving as third-party neutrals. Lawyer-neutrals may also be subject to various codes of ethics, such as the Code of Ethics for Arbitration in Commercial Disputes prepared by a joint committee of the American Bar Association and the American Arbitration Association or the Model Standards of Conduct for Mediators jointly prepared by the American Bar Association, the American Arbitration Association and the Society of Professionals in Dispute Resolution.

[3] Unlike nonlawyers who serve as third-party neutrals, lawyers serving in this role may experience unique problems as a result of differences between the role of a third-party neutral and a lawyer's service as a client representative. The potential for confusion is significant when the parties are unrepresented in the process. Thus, paragraph (b) requires a lawyer-neutral to inform unrepresented parties that the lawyer is not representing them. For some parties, particularly parties who frequently use dispute-resolution processes, this information will be sufficient. For others, particularly those who are using the process for

the first time, more information will be required. Where appropriate, the lawyer should inform unrepresented parties of the important differences between the lawyer's role as third-party neutral and a lawyer's role as a client representative, including the inapplicability of the attorney-client evidentiary privilege. The extent of disclosure required under this paragraph will depend on the particular parties involved and the subject matter of the proceeding, as well as the particular features of the dispute-resolution process selected.

[4] A lawyer who serves as a third-party neutral subsequently may be asked to serve as a lawyer representing a client in the same matter. The conflicts of interest that arise for both the individual lawyer and the lawyer's law firm are addressed in Rule 1.12.

[5] Lawyers who represent clients in alternative dispute-resolution processes are governed by the Rules of Professional Conduct. When the dispute-resolution process takes place before a tribunal, as in binding arbitration (see Rule 1.0(m)), the lawyer's duty of candor is governed by Rule 3.3. Otherwise, the lawyer's duty of candor toward both the third-party neutral and other parties is governed by Rule 4.1.

ADVOCATE
RULE 3.3 Candor Toward the Tribunal
(a) A lawyer shall not knowingly:

(1) make a false statement of fact or law to a tribunal or fail to correct a false statement of material fact or law previously made to the tribunal by the lawyer;

(2) fail to disclose to the tribunal legal authority in the controlling jurisdiction known to the lawyer to be directly adverse to the position of the client and not disclosed by opposing counsel; or

(3) offer evidence that the lawyer knows to be false. If a lawyer, the lawyer's client, or a witness called by the lawyer, has offered material evidence and the lawyer comes to know of its falsity, the lawyer shall take reasonable remedial measures, including, if necessary, disclosure to the tribunal. A lawyer may refuse to offer evidence, other than the testimony of a defendant in a criminal matter, that the lawyer reasonably believes is false.

(b) A lawyer who represents a client in an adjudicative proceeding and who knows that a person intends to engage, is engaging or has engaged in criminal or fraudulent conduct related to the proceeding shall take reasonable remedial measures, including, if necessary, disclosure to the tribunal.

(c) The duties stated in paragraphs (a) and (b) continue to the conclusion of the proceeding, and apply even if compliance requires disclosure of information otherwise protected by Rule 1.6.

(d) In an ex parte proceeding, a lawyer shall inform the tribunal of all material facts known to the lawyer that will enable the tribunal to make an informed decision, whether or not the facts are adverse.

TRANSACTIONS WITH PERSONS OTHER THAN CLIENTS
RULE 4.1 Truthfulness in Statements to Others
In the course of representing a client a lawyer shall not knowingly:

(a) make a false statement of material fact or law to a third person; or

(b) fail to disclose a material fact to a third person when disclosure is necessary to avoid assisting a criminal or fraudulent act by a client, unless disclosure is prohibited by Rule 1.6.

COMMENT
Misrepresentation
[1] A lawyer is required to be truthful when dealing with others on a client's behalf, but generally has no affirmative duty to inform an opposing party of relevant facts. A misrepresentation can occur if the lawyer incorporates or affirms a statement of another person that the lawyer knows is false. Misrepresentations can also occur by partially true but misleading statements or omissions that are the equivalent of affirmative false statements. For dishonest conduct that does not amount to a false statement or for misrepresentations by a lawyer other than in the course of representing a client, see Rule 8.4.

Statements of Fact
[2] This Rule refers to statements of fact. Whether a particular statement should be regarded as one of fact can depend on the circumstances. Under generally accepted conventions in negotiation, certain types of statements ordinarily are not taken as statements of material fact. Estimates of price or value placed on the subject of a transaction and a party's intentions as to an acceptable settlement of a claim are ordinarily in this category, and so is the existence of an undisclosed principal except where nondisclosure of the principal would constitute fraud. Lawyers should be mindful of their obligations under applicable law to avoid criminal and tortious misrepresentation.

Crime or Fraud by Client
[3] Under Rule 1.2(d), a lawyer is prohibited from counseling or assisting a client in conduct that the lawyer knows is criminal or fraudulent. Paragraph (b) states a specific application of the principle set forth in Rule 1.2(d) and addresses the situation where a client's crime or fraud takes the form of a lie or misrepresentation. Ordinarily, a lawyer can avoid assisting a client's crime or fraud by withdrawing from the representation. Sometimes it may be necessary for the lawyer to give notice of the fact of withdrawal and to disaffirm an opinion, document, affirmation or the like. In extreme cases, substantive law may require a lawyer to disclose information relating to the representation to avoid being deemed to have assisted the client's crime or fraud. If the lawyer can avoid assisting a client's crime or fraud only by disclosing this information, then under paragraph (b) the lawyer is required to do so, unless the disclosure is prohibited by Rule 1.6.

TRANSACTIONS WITH PERSONS OTHER THAN CLIENTS
RULE 4.4 Respect for Rights of Third Persons
(a) In representing a client, a lawyer shall not use means that have no substantial purpose other than to embarrass, delay, or burden a third person, or use methods of obtaining evidence that violate the legal rights of such a person.

(b) A lawyer who receives a document relating to the representation of the lawyer's client and knows or reasonably should know that the document was inadvertently sent shall promptly notify the sender.

COMMENT
[1] Responsibility to a client requires a lawyer to subordinate the interests of others to those of the client, but that responsibility does not imply that a lawyer may disregard the rights of third persons. It is impractical to catalogue all such rights, but they include legal restrictions on methods of obtaining evidence from third persons and unwarranted intrusions into privileged relationships, such as the client-lawyer relationship.

[2] Paragraph (b) recognizes that lawyers sometimes receive documents that were mistakenly sent or produced by opposing parties or their lawyers. If a lawyer knows or reasonably should know that such a document was sent inadvertently, then this Rule requires the lawyer to promptly notify the sender in order to permit that person to take

protective measures. Whether the lawyer is required to take additional steps, such as returning the original document, is a matter of law beyond the scope of these Rules, as is the question of whether the privileged status of a document has been waived. Similarly, this Rule does not address the legal duties of a lawyer who receives a document that the lawyer knows or reasonably should know may have been wrongfully obtained by the sending person. For purposes of this Rule, "document" includes e-mail or other electronic modes of transmission subject to being read or put into readable form.

[3] Some lawyers may choose to return a document unread, for example, when the lawyer learns before receiving the document that it was inadvertently sent to the wrong address. Where a lawyer is not required by applicable law to do so, the decision to voluntarily return such a document is a matter of professional judgment ordinarily reserved to the lawyer. See Rules 1.2 and 1.4.

LAW FIRMS AND ASSOCIATIONS
RULE 5.6 Restrictions on Right to Practice
A lawyer shall not participate in offering or making:

(a) a partnership, shareholders, operating, employment, or other similar type of agreement that restricts the right of a lawyer to practice after termination of the relationship, except an agreement concerning benefits upon retirement; or

(b) an agreement in which a restriction on the lawyer's right to practice is part of the settlement of a client controversy.

COMMENT
[1] An agreement restricting the right of lawyers to practice after leaving a firm not only limits their professional autonomy but also limits the freedom of clients to choose a lawyer. Paragraph (a) prohibits such agreements except for restrictions incident to provisions concerning retirement benefits for service with the firm.

[2] Paragraph (b) prohibits a lawyer from agreeing not to represent other persons in connection with settling a claim on behalf of a client.

[3] This Rule does not apply to prohibit restrictions that may be included in the terms of the sale of a law practice pursuant to Rule 1.17.

MAINTAINING THE INTEGRITY OF THE PROFESSION
RULE 8.3 Reporting Professional Misconduct
(a) A lawyer who knows that another lawyer has committed a violation of the Rules of Professional Conduct that raises a substantial question as to that lawyer's honesty, trustworthiness or fitness as a lawyer in other respects, shall inform the appropriate professional authority.

(b) A lawyer who knows that a judge has committed a violation of applicable rules of judicial conduct that raises a substantial question as to the judge's fitness for office shall inform the appropriate authority.

(c) This Rule does not require disclosure of information otherwise protected by Rule 1.6 or information gained by a lawyer or judge while participating in an approved lawyers assistance program.

COMMENT
[1] Self-regulation of the legal profession requires that members of the profession initiate disciplinary investigation when they know of a violation of the Rules of Professional Conduct. Lawyers have a similar obligation with respect to judicial misconduct. An

apparently isolated violation may indicate a pattern of misconduct that only a disciplinary investigation can uncover. Reporting a violation is especially important where the victim is unlikely to discover the offense.

[2] A report about misconduct is not required where it would involve violation of Rule 1.6. However, a lawyer should encourage a client to consent to disclosure where prosecution would not substantially prejudice the client's interests.

[3] If a lawyer were obliged to report every violation of the Rules, the failure to report any violation would itself be a professional offense. Such a requirement existed in many jurisdictions but proved to be unenforceable. This Rule limits the reporting obligation to those offenses that a self-regulating profession must vigorously endeavor to prevent. A measure of judgment is, therefore, required in complying with the provisions of this Rule. The term "substantial" refers to the seriousness of the possible offense and not the quantum of evidence of which the lawyer is aware. A report should be made to the bar disciplinary agency unless some other agency, such as a peer review agency, is more appropriate in the circumstances. Similar considerations apply to the reporting of judicial misconduct.

[4] The duty to report professional misconduct does not apply to a lawyer retained to represent a lawyer whose professional conduct is in question. Such a situation is governed by the Rules applicable to the client-lawyer relationship.

[5] Information about a lawyer's or judge's misconduct or fitness may be received by a lawyer in the course of that lawyer's participation in an approved lawyers or judges assistance program. In that circumstance, providing for an exception to the reporting requirements of paragraphs (a) and (b) of this Rule encourages lawyers and judges to seek treatment through such a program. Conversely, without such an exception, lawyers and judges may hesitate to seek assistance from these programs, which may then result in additional harm to their professional careers and additional injury to the welfare of clients and the public. These Rules do not otherwise address the confidentiality of information received by a lawyer or judge participating in an approved lawyers assistance program; such an obligation, however, may be imposed by the rules of the program or other law.

MAINTAINING THE INTEGRITY OF THE PROFESSION
RULE 8.4 Misconduct

It is professional misconduct for a lawyer to:

(a) violate or attempt to violate the Rules of Professional Conduct, knowingly assist or induce another to do so, or do so through the acts of another;

(b) commit a criminal act that reflects adversely on the lawyer's honesty, trustworthiness or fitness as a lawyer in other respects;

(c) engage in conduct involving dishonesty, fraud, deceit or misrepresentation;

(d) engage in conduct that is prejudicial to the administration of justice;

(e) state or imply an ability to influence improperly a government agency or official or to achieve results by means that violate the Rules of Professional Conduct or other law; or

(f) knowingly assist a judge or judicial officer in conduct that is a violation of applicable rules of judicial conduct or other law.

COMMENT

[1] Lawyers are subject to discipline when they violate or attempt to violate the Rules of Professional Conduct, knowingly assist or induce another to do so or do so through the acts of another, as when they request or instruct an agent to do so on the lawyer's behalf. Paragraph (a), however, does not prohibit a lawyer from advising a client concerning action the client is legally entitled to take.

[2] Many kinds of illegal conduct reflect adversely on fitness to practice law, such as offenses involving fraud and the offense of willful failure to file an income tax return. However, some kinds of offenses carry no such implication. Traditionally, the distinction was drawn in terms of offenses involving "moral turpitude." That concept can be construed to include offenses concerning some matters of personal morality, such as adultery and comparable offenses, that have no specific connection to fitness for the practice of law. Although a lawyer is personally answerable to the entire criminal law, a lawyer should be professionally answerable only for offenses that indicate lack of those characteristics relevant to law practice. Offenses involving violence, dishonesty, breach of trust, or serious interference with the administration of justice are in that category. A pattern of repeated offenses, even ones of minor significance when considered separately, can indicate indifference to legal obligation.

[3] A lawyer who, in the course of representing a client, knowingly manifests by words or conduct, bias or prejudice based upon race, sex, religion, national origin, disability, age, sexual orientation or socioeconomic status, violates paragraph (d) when such actions are prejudicial to the administration of justice. Legitimate advocacy respecting the foregoing factors does not violate paragraph (d). A trial judge's finding that peremptory challenges were exercised on a discriminatory basis does not alone establish a violation of this rule.

[4] A lawyer may refuse to comply with an obligation imposed by law upon a good faith belief that no valid obligation exists. The provisions of Rule 1.2(d) concerning a good faith challenge to the validity, scope, meaning or application of the law apply to challenges of legal regulation of the practice of law.

[5] Lawyers holding public office assume legal responsibilities going beyond those of other citizens. A lawyer's abuse of public office can suggest an inability to fulfill the professional role of lawyers. The same is true of abuse of positions of private trust such as trustee, executor, administrator, guardian, agent and officer, director or manager of a corporation or other organization.

Table of Online Resources

Table of Rules and Statutes

Statute   Page

Table of Cases

Collected References

AARON, David (1999). "Ethics, Law Enforcement, and Fair Dealing: A Prosecutor's Duty to Disclose Non-Evidentiary Information," 67 *Fordham L. Rev.* 3005.

ABA SECTION OF LITIGATION (2002). "Ethical Guidelines for Settlement Negotiations," available at *http://www.abanet.org/litigation/ethics/settlementnegotiations.pdf.*

ADLER, Robert S. (2005). "Flawed Thinking: Addressing Decision Biases in Negotiation," 20 *Ohio St. J. on Disp. Resol.* 683.

ADLER, Robert S., Benson ROSEN & Elliot M. SILVERSTEIN (1998). "How to Manage Fear and Anger," 14 *Negot. J.* 161.

ADLER, Robert S. & Elliot M. SILVERSTEIN (2000). "When David Meets Goliath: Dealing with Power Differentials in Negotiations," 5 *Harv. Negot. L. Rev.* 1.

ALBIN, Cecilia (1993). "The Role of Fairness in Negotiation," 9 *Negot. J.* 223.

ALFINI, James J. (1991). "Trashing, Bashing, and Hashing It Out: Is This the End of 'Good Mediation'?," 19 *Fla. St. U. L. Rev.* 47.

ALLRED, Keith G., John S. MALLOZZI, Fusako MATSUI & Christopher P. RAIA (1997). "The Influence of Anger and Compassion on Negotiation Performance," 70 *Organizational Behav. & Hum. Decision Processes* 175.

ANGIER, Natalie (2002). "Why We're So Nice: We're Wired to Cooperate," *N.Y. Times*, July 23, at F1.

APPLBAUM, Arthur Isak (1996). "Rules of the Game, Permissible Harms, and the Principle of Fair Play," in Richard J. Zeckhauser, Ralph L. Keeney & James K. Sebenius, eds., *Wise Choices: Decisions, Games, and Negotiations*. Boston: Harvard Business School Press.

ARENDT, Hannah (1958). *The Human Condition*. New York: Doubleday.

ARNOLD, Tom (1995). "20 Common Errors in Mediation Advocacy," 13 *Alternatives to High Cost Litig.* 69.

AVRUCH, Kevin (2004). "Culture as Context, Culture as Communication: Considerations for Humanitarian Negotiators," 9 *Harv. Negot. L. Rev.* 391.

_____ (2000). "Culture and Negotiation Pedagogy," 16 *Negot. J.* 339.

AVRUCH, Kevin & Peter BLACK (1991). "The Culture Question and Conflict Resolution," 16 *Peace & Change* 22.

AXELROD, Robert (1984). *The Evolution of Cooperation*. New York: Basic Books.

AYRES, Ian (1995). "Further Evidence of Discrimination in New Car Negotiations and Estimates of Its Cause," 94 *Mich. L. Rev.* 109.

_____ (1991). "Fair Driving: Gender and Race Discrimination in Retail Car Negotiations," 104 *Harv. L. Rev.* 817.

AYRES, Ian & Barry J. NALEBUFF (1997). "Common Knowledge as a Barrier to Negotiation," 44 *UCLA L. Rev.* 1631.

BABBITT, Eileen F. (1999). "Challenges for International Diplomatic Agents," in Robert H. Mnookin, Lawrence E. Susskind, eds., with Pacey C. Foster, *Negotiating on Behalf of Others: Advice to Lawyers, Business Executives, Sports Agents, Diplomats, Politicians, and Everybody Else.* Thousand Oaks, Cal.: Sage Publications.

BABCOCK, Linda & Sara LASCHEVER (2003). *Women Don't Ask: Negotiation and the Gender Divide.* Princeton: Princeton University Press.

BABCOCK, Linda & George LOEWENSTEIN (1997). "Exploring Bargaining Impasses: The Role of Self-Serving Biases," 11 *J. Econ. Persp.* 109.

BARON, Robert A. (1990). "Environmentally Induced Positive Affect: Its Impact on Self-Efficacy, Task Performance, Negotiation, and Conflict," 20 *J. Applied Soc. Psychol.* 368.

BARRY, Bruce & Richard L. OLIVER (1996). "Affect in Dyadic Negotiations: A Model and Propositions," 67 *Org. Behav. & Hum. Decision Processes* 127.

BASTRESS, Robert M. & Joseph D. HARBAUGH (1990). *Interviewing, Counseling, and Negotiating: Skills for Effective Representation.* Boston: Little, Brown.

BATSON, C. Daniel & Nadia AHMAD (2001). "Empathy Induced Altruism in a Prisoner's Dilemma II: What if the Target of Empathy Has Defected?," 31 *Eur. J. Soc. Psychol.* 25.

BAZERMAN, Max H. & Margaret A. NEALE (1992). *Negotiating Rationally.* New York: Free Press.

BAZERMAN, Max H., Ann E. TENBRUNSEL & Kimberly WADE-BENZONI (1998). "Negotiating with Yourself and Losing: Making Decisions with Competing Internal Preferences," 23 *Acad. Mgmt. Rev.* 225.

BECKER, Gary (1971). *The Economics of Discrimination* (2d ed.) Chicago: University of Chicago Press.

BEGLEY, Sharon (2000). "The Stereotype Trap," *Newsweek*, Nov. 6, at 66-68.

BENEDICT, John. E. (1987). Note, "It's a Mistake to Tolerate the Mary Carter Agreement," 87 *Colum. L. Rev.* 368.

BERCOVITCH, Jacob, ed. (1996). *Resolving International Conflicts: The Theory and Practice of Mediation.* Boulder, Colo.: Lynne Rienner Publishers.

BEZANSON, Randall P., Gilbert CRANBERG & John SOLOSKI (1987). *Libel Law and the Press: Myth and Reality.* New York: Free Press.

BIBAS, Stephanos (2004). "Plea Bargaining Outside the Shadow of Trial," 117 *Harv. L. Rev.* 2463.

BIBAS, Stephanos & Richard A. BIERSCHBACH (2004). "Integrating Remorse and Apology into Criminal Procedure," 114 *Yale L.J.* 85.

BINDER, David A., Paul BERGMAN, Susan C. PRICE & Paul K. TREMBLAY (2004). *Lawyers as Counselors: A Client-Centered Approach* (2d ed.). St. Paul: West Group.

BINGHAM, Lisa B. (2003). "Mediation at Work: Transforming Workplace Conflict at the United States Postal Service." Washington, D.C.: IBM Center for The Business of Government, available at *http://www.businessofgovernment.org/pdfs/Bingham_Report.pdf.*

BIRKE, Richard (1999). "Reconciling Loss Aversion and Guilty Pleas," 1999 *Utah L. Rev.* 205.

BLAKE, Robert R., Herbert A. SHEPARD & Jane S. MOUTON (1964). *Managing Intergroup Conflict in Industry.* Houston: Gulf Publishing.

BOTTOM, William P., Kevin GIBSON, Steven E. DANIELS & J. Keith MURNIGHAN (2000). "When Talk Is Not Cheap: Substantive Penance and Expression of Intent in Rebuilding Cooperation," 13 *Org. Sci.* 497.

BRAITHWAITE, John (2003). "Restorative Justice and Social Justice," 63 *Saskatchewan L. Rev.* 194.

BRAMS, Steven J. (forthcoming 2006). "Fair Division," in Barry R. Weingast & Donald Wittman, eds., *Oxford Handbook of Political Economy.* New York: Oxford University Press.

BRAMS, Steven J. & Alan D. TAYLOR (1996). *Fair Division: From Cake-Cutting to Dispute Resolution.* New York: Cambridge University Press.

BRAZIL, Wayne D. (1998). "Protecting Confidentiality of Settlement Negotiations," 39 *Hastings L.J.* 955.

BRETT, Jeanne M. (2001). *Negotiating Globally: How to Negotiate Deals, Resolve Disputes, and Make Decisions Across Cultural Boundaries*. San Francisco: Jossey-Bass Publishers.

BROOKE, James (2005). "Fighting to Protect Her Gift to Japanese Women," *N.Y. Times*, May 28, at A4.

_____ (2005). "Relations Fray as Japan Criticizes Chinese Official's Snub," *N.Y. Times*, May 25, at A10.

BROWN, Jennifer Gerarda (2004). "Creativity and Problem-Solving," 87 *Marq. L. Rev.* 697.

_____ (2004). "The Role of Apology in Negotiation," 87 *Marq. L. Rev.* 665.

_____ (1997). "The Role of Hope in Negotiation," 44 *UCLA L. Rev.* 1661.

BROWN, Jennifer Gerarda, Marcia Caton CAMPBELL, Jayne Seminare DOCHERTY & Nancy WELSH (2004). "Negotiation as One Among Many Tools," 87 *Marq. L. Rev.* 853.

BURGER, Warren E. (1971). "The Necessity for Civility," 52 *F.R.D.* 211.

BURTON, John W. (1987). *Resolving Deep-Rooted Conflict: A Handbook*. Lanham, Md.: University Press of America.

BUSH, Robert A. Baruch (2002). "Substituting Mediation for Arbitration: The Growing Market for Evaluative Mediation, and What It Means for the ADR Field," 3 *Pepp. Disp. Resol. L.J.* 111.

BUSH, Robert A. Baruch & Joseph P. FOLGER (2004). *The Promise of Mediation: The Transformative Approach to Conflict* (rev. ed.). San Francisco: Jossey-Bass.

_____ (1994). *The Promise of Mediation: Responding to Conflict Through Empowerment and Recognition* (1st ed.). San Francisco: Jossey-Bass Publishers.

CAMERER, Colin F. & Teck H. HO (2001). "Strategic Learning and Teaching," in Stephen J. Hoch & Howard C. Kunreuther, eds., with Robert E. Gunther, *Wharton on Making Decisions*. New York: John Wiley & Sons.

CANBY, William C., Jr. (2000). "A Senior Judge's Foray into Diplomacy," 10 *Experience* 20.

CARNEVALE, Peter J.D. & Alice M. ISEN (1986). "The Influence of Positive Affect and Visual Access on the Discovery of Integrative Solutions in Bilateral Negotiation," 37 *Organizational Behav. & Hum. Decision Processes* 1.

CARTER, Jimmy (1982). *Keeping Faith: Memoirs of a President*. Toronto: Bantam Books.

CENTER FOR CONFLICT RESOLUTION (1978). *A Manual for Group Facilitators*. Madison, Wis.: Center for Conflict Resolution.

CHAYES, Abram J. (1999). Preface to Robert H. Mnookin & Lawrence E. Susskind, eds., with Pacey C. Foster, *Negotiating on Behalf of Others: Advice to Lawyers, Business Executives, Sports Agents, Diplomats, Politicians, and Everybody Else*. Thousand Oaks, Cal.: Sage Publications.

CHEW, Pat (2004). "The Pervasiveness of Culture in Conflict," 54 *J. Legal Educ.* 60.

CIALDINI, Robert B. (1993). *Influence: The Psychology of Persuasion* (rev. ed.). New York: William Morrow.

COFFEE, John C., Jr. (1995). "Class Wars: The Dilemma of the Mass Tort Class Action," 95 *Colum. L. Rev.* 1343.

COGLIANESE, Gary (1997). "Assessing Consensus: The Promise and Performance of Negotiated Rulemaking," 46 *Duke L.J.* 1255.

COHEN, Jonathan R. (2005). "The Immorality of Denial," 79 *Tul. L. Rev.* 903.

_____ (2004). "Toward Candor After Medical Error: The First Apology Law," 5 *Harv. Health Poly. Rev.* 21.

_____ (2003). "Adversaries? Partners? How About Counterparts? On Metaphors in the Practice and Teaching of Negotiation and Dispute Resolution," 20 *Conflict Resol. Q.* 433.

_____ (2002). "Legislating Apology: The Pros and Cons," 70 *U. Cinn. L. Rev.* 819.

_____ (2001). "When People Are the Means: Negotiating with Respect," 14 *Geo. J. Legal Ethics* 739.

_____ (2000). "Apology and Organizations: Exploring an Example from Medical Practice," 27 *Fordham Urb. L.J.* 1447.

_____ (1999). "Advising Clients to Apologize," 72 *Cal. L. Rev.* 1009.

COHEN, Stephen B. (forthcoming 2005). "Misassigning Income: The Supreme Court and Attorney's Fees," Georgetown U. Law Ctr., Working Paper No. 799964, available at *http://papers.ssrn.com/sol3/papers.cfm?abstract_id=799964*.

COHEN, Stephen B. & Laura SAGER (2000). "How the Income Tax Undermines Civil Rights Law," 73 *S. Cal. L. Rev.* 1075.

_____ (1998). "Discrimination Against Discrimination Damages," 35 *Harv. L. Legis.* 447.

COLEMAN, Jules & Charles SILVER (1986). "Justice in Settlements," 4 *Soc. Phil. & Poly.* 102.

COLEMAN, Peter T. (2000). "Power and Conflict," in Morton Deutsch & Peter T. Coleman, eds., *The Handbook of Conflict Resolution: Theory and Practice.* San Francisco: Jossey-Bass Publishers.

CONDLIN, Robert J. (1992). "Bargaining in the Dark: The Normative Incoherence of Lawyer Dispute Bargaining Role," 51 *Md. L. Rev.* 1.

_____ (1985). "'Cases on Both Sides': Patterns of Argument in Legal Dispute-Negotiation," 44 *Md. L. Rev.* 65.

CORTINA, Lilia M. et al. (2002). "What's Gender Got to Do with It? Incivility in the Federal Courts," 27 *Law & Soc. Inquiry* 235.

COX, Archibald (1958). "The Duty to Bargain in Good Faith," 71 *Harv. L. Rev.* 1401.

CRAVER, Charles B. & David W. BARNES (1999). "Gender, Risk Taking, and Negotiation Performance," 5 *Mich. J. Gender & L.* 299.

CROCKER, Chester A., Fen Osler HAMPSON & Pamela AALL, eds. (2001). *Turbulent Peace: The Challenges of Managing International Conflict.* Washington, D.C.: United States Institute of Peace Press.

_____ (1999). *Herding Cats: Multiparty Mediation in a Complex World.* Washington, D.C.: United States Institute of Peace Press.

CROSON, Rachel & Robert H. MNOOKIN (1997). "Does Disputing Through Agents Enhance Cooperation? Experimental Evidence," 26 *J. Legal Stud.* 331.

CRUMP, Larry (2005). "For the Sake of the Team: Unity and Disunity in a Multiparty Major League Baseball Negotiation," 21 *Negot. J.* 317.

CRYSTAL, Nathan (1999). "The Lawyer's Duty to Disclose Material Facts in Contract or Settlement Negotiations," 87 *Ky. L.J.* 1055.

CURHAN, Jared R., Margaret A. NEALE & Lee ROSS (2004). "Dynamic Valuation: Preference Changes in the Context of Face-to-Face Negotiation," 40 *J. Experimental Psychol.* 142.

CURRAN, Daniel, James K. SEBENIUS & Michael WATKINS (2004). "Two Paths to Peace: Contrasting George Mitchell in Northern Ireland with Richard Holbrooke in Bosnia-Herzegovina," 20 *Negot. J.* 513.

DAICOFF, Susan (1997). "Lawyer, Know Thyself: A Review of Empirical Research on Attorney Attributes Bearing on Professionalism," 46 *Am. U. L. Rev.* 1337.

DALY, Joseph P. (1991). "The Effects of Anger on Negotiations over Mergers and Acquisitions," 7 *Negot. J.* 31.

DAMASIO, Antonio (1994). *Descartes' Error: Emotion, Reason, and the Human Brain.* New York: G.P. Putnam.

DAUGHETY, Andrew F. & Jennifer F. REINGAMUM (2005). "Economic Theories of Settlement Bargaining," 1 *Ann. Rev. L. & Soc. Sci.* 35.

DE BONO, Edward (1999) *Six Thinking Hats* (rev. ed.). Boston: Little, Brown.

DEASON, Ellen E. (2001) "Enforcing Mediated Settlement Agreements: Contract Law Collides with Confidentiality," 35 *U.C. Davis L. Rev.* 33.

DEMOTT, Deborah A. (1998). "A Revised Prospectus for a Third Restatement of Agency," 31 *U.C. Davis L. Rev.* 1035.

DENOON, David B.H. & Steven J. BRAMS (1997). "Fair Division: A New Approach to the Spratly Islands Controversy," 2 *Intl. Negot.* 303.

DEUTSCH, Morton (1973). *The Resolution of Conflict: Constructive and Destructive Processes.* New Haven: Yale University Press.

DICKENS, Charles (1853). *Bleak House* (1956 ed.). Boston: Houghton Mifflin.

DINERSTEIN, Robert D. (1990). "Client-Centered Counseling: Reappraisal and Refinement," 32 *Ariz. L. Rev.* 501.

DOCHERTY, Jayne Seminare (2004). "Culture and Negotiation: Symmetrical Anthropology for Negotiators," 87 *Marq. L. Rev.* 711.

_____ (2004). "Power in the Social/Political Realm," 87 *Marq. L. Rev.* 861.

_____ (2001). *Learning Lessons from Waco: When Parties Bring Their Gods to the Negotiation Table.* Syracuse, N.Y.: Syracuse University Press.

DOCHERTY, Jayne Seminare & Marcia Caton CAMPBELL (2004). "Teaching Negotiators to Analyze Conflict Structure and Anticipate the Consequences of Principal-Agent Relationships," 87 *Marq. L. Rev.* 655.

DOERRE, Sharon (2001). "Negotiating Gender and Authority in Northern Syria," 6 *Intl. Negot.* 251.

DONAHUE, John J. (1991). "Opting for the British Rule, or if Posner and Shavell Can't Remember the Coase Theorem, Who Will?," 104 *Harv. L. Rev.* 1093.

DONNELL, Susan M. & Jay HALL (1980). "Men and Women as Managers: A Significant Case of No Significant Difference," *Org. Dynamics* (Spring) at 76.

DONOHUE, William A. & Anthony J. ROBERTO (1993). "Relational Development as Negotiated Order in Hostage Negotiation," 20 *Hum. Comm. Res.* 175.

DUVIN, Robert. P. (1964). "The Duty to Bargain: Law in Search of Policy," 64 *Colum. L. Rev.* 248.

EDMONDS, David & John EIDINOW (2001). *Wittgenstein's Poker: The Story of a Ten-Minute Argument Between Two Great Philosophers.* New York: Ecco.

ELLMANN, Stephen (1987). "Lawyers and Clients," 34 *UCLA L. Rev.* 717.

ELSTER, Jon (1995). "Strategic Uses of Argument," in Kenneth J. Arrow et al., eds., *Barriers to Conflict Resolution.* New York: W.W. Norton.

EPSTEIN, Lynn (1997). "Post-Settlement Malpractice, Undoing the Done Deal," 46 *Cath. U. L. Rev.* 453.

ERTEL, Danny (1999). "Turning Negotiation into a Corporate Capability," *Harv. Bus. Rev.* May-June 1999.

"Fair Dinkum" (2005). "Australia and East Timor: Australia, at Long Last, Does the Right Thing by East Timor," *The Economist*, May 21, at 46.

FALK, David B. (1992). "The Art of Contract Negotiation," 3 *Marq. Sports L.J.* 1.

FASSINA, Neil E. (2004). "Constraining a Principal's Choice: Outcome Versus Behavior Contingent Agency Contracts in Representative Negotiations," 20 *Negot. J.* 435.

FEDERAL JUDICIAL CENTER (1985). *Manual for Complex Litigation* (2d ed.). St. Paul: West Pub. Co.

FELSTINER, William L. F., Richard L. ABEL & Austin SARAT (1980-1981). "The Emergence and Transformation of Disputes: Naming, Blaming, Claiming...," 15 *Law & Socy. Rev.* 631.

FELSTINER, William L. F. & Austin SARAT (1992). "Enactments of Power: Negotiating Reality and Responsibility in Lawyer-Client Interactions," 77 *Cornell L. Rev.* 1447.

FICK, B. J. (1989). "Negotiation Theory and the Law of Collective Bargaining," 38 *Kan. L. Rev.* 426.

FISHER, Roger (1989). "Negotiating Inside Out: What Are the Best Ways to Relate Internal Negotiations with External Ones?," 5 *Negot. J.* 33.

_____ (1969). *International Conflict for Beginners.* New York: Harper & Row.

FISHER, Roger & Andrea Kupfer SCHNEIDER, Elizabeth BORGWARDT & Brian GANSON (1997). *Coping with International Conflict: A Systematic Approach to Influence in International Negotiation.* Upper Saddle River, N.J.: Prentice Hall.

FISHER, Roger & Wayne H. DAVIS (1987). "Six Basic Interpersonal Skills for a Negotiator's Repertoire," 3 *Negot. J.* 117.

FISHER, Roger, Elizabeth KOPELMAN & Andrea Kupfer SCHNEIDER (1994). *Beyond Machiavelli: Tools for Coping with Conflict.* Cambridge: Harvard University Press.

FISHER, Roger & Daniel SHAPIRO (2005). *Beyond Reason: Using Emotions as You Negotiate.* New York: Viking Penguin.

FISHER, Roger, William URY & Bruce PATTON (1991). *Getting to YES: Negotiating Agreement Without Giving In* (2d ed.). Boston: Houghton Mifflin.

FISS, Owen M. (1984). "Against Settlement," 93 *Yale L.J.* 1073.

FOLLETT, Mary Parker (1995). "Constructive Conflict," in Pauline Graham, ed., *Mary Parker Follett — Prophet of Management: A Celebration of Writings from the 1920s.* Boston: Harvard Business School Press.

FONG, Archon & Erik Olin WRIGHT (2003). *Deepening Democracy: Institutional Innovations in Empowered Participatory Governance.* New York: Verso.

FOREST, Heather (1996). *Wisdom Tales from Around the World.* Little Rock, Ark.: August House Publishers.

FORGAS, Joseph P. (1998). "On Feeling Good and Getting Your Way: Mood Effects on Negotiator Cognition and Bargaining Strategies," 74 *J. Personality & Soc. Psychol.* 565.

FREEMAN, Jody (1997). "Collaborative Governance in the Administrative State," 45 *UCLA L. Rev.* 1.

FREEMAN, Jody & Laura I. LANGBEIN (2000). "Regulatory Negotiation and the Legitimacy Benefit," 9 *N.Y.U. Envtl. L.J.* 60.

FRESHMAN, Clark, Adele HAYES & Greg FELDMAN (2002). "The Lawyer-Negotiator as Mood Scientist: What We Know and Don't Know About How Mood Relates to Successful Negotiation," 2002 *J. Disp. Resol.* 1.

FRIEDMAN, Gary & Jack HIMMELSTEIN (2004). "The Understanding-Based Approach to Mediation." The Center for Mediation in Law, available at *http://www.mediationinlaw.org/about.html.*

FUKUYAMA, Francis (1992). *The End of History and the Last Man.* New York: Free Press.

FULLER, Lon L. (1971). "Mediation — Its Forms and Functions," 44 *S. Cal. L. Rev.* 305.

GALTON, Eric (2000). "Mediation of Medical Negligence Claims," 28 *Cap. U. L. Rev.* 321.

GASTIL, John & Peter LEVINE, eds. (2005). *The Deliberative Democracy Handbook.* San Francisco: Jossey-Bass.

GAUTHIER, David (1986). *Morals by Agreement.* Oxford: Clarendon Press.

GIFFORD, Donald G. (1985). "A Context-Based Theory of Strategy Selection in Legal Negotiation," 46 *Ohio St. L.J.* 41.

_____ (1987). "The Synthesis of Legal Counseling and Negotiation Models: Preserving Client-Centered Advocacy in the Negotiation Context," 34 *UCLA L. Rev.* 811.

GILLIGAN, Carol (1982). *In a Different Voice: Psychological Theory and Women's Development.* Cambridge: Harvard University Press.

GILSON, Ronald J. (1994). "Disputing Through Agents: Cooperation and Conflict Between Lawyers in Litigation," 94 *Colum. L. Rev.* 509.

_____ (1984). "Value Creation by Business Lawyers: Legal Skills and Asset Pricing," 94 *Yale L.J.* 239.

GINSBURG, Tom & Richard H. McADAMS (2004). "Adjudicating in Anarchy: An Expressive Theory of International Dispute Resolution," 45 *Wm. & Mary L. Rev.* 1229.

GLADWELL, Malcolm (2005). *Blink: The Power of Thinking Without Thinking.* New York: Little, Brown and Co.

GLASER, Connie & Barbara SMALLEY (2003). *What Queen Esther Knew: Business Strategies from a Biblical Sage.* Emmaus, Penn.: Rodesdale.

GLICK, Steven & Rachel CROSON (2001). "Reputations in Negotiation," in Stephen J. Hoch & Howard C. Kunreuther, eds., with Robert E. Gunther, *Wharton on Making Decisions.* New York: John Wiley & Sons.

GOLDSTEIN, Joseph & Jay KATZ (1965). *The Family and the Law: Problems for Decision in the Family Law Process.* New York: Free Press.

GOODPASTER, Gary (1996). "A Primer on Competitive Bargaining," 1996 *J. Disp. Resol.* 325.

GOODWYN, Wade (2002). "Southwest Airlines Soars Above Industry's Turbulence," *National Public Radio,* December 4, available at *http://www.npr.org/templates/story/story.php?storyId=865383.*

GORDON, Beate Sirota (1997). *The Only Woman in the Room: A Memoir* (1st ed.). New York: Kodansha.

GRAY, Barbara (1989). "The Impetus to Collaborate," in *Collaborating: Finding Common Ground for Multiparty Problems.* San Francisco: Jossey-Bass.

GREENBERG, Melanie C., John H. BARTON & Margaret E. McGUINNESS, eds. (2000). *Words over War: Mediation and Arbitration to Prevent Deadly Conflict.* Lanham, Md.: Rowman & Littlefield Publishers.

GREENHALGH, Leonard (1987). "Relationships in Negotiation," 3 *Negot. J.* 235.

_____ (1987). "The Case Against Winning in Negotiations," 3 *Negot. J.* 167.

GROSS, Samuel & Kent D. SYVERUD (1991). "Getting to No: A Study of Settlement Negotiations and the Selection of Cases for Trial," 90 *Mich. L. Rev.* 319.

GULLIVER, Phillip H. (1979). *Disputes and Negotiations: A Cross-Cultural Perspective.* New York: Academic Press.

GURR, Ted Robert (2000). "Ethnic Warfare on the Wane," 79 *Foreign Affairs* 52.

____ (1994). "Peoples Against States: Ethnopolitical Conflict and the Changing World System: 1994 Presidential Address," 38 *Intl. Stud. Q.* 347.

GUTHRIE, Chris (2004). "Principles of Influence Negotiation," 87 *Marq. L. Rev.* 829.

____ (2003). "Panacea or Pandora's Box?: The Costs of Options in Negotiation," 88 *Iowa L. Rev.* 601.

GUTHRIE, Chris & David SALLY (2004). "The Impact of the Impact Bias on Negotiation," 87 *Marq. L. Rev.* 817.

HABERMAS, Jürgen (1989). *The Structural Transformation of the Public Sphere: An Inquiry into a Category of Bourgeois Society.* Trans. Thomas Burger with Frederick Lawrence. Cambridge: MIT Press.

HACKETT, Donald & Charles L. MARTIN (1993). *Facilitation Skills for Team Leaders.* Menlo Park, Cal.: Crisp Publications.

HAMILTON, Alexander (1961). "The Federalist No. 70," in Clinton Rossiter, ed., *The Federalist Papers.* New York: New American Library.

HAMPSHIRE, Stuart (2000). *Justice Is Conflict.* Princeton: Princeton University Press.

HARR, Jonathan (1995). *A Civil Action.* New York: Random House.

HART, Henry M., Jr. & Albert M. SACKS (1958, 1994). *The Legal Process: Basic Problems in the Making and Application of Law* (William N. Eskridge, Jr. & Philip P. Frickey, eds.). Mineola, N.Y.: Foundation Press.

HARTER, Philip J. (2000). "Assessing the Assessors: The Actual Performance of Negotiated Rule-making," 9 *N.Y.U. Envtl. L.J.* 32.

____ (1982). "Negotiating Regulations: A Cure for Malaise," 71 *Geo. L.J.* 1.

HAWKINS, Lee, Jr. (2004). "GM's Finance Arm Is Close to Settling Racial-Bias Lawsuit," *Wall St. J.*, January 30, at A1.

HAZARD, Geoffrey C., Jr. (1978). "Lawyer for the Situation," in *Ethics in the Practice of Law.* New Haven: Yale University Press.

HEGLAND, Kenny (1982). "Why Teach Trial Advocacy? An Essay on Never Ask Why," in Jack Himmelstein & Howard Lesnick, eds., *Humanistic Education in Law.* New York: Columbia University School of Law.

HINDLE, Tim (1998). *Managing Meetings.* London: Dorling Kindersley.

HOFSTADTER, Douglas R. (1985). *Metamagical Themas: Questing for the Essence of Mind and Pattern.* New York: Basic Books.

HONEYMAN, Christopher (2004). "The Physics of Power," 87 *Marq L. Rev.* 871.

HUGHES, James W. & Edward A. SNYDER (1995). "Litigation and Settlement Under the English and American Rules: Theory and Evidence," 38 *J. L. & Econ.* 225.

HUNTINGTON, Samuel P. (1996). *The Clash of Civilizations and the Remaking of World Order.* New York: Simon & Schuster.

____ (1994). "The Clash of Civilizations?," in Armand Clesse, Richard Cooper & Yoshikazu Sakamoto, eds., *The International System After the Collapse of the East-West Order.* Dordrecht, Netherlands.: Martinus Nijhoff Publishers.

HURT, Christine (2005). "No Harm Intended: Teaching a Torts Class Offered Endless Opportunity for Dark Humor—Until it Became No Laughing Matter," *Chron. Higher Educ.*, May 27, 2005, at C3.

IGNATIEFF, Michael (1994). *Blood and Belonging: Journeys into the New Nationalism* (1st Am. ed.). New York: Farrar, Straus & Giroux.

IKLÉ, Fred Charles (1964). *How Nations Negotiate.* New York: Harper & Row.

ISEN, Alice M., Kimberly A. DAUBMAN & Gary P. NOWICKI (1987). "Positive Affect Facilitates Creative Problem Solving," 52 *J. Personality & Soc. Psychol.* 112.

ISEN, Alice M., P.M. NIEDENTHAL & N. CANTOR (1992). "Positive Affect Facilitates Creative Problem Solving: An Influence of Positive Affect on Social Categorization," 16 *Motivation & Emotion* 65.

JANIS, Irving L. (1982). *Groupthink: Psychological Studies of Policy Decisions and Fiascoes* (2d ed.). Boston: Houghton Mifflin.

JOHNSTON, Jason Scott & Joel WALDFOGEL (2002). "Does Repeat Play Elicit Cooperation? Evidence from Federal Civil Litigation," 31 *J. Legal Stud.* 39.

KAHNEMAN, Daniel (1999). "Objective Happiness," in Daniel Kahneman, Ed Diener & Norbert Schwartz, eds., *Well Being: The Foundations of Hedonic Psychology*. New York: Russell Sage Foundation.

KAHNEMAN, Daniel & Amos TVERSKY (1995). "Conflict Resolution: A Cognitive Perspective," in Kenneth J. Arrow et al., eds., *Barriers to Conflict Resolution*. New York: W.W. Norton.

KAPLOW, Louis & Steven SHAVELL (2004). *Contracting*. New York: Foundation Press.

KARRASS, Chester L. (1970). *The Negotiating Game*. New York: Crowell.

KELMAN, Herbert C. (1993). "Coalitions Across Conflict Lines: The Interplay of Conflicts Within and Between the Israeli and Palestinian Communities," in Stephen Worchel & Jeffrey A. Simpson, eds., *Conflicts Between People and Groups*. Chicago: Nelson-Hall.

____ (1972). "The Problem-Solving Workshop in Conflict Resolution," in Richard L. Merritt, ed., *Communication in International Politics*. Urbana: University of Illinois Press.

KEPNER, Tyler (2005). "A Careful Apology from Giambi," *N.Y. Times*, Feb. 11, at D-1.

KISSINGER, Henry (1979). *The White House Years*. Boston: Little, Brown.

KLONOFF, Robert H. & Edward K.M. BILICH (2000). "Resolution of Class Actions," in *Class Actions and Other Multi-Party Litigation: Cases and Materials*. St. Paul: West Group.

KOLB, Deborah M. (2000). "More than Just a Footnote: Constructing a Theoretical Framework for Teaching About Gender in Negotiation," 16 *Negot. J.* 347.

____ (2000). *The Shadow Negotiation: How Women Can Master the Hidden Agendas in Bargaining* (rev. ed.) San Francisco: Jossey-Bass.

KOLB, Deborah M. & Gloria COOLIDGE (1991). "Her Place at the Table: A Consideration of Gender Issues in Negotiation," in J. William Breslin & Jeffrey Z. Rubin, eds., *Negotiation Theory and Practice*. Cambridge: Program on Negotiation at Harvard Law School.

KOLB, Deborah M. & Judith WILLIAMS (2003). *Everyday Negotiation: Navigating the Hidden Agendas in Bargaining* (rev. ed.). San Francisco: Jossey-Bass.

KOLB, Deborah M., Judith WILLIAMS & Carol FROHLINGER (2004). *Her Place at the Table: A Woman's Guide to Negotiating Five Key Challenges to Leadership Success*. San Francisco: Jossey-Bass.

KONIAK, Susan (1995). "*Feasting While the Widow Weeps:* Georgine v. Amchem Products," 80 *Cornell L. Rev.* 1045.

KORNHEISER, Tony (1977). "Borg Ends Dominance by Connors," *N.Y. Times*, Jan. 24, at 34.

KOROBKIN, Russell (2005). "The Role of Law in Settlements," in Michael L. Moffitt & Robert C. Bordone, eds., *The Handbook of Dispute Resolution*. San Francisco: Jossey-Bass.

____ (2004). "Bargaining Power as Threat of Impasse," 87 *Marq. L. Rev.* 867.

____ (2000). "A Positive Theory of Legal Negotiation," 88 *Geo. L.J.* 1789.

KOROBKIN, Russell & Chris GUTHRIE (2004). "Heuristics and Biases at the Bargaining Table," 87 *Marq. L. Rev.* 795.

____ (1994). "Psychological Barriers to Litigation Settlement: An Experimental Approach," 93 *Mich. L. Rev.* 107.

KOROBKIN, Russell, Michael MOFFITT & Nancy WELSH (2004). "The Law of Bargaining," 87 *Marq. L. Rev.* 839.

KRAMER, Roderick M., E. NEWTON & P.L. POMMERENKE (1993). "Self-Enhancement Biases and Negotiator Judgment: Effects of Self-Esteem and Mood," 56 *Org. Behav. & Hum. Decision Processes* 110.

KRAY, Laura J., Adam D. GALINSKY & Leigh THOMPSON (2002). "Reversing the Gender Gap in Negotiations: An Exploration of Stereotype Regeneration," 87 *Org. Behav. & Hum. Decision Processes* 386.

KRITEK, Phyllis Beck (1994). *Negotiating at an Uneven Table: A Practical Approach to Working with Difference and Diversity*. San Francisco: Jossey-Bass Publishers.

KRITZER, Herbert (1992). "The English Rule," 78 *A.B.A. J.* 54.

LANDAU, Sy, Barbara LANDAU & Daryl LANDAU (2001). *From Conflict to Creativity: How Resolving Workplace Disagreements Can Inspire Innovation and Productivity*. San Francisco: Jossey-Bass Publishers.

LANGEVOORT, Donald (1999). "Half-Truths: Protecting Mistaken Inferences by Investors and Others," 52 *Stan. L. Rev.* 88.

LAWLER, Edward J. (1992). "Power Process in Bargaining," 33 *Soc. Q.* 17.

LAX, David A. & James K. SEBENIUS (1986). *The Manager as Negotiator: Bargaining for Cooperation and Competitive Gain*. New York: Free Press.

_____ (1986). "Interests: The Measure of Negotiation," 2 *Negot. J.* 73.

LEDERACH, John Paul (2003). "Cultivating Peace: A Practitioner's View of Deadly Conflict and Negotiation," in John Darby & Roger MacGinty, eds., *Contemporary Peacemaking: Conflict, Violence and Peace Processes*. New York: Palgrave MacMillan.

LEE, Ilhyung (2005). "In re Culture: The Cross-Cultural Negotiations Course in the Law School Curriculum," 20 *Ohio St. J. on Disp. Resol.* 375.

LEHMAN, Warren (1979). "The Pursuit of a Client's Interest," 77 *Mich. L. Rev.* 1078.

LESTER, Brandon J. (2005) "System Failure: The Case for Supplanting Negotiation for Mediation in Plea Bargaining," 20 *Ohio St. J. Disp. Res.* 563.

LEWICKI, Roy J. & Barbara Benedict BUNKER (1995). "Trust in Relationships: A Model of Development and Decline," in Barbara Benedict Bunker, Jeffrey Z. Rubin et al., eds., *Conflict, Cooperation & Justice: Essays Inspired by the Work of Morton Deutsch*. San Francisco: Jossey-Bass Publishers.

LEWICKI, Roy J. & Carolyn WIETHOFF (2000). "Trust, Trust Development & Trust Repair," in Morton Deutsch & Peter T. Coleman, eds., *The Handbook of Conflict Resolution: Theory and Practice*. San Francisco: Jossey-Bass Publishers.

LEWIS, Michael (1989). *Liar's Poker: Rising Through the Wreckage on Wall Street*. New York: W.W. Norton.

_____ (2003). *Moneyball: The Art of Winning an Unfair Game*. New York: W.W. Norton.

LONGAN, Patrick Emery (2001). "Ethics in Settlement Negotiations," Foreword, 52 *Mercer L. Rev.* 807.

LOVE, Lela P. (1993). "Glen Cove: Mediation Achieves What Litigation Cannot," 20 *Consensus* 1.

LOVE, Lela P. & Cheryl B. McDONALD (1997). "A Tale of Two Cities: Day Labor and Conflict Resolution for Communities in Crisis," *Disp. Resol. Mag.* 8 (Fall).

LUBAN, David (1995). "Settlements and the Erosion of the Public Realm," 83 *Geo. L.J.* 2619.

_____ (1987). "Some Greek Trials: Order and Justice in Homer, Hesiod, Aeschylus and Plato," 43 *Tenn. L. Rev.* 279.

LUBET, Steven (1996). "Notes on the Bedouin Horse Trade or 'Why Won't the Market Clear, Daddy?,'" 74 *Tex. L. Rev.* 1039.

LYNCH, Eugene F. (2005). *Negotiation and Settlement* (2d ed.). Eagan, Minn.: Thomson/West.

MACFARLANE, Julie (2004). "Experience of Collaborative Law: Preliminary Results from the Collaborative Lawyering Research Project," 2004 *J. Disp. Res.* 179.

MACHIAVELLI, Niccolò (1998). *The Prince* (2d ed.). Trans. Harvey C. Mansfield. University of Chicago Press.

MAUTE, Judith L. (1991). "Public Values and Private Justice: A Case for Mediator Accountability," 4 *Geo. J. Legal Ethics* 503.

McCORMICK, Charles Tilford (1935). *Handbook on the Law of Damages*. St. Paul: West Pub. Co.

MELTSNER, Michael & Philip G. SCHRAG (1974). "Negotiation," in *Public Interest Advocacy: Materials for Clinical Legal Education*. Boston: Little, Brown.

MENKEL-MEADOW, Carrie (2005). "Is the Adversary System Really Dead? Dilemmas of Legal Ethics as Legal Institutions and Roles Evolve," in Jane Holder, Colm O'Cinneide & Michael Freeman, eds., *Current Legal Problems 2004*. New York: Oxford University Press.

_____ (2005). "Legal Negotiation in Popular Culture: What Are We Bargaining For?," in Michael Freeman, ed., *Law and Popular Culture*. New York: Oxford University Press.

_____ (2005). "Roots and Inspirations: A Brief History of the Foundations of Dispute Resolution," in Michael L. Moffitt & Robert C. Bordone, eds., *The Handbook of Dispute Resolution*. San Francisco: Jossey-Bass.

_____ (2004/2005). "The Lawyer's Roles in Deliberative Democracy," 5 *UNLV L. Rev.* 347.

_____ (2004). "What's Fair in Negotiation? What Is Ethics in Negotiation?," in Carrie Menkel-Meadow & Michael Wheeler, eds., *What's Fair: Ethics for Negotiators*. San Francisco: Jossey-Bass Publishers.

_____ (2003). "Conflict Theory," in Karen Christensen & David Levinson, eds., 1 *Encyclopedia of Community: From the Village to the Virtual World*. 4 vols. Thousand Oaks, Cal.: Sage Publications.

____ (2003). "Correspondences and Contradictions in International and Domestic Conflict Resolution: Lessons from General Theory and Varied Contexts," 2003 *J. Disp. Resol.* 319.

____ (2003). "Introduction: From Legal Disputes to Conflict Resolution and Human Problem Solving," in Carrie Menkel-Meadow, *Dispute Processing and Conflict Resolution: Theory, Practice and Policy*. Aldershot, England: Ashgate/Dartmouth.

____ (2002). "Ethics, Morality and Professional Responsibility in Negotiation," in Phyllis Bernard & Bryant Garth, eds., *Dispute Resolution Ethics: A Comprehensive Guide*. Washington, D.C.: ABA Section of Dispute Resolution.

____ (2001). "Aha? Is Creativity Possible in Legal Problem Solving and Teachable in Legal Education?," 6 *Harv. Negot. L. Rev.* 97.

____ (2001). "Can They Do That? Legal Ethics in Popular Culture: Of Character and Acts," 48 *UCLA L. Rev.* 1305.

____ (2001). "Introduction," in Carrie Menkel-Meadow, ed., *Mediation: Theory, Policy and Practice*. Burlington, Vt.: Ashgate.

____ (2000). "Teaching About Gender and Negotiation: Sex, Truths and Video Tape," 16 *Negot J.* 357.

____ (1999). "The Art and Science of Problem Solving Negotiations," *Trial Mag.*, June at 48.

____ (1996). "The Trouble with the Adversary System in a Postmodern, Multicultural World," 38 *Wm. & Mary L. Rev.* 5.

____ (1995). "Ethics and the Settlements of Mass Torts: When the Rules Meet the Road," 80 *Cornell L. Rev.* 1159.

____ (1995). "Whose Dispute Is It Anyway?: A Philosophical and Democratic Defense of Settlement (in Some Cases)," 83 *Geo. L.J.* 2663.

____ (1993). "Public Access to Private Settlements: Conflicting Legal Policies," 11 *Alternatives to High Cost Litig.* 85.

____ (1985). "Feminist Discourse, Moral Values, and the Law — A Conversation," 34 *Buff. L. Rev.* 11.

____ (1984). "Toward Another View of Legal Negotiation: The Structure of Problem Solving," 31 *UCLA L. Rev.* 754.

____ (1983). "Legal Negotiation: A Study of Strategies in Search of a Theory," 1983 *Am. Bar. Found. Res. J.* 905.

MENKEL-MEADOW, Carrie & David BINDER (1983). *The Stages and Phases of Negotiation*. Washington, D.C.: ABA Lawyering Skills Institute.

MENKEL-MEADOW, Carrie, Lela LOVE & Andrea Kupfer SCHNEIDER (2006). *Mediation: Practice, Policy, and Ethics*. New York: Aspen Publishers.

MENKEL-MEADOW, Carrie, Lela LOVE, Andrea Kupfer SCHNEIDER & Jean STERNLIGHT (2005). *Dispute Resolution: Beyond the Adversarial Model*. New York: Aspen Publishers.

METCALF, Nelson, Jr. (1992). "The Kid in Upper 4," *Harv. Mag.*, Jan.-Feb. 1992, at 76.

MIALL, Hugh (1992). *The Peacemakers: Peaceful Settlement of Disputes Since 1945*. New York: St. Martin's Press.

MITCHELL, George J. (1999). *Making Peace*. New York: Knopf.

MNOOKIN, Robert H. (2003). "Strategic Barriers to Dispute Resolution: A Comparison of Bilateral and Multilateral Negotiations," 159 *J. Institutional & Theoretical Econ.* 199.

____ (2003). "When Not to Negotiate: A Negotiation Imperialist Reflects on Appropriate Limits," 74 *U. Colo. L. Rev.* 1077.

____ (1993). "Why Negotiations Fail: An Exploration of Barriers to the Resolution of Conflict," 8 *Ohio St. J. on Disp. Resol.* 235.

MNOOKIN, Robert H. & Lewis KORNHAUSER (1979). "Bargaining in the Shadow of the Law: The Case of Divorce," 88 *Yale L.J.* 950.

MNOOKIN, Robert H., Scott R. PEPPET & Andrew S. TULUMELLO (2000). *Beyond Winning: Negotiating to Create Value in Deals and Disputes*. Cambridge: Belknap Press of Harvard University Press.

MOFFITT, Michael L. (2005). "Disputes as Opportunities to Create Value," in Michael L. Moffitt & Robert C. Bordone, eds., *The Handbook of Dispute Resolution*. San Francisco: Jossey-Bass.

_____ (2004). "'Contingent Agreements: Agreeing to Disagree About the Future,'" 87 *Marq. L. Rev.* 691.

MOFFITT, Michael L. & Robert C. BORDONE, eds., (2005). *The Handbook of Dispute Resolution.* San Francisco: Jossey-Bass.

MOFFITT, Michael L. & Scott R. PEPPET (2004). "Action Science and Negotiation," 87 *Marq. L. Rev.* 649.

MORAWETZ, Nancy (1993). "Bargaining, Class Representation, and Fairness," 54 *Ohio St. L.J.* 1.

MORRIS, Michael, Janice NADLER, Terri KURTZBERG & Leigh THOMPSON (2002). "Schmooze or Lose: Social Friction and Lubrication in E-Mail Negotiations," 6 *Group Dynamics* 89.

NADLER, Janice (2004). "Rapport in Legal Negotiation: How Small Talk Can Facilitate E-Mail Dealmaking," 9 *Harv. Neg. L. Rev.* 223.

_____ (2004). "Rapport in Negotiation and Conflict Resolution," 87 *Marq. L. Rev.* 875.

NALEBUFF, Barry & Ian AYRES (2003). *Why Not? How to Use Everyday Ingenuity to Solve Problems Big and Small.* Boston: Harvard Business School Press.

NEALE, Margaret A. & Max H. BAZERMAN (1983). "The Role of Perspective Taking Ability in Negotiating Under Different Forms of Arbitration," 34 *Indus. & Lab. Rel. Rev.* 378.

NELKEN, Melissa L. (1996). "Negotiation and Psychoanalysis: If I'd Wanted to Learn About Feelings, I Wouldn't Have Gone to Law School," 46 *J. Legal Educ.* 420.

"Nigerian Women Show Their Power," *NEWS24.com,* July 19, 2002, available at *http://www.news24.com/News24/Africa/Features/0,,2-11-37_1216228,00.html.*

NOESNER, Gary W. & Mike WEBSTER (1997). "Crisis Intervention: Using Active Listening Skills in Negotiations," *FBI L. Enforcement Bull.*, August 1, at 13.

NOLEN-HOEKSEMA, Susan & Cheryl L. RUSTING (1999). "Gender Differences in Well-Being," in Daniel Kahneman et al., eds., *Well-Being: The Foundations of Hedonic Psychology.* New York: Russell Sage Foundation.

O'CONNOR, Kathleen & Catherine TINGSLEY (forthcoming). "Looking for a Strategic Advantage? Cultivate a Reputation for Mutually Beneficial Dealmaking." Working Paper International Academy of Conflict Management.

OESCH, John M. & Adam D. GALINSKY, "First Offers in Negotiations: Determinants and Effects," 16th Annual IACM Conference, Melbourne, Australia, available at *http://ssrn.com/abstract=399722.*

PATTON, Bruce, Douglas STONE & Sheila HEEN (1993). *Discussion Problems on Difficult Conversations.* Cambridge, Mass.: Program on Negotiation, Harvard University.

PEPPET, Scott R. (2005). "Lawyer's Bargaining Ethics, Contract, and Collaboration: The End of the Legal Profession and the Beginning of Professional Pluralism," 90 *Iowa L. Rev.* 475.

_____ (2005). "Six Principles for Using Negotiating Agents to Maximum Advantage," in Michael L. Moffitt & Robert C. Bordone, eds., *The Handbook of Dispute Resolution.* San Francisco: Jossey-Bass.

_____ (2004). "Contract Formation in Imperfect Markets: Should We Use Mediators in Deals?," 19 *Ohio St. J. on Disp. Resol.* 283.

PERSCHBACHER, Rex (1985). "Regulating Lawyer's Negotiations," 27 *Ariz. L. Rev.* 75.

PETERS, Don (1993). "Forever Jung: Psychological Type Theory, the Myers-Briggs Type Indicator and Learning Negotiation," 42 *Drake L. Rev.* 1.

PINKLEY, Robin L. & Gregory B. NORTHCRAFT (2000). *Get Paid What You're Worth: The Expert Negotiator's Guide to Salary and Compensation.* New York: St. Martin's Press.

PLOUS, Scott (1993). *The Psychology of Judgment and Decision Making.* Philadelphia: Temple University Press.

POSNER, Richard A. (1978). "Adjudication as a Private Good," 8 *J. Leg. Stud.* 235.

POUNDSTONE, William (2003). *How Would You Move Mount Fuji?* Boston: Little, Brown.

POWELL, Gary N. (1990). "One More Time: Do Female and Male Managers Differ?," 4 *Acad. Mgmt. Exec.* 68.

PRIEST, George L. & Benjamin KLEIN (1984). "The Selection of Disputes for Litigation," 13 *J. Leg. Stud.* 1.

PRUITT, Dean G. (1983). "Achieving Integrative Agreements," in Max H. Bazerman & Roy J. Lewicki, eds., *Negotiating in Organizations.* Beverly Hills: Sage Publications.

_____ (1981). *Negotiation Behavior.* New York: Academic Press.

PRUITT, Dean G. & Steven A. LEWIS (1977). "The Psychology of Integrative Bargaining," in Daniel Druckman, ed., *Negotiations: Social-Psychological Perspectives*. Beverly Hills: Sage Publications.

PUBLIC CONVERSATIONS PROJECT (2003). "Constructive Conversations About Challenging Times: A Guide to Community Dialogue" (version 3.0). Public Conversations Project, available at *http://www.publicconversations.org/pcp/uploadDocs/CommunityGuide3.0.pdf*.

PUTNAM, Linda L. (1994). "Challenging the Assumptions of Traditional Approaches to Negotiation," 10 *Negot. J*. 337.

PUTNAM, Robert D. (1993). "Diplomacy and Domestic Politics: The Logic of Two-Level Games," in Peter B. Evans, Harold K. Jacobson & Robert D. Putnam, eds., *Double-Edged Diplomacy: International Bargaining and Domestic Politics*. Berkeley: University of California Press.

RAIFFA, Howard (1985). "Post-Settlement Settlements," 1 *Negot. J*. 9.

_____ (1982). *The Art and Science of Negotiation*. Cambridge, Mass.: Belknap Press of Harvard University Press.

RAIFFA, Howard with John RICHARDSON & David METCALF (2002). *Negotiation Analysis: The Science and Art of Collaborative Decision Making*. Cambridge: Belknap Press of Harvard University Press.

RAVEN, Bertran H. (1993). "The Bases of Power: Origins and Recent Developments," 49 *J. Soc. Issues* 227.

RAWLS, John (1971). *A Theory of Justice*. Cambridge, Mass.: Belknap Press of Harvard University Press.

RAY, Douglas, Calvin William SHARPE & Robert STRESSFED (1999). *Understanding Labor Law*. New York: M. Bender.

REICH, Charles (1964). "The New Property," 73 *Yale L.J*. 733.

REILLY, Peter (2005). "Teaching Law Students How to Feel: Using Negotiations Training to Increase Emotional Intelligence," 21 *Negot. J*. 303.

REYES, Robert M., William C. THOMPSON & Gordon H. BOWER (1980). "Judgmental Biases Resulting from Differing Availabilities of Arguments," 39 *J. Personality & Soc. Psychol*. 2.

RISKIN, Leonard L. (2003). "Decisionmaking in Mediation: The New Old Grid and the New New Grid System," 79 *Notre Dame L. Rev*. 1.

_____ (1994). "Mediator Orientations, Strategies and Techniques," 12 *Alternatives to High Cost Litig*. 111.

ROBBENNOLT, Jennifer K. (2003). "Apologies and Legal Settlement: An Empirical Examination," 102 *Mich. L. Rev*. 460.

ROBBENNOLT, Jennifer K. & Christine A. STUDEBAKER (1999). "Anchoring in the Courtroom: The Effects of Caps on Punitive Damages," 23 *Law & Hum. Behav*. 353.

ROBINSON, Robert, Dacher KELTNER, Andrew WARD & Lee ROSS (1995). "Actual Versus Assumed Differences in Construal: 'Naïve Realism' in Intergroup Perception and Conflict," 68 *J. Personality & Soc. Psychol*. 404.

ROSE, Carol M. (1995). "Bargaining and Gender," 18 *Harv. J. L. & Pub. Poly*. 547.

ROSENTHAL, Robert & Lenore JACOBSON (1968). *Pygmalion in the Classroom: Teacher Expectations and Pupils' Intellectual Development*. New York: Holt, Rinehart & Wilson.

ROSS, Dennis (2004). *The Missing Peace: The Inside Story of the Fight for Middle East Peace*. New York: Farrar, Straus and Giroux.

ROSS, Lee (1995). "Reactive Devaluation in Negotiation and Conflict Resolution," in Kenneth J. Arrow et al., eds., *Barriers to Conflict Resolution*. New York: W.W. Norton.

ROSS, Rick (1994). "The Ladder of Inference," in Peter M. Senge et al., eds., *The Fifth Discipline Fieldbook*. New York: Doubleday.

RUBIN, Jeffrey Z. & Frank E.A. SANDER (1991). "Culture, Negotiation, and the Eye of the Beholder," 7 *Negot. J*. 249.

_____ (1988). "When Should We Use Agents? Direct vs. Representative Negotiation," 4 *Negot. J*. 395.

SALACUSE, Jeswald W. (1998). "Ten Ways That Culture Affects Negotiating Style: Some Survey Results," 14 *Negot. J*. 221.

SALLY, David (2004). "Game Theory Behaves," 87 *Marq. L. Rev*. 783.

SANDER, Frank E.A. & Jeffrey Z. RUBIN (1988). "The Janus Quality of Negotiation: Dealmaking and Dispute Settlement," 4 *Negot. J*. 109.

SAX, Joseph (1967). "Slumlordism as a Tort," 65 *Michigan L. Rev.* 869.

SCARDILLI, Frank J. (1997). "*Sisters of the Precious Blood v. Bristol-Meyers Co.*: A Shareholder-Management Dispute," reprinted in Leonard L. Riskin & James E. Westbrook, *Dispute Resolution and Lawyers* (2d ed.). St. Paul: West Group.

SCHELLING, Thomas C. (1960). *The Strategy of Conflict.* Cambridge: Harvard University Press.

SCHILTZ, Patrick J. (1999). "On Being a Happy, Healthy, and Ethical Member of an Unhappy, Unhealthy, and Unethical Profession," 52 *Vand. L. Rev.* 871.

SCHNEIDER, Andrea Kupfer (2005). "Public and Private International Dispute Resolution," in Michael L. Moffitt & Robert C. Bordone, eds., *The Handbook of Dispute Resolution.* San Francisco: Jossey-Bass.

SCHNEIDER, Andrea Kupfer (2004). "Aspirations in Negotiation," 87 *Marq. L. Rev.* 675.

____ (2002). "Shattering Negotiation Myths: Empirical Evidence on the Effectiveness of Negotiation Style," 7 *Harv. Negot. L. Rev.* 143.

____ (1999). "Getting Along: The Evolution of Dispute Resolution Regimes in International Trade Organizations," 20 *Mich. J. Intl. L.* 697.

____ (1994). "Effective Responses to Offensive Comments," 10 *Negot. J.* 107.

SCHNEIDER, Andrea Kupfer & Christopher HONEYMAN, eds., (2006). *The Negotiator's Field Guide.* Washington, D.C.: ABA Section of Dispute Resolution.

SCHWARTZ, Theodore (1992). "Anthropology and Psychology: An Unrequited Relationship," in Theodore Schwartz, Geoffrey White & Catherine A. Lutz, eds., *New Directions in Psychological Anthropology.* New York: Cambridge University Press.

SEBENIUS, James K. (2002). "Caveats for Cross-Border Negotiations,"18 *Negot. J.* 122.

____ (2001). "Solving Teddy Roosevelt's Negotiation Problem," in "Six Habits of Merely Effective Negotiators," Harv. Bus. Rev., April 2001, at 92-93.

____ (1996). "Sequencing to Build Coalitions: With Whom Should I Talk First?," in Richard J. Zeckhauser, Ralph L. Keeney & James K. Sebenius, eds., *Wise Choices: Decisions, Games, and Negotiations.* Boston: Harvard Business School Press.

SEDONA CONFERENCE (2005). "Sedona Guidelines: Best Practices Addressing Protective Orders, Confidentiality and Public Access in Civil Cases," available at *http://www.thesedonaconference.org/content/miscFiles/wg2may05draft2.*

SENGER, Jeffrey M. (2004). "Decision Analysis in Negotiation," 87 *Marq. L. Rev.* 723.

SEUL, Jeffrey R. (2005). "Settling Significant Cases," 79 *Wash. L. Rev.* 881.

____ (1999). "How Transformative Is Transformative Mediation?: A Constructive-Developmental Assessment," 15 *Ohio St. J. on Disp. Resol.* 135.

SEVENTH FEDERAL JUDICIAL CIRCUIT (1991). "Final Report of the Committee on Civility of the Seventh Federal Judicial Circuit," 143 *F.R.D.* 441.

____ (1991). "Interim Report of the Committee on Civility of the Seventh Federal Judicial Circuit," 143 *F.R.D.* 371.

SHAPIRO, Daniel L. (2004). "Emotions in Negotiation: Peril or Promise?," 87 *Marq. L. Rev.* 737.

SHAVELL, Steven (1982). "Suit, Settlement, and Trial: A Theoretical Analysis Under Alternative Methods for Allocation of Legal Costs," 11 *J. Legal Stud.* 55.

SHELL, G. Richard (2001). "Electronic Bargaining: The Perils of E-Mail and the Promise of Computer-Assisted Negotiations," in Stephen J. Hoch & Howard C. Kunreuther, eds., with Robert E. Gunther, *Wharton on Making Decisions.* New York: John Wiley & Sons.

____ (1999). *Bargaining for Advantage: Negotiation Strategies for Reasonable People.* New York: Viking.

SHERMAN, Edward F. (1998). "From 'Loser Pays' to Modified Offer of Judgment Rules: Reconciling Incentives to Settle with Access to Justice," 76 *Tex. L. Rev.* 1863.

SHOEMAKER, Paul J.H. & J. Edward RUSSO (2001). "Managing Frames to Make Better Decisions," in Stephen J. Hoch & Howard C. Kunreuther, eds., with Robert E. Gunther, *Wharton on Making Decisions.* New York: John Wiley & Sons.

SILBEY, Susan S. & Sally E. MERRY (1986). "Mediator Settlement Strategies," 8 *Law & Poly.* 7.

SIMONSON, Itamar & Amos TVERSKY (1992). "Choice of Contest: Tradeoff Contrast and Extremeness Aversion," 29 *J. Marketing Res.* 281.

SPILLENGER, Clyde (1996). "Elusive Advocate: Reconsidering Brandeis as People's Lawyer," 105 *Yale L.J.* 1445.

SPINNEY, Laura (2004). "Why We Do What We Do," 183 *New Scientist*, July 31, at 32.

ST. ANTOINE, Theodore J., Charles C. CRAVER & Marion CRAIN (1999). *Labor Relations Law: Cases and Materials* (10th ed.). Charlottesville, Va.: Lexis Law Pub.

STEELE, Walter W., Jr. (1986). "Essay: Deceptive Negotiation and High-Toned Morality," 39 *Vand. L. Rev.* 1387.

STILLINGER, Constance, Michael EPELBAUM, Dacher KELTNER & Lee ROSS (1990). "The 'Reactive Devaluation' Barrier to Conflict Resolution" (unpublished manuscript, on file with Stanford University).

STONE, Douglas, Bruce PATTON & Sheila HEEN (1999). *Difficult Conversations: How to Discuss What Matters Most.* New York: Viking.

STRAUS, David A. (1999). "Managing Meetings to Build Consensus," in Lawrence Susskind, Sarah McKearnan & Jennifer Thomas-Larmer, eds., *The Consensus Building Handbook: A Comprehensive Guide to Reaching Agreement.* Thousand Oaks, Cal.: Sage Publications.

STUNTZ, William J. (2004). "Plea Bargaining and Criminal Law's Disappearing Shadow," 117 *Harv. L. Rev.* 2548.

SUNSTEIN, Cass R. (2000). "Deliberative Trouble? Why Groups Go to Extremes," 110 *Yale L.J.* 71.

SUSSKIND, Lawrence, Sarah McKEARNAN & Jennifer THOMAS-LARMER (1999). "An Alternative to Robert's Rules of Order for Groups, Organizations, and Ad Hoc Assemblies That Want to Operate by Consensus," in Lawrence Susskind, Sarah McKearnan & Jennifer Thomas-Larmer, eds., *The Consensus Building Handbook: A Comprehensive Guide to Reaching Agreement.* Thousand Oaks, Cal.: Sage Publications.

SUSSKIND, Lawrence, Robert MNOOKIN, Lukasz ROZDEICZER & Boyd FULLER (2005). "What We Have Learned About Teaching Multiparty Negotiation," 21 *Negot. J.* 395.

TAFT, Lee (2000). "Apology Subverted: The Commodification of Apology," 109 *Yale L.J.* 1135.

TANNEN, Deborah (1998). *The Argument Culture: Moving from Debate to Dialogue.* New York: Random House.

TEMKIN, Barry (2004). "Misrepresentations by Omission in Settlement Negotiations: Should There Be a Silent Safe Harbor?," 18 *Geo. J. Legal Ethics* 179.

THALER, Richard H. (1980). "Toward a Positive Theory of Consumer Choice," 1 *J. Econ. Behav. & Org.* 39.

THOMAS, Kenneth (1976). "Conflict and Conflict Management," in Marvin D. Dunnette, ed., *Handbook of Industrial and Organizational Psychology.* Chicago: Rand McNally College Publishing.

THOMPSON, Leigh (2005). *The Mind and Heart of the Negotiator* (3d ed.). Upper Saddle River, N.J.: Prentice Hall.

THOMPSON, Leigh, Janice NADLER & Peter H. KIM (1999). "Some Like It Hot: The Case for the Emotional Negotiator," in Leigh L. Thompson, John M. Levine, & David M. Messick, eds., *Shared Cognition in Organizations: The Management of Knowledge.* Mahwah, N.J.: L. Erlbaum.

TIERNEY, John (2005). "The Urge to Win," *N.Y. Times*, May 31, at A19.

_____ (2005). "What Women Want," *N.Y. Times*, May 24, at A25.

TINSLEY, Cathy, Kathleen O'CONNER & Brandon A. SULLIVAN (2001). "Tough Guys Finish Last," 88 *Org. Behav & Hum. Decision Processes* 621.

TONN, Joan C. (2003). *Mary P. Follett: Creating Democracy, Transforming Management.* New Haven: Yale University Press.

TYLER, Tom (1990). *Why People Obey the Law.* New Haven: Yale University Press.

TYLER, Patrick E. (2004). "Blair Offers an Apology, of Sorts, Over Iraq," *N.Y. Times*, Sept. 29, at A10.

URY, William (1991). *Getting Past No: Negotiating with Difficult People.* New York: Bantam Books.

VOLTAN, Vamik (1997). *Blood Lines: From Ethnic Pride to Ethnic Terrorism.* New York: Farrar, Straus & Giroux.

WALSH, Elsa (1996). "The Negotiator," *The New Yorker*, March 18, at 86-97.

WATSON, Carol (1994). "Gender Versus Power as a Predictor of Negotiation Behavior and Outcomes," 10 *Negot. J.* 117.

WEINSTEIN, Janet & Linda MORTON (2003). "Stuck in a Rut: The Role of Creative Thinking in Problem Solving and Legal Education," 9 *Clinical L. Rev.* 835.

WELSH, Nancy A. (2001). "Making Deals in Court-Connected Mediation: What's Justice Got to Do with It?," 79 *Wash. U. L.Q.* 787.

WETLAUFER, Gerald B. (1996). "The Limits of Integrative Bargaining," 85 *Geo. L.J.* 369.

____ (1990). "The Ethics of Lying in Negotiations," 75 *Iowa L. Rev.* 1219.

WHITE, James J. (1980). "Machiavelli and the Bar: Ethical Limitations on Lying in Negotiation," 1980 *Am. B. Found. Res. J.* 926.

WILLIAMS, Gerald R. (1996). "Negotiation as a Healing Process," 1996 *J. Disp. Resol.* 1-65.

____ (1983). *Legal Negotiation and Settlement.* St. Paul: West Group.

WU, Jianzhong & Robert AXELROD (1995). "How to Cope with Noise in the Iterated Prisoner's Dilemma," 39 *J. Conflict Resol.* 183.

ZARTMAN, I. William (2003). "The Timing of Peace Initiatives: Hurting Stalemates and Ripe Moments," in John Darby & Roger MacGinty, eds., *Contemporary Peacemaking: Conflict, Violence and Peace Processes.* New York: Palgrave Macmillan.

ZARTMAN, I. William & Maureen R. BERMAN (1982). *The Practical Negotiator.* New Haven: Yale University Press.

Index